Government and Politics in Florida

UNIVERSITY PRESS OF FLORIDA

Florida A&M University, Tallahassee
Florida Atlantic University, Boca Raton
Florida Gulf Coast University, Ft. Myers
Florida International University, Miami
Florida State University, Tallahassee
New College of Florida, Sarasota
University of Central Florida, Orlando
University of Florida, Gainesville
University of North Florida, Jacksonville
University of South Florida, Tampa
University of West Florida, Pensacola

Government and Politics in Florida

Third Edition

Edited by J. Edwin Benton

Foreword by Governor Reubin O'Donovan Askew

University Press of Florida
Gainesville/Tallahassee/Tampa/Boca Raton
Pensacola/Orlando/Miami/Jacksonville/Ft. Myers/Sarasota

12   11   10   09   08   07   6   5   4   3   2   1

Library of Congress Cataloging-in-Publication Data
Government and politics in Florida / edited by J. Edwin Benton ; foreword by Reubin O'Donovan Askew. — 3rd ed.
p. cm.
Includes bibliographical references and index.
ISBN 978-0-8130-3169-9 (cloth : alk. paper) — ISBN 978-0-8130-3170-5
(pbk. : alk. paper)
1. Florida—Politics and government—1951– I. Benton, J. Edwin, 1950–
JK4416.G38 2008
320.9759—dc22
2007031681

The University Press of Florida is the scholarly publishing agency for the
State University System of Florida, comprising Florida A&M Univer-
sity, Florida Atlantic University, Florida Gulf Coast University, Florida
International University, Florida State University, New College of Florida,
University of Central Florida, University of Florida, University of North
Florida, University of South Florida, and University of West Florida.

University Press of Florida
15 Northwest 15th Street
Gainesville, FL 32611-2079
www.upf.com

Dedicated
to
my mother
Betty Blakely Benton

Contents

Figures

Tables

Foreword

Change has been synonymous with the demographics and politics of Florida for over a half century. Since the end of World War II, there has been a steady stream of people to the Sunshine State. But unlike many of those who came in the early years, a larger proportion of those who come to Florida today do not necessarily view it as a place to retire or spend the winter months or enjoy a family vacation. Today, more of those coming to the state view it as a place to find employment in the vastly growing service sector, establish a career and raise a family, take advantage of what Florida's "good life" has to offer, and then perhaps retire. And while they still come from the other forty-nine states, they also come from many of the countries in the Caribbean, Central and South America, Europe, Asia, and Africa. As a result, the state's population has increased exponentially. Once small, sleepy, and primarily agricultural areas are now bustling centers of business and commerce. Moreover, the state's population is much more heterogeneous, cosmopolitan, and eclectic than was the case in the 1950s and 1960s.

The tremendous and rapid growth in the state's population has meant that government and politics in the Sunshine State have had to change as well. For the most part, much of the state's earlier resemblance to Old Dixie has faded, while progressive elements of reformism, good-government initiatives, and modern, efficient, effective, and responsive ways of conducting business within the public sector have emerged. In this regard, the state can be seen as an innovator in some areas but almost always considerably ahead of other southern states. And, of course, the state government and its local governments have been forced to respond to the unprecedented (and sometimes overwhelming) demand for new and expanded services. It has been in this area that government has been challenged most often and most profoundly, as the state government and its municipalities, counties, special districts, and school districts have had to generate additional revenue in what continues to be a fiscally conservative political environment.

Like most texts devoted to state and local government and politics, the chapters in the third edition of *Government and Politics in Florida* cover the basics—that is, the division of powers and legal responsibilities, the structure of government, the state's political culture and public opinion, individual and mass political behavior (e.g., voting behavior and elections, interest groups, and political parties), political institutions (legislative, executive, and judicial branches), revenue sources and constraints, and policy issues (e.g., education, health care, welfare, growth management and the environment). Each contributor has done an excellent job of capturing the reality and challenges of efficient operation of government in the third fastest-growing state in the United States. Chapter 1 sets the tone for the remainder of the book by providing the context that underlies and influences the practice of politics and the functioning of governmental institutions. The authors of each chapter seek to describe what exactly the state's government, 67 counties, 412 municipalities, 67 school districts, and innumerable special districts and legislative authorities do, what motivates them to do what they do and how they do it, and what the political, economic, and social consequences are of their actions.

Given the thrust and purpose of *Government and Politics in Florida*, who should be interested in reading it? The most obvious candidates would be college undergraduate students taking courses that focus on the operation of government and practice of politics in the state of Florida. Indeed, this book has been the staple text in most such courses at Florida colleges and universities and, until recently, was the only such text available that covers this subject. The book should also be of interest to graduate students and political science and public administration faculty who teach graduate and undergraduate courses on state and local government and politics at colleges and universities both within and outside of Florida. An understanding of political activity and governmental actions in Florida is relevant to an understanding of what is happening in other states; the state is rapidly becoming—or perhaps already is—a microcosm of the nation and a reasonably accurate bellwether for predicting regional and national political outcomes.

In addition, the book should be of value and interest to those outside academia. For instance, those in the media should find the book to be a useful guide and valuable commentary as they endeavor to accurately report on political news in Florida and provide an accurate context for political events. Individuals who play vital roles in government and politics in Florida (e.g., elected and appointed officials or people and groups who try to influence elections or policy decisions) should find the book instructive and valuable. Federal officials and public officials in other states who interact with various governmental units in Florida or their political counterparts in the state will find invaluable insights in this volume that should serve them well. Finally, the average Florida citizen or even new residents of the state could learn a great deal from reading this book. It should help them better understand how their state government and the local governments that serve them function and, perhaps most important, how they can provide an effective voice on issues of vital concern to them.

Reubin O'D. Askew
Professor, Askew School of Public Administration and Policy
Florida State University
Tallahassee, Florida
Governor of the State of Florida, 1971–1979

Preface

When I agreed to become the new editor of the third edition of *Government and Politics in Florida* about two and a half years ago, I was understandably awestruck about being asked to lead such an effort and immediately realized that a significant and challenging task lay ahead of me. On the one hand, I recognized the necessity of maintaining the rich tradition and the legacy of this volume that had been fashioned in earlier editions. On the other hand, I had a strong desire to take the book to a higher level and in some different directions and leave my own imprint on it. It is my earnest hope that I, along with the contributors to this volume, have been able to realize both goals and that teaching faculty who adopt the book for classroom instruction and students who seek to learn how government and politics plays out in the nation's fourth most populous state will not come away disappointed after reading it.

From the outset, I also recognized that as editor I had some very big shoes to fill. The editor of a forerunner to this volume (the late Manning Dauer) as well as the original editor of the present book (Robert J. Huckshorn) were tough acts to follow; not only were they highly visible political scientists but one was a well-known and respected icon among state and local officials in Florida. What is there to say that has not been said and what accolade has not been used to characterize the storied career and life of Manning Dauer, known to many of us as "Mr. Florida Political Science"? Professor Dauer was distinguished service professor at the University of Florida and the preeminent member of the discipline in the state for many years. Professor Huckshorn (now retired) was professor of political science at Florida Atlantic University and the vice president of that university's northern campuses and is still a widely quoted and respected authority on state government and politics and political parties. He was a charter member of the Florida Election Commission and served on it for sixteen years, two of them as chair.

With the cooperation of a number of colleagues in the public and private universities and colleges and some practitioners of government in the state, Professor Dauer published the first edition of *Florida Politics and Government* in 1980. The University Press of Florida published a revised edition three years later and a second edition in 1984. After Professor Dauer's death in 1986, Professor Huchshorn was asked to revise the book for a third edition, but he agreed to do so only if he was permitted to create an entirely new book with a different format and new authors. The editors of the University Press of Florida agreed to this condition and subsequently published the first edition of *Government and Politics in Florida* in 1991. The book's second edition was published in 1998.

A quick perusal of the table of contents of the third edition of *Government and Politics in Florida* reveals that all of the subject matter of the chapters of the second edition has been retained, although over half of the chapters have new authors. But one will also notice that the third edition includes new chapters covering the three critical policy areas of education, public welfare, and health care and that a chapter on intergovernmental relations has been added. Furthermore, a chapter in the second edition that previously covered the topics of public opinion and interest groups has been divided into two chapters; one that focuses on political culture and political attitudes and another that focuses on interest groups. A final, concluding new chapter ties together the previous sixteen chapters and speculates about the future of government and politics in the Sunshine State.

Acknowledgments

There are countless people to thank when a book of the magnitude and scope of this edited volume has been completed. As trite as it may sound, there is simply no way for this project to have been carried out without the hard work and dedication of a host of people who gave unselfishly and tirelessly of their time and talents. Different people contributed different skills, performed varied tasks, and carried out vital assignments. Most of the people who in some way contributed to this project were well aware of the part they played; others will learn of their invaluable contribution when they read this preface; still others, unfortunately, will never know of the inspiration they provided since they have passed away. And, of course, there will be some who will have been unintentionally overlooked. To them, I offer my sincere apology in advance while thanking them for their contribution.

First, I wish to express my sincere appreciation to the stellar group of authors who agreed to participate in this major undertaking. They are truly the most gifted and knowledgeable authorities and scholars on the subject of Florida government and politics. It was a sheer delight to collaborate with all of them. They never said "no" when I asked anything of them, whether it was to make changes in their original draft, review another author's chapter, or adhere to deadlines. Furthermore, I appreciate their patience with and understanding of me as I endeavored to readapt myself to the role of an editor (I had not played this role since 1986) that, at times, could be compared to the task of continually rounding up a herd of stray cats!

Second, I need to recognize an all-star cast of colleagues and talented scholars in their own right who liberally gave of their time and expertise to serve as blind reviewers for each of the chapters in this volume. The following individuals performed this invaluable service: John Kincaid (Lafayette College), Russell Dalton (University of California—Irvine), Gerald C. Wright Jr. (Indiana University), Rodney Hero (University of Notre Dame), Paul Allen Beck (Ohio State University), Douglas St. Angelo (professor emeritus, Florida State University), Allen Cigler (University of Kansas), Wayne L. Francis (professor emeritus, University of Florida), Alka Sapat (Florida Atlantic University), Steven Tauber (University of South Florida), Donald C. Menzel (University of South Florida—Sarasota-Manatee and professor emeritus, Northern Illinois University), Thomas P. Lauth (University of Georgia), Robert Crew (Florida State University), Gregory Strieb (Georgia State University), and Alvin W. Wolfe (professor emeritus, University of South Florida).

Third, special recognition is due to several people at the University Press of Florida. John Byram, editor-in-chief of the press, is absolutely the most understanding, considerate, and supportive person I have had the opportunity to work with. He made an extremely memorable and rewarding experience out of what could have been a gut-wrenching ordeal. Moreover, he offered me patience when mine seemed to be depleted, hope when mine had dissipated, encouragement in the face of discouragement, and ideas when I was out of ideas. He is truly a master at what he does. Jen Graham, acquisitions assistant at the press, was also extremely helpful in getting all of the figures ready for production, while Susan Albury and Kate Babbitt did a masterful job in the copyediting process.

Others who made important contributions to this volume include three former graduate assistants, Eric Wolters, Matt Kohen, and Mandy Ransome, who proofed parts of the manuscript, dug up little-known facts for me, and assisted in preparing the index. Rick Feiock of FSU was more than a co-author with me, for he helped line up authors and offered advice and shared ideas with me at various stages during preparation of this book. And Mohsen Milani, my department chair at USF and my friend, warrants special recognition because he is the epitome of the ideal departmental chair. He has always offered unwavering encouragement in all of my research endeavors, but most important, he has provided a supportive and congenial work environment for me and my colleagues so that we can reach our potential as productive and visible scholars.

I also need to acknowledge the importance of two other individuals, neither of whom was connected to preparation and production of this book. Thomas R. Dye, formerly McKenzie Professor of Government at Florida State University and my dissertation director, has had a tremendous influence on my development as a scholar. In addition to being an exemplary role model, he always had time to offer commentary and advice on my research and never missed the opportunity to promote my candidacy for jobs when I was a young assistant professor. A few years ago, he graciously wrote that I and several other fellow FSU graduate students to whom he was a mentor "contributed most to [his] education." However, we learned more from him than he learned from us. And I cannot forget to pay tribute to Anne E. Kelley, my late colleague in the Department of Government and International Affairs at the University of South Florida. She was my tacit "professional mother" and helped socialize me into academia during the early impressionable years of my career. Everyone needs an Anne Kelley in their life who will give candid and sound advice, offer unswerving support and encouragement, and settle for nothing less than excellence, integrity, and professionalism in academia.

Lastly, I would be remiss if I did not single out my adult children, James Edwin Benton II (Jamie) and Brittany Nicole Benton, for the understanding and support they have and continue to give me. While they do not necessarily share my passion for the study of government and politics, they do share my enthusiasm for what it is I do. But, most important, they have made parenthood the joy it should be.

1

Introduction

J. EDWIN BENTON

When people think of Florida, they are likely to associate the state with things such as theme parks (e.g., Disney World, MGM Studios, Busch Gardens, Sea World), NASA space launches, winter/vacation resorts, massive groves of citrus fruit trees, devastating hurricanes (Charlie, Francis, Jeanne, and Ivan made unwelcome visits to the state in 2004), senior citizen/retirement villages, spring break destinations for high school and college students, or perhaps the Suwannee River in North Florida that served as the inspiration for Stephen Foster's song "Old Folks At Home." People are also likely to associate the state with sports—NASCAR in Daytona Beach, NCAA postseason football bowl games, pro sports champions (e.g., the Florida Marlins, 2003 World Series champions; the Tampa Bay Buccaneers, 2002 Super Bowl champions; the Tampa Bay Lightning, 2004 Stanley Cup champions), and baseball spring training camps. In addition, people are likely to be familiar with the state's major, rapidly growing, and vibrant metropolitan areas (Orlando, Tampa–St. Petersburg, Miami, Fort Lauderdale, Jacksonville, Sarasota-Bradenton, Fort Myers, Tallahassee, Pensacola, Daytona Beach, West Palm Beach), vast coastlines touching the Atlantic Ocean and Gulf of Mexico, the Everglades, prominent military installations (MacDill Air Force Base—home to the Central Command—and Pensacola and Mayport Naval Stations), and some of the state's most recognizable universities (University of Florida, Florida State University, and the University of Miami).

On the political scene, the state has had its share of notable political personalities and events. It has been represented in Congress by such persons as the great-grandson and namesake of the original owner of the Philadelphia Phillies baseball team, former Senator Connie Mack; the brother-in-law of the *Washington Post*'s Katherine Graham, former Senator Bob Graham; senior citizen advocate Rep. Claude Pepper; and Senator Bill Nelson, a member of Congress who has gone on a space shuttle mission. The former governor of the state is the son of a former president and brother of the present president (Jeb Bush). And the state is remembered for what some have called the 2000 presidential election debacle that led to the election of George W. Bush as president.

Yet as recently as the late 1940s, a visitor to the state would not have found most of these familiar sites and features that seem to be commonly identified with the Sunshine State today, and the state was a small-time player in the presidential sweepstakes with only seven electoral college votes—one more than the state of South Carolina has today.

As recent as the late 1930s, Florida could be accurately described as "an isolated, swampy, disease-ridden, sparsely settled collection of rural towns, fishing camps, American Indian settlements, and small land holdings." A substantial proportion of the state's inhabitants lived a life of subsistence and struggled to make a living from agricultural pursuits "in some of the most uncomfortable summer weather in the United States" (Huckshorn 1998, 1). In 1940, less than 2 million people called Florida home. This made Florida the smallest of the southern states and, and it ranked only 27th among forty-eight states nationally. In the 1950s, middle- and upper-class residents of the northeastern and midwestern sections of the country were attracted by the mild winter weather and a number of well-known vacation resorts, while poor (mainly Hispanic) migrant workers flocked to the state in the 1960s and 1970s to help harvest winter crops of vegetables and fruits and cultivate the fields. As late as the early 1960s, the state's population could still be described as politically conservative, provincial, and strongly allied with the southern wing of the Democratic Party. For the most part, government power and political influence continued to be located in the state's Panhandle region, that northern tier of two dozen sparsely populated counties that runs from east—Duval County (Jacksonville)—to west—Escambia County (Pensacola)—across the top of the state. Politicians from this region, known as the "Pork Chop Gang," often controlled the legislature and the executive branch of Florida government.

During the last four decades of the twentieth century, the political, economic, and social complexion of Florida changed dramatically. The old-family establishment in northern Florida lost its strong grip of influence over the legislature, the governorship, the cabinet, most of the court system, and a large proportion of the wealth in the state (Huckshorn 1998). Political power was not transferred to any one group of people or part of the state. Instead, it was dispersed throughout the state; no particular region, party, or group was able to dictate the outcome of policy decisions. The state's population not only increased significantly but also became truly heterogeneous, more moderate, and Republican.

The Context for Politics in Florida

The Florida one finds today is not the Florida one would have found in the early 1940s. The most dramatic change has been the tremendous growth in the state's population since the end of World War II. From 1945 to 1960, the state's population more than doubled, from approximately 2.3 million to nearly 5 million people. Over the next four decades, Florida's population increased by 37 (1960s), 44 (1970s), 33 (1980s), and 24 (1990s) percent. Presently, Florida's population stands at about 18 million people. Although the state's rate of population growth has declined slightly over the last decade, the Bureau of Economic and Business Research (2004) at the University of Florida predicts that the number of people who call Florida home will grow to 19.7 million in 2010, to around 23 million in 2020, and to approximately 26 million by 2030 (see Figure 1.1). During the 1970s and 1980s, the state's population grew at a rate of around 350,000 per year, or about 963 persons per day (State Comprehensive Plan Committee 1987). This is equivalent to the approximate combined populations of the cities of St. Petersburg and Clearwater or the size of Brevard County (home to Titusville, Cape Canaveral, Cocoa Beach). Currently, the net daily population increase is around 700 people. By the early 1990s, a majority of Floridians had been born somewhere else. According to the latest U.S. census figures, the largest number of annual in-migrants came from New York, followed by New Jersey, Massachusetts, and Pennsylvania. By 2005, Florida was the fourth most populous state in the nation, surpassed only by California, New York,

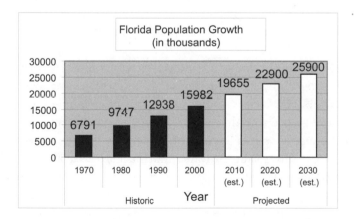

Figure 1.1. Historic and Projected Population Growth in Florida, 1970–2030.

and Texas. Moreover, it was the third fastest growing state, outpaced only by California and Texas.

Of equal importance to the sheer magnitude of the population growth in Florida has been where it has occurred. Newcomers to Florida as well as Floridians who have moved within the state increasingly have chosen to settle in the unincorporated parts of the state's sixty-seven counties. Prior to 1990, over half of all Floridians resided in the state's 395 municipalities at the time (that is, incorporated areas). As recent as 1960, about two out of every three Floridians (68 percent) lived in one of the state's municipalities. But the proportion of city dwellers had decreased to 60 percent by 1970 and to 54 percent by 1980. The 1990 census marked the first time that more than half of the state's residents (51 percent) lived outside the boundaries of the state's municipalities. The unincorporated proportion increased to 53 percent by 2005 and is estimated to rise to 55 by 2010. Currently, over 65 percent of all persons residing in the state's rural counties as well as in twenty-three counties with populations of 50,000 or more live in the unincorporated area of their county. A number of these counties (Collier, Escambia, Hillsborough, Manatee, Marion, Orange, Osceola, Pasco, Polk, and Sarasota) are substantial in size.

The population growth the state has experienced is the consequence of three primary migration streams. The first group of migrants came in the 1950s and was made up of largely upper-middle-class, prosperous, educated, mostly Protestant retirees from large northern and midwestern cities and small New England and midwestern towns who were attracted by the warm winter climate and comprehensive retirement housing developments. They typically settled on the southeast (Dade, Broward, and Palm Beach counties) and southwest (Collier, Lee, Sarasota, and Manatee counties) coasts of the state.

The second group—primarily blue-collar midwesterners and northerners of a variety of ethnic subgroups, including thousands of Catholics and Jews, arrived in the 1960s and 1970s but were not necessarily of retirement age. They were mostly middle-aged, and they were looking for blue-collar, clerical, and service-sector jobs as well as the opportunity to establish their own businesses in southeast Florida (Dade, Broward, Martin, and St. Lucie counties) and on the Gulf Coast (Pinellas, Hillsborough, Pasco, and Hernando counties).

The last group to migrate to Florida were the most controversial and perhaps the least accepted by both native Floridians and new transplants from the Northeast and Midwest—Cubans, Haitians, Dominican Republicans,

Nicaraguans, Colombians, and virtually all other Central and South American nationalities. They were usually poor, much less educated, culturally different, and they spoke very little or no English. However, they saw Florida and America as the land of opportunity and hoped for better lives both economically and politically. The Cubans arrived in two waves: an early 1960s group that was fleeing from the initial Castro takeover and the failed Bay of Pigs military operation and a 1970s group that included the people of the Mariel boatlift. Others from Central and South America and the Caribbean filtered into Florida during the 1970s, 1980, and 1990s.

Overlaying these three migration streams has been the readily noticeable "graying" of the state's population. Today, Florida ranks first among the fifty states in the median age of its population and the proportion of its residents who are over 65 years of age. The aging of the state population over the last fifty years coupled with the influx of retired persons means that nearly one-fifth of the state's population is elderly. Senior citizens are mainly white and, as a result of rising Social Security benefits (and their indexation above the rate of inflation) and Medicare, are usually less poor than the young. Seniors are also the most conservative group in the state. Traditionally, seniors oppose government taxing (particularly property taxes) and spending programs that do not promise immediate benefits to the elderly population (e.g., see Rosenbaum and Button 1995; MacManus 1996, 1995). Senior citizens are the most likely group of Floridians to vote—voter turnout among persons 65 and over typically exceeds 75 percent—in order to advance a very potent senior citizens' agenda in state and local politics in Florida.

As a result of this massive in-migration and other demographic trends, Florida's population has become one of the most diverse in the nation. Moreover, this diversity is spread out over several major clusters throughout the state and has produced what Thomas R. Dye (1998, 6) has called a "fractured political geography." The Panhandle region is anchored by Jacksonville in the east and Pensacola in the west. Although the Jacksonville area is a booming center for business and international trade, its workforce is overwhelmingly blue collar. Likewise, the Pensacola area (although it is smaller than Jacksonville) is basically driven by a blue-collar economy and a strong military presence (Pensacola Naval Air Station and Eglin Air Force Base). In many respects, this region is still part of the Bible Belt (home to many Christian fundamentalists) and resembles Old Dixie politically. Conservative whites still dominate the region, but their political allegiance has steadily shifted from the southern wing of the Democratic Party to the Republican Party. In spite of the fact that voters of this region may continue to register Democratic, they often vote Republican. However, the areas around Tallahassee, with its state bureaucrats, and Gainesville, with its state university presence, provide exceptions to this otherwise conservative region.

The western peninsula of Florida (sometimes referred to as the Gulf Coast) can be divided into two distinguishable regions—the northwest and southwest Gulf coasts. Hillsborough (Tampa) and Pinellas (St. Petersburg-Clearwater) counties constitute the nucleus of the northwest Gulf Coast region. Voters in these two counties as well as those in Pasco, Hernando, and Citrus counties to the north are generally conservative and Republican, but this region's large number of retirees is very protective of social services such as Social Security and Medicare. The southwest Gulf Coast region, extending from the Bradenton/Sarasota area to Fort Myers and Naples, is mainly a resort and retirement area. Its retirees are typically more affluent and more educated than those in the northwest Gulf Coast region and, unless given a good reason not to do so, they are more apt to vote Republican.

The southeast region, which includes Miami-Dade County, Fort Lauderdale and Broward county communities, and Palm Beach County, is the most populous region of the state and is truly a mix of many cultures. For instance, one finds numerous wealthy, upper-class, white Anglo-Saxon Protestant (WASP) neighborhoods in Palm Beach; distinctly Jewish enclaves in Miami, Miami Beach, Hollywood, and Boca Raton, large African-American communities in Miami, Fort Lauderdale, and Rivera Beach; innumerable Cuban-American neighborhoods in Miami and Hialeah, and Coral Gables; and a hodgepodge of fast-growing Haitian communities in Miami, Fort Lauderdale, and Palm Beach. In fact, New York transplants outnumber native Floridians in this region. Broward County normally gives Democratic candidates for statewide office their greatest political support, while Miami-Dade County has become a political testing ground for conservative Republican Cubans, generally liberal and Democratic African Americans, liberal Jews, and conservative business interests.

The Central Florida region, or the state's midsection, extends along the Interstate 4 corridor from Daytona Beach/Titusville/Vero Beach (Space Coast) to the Tampa-St. Petersburg area and is the fastest-growing area of the state. While the economy of the Space Coast depends on a combination of tourism and the space industry, the Orlando area is rapidly becoming a world mecca of family entertainment through its many theme parks, such as Walt Disney World, Walt Disney World Resort-Epcot, Sea World, and two movie-oriented centers built by Disney and Universal Studios. By contrast, the Winter Haven/Lakeland area, while still known for citrus, cattle, and the phosphate industry, is rapidly becoming a major distribution center for food stores, auto parts, mobile homes, and food manufactures. This region contains a growing number of both working-class families and retirees, and like the northwest Gulf Coast region, its residents are mainly conservative and increasingly Republican. However, its large retiree population remains very protective of federal entitlement programs such as Social Security and Medicare.

The "fractured political geography" of Florida has meant that there is no homogeneous image of the state. No particular city, whether it is Miami, Tampa, St. Petersburg, Orlando, Jacksonville, Fort Lauderdale, West Palm Beach, Tallahassee, or Pensacola, or region (Panhandle, northwest and southwest Gulf Coasts, Southeast, Space Coast, Central) can truly capture the essence of Florida and its politics. It is as though there are many different Floridas (small, medium, and large), and, like the geometry principle, the state is equal to the sum of its parts. For the most part, Floridians do not think of themselves as Floridians. As one longtime observer of Florida (Dye 1998, 8) has noted, "Floridians are likely to look to city and regional newspapers and television stations for whatever sense of community they may develop."[1]

Growth and Political Rootlessness

The explosive growth the state has experienced as a result of in-migration has produced both positive and negative consequences. On the positive side, the state has seen a substantial increase in international businesses, other commercial ventures, and tourism; the development of a space center; and an expanding high-tech industrial base and higher education system. The increase in population has also meant a greater voice for the state's citizens in the policy positions of the Democratic and Republican parties, representation and presence in Congress, and influence on the outcome of presidential races. And, of course, there is the prestige of being one of the most populous states.

On the negative side, there has been an alarming increase in international drug traffic, a soaring rate of crime and incarceration, deteriorating air and water quality and other environmental concerns, water shortages, shrinkage of green space, and snarled highway traffic. To compound matters, the state's inadequate political structure, mechanisms, and processes for dealing with rapid growth have caused what amounts to a partial breakdown of Florida's government. The state government has looked to local governments to seize the initiative in meeting the challenges posed by rapid growth, while the state's municipal and county officials have insisted that political leadership and financial assistance should come from Tallahassee. In 1987, the State

Comprehensive Plan Committee estimated that it would take $52.9 billion to catch up with the backlog of local government infrastructure needs. Moreover, the social and economic dislocations have tended to cast a dark overshadow over the prospects for boom times. Some would argue that the increase in tax revenues and the prestige of being a populous and diverse state has come with a price, a decrease in the quality of life for both present and future generations. Debates over growth-related issues and between pro- and anti-growth groups continue to dominate the state's politics and government.

For good or bad, the massive influx of newcomers to Florida has produced a sense of political rootlessness within the state. Two clear effects can be seen. First, lacking the traditional political references that they were accustomed to in their former city, county, state, or country of origin (e.g., long-standing church memberships, labor unions, professional group affiliations, old neighborhoods, family, friendship, and social ties), newcomers to Florida are potentially more susceptible to political cues from newspapers and television. According to Dye (1998, 5), this means that newcomers may be may be more open to "slick television advertisements, snappy campaign slogans, and charismatic candidates." Consequently, newcomers tend to change party and candidate allegiances from election to election, which virtually guarantees enough swing votes in most elections to make the outcomes uncertain.

Second, a spirit of rootlessness among newcomers also may be responsible for a mind-set that poses a significant challenge to state and local officials. Both empirical and anecdotal evidence (Benton and Daly 1992; Beck and Dye 1982) indicates that newcomers want an expansion in the number and level of services but are opposed to the increases in taxes or fees that would be required. It is as though newcomers do not have a firm grip on political and fiscal reality. Indeed, these paradoxical views associated with both the menu and scope of state and local services suggest that newcomers lack a sense of attachment to the government and political institutions of their adopted state. This lack of attachment has been responsible for a decidedly conservative fiscal posture among newcomers and reinforces the fiscal conservatism generally found among native Floridians. In short, this makes it even more difficult for public officials to "sell" Floridians (both natives and migrants) on the need to raise more revenue to fund the cost of new and expanded services.

Politics and Policy Making: The Influence of the State's Constitution

A state's constitution can set the tone for the practice of politics and policy making. Simply stated, the constitution is the instrument by which a society decides what powers will be given to its government and what powers will be kept by the people and expressly denied its government. Moreover, the constitution embodies what David Easton (1965) has called the "regime rules" or "rules of the game" of a political system. Regime rules set the parameters of what governments can and cannot do and, perhaps just as important, how government officials are selected and how governments are to go about the business of making decisions that are binding on the governed.

Florida has had six constitutions; the most recent one went into effect in 1968. Although this constitution lays out the rules by which state policy is made (and provides for local governments and their responsibilities and authority), it is not without external limits. First, it is always subject to being amended, revised, or even replaced by the state's citizens. Indeed, the latest constitution is less than forty years old. Efforts to amend the 1968 constitution have been less frequent than was the case with previous constitutions. To date, 110 amendments to the present constitution have been proposed and 81 have been ratified. That averages out to around six proposed and five ratified amendments every biennial election, meaning that the voters approve most proposals. Most proposals have involved reorganization of government, finance and taxation, education, apportionment, and gambling.

Second, the state's constitution, statutes, and local ordinances are limited in the sense that they are subordinate to the U.S. Constitution, federal laws (i.e., laws enacted by Congress), and federal treaties. More specifically, Article VI of the U.S. Constitution provides for the supremacy of the Constitution as well as federal laws and treaties in the event that state constitutions and statutes and local ordinances conflict with them. In addition, the U.S. Supreme Court has the authority to strike down all or parts of state constitutions, state statutes, and local ordinances and overturn decisions of the state courts.

These limitations notwithstanding, Florida's constitution has a tempering affect on how politics is practiced and eventually on the content of policy decisions. The constitution is a part or final element of the context of government and politics in Florida. Space restrictions do not permit us to elaborate on even a modest sampling of the most relevant parts of the Florida constitution that are important for understanding politics and policy decisions in Florida. Therefore, what follows is a brief comparison of Florida's constitution with the U.S. Constitution and a look at how Florida's constitutions can be changed.

The 1968 constitution is strikingly different from the Constitution of the United States. The latter is approximately twenty to twenty-five pages long, including the original document, the Bill of Rights, and amendments. In contrast, Florida's constitution contains forty double-columned pages of small print (plus a 24-page index). It incorporates its dozens of amendments in the body of the document rather than listing them separately at the end, as the U.S. Constitution does.

Florida's constitution, however, does not differ noticeably from those of other states. The U.S. Constitution only briefly outlines general provisions of governmental power and structure, leaving the details and interpretation to Congress, the executive branch, the courts, and the states. Such a system assumes that the states will implement their powers through constitutional provision and law. As a consequence, state constitutions usually are excessively long, comprehensively detailed and wordy, and subject to frequent amendment.

The Florida constitution can be amended in five ways. Regardless of how amendments are proposed, ratification ultimately requires a majority vote of the citizens. All methods have been used at least one time; the typical general election ballot includes an average of six or seven proposed amendments.

In the first method, amendments (which are presented one or more at a time) result from resolutions adopted jointly by both houses of the legislature by a margin of three-fifths of the membership of each house. Since they are joint resolutions, these proposals are not sent to the governor. Rather, they go directly to the voters at the next general election. The second method (which is limited to a single amendment or revision at a time) requires a joint resolution approved by a three-fourths vote of each house of the legislature followed by a special vote of the citizenry before the next general election.

The third method of amendment entails an initiative petition. The proposed amendment appears at the head of petition forms requesting that it be placed on the ballot at the next general election. Supporters pass around the petitions to collect signatures of registered voters. For the proposed amendment to make it to the ballot, however, the number of signatories must equal 8 percent of the number of Floridians who voted in the most recent presidential election, including 8 percent of the number of voters in at least half the U.S. congressional districts. The offices of county supervisors of elections confirm the signatures against voter registration lists.

The fourth amendment method begins with recommendations that result from the deliberations of the Constitutional Revision Commission. (The commission met in the tenth year following the adoption of the 1968 constitution and will meet every twentieth year thereafter.) The recommendations of the commission can vary from a complete revamping of the constitution to minor changes with individual provisions.

Finally, a constitutional convention may recommend amendments in an awkward six-year procedure that has not been used since 1885. Such a convention begins with a voter petition after signatures equaling at least 15 percent of the number who voted in the last presidential election in the state *and* 5 percent of the number who voted in half the congressional districts have been collected. After offices of county supervisors of elections verify the signatures, the call for a convention appears on the ballot of the next general election. If the proposal is approved, candidates for convention seats campaign in each legislative house district and are elected at the next general election. Then the convention assembles, and any proposed amendments that result from this body's deliberations are placed on the ballot at the next general election.

Experiments in Government

Regardless of the fact that it is located in the conservative South, in a number of instances Florida has been progressively bold and has led the way in experimenting with governmental structure and pro-democracy activities. It was the first state to adopt a presidential primary (although Wisconsin also claims this distinction). Florida originated the concept of sunshine laws that require public officials to hold meetings in the open so the public and the press may attend. Sunshine laws also require all public documents and papers to be open to public inspection. Florida was also ahead of other states in adopting a "resign to run" law, which requires all state, county, or local officials to resign before the end of their terms if they choose to run for another office. The law effectively ended the practice of officials elected to four-year terms running for a different office after two years, relying on their incumbency for security in case of defeat. The Florida legislature became widely known in the late 1970s and early 1980s for its efforts to modernize the legislative process by massive computerization, expanded member and committee staffs, and up-to-date offices for legislators in Tallahassee and their home districts. In addition, by the early 1990s, the state was on the cutting edge of welfare reform, and much of what the state was doing—particularly with regard to work expectations, parental responsibility, and time limits on program eligibility connected to the Aid to Families with Dependent Children (AFDC) program (subsequently renamed Temporary Assistance to Needy Families, TANF)—was used as a template for the Personal Responsibility and Work Opportunity Reconciliation Act that Congress enacted in 1996.

Florida's cabinet system, which was abolished in 1999, was unique among the states. The system was thought to substantially weaken the office of governor by forcing her/him to share executive power with six other elected officials, all chosen for four-year terms but eligible for reelection for an additional four years. The cabinet would meet weekly and voted on all major issues of policy. Each cabinet official—the secretary of state, commissioner of education, attorney general, comptroller, commissioner of agriculture, and treasurer/insurance commissioner—headed an executive department and had an equal voice in cabinet decisions. With the governor, the cabinet members also constituted a number of important state boards, such as the state board of education and state pardon board.

Florida in the Twenty-First Century

The Florida of today probably would not be recognizable to those who lived in the state in the late 1940s or early 1950s. And the Florida of today probably will be barely recognizable to those living here sixty or seventy years from now. The demographics of the state have changed radically since the end of World War II. Large, sprawling, and densely populated urban centers have replaced the isolated, swampy, sparsely settled collection of rural towns, fishing villages, and American Indian settlements and small land holdings characteristic of the state in the late 1940s. Thousands of acres of land that once were the site of cattle and dairy ranches, citrus groves, and pristine forests and open areas have been transformed into large shopping malls, massive housing developments and condominiums, business-office complexes, and a maze of new highways and roads, schools, and government office buildings and facilities. Challenges posed by pollution, water shortages, sewage and solid waste disposal, and the lack of green space have ensued.

If the demographics of the state have changed, so has the political landscape. The two-party system continues to evolve, while Republican control of the legislature seems to be a fixture for the immediate future. Floridians are increasingly inclined to vote Republican in national and local elections. In addition, a number of new activist voting groups (e.g., Cuban-Americans, Haitians, senior citizens, anti-growth activists, and gays and lesbians) have emerged around the state. They vote in large numbers and often show up to lobby and speak out at legislative committee hearings and city, county, and special and school district meetings. Moreover, the growth in size, number (in the case of cities), and complexity of local governments has created the potential for both cooperation and conflict in the intergovernmental arena. Cities and counties seek greater autonomy and flexibility from the state government as their service responsibilities grow, and they are interacting more frequently with the federal government and governments of other countries.

These and other unparalleled changes set Florida apart from other states and communities around the nation. It probably can be said that the only constant in Florida is change. The authors of this book do not claim to have a crystal ball that permits them to look very far into the future of government and politics in Florida, for predicting the future of a rapidly growing and ever-changing state like Florida is probably a futile exercise. However, as good social scientists, we do hope to provide a clear description of what the state government and local governments, public officials, and involved citizens in Florida do, why they do it, and what the social, economic, and political consequences of their actions are.

Organization of This Book

To that end, the chapters that follow can be divided into four categories. First, Chapters 2–6 are devoted to mass political behavior and the electoral process. Suzanne Parker and Terri Toner (Chapter 2) provide a setting for politics in Florida by painting a picture of the state's political culture and the resultant political attitudes Floridians hold on a wide range of issues, while Stephen Craig and Roger Austin (Chapter 3) recount and analyze election outcomes—especially partisan changes—that have occurred within the context of Florida's political culture, which seems to be changing with the arrival of more and more new residents. The next three chapters consider the roles of some of the more visible players in the political system. This begins in Chapter 4 where Kevin Hill and Dario Moreno provide a detailed and systematic account of the political behavior of African Americans and Hispanics in Florida, followed by Thomas Carsey and J. B. Nelson's (Chapter 5) and Matthew Corrigan and J. Edwin Benton's (Chapter 6) examination of political-party and interest-group participation and behavior in state politics and governance.

Chapters 7, 8, and 9 can be thought of as another major division of the book. In these chapters, the authors focus on what scholars typically refer to as the political institutions, or the three branches, of government. In

Chapter 7, Kevin Wagner and Eric Prier describe the foundations of legislative government, what citizens expect from the state legislature, how the legislature goes about its work, and implications for state policy. Richard Scher (Chapter 8) provides a historical perspective on Florida's executive branch (with particular emphasis on the governor) and the prospects for enhanced gubernatorial leadership after Jeb Bush. Finally, Chapter 9, by Drew Lanier and Roger Handberg, present an insightful overview of the structure of Florida judiciary and an analysis of the important—but frequently overlooked—role that courts in Florida play as enforcers of norms and, at times, critical policy makers.

Two other chapters constitute a third part of the book and focus on local governments and intergovernmental relations in Florida. The authors of Chapter 10 (J. Edwin Benton and Richard Feiock) present a summary of the history, legal status, and structure of counties, municipalities, and special districts as well as the role that each plays as front-line service providers to a burgeoning population. Robert Bradley and J. Edwin Benton (Chapter 11) lay out a context for understanding and analyzing the often-changing intergovernmental dynamics in Florida and the opportunity for both cooperation and conflict in adopting and implementing policy decisions.

A final set of chapters (12–16) concentrates on public policy matters—that is, the outputs or products of the political system in general and the political institutions in particular. Recognizing that almost all policy decisions require fiscal resources for implementation, Susan MacManus (Chapter 12) provides a comprehensive and realistic assessment of the political and economic context for state and local revenue policy in Florida as well as a thorough review of the varying types of revenue sources the state and its local governments tap. The other four chapters in this section deal with "tough choices" policy issues that continue to command the attention of policy makers and the public alike. Lynne Holt and Babak Lotfinia (Chapter 13) and Carol and William Weissert (Chapter 14) offer eye-opening evaluations of the state's education and health care policies and programs, respectively, and the funding challenges that will arise if things are to be turned around. Renee Johnson and David Hedge (Chapter 15) and Lance deHaven-Smith (Chapter 16) convincingly remind us of the unfinished business that awaits the state and its citizens with regard to public welfare reform, environmental protection, and growth management and the social, political, and monetary costs associated with each of these issues.

The final chapter of the book takes a brief look back to understand the present political climate and state of affairs in Florida. It concludes with some realistic projections—that is, specific things to pay close attention to and look for—for the future and vitality of government and politics in the Sunshine State.

Notes

1. See also Hill, MacManus, and Moreno (2004) for a thorough discussion of the diversity of political views and information across the various regions or media markets in Florida and subsequent policy impacts.

References

Beck, Paul Allen, and Thomas R. Dye. 1982. "Sources of Public Opinion on Taxes: The Florida Case." *Journal of Politics* 44, no. 1: 172–82.

Benton, J. Edwin, and John L. Daly. 1992. "The Paradox of Citizen Service Evaluations and Tax/Fee Preferences: The Case of Two Small Cities." *American Review of Public Administration* 22, no. 4: 271–87.

Bureau of Economic and Business Research. 2004. *Florida Statistical Abstract, 2004.* Gainesville: University of Florida.

Dye, Thomas R. 1998. *Politics in Florida.* Upper Saddle River, N.J.: Prentice Hall.

Easton, David. 1965. *A Framework for Political Analysis.* Englewood Cliffs, N.J.: Prentice Hall.

Hill, Kevin A., Susan A. MacManus, and Dario Moreno, eds. 2004. *Florida's Politics: Ten Media Markets, One Powerful State.* Tallahassee: Florida Institute of Government.

Huckshorn, Robert J. 1998. "Introduction." In *Government and Politics in Florida*, edited by Robert J. Huckshorn, 2nd ed., 1–9. Gainesville: University Press of Florida.

MacManus, Susan A. 1995. "Taxing and Spending Policies: A Generational Perspective." *Journal of Politics* 57, no. 3: 607–29.

———. 1996. *The Widening Gap between Florida's Public Schools and Their Communities.* Tallahassee: James Madison Institute.

Rosenbaum, Walter, and James Button. 1995. "Is There a Gray Peril? Retirement Politics in Florida." *Gerontologist* 29, no. 3: 300–306.

State Comprehensive Plan Committee. 1987. *Keys to Florida's Future: Winning in a Competitive World.* Tallahassee: State Comprehensive Plan Committee to the State of Florida.

2

Political Culture and Political Attitudes in Florida

SUZANNE L. PARKER AND TERRI L. TOWNER

Discussions of political culture have a long tradition in the United States dating back to Alexis de Tocqueville's (1999) visit to describe democracy in America in 1831. He was surprised at the degree to which equalitarianism pervaded the country and affected social interactions as well as political discourse. The citizenry he described was engaged in politics, taking part in town meetings that made major civic decisions. Other accounts of early America make similar observations about the equality among citizens in their social and political interactions (see Lipset 1979, Chapter 3). More recently, studies of political culture have fallen into two camps. The first of these emphasizes the attitudes, opinions, and behaviors of citizens as constituting political culture. The second camp emphasizes the relationship of the citizenry to the government, expectations about government, and practices in policy making. This research focuses on regional differences rather than individual differences (Erikson, Wright, and McIver 1996).

One of the earliest attempts to systematically examine political culture using public opinion data was Gabriel Almond's and Sidney Verba's *The Civic Culture* (1965). In the aftermath of World War II, they were motivated to study the issue of stable democracy and what population characteristics contributed to the stability of countries such as Great Britain and the United States. They questioned why democracy in Germany and Italy had not withstood the challenges of the 1920s and 1930s as the other two democracies had. To examine this problem, they conducted surveys of the population in five democracies (adding Mexico to the four countries mentioned previously).

The authors traced the origins of the concept of a "civic culture" over time, including the earliest civilizations, the Greeks (Plato and Aristotle), the Enlightenment and liberal thought, and the twentieth-century additions to the study of the social sciences including sociology and social psychology (Almond and Verba 1980). They coupled theories of stable democracy with modern survey methodology to research the relationship between citizens and their political systems. Their underlying idea is that the psychological orientations people hold about the political system are important in determining the stability of democratic systems: "The term 'political culture' thus refers to the specifically political orientations—attitudes toward the political system and its various parts, and attitudes toward the role of the self in the system." (Almond and Verba 1965, 12).

In the course of their research, they assessed such attitudes and behaviors as awareness and interest in politics, feelings and expectations about government, attitudes toward political parties and their supporters, a sense of civic obligation and competence, and allegiance. Subsequent research expands the definition of political culture to include behaviors that are related to values and support for the political system: "Political culture . . . is a historical system of widespread, fundamental, behavioral, political values . . . held by system members" (Devine 1972, 17–18). The work of David Easton (1965) added to our understanding of the idea of support for the political system. According to Easton, political culture underlies the political system and maintains a reservoir of support for the government so that it can take unpopular policy actions without risking overthrow or revolt. Two types of support are relevant—specific support and diffuse support. Specific support is trust in political officials who currently hold office. Diffuse support is directed toward the political system and the political institutions that constitute that system. It reflects an individual's support for the institutions and rules that make up the political system and demonstrates the belief that they are legitimate and deserving of trust. This type of support is most important to maintaining political stability. Easton (1965) defines supportive political behaviors as signs of overt support for the political system.

Daniel J. Elazar (1984) offers the second approach to the study of political culture. He expands on the concept by asserting that because our constitution limits the exercise of power by the federal government and because of the nature of our federal system, state governments have developed and operated within their own political cultures. His research identifies three distinctive political cultures that vie for dominance in the states—moralistic, individualistic, and traditionalistic. These cultures differ from one another in several ways, including the goals of government action, who should participate in politics, the role of parties, and the discourse at elections.

In a moralistic political culture, Elazar explains, government is seen as a means of achieving a good society. This goal is accomplished through direct government action. Politics are a civic responsibility in this orientation, and the role of elected officials is to serve the general good. It is everyone's civic obligation to participate in government. At elections, parties compete for office on the basis of issues.

In an individualistic political culture, competition between the parties is not about issues but about the distribution of benefits from government. Politicians are expected to pursue their own interests and those of their supporters. The goal of the political system is to clear the way for individuals to pursue their own self-interest. Government does not take an activist stance in the sense that it does not take the initiative to propose policy; instead, it waits for significant public demands for extra services from citizens.

In the traditionalistic culture, the government's goal is to maintain the existing social, political, and economic power structure. This is an elitist orientation in which government initiates only the policies designed to promote the interests of the governmental and economic elite. In this perspective, politics is viewed negatively and participation is a privilege rather than a right. Only the elite should be allowed to participate in politics in a traditionalistic political culture.

According to Elazar (1984), southern states adopted a traditionalistic culture that discouraged large portions of the population from participating in elections. Both whites and blacks were disenfranchised to ensure that elites would control government and politics. However, because of migration to southern states by citizens who carried their own political orientations with them from other places, most southern political cultures show a mix of political orientations. Hence, Elazar characterizes the political culture of Florida as a mixture of traditionalistic and individualistic cultures.

According to the individualistic and traditionalistic perspectives, politics is viewed as negative at best and as corrupt at worst. It is not expected that government will make life easier for the poor or minorities. Neither perspective supports an activist role for government; both prefer limited government. Both perspectives see politicians as self-interested individuals who promote the interests of a limited segment of the population rather than the general good of the entire population. According to Elazar, individualistic and traditionalistic perspectives both tend to promote the interests of upper-status groups.

If Elazar's description of Florida's political culture is accurate, it would be expected that the majority of Floridians would hold mostly negative attitudes about government and politics. The majority would be expected to be distrusting of both state and federal governments. Floridians would not be expected to hold politicians in high regard because elected officials would be expected to act primarily in their own best interest. Since legislative bodies would comprise primarily self-seeking individuals, we would not expect Floridians to view them very positively either.

Most conceptualizations of government expect political culture to remain fairly stable because it is assumed that the attitudes that constitute political culture are taught when children learn other attitudes. That is, political attitudes are passed from generation to generation—through parents, teachers, schools, and the media to children. Public schools are particularly influential in passing on political values and attitudes that promote allegiance to the political system. The fact that political support is taught and that values are passed from one generation to the next gives great stability to a democracy because it assures continuity in beliefs and assures that there will be little conflict over basic values. We examine these attitudes because despite the tendency toward stability, events, policies, and people can change even consensual values and attitudes. For that reason, it is also possible for citizens' attitudes about government and elected officials to change substantially.

Since 1950, southern states have undergone significant changes in population; large numbers of people have migrated in and out of the region. The rules about who was and who was not allowed to participate in government and make political decisions have changed dramatically. The attitude of the federal government toward southern state governments changed in important ways over that time period. The federal government's intervention in the matter of race relations, an area that previously was considered to be strictly the domain of state politics, caused much resentment among southerners. With this action, the federal government significantly changed the relationship between state governments and their citizens, especially black and other minority citizens. It changed how the political parties appealed to southern voters, and over the course of these decades, changes in the parties' stands led to an alteration in partisan attachments in the South. Many of these changes were imposed on a reluctant white population. The civil rights movement, the Civil Rights Act, and the Voting Rights Act changed relationships between black and white southerners and changed the rules of the political game in the South.

Florida has been as subject to these changes as other southern states. The population of the state has doubled since the 1980s due in large part to the in-migration from other parts of the United States, Central and South America, and the Caribbean. The civil rights movement significantly altered the role of blacks in society and politics in Florida, just as it did in other parts of the south. Blacks had previously been segregated and disenfranchised in Florida, just as they had been in other southern states, and the Civil Rights Act and the Voting Rights Act altered those restrictions. In light of these changes in the relationship of southern citizens to southern state and local governments and of the federal intervention to bring about these changes, it is very likely that the attitudes that reflect the political culture of the state have been in flux. Stable attitudes such as party identification appear to have changed significantly during this time period. For this reason it is important to examine the attitudes that constitute what has been defined as "political culture"—attitudes about government, elected officials, political parties, values, and issues dealing with the scope of government action.

This chapter first looks at public opinion on key questions for Florida's political culture. The question of whether Floridians trust the state and federal government is addressed in the first section. The chapter then moves to an examination of citizens' evaluations of the performance of federal and state government and legislative institutions such as the U.S. Congress and the state legislature and evaluations of elected officials between 1980 and 2003. Citizen behaviors and attitudes that show support for the political system, such as political participation and interest in politics, serve in this chapter as indicators of citizen involvement in government and politics. The chapter's examination of public opinion in Florida shifts to changes over the last two decades in partisanship, ideology, stances on issues, and attitudes toward taxes. When possible, Floridians' attitudes are compared to those of all Americans. Relevant differences between Florida regions are examined as well. The goal of this chapter is to evaluate the changes that have taken place in the political culture of Florida since 1980 by tracing the development of citizen attitudes and behaviors over time.

The data in this chapter come from annual statewide public opinion surveys with Florida residents eighteen and older conducted from 1980 through 2003 (excluding 1998) by the Survey Research Laboratory at Florida State University. The telephone interviews were conducted with randomly selected respondents by paid interviewers calling from a central site.[1]

Floridians' Views of Government and Public Officials

To measure feelings of support for and alienation from government, a question was developed to measure diffuse support for the political system. It asks how frequently the individual trusts the state/federal government in Tallahassee/Washington, D.C., to do what is right. The provided response categories are "almost always," "most of the time," "only some of the time," and "never." The questions about the performance of specific politicians use the same format.

When the questions about trust that the University of Michigan used to

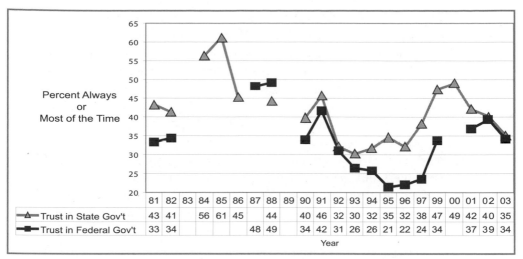

Figure 2.1. Floridians' Trust in Florida State Government and the Federal Government, 1981–2003.
Question: How much of the time do you think you can trust the Florida state/Federal government to do what is right: just about always, most of the time, only some of the time, never? *Source:* Florida Annual Policy Surveys, Survey Research Laboratory, Florida State University.

measure Americans' support for the federal government in the American National Election Studies (ANES) surveys are tracked over time, a significant decline in trust can be detected by 1972. Prior to 1974, from 53 (1972) to 76 percent (1964) of the U. S. public said they trusted the federal government to do what is right almost always and most of the time. Prior to 1974 (1958–1972), on average 64 percent of the American public trusted the federal government almost always or most of the time; after 1972, trust levels fell to the 35 percent range. Trust levels have never recovered to the pre-1974 levels, but in 2002, after the 9/11 incident, the percent of Americans who said that they trusted the federal government almost always or most of the time rose to 56 percent. It is apparent this was a temporary spike, however, since trust levels declined once again to 47 percent in 2004 (American National Election Studies 2006).

Among Florida residents, the trends in trust in the federal government and trust in the state government are quite similar (Parker 1998). In the 1980s, an average of 41 percent of Floridians trusted the federal government always or most of the time; this dropped to an average of 29 percent of Floridians who expressed that level of trust in the 1990s and then rebounded in the 2000s to an average of 37 percent (see Figure 2.1). In the 1990s, trust in the federal government was on average 8 percentage points lower than trust in state government. The high points for trust in the federal government were in 1987 and 1988, at the end of Ronald Reagan's second term.

The comparable national averages for all Americans can be found in the American National Election Studies. In the 1980s, 36 percent of Americans said that they trusted the federal government always or most of the time. This figure dropped to 30 percent in the 1990s and rose to 49 percent in the 2000s. Thus, during the 1980s and 1990s the percentage of Floridians who expressed high levels of trust in the federal government was similar to the comparable national average. The percentages expressing high levels of support in the 2000s were 12 percentage points higher among all Americans than among Floridians. However, the data in 2002 show an extremely high level of trust followed by a decline in 2004. This may be the result of the patriotic feelings engendered by 9/11 (Parker 1995).

Floridians grew more cynical and alienated from state government in the 1990s and 2000s, just as they did about the federal government: An average of 49 percent of state residents said they trusted the state government always or most of the time to do what is right during the 1980s, but only an average of 37 percent felt that way in the 1990s; that statistic increased slightly to 42 percent in the 2000s (see Figure 2.1). Observing the patterns over time reveals that the period of the highest levels of trust occurred during Bob Graham's second term as governor in 1984 and 1985. The next-highest levels of trust in state government were recorded during Jeb Bush's first term as governor in 1999 and 2000.

Floridians also tended to trust political leaders more than political institutions to do the right thing. For example, in 1988, the Florida Annual Policy Survey included questions designed to measure trust in specific public officials and national institutions; they showed that a larger proportion of the public trusted U. S. senator Bob Graham (73 percent trusted him always or most of the time), their U.S. representative (67 percent trusted him or her always or most of the time), and President Reagan (61 percent trusted him always or most of the time) to do what was right. These figures were higher than the comparable statistics measuring trust in most political institutions. The U.S. Supreme Court secured the highest level of trust (67 percent trusted it almost always or most of the time), the executive branch the second highest level (50 percent), and Congress the lowest (44 percent always or most of the time).

Next we turn to evaluations of the performance of elected officials, the Florida legislature, and the U.S. Congress. Here citizens were asked to rate the performance of the elected official or institution as excellent, good, fair, or poor. Performance evaluations are measures of specific rather than diffuse

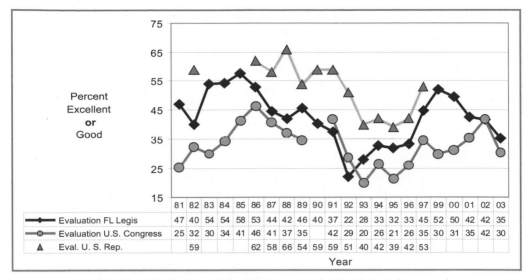

	81	82	83	84	85	86	87	88	89	90	91	92	93	94	95	96	97	99	00	01	02	03
Evaluation FL Legis	47	40	54	54	58	53	44	42	46	40	37	22	28	33	32	33	45	52	50	42	42	35
Evaluation U.S. Congress	25	32	30	34	41	46	41	37	35		42	29	20	26	21	26	35	30	31	35	42	30
Eval. U. S. Rep.		59				62	58	66	54	59	59	51	40	42	39	42	53					

Year

Figure 2.2. Floridians' Evaluations of the U.S. Congress, the Florida Legislature, and Florida's U. S. Representatives, 1981–2003.
Questions: How would you rate the job the U.S. Congress/Florida Legislature is doing? How would you rate the job your representative in the U.S. House of Representatives has been doing: excellent, good, fair, or poor? *Source:* Florida Annual Policy Surveys, Survey Research Laboratory, Florida State University.

support since they focus on specific behavior over a measurable time period. They focus on the current officials holding office. Easton (1965) suggests that specific support has different consequences than diffuse support does. If specific support for incumbent officials declines, people will be motivated to vote those officials out of office. If diffuse support decreases and alienation increases, people may be motivated to replace the current governmental structures.

Since 1980, less than half the public evaluated the performance of the Florida legislature and the U.S. Congress as excellent or good, although in the 1980s the Florida legislature was generally held in higher regard than Congress (see Figure 2.2). Between 1980 and 1989, an average of 49 percent of the Florida public rated the state legislature's performance as excellent or good. According to the American National Election Studies, however, the national average in the 1980s for approval of the performance of Congress was higher (51 percent) than the same evaluation by Floridians (36 percent). After 1990, the trend changed in Florida and at the national level. Floridians' evaluations of legislative institutions fell sharply, and evaluations of the two institutions began to converge; an average of 36 percent of the public rated the Florida legislature positively and 29 percent rated the U.S. Congress favorably. An average of 58 percent of all Americans reported that they disapproved of the performance of Congress during the 1990s. During the 2000s, the evaluations of Congress surged after the 9/11 terrorist incident; 42 percent of Floridians and 65 percent of Americans gave it positive evaluations in 2002 (the year the first surveys were completed after 9/11). However, these ratings declined to more normal levels in 2003 in Florida (30 percent evaluating congressional performance positively) and at the national level (53 percent) (American National Election Studies 2006).

Following a tendency observed on the national level, Florida residents evaluated the performance of their own representatives more highly than they did the institution of Congress (Parker 1986). For example, 59 percent of residents in 1982 rated the job done by their representatives as excellent or good, but only 30 percent rated the performance of Congress as high. Rating the performance of the state's representatives higher than the performance of Congress is a consistent trend among Floridians. This seeming paradox can be explained by observing that people use different criteria to evaluate Congress and their representatives (Parker and Davidson 1979; Parker 1986; Hibbing and Theiss-Morse 1995). "Congressmen are expected to serve and communicate with constituents, but for Congress as an institution, citizens expect the resolution of pressing national problems" (Parker 1986, 3). Floridians who rated Reagan's job performance as excellent or good tended to rate Congress similarly. It appears that if Reagan had been less popular in the state during this time period, the ratings of Congress might have been even lower (Parker 1986). In sum, while the performance of incumbent officials generally received high ratings, Floridians generally rated the performance of legislative institutions as fair or poor. The public apparently applies different standards to public institutions and to public officials.

Among Floridians, President Ronald Reagan and Governor Bob Graham were the two most highly evaluated incumbents since 1980 (see Figure 2.3). An average of 62 percent of the Florida public evaluated Reagan's performance as excellent or good; similarly, 61 percent of the Florida public gave George H. W. Bush positive ratings. The ratings for Bill Clinton contrasted sharply with those for Reagan and Bush; an average of only 39 percent of the Florida public rated Clinton as excellent or good. Some caution should be used in assessing evaluations of Clinton, however, since there are no evaluations for 1998–2000. It is possible that focusing on his first term and the absence of evaluations of three years of his second term biased his evaluations downward.

Finally, evaluations of George W. Bush's performances are lower than those for Reagan and George H. Bush but higher than evaluations of Clin-

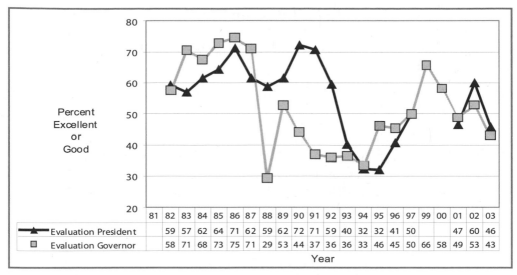

	81	82	83	84	85	86	87	88	89	90	91	92	93	94	95	96	97	99	00	01	02	03
▲ Evaluation President		59	57	62	64	71	62	59	62	72	71	59	40	32	32	41	50			47	60	46
☐ Evaluation Governor		58	71	68	73	75	71	29	53	44	37	36	36	33	46	45	50	66	58	49	53	43

Year

Figure 2.3. Floridians' Performance Ratings of the U.S. President and Florida's Governor, 1982–2003.
Question: How would you rate the job that (NAME OF PERSON) is doing as president/ governor: excellent, good, fair, or poor? *Note:* Positive evaluations during 1990, 1991, and 2002 may be inflated because these surveys were conducted during a war or after the 9/11 terrorist incident. *Source:* Florida Annual Policy Surveys, Survey Research Laboratory, Florida State University.

ton. An average of 54 percent of Floridians evaluated George W. Bush's performance as president as excellent or good between 2001 and 2003. These figures might be inflated because the 2002 evaluation came soon after the 9/11 terrorist attack, which significantly elevated his evaluations. (The same was true during his father's term in 1990 and 1991 during the Gulf War. His evaluations in this period were exceptionally high but dropped at the end of the conflict. By 1993, his ratings were more similar to the period prior to the start of the war.) In 2001 and 2003, George W. Bush's evaluations were about 14 percentage points lower than in 2002. John Mueller (1970) calls the inflation of a president's popularity during national crises a "rally around the flag" effect. It has been shown to reflect patriotism and support for the country rather than evaluations of actual presidential performance (Parker 1995).

Floridians have given Florida's governors differing evaluations as well. Governor Bob Graham's rating, for instance, was markedly higher than that of his successors. An average of 69 percent of Floridians rated Graham's performance positively (1980–1987 in Figure 2.3, where the 1987 rating is a review of the previous four years). By contrast, only 41 percent of Florida's public gave positive ratings to Bob Martinez's performance (1987–1991, where 1991 was a review of his four years in office) and 41 percent to Lawton Chiles during his term (1992–1997 surveys). Jeb Bush has been given significantly higher evaluations by the Florida public than his two predecessors—an average of 54 percent of the Florida public ranked his performance as excellent or good (1999–2003).

The trends in all the time series examined here were similar. The most positive ratings were given in the 1980s and evaluations were significantly lower in the 1990s. Most measures showed some recovery in the late 1990s but declined again after that. The second half of the 1990s were the low points for all the measures examined—the lowest trust levels, the lowest evaluations for institutions and officials. The second trend in this data is that elected officials received higher evaluations and support than political institutions. Levels of support for institutions are under 45 percent over the entire period (1981–2003). This means that a sizeable majority of individuals in the state expressed lack of support for political institutions. In sum, on most of the measures investigated thus far, support of political institutions and the political system are not particularly high. It is clear that overwhelming levels of support are not necessary to create stability in political systems.

Floridians' Interest in and Participation in Politics

Another measure of the health of a political system is the degree to which citizens are motivated to become involved in politics. This would correspond to Easton's (1965) concept of overt support for the political system. The first measure Easton examined, voter registration, has been a significant obstacle to participation in elections. Participation rates in elections in the United States are lower than in most democracies worldwide. Part of the cause of the low participation rates is the elaborate registration system most state governments use; these systems tend to discourage individuals with lower socioeconomic status and those with low interest in politics from participating in elections.

After the 1992 election, legislation allowing voter registration at state motor vehicle offices was designed to reduce the burden of registration. The trend in this measure should show an increase over time if this legislation encouraged participation, and registration did climb over the period. The mean percentage of Floridians registered in the 1980s was 75 percent; that figure rose to 80 percent in the 1990s and to 83 percent in the 2000s. There appears to be a significant increase in registration in the state that coincides with the implementation of the new legislation. Registration rates in Florida

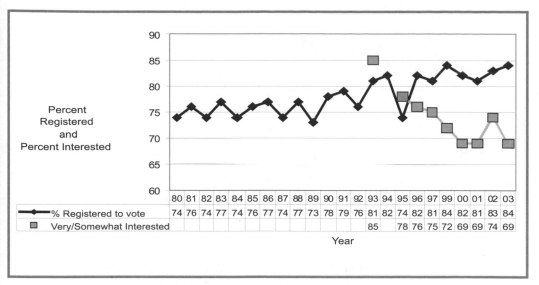

Figure 2.4. Percent of Floridians Who Registered to Vote and Were Interested in Politics, 1980–2003.
Questions: Some people seem to follow what's going on in government and public affairs most of the time, and others aren't that interested. How interested are you in the national government in Washington, and national politics: very interested, somewhat interested, a little interested, or not at all interested? At present are you registered to vote in Florida? *Source:* Florida Annual Policy Surveys, Survey Research Laboratory, Florida State University.

are at all-time highs compared to earlier decades. Nationally, registration rose after 1992, when new laws made it easier to register, to an average of 83 percent of Americans registered after the passage of the so-called motor-voter registration laws (American National Election Studies 2006). The results of that law are even more visible in the national average for the 2000s, when 86 percent of Americans had registered to vote. This is 3 percentage points higher than in Florida for a similar time period.

Paradoxically, interest in politics declined over this time period as well. In the 1990s, a mean of 77 percent of the Florida public responded that they were very or somewhat interested in national politics (see Figure 2.4). In the 2000s, this dropped to 70 percent who expressed an interest in national politics. Surveyors asked respondents about their level of interest in state politics much less frequently than they asked about interest in national politics, but in the years this question was asked, the trend was similar to interest in national politics. According to the Florida Annual Policy Surveys

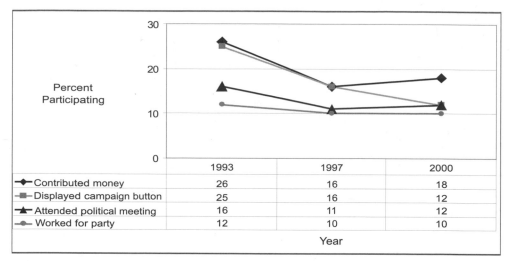

Figure 2.5. Percent of Floridians Who Participated in Political Campaigns, 1993, 1997, and 2000.
Questions: Have you contributed money to or bought tickets to help a political party or candidate? Have you worn a campaign button or put a campaign sticker on your car? Attended a political meeting, dinner, or rally? Have you done any other work for a party, candidate, or issue? *Source:* Florida Annual Policy Surveys, Survey Research Laboratory, Florida State University.

in 1999 and 2000, 68 percent were very or somewhat interested in state politics; in 2002, 67 percent were very or somewhat interested; and in 2003, 59 percent were very or somewhat interested in state politics.

Another measure of overt behavior that is supportive of the political system is involvement in political campaigns. Because this type of activity takes far more time and commitment than registering to vote, it is to be expected that a much smaller proportion of the population will be engaged in this activity than will be registered to vote or than will actually vote. These activities were measured less frequently over time than registration was; there are only three time points that can be compared—1993, 1997, and 2000 (see Figure 2.5). Of the four measures of campaign activity, two declined significantly between 1993 and 2000: the percent of people who contributed money to a candidate or political party and the percent who displayed a campaign button or bumper sticker. The percent who attended a political meeting or rally dropped, but this decline may not be statistically significant. The percent of those who worked for a candidate or party remained stable. While voter registration went up over the last two and a half decades, other measures of political involvement declined or held steady.

Party Identification, Ideology, Stands on Ideas, and Attitudes toward Taxing

Another aspect of political culture is the degree to which consensus exists about political attitudes and political loyalties. Conflict, polarization, and declining support mark political systems under stress because of political divisions. For example, party identification can either unite or divide the public; when there is consensus on party identification, one political party generally dominates politics, as the Democrats did in southern states from the end of the Civil War to the 1980s. A decline in support for the dominant party can lead to greater volatility in elections and political outcomes. When partisan divisions also coincide with ideological differences, the conflict and volatility in politics can be exacerbated. Finally, conflict within the populace may be caused by particular issues that divide supporters and opponents into opposing camps. Issues such as abortion, school prayer, assistance to minorities, and government assistance have the potential to be very divisive. Any analysis of political culture that did not include a discussion of partisanship, ideology, and the stands people take on issues would not be complete.

Additionally, policy preferences affect legislation passed nationally and at the state level and provide insight into future actions. Public officials find it difficult to ignore the public when legislation is created in areas where citizens hold strong opinions. Several studies have demonstrated the effects of public opinion on policy at the state and national levels (for example, Erikson 1976; Page and Shapiro 1983; Erikson, Wright, and McIver 1996); some have shown that changes in the public's preferences bring about policy changes (Page and Shapiro 1983). However, these studies caution that public attitudes are most likely to influence issues that are widely known and important to the public. In addition, substantial and sustained shifts in attitudes are most likely to bring about policy changes (Page and Shapiro 1983).

The relative ease with which the public can make their preferences known through the amending process in Florida means that if politicians disregard public opinion for too long, policy decisions can be taken out of their hands. Since 1980, the amending process has been used for a variety of purposes, including to mandate English as the official language, to assign responsibility for the cleanup of the Everglades, to institute a three-day waiting period for handgun purchases, to change the dates for convening the legislature, to set the size of nets and the areas that can be used by commercial fishermen, to set term limits on elected officials, and to set class sizes for primary and secondary schools. Unsuccessful attempts have been made to use the amending process to legalize casino gambling and restrict abortion. As this illustrates, elected officials and those who seek to influence policy operate within the confines of public opinion and ignore it at their peril. Clearly, whichever party commands the largest number of adherents affects who wins elections, and what Floridians think about policy issues influences the decisions that are made. This section focuses on the Florida public's attachment to the political parties, ideological stances, and attitudes on political issues facing the state and nation.

Partisan Preferences

Political scientists have described party identification as a psychological attachment to a political party (Campbell, Converse, Miller, and Stokes 1960; Green, Palmquist, and Schickler 2002). Once an individual develops this bond, it tends to remain fairly stable over his or her lifetime. That is, such orientations do not change much under normal circumstances. Yet significant changes in the party identifications of Floridians appeared during the 1980s that have persisted into the 1990s and 2000s (see Table 2.1). In looking at party identification, we compare changes among all Floridians at the beginning and at the end of the series (1980 and 2003). We also compare the average percent of Floridians who are Republicans and Democrats in each ten-year interval—1980s, 1990s, 2000s.

The percentage of Floridians who identified themselves as Republicans grew between 1980 and 2003 from 21 percent Republican in 1980 to 31 percent Republican in 2003 (see Table 2.1). The average percentage of Republicans in Florida was 33 percent in the 1980s, 36 percent in the 1990s, and 33 percent in the 2000s. At the same time, the percentage of Democrats decreased between 1980 and 2003. The average percentage of Democrats in the 1980s was 38 percent, 31 percent in the 1990s, and 35 percent in the 2000s. About a third of the public said they were independents during this period.

Thus, at the beginning of the 1980s, prior to the election of Ronald Reagan, Florida Democrats enjoyed a two-to-one advantage over Republicans among all Floridians (21 percent Republican to 45 percent Democrat). The shift to parity in the number of Democrats and Republicans led to close elections and divided control of the state legislature in the early 1990s. Both houses of the legislature came under Republican control after the 1996 election, a historic turnabout. And in 1998, Jeb Bush was elected governor, giving Republicans control of both the executive and legislative branches for

Table 2.1. Party Identification in Florida, 1980–2003, by Percent

Question: Generally speaking, do you think of yourself as a Republican, a Democrat, an independent, or what?[1]

Year	All Floridians			White Floridians			Black Floridians		
	Rep	Ind	Dem	Rep	Ind	Dem	Rep	Ind	Dem
1980	21	34	45	23	35	42	4	21	76
1981	29	31	40	30	33	37	8	19	73
1982	33	27	41	34	28	37	8	12	80
1983	29	29	42	62	30	38	4	22	74
1984	30	30	40	32	32	36	4	14	82
1985[2]	36	29	36	38	31	32	9	9	83
1986	38	30	32	41	30	29	6	29	65
1987	37	31	33	40	34	27	9	8	83
1988	35	30	35	38	31	31	10	17	74
1989	42	24	33	46	25	29	6	23	72
1990	40	28	32	43	29	29	13	23	64
1991	32	36	32	36	37	27	2	27	70
1992	37	36	28	39	35	25	8	40	52
1993	33	35	32	36	36	29	9	30	61
1994	33	34	32	36	35	29	11	26	64
1995	39	34	27	43	33	24	8	35	57
1996	40	29	32	44	27	29	7	35	58
1997	36	31	33	40	31	29	2	30	68
1999	35	31	35	39	30	31	6	32	63
2000	35	30	35	39	31	30	4	26	70
2001	30	30	40	34	31	36	4	18	78
2002	35	32	33	41	29	30	3	36	61
2003	31	35	34	34	35	30	7	30	63
Average									
1980–89	33		38						
1990–99	36		31						
2000–03	33		35						

Source: Florida Annual Policy Surveys, Survey Research Laboratory, Florida State University.
Notes: 1. Those who mentioned some other party or who said they didn't know were excluded from the analysis.
2. The 1985 data are weighted to provide a representation of blacks that is similar to those of previous years.

the first time since Reconstruction. Yet the continued competitiveness of Florida politics was demonstrated in the 2000 presidential election.

Floridians' attitudes were consistent with national samples that reported 23 percent of Americans identifying as Republicans in 1980, increasing to 30 percent in 2002, while those identifying as Democrats dropped from 42 percent in 1980 to 33 percent in 2004. The average percentage of Republicans was 26 percent in the 1980s, 27 percent in the 1990s, and 24 percent in the 2000s. The average percentage of Democrats in the 1980s was 40 percent,

37 percent in the 1990s, and 33 percent in the 2000s. Americans identifying as independents remained stable during this period—34 percent in the 1980s, 36 percent in the 1990s, and 38 percent in the 2000s (American National Election Studies 2006).

The changes in party attachments in Florida over the last twenty years have sparked speculation about their causes and long-term consequences. Some in the state believe that these changes mark the beginning of a realignment of party loyalty that would give the advantage to Republicans in state politics in much the same way that Democrats had been favored from the Civil War until the 1980s. Many of the changes in Florida reflect trends common to the South, where the Republican Party has become more competitive (Black and Black 2002). However, as political scientist V. O. Key Jr. (1949), pointed out in the 1940s, voters in Florida characteristically display political behavior that differs from that of their southern neighbors: They practice candidate-centered politics and respond more to personalities and promises than to party loyalty or platforms.

An example of this difference is evident in Figure 2.6, which shows the growth in the percentage of those who identified as Republican in Florida and Georgia and in the United States as a whole. During the 1990s the percent of those who identified as Republican in Florida ranged from 31 to 38, whereas in neighboring Georgia the percent of Republican identifiers did not reach 30 until 2001. The growth was greater and occurred earlier in Florida, which is considered part of the periphery south, than it did in Georgia, which is considered part of the Deep South. (See Black and Black 2002 for changes in partisanship in the periphery and Deep South.) In Florida, the percentage of Republican identifiers reached one-third of the population in the 1980s (See Figure 2.6). By the last time point that has been measured (2004), the percent of Republican identifiers in Florida and Georgia had converged with the corresponding percent in the country as a whole—around one-third of the population.

Another indicator that Key's observation still applies is apparent in a comparison of the outcomes of state and national elections. Floridians have elected both Republican (Martinez and Jeb Bush for two terms) and Democratic (Graham and Chiles for two terms each) governors since the 1980s, and they have divided their votes for senator between Democrats (Graham and Nelson) and Republicans (Hawkins, Mack, and Martinez). Thus, caution should be used in ascribing the recent changes in party identification to a realignment of party loyalties. The Republican victory in the legislature in the 1996 election came at the same time that the state's electoral votes went to a Democratic presidential candidate. Four years later, the 2000 presi-

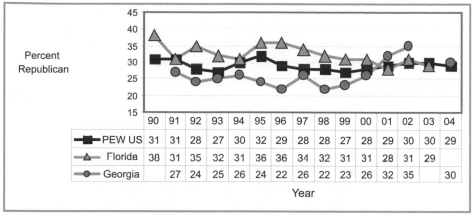

	90	91	92	93	94	95	96	97	98	99	00	01	02	03	04
PEW US	31	31	28	27	30	32	29	28	28	27	28	29	30	30	29
Florida	38	31	35	32	31	36	36	34	32	31	31	28	31	29	
Georgia		27	24	25	26	24	22	26	22	23	26	32	35		30

Figure 2.6. Percent of U.S., Florida, and Georgia Voters Who Are Republican, 1990–2004. Questions: For Florida and the Pew survey: Generally speaking, do you think of yourself as a Republican, a Democrat, an Independent or what? For Georgia: Do you usually think of yourself as a Democrat, a Republican, an Independent, or something else? *Source:* The U.S. data are from The Pew Research Center for the People and the Press, The Pew Research Center. The Georgia data are from The Georgia Poll, Survey Research Center, University of Georgia. The Florida data are from the Florida Annual Policy Survey, Survey Research Laboratory, Florida State University.

dential race was so close that in the end the election was decided by the U.S. Supreme Court. It seems unlikely this is a realigned electorate, since the percentage of the electorate who self-identifies as independent remains high, even among such party-loyal groups as blacks (who identified as independents at an average rate of 31 percent in the 1990s and 27 percent in the 2000s, compared to an average of 17 percent in the 1980s). These numbers seem to portend competitive races well into the future. At this point, neither party can command a majority on the basis of the number of their party adherents alone, and each must appeal to independents to secure a victory. Republicans grew more adept at doing this in the 1990s and 2000s on both the state and national levels

In examining the changes in party identification, it is useful to compare the party preferences of black and white Floridians because the changes in each group over the decades have differed significantly (see Table 2.1). The growth of Republicanism among whites has been notable. Even among blacks, who have been strong Democrats since at least the 1960s, preferences have changed. During the 1980s an overwhelming majority identified with the Democrats, but in the 1990s and into the 2000s, the percentage of independent blacks has grown substantially. The percentage of Democrats among blacks declined 13 points between 1980 and 2003.

A study of the sources of change in party identification among whites in the state suggests that the shifts occurred across income, education, and ideological groups and among migrants as well as those born in the United States (Parker 1988, 1992). Patterns in party identification indicate that strong forces during the period drove all groups in the white population toward the Republican Party. Reagan's popularity among whites in the 1980s was a major factor behind the changes. The economic problems of the early 1980s appear to have affected Reagan's early evaluations, but after 1983, the percentage of white Floridians who rated his job performance as excellent or good never dropped below 50. In 1989, 61 percent of Floridians said they thought Reagan had done an excellent or good job in his last four years in office. (Ronald Reagan and Dwight D. Eisenhower are the only recent U.S. presidents who were as popular with the American public when they left office as they were when they were inaugurated.)

These high evaluations are significantly related to the increase in the number of Floridians who identified themselves as Republicans (Parker 1988, 1992). That is, not only did people who gave Reagan top evaluations tend to identify with the Republican Party, but the tie grew so strong during the Reagan years that it was the most important factor influencing citizens' choice of party during the decade. As Black and Black (2002) note, Reagan made it respectable for southerners to call themselves Republicans. The growth in Republican identifiers reached its nadir in the first year of George H. W. Bush's term (42 percent identified as Republican in 1989 among the entire population and 46 percent among whites only). Since that time, growth in the percentage of the Florida populace that identifies as Republican has stalled (see Table 2.1).

An additional contributing factor to the decline in the percentage of Floridians who identify as Democrats was the migration to Florida of people from other areas of the United States. Florida's in-migrants since 1960 have tended to be more Republican than Democratic in their identification, while those who moved to the state before 1960 were more attached to the Democratic than to the Republican Party in the 1980s. Further, the large number of new state residents during the 1980s reduced the proportion of total citizens who identified more strongly with Democrats, long-term residents (those who relocated prior to 1960) and native Floridians, those born and raised in Florida (Parker, 1988, 1992; Sly, Serow, and Calhoun 1989). Both the influx of new residents, who were more Republican, and the decline in the proportion of the population displaying the strongest ties to the Democrats reduced the number of people in the state who identify with the Democratic Party.

Recent immigrants have exerted less of an influence on party politics

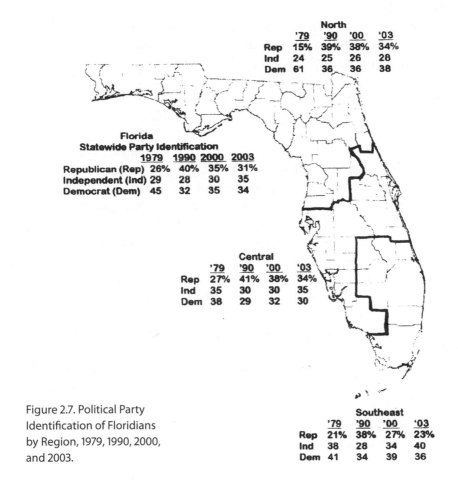

North

	'79	'90	'00	'03
Rep	15%	39%	38%	34%
Ind	24	25	26	28
Dem	61	36	36	38

Florida
Statewide Party Identification

	1979	1990	2000	2003
Republican (Rep)	26%	40%	35%	31%
Independent (Ind)	29	28	30	35
Democrat (Dem)	45	32	35	34

Central

	'79	'90	'00	'03
Rep	27%	41%	38%	34%
Ind	35	30	30	35
Dem	38	29	32	30

Southeast

	'79	'90	'00	'03
Rep	21%	38%	27%	23%
Ind	38	28	34	40
Dem	41	34	39	36

Figure 2.7. Political Party Identification of Floridians by Region, 1979, 1990, 2000, and 2003.

than their numbers might have warranted because of their tendency not to participate. "[O]ne needs to bear in mind that actual numbers (as well as percents) are important. Thus, with the number of natives and early migrants who are registered to vote outnumbering those among recent and midterm migrants by more than 2.6 to 1, the impact of the recent upturn in Republican and Independent registration among migrants is minimized" (Sly, Serow, and Calhoun 1989, 9).

One final trend in party identification should be noted. The rate of Republican identification has varied around the state. The northern part of Florida is more rural and displayed a strong tendency toward conservative Democratic leanings well into the 1980s. As Figure 2.7 illustrates, in north Florida in 1979 the ratio of those who identified with the Democratic Party to those who identified with the Republican Party was 4 to 1. The panhandle counties display the strongest ties to the old south, as this area in the past was most conducive to plantations and had high concentrations of blacks in several panhandle counties (classified by V. O. Key as Black Belt counties). This area also proved receptive to the conservative message of the Republican Party, as shown in the growth of those who identified as Republican: Democrats fell from a 4-to-1 advantage over Republicans to parity in the 1990s and 2000s.

The central portion of the state was more Republican in 1979 (27 percent identified as Republican) than the north (15 percent) and the southeastern (21 percent) portions of the state. The central and northern regions showed similar trends in the 1990s and 2000s. The one region to show a decline in Republicans was the southeast, where the percentage of those who identified as Republican dropped from 38 in 1990 to 23 in 2003. The pattern for all regions was that the percentage of those who identify as Republican grew from 1979 to 1990 and then showed no further growth in the 2000s. By 2004, Republican identifiers were about one-third of the population in all regions of the state.

The fact that both the Republicans and Democrats fail to claim a majority of identifiers in the state means that elections are closely contested. It also signals that the Republicans have become a competitive party in the state. To win elections, both the Republicans and Democrats must persuade independents to vote for their ticket or they will not win.

Ideological Orientations

The percent of Floridians that classified themselves as ideological conservatives over the period 1980–2003 remained fairly constant—ranging in the 1980s from 34 percent to 42 percent with a median (the score in the middle of this distribution)of 41 percent; ranging in the 1990s from 38 percent to 47 percent with a median of 43; and ranging from 37 percent to 42 percent in the 2000 with a median of 39 percent (see Figure 2.8). A similar proportion (a median of 43 percent in the 1980s, 41 percent in the 1990s, and 41 percent in the 2000s) identified themselves as middle of the road ideologically. Liberals constitute the smallest proportion of Floridians-a median of 16.5 percent in the 1980s, a median of 17 in the 1990s, and a median of 21 percent in the 2000s. (About one-third of the Florida public says they do not think in ideological terms; they are excluded from these calculations.) According to American National Election Studies, Floridians are similar ideologically to the American public as a whole. Americans who classify themselves as ideological conservatives constitute the largest proportion—41 percent in the

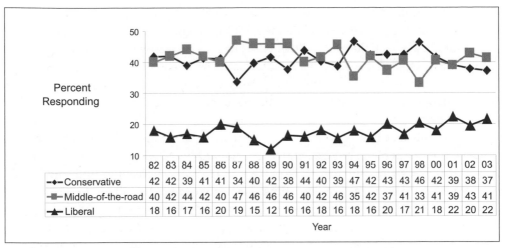

Figure 2.8. Percent of Floridians Who Identified with Conservative, Middle-of-the-Road, and Liberal Political Ideology, 1982–2003.
Question: In politics today, do you think of yourself as a liberal, a conservative, or as middle-of-the-road, or don't you think of yourself in these terms. People saying they do not think in ideological terms are excluded. *Source:* Florida Annual Policy Surveys, Survey Research Laboratory, Florida State University.

1980s, 42 percent in the 1990s, and 42 percent in the 2000s. Americans who identify as ideological liberals constitute the smallest proportion; 24 percent in the 1980s, 23 percent in the 1990s, and 28 percent in the 2000s. Those who identify as middle of the road ideologically have remained stable—32 percent in the 1980s, 34 percent in the 1990s, and 31 percent in the 2000s (American National Election Studies 2006).

In short, while Floridians' political party identification has changed significantly, their political ideology has not. A significant percentage of citizens increasingly identify with the Republican Party, and the bulk of residents remain middle of the road or conservative. Some of the changes in party identification are the result of the influx of new residents, but the most significant cause was the popularity of Ronald Reagan and George Bush in Florida during the 1980s.

Public Opinion on National and State Issues

If a conservative revolution or realignment were under way in Florida, we might expect to see some evidence of it in changes in Floridians' opinions on issues that historically divide liberals from conservatives and that currently divide Republicans and Democrats. However, citizens' attitudes on issues such as abortion, school prayer, and assistance to the poor and minorities indicate that support for moderate positions has grown while the percentage of those who hold conservative views has decreased over time. This is not what would be expected if a Republican realignment were occurring.

Between 1981 and 1995, for example, positions of Florida residents changed on whether the federal government should see to it that all citizens have a job and a good standard of living. Although the percentage of the populace that supports government assistance remained relatively constant, the percentage who felt that individuals should get ahead on their own dropped significantly, from 54 percent in 1981 to 33 percent in 1995 and 35 percent in 1997. At the same time, the percentage of Floridians who chose the middle position on the issue rose from 22 percent (1981) to 40 percent (1995) and 37 percent (1997). The national sample of American attitudes toward government assistance and standard of living differed from the attitudes of Floridians. Americans who felt that individuals should get ahead on their own changed from 49 percent in 1980 to 43 percent in 1990 and 55 percent in 2000. The percentage of individuals who held the middle position decreased slightly from 21 in 1980 and 1990 to 19 in 2000 (American National Election Studies 2006). In Florida, opposition to government help to improve the social and economic positions of blacks and other minorities changed from 38 percent in 1981 to 23 percent in 1995 and 25 percent in 1997. In contrast, American National Election Studies samples report that opposition to government aid for blacks and other minorities has risen from 48 percent in 1980 and 1990 to 55 percent in 2000. The percentage of Floridians that support the idea of government help dropped to 19 in 2000 from 26 in 1990, the highest percentage reported in the 1990s. The percentage of Floridians that support school prayer declined from 70 percent in 1981 to 60 percent in 1987, where it remained in 1995.

On abortion rights, in 1986 and again in 1990 a sizable portion of respondents asked about the conditions under which legal abortion should be available supported legal abortions for "physical" reasons—if the mother's life was seriously endangered (91 and 92 percent), if the pregnancy was the result of rape (84 and 90 percent), or if there was a chance of a defect in the baby (81 and 85 percent) (Osmond and Pavalko 1986). Floridians' attitudes concerning these conditions were similar to those nationwide and in the South as a whole. In the circumstance where the mother's health was endangered, 89 percent in both the United States and in the South supported abortion; when the pregnancy was the result of rape, 81 percent in both the United States and the South supported it; and in the case of possible birth defect, 78 percent supported it in the United States and 75 percent did so in the South.

Floridians in 1986 were more supportive of legal abortions under other conditions than the samples for the nation or the South were. For example in 1986, 54 percent of Florida residents supported legal abortions if the family was poor and could not afford more children, compared to 39 percent of in the South and 44 percent in the United States. In 1990, 64 percent of Florida's public supported abortion under these circumstances. This represented an increase of 10 percentage points over the four years from 1986 to 1990. The same pattern was repeated in 1986 and 1990 for scenarios in which the woman is unwed and does not want to marry or is married and wants no more children and for abortions for any reason (Osmond and Pavalko 1986). In 1997, when respondents were asked if they supported laws limiting a woman's ability to obtain an abortion, 63 percent opposed limitations. Over the last twenty years, a substantial majority of Floridians have consistently supported a woman's ability to get an abortion.

Regions of the state differed in their support for abortion in various circumstances. For instance, support for legal abortions was more widespread in the southeastern part of the state than in the central or northern areas. Differences were most pronounced for the "nonphysical" reasons for abortion (the mother is too poor or is not married). Residents of North Florida were least supportive of legal abortions, particularly for nonphysical reasons.

Osmond and Pavalko (1986) found that the only significant differences in support for abortion according to one's social group appeared among income and racial groups. High-income residents (those earning more than $30,000 in the 1980s) were significantly more supportive of abortion for any reason (58 percent) than were low-income residents (those earning under $15,000, 43 percent). By 1997, this difference was still significant, but the relationship was weak. In the original research, whites were more supportive than blacks of abortion for any reason (51 and 33 percent, respectively). The Florida Annual Policy Survey in 1997 shows that the relationship had disappeared by 1997, when both whites and blacks were equally opposed to restrictions on a woman's right to an abortion. Ideological and religious beliefs had the strongest impact on attitudes toward abortion; those least supportive of abortion classified themselves as conservatives and born-again Christians, two characteristics that proved more important than gender, age, marital status, income, or race (Osmond and Pavalko 1986).

Thus, Floridians' stands on national issues became more moderate and less conservative over the 1980s and 1990s, despite the shift in party identification among whites to the Republican Party. The trends in issue positions match the relative stability of ideological classifications. On the abortion issue, Floridians' attitudes tended to be similar to those held in the United States and in the South when physical circumstances for an abortion were considered, but they were more liberal than these two populations regarding social reasons for abortion.

Most Important Problems

A good indicator of the degree of consensus on what state issues are important is a question that asks respondents to spontaneously choose the most important problem facing the state (see Table 2.2). Over the last two decades when Floridians have been asked to do this, three areas have consistently been among the top four problems mentioned—crime, economic problems, and development issues. The general pattern has been that most problem areas concern the public for a period of time and then drop down on the list of concerns, sometimes because policies are enacted to address the problems and sometimes because other problems have become more pressing. As an example, economic problems were ranked among the top four problems in eighteen of the twenty-three Florida Annual Policy Surveys between 1980 and 2003, but this area was of greatest concern during the recessions in 1980–1984 and 1991–1994. When the economy improved, economic problems dropped so far down on the list of concerns that it was not ranked among the top four problems from 1999 through 2002. (Over the last twenty years, between 6 and 15 percent of the public per year have not been able to identify any problems facing the state.)

During the 1980s, Floridians worried about economic problems, crime, and growth. As Jimmy Carter's term ended and Ronald Reagan's term began, large numbers of respondents mentioned problems such as inflation and unemployment in 1980 and 1981. The recession of 1982 brought economic issues to the forefront again, and 39 percent of residents mentioned such problems as the most important facing the state in 1983. An improved economy in 1983 led economic issues to loom less large, a decline that lasted the rest of the decade. By 1989, a low percentage of respondents mentioned such concerns. Economic anxiety rose again with the recession in 1992; 23 percent mentioned economic problems in 1993. Worry over the economy did not begin to subside again until 1995.

Concern over rapid growth and the problems accompanying a mushrooming population dominated five of the six years after 1983, including

Table 2.2. Floridians' Rankings of the Four Most Important Categories of Problems Facing the State, 1980–2003, by Percent

Question: What do you think are the most important problems facing the state of Florida?

	1980	1981	1982	1983	1984	1985	1986	1987	1988	1989	1990	1991	1992	1993	1994	1995	1996	1997	1999	2000	2001	2002	2003
Crime	—	10	23	13	11	13	17	21	15	27	23	13	10	18	45	36	30	27	26	24	11	—	—
Economic	21	25	16	39	19	12	—	13	14	10	7	18	19	23	15	9	13	12	—	—	—	—	13
Social	9	17	21	10	—	10	10	—	—	10	—	—	—	14	13	20	28	16	13	18	11	12	—
Community Development	18	16	11	12	21	29	24	23	26	20	21	16	—	—	—	—	—	—	21	18	17	12	16
Environment	—	—	—	—	10	10	10	11	—	10	20	13	—	—	—	—	—	—	—	—	15	—	—
Education	—	—	—	—	—	—	—	—	—	—	—	—	26	16	9	11	22	19	23	19	26	40	40
Government	—	—	—	—	—	—	—	—	9	—	—	—	15	—	—	—	—	—	—	—	—	12	10
Energy	14	—	—	—	—	—	—	—	—	—	—	—	—	—	—	—	—	—	—	—	—	—	—

Source: Florida Annual Policy Surveys, Survey Research Laboratory, Florida State University.

complaints about traffic congestion, too many people, and too much development. The percentage of people mentioning growth jumped after 1983. In
each year that respondents were asked how big a problem they considered
growth to be, about two-thirds thought it was a problem, whether major
or minor, where they lived. Central and Southeast Florida expressed most
concern, and those in the northern region of the state expressed the least
concern. As growth tapered off in the 1990s, so did the percentage of people
mentioning this problem.

As concern over growth and its consequences grew, so did support for
exercising government control over it. In 1988, for instance, 72 percent of
the public wanted stricter laws on what a developer could do with land being developed, and about two-thirds supported the state's program to purchase endangered lands. The desire to control growth has fluctuated over
the decade: Support for regulation was higher in 1985 than in 1989 (a shift
from 70 to 54 percent who thought growth should be limited or stopped)
but rebounded in 1990 (86 percent who thought growth should be limited
or stopped). Sentiment for this option declined in the 2000s; only 64 percent of the public favored government control of growth in 2001. In a pattern similar to concern about population growth, support for limiting it was
highest in the southeastern and central regions of the state and lowest in the
north.

The problem mentioned with the greatest frequency in the twenty-three
surveys conducted between 1980 and 2003 was crime; it was among the top
four problems in every survey during this period but three (1980, 2002, and
2003). The period in which citizens expressed the greatest concern over
crime was between 1994 and 2000, when it ranked first in every year during
the time period. In most other time periods it was the second or third most
frequently mentioned problem. The percentage of residents mentioning
crime as the most important problem facing the state fluctuated frequently
between 1981 and 2000 (see Table 2.2).

Education emerged as a problem over the 1990s; starting in 1992, the
public named it as the top concern. This concern coincided with complaints
about overcrowding in South and Central Florida schools. In fact, the public
became concerned enough with education to pass a constitutional amendment in 2002 that reduced the number of students per classroom in the
state's primary and secondary schools. Along with complaints about overcrowding were concerns about the quality of educational instruction and
achievement, teachers' salaries, and teacher shortages. In 2002 and 2003,
40 percent of the public ranked education as the number one problem facing the state, suggesting that residents are not satisfied with education reforms.

Spontaneous accounts of the most important problems give a clue to what issues have captured the attention of the public. Crime, economic problems, and development dominated public concerns in the 1980s. Residents continued to worry about crime and economic problems during the 1990s, but worry about development and the environment began to wane. These problems were replaced by concern over education. In the 2000s, economic concerns are subsiding, but development reemerged as a problem in 1999 after a seven-year hiatus. It appears that concern over crime rarely recedes enough for it to drop from the list of top concerns.

Attitudes toward Taxing

The last indicator of the health and stability of a political system, be it national or state, is citizens' evaluations of taxes. Floridian's attitudes about taxing grew more moderate between 1980 and 1995, especially antitax sentiment. Anti-tax sentiment was at its height in 1979, when 32 percent of Floridians wanted taxes cut even if public services had to be cut as a result, while 60 percent supported maintaining services even if it meant paying the same taxes. By 1995, 19 percent favored reducing taxes and 71 percent preferred maintaining services; in 1996, 69 percent of the public supported maintaining services and 18 percent preferred cutting taxes.

Florida is one of the few states that has not enacted a state income tax to generate revenues to fund state government, and public support for such a measure remained low throughout the period of this study. For example, in 1982 and again in 1986, only about one-quarter of the public said they favored a state income tax. When respondents were asked the best way for the state to raise taxes if it needed to do so, 19 percent selected establishing a state income tax in 1989; this number had dropped to 11 percent by 1995. In 1989, 37 percent supported raising the sales tax and 32 percent supported extending the tax to services such as haircuts, lawyers' fees, and accounting fees, a percentage that increased to 47 percent in 1995.

Strong support for using the sales tax as a major revenue source was also reflected in the large percentage of people who felt that it was at "about the right level"; 73 percent supported this statement in 1988 just after a sales-tax increase. The percentage increased to 81 in 1980, 1983, and 1987. (The average percent of those who felt that the sales tax was at the right level in the 1980s was 78.) Between 1990 and 1999, satisfaction with the sales tax ranged from 70 to 77 percent and averaged 72 percent. However, support for this popular tax began to show declines in the 2000s, when the average percent who said the sales tax was at the right level was 70.

The percentage of the public that rated the property tax as at about the right level was significantly smaller than those who said the sales tax was at the right level, ranging from 40 to 58 percent in the 1980s (averaging 52 percent in that decade). In the 1990s and 2000s, this average declined to 46 percent who said it was at the right level.

Compared to sales and property taxes, on average fewer Floridians thought the gasoline tax was at the right level: 58 percent in the 1980s and 46 percent in the 1990s. Support for this tax has continued to decline into the 2000s. The mean level of support for the gas tax between 2000 and 2003 fell to an average of 27 percent of people who said that it was at the right level.

Many more Floridians feel that federal taxes are wasted than those who feel that state taxes are being used inefficiently. The more-limited time series for this spans from 1992 to 1997; the percentage of Floridians for this period who said the federal government wasted all or most of their tax money averaged 44 percent. In contrast, the percentage of people who thought that the state government wasted all or most of their tax dollars was considerably lower—in the 1980s the average was 14 percent. However, this number had doubled by the 1990s, when 33 percent of the Florida public said all or most of their state tax dollars were wasted. Therefore, the perception that state taxes are at the right level has been declining at the same time that the perception that taxes are being wasted has risen.

Conclusion

In this chapter we examined three types of indicators of the health of Florida's political system: support for political institutions and elected officials; consensus on partisanship, ideology, and issues; and support for the lifeblood of government, taxing. Some patterns in these indicators are noteworthy. First, consensus was higher in the earlier years (1980s) of the study than in the later years. Trust in political institutions was higher, evaluations of public officials were more positive, interest in politics was higher, partisanship was distinctly more Democratic, and satisfaction with the level of taxes was higher.

Second, as partisanship began to shift in the late 1980s, consensus declined on this and other issues. The changes in party identification in the state have had a measurable impact on elections. Republicans were far more successful in the late 1980s in state politics than in any period since Reconstruction, and in the 1990s they were able to secure a majority in both houses of the Florida legislature and control the governorship for the first time. However, the fairly even split in those who identify with a political party is also reflected in split election results. Elections became closer and election results became split between the parties, culminating in the divisive results of the 2000 presidential election. In short, the political system in Florida became much more competitive than it had been at any time previously.

Since competition is generally viewed as a sign of a healthy political system, giving citizens the widest range of choices and giving voice to many more interests than under a less competitive system, it is ironic that as competition increased, the other signs of a healthy political system began to decrease. That is, trust in the political system declined over the 1990s, and the rise in this measure in the early 2000s may have been an artifact of the 9/11 incident. The last point in the time series that measures trust suggests that levels are declining once again. Satisfaction with the performance of elected officials and institutions also declined as political competition increased, and interest in politics declined as well. This suggests that greater political competition may lead to less satisfaction with the functioning of the political system. One consequence of the greater competitiveness of the Republican Party is less inclination to compromise on policy or ideology. Since most Floridians either do not think ideologically or are moderates, this unwillingness to find middle ground can cause greater dissatisfaction with the performance and outcomes of government.

Close elections are likely to continue as long as party identification remains relatively evenly divided between adherents of the two parties and the state continues to have many independents. Contentious fights over policy are also likely to continue as Republicans and Democrats struggle to build a large enough core of adherents to make election successes easier to accomplish on a regular basis. This suggests that lower levels of trust and smaller percentages who rate performance as high are likely to continue in the future. It also may mean more moves to alter some of the basic structures of government in the state, such as those that have been undertaken in the last twenty years: changing how cabinet members attain office, ending affirmative action in the state bureaucracy, instituting new policies for the administration of education in the state, abolishing state agencies.

The lowered levels of satisfaction with government, however, do not appear to threaten the stability of the Florida political system. There may be growing dissatisfaction, but that does not necessarily guarantee that citizens will mobilize to change the basic structures of government because of that dissatisfaction. It appears that political systems can continue to function without high levels of political support. This is the case in Florida, where there is continuing distrust and dissatisfaction with government among over half of the population.

Notes

1. The following table lists the year, the dates the survey was conducted, and the number of people interviewed. The sampling error for all surveys but 1996 and 1999 is +/- 4%.

Tax Surveys

Year	Dates	Sample Size
1979	Oct '79-Jan0 '80	854
1980	Mar-Apr	848
1981	Jan-Feb	1019
1982	Jan-Feb	1086
1983	Jan-Feb	923
1984	Feb	911
1985	Feb-Mar	983
1986	Feb-Mar	929
1987	Feb-Mar	901
1988	Jan-Feb	989
1989	Jan-Mar	1084
1990	Jan-Mar	955
1991	Nov '90-Feb '91	914*
1992	Sept '91-Jan '92	1013
1993	Nov '92-Apr '93	952
1994	Oct '93-Jan '94	1024
1995	Nov '94-Mar '95	922
1996	May-Jun	541
1997	Jan-Apr	1083
1999	Mar-Jun	676
2000	Nov '99-Apr '00	951
2001	Jul-Sept 10, 2001	1085
2002	Sept-Dec	1011
2003	Nov '03-Apr '04	967

*Persian Gulf War

Note: In the tables, figures, and analysis, "don't know" and "refused" responses are excluded. The one exception to this is figure 2.6. The marginals for the comparison data from Pew and the Georgia Poll are reported with "don't know" responses included. For comparability purposes, the Florida data in figure 2.7 do include these responses as well. Hence the percent of people reporting Republican identification in figure 2.6 will vary by a small amount from the percents reported in Table 2.1 where "don't know" responses have been excluded.

References

Almond, Gabriel A., and Sidney Verba. 1965. *The Civic Culture: Political Attitudes and Democracy in Five Nations*. Boston: Little, Brown and Company.

———. 1980. *The Civic Culture Revisited*. Boston: Little, Brown and Company.

American National Election Studies. 2006. *The ANES Guide to Public Opinion and Electoral Behavior*. Ann Arbor: University of Michigan, Center for Political Studies. <www.electionstudies.org/nesguide/nesguide.htm> (accessed 2 March 2007).

Black, Earl, and Merle Black. 2002. *The Rise of Southern Republicans*. Cambridge, Mass.: Harvard University Press.

Campbell, Angus, Philip E. Converse, Warren E. Miller, and Donald E. Stokes. 1960. *The American Voter*. New York: John Wiley.

Devine, Donald J. 1972. *The Political Culture of the United States: The Influence of Member Values on Regime Maintenance*. Boston: Little, Brown and Company.

de Tocqueville, Alexis. 1999. *Democracy in America*. New York: Westvaco.

Easton, David. 1965. *A Systems Analysis of Political Life*. New York: John Wiley.

Elazar, Daniel J. 1984. *American Federalism: A View from the States*. New York: Harper and Row.

Erikson, Robert S. 1976. "The Relationship between Public Opinion and State Policy: A New Look Based on Some Forgotten Data." *American Journal of Political Science* 20, no. 1: 25–36.

Erikson, Robert S., Gerald C. Wright, and John P. McIver. 1996. *Statehouse Democracy: Public Opinion and Policy in the American States*. New York: Cambridge University Press.

Green, Donald, Bradley Palmquist, and Eric Schickler. 2002. *Partisan Hearts and Minds: Political Parties and Social Identities of Voters*. New Haven, Conn.: Yale University Press.

Hibbing, John R., and Elizabeth Theiss-Morse. 1995. *Congress as Public Enemy: Public Attitudes toward American Political Institutions*. New York: Cambridge University Press.

Key, V. O., Jr. 1949. *Southern Politics in State and Nation*. New York: Vintage.

Lipset, Seymour Martin. 1979. *The First New Nation: The United States in Historical and Comparative Perspective*. New York: W. W. Norton and Company.

Mueller, John. 1970. "Presidential Popularity from Truman to Johnson." *American Political Science Review* 64 (March): 18–34.

Osmond, Marie, and Eliza Pavalko. 1986. "Attitudes towards Abortion Challenge Dichotomous Positions." *Florida Public Opinion* 2, no. 1: 5–12.

Page, Benjamin L., and Robert Y Shapiro. 1983. "The Effects of Public Opinion on Policy." *American Political Science Review* 77, no. 1: 175–89.

Parker, Glenn R. 1986. "Legislatures and Legislators: How They Rate with Floridians." *Florida Public Opinion* 2, no. 1: 2–5.

Parker, Glenn R., and Roger Davidson. 1979. "Why Do Americans Love Their Congressmen So Much More Than Their Congress?" *Legislative Studies Quarterly* 4, no. 1: 53–61.

Parker, Suzanne L. 1988. "Shifting Party Tides in Florida: Where Have All the Democrats Gone?" In *The South's New Politics: Realignment and Dealignment*, edited by Robert H. Swansbrough and David M. Brodsky, 22–37. Columbia: University of South Carolina Press.

———. 1992. "Florida, a Polity in Transition." In *Party Realignment in the American States*, edited by Maureen Moakley, 106–26. Columbus: Ohio State University Press.

———. 1995. "Toward an Understanding of 'Rally' Effects: Public Opinion in the Persian Gulf War." *Public Opinion Quarterly* 59, no. 4: 526–46.

———. 1998. "The Depths of Floridians' Distrust of Government." In *Building a Sense of Statewide Community in Florida Amid Political, Cultural, and Civil Diversity*, edited by Lance DeHaven-Smith, 127–62. Gainesville: University Press of Florida.

Sly, David F., William J. Serow, and Shannon Calhoun. 1989. "Migration and the Political Process in Florida." *Florida Public Opinion* 4, no. 1: 8–11.

3

Elections and Partisan Change in Florida

STEPHEN C. CRAIG AND ROGER AUSTIN

The year 1998 was an extremely good one for the Republican Party in Florida. Jeb Bush was elected governor, thereby giving the GOP control of both legislative and executive branches of government for the first time since Reconstruction. After decades of massive population growth and political change, Florida had finally become a true two-party state by the late 1980s. Then, in the decade that followed, continued gains in voter registration and the number of elected officials enabled Republicans to achieve a majority of the state congressional delegation in 1989, parity in the state senate in 1992 (followed by outright control two years later), and capture of the state house in 1996. The party takeover became complete with Bush's election as governor in 1998. The future looked very bright for Republicans. If they could maintain their legislative majorities in 2000, they would control the reapportionment process in 2002 and, as a result, be able to consolidate their gains and perhaps maintain their advantage for many years to come.

The Democrats, however, who had dominated the state politically for over a century, were not to be counted out just yet. Florida, which had been predominantly Republican at the presidential level for several decades, gave its electoral votes to Bill Clinton in 1996, and Al Gore battled George W. Bush to a virtual tie in the infamous 2000 election (Ceaser and Busch 2001). Further, Floridians elected Bob Graham to his third term in the U.S. Senate in 1998 with over 62 percent of the vote, and fellow Democrats won reelection to three of the six seats in what then constituted the Florida cabinet. Two years later, Insurance Commissioner Bill Nelson won the open U.S. Senate seat that had been held since 1988 by Republican Connie Mack. To paraphrase Mark Twain, rumors of the Democratic Party demise appeared to be greatly exaggerated.

As the 2002 elections approached, Florida Democrats had reason to be optimistic despite the unprecedented Republican gains of recent years: They had a plurality of registered voters in the state (see Tables 3.1 and 3.2), control of both U.S. Senate seats, theoretical momentum from what many per-

Table 3.1. Voter Registration in Florida, October 2004

County	Democrats	Percent	Republicans	Percent	Other	Percent
Alachua	71,948	50.5	39,605	27.8	30,805	21.6
Baker	8,926	69.3	3,126	24.3	835	6.5
Bay	39,707	39.2	44,751	44.2	16,857	16.6
Bradford	9,039	61.4	4,168	28.3	1,514	10.3
Brevard	123,578	36.6	151,535	44.8	63,082	18.7
Broward	533,976	50.5	283,736	26.8	240,357	22.7
Calhoun	6,879	82.4	993	11.9	478	5.7
Charlotte	36,306	31.9	51,110	44.9	26,392	23.2
Citrus	35,340	38.9	37,653	41.5	17,787	19.6
Clay	27,282	25.6	60,192	56.5	18,990	17.8
Collier	41,082	24.4	89,559	53.1	38,032	22.5
Columbia	19,374	56.5	10,737	31.3	4,171	12.2
Dade	453,631	42.8	368,334	34.8	236,836	22.4
DeSoto	8,838	59.3	3,787	25.4	2,276	15.3
Dixie	7,495	77.5	1,454	15.0	727	7.5
Duval	238,264	46.2	190,111	36.9	86,827	16.9
Escambia	77,250	40.7	83,165	43.8	29,418	15.5
Flagler	17,940	38.1	19,179	40.7	9,949	21.1
Franklin	5,893	77.3	1,212	15.9	515	6.8
Gadsden	22,280	82.9	3,012	11.2	1,592	5.9
Gilchrist	5,295	58.6	2,750	30.4	990	11.0
Glades	3,867	64.8	1,479	24.8	617	10.3
Gulf	6,464	67.1	2,557	26.6	606	6.3
Hamilton	6,029	78.9	1,140	14.9	476	6.2
Hardee	6,630	63.8	2,779	26.7	990	9.5
Hendry	9,688	56.5	5,279	30.8	2,177	12.7
Hernando	42,554	38.8	45,266	41.3	21,836	19.9
Highlands	23,939	39.8	26,752	44.5	9,485	15.8
Hillsborough	258,882	41.7	217,766	35.1	144,553	23.3
Holmes	7,988	72.7	2,344	21.3	650	5.9
Indian River	24,515	30.0	41,866	51.3	15,262	18.7
Jackson	19,411	71.5	5,962	22.0	1,765	6.5
Jefferson	6,726	72.3	1,929	20.7	645	6.9
Lafayette	3,570	82.8	570	13.2	169	3.9
Lake	55,258	34.3	76,387	47.4	29,624	18.4
Lee	90,716	29.7	144,948	47.5	69,273	22.7
Leon	97,672	57.1	45,578	26.6	27,932	16.3
Levy	13,503	59.7	6,241	27.6	2,873	12.7
Liberty	3,597	88.3	320	7.9	158	3.9
Madison	9,042	79.5	1,695	14.9	634	5.6
Manatee	63,305	33.0	84,804	44.3	43,526	22.7
Marion	73,168	39.7	79,572	43.2	31,517	17.1
Martin	27,203	27.5	51,869	52.5	19,785	20.0
Monroe	18,563	36.1	19,874	38.7	12,940	25.2
Nassau	15,218	36.8	20,300	49.1	5,835	14.1
Okaloosa	31,526	24.7	72,885	57.2	23,044	18.1
Okeechobee	10,891	58.5	5,537	29.7	2,199	11.8
Orange	213,702	40.2	186,614	35.1	131,458	24.7
Osceola	52,064	40.2	42,462	32.8	34,961	27.0

continued

Table 3.1.—*Continued*

County	Democrats	Percent	Republicans	Percent	Other	Percent
Palm Beach	329,232	45.1	233,495	32.0	166,848	22.9
Pasco	99,272	37.3	106,649	40.1	60,053	22.6
Pinellas	223,544	37.8	231,652	39.2	135,793	23.0
Polk	125,870	42.6	115,211	39.0	54,661	18.5
Putnam	26,184	57.7	12,728	28.1	6,432	14.2
St. Johns	31,051	28.3	58,436	53.3	20,148	18.4
St. Lucie	57,128	41.4	50,436	36.6	30,387	22.0
Santa Rosa	27,083	28.1	53,853	55.9	15,423	16.0
Sarasota	74,986	31.2	115,317	47.9	50,289	20.9
Seminole	77,964	32.3	107,613	44.6	55,653	23.1
Sumter	16,553	40.8	17,631	43.5	6,339	15.6
Suwanee	13,941	63.6	5,885	26.8	2,104	9.6
Taylor	8,679	75.6	2,170	18.9	632	5.5
Union	5,331	75.5	1,291	18.3	441	6.2
Volusia	126,405	40.8	111,372	35.9	72,153	23.3
Wakulla	10,293	66.9	3,730	24.2	1,373	8.9
Walton	12,051	36.8	16,413	50.1	4,313	13.2
Washington	9,668	67.0	3,666	25.4	1,087	7.5
State	4,261,249	41.4	3,892,492	37.8	2,147,549	20.8

Source: Division of Elections, Florida Department of State, Tallahassee.

Table 3.2. Major-Party Voter Registration in Florida, 1952–2004

Year	Registered	Democrats	Percent	Republicans	Percent
1952	1,207,597	1,119,361	92.7	88,236	7.3
1956	1,595,244	1,384,447	86.8	210,797	13.2
1960	1,994,363	1,656,023	83.0	338,340	17.0
1964	2,467,998	2,009,842	81.4	458,156	18.6
1968	2,709,849	2,090,787	77.2	619,062	22.8
1972	3,369,603	2,394,604	71.1	974,999	28.9
1976	3,889,474	2,750,723	70.7	1,138,751	29.3
1980	4,517,072	3,087,427	68.4	1,429,645	31.6
1984	5,209,010	3,313,073	63.6	1,895,937	36.4
1988	5,624,539	3,264,105	58.0	2,360,434	42.0
1992	5,991.547	3,318,579	55.4	2,672,968	44.6
1996	7,037,618	3,728,513	53.0	3,309,105	47.0
2000	7,233,319	3,803,081	52.6	3,430,238	47.4
2004	8,153,741	4,261,249	52.3	3,892,492	47.4

Source: Division of Elections, Florida Department of State, Tallahassee.
Note: Totals and percentages refer to registered Democrats and Republicans only; independents and minor party supporters are excluded. These accounted for a combined 20.8 percent of all registrants in 2004, up from 8.4 percent in 1992 and 7.0 percent in 1988.

ceived to have been an unjust result in the 2000 presidential debacle, and a party that was mostly united behind gubernatorial nominee Bill McBride. With Jeb Bush's less-than-stellar polling numbers at the time and McBride seemingly within striking distance, Democratic National Committee chairman Terry McAuliffe not only made Bush the party's number-one target nationally, but he went so far as to confidently (and not altogether unreasonably) predict victory. However, as September turned into October and the race heated up, Bush's political savvy and prior campaign experience proved to be too much for first-time candidate McBride. Just as Bush himself had faltered at the end in his bid to unseat incumbent governor Lawton Chiles eight years earlier, McBride made some costly mistakes and was unable to keep pace with his well-organized and well-financed opponent.

Jeb Bush won by 56 to 43 percent, becoming the first Republican governor ever reelected in Florida. The GOP also managed to consolidate or even enhance its earlier gains in Congress and the state legislature, due in part to the party's control of the reapportionment that took place following the 2000 census. Then, in 2004, George W. Bush turned back a strong challenge from Democratic presidential nominee John Kerry, and the Republicans again maintained their legislative and congressional majorities while at the same time picking up the U.S. Senate seat left open by Bob Graham's retirement.

What remains to be seen is whether this most recent Republican surge will produce the kind of overwhelming and long-lasting dominance the Democrats held for so long in Florida politics. The GOP has had breakthrough years in the past, only to have the Democrats come back and slow their momentum. For example, when political analyst Kevin Phillips (1969) declared that an emerging [national] Republican majority" was unfolding in the late 1960s, Florida appeared to be representative of the overall trend: The state elected its first Republican governor since Reconstruction (Claude Kirk) in 1966 and a Republican U.S. senator (Ed Gurney) in 1968, and seemed poised for even greater success in future elections. The Democrats rebounded in 1970, however, by recapturing the governorship (when Reuben Askew defeated Kirk), retaining an open U.S. Senate seat (underdog Lawton Chiles bested respected Congressman Bill Cramer), and maintaining their sizable advantage in both the cabinet and state legislature. Other notable Republican victories occurred when Paula Hawkins was elected to the U.S. Senate in 1980 and Bob Martinez captured the governorship in 1986, yet neither was able to win a second term.

Much has changed over the past two decades, of course, and there is little doubt that Republicans have finally gained the upper hand. Nevertheless, the future is not altogether clear. Although the Democrats' stranglehold on

voter loyalties obviously is a thing of the past, Florida remains at least potentially more competitive than the current distribution of major elective offices might lead one to believe. Heading into the 2006–2008 election cycles,
both parties are on virtually equal footing in terms of voter registration, and
each is looking for a fresh face because their historic and proven vote-getters
are no longer available. Interestingly, just as Lawton Chiles and Bob Graham
(both of whom served two terms as governor and three terms as members of
the U.S. Senate) personified Democratic dominance during the latter third
of the twentieth century, the Bush family has lately been something of a
dynasty on the Republican side. Between 1980 and 2004, a Bush (George
H. W., George W., or Jeb) was on the Florida ballot in nine of thirteen general elections and was victorious in eight of those nine races (losing only to
Chiles in 1994). All of these political icons are now gone from the scene and
a new generation of leaders scrambling to take their place, Republicans and
Democrats alike are faced with both opportunities and challenges in a state
where social and political change continues to be the norm.

Florida politics cannot be properly understood without taking into account the massive population growth that has occurred since World War
II. Over the past sixty years, Florida's population has risen by roughly 14
million. Wave after wave of new residents has arrived from other states and
other countries, an influx that has profoundly altered the demographic, economic, ethnic, and political character of the state. Whereas the Democratic
primary once meant everything, now a competitive two-party system exists
and there are enough nonaligned voters that neither major party has (thus
far) been able to claim a consistent and enduring advantage. Before looking to the future, however, we should examine the past, including some of
the ways in which Florida differed from other states in the old Confederate
South in terms of its potential for political change. Those differences made
the Sunshine State as fertile a breeding ground for Republicanism as existed
anywhere in Dixie and contributed to Florida's evolution from a one-party
system dominated by the Democrats to the independent-minded but Republican-leaning state that it is today.

Electoral Change in Florida

The Era of Democratic Dominance

In Florida, as in much of the South, Republicans reigned during the Reconstruction era that followed the Civil War. After 1876, Republicans became
virtually nonexistent and the Democratic Party ruled what became known

as the Solid South for the better part of a century. Yet to say that the Democrats dominated the state and had a virtual monopoly on elective offices at all levels does not mean there was a lack of political competition. On the contrary, competition was often intense; it simply was concentrated among Democrats facing each other in primaries rather than between Democrats and Republicans running in general elections.

In his classic study of southern politics, V. O. Key Jr. (1949, 82) described elections in Florida as:

almost literally [a matter of] every candidate for himself. Ordinarily each candidate for county office runs without collaboration with other local candidates. He hesitates to become publicly committed in contests for state office lest he fall heir to all the local enemies of the statewide candidate. Each candidate for the half dozen or so minor elective state offices [i.e., cabinet] tends to his own knitting and recruits his own following. Senators and Representatives hoe their own row and each of the numerous candidates for governor does likewise. With each successive campaign different divisions within the electorate develop. Few politicians exert real influence beyond their own county, and those who can deliver their home county are few. Florida is not only unbossed, it is also unled. Anything can happen in elections, and does.

Key described Florida as having "no political organization in the conventional sense of the term" (1949, 87) and explained that political organization is important because it provides a source of leadership, facilitates the ability of officeholders to work together to enact programs, and gives citizens a basis for knowing whom to blame or praise for the results of those programs (1949, 87). It is clear from Key's analysis that effective political organization, partisan or otherwise, simply did not exist in Florida during the era of Democratic dominance. In its place was a governing system characterized by multiple and shifting factions, issueless campaigns, and widespread voter confusion (as well as very low turnout rates on Election Day). The result was a political structure that left many citizens feeling uninterested, uninvolved, and unrepresented when important decisions were being made.

At the same time, conditions were present that eventually led to dramatic changes in Florida politics. In addition to having a diverse economy and relatively high urbanization compared with the rest of the South, two other factors differentiated Florida from other states in the region: growth and race (the latter of which was a less prominent, and hence less corrosive, force than was typical in southern politics generally). First, the state was already beginning to experience the explosive population growth that continues to exert a major impact today. In 1940, Florida was the 27th-largest state, with under 2 million residents; it is currently the 4th-largest, with close to 17 million (see Chapter 1 in this volume). Many newcomers were lifelong Republicans who often settled in the larger cities and suburban towns of Central and South Florida. Although it was not uncommon for these newcomers to register as Democrats in deference to local realities and to vote Democratic in the general election (either because the GOP did not field a candidate or because their party's nominee had little chance of winning), they nonetheless managed to establish several small pockets of Republicanism that emerged first at the presidential level and then, over the ensuing decades, in other races as well.

Brief glimpses into Florida's political future were provided by the 1928 and 1948 presidential elections. In 1928, Republican Herbert Hoover was opposed by Democrat Al Smith, the governor of New York and the first Catholic nominated by either party. Though not a liberal by today's standards, Smith was opposed to Prohibition and more closely identified with the urban, ethnic, immigrant milieu of the Northeast than with the traditional, rural, and small-town Protestant values of the South (Sundquist 1983). While the Hoover-Smith contest was not about race, racial factors played a significant role in shaping the voting behavior of southern states. As described by Key (1949, 318–29), areas with a higher proportion of black residents (the so-called Black Belt) remained Democratic by virtue of their "common tradition and anxiety about the Negro." In contrast, whites who lived in areas with fewer blacks "could afford the luxury of voting their convictions on the religious and prohibition issues." Partly because blacks have always constituted a relatively small share of the overall population in Florida, racial demagoguery by Democratic leaders and the systematic exclusion of blacks from participation in the electoral process through such means as poll taxes, literacy tests, and the whites-only Democratic primary were never as intense or as widespread as they were elsewhere in the South during the days of Jim Crow. Thus, in 1928, many white Floridians set race aside and did the previously unthinkable: They voted for a Republican candidate for president. Blacks were still mainly Republicans at the time, so their high levels of support for Hoover were to be expected.

The lesser importance of race in Florida politics became evident once again in the 1948 presidential contest, which pitted incumbent Harry Truman against Republican governor Thomas Dewey of New York, who also had been the GOP nominee against Franklin Roosevelt four years earlier. Dewey was not a serious threat to carry the state on his own, but Truman's position was made precarious when a splinter group, the States Rights Democrats (or Dixiecrats), bolted the national convention after it adopted a platform that committed the party to eradicating "all racial, religious and economic discrimination" in such areas as voting rights, employment, personal security, and treatment of members of the armed forces (see Key 1949, 335). The insurgents later met in Birmingham, where their own presidential nominee, Governor Strom Thurmond of South Carolina, declared that "there's not enough troops in the army to force the southern people to break down segregation and admit the Negro race into our theaters, into our swimming pools, into our homes, and into our churches" (Cohodas 1993, 177). Truman won the election, but the Dixiecrats carried four Deep South states where they appeared on the ballot as the official Democratic ticket. Although Florida was not one of those states, voter dissatisfaction with the national Democratic Party—including its positions on issues that had nothing to do with race or civil rights—helped Dewey do slightly better than he had against Roosevelt four years earlier (see Table 3.3). The existence of the Dixiecrats

Table 3.3. Number and Percent of Major-Party Votes in Presidential Elections, Florida, 1928–2004

Year	Democrats	Percent	Republicans	Percent	Other	Percent
1928	100,721	41.1	144,168	58.9	—	—
1932	206.307	74.9	69,170	25.1	—	—
1936	249,117	76.1	78,248	23.9	—	—
1940	359,334	74.0	126,158	26.0	—	—
1944	339,377	70.3	143,215	29.7	—	—
1948	281,988	49.8	194,280	34.3	89,755	15.9
1952	444,950	45.0	544,036	55.0	—	—
1956	480,371	42.7	643,849	57.3	—	—
1960	748,700	48.5	795,476	51.5	—	—
1964	948,540	51.1	905,941	48.9	—	—
1968	676,794	30.9	886,804	40.5	624,207	28.5
1972	718,117	27.9	1,857,759	72.1	—	—
1976	1,636,000	52.7	1,469,531	47.3	—	—
1980	1,419,475	38.8	2,046,951	56.0	189,692	5.2
1984	1,448,816	34.7	2,730,350	65.3	—	—
1988	1,656,701	38.7	2,618,885	61.3	—	—
1992	2,072,698	39.1	2,173,310	41.0	1,053,067	19.9
1996	2,546,870	48.3	2,244,536	42.5	483,870	9.2
2000	2,912,253	49.2	2,912,790	49.2	97,488	1.6
2004	3,583,544	47.5	3,964,522	52.5	—	—

Source: Division of Elections, Florida Department of State, Tallahassee.
Note: Percentages are based on the two-party vote except in 1948 (when Strom Thurmond ran for the States Rights Democrats), 1968 (when George Wallace ran for the American Independent Party), 1980 (when John Anderson ran as an independent), 1992 and 1996 (when Ross Perot ran as an independent [1992] and as the nominee of the Reform Party [1996]), and 2000 (when Ralph Nader ran for the Green Party).

pointed to growing tensions between the South and other elements of the Democratic coalition.

For the South as a whole, the same Black Belt areas that had loyally stayed with Al Smith in 1928 were the most likely to support Thurmond and the Dixiecrats in 1948. The message was clear: As long as segregationist whites saw the Democrats as their best hope for maintaining the racial status quo, they would continue to vote accordingly at all levels, but when the party evidenced too much sympathy for the cause of black civil rights, all bets were off. The same underlying pattern could be seen in Florida as well, even if the state's small black population and limited preoccupation with matters of race allowed it to escape much of the turmoil that was being experienced elsewhere as segregationist institutions came under increasing attack. There were areas—the Panhandle and less urbanized north, for example—where blacks were more numerous and race counted for a great deal among many white voters, and as the Democratic Party came to embrace the goal of racial equality more openly, the potential for defection from traditional loyalties grew stronger each year. Combined with the continued influx of Republican newcomers from other parts of the country, these circumstances created a situation that made major political change inevitable.

The 1950s and 1960s: A Republican Beginning

The shift to presidential Republicanism became clear in 1952 and 1956, when Florida joined with most of the country to elect Dwight D. Eisenhower president, and again in 1960, when Richard Nixon captured the state's electoral votes in his narrow loss nationally to John F. Kennedy. In all three races, GOP strength was concentrated less in the Black Belt northern counties that had earlier been receptive to the Dixiecrats and more in what has been described as "an urban horseshoe, with one leg beginning at Fort Lauderdale and Palm Beach, running up the east coast to Daytona Beach, then inland to Orlando and curving to St. Petersburg on the west coast and descending to Fort Myers and Naples" (Bass and DeVries 1976, 117).

This pattern began to change somewhat with the 1964 race between President Lyndon Johnson and Senator Barry Goldwater of Arizona, one of only three Republican candidates not to carry Florida since 1948. In the final analysis, Goldwater's willingness to reform the Social Security system and his rigid conservatism on a broad range of other issues cost him a measure of traditional Republican support and contributed to his relatively poor showing in the state overall. Yet this same conservatism, especially his opposition to the Civil Rights Act of 1964 (on what he said were constitutional grounds; specifically, that such matters should be dealt with by the state governments), attracted many white voters who for decades had supported the Democrats. In his defense, it must be noted that Goldwater did not openly appeal to racist sentiments during the campaign. He did, however, adopt a "southern strategy" that sought the backing of disaffected white Democrats in the region. He also assumed (correctly) that there was little use in trying to mollify black and liberal white voters, who would not vote for him anyway. While this strategy doomed Goldwater, it is now clear that the 1964 election marked an important turning point in the growth of Republicanism throughout the South.

When Richard Nixon employed a modified southern strategy four years later, he was able to win both in Florida and nationwide despite a strong third-party challenge from the right by former Governor George Wallace of Alabama. Although it was the segregationist Wallace more than Nixon who inherited the Black Belt Dixiecrat vote, the Wallace candidacy may have served as a "halfway house" for conservative whites who were disenchanted with their old party but not yet ready to become full-fledged presidential Republicans. In the meantime, Nixon won back most of the mainstream Republicans who had been scared off by Goldwater's apparent extremism in 1964, and with his successful bid for reelection in 1972, he succeeded in merging the two groups into what ultimately became a rather formidable coalition. Since the Goldwater debacle, Jimmy Carter in 1976 and Bill Clinton in 1996 have been the only Democratic nominees who have drawn enough white votes to defeat this coalition (the latter was probably helped, as in 1992 when he ran a close second behind George Bush, by independent candidate Ross Perot's presence on the ballot).

The 1960s also were a time of growth for Florida Republicans below the presidential level. Claude Kirk's unexpected victory in the 1966 gubernatorial race came at the expense of liberal Mayor Robert King High of Miami, who had unseated the more conservative incumbent Governor Haydon Burns in a bitter Democratic primary earlier that year. Burns and many of his supporters refused to endorse High, thereby opening the door to businessman Kirk, who took advantage of the growing split within Democratic ranks by attacking High for his racial attitudes and linking him to the increasingly unpopular administration of President Lyndon Johnson. Kirk won the election with 55 percent of the vote, doing well in several North Florida and Panhandle counties where the Democrats traditionally racked up large majorities.

Another GOP breakthrough occurred in the 1968 U.S. Senate contest, as Congressman Edward Gurney defeated former Governor LeRoy Collins. The latter was burdened by the effects of yet another divisive Democratic primary and by the public's antipathy toward the party's national ticket that year. A racial moderate, Collins was an advocate of civil rights reform during the late 1950s and early 1960s, but his progressive record ultimately did him more harm than good in the Senate race. Opponents dubbed him "Liberal LeRoy," and in some of the rural Black Belt counties of North Florida, a photograph was circulated showing Collins walking alongside Rev. Martin Luther King Jr. at a 1965 protest march in Selma, Alabama. By way of contrast, Gurney portrayed himself as a strong advocate of law and order and "as a fighter, a man of action, an effective leader" (Bass and DeVries 1976, 122–23). In fact, Republican candidates ran stronger at all levels in 1968 despite a continuing edge for the Democrats in voter loyalties. If nothing else, the back-to-back triumphs of Kirk and Gurney had many voters thinking for the first time about the possibility of genuine two-party competition in Florida politics (Bass and DeVries 1976, 121).

The Democrats Strike Back

According to political analysts Jack Bass and Walter DeVries, Kirk "created an exciting atmosphere with his politics of confrontation, flow of creative ideas, and personal flamboyance. He fought to get a new [state] constitution and brought fresh faces into state government, many of them appointments of high quality." Unfortunately, there also were problems. Today Claude Kirk is remembered less for his leadership than "for lavish parties at the governor's mansion, for jetting around the country at state Republican Party expense, and for hiring a Madison Avenue firm with state funds to promote himself for the 1968 vice-presidential nomination" (Bass and DeVries 1976, 118–19). Kirk lost his 1970 reelection bid to state senator Reubin Askew of Pensacola, who campaigned on a platform calling for tax reform, adoption of a corporate income tax, environmental protection, and financial disclosure for elected officials. Askew's victory resulted largely from a strong showing in those areas of North Florida and the Panhandle that had demonstrated a willingness to vote for conservative Republicans in 1966 and 1968. By also faring well among blacks and, to a lesser extent, among moderate whites living in urban areas south of the frost line, Askew provided a formula that Democratic candidates would use with success throughout the remainder of the 1970s and into the 1980s.

The same can be said of Lawton Chiles. Kirk's problems aside, the Republicans were thought to have a good chance of capturing the U.S. Senate seat left open in 1970 by the retirement of Spessard Holland. Not only were the Democrats in obvious disarray (Lamis 1988, 183), but the GOP had a strong candidate in Congressman William Cramer from St. Petersburg, a man often referred to as "Mr. Republican" of Florida politics and the first member of his party to have been elected to Congress from the state in the twentieth century. Cramer was damaged, however, in the Republican primary when Kirk and Gurney found a challenger for him in their attempt to gain control of the state party organization (Bass and DeVries 1976, 124). Although Cramer prevailed, his campaign divided Republicans at a time when unity was essential. Democratic nominee Lawton Chiles was less willing than Askew to take left of center positions on issues (Lamis 1988, 192), but he nonetheless managed to project an "aw shucks" populist image by walking 1,000 miles from one end of the state to the other and by stressing his ties to the working people of Florida. The state senator from Lakeland won fairly handily; like Askew, he did better than anticipated in North Florida while also pulling in enough votes from the rest of the state to beat the favored Cramer. As Chiles later noted, "when you give [the people in North Florida] a Democrat they can accept, they'll vote for him" (quoted in Lamis 1988, 185).

For the next several statewide elections, Democrats proved to be fairly adept at nominating candidates the swing voters in the north could support. Askew suffered some erosion there in his 1974 reelection campaign, probably due to memories of his opposition to an anti-busing referendum on the 1972 presidential primary ballot (it passed with 74 percent approval), but he balanced that by running well in some of the Central and South Florida urban areas that normally favored Republicans (Lamis 1988, 187). He was succeeded as governor by Bob Graham, a state senator from Miami Lakes, who won an upset victory in the 1978 Democratic primary. One key ingredient of the Graham campaign was a gimmick known as "workdays": The candidate spent 100 days working 100 different jobs ranging from bartender to garbage collector to schoolteacher, the idea being to demonstrate a connection to working people in the state (Lamis 1988, 188). Graham also was helped by the selection of veteran panhandle legislator Wayne Mixson from Marianna as his running mate and won comfortably with almost 56 percent of the vote.

That gubernatorial election, according to Alexander Lamis, generally fit the pattern of other statewide races during the same period: "When the Democrats field a candidate who can hold together the traditional North Florida Democratic vote with a coalition of blacks and blue-collar whites in the large urban centers, plus the heavily Democratic areas of South Florida, they are usually able to win with a modest statewide majority" (Lamis 1988, 188–89). By the end of the 1970s, Democrats controlled the governorship, both seats in the U.S. Senate, 12 of 15 seats in the U.S. House, all six cabinet positions, 29 of 40 seats in the Florida Senate, and 89 of 120 seats in the Florida House of Representatives. Republican growth had not been stopped by any means, but intra-party strife set the party back at times and made the task of challenging for majority status more difficult than it otherwise might have been. Meanwhile, by nominating Reubin Askew and Lawton Chiles in 1970, the Democrats began turning to a new generation of leaders who appealed to many voters regardless of their partisan leanings.

Democrats also benefited from the diminished importance of race, which had flared up in the mid to late 1960s and contributed to the success of conservative Republican candidates such as Kirk and Gurney. Nationally as well as in Florida, the opportunities for GOP gains were further limited by the Watergate scandal and by growing concern about the economy during the administration of President Gerald Ford. Nevertheless, while Democrats continued to hold better than a 2-to-1 edge in voter registration among Floridians, the period after 1964 left little doubt that the state's political landscape (and that of the South as a whole) had changed dramatically since the days when Democrats had things to themselves. Republican activists and leaders at the state and local levels were becoming increasingly effective at recruiting strong candidates, raising the large sums of money often necessary to run a credible race, and building a party apparatus that in some areas had the Democrats playing catch-up (Bass and DeVries 1976, 125). The GOP did not always win, of course, but the effort was there and public opinion was clearly beginning to shift in the Republicans' favor. Then came the pivotal election of 1980.

The 1980s: The Reagan Years

In 1980, Ronald Reagan handily defeated Jimmy Carter in Florida by 56 to 39 percent, with 5 percent going to independent John Anderson. According to Alexander Lamis, "National factors were chiefly responsible for this result, although Reagan campaigned effectively and extensively in the state, paying attention to matters of local interest." Unlike Goldwater, for example, he appealed to Florida's older voters by stressing his commitment to the Social Security system; and in South Florida, "where Cuban refugees were the source of local concern," Reagan criticized his opponent for trying to shift the burden of what was essentially a national problem "onto the backs of Florida residents" (Lamis 1988, 189). When these elements were added to the bad economy and Carter's overall image as a weak leader, any chance the president had of carrying Florida quickly vanished.

Reagan's huge win also helped elect Republican Paula Hawkins of Winter Park to the U.S. Senate in 1980. A former member of the Florida Public Service Commission, Hawkins defeated state insurance commissioner and former Congressman Bill Gunter, winner of a typically bruising Democratic primary over incumbent Richard Stone. With the Democrats divided, Hawkins ran strongest in Central Florida, the Gold Coast (from North Palm Beach down through Boca Raton, Fort Lauderdale, and Hollywood), and "in just about every county with a sizable portion of immigrants from the North" (Barone and Ujifusa 1981, 209). She received 52 percent of the vote statewide and became only the second Republican elected to the Senate from Florida in the twentieth century.

Although the GOP began to make significant gains in voter registration after 1980, the Democrats held their own in 1982 by easily reelecting Governor Graham (65 percent against Congressman Skip Bafalis) and Senator Chiles (62 percent against state Senator Van Poole) and by retaining their healthy edge in congressional and state legislative seats. With no statewide races on the ballot, they also fared reasonably well two years later, despite Reagan's rout of Walter Mondale in the 1984 presidential contest.

Such inconsistent outcomes reinforced the idea that Florida, with its steady stream of new residents who lacked "any permanent connection with the civic culture of the state" (Barone and Ujifusa 1989, 242), was becoming unusually volatile and unpredictable, subject to wide voting swings from one election to the next or even across a range of offices within the same election year. In fact, 30 percent of all U.S.-born whites residing in Florida in 1950 had been born outside the South, a figure that rose to more than 50 percent over the next thirty years (Black and Black 1987, 17). The sheer size of the state (it is almost 800 miles from Pensacola to Key West) made it difficult for candidates to communicate with voters except through the costly and mostly superficial medium of television—which, in turn, tended to focus attention on individual candidates rather than on the entire party ticket. When V. O. Key cited a similar phenomenon (that "anything can happen in elections, and does") in his analysis of Florida politics during the 1930s and 1940s, the instability was limited to the Democratic side because Republicans did not yet pose a serious threat. Voters in the modern era frequently sent mixed signals by supporting Republican candidates for some offices and Democratic candidates for others. Well-known incumbents occasionally lost because they were unable to win support from an electorate that, because of new arrivals and high turnover among the large elderly population, was quite different from the one that put them into office in the first place. Wounds that developed in the heat of an intense primary campaign did not always have time to heal during the short period separating the first primary (late August or early September) and runoff (late September or early October)[1] from the general election (November).

The 1986 off-year elections provided a vivid example of several of these factors: a vulnerable incumbent, widespread ticket-splitting, divisive primaries, and candidate-centered campaigns. For the U.S. Senate, incumbent Paula Hawkins faced Governor Bob Graham in one of the nation's glamour races. Hawkins associated herself closely with President Reagan and attempted to connect Graham with the failed administration of Jimmy Carter. She was hurt, though, by persistent health problems, a series of gaffes, and a reputation for ineffectiveness. All of this contrasted sharply with Graham's "image of competence built on a record of accomplishment" during his eight years as governor (Ehrenhalt 1987, 288). The challenger also won support from conservatives with his stands in favor of capital punishment, stiffer penalties for drug dealers, and continued U.S. funding for the Contra rebel movement in Nicaragua. On Election Day, Graham won with a comfortable 55 percent and Hawkins became the third consecutive holder of that particular Senate seat (following Gurney and Stone) to leave office after just six years.

The gubernatorial race was an altogether different story. State representative Steve Pajcic eked out a close win over Attorney General Jim Smith in the Democratic runoff but was weakened by Smith's portrayal of him as an unrepentant liberal whose sympathy for higher taxes, pornography, and abolition of the death penalty placed him "totally out of step with Florida's mainstream" (Lamis 1988, 293). Loser Smith refused to endorse Pajcic in the general election and shortly afterward switched his affiliation to the Republican Party. The GOP nominated Bob Martinez, who picked up on many of Smith's anti-Pajcic themes while also pointing to his own administrative experience as mayor of Tampa during the early 1980s. By capturing just under 55 percent of the vote, Martinez became Florida's first Hispanic governor.

It is interesting to note that in each of the two major statewide races in 1986, the winner (one Democrat, one Republican) outpaced the loser by a margin of approximately 1.85 million to 1.55 million votes—discrepant outcomes that could only occur as a result of frequent ticket-splitting among voters. Both of these contests also were marked by high campaign costs, heavy reliance on television ads (many of them hard-hitting attacks on the opposition), and input from professional consultants whose main goal was to ensure the success of their clients regardless of what happened to the rest of the party. When Key (1949, 82) described Florida politics as a matter of "every candidate for himself," he could as easily have been talking about the 1980s as about the period during and after the Great Depression.

Below the top level, Democrats did not fare badly in 1986. They won all six cabinet positions, twelve of the nineteen U.S. House seats, and a majority in both houses of the state legislature (though a post-election coalition of Republicans and conservative Democrats was able to successfully challenge the progressive/liberal faction for control of the Senate). Taken as a whole, these results underscored the fact that the specific mix of candidates, issues, and circumstances in a race could sometimes override any predisposition that citizens might have to favor one party or the other. Yet despite the electoral volatility that has been part of the state's political tradition for over half a century, a trend toward the GOP was evident throughout the decade of the 1980s. Republican gains can be seen in the registration figures shown in Table 3.2 and with even greater clarity in the events of the late 1980s and early 1990s—a period when Florida increasingly began to look like a state in the midst of a fundamental partisan realignment.

1988 to 1996: A Split Decision

Although George Bush won Florida by a comfortable margin over Michael Dukakis in the 1988 presidential race, the most significant developments that year were taking place elsewhere. When three-term incumbent Lawton Chiles decided to retire from the U.S. Senate, Republicans initially rejoiced. However, when former governor Reubin Askew immediately announced his candidacy to succeed Chiles, Democrats felt confident they could retain the seat—at least until Askew, leading in all polls, dropped out himself the following May, citing his distaste for fund-raising. With the primary just four months away, other prospective Democratic candidates were left with little time to build an organization, raise money, and develop an effective message that they could communicate to voters. A typically nasty intra-party battle ensued, with centrist congressman Buddy MacKay earning the nomination in an upset over Bill Gunter.

On the Republican side, Congressman Connie Mack III of Cape Coral won handily against former U.S. Attorney Robert "Mad Dog" Merkle in the primary and then spent the next several weeks trying to link his opponent in the general election to unpopular Democratic policies. Apart from talking about his own commitment to "less taxes, less spending, less government, and more freedom," Mack ran numerous attack ads that ended with the tag line, "Hey, Buddy, you're a liberal." Mack, in turn, proved vulnerable to Democratic charges that he was insufficiently committed to protecting Social Security benefits for elderly citizens (Barone and Ujifusa 1989, 246–47). The final tally was extraordinarily close, but Mack prevailed when a sophisticated GOP absentee-ballot campaign turned apparent defeat into a winning margin of 35,000 votes (out of more than 4 million cast statewide). Had Dukakis not conceded Florida's electoral votes early and left the state, Bush's margin of almost 1 million votes in the presidential race would have likely been less and Buddy MacKay would probably have been a senator.

Mack's narrow win was by no means the only bright spot for Republicans in 1988. They also captured two cabinet posts (Secretary of State Jim Smith, who by then had switched parties, and Insurance Commissioner Tom Gallagher), plus nine of nineteen U.S. House seats; the Democratic advantage in Tallahassee fell to 23 to 17 in the Senate and 73 to 47 in the House. The GOP gained added strength in early 1989 when Bill Grant, a Democratic congressman from the Panhandle who had been reelected without opposition, decided to switch to the other side. This gave Republicans an unprecedented 10-to-9 lead that swelled to 11 to 8 after Ileana Ros-Lehtinen (the first Cuban American ever to serve in Congress) won a special election following the death of Miami's venerable Claude Pepper. One Democratic state legislator also switched parties in midyear, while several of his colleagues and a smattering of local officials from around the state teetered on the brink of doing the same—a clear sign that the time was passing when someone might run for office as a Democrat simply because that was where the action happened to be.

In the 1990 and 1992 elections, the pace of change in state government slowed a little. Democrats managed to recapture the governorship in 1990, when Lawton Chiles came out of retirement to unseat Bob Martinez by the surprisingly comfortable margin of 57 to 43 percent. Martinez, who shortly after taking office had supported passage of a state tax on services, never quite recovered from the adverse public reaction to that tax—or from the weak leadership image he conveyed by also backing those who (successfully) worked for its repeal the following year. The governor's presence at the top of the ticket in 1990 proved to be a drag on other GOP candidates, thereby helping the Democrats retain control of the cabinet and both houses of the state legislature. They even picked up one seat in the state House and one in Congress as party-switcher Grant was defeated by the Democratic challenger, former Vietnam POW Pete Peterson.

Democrats survived in 1992 as well. Bill Clinton did reasonably well in the presidential race, losing by just 100,000 votes, and Bob Graham won a second term in the U.S. Senate by defeating Bill Grant with 65 percent of the vote. Republicans continued to improve their performance in legislative races, however, and achieved an historic 20-20 split with Democrats in the

Florida Senate. Reapportionment yielded four new congressional seats due to growth, and the Republicans emerged with a 15-to-8 advantage. This set the stage for 1994, a year in which the GOP made huge gains nationwide: in Congress (capturing control of both chambers for the first time since 1952), governorships (including the election of George W. Bush in Texas), and the various state legislatures. In Florida, they won three of the six cabinet positions, fifteen of twenty-three seats in the U.S. House, and outright control of the Florida Senate (21 to 19), and they closed the Democrats' advantage in the Florida House to 63 to 57 by picking up eight seats. Connie Mack easily won reelection to the U.S. Senate against political newcomer (and brother of the First Lady) Hugh Rodham.

One of the few bright spots for the Democrats in 1994 came in the race for governor, where Lawton Chiles narrowly survived a strong challenge from presidential son and Miami businessman Jeb Bush. Chiles initially looked vulnerable; he had been elected four years earlier on the promise of reforming state government and "right-sizing" the bureaucracy but had later called for $1.3 billion in new taxes and proposed a health care reform package that was rejected by the legislature. Bush championed a conservative agenda that included welfare reform, school choice, and speedier executions for death-row inmates, and most polls showed him with an early double-digit lead. The governor, however, responded with a negative attack (most notably concerning his opponent's alleged ties with the savings-and-loan industry) and began to emphasize his own southern "cracker" roots in an effort to attract support from conservative Democrats, especially in North Florida (Barone and Ujifusa with Cohen 1995, 291–92). On Election Day, he prevailed by the margin of 51 to 49 percent.

Chiles, once again having shown Democrats how to hold a coalition together and prevail statewide, provided inspiration to Bill Clinton in 1996. Deemed "irrelevant" by many pundits and politicians after the 1994 national debacle (for which he and his party were blamed in the wake of their failure to enact national health care reform and other key legislation), Clinton crafted a brilliant national strategy and turned his 100,000-vote loss to George H. W. Bush in Florida in 1992 into a 300,000-vote win over the hapless Bob Dole in 1996. Nevertheless, even as Clinton was becoming only the third Democrat to win Florida's electoral votes since 1948, there were few other bright spots for the Democrats. Republicans maintained their 15-to-8 lead in the congressional delegation, increased their state Senate margin to 23 to 17, and, in another historic moment, took 61-to-59 control in the Florida House of Representatives.

1998 and Beyond: Republican Ascendance

The 1998 elections featured spirited gubernatorial and U.S. Senate contests that ended in a split between the parties. Jeb Bush was once again the Republican nominee for governor, facing off against Lieutenant Governor Buddy MacKay. Bush won by the comfortable margin of 55 to 45 percent, racing ahead to an early lead (just as he had four years earlier) and then cruising to victory over an opponent who lacked Chiles's personal magnetism and failed repeatedly to craft a compelling message that might attract supporters to his cause. The GOP's ascendance in state politics in the late 1990s was such that many Republicans believed (or at least hoped) that Bob Graham also might be vulnerable. Instead, Graham coasted to his third term in the U.S. Senate over state senator Charlie Crist with 62 percent of the vote. Once again, the results indicated widespread ticket-splitting on Election Day and provided a ray of hope for the beleaguered Democrats. Even as Republicans were taking complete control over state government for the first time in over a century, Graham continued to thrive by using the old Democratic formula that had worked so well earlier for Chiles and others; he carried, for example, 26 of 28 counties in North Florida and the Panhandle, while Bush was winning 25 of the same counties in the governor's race. The Graham victory aside, however, Republicans held their 15-to-8 congressional majority and maintained control of the state legislature by sizable margins (25 to 15 in the Senate and 72 to 48 in the House, the latter figure including two party switches by Democratic incumbents).

In 2000, Florida unexpectedly became the focal point for one of the longest and most confusing elections in our nation's history, but this was only part of the story. On the one hand, Republicans held on to or increased (moving to 77 to 43 in the state house) their congressional and state legislative majorities. On the other hand, Insurance Commissioner Bill Nelson won back a U.S. Senate seat for the Democrats following the retirement of two-term incumbent Connie Mack. Nelson, who was the undisputed choice of most party leaders around the state and had no significant primary opposition, was widely known as a centrist Democrat in the mold of Senator Graham. His opponent, Congressman Bill McCollum, also won his primary without a serious challenge (in part because Jeb Bush and GOP party officials persuaded Education Commissioner Tom Gallagher to step aside) but went into the fall campaign with two serious disadvantages: modest name recognition and a reputation for being too conservative even for many Republicans in the state. Although he eventually fared better than some had expected (losing by just 51 to 46 percent), McCollum was never able to overcome Nelson's initial advantage. Once again, the results demonstrated the willingness of Florida voters to support certain kinds of Democrats under the right circumstances.

This point was reinforced in the presidential race, which culminated in a 36-day standoff between George W. Bush and Al Gore that was not resolved until the U.S. Supreme Court issued a ruling that effectively precluded any further vote recounts from taking place. The story is well known and need not be considered in detail here (see, for example, Ceaser and Busch 2001). What is important for our purposes is that Florida—which was increasingly tilting toward the Republican Party at the state level and was once described as "the safest Republican big state in presidential elections" (Barone and Ujifusa 1989, 247)—was now showing clear signs of being up for grabs. For all intents and purposes, the presidential race was a statistical tie, with an official total of 537 votes (out of almost 6 million cast) separating the two major candidates. It no longer seemed that Florida could be counted as falling safely in the Republican presidential column.

Thus, although the GOP won most of its targeted races in 2000, the presidential near-miss and Nelson's Senate victory left the Democrats feeling confident going into the 2002 election cycle. Many felt that Governor Jeb Bush, who was seeking reelection, was especially vulnerable due to the controversial role he had played during the presidential imbroglio two years earlier.[2] His principal challengers on the Democratic side were Janet Reno, former attorney general during the Clinton administration, and Tampa attorney Bill McBride, who was making his first bid for public office. Although Reno began the race as a prohibitive favorite, her health (she suffered from Parkinson's disease and shook noticeably when speaking) and liberal views eventually became liabilities for some Democratic primary voters, who did not feel that she would give the party its best chance of unseating Bush in November. Reno also was hurt by the presence of state Senator Daryl Jones, an African American from South Florida, in the race. Jones captured about 11 percent of the primary vote, most of which might otherwise have gone to Reno, and thereby paved the way for McBride to win by a margin of less than 5,000 votes.

While the Democrats (including Reno) quickly united behind their nominee, his lack of political experience increasingly became a problem as the campaign wore on. The stakes were high for both parties, not only because Republicans wanted to maintain their momentum in Florida politics but also because, with the 2004 presidential election looming, a loss by the president's brother might be seen as a harbinger of things to come. As a result, the Bush-McBride match-up became one of the nation's most closely watched, and most expensive, races in the off year. McBride managed to stay close into October, but a weak performance in the last of three debates served to highlight his inexperience and raise questions about his grasp of key issues. With virtually all of those who had remained undecided moving to Bush in the closing days, the governor won a second term by 56 to 43 percent. Following reapportionment, with Republicans controlling the process for the first time since Reconstruction, the GOP increased its majorities in both Congress (18 to 7 after Florida received two new seats that reflected the state's continued growth) and the state house (81 to 39), and maintained its 25-to-15 advantage in the state senate.

Despite these results, the Democrats remained hopeful heading into 2004. They received a setback when Bob Graham (who had unsuccessfully sought his party's presidential nomination) decided to retire after serving eighteen years in the U.S. Senate. In a typically bruising primary fight, former Commissioner of Education and state Senator Betty Castor of Tampa dispatched two politicians from South Florida, Congressman Peter Deutsch of Broward County and Miami-Dade Mayor Alex Penelas. Her Republican opponent was Mel Martinez, a former Orange County (Orlando) chairman and secretary of Housing and Urban Development during President Bush's first term. Martinez's ties to the administration (including the widespread belief that he was the president's choice in this race) helped him defeat Bill McCollum and several others in an uncharacteristically nasty Republican primary—so nasty, in fact, that the *St. Petersburg Times* actually withdrew its endorsement of Martinez and McCollum initially refused to endorse him at all (and later did so only tepidly). With the removal of the runoff election in 2002, however (see note 1), the GOP had two months rather than one to heal their wounds and prepare for the general election campaign.

Early polls showed the two contenders running neck and neck, and that is how it stayed right up through Election Day. Martinez's White House connections were a double-edged sword given the closeness of the presidential race; while he played them up at every opportunity, Castor tried to link him to unpopular Bush policies (most notably tax cuts for the wealthy). Martinez, for his part, picked up on one of the charges leveled against Castor during the Democratic primary, specifically, that she was soft on terrorism.[3] The race was so close that Martinez was not declared the winner until the day after the election, and Castor did not formally concede until the day after that. The final margin separating the two was approximately 82,000 out of 7.5 million votes cast. Just as had been true for Connie Mack in 1988, this particular GOP Senate victory might not have happened except for the coattails provided by a presidential candidate named Bush.

As expected, the presidential race between George W. Bush and Democrat John Kerry was hotly contested. Unlike 2000, however, both parties knew the stakes from the beginning and recognized that Florida could once again be the battleground state that decided the winner. Although polls taken late in the campaign showed the election to be a toss-up, the priority voters gave to national security, foreign policy, and moral issues such as abortion and gay marriage (as opposed to unemployment and traditional social welfare concerns; see Ceaser and Busch 2005) worked to the Republicans' advantage. Bush won by a surprisingly comfortable margin (just over 380,000 votes, 52 to 47 percent), while the GOP preserved its margins in Congress and the state senate and picked up three additional seats in the state house (giving them an 84-to-36 edge). All in all, 2004 was a very good year for the Republican Party in Florida.

The Realignment of Florida Politics

Florida has experienced dramatic changes, politically as well as socially, over the past several decades. As recently as the 1950s, approximately 90 percent of registered voters and virtually all elected officials in the state were Democrats. In 2004, however, voter registration was almost evenly divided between the parties (41 percent Democrat, 38 percent Republican, 21 percent other or no party preference; see the last set of entries in Table 3.1), while the GOP held every statewide office except one (U.S. Senator Bill Nelson is a Democrat) and dominated both the state legislature and, in some areas, local government to an unprecedented degree.

Geographically, Florida contains four politically distinct regions: Southeast, Southwest, North Florida, and the so-called I-4 corridor (see Hill, MacManus, and Moreno 2004). Southeast Florida includes Miami-Dade, Monroe, Broward, and Palm Beach counties. About one-third of all voters live in this region and, apart from Cuban Americans, it is the heart and soul of Florida's Democratic Party today. Broward County (including Fort Lauderdale), in particular, plays a critical role; for example, it gave Kerry-Edwards a 200,000-plus vote margin over Bush-Cheney (64 to 35 percent) in the 2004 presidential race. If they are to have any chance of winning a statewide election, the Democrats must do well in the Southeast in order to offset the GOP's numerical advantages elsewhere.

Southwest Florida begins with Naples on the west coast and moves northward to the St. Petersburg-Tampa area. It has become increasingly Republican over the years and is home to some of the party's wealthiest supporters. North Florida has some of the last vestiges of the Old South in the Sunshine

State. The urban areas of Jacksonville in the east and Pensacola in the west anchor this large expanse of territory, where one can still find a fair number of Dixiecrat voters who remain willing (at times) to support Democrats for local and statewide office but who have, for the most part, been presidential Republicans since the 1960s. Newer and younger residents, in contrast, tend to favor the GOP at all levels. As noted earlier, Democratic strategists generally believe that the key to winning statewide is to choose a candidate (such as Lawton Chiles) who can build a coalition that includes both North Florida Dixiecrats and the party's more traditional base living in the condominiums of Southeast Florida.

The urban and suburban bedroom communities of Central Florida represent one of the fastest-growing areas of the state. Dubbed the I-4 corridor after the interstate highway that travels from west to east across it and connects Tampa, Orlando, and Daytona Beach, this region contains many of Florida's true swing voters. Although it is home to the state's Christian Coalition organization and to some of the religious right's most ardent supporters, the I-4 corridor also has many voters (especially among newer arrivals) who lean Republican but are not firmly attached to either party. The results of recent elections suggest that no candidate is likely to win statewide office without at least a reasonably strong showing along the I-4 corridor.

Overall, the trend in voter registration depicted in Table 3.2 provides clear evidence of Florida's transformation from a Democratic bastion to what some analysts have described as a "competitive red-blue state" (MacManus 2004, 12).[4] The same transformation can be seen in Table 3.4, which tracks changes over time in citizens' psychological attachments to one party or the other. Because some people choose their party registration (including, in states with closed primaries, deciding whether to register with a party at all) based on strategic considerations, such attachments often are a better gauge of an individual's true leanings and, in the aggregate, are a leading indicator of partisan change that may be taking place in the electorate. A partisan realignment is said to occur only when there is a durable (not temporary) shift in the distribution of party loyalties (not simply vote preference or registration) among the general public. Short-term forces may occasionally conspire to produce an uncharacteristic result—for example, the defection of many Democrats to Eisenhower and the GOP in 1952 and 1956 or, in state races, the election of Claude Kirk as governor and Ed Gurney to the U.S. Senate in 1966 and 1968, respectively. This kind of result does not constitute a realignment unless it is accompanied (as it was not in the 1950s or 1960s) by changes in the pattern of underlying predispositions and long-term voting habits among large numbers of citizens.

Table 3.4. Party Identification in Florida, 1980–2005, by Percent

Question: Generally speaking, do you usually think of yourself as a Republican, a Democrat, an independent, or what?

	1980	1984	1988	1992	1995	2001	2004	2005
Republican	21	35	35	37	38	30	31	37
Democrat	44	36	35	28	28	40	34	35
Independent	35	29	30	36	34	30	35	28

Source: Survey Research Laboratory, Florida State University, Tallahassee (1980–2004); Bureau of Economic and Business Research, University of Florida, Gainesville (2005).
Note: Minor-party identifiers and those who answered "don't know" to the original question are omitted from calculations. Independents who responded to a follow-up question by saying that they felt closer to one party are nevertheless classified as independents. In 2005, those who said they had "no preference" between the parties were coded as independents. Interviews for the 2004 survey were conducted from November 3, 2003 to April 4, 2004. Results for 2005 are the combined totals for monthly surveys conducted from January through April of that year.

The figures in Table 3.4 reveal that there has indeed been a reshuffling of basic loyalties in Florida since the early 1980s. Their enthusiasm for Ronald Reagan notwithstanding, voting-age adults preferred the Democrats over-all by a formidable 44 to 21 percent in the spring of 1980; yet within just four years the GOP had managed to achieve parity and by 1992 Republicans actually had pulled ahead by a margin of 37 to 28 percent. The numbers have fluctuated back and forth since then, with Democrats regaining the advantage in 2001 (prior to September 11th) before losing it again in 2004–2005,[5] but the bottom line is clear enough: Florida, like much of the South (Black and Black 2002), has experienced a partisan realignment. Although Democrats remain more competitive in Florida than in some other southern states, the political landscape has nonetheless changed in a fundamental and (presumably) enduring way.

It should be understood, by the way, that Republican identification and voting is primarily a white phenomenon. Race never played as central a role in Florida politics as it did elsewhere in the region, but there can be little doubt that the end of de jure segregation and the greater reliance of today's Democratic politicians on African-American votes are developments that have helped to boost GOP fortunes among conservative whites. In particular, the southern strategy Barry Goldwater and Richard Nixon used in the 1960s attracted "the most reactionary elements" and forced out moderate leadership in many states (Bass and DeVries 1976, 29). Now that the party's base is broader in Florida, this is less of a problem than it used to be. Republican candidates seldom appeal overtly for support on the basis of race, and, in fact, party leaders in Washington and Tallahassee (including George W. and Jeb Bush, each of whom has tried to reach out to black voters in recent elections) claim to be searching for ways to cut into the black Democratic vote, which runs at 85 to 90 percent in most contests.[6] It continues to be an uphill battle, however, despite some evidence suggesting that racial issues per se may not be as important as is often assumed in distinguishing Republican identifiers from Democratic identifiers in Florida politics (Lublin 2004; but see Black and Black 2002).

Republicans, of course, deny that their success is primarily (or even substantially) a result of white backlash against the racial liberalism of the Democratic Party. To the contrary, GOP leaders prefer to believe that they have gained adherents due to rising conservatism on a range of issues (economic, moral, foreign policy, national security) that have little or nothing to do with race and that Democrats have moved too far toward the ideological left on many of these same issues. The relative centrism of "New Democrat" Bill Clinton notwithstanding, there is no question that the Democratic Party, both nationally and in Florida, has become more liberal since the 1960s, in large part due to the steady exodus of its conservative southern wing. Less certain is the notion that voters have moved to any significant degree in the opposite direction. The proportion of citizens who label themselves "conservatives" does not appear to have changed much over the years, and public opinion generally is something of a mixed bag.[7] In a 2004 survey of registered voters (see note 5), for example,

- 52 percent said that the government should "provide more services to citizens even if it means an increase in spending" (versus just 27 percent who felt that "the government should provide fewer services, even in areas such as health and education, in order to reduce spending");
- 60 percent believed that "we need a strong government to handle today's complex economic problems" (versus 21 percent who said that "the free market can handle these problems without government being involved"); and
- solid majorities expressed either "generally" or "extremely" positive feelings toward the idea that government should "ensure that every citizen has adequate medical insurance" (78 percent), "provide programs to help homeless people find a place to live" (62 percent), "provide programs that improve the standard of living of poor Americans" (69 percent), "see to it that everyone who wants a job has one" (66 percent), and "provide child care programs to assist working parents" (63 percent).

All of this aside, it probably is fair to say that southerners in general and Floridians in particular are more conservative, on balance, than people living in other areas of the country. It does not necessarily follow, however, that they are substantially more conservative than they used to be or that ideology has been the main force driving recent increases in Republican partisanship. Much of the change is a result of the continued in-migration of citizens from non-southern states (including, for example, professionals of various types, young two-wage-earner families who are moving to the suburbs, and military veterans; see MacManus 2004) who are disproportionately Republican in their partisanship but are not always more conservative than native Floridians. A second factor is the conversion of voters from Democrat to Republican, especially as some of those who were more conservative in the first place responded to the polarization of national party elites during the 1980s and 1990s (Fiorina with Abrams and Pope 2005) by bringing their partisan attachments into line with their policy preferences (Abramowitz and Saunders 1998). Partisan change also has been facilitated by the GOP's growing competitiveness in state and local elections (thereby removing an incentive for some Republican-leaning voters to side with the Democrats so they would be eligible to participate in that party's primary), the personal popularity of Republican leaders (most notably Ronald Reagan, who won the support even of some who did not share his staunchly conservative views), and shifting perceptions about which party was better able to handle the most important problems facing the country (managing the economy in the 1980s, national security and foreign affairs in the post–September 11 era).

But what about the future? Is Florida politics likely to take on an increasingly Republican hue in the years ahead or can the Democrats remain competitive, at least (given the GOP's control of redistricting) in presidential and statewide elections? Whereas earlier we saw evidence of a pro-Republican *realignment*, it is important to note that Florida (along with the rest of the country) also has experienced aspects of partisan *dealignment* in recent decades; that is, "a durable weakening of individual partisan attachments, either a switch from identifying with parties to independence or a reduction in the connection between identifying with a party and voting for the party's candidates" (Stanley and Castle 1988, 241). As shown in Table 3.4, roughly one-third of Floridians identify themselves as political independents (though many admit that they feel "closer" to one party or the other). Perhaps more impressively, an increasing number of voters are choosing to formally register as something other than Democrats or Republicans,[8] a fairly strong statement given that the state still has a semi-closed primary system. Table 3.5 depicts changes in party registration that occurred in twenty-two selected counties between 1988 and 2004. What we see from the table, first, is that Democrats lost ground (proportionally) in each of these counties,

Table 3.5. Changes in Voter Registration in Selected Counties, 1988–2004

County	Percent Democratic 2004	Change	Percent Republican 2004	Change	Percent Other 2004	Change
Alachua	50.5	−14.9	27.8	−0.7	21.6	+15.6
Brevard	36.6	−9.9	44.8	−1.9	18.7	+11.9
Broward	50.5	−5.6	26.8	−9.1	22.7	+14.7
Clay	25.6	−28.2	56.5	+16.6	17.8	+11.6
Dade	42.8	−13.8	34.8	−0.9	22.4	+14.7
Duval	46.2	−20.0	36.9	+8.7	16.9	+11.3
Escambia	40.7	−26.2	43.8	+14.7	15.5	+11.5
Highlands	39.8	−15.9	44.5	+3.2	15.8	+12.6
Hillsborough	41.7	−16.6	35.1	+0.6	23.3	+16.0
Lee	29.7	−10.8	47.5	−4.9	22.7	+15.7
Marion	39.7	−16.3	43.2	+6.1	17.1	+10.2
Monroe	36.1	−21.5	38.7	+4.4	25.2	+17.1
Okaloosa	24.7	−30.0	57.2	+16.6	18.1	+13.4
Orange	40.2	−6.3	35.1	−11.9	24.7	+18.3
Palm Beach	45.1	−4.0	32.0	−8.8	22.9	+12.8
Pasco	37.3	−12.7	40.1	−2.9	22.6	+15.6
Pinellas	37.8	−4.9	39.2	−8.3	23.0	+13.2
Polk	42.6	−19.4	39.0	+3.4	18.5	+15.9
St. Johns	28.3	−29.7	53.3	+16.0	18.4	+13.7
Sarasota	31.2	−2.1	47.9	−12.2	20.9	+14.3
Seminole	32.3	−6.9	44.6	−8.7	23.1	+15.6
Volusia	40.8	−13.0	35.9	−3.7	23.3	+16.7

Source: Division of Elections, Florida Department of State, Tallahassee.
Note: The degree of change for 2004 indicates shifts in registration between October 1988 and October 2004.

ranging from a low of 2.1 points in Sarasota County to a high of 30.0 points in Okaloosa. Republicans, in contrast, increased their share of the electorate in ten of the twenty-two counties but lost at least some ground, relatively speaking, in the remaining twelve. The consistent winner here is the minor-party/no-affiliation category, which recorded double-digit gains across the board (including statewide; see Table 3.2) during the sixteen-year period under examination. These are the true swing voters in Florida politics (Mac-Manus 2004, 13), and their numbers are large enough that neither party can be successful over the long term without winning the lion's share of their votes.

Some further clues as to what the future might hold can be found by looking at the parties' respective support coalitions in the electorate. Most of the group differences evident in Table 3.6 are familiar and similar to patterns seen in national surveys (Abramson, Aldrich, and Rohde 2003).[9]

- Gender: Men are more likely to be Republicans; women are more likely to be Democrats.
- Class: Society's haves (relatively speaking, measured in terms of income and education) are more likely to be Republicans than have-nots.
- Race: A plurality of whites are Republicans; an overwhelming majority of blacks are Democrats.
- Politics and religion: Protestants (especially those belonging to fundamentalist denominations) tilt Republican and Catholics represent an important swing bloc of voters, while both Jews and the nonreligious prefer Democrats.

At least two other aspects of Table 3.6 are worth noting. First, the Hispanic population is currently divided, with Cuban Americans favoring the GOP (older voters more than younger; see Scicchitano and Scher 2003) and other groups either leaning Democratic or remaining independent. As these groups continue to grow in size in Florida and nationwide, both parties will be competing aggressively for their support; for now, though, the jury is still out. Second, much the same thing is true for younger voters. Floridians who came of voting age during the Reagan era were disproportionately Republican, while those who entered the electorate while Bill Clinton was president were more Democratic in their allegiances (Craig 1998). Although many younger citizens may end up changing their outlooks (and those who have not yet come of voting age will form theirs) in response to major events and shifting political tides, at least for now it seems that the GOP has regained the upper hand with the voters of tomorrow.

Conclusion

Numerous factors have contributed to political change and, specifically, to the emergence of genuine two-party competition in Florida over the past several decades, including explosive population growth, relatively high levels of economic diversity and urbanization compared with the rest of the South, the political mobilization of black voters, a significant (and growing) Hispanic presence, the ideological polarization of national party elites, the establishment of strong state and local party organizations (especially on the Republican side), the personal popularity of Ronald Reagan in the 1980s, and attitudinal changes among the general public (including skepticism toward the parties and a heightened sense of independence from both; see Craig

Table 3.6. Party Identification by Gender, Age, Education, Income, Race/Ethnicity, and Religion in Florida, 2004, by Percent

Question: Generally speaking, do you usually think of yourself as a Republican, a Democrat, an independent, or what?

	Republican	Democrat	Independent
Total Sample	36.7	36.6	26.7
Gender			
Men	37.6	33.0	29.4
Women	36.0	39.6	24.4
Age			
18–34	41.0	32.8	26.2
35–49	42.5	30.0	27.5
50–64	31.8	38.8	29.3
65–plus	36.7	38.6	24.7
Education			
High School or less	31.2	44.8	23.9
Some College	36.7	33.2	30.0
College Graduate	41.5	32.2	26.3
Income			
Less than $30,000	29.0	46.0	25.0
$30,000 to $50,000	36.1	34.1	29.8
$50,000 and above	42.4	32.2	25.5
Race/Ethnicity			
White	39.6	33.4	27.0
Black	4.4	77.8	17.7
Hispanic	31.3	37.4	31.3
Religion			
Traditional Protestant	41.7	35.0	23.3
Evangelical Christian/Fundamentalist	50.9	27.3	21.8
Catholic	35.4	36.3	28.3
Jewish	16.3	61.8	21.9
No Affiliation	22.3	33.9	43.8

Source: Pooled data from four statewide surveys of registered voters conducted by the Florida Voter polling organization between October 2000 and June 2004 (valid N = 2,412; see note 9). Note: Minor-party identifiers and those who answered "don't know" to the original question are omitted from calculations. Independents who responded to a follow-up question by saying that they felt closer to one party are nevertheless classified as independents.

1998). The end result is that not only have Republicans become a viable force in Florida politics, they actually appear to have replaced the Democrats as the state's dominant party. However, keeping in mind recent Democratic victories and near-misses in presidential and state races, it would be a mistake to write the Democratic Party off completely. Considering the large number of voters who are willing to support strong leaders on both sides of the aisle, the Sunshine State's long tradition of candidate-oriented campaigns and electoral volatility may yet survive what has thus far been nearly half a century of dramatic political change.

Notes

1. The Florida legislature temporarily eliminated its runoff primary in 2002 and made the change permanent in 2005; party nominees are now determined by plurality vote in a single primary election.

2. The day after the election, Bush recused himself from any active involvement in state actions relating to the vote-count controversy. Nevertheless, partisans either hoped (Republicans) or feared (Democrats) that he was playing a role behind the scenes—perceptions that were encouraged by the fact that Secretary of State Katherine Harris, whose office had responsibility for certifying the election outcome, had been a titular head (along with current U.S. Senator Mel Martinez) of George W. Bush's presidential campaign in Florida.

3. As president of the University of South Florida from 1994 to 1999, Castor suspended but did not fire a professor with alleged ties to Middle East terrorist groups.

4. Reflecting the colors used by television networks to portray the distribution of electoral votes in presidential elections, the distinction between red and blue states has become a shorthand way of describing the political leanings of different states and regions throughout the country; see <www.answers.com/topic/red-state-vs-blue-state-divide>.

5. The sampling frames represented in Table 3.4 are voting-age adults (1980–2004) and households (2005). A statewide survey conducted in May–June 2004 by the Florida Voter polling organization also revealed an even split among registered voters: 39 percent Democrat, 39 percent Republican, and 21 percent independent. Further information about this and other Florida Voter surveys used in the present chapter (see Table 3.6) can be obtained from the Graduate Program in Political Campaigning at the University of Florida.

6. While the preferences of African Americans are solidly Democratic, their turnout rates fluctuate widely from election to election (MacManus 2004, 8). This obviously places a premium on voter mobilization, which is not something that Democrats always do well.

7. Among Floridians who profess an explicit ideological preference (as many as 40 percent do not), conservatives outnumbered liberals by 42 to 18 percent in 1982, by

40 to 18 percent in 1992, and by 37 to 22 percent in 2003–2004 (data provided by the Survey Research Laboratory, Florida State University).

8. This includes registration with one of several minor parties (e.g., Libertarian, Green, Reform, Independent) or, most commonly, designation as "no party affiliation" at all (1,886,013 in October 2004).

9. As indicated, Table 3.6 is based on pooled data from four surveys (of registered voters, who matter the most at election time) conducted between 2000 and 2004. This was a period of very little aggregate change in partisanship among Florida voters, so the extended time frame has been used in an effort to increase both sample size and the accuracy of our estimates of intergroup differences.

References

Abramowitz, Alan I., and Kyle L. Saunders. 1998. "Ideological Realignment in the U.S. Electorate." *Journal of Politics* 60, no. 3: 634–52.

Abramson, Paul R., John H. Aldrich, and David W. Rohde. 2003. *Change and Continuity in the 2000 and 2002 Elections.* Washington, D.C.: CQ Press.

Barone, Michael, and Grant Ujifusa. 1981. *The Almanac of American Politics, 1982.* Washington, D.C.: National Journal Group.

———. 1989. *The Almanac of American Politics, 1990.* Washington, D.C.: National Journal Group.

———, with Richard E. Cohen. 1995. *The Almanac of American Politics, 1996.* Washington, D.C.: National Journal Group.

Bass, Jack, and Walter DeVries. 1976. *The Transformation of Southern Politics: Social Change and Political Consequences since 1945.* New York: Basic Books.

Black, Earl, and Merle Black. 1987. *Politics and Society in the South.* Cambridge, Mass.: Harvard University Press.

———. 2002. *The Rise of Southern Republicans.* Cambridge, Mass.: Harvard University Press.

Ceaser, James W., and Andrew E. Busch. 2001. *The Perfect Tie: The True Story of the 2000 Presidential Election.* Lanham, Md.: Rowman and Littlefield.

———. 2005. *Red over Blue: The 2004 Elections and American Politics.* Lanham, Md.: Rowman and Littlefield.

Cohodas, Nadine. 1993. *Strom Thurmond and the Politics of Southern Change.* New York: Simon and Schuster.

Craig, Stephen C. 1998. "Elections and Partisan Change." In *Government and Politics in Florida,* edited by Robert J. Huckshorn. 2nd ed. 30–65. Gainesville: University Press of Florida.

Ehrenhalt, Alan, ed. 1987. *Politics in America: The 100th Congress.* Washington, D.C.: CQ Press.

Fiorina, Morris P., with Samuel J. Abrams and Jeremy C. Pope. 2005. *Culture War? The Myth of a Polarized America.* New York: Pearson Longman.

Hill, Kevin A., Susan A. MacManus, and Dario Moreno, eds. 2004. *Florida's Politics: Ten Media Markets, One Powerful State.* Tallahassee: Florida Institute of Government.

Key, V. O., Jr. 1949. *Southern Politics in State and Nation.* New York: Knopf.

Lamis, Alexander P. 1988. *The Two-Party South.* Exp. ed. New York: Oxford University Press.

Lublin, David. 2004. *The Republican South: Democratization and Partisan Change.* Princeton, N.J.: Princeton University Press.

MacManus, Susan A. 2004. "Florida Overview: Ten Media Markets—One Powerful State." In *Florida's Politics: Ten Media Markets, One Powerful State,* edited by Kevin A. Hill, Susan A. MacManus, and Dario Moreno, 1–64. Tallahassee: Florida Institute of Government.

Phillips, Kevin P. 1969. *The Emerging Republican Majority.* New Rochelle, N.Y.: Arlington House.

Scicchitano, Michael J., and Richard K. Scher. 2003. "Florida: Political Change, 1950–2000." In *The New Politics of the Old South: An Introduction to Southern Politics,* edited by Charles S. Bullock III and Mark J. Rozell. 2nd ed. 247–65. Lanham, Md.: Rowman and Littlefield.

Stanley, Harold W., and David S. Castle. 1988. "Partisan Changes in the South: Making Sense of Scholarly Dissonance." In *The South's New Politics: Realignment and Dealignment,* edited by Robert H. Swansbrough and David M. Brodsky. 238–52. Columbia: University of South Carolina Press.

Sundquist, James L. 1983. *Dynamics of the Party System: Alignment and Realignment of Political Parties in the United States.* Rev. ed. Washington, D.C.: Brookings Institution.

4

Politics and Ethnic Change in Florida

KEVIN A. HILL AND DARIO A. MORENO

The election of Mel Martinez to the U.S. Senate was the culmination of twenty-five years of Hispanic political empowerment in Florida. Although Hispanics have played a prominent role in Florida politics in the past (for example, Florida's first delegate to the U.S. Congress was Joseph Marion Hernandez), the empowerment of Latinos is a very recent phenomenon there. Hispanics did not become a factor in modern state politics until the 1980s. Martinez's election is symbolic of the rapid empowerment of Florida's growing Hispanic population. Today it is impossible to understand Florida politics without taking into account Hispanic political clout. Florida's role as a swing state in presidential elections, combined with the fund-raising muscle and bloc voting of Miami's Cuban Americans and the rapid growth of the state's Puerto Rican population along the I-4 corridor, make the state's Hispanic community one of the most influential Latino populations in the country. In fact, Florida's Hispanics have as much national political power as much larger and more established Hispanic communities in California and Texas.

In sharp contrast, Florida's black voters remain largely marginalized in state politics. Although African Americans have dramatically increased their representation in both Tallahassee and Washington, these gains have been offset by the surging power of the Republican Party in Florida. Republican political ascendancy and the conservative Democratic agenda has placed the interests of black Floridians far from the state's ideological mainstream. However, African Americans have been able to push their agenda in alliances with other liberal groups using Florida's progressive constitutional amendment process. In 2002, despite the opposition of Governor Jeb Bush and the legislative leadership, Florida voters approved a statewide constitutional amendment limiting classroom size. The campaign to reduce classroom size was spearheaded by Congressman Kendrick Meek (D-Miami) in concert with Florida's teachers' unions. Despite this victory, black Floridians remain frustrated with the elusiveness of African American political power;

this contrasts markedly with Hispanics' perception of their own political prominence. Because the Democratic Party is a small and dwindling part of the political landscape in Tallahassee, the prospects for black (Democratic) political power in the near future are dim.

Current demographic trends confirm the confidence of Hispanics in their growing influence over state politics. Hispanics are now the largest minority group in Florida. According to 2000 census, they constituted 16.8 percent (2,682,715) of the Sunshine State's population. This is remarkable growth, considering that as late as 1980 there were only 860,000 Latinos in Florida, just 8.9 percent of the population. The 1990 census showed a remarkable 83 percent growth in the Hispanic population to 1,574,000, or 12.1 percent of the total. The Hispanic population grew by an impressive 70.4 percent from 1990 to 2000. More recent U.S. Bureau of the Census (2003) estimates, from the 2003 American Community Survey, put the Hispanic population of Florida at 3,108,578, or 18.7 percent of the state's population. Given the rapid pace of growth in the Hispanic population, Latino political power in Florida should continue to grow for the foreseeable future.

African American population growth has been relatively stable since 1980. Today, according to the 2000 census, they are 2,234,404 African Americans in Florida, constituting 14.6 percent of the state's population (U.S. Bureau of the Census 2003). In 1990, blacks constituted 13.6 percent of Florida's population, with a total population of 1,759,500. The size of Florida's black population grew 26.9 percent from 1990 to 2000, a total net gain of 474,904 people. These figures are almost identical to the growth of the state's African American population from 1980 to 1990, when the black population grew by 416,800, a rate of 31 percent. The dramatic growth of the state's Hispanic population over the last two decades in contrast to the relative stability of its African American population shapes the perception of both groups as they compete for political power in Florida.

Hispanic Political Empowerment

Hispanic political power has increased with every election cycle. In 1980, only one Latino served in the Florida legislature; Elvin Martinez represented the traditional Hispanic area of West Tampa in the Florida House of Representatives. Today, there are seventeen Hispanic members of the legislature, fourteen in the Florida House (twelve Republicans and two Democrats), and three in the Florida Senate (all Republicans).

The rapid political empowerment of Hispanics was made possible by a convergence of forces unique to Florida politics. Four factors have contributed to this change. The first is the extreme concentration of the U.S. Cuban population. Over two-thirds of all Cubans in the United States live in Florida, and of the 833,120 Cubans who live there, a remarkable 650,601 reside in Miami-Dade County. In other words, over half of all Cubans in the United States (52 percent) and over three-fourths (78 percent) of all Cubans in Florida live in just one county. This extraordinary concentration of Cubans in South Florida has been a critical factor contributing to Cuban political influence in the United States. This heavy concentration in Florida means that Cuban-Americans constitute 8 percent of Florida's electorate.[1] Florida's close partisan divide has made Cuban Americans the decisive voters in at least three statewide elections. Overwhelming Cuban support for Connie Mack (R-Florida) was instrumental in his narrow victory in the 1988 election for the U.S. Senate. Mack edged out Buddy McKay by only 33,612 votes out of over 4,065,046 votes cast. Similarly, Cuban Americans provided the critical margin of victory in two presidential races, for President George H. Bush in 1992 and for George W. Bush in the controversial 2000 election.

Miami-Dade County is still the epicenter of Hispanic politics in Florida due to the heavy concentration of Cubans and other Latinos there (Moreno 2004, 84). Miami-Dade is the only Florida county that is majority Hispanic; it has a total Latino population of 1,291,737, or 58 percent. Nearly half (48.1 percent) of all Hispanics in Florida live in Miami-Dade. Neighboring Broward County has the second-largest Hispanic population in the state, with 189,347. Combined, the two Southeast Florida counties have 55.2 percent of the total Hispanic population in the state. Not surprisingly, Hispanics control nearly every major political institution in Miami-Dade County. The county mayor is Cuban American, as are seven of the thirteen members of the county commission, five out of the nine school board members, and the state attorney. The mayors of the two largest cities—Miami and Hialeah—are also Cuban American.

The concentration of Hispanics in South Florida combined with the advent of single-member state legislative districts in 1982 created the political conditions for Latino political empowerment. Table 4.1 shows the rapid growth of Florida's Hispanic representation in both the state legislature and the U.S. Congress since 1980. Given the continuous concentration of Hispanics in South Florida (according to the U.S. Census 2003 estimates, Miami-Dade is now 61 percent Hispanic and Broward is 20 percent Hispanic) and the creation of new Hispanic communities in Central Florida (Orange County is 22 percent Hispanic and Osceola County is 30 percent Hispanic), this trend of growing political influence should continue well into the next century.

Table 4.1. Hispanic Political Empowerment in Florida, 1980–2004

Year	Florida House	Florida Senate	Congressional U.S. House Delegation	Florida Statewide Office
1980	1	0	0	0
1982	4	0	0	0
1984	8	0	0	0
1986	8	1	0	1
1988	8	3	0	1
1990	8	3	1	0
1992	10	3	2	0
1994	11	3	2	0
1996	11	3	2	0
1998	11	3	2	0
2000	11	3	2	0
2002	14	3	3	0
2004	14	3	3	1

Source: Florida Deparment of State, Division of Election, 1980–2006.

Florida's twenty-seven electoral votes and its partisan competitiveness also amplify the importance of the state's Hispanics in national politics. Florida's critical role in national politics has been underscored by the fact that since the 1992 election, Florida has been a so-called battleground state. Florida is the most competitive of the large states whose party orientation was decided by a margin of less than 5.2 percent in the last four presidential elections, including the controversial 537-vote victory it gave President Bush in 2000. As a result of these election-year results, candidates from both parties pander to Cubans' desire to strengthen the anti-Castro policy of the United States. Ronald Reagan, the first presidential candidate to court the Cuban vote, was rewarded with over 80 percent of that vote. He easily won Florida's electoral votes in 1980 and 1984 and approved the establishment of Radio and TV Marti in part to reward his Cuban supporters (Moreno and Warren 1992, 134). During the 1992 presidential election, Bill Clinton was the first Democratic presidential nominee to campaign in Miami's Cuban neighborhoods. He endorsed the Torricelli bill, which tightened the economic embargo against Cuba before his Republican opponent, President Bush, did so. This strong anti-Castro stance allowed him to establish important inroads with Cubans, although he received only 25 percent of the Cuban vote in 1992 (Moreno and Warren 1996, 174–75). Clinton dramatically improved his standing with Cuban voters after he signed the Helms-Burton bill, which codified the embargo. He received nearly 40 percent of Miami's Cuban vote in the 1996 presidential election (Moreno and Hill 2005, 231–32). However, these significant gains by the Democrats were lost as a consequence of the Elián González affair. Cuban Americans angered by the Clinton administration's return of the young boy to Castro's Cuba solidly rejected the Democratic candidates in both the 2000 presidential and 2002 gubernatorial elections (Moreno and Hill 2005, 217–20). In both those elections, Republican candidates received well over 80 percent of the Cuban vote.

Further, while most Hispanics who live in Central Florida are of Puerto Rican origin, they are not as overwhelmingly Democratic as Puerto Ricans in other parts of the country, especially New York. While the plurality of Central Florida's Hispanic voters are indeed registered Democrats, Jeb Bush won the majority of the Puerto Rican vote in Florida in the 2002 gubernatorial election, while George W. Bush closely split the Puerto Rican vote in 2004 with John Kerry. Also, the only Hispanic state representative from Central Florida, John Quiñones, is a Republican.

The concentration of so many Hispanics in a vital presidential swing state led both parties to mount aggressive campaigns to woo Florida Hispanics during the 2004 presidential election. The Democrats developed a three-prong strategy to improve their showing among Latinos in the state. First, they invested considerable resources to replicate Al Gore's strong showing among Hispanics in Central Florida and Hillsborough County in 2000. The party used many Hispanic 527 advocacy groups organized as to organize registration and get-out-the-vote drives among the mostly non-Cuban Latinos living along the I-4 corridor. Spearheaded by the New Democrat Network, the party also invested heavily in trying to significantly reduce Cuban American support for the Republican ticket. Democrats hired two experts on the Cuban community— former executive director of the Cuban-American National Foundation Joe Garcia and pollster Sergio Bendixen—to court the Cuban vote. Democrats also established a physical presence in the Cuban community by opening a campaign headquarters in Little Havana. Their message to Cuban Americans was simple: Republican promises to liberate Cuba are insincere, and what really matters are domestic issues such as providing access to health insurance, decreasing the cost of prescription drugs, and expanding the Medicare program.[2] Finally, Democrats hoped to improve their image among Florida's Hispanics by running young Latino candidates for state legislative seats. Barbra Herrera-Hill in Broward County and Israel Mercado in Orange County were viewed as the future of the Democratic Party among the state's Hispanics. Almost all Democratic efforts focusing on the Hispanic vote failed in 2004. In fact, the state Democratic Party did not even have a database of registered voters that identified which voters were Hispanic, something easily obtained for a small fee from supervisors of elections.

The Republican campaign countered with a two-pronged strategy. First, they reminded Cuban voters that President Bush was pursuing a robust strategy to hasten democratization in Cuba, including tougher travel restrictions to the island and restrictions on the amount of remittances that exiles can send to Cuba. The Bush campaign also stressed the administration's policy of spending money to help organizations that protect Cuban dissidents and promote human rights. Second, the president's campaign encouraged the candidacy and nomination of Mel Martinez for U.S. Senate. Republicans hoped that Martinez's candidacy would mobilize a historic turnout among his co-nationals in Miami-Dade. Because Martinez was the former mayor of Orange County, his candidacy might serve to encourage his former Latino constituents in Central Florida to vote for the Republican ticket. Finally, Republicans organized a strong get-out-the-vote campaign in the traditional Cuban neighborhoods of Miami-Dade County.

The Republican strategy was successful; Bush carried Florida by 380,978 votes. This was the largest Republican margin in Florida since the 1988 presidential election, when the GOP won the state by 962,184 votes. Hispanic voters were an important segment of the president's winning coalition. Despite the efforts of the Kerry campaign and the New Democratic Network, Cuban Americans supported the president nearly four to one. Cuban American support for Bush dropped from 82 percent in 2000 to 77 percent in 2004, but this can be attributed to the unusual anti-Democratic sentiment in Miami after the Elián González affair in 2000.[3] President Bush improved his showing in Central Florida; he split the Hispanic vote with Senator Kerry 50-50. This signifies a 10 percent improvement from the president's performance among Central Florida Hispanics in 2000.

The concentration of such large numbers of Hispanics in South Florida has led to the development of the region's most distinctive political, social, and economic feature: the South Florida Hispanic enclave, a network of small businesses that caters to the large and ever-growing Latin market in South Florida. The economic enclave is the second factor that has contributed to the rapid political empowerment of Florida's Hispanics. These businesses and professional services, originally established by Cubans fleeing the Castro regime, now serve both the common taste and particular national preferences of the South Florida Hispanic community. The most important characteristic of the enclave, according to sociologist Lisandro Perez (1992, 90–93), is "institutional completeness," the fact that the enclave provides all the goods and services (supermarket, medical, legal, financial, restaurants, communications) necessary to survive in North American society. This self-sufficiency allows many Hispanics in South Florida to live their lives using their native language and largely avoid assimilation.

The protection the enclave provides for immigrants partly explains the economic success of South Florida Hispanics. The Miami–Fort Lauderdale metropolitan area has the largest number of Latino-owned businesses in the United States. Hispanics in South Florida are far more likely to own their own businesses than their counterparts in California, New York, or Texas. South Florida Hispanics' high rate of business ownership is often cited as a model for other minority groups. Similarly, the 2000 census reports that South Florida Hispanics have the highest rate of homeownership of any Latino group in the nation. In fact, Cuban Americans in Broward County have the highest rate of homeownership—77 percent—of any ethnic group in the four South Florida counties, including non-Latin whites. Cuban American homeownership in Miami-Dade County is 61 percent, compared to a national Hispanic average of 46 percent (U.S. Bureau of the Census 2003).

Sociologists Alejandro Portes and Alex Stepick (1992) argue that the self-sufficiency of the Hispanic enclave in South Florida allows the community to pursue other strategies in contrast to the traditional policy of assimilation. "This was no mere immigrant neighborhood, but a 'moral community' standing for the values of old Cuban society and against the new order imposed by Castroism," they argue (Portes and Stepick 1992, 107). Throughout the 1970s, this project continued at a rapid pace. The rhetoric was one of return to Cuba, but the reality was one of consolidation. Consolidation of the Cuban American population in South Florida continued through the 1970s, despite the objections of white elites. Over time, Miami took on the character of a second Havana (Portes and Stepick 1992, 107).

This network of Hispanic businessmen and professionals became a funding source for political campaigns. Cuban businessmen in the development sector (construction, real estate, financing) became instrumental in electing pro-development Cubans to local offices. The willingness of Miami's Hispanic business community to raise large sums of money for their candidates has reshaped Miami politics; for example, Alex Penelas raised over $3 million for his 1996 county mayor's race and Manny Diaz raised an unprecedented $1.5 million for his 2001 city of Miami mayor campaign. The Cuban business community has used its financial resources far beyond Miami. The sugar-growing Fajul family is a major contributor to both political parties, while the Free Cuba Political Action Committee, operated by the Cuban American National Foundation, raises money for congressional candidates.

The Cuban community's fund-raising strength is a major factor in their political success.

Third, the existence of well-established and concentrated Hispanic neighborhoods in South Florida combined with the extraordinary fund-raising capacity of the enclave has created a network of campaign technicians. This network of political activists, consultants, pollsters, and public relations and media experts gives South Florida Hispanics the expertise to run sophisticated political campaigns. The professionalism of Cuban electoral campaigns partially explains why Cuban Americans turn out to vote in greater numbers than any other Latino group in the United States. In fact, Cuban Americans in Miami-Dade County regularly vote at a greater rate than non-Latin whites in local elections. The creation of an ethnic political machine is an important factor in explaining the success of Cuban Americans in the U.S. political system.

The final factor contributing to the rapid and successful empowerment of Florida's Hispanics is the partisan and ideological cohesion of the Cuban community in the United States. Because of their unity on Cuban policy, ethnic bloc voting by Cuban Americans increases their political capital. The strong anti-Castro consensus among Cuban Americans has translated into strong support for the U.S. economic embargo against Cuba, the travel ban, and the Republican Party. Although recent polls have indicated some erosion of support for the embargo among the general Cuban American population, there is almost universal support for maintaining the economic embargo among likely Cuban American voters. This ideological cohesion has translated into strong support for the conservative foreign policy of the Republican Party.

Other Hispanic groups in South Florida share the anti-communist attitudes of Cuban Americans. Nicaraguans, who fled the leftist Sandinista regime, also tend to support a hard-line foreign policy toward Latin American revolutionaries. Venezuelans, many of whom recently settled in Broward County after becoming disenchanted with the populist left-leaning policy of Hugo Chavez, also support a conservative U.S. policy toward Latin American. Similarly, Colombians and Peruvians, many who came to Miami-Dade and Broward counties fleeing leftist political violence in their countries, support U.S. military assistance to their homeland to defeat left-wing guerillas and terrorists.

Hispanics in South Florida, in sharp contrast to U.S. Latinos elsewhere, tend to support a hard-line foreign policy. Cuban Americans and South Florida Hispanics have supported GOP nominees in every presidential and gubernatorial election but one since 1980. Moreover, in all but two of these elections, South Florida Hispanics have given the Republican candidates at least 70 percent of their votes. The growing Puerto Rican population of Central Florida, which shows an inclination to split its votes between Democrats and Republicans (many times in favor of Republicans), is another reason why Hispanic political power in Florida is more considerable than population percentages would suggest. After all, Florida's Hispanic population percentage is not much above the national average and nowhere near the percentages seen in Texas, New Mexico, California, or Arizona. But for the four reasons cited above, Florida Hispanic political power benefits from a tremendous multiplier effect not seen in any other state. The same can most definitely *not* be said for Florida's black voters.

The Black Struggle for Political Power

African Americans have been historically underrepresented in Florida politics. Like the rest of the old Confederacy, Florida severely limited the ability of its black citizens to participate in politics. From the end of Reconstruction in 1877 to the advent of the civil rights movement in the 1950s, black Floridians were essentially shut out of the state's political life. Florida used the Jim Crow legal system of white Democratic primaries, literacy tests, segregated public facilities, poll taxes, and violence to disenfranchise its black citizens. Florida did not have a black member of the state legislature until 1968, when Miami schoolteacher John Lang Kershaw became the first African American elected to the state house of representatives since Reconstruction (Dunn 1997, 200).

However, within this context of a history of southern racism, it should be pointed out that the development of African American politics in Florida was significantly different from that development in the rest of the South. The death of the cotton industry in the 1910s led to a mass exodus of up to half of the black population in the rural south—but not in Florida, where the cotton industry was relatively small. Rather, a massive influx of whites in the 1920s radically transformed the racial balance in Florida, not an outflow of blacks (Hill 2004, 65). Back in 1900, blacks were 45 percent of the state's population; today, the state's black population hovers around 15 percent of all Floridians.

According to the 2000 U.S. census, only Texas (2,404,566, or 12 percent) and Georgia (2,349,542, or 29 percent) had larger black populations among the southern states than Florida's 15 percent. Therefore, Florida has at the same time one of the largest black populations *by number* in the South yet at

Table 4.2. Black Population of Florida by County, 2000

1. Counties over 25 percent black

County	Black Population	Percent Black	Percent of Statewide Black Population
Gadsden	25,768	57	< 1
Madison	7,543	40	< 1
Jefferson	4,934	38	< 1
Hamilton	5,017	38	< 1
Leon	70,296	29	3
Duval	218,829	28	9
Jackson	12,485	27	< 1

2. Counties with over 100,000 black residents

County	Black Population	Percent Black	Percent of Statewide Black Population
Miami-Dade	448,173	20	19
Broward	349,610	22	15
Duval	218,829	28	9
Orange	166,815	19	7
Palm Beach	163,774	15	7
Hillsborough	150,173	15	6

Source: Florida Deparment of State, Division of Election, 2000–2006.

15 percent one of the smallest black populations *by proportion* to the entire state.

These overall statistics are misleading, since the bulk of Florida's black population is concentrated in just a few areas. Three urban counties—one northern and two southern—contain 43 percent of the entire black population of the state: there are 443,173 blacks in Miami-Dade County, 349,610 in Broward County, and 218,829 in Duval County. What is striking about these numbers is that blacks form nowhere near a majority of the population in the counties where they are most concentrated. Blacks are 19 percent of Miami-Dade's population, 22 percent of Broward's, and 28 percent of Duval's. This is consequential to the countywide success of black candidates in these urban areas.

Blacks are the majority of the population in only one county—Gadsden, which has a population of less than 50,000 people. Over a dozen cities in Miami-Dade and Broward have a higher population than this Panhandle county. Blacks constitute over 30 percent of the population in only three other small rural counties—Madison (40 percent), Jefferson (38 percent), and Hamilton (38 percent). Madison, the largest of these counties, had only 18,733 inhabitants in 2000. Table 4.2 lists the counties with the highest black populations by number and percent. In Florida, blacks are concentrated in areas where they are a minority; they form a majority or a large minority

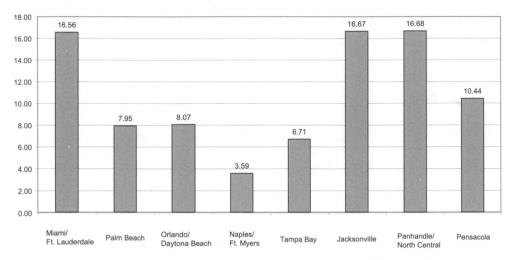

Figure 4.1. Percent Black Registered Voters in Florida by Region, 2004. *Source:* Florida Department of State, Division of Elections, 1980-2006.

only in a few small Panhandle counties. This demographic does not predict political success for black candidates in counties or in the state in light of Florida's history of racially polarized voting.

Figure 4.1 shows the percentage of black registered voters by media market in Florida. Interestingly, at their highest rates, blacks constitute between 16 percent and 17 percent of all registered voters in the Miami–Fort Lauderdale, Jacksonville, and Panhandle/North Central media markets. This means that blacks constitute no more than about one-sixth of registered voters *at the most* in any one region of Florida. On the other extreme, black voters are less than 4 percent of all voters in Southwest Florida and in the much larger regions of Tampa Bay and Orlando/Space Coast, no more than 8 percent of all registered voters.

As more and more white and Hispanic voters in Florida have registered as either Republicans or independents, black voters have become an increasing percentage of the Democratic electorate in Florida. Therefore, in areas of high Democratic concentration, blacks are a disproportionate number of the electors in Democratic primaries, which are often decisive in elections. Black voters are most highly concentrated in the Miami–Fort Lauderdale, Jacksonville-Northeast, and Panhandle–North Central Florida media markets. But these numbers mask one important factor: blacks are overwhelmingly registered as Democrats in the state of Florida. In 2000, 791,775, or

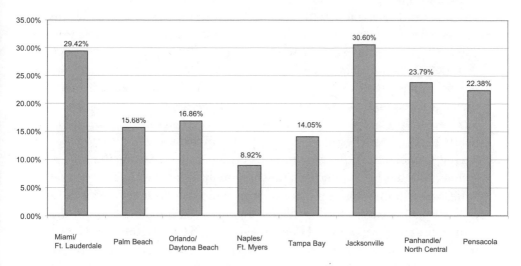

Figure 4.2. Blacks as a Percentage of Registered Democrats in Florida, 2004. Source: Florida Department of State, Division of Elections, 1980–2006.

85 percent, of the 933,645 black registered voters in Florida were registered Democrats. This means that over 20 percent of all registered Democrats in Florida are black. When combined with the fact that many whites who register as Democrats—especially in North Florida—are really Republican voters, the landscape for black electoral influence expands dramatically.

Figure 4.2 presents the percentage of registered *Democrats* in Florida regions who are black. In South Florida and Jacksonville, this statistic essentially doubles the concentration of black voters when compared to the statistic of percentage of registered black *voters* by region. While about 17 percent of all registered voters in the Miami–Fort Lauderdale media market are black, nearly 30 percent of all registered Democrats are black. When one realizes that South Florida is often the bedrock of any statewide Democratic candidacy, this figure alone increases the potential impact of black bloc voting. Since many single-member districts in South Florida are overwhelmingly Democratic, the effect of black voting increases sharply there. Further, three state legislative districts in South Florida are over 35 percent black in voter registration, and all are represented by black Democrats (Edward Bullard, Larcenia Bullard, and Phillip Brutus). Likewise, nearly 31 percent of all registered Democrats in the Jacksonville-Northeast media market are black voters, while nearly 25 percent of Democrats in the Panhandle are black; in the West Florida media market, this statistic is 22 percent.

As the population of Florida relocates within the state, the impact of black voters on the Democratic Party may well increase. Broward, Leon, and Palm Beach counties are each solidly Democratic counties that have experienced black growth rates in excess of 50 percent since 1990. These are also large counties. Broward County, the backbone of the Democratic Party in Florida, particularly stands out. This county has over 1 million registered voters, the largest voter base in the state of Florida, larger than even Miami-Dade. Since 1990, its black population has nearly doubled; blacks now constitute nearly 15 percent of the registered voters in Broward and 27 percent of registered Democrats. If this growth rate continues at even a fraction of the 1990–2000 rate, black voters will fundamentally transform the Democratic landscape of Broward County, probably even more in the immediate future than Hispanic voters, who face citizenship obstacles and do not vote at the same rate as blacks in Broward County. Palm Beach County, the third largest in the state, is another example of demographic change that favors a greater impact from black voters. The rate of growth of its black population was 50 percent in the 1990s. Although only 8 percent of the county's residents are registered voters, blacks constitute 17 percent of all Democrats there.

Second, the national-origin composition of Florida's black population is also unique. The economic and social deprivation that blacks suffered in the Bahamas created a significant influx of blacks to the Florida Keys and South Florida in the nineteenth century, and South Florida witnessed a large in-migration of black Bahamians beginning in the second half of the century. Marvin Dunn (1997, 16) described the Bahamian migration:

> As white farmers began to trickle down to the wilderness on Biscayne Bay in the 1870s, black Bahamians migrated seasonally to the South Florida area to find farm work. By the time the City of Miami was founded in 1896, there was a growing Bahamian population permanently settled in various parts of Dade County. When Miami was established more than 40 percent of its black population was Bahamian.

Bahamian blacks played a critical role in the development of African American politics in South Florida. The two first African Americans elected to the Florida legislature were of Bahamian descent: Joe Lang Kershaw and Gwendolyn Cherry. Cherry was the daughter of Dr. W. B. Sawyer, a physician and one of the original Bahamian pioneers in Florida.

Today, this connection between the Caribbean and South Florida's black population is still a defining characteristic of black politics in the state. The connection was reinforced with a recent and dramatic (though not well doc-

umented) new migration of blacks from the Caribbean that altered the national-origin profile of Florida's blacks (Hill 2004, 65). The Caribbean influx
rapidly accelerated during the last two decades of the twentieth century with
large migrations from Haiti and the English-speaking Caribbean, most notably Jamaica. There are now two Haitian Americans in Miami-Dade County's
state legislative delegation: Yolly Roberson and Phillip Brutus. Moreover,
Haitians have become an influential force in two Miami-Dade municipalities, North Miami and El Portal. Similarly, until March 2005 a majority of
the city commission was composed of Jamaican Americans in one Broward
County city, Miramar, although only 20 percent of its population is from the
island. Caribbean blacks have been elected to municipal office in three other
Broward cities: Southwest Ranches, Lauderhill, and Lauderdale Lakes. The
unique composition of South Florida's black population portends a different style of African American politics. A sign of potential future intra-black
political struggles occurred in 2002, when an African American, a Jamaican
American, and a Haitian American competed for the same state legislative
seat in central Broward County (the African American incumbent barely
won). In 2005, in the city of Miramar, every contested city commission election featured at least one African American running against at least one
Jamaican American. As the Caribbean population of Florida increases and
as the African American population remains stable, these types of political
battles will become more frequent in the years to come.

This national origin-based diversity in the black population is not confined
to Miami-Dade and Broward counties. Not surprisingly, the Miami–Fort
Lauderdale media market has the highest ratio of Haitians and Jamaicans to
overall black population. In 2000, 29 percent of the black population identified as having Jamaican ancestry in Miami-Dade, Broward, and Monroe
counties, while nearly 20 percent identified as Haitian. This is the highest
concentration of Caribbean-descended blacks in Florida. Yet over 15 percent
of blacks in the Palm Beach–Treasure Coast market identify as Haitian, as
do 16 percent of blacks in Southwest Florida. Clearly, Caribbean-descended
blacks are demographically expanding throughout all regions of southern
Florida, portending great change in black and overall politics throughout
this part of the state.

Haitians and Jamaicans are getting elected to office in Miami-Dade and
Broward in rates out of proportion to their numbers. The fact that Miami-
Dade has two state representatives who were born in Haiti is impressive,
given that there are only four majority-black state representative districts
in the county. Overall, Miami-Dade County has 95,669 people who claim
Haitian ancestry and 41,576 who claim Jamaican ancestry. Broward County

hosts 62,342 and 71,766, respectively. In 2000, there were 16,473 Haitians and 10,904 Jamaicans in Orange County. Palm Beach hosts 30,958 Haitians and 13,678 Jamaicans. One of the major stories in ethnic politics in the 2000s in Florida will surely be the continuing political ascendancy of these two Caribbean national-origin groups and any potential tensions that might emerge between African American–, Haitian American–, and Jamaican American–backed candidates for office.

Not surprisingly, the ratio of Haitian and Jamaican ancestry to overall black population is very low in the Jacksonville–Northeast media market. Less than 3 percent of the black population in this major area of black concentration outside South Florida identifies with one of these national origin groups. Likewise, fewer than 4 percent of blacks in the Panhandle and North Central Florida claim Haitian or Jamaican ancestry. If the black population of North Florida remains overwhelmingly African American as the black population of the southern Florida regions become more diverse, it will be very interesting to see the political dynamics in the black caucuses of the state legislature. The fact that a relatively large number of Haitian American voters in South Florida is starting to register as Republican while many Jamaicans register as independent in Broward County will also have an unpredictable effect on intra-party and inter-party ethnic politics in the state for years to come.

The third characteristic of African American politics in Florida is the fact that the change of the status in the Democratic Party there over the past several decades has increased the power of blacks within an increasingly weak party. Fifty percent of the Democrats in the state senate, over 45 percent of the Democrats in the state house, and more than 40 percent of the state's Democratic congressional delegation is African American. For the 2005–2006 state legislative session, the Democratic leaders of both the house (Chris Smith of Fort Lauderdale) and senate (Les Miller of Tampa) were African Americans. Moreover, as more white and Hispanic Floridians register as either Republicans or independents, black voters are becoming an increasing percentage of the Democratic electorate. In areas of high Democratic concentration, blacks are a disproportionate number of the electors in Democratic primaries (Hill 2004, 67). For example, in South Florida and in the Jacksonville area, blacks now constitute nearly 30 percent of the Democratic electorate.

Impact on Legislative Politics

The rapid political empowerment of Hispanics and the dramatic increase in the number of African American legislators has profoundly transformed legislative politics in Florida. In Tallahassee, Hispanic (Republican) legislators have emerged as an important voice on such diverse issues as the selection of state legislative leaders, health care reform, educational reform, taxes, and state spending. African American and Hispanic legislators were able to take advantage of two historical changes in Florida politics to increase their influence. The first was the dramatic shift in both the Florida Senate and Florida House from Democratic control to Republican ascendancy. In barely twenty years, the Democrats' near-hegemonic control of the Florida House and Senate has given way to Republican domination. In 1976, Republicans controlled only 29 of the 120 seats in the Florida House and 9 of the 40 seats in the Florida Senate. By 2006, Republicans controlled 85 of the 120 seats in the house and 26 of the 40 seats in the senate. This partisan shift has made African Americans indispensable to what is left of the Democratic Party in Tallahassee and reinforced the importance of Cuban Americans to the governing Republican coalition. Second, both Hispanic and African American legislators have forged issue-specific coalitions with urban liberals to challenge northern Florida's longtime rural/agrarian dominance of the legislature. The coalition deals with urban, education, and poverty issues as well as issues involving minority empowerment and representation.

Initially, Hispanic legislators had little say about Florida public policy. At first, as a minority group within the Republican Party minority in the legislature, Cuban Americans had little impact on state policy. That they shared little with their fellow Republicans except party identification only sharpened their frustration. Most Republicans represented suburban or rural districts, while all the Hispanics came from urban areas. The socioeconomic needs of the older first-generation Hispanic immigrants mandated policies more closely akin with those of liberal urban Democrats than those of their Republican colleagues. The first generation of Hispanic legislators in Tallahassee found themselves ignored by their more conservative rural colleagues.

Cuban influence began growing in 1986 when the seven Cubans Americans in the state house of representatives organized a Cuban caucus. The legislative power of the Cuban caucus increased dramatically when it defied the Republican leadership in the legislature and supported Representative Tom Gustafson (D-Fort Lauderdale) for speaker of the Florida House. The Republican leaders were backing conservative Democrat Carl Carpenter

(D-Plant City) for speaker. The defection of seven Cuban representatives assured Gustafson of the speaker's position. He named all seven Cubans to the critical appropriations committee, which helps set the Florida state budget. The Cubans used their newfound clout to obtain state funding for an array of special projects for their districts. There was $50,000 for a Bay of Pigs museum, $170,000 for a park named after a Cuban war hero, $400,000 for a nutrition center in Little Havana, $275,000 for a day-care center at a hospital in Hialeah, and $30,000 for a history and archives project for Cuban exiles (Moreno and Hill 2002).

Cuban Americans' support for the Democratic leadership during the next two legislative sessions (1988–1992) ensured that they were able to deliver pet projects to their constituents. The Cuban caucus used its position to push for local projects that provided more programs at local universities, medical and meal programs for elderly Hispanics, and more money for urban school districts and made it easier for Cuban doctors and dentists to receive Florida medical licenses. Cuban Americans were able to defy the party leadership because of their extraordinary unity. The seven-member Cuban caucus was the most cohesive group in the state legislature in the 1988–1992 sessions. The standard deviation for Cuban members on 122 contested votes was remarkably low (.02574972); this compared favorably with the same statistic for the African American caucus (.03920432), the Republican caucus (.06295647), and the Democratic caucus (.06317288). In this case, the standard deviation is a measure of the dispersal of the scores for each individual legislator from the mean for all legislators in that category. So, the lower the standard deviation, the more cohesively the group voted as a bloc. Two factors explained this high level of cohesion. First, unlike members of the other caucuses who came from all over the state, the Cubans all came from Dade County and knew each other well. The Cuban members all shared an urban agenda and favored policies that would shift state resources and programs from North to South Florida. Second, the Cuban Americans were the only group in the legislature to impose a rule on its members that caucus positions were binding.

The bitter fight over reapportionment in 1992 shattered the liberal Democrat–Cuban coalition in the state legislature. The Democratic leadership in the senate refused to create a second majority-Cuban congressional district in Miami-Dade County. This gave the Republican Party a vehicle through which to rebuild its tenuous ties with Cuban American leaders. The Republican reapportionment effort paid off when the 1992 elections produced an evenly divided senate chamber—twenty Democrats and twenty Republicans. The Democrats again attempted to lure the three Cuban senators (with promises of key committee assignments) to support their leader Pat Thomas for the president of the senate. But the legacy of the reapportionment battle and the Democrats' previous betrayal had made Cubans distrustful of the Democratic leadership. In sharp contrast to the 1980s, Cubans supported the Republicans in the leadership battle, creating another deadlock in the senate. Democrats were forced to agree to a compromise in which Republicans elected a president for the first year of the session and Democrats elected the president for the second year.

In the 1990s, Cuban American lawmakers achieved positions of prominence and influence in the state legislature. As the Republicans captured both the senate and house, they promoted Cubans to leadership positions. State senator Mario Diaz Balart was selected by the Republican leadership to chair the appropriations committee. In the House, both Rudy Garcia (1996–1998) and Carlos Lacasa (2000–2002) served as chair of the powerful committee. In the 2002 session of the Florida legislature, Alex Diaz de la Portilla was elected president pro tempore of the senate and Marco Rubio was selected majority leader of the house. In 2004, Gaston Cantens became the first Cuban American to run for house speaker. Although his effort ultimately failed, he came close enough to ensure that Marco Rubio was the front runner for the speaker's chair in 2006. Ironically, the success of individual members created tensions within the Cuban delegation that is eroding the unity that was the hallmark of Cuban success in the 1980s. While Cuban American legislators are still bound together by the needs of a conservative urban constituency, intra-group rivalry for political leadership and influence has destroyed the unity that made them the most successful caucus in Tallahassee.

As part of the Republican majority in Tallahassee, Cuban Americans are expected to faithfully support the party's legislative agenda. The freedoms many individual Hispanic members enjoyed when they were part of the minority and could form coalitions with like-minded Democratic members are largely gone. The pressure to conform to the party line has increased as Hispanics have risen in the legislative leadership. As speaker-designate of the Florida House of Representatives for 2007–2008, Marco Rubio is responsible for assuring the loyalty of the South Florida delegation. Alex Villalobos, who is slated to be the first Hispanic president of the Florida Senate in 2008–2010, leads a legislative caucus that is far more conservative than he is.

Majority status forced the reconfiguration of the Cuban caucus during the 2002–2004 legislative session. First, in recognition of the diversity of Hispanic legislators, the caucus changed its name to the Florida Hispanic Legislative Caucus. Three non-Cuban members had been elected to the Florida House during the 2002 election cycle: Susan Bucher, a Mexican American Democrat from West Palm Beach; John Quinones, a Puerto Rican Republican from Orlando; and Juan Carlos Zapata, a Colombian American Republican from Miami. The new caucus also dropped the rule that made caucus decisions binding. Hispanic members realize that the rule was impractical given the diversity of the caucus. Members had largely ignored the rule, and that had led to disputes within the caucus. Despite the fact that twelve of its fourteen members are Republicans, the caucus has on occasion defied the legislative leadership. In 2003, The Hispanic Legislative Caucus joined with the Democratic minority in opposing Republican efforts to restrict the ability of local jurisdictions to pass living-wage ordinances. These living-wage measures enjoy wide support among South Florida blacks and Hispanics; both the Broward and Miami-Dade county commissions have passed such ordinances. The Hispanic Caucus also fought Republican efforts to repeal the district differential that gave school districts in urban areas more money per pupil than those in rural areas of Florida. The district differential is important for school districts in urban South Florida, where the cost of living is much higher than in rural North Florida. The legislative leadership tolerated the defection of Hispanic Republicans on these two issues because they were important to their Hispanic constituents and because they ultimately failed.

Finally, what about the interaction between the Republican surge of the 1990s in statewide politics and the fact that blacks continue to vote overwhelmingly Democratic? Republican growth among whites (and to a certain extent among Hispanics) has produced a state legislature that is nearly 75 percent Republican, and Florida's delegation to the U.S. Congress, as of 2006, stands at 72 percent (18 out of 25) Republican. The flight of whites from the Democratic Party has combined with successful Republican partisan redistricting in 2002 to create a situation in which a disproportionate percentage of Democrats elected to state and federal offices are black.

Half of the fourteen Democratic state senators in the 2005–2006 legislature are African American. The fact that two have been elected from districts that are not majority black (Larcenia Bullard and Gary Siplin) is testimony to the fact that blacks are the key component in getting candidates of choice elected to state office. Likewise, of the state's seven Democratic congresspersons, three (or 43 percent) are African Americans. In the end, although the Republican Party transformed statewide politics in Florida in the 1990s and 2000s with its unprecedented electoral successes, African American loyalties to the Democratic Party will continue to transform the remnant of Florida's oldest political organization. But as long as Florida's blacks remain overwhelmingly concentrated in a dwindling political party with almost no power in Tallahassee, the influence of black Floridians on politics in the state legislature will remain very low.

Looking Ahead

Predicting the future is always a risky venture in politics. In a state such as Florida, which continues to grow at a rapid pace, predictions are all the more difficult. However, looking back on the trends of the past few years, one can make some educated guesses about what role blacks and Hispanics will play in the state in the next few years. First, there is no sign that the growth of Florida's Hispanic population will abate anytime soon. As more and more Hispanics come to Florida from other parts of the United States and overseas, that population is likely to become more diverse in terms of national origin. For example, as of the 2000 census, Broward County was 16 percent Hispanic. In just four years, the percentage of Hispanics in Broward grew to 21. Almost all of this growth came from South Americans, mostly from Venezuela and Colombia (U.S. Bureau of the Census 2000; American Community Survey 2004). Miami-Dade was 57 percent Hispanic in 2000 but was 61 percent Hispanic in 2004, also according to the American Community Survey. That study also found that for the first time, non-Hispanic whites were a minority of the population in politically critical Orange County.

The black population of Florida is not growing nearly as fast, particularly in the Panhandle and the Jacksonville area. There is also no evidence of black population growth in Miami-Dade County. Actually, according to purely anecdotal evidence collected by the authors, many Miami-Dade blacks, especially Haitians and Jamaicans, are moving into Broward County and out of Miami-Dade. Broward County is now 25 percent black; that county was barely 20 percent black in 2000 (Census, 2000). When we think of mobility in Florida, we usually think of people moving into the state from elsewhere. However, social scientists, and politicians for that matter, cannot ignore migration within the state. As people move from one part of Florida to another, even if they only move across a county line, they may well dramatically and quickly influence the politics of that area.

Even though predicting the future of Florida politics with any accuracy is difficult, especially when dealing with the diverse black and Hispanic populations of the state, several things are certain. Blacks and Hispanics will continue to come to Florida, they will continue to move from one place to another in Florida, and they will have foreseen and unforeseen impacts on the political development of the state.

Notes

1. It should be noted that 85.8 percent of the Cuban vote, 28.8 percent of the Puerto Rican vote, 73.2 percent of the Colombian vote, 92.2 percent of the Nicaraguan vote, and 24 percent of the Mexican vote is concentrated in South Florida.

2. New Democrat Network advertisement: "Cuban Woman." <www.noticias.info/Archivo/2004>.

3. Polls conducted by Campaign Data, Inc., in Miami-Dade showed between 78 and 81 percent Cuban support for maintaining the economic embargo. The polls were conducted in February 2000 and July 2002.

References

Dunn, Marvin. 1997. *Black Miami in the Twentieth Century*. Gainesville: University Press of Florida.

Hill, Kevin. 2004. "Florida's Black Voters: Regional Concentration, National Origin Diversity, and Partisanship." In *Florida Politics: Ten Media Market, One Powerful State*, edited by Kevin Hill, Susan MacManus, and Dario Moreno, 65–82. Tallahassee: Florida Institute of Government.

Moreno, Dario. 2004. "Florida Hispanic Voters: Growth, Immigration, and Political Clout." In *Florida Politics: Ten Media Markets, One Powerful State*, edited by Kevin Hill, Susan MacManus, and Dario Moreno. 83–100. Tallahassee: Florida Institute of Government.

Moreno, Kevin, and Kevin Hill. 2002. "A Community or a Crowd? Racial, Ethnic, and Regional Bloc Voting in the Florida House of Representatives 1989–98." *Politics and Policy* 30:90–113.

———. 2005. "Battleground Florida." In *Muted Voices: Latinos and the 2000 Election*, edited by Rudolfo O. De la Garza and Louis DeSipio. 213–27. Oxford, Md.: Rowman and Littlefield.

Moreno, Dario, and Christopher L. Warren. 1992. "The Conservative Enclave: Cubans in Florida." In *From Rhetoric to Reality: Latino Politics in the 1988 Election*, edited by Rudolfo O. de la Garza and Louis DeSipio. 127–46. Boulder, Colo.: Westview Press.

———. 1996. "The Conservative Enclave Revisited: Cuban-Americans in Florida." In *Ethnic Ironies: Latino Politics in the 1992 Elections*, edited by Rudolfo O. De la Garza and Louis DeSipio. 169–84. Boulder, Colo.: Westview Press.

———. 1999. "Pragmatism and Strategic Realignment in the 1996 Election: Florida's Cuban Americans." In *Awash in the Mainstream: Latino Politics in the 1996 Election*, edited by Rudolfo O. De la Garza and Louis DeSipio. 211–37. Boulder, Colo.: Westview Press.

Perez, Lisandro. 1992. "Cuban Miami." In *Miami Now: Immigration, Ethnicity, and Social Change*, edited by Guillermo Grenier and Alex Stepick. 67–79. Gainesville: University Press of Florida.

Portes, Alejandro, and Alex Stepick. 1992. *City on the Edge: The Transformation of Miami*. Berkeley: University of California Press.

U.S. Census Bureau. 2000. Census. Washington, D.C.: Government Printing Office.

U.S. Census Bureau. 2002. 2000 Census. Washington, D.C.: Government Printing Office.

U.S. Census Bureau. 2003. American Community Survey. Washington, D.C.: Government Printing Office.

5

Political Parties in Florida

THOMAS M. CARSEY AND J. P. NELSON

The 2004 and especially the 2000 presidential elections drew national attention to campaigns, parties, and elections in the state of Florida. Because Florida is considered to be a swing state in which the vote in presidential races could go to either major-party candidate, both parties have made conscious efforts to seek out and mobilize Floridians in recent years. Interestingly, this added attention from the national parties and their presidential candidates has not translated into an increase the number of Floridians who are willing to register as members of one of the two major parties. While the percentage of registered voters in Florida who register as Democrats or Republicans is high, a growing minority—up to about 21 percent in 2004—are registering as independents or as members of some other political party. While many Floridians are not party members, both national parties have a noticeable presence and strong electoral prospects in Florida.

Florida's state political parties have also undergone change in recent decades. Like other states in the South, Florida has witnessed a transformation from one-party dominance by the Democrats to a competitive two-party system and now is showing signs that the Republican Party holds a consistent upper hand. The state party organizations, particularly on the GOP side, have also become increasingly professionalized and organized. Finally, several developments within state government have reinforced the importance of Florida's political parties in governing the state. Florida's political parties play an increasingly important role in both state and national politics. In this chapter, we turn our attention to understanding this role, how it has come about, and what it means for party politics in the state.

Throughout U.S. history, political parties have played a central role in organizing individuals united by common interests for the purpose of governing. Political parties were once characterized as "the makers of democratic government" (Schattschneider 1942, 1). In making democracy work, parties perform a number of functions (see Aldrich 1995; Hershey 2005 for overviews). Parties help select candidates for office from among a group of ambitious rivals and help recruit candidates where they would not otherwise emerge. Parties select positions on issues from among various alternatives to advocate as party doctrine. Parties play a principle role in organizing elections and the resulting competition for voters. Parties also play a central role in coordinating the process of governing after an election. Finally, parties provide a means for voters to gather and evaluate information quickly and efficiently; voters can predict fairly accurately what a candidate stands for simply by knowing her/his party affiliation (Downs 1957). More generally, this collection of functions means that parties provide important information and coordination within a representative democracy. The layers of government, separation of powers, checks and balances, and multi-staged lawmaking processes of a representative democracy are all subject to the review of a sometimes-fickle electorate with limited information and are designed to slow down decision making. Political parties are the primary organizations that bridge gaps between institutions, the challenges of coordination, and the limits of available information.

We should also place this general framework of the role of political parties in representative governments within the context of three major trends among parties in the United States that have occurred over the past several decades. First, political parties in the United States have gone through a cycle of decline in importance followed by a more recent resurgence (see Cohen, Fleisher, and Kantor 2001). The decline occurred across the board— parties became less influential in campaigns and elections in the 1970s and 1980s in the face of more candidate-centered politics. Party discipline in Congress significantly declined during the same period, and the proportion of citizens who were willing to identify with a particular political party or vote a straight party ticket on Election Day steadily declined as well. This all began to change in the late 1980s and through the 1990s, and scholars more recently have announced the resurgence of parties at both the mass and elite levels (e.g., Herrnson and Green 2003; Bartels 2000; Bond and Fleisher 2000).

Second, the Democratic and Republican parties have become increasingly polarized since 1980. By this, we mean that both elected officials and citizens who identify with the Republican Party are increasingly farther apart ideologically from elected officials and citizens who identify with the Democratic Party than they were in 1980. This polarization has occurred with cultural issues such as abortion rights, prayer in school, and gay rights that have emerged as new issues in the last few decades, but it has also happened with racial issues that emerged in the 1950s and 1960s as well as issues regarding the role of government in providing for the social welfare of its citizens that emerged during President Roosevelt's New Deal in the 1930s. Layman and Carsey (2002) describe this process as one of partisan "conflict extension."

Third, the entire South has experienced a significant shift away from Democratic Party dominance that once characterized the region (Petrocik 1987; Stanley 1988; Schreckhise and Shields 2003; Knuckey 2005), and Florida has been no exception (Beck 1982). What once was the solid Democratic South gave way to vibrant two-party competition at the national level beginning in earnest in the 1960s, followed in the 1970s and 1980s at the state level. More recently, the Republican Party has enjoyed a significant advantage throughout much of the region, including Florida, but the GOP has not achieved the one-party dominance the Democrats enjoyed two generations ago.

Full treatments of the decline and resurgence of U.S. parties, the increased polarization between partisans, and the partisan realignment of the South as a region are beyond the scope of this chapter. Interested readers should consult the works cited above. However, these national trends are important to note because they characterize aspects of the party system in Florida in recent years.

Parties in Action

Political parties serve many functions within the U.S. system at both the state and the national levels. First and foremost, political parties are aggregations of people who work to get like-minded individuals elected to office so they can enact their policy preferences. Factional conflict sometimes occurs within political parties, but the parties have effective mechanisms for determining which candidates to nominate and which platform to adopt. While political parties engage in many other activities, everything they do revolves around electoral competition for the control of government. While the pragmatic consideration of a candidate's electoral prospects comes into play during the nomination process, ideological commonalities are central to whether party members will support a particular candidate for nomination to begin with. Thus, parties consider both ideology and electability when choosing candidates to nominate for offices.

Parties are highly involved in getting their candidates elected, and, in partnership with some nonparty interest groups, they conduct door-to-door canvassing, place calls to constituents, and post information on their Web sites to inform people of how they can register to vote. For example, Florida's Republican and Democratic parties both have links on their Web sites through which visitors can register to vote.[1]

Direct mail and other information the political parties provide to voters are known for being strongly biased toward their candidates, but other information parties convey to the voters is much more valuable. By simply mentioning their party affiliation, candidates convey a great deal of pertinent information about themselves to voters. Even if voters do not identify with a particular party, they have a general idea of where the parties stand on issues. They know that Democrats are more liberal than Republicans and that Republicans, conversely, are more conservative than Democrats. Thus, instead of finding out candidates' positions on a multitude of different issues, voters can observe whether candidates have an (R) or a (D) next to their names and get a rough approximation of what they stand for.

In this manner, political parties make it easier for voters to make informed choices and vote for a candidate whose political beliefs are close to their own. When the costs to voters of information-gathering, which include time spent locating information and resources in acquiring and absorbing it, are weighed against the benefits to voters that result from those efforts, learning a candidate's party affiliation is a very efficient way for voters to learn about a candidate (Downs 1957).

Party Organization in Florida

As in most states, the Democratic and Republican parties in Florida are organized in multiple layers. Both parties have official organizations in each of Florida's sixty-seven counties, and within each county, the parties are organized around precincts. At every level, the parties choose delegates to send to their meetings and conventions at the next level, ultimately culminating in the selection of delegates to each respective party's national convention. Only national conventions attract the attention of most citizens. To the passive viewer, the national conventions are mere media spectacles designed to showcase the parties' best speakers on national television. However, national conventions do much more than this; they approve new party platforms, nominate candidates for the presidency and vice presidency, and allow delegates to commingle with like-minded politically active individuals.

Many of the activities of political parties involve attempts to get their candidates elected, but some offices bring more power to a party than others. Also, once their candidates are elected, parties must find ways to effectively exercise and maintain their power. The ways parties do so in Florida are affected by the structure of state government. Up until the time Jeb Bush first took office as governor in 1998, Florida's state constitution and state statutes produced a relatively weak executive branch in which power was shared by the governor and six other elected officials (Prier 1997, 53). This attribute of the Florida governorship made pursuing that office a less effective way for parties to gain power in Florida than it would be in many other states. However, under Bush's tenure, the office of the governor has been strengthened. A number of upper-level staff positions have been converted from civil service jobs to jobs appointed at the discretion of the governor and/or his top political appointees under Bush's 2001 Service First initiative. Now the only state executive offices that are filled by election are the attorney general, the state treasurer, and the state agricultural commissioner. At the same time, several features of Florida's legislature (to be discussed below) have made it relatively weak compared to the governor's office in recent years.

Figure 5.1 reveals that these changes have resulted in a perception that power has shifted between the legislature and the governor in Florida. Figure 5.1 plots the perceived power of the governor relative to his/her state's legislature over time. The data comes from the American State Administrators Project directed by Deil S. Wright, Nelson C. Dometrius, and Cynthia J. Bowling.[2] The measure is taken from a regularly conducted survey of state agency heads and top executives within each state's government at various times. Respondents are asked whether the governor or the legislature exerts more control and influence in state politics. Responses are coded +1 for those who say the governor has more influence, −1 for those who say the legislature exerts greater control, and 0 if both are viewed as having about the same influence. Taking a simple mean of this measure provides one indication of the relative influence governors have in the eyes of political insiders in their states.

As Figure 5.1 shows, the average governor across all states enjoys a slight advantage over the state legislature in perceived influence over the entire period covered by these surveys. The same does not hold true for Florida. From the 1960s through the 1990s, Floridians viewed the legislature as relatively more powerful than the governor. In the public's perception, Florida's governor was noticeably less powerful relative to the average governor from other states. Figure 5.1 documents a dramatic upswing in the perceived influence of the governor in Florida under Jeb Bush. In fact, by 2004, perceptions of Bush's influence in Florida surpassed the average perceived influence of his gubernatorial counterparts across all states. Clearly, survey respondents in Florida believe that Jeb Bush has strengthened his hand while in office.

The structure of the legislature also has an impact on how state party organizations in Florida conduct business. New presiding officers are selected in both houses of the Florida legislature biennially. Both of these officers are elected by legislators who serve in the term prior to the one during which

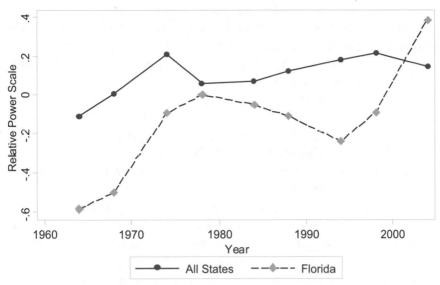

Figure 5.1. Perceptions of the Relative Power of State Governors and State Legislatures, in the United States and Florida, 1960–2000.

they will lead. This gives parties an incentive to press even retiring members of the legislature to choose their preferred candidate for president of the senate or speaker of the house. Also, would-be speakers must gather coalitions of support to reach their goal (Prier 1997, 62). This is true of any leadership position in a legislative body, but the mobilization of these coalitions must occur frequently in the Florida legislature because of the two-year terms of its leaders. Clearly, a candidate's co-partisans constitute the key members of such coalitions, leaving parties and their leaders to play an important role in determining formal leadership in the house and senate.

Traditionally, the presiding officer of each house leaves the Florida legislature after serving a single two-year term in that position, often turning to a fruitful lobbying career in the Florida legislature after he or she departs (Prier 1997, 61). This means that nearly every presiding officer in the Florida State legislature is effectively a lame-duck during their tenure. The lame-duck status of presiding officers should provide them with at least the opportunity for more independence from their party organizations than legislators who would be seeking reelection. However, those who are planning careers as lobbyists or hoping to run for higher offices in the state must still keep in mind the need to maintain the loyal support of their fellow partisans. It is also the case that individuals are unlikely to rise to leadership positions within the legislature unless they can be expected to lead the party in the direction members of the party want to go. Thus, the typical house speaker and senate president can be expected to toe the party line in most circumstances rather than break with their party on any important policy matter. One recent exception was senate president John McKay, who in 2001 broke with the GOP to support an overhaul of the state sales tax code with the objective of eliminating many of the hundreds of exemptions that exist (Salinero 2001, 1). This break with his party, however, was not successful as no major revisions were adopted.

Another key aspect to understanding the role of parties in the state legislature centers on the issue of term limits. Term limits for state representatives in Florida were adopted in 1992 and went into effect in 2000 (Dunkelberger 2004). Currently, members of the Florida House are allowed to serve four two-year terms and members of the state senate are allowed to serve two four-year terms. Term limits for legislators have been adopted by more than half the states in the United States in one form or another. While there is some disagreement about their impact, the general consensus is that term limits weaken the legislature relative to other participants in the policy-making process, particularly the executive branch and lobbyists. Term limits result in a legislature loaded with relatively inexperienced legislators who must seek advice and support as they learn to navigate the waters of state government.

While much more could be said about term limits, one often-overlooked point is that term limits create the opportunity for political parties to become more influential. This happens for two reasons. First, the more-frequent turnover among the membership of the legislature places a greater demand on the parties to recruit and groom new candidates for these offices at the local level. Parties cannot afford to simply wait for strong candidates to develop while an entrenched incumbent serves for twenty years or more—they have to be more proactive in seeking candidates within a shorter time frame. Second, one of the places newly elected members of the legislature turn for guidance while in office is the leadership within their party. Thus, term limits may contribute to more party-line voting in the legislature and a greater concentration of real power among party/legislative leaders.

In summary, the last eight to ten years have witnessed the emergence of an environment in which Governor Bush effectively used party loyalty to push his agenda through the state legislature. Power shifted toward the executive branch, and within the legislature, power shifted toward party leaders (see

Benton 2007). Thus, we believe that in Florida a confluence of institutional changes in both the executive and legislative branches has strengthened the role of the party and its leaders in state politics. This is evident in the increasing frequency of voting along party lines in the state legislature, where the GOP majority remains largely united against the Democratic minority on most issues. Bipartisanship emerges when Democrats agree to fall in line with Republicans, but the frequency with which bills are passed with significant bipartisan support over the objection of bipartisan opposition has decreased significantly. It remains to be seen whether the party's impact will remain high under these current institutional arrangements now that Bush has left office and been replaced by current Republican Governor Charlie Crist.

Party Behavior within the State

The political climate of Florida has undergone some major changes since the Reconstruction period. The state's party system has progressed from one in which Democrats were the dominant party to a more competitive system and then to a system that leans toward the Republican Party, at least in terms of electoral success. Between 1876 and 1944, the state of Florida awarded its electoral votes to a Republican presidential candidate only twice—in the elections of 1876 and 1928 (Key 1949, 10). However, between 1992 and 2004, Florida's electoral votes were won by Republican presidential candidates in three of four races—George H. W. Bush won Florida in 1992 but lost the national election, while his son, George W. Bush, won both Florida and the presidency in 2000 and 2004.[3]

The pattern in Florida mirrors that of the rest of the states in the South. The entire region of the South lacked two-party competition in the mid-twentieth century. As a result, political disputes existed between the Democratic Party's factions (Key 1949, 11). This factionalism is no longer a characteristic of Florida politics and has been replaced by two-party competition.

Currently, the South is a region where the Republicans have an electoral advantage. Republicans have realized most of their electoral gains at the state level in Florida and across the South since 1990, but the underlying transformation of southern politics that made these gains possible was set in motion decades earlier. The trend began long before the Republic Party's "Contract with America" that framed the 1994 midterm elections and brought significant Republican gains in the South. It also began long before the outrage conservatives expressed over the U.S. Supreme Court's *Roe v. Wade* decision in 1973 that provided protection for abortion rights. The trend really began when relatively affluent southern whites began leaving the Democratic Party for the Republican Party during the 1930s as a result of President Roosevelt's New Deal (Black and Black 2002, 256). The civil rights movement of the 1950s and 1960s, coupled with President Johnson's support of the Voting Rights Act of 1965 and the Civil Rights Act of 1964, sparked additional movement of conservative whites in the South away from the Democratic Party and its candidates (Carmines and Stimson 1989). This is most evident in the support Barry Goldwater received in the South for his presidential candidacy in 1964 and George Wallace received in his run for the White House in 1968. However, even with the push of racial issues, the shift toward the GOP in the South among whites moved down the socioeconomic ladder very slowly. By 1976, more than four decades after Roosevelt was elected the first time, "only 30 percent of conservative white southerners were Republicans" (Black and Black 2002, 222). The emergence of cultural issues such as abortion, women's rights, and gay rights in the 1970s and 1980s and the presidency of Ronald Reagan helped cement the movement of most conservative whites across all social classes toward the GOP. As a result, by 1988, 60 percent of conservative white southerners considered themselves to be Republicans. The transition of conservative white southerners from the Democratic Party to the Republican Party was not a knee-jerk response to any single divisive issue such as school integration or abortion. It was a gradual process that lasted half a century. This constituency is now a key component of the Republican Party.

In recent years, Florida's political system has mirrored the rest of the South and become more competitive. This development has enabled the Republican Party to become more powerful than it was in the Democrat-dominated Solid South. Even so, the Republican Party does not have the same hold over the southern states that the Democratic Party once had, particularly in Florida. In recent presidential elections, Florida has been a battleground state in which both major political parties have fought hard to acquire electoral votes. It is neither a "red state" nor a decidedly "blue state." Thus, in contemporary Florida politics, the battles between factions within the Democratic Party for control of the state have been replaced by battles between strong and increasingly homogeneous Democratic and Republican parties.

In fact, Florida's party system is considered to be among the most competitive, and the state has been portrayed as "a microcosm of the nation" (Knuckey 2003, 128). The greater degree of competition among Florida's political parties in recent years is reflected in voter registration data and election returns from the state. In every election year from 1994 to 2004,

Table 5.1. Major-Party Registration in Florida by Number and Percent, 1994–2004

Date	Republican	Democratic	Total	Percent Republican	Percent Democratic
October 11, 1994	2,747,074	3,245,518	6,559,598	41.88	49.48
October 7, 1996	3,309,105	3,728,513	8,077,877	40.97	46.16
October 5, 1998	3,292,589	3,691,742	8,220,266	40.05	44.91
October 10, 2000	3,430,238	3,803,081	8,752,717	39.19	43.45
October 7, 2002	3,599,053	3,958,910	9,302,360	38.69	42.56
October 4, 2004	3,892,492	4,261,249	10,301,290	37.79	41.37

Source: Florida Department of State, Division of Elections, "Voter Registration Statistics," available online at http://elections.dos.state.fl.us/votereg/index.shtml.

and undoubtedly throughout much of Florida's history, the state has had a higher percentage of registered Democrats than registered Republicans (see Table 5.1). This gap, however, is noticeably smaller than it was a little over a decade ago. In 1994, Democrats still held an edge over Republicans in party registration of nearly nine percentage points, but that gap had shrunk to less than four percentage points by 2004. Given the tendency for Democratic voters to turnout at somewhat lower rates, and to be somewhat more likely than their Republican counterparts to vote for candidates from the opposing party, the advantage Democrats held in the state for much of its history has effectively disappeared.

The geography of party registration in Florida is quite interesting, as the relative advantage one party holds over the other varies substantially across the state. Figure 5.2 highlights this. Figure 5.2 depicts which counties have significantly higher voter registration with the Republican Party, which counties have significantly higher registration with the Democratic Party, and which counties were characterized by a fairly even match between the two parties in 2004. Democrats continue to maintain their strongest advantage in the greater Big Bend area of North Florida. The Republican advantage is concentrated on the southern Gulf Coast, the northeast coast surrounding Jacksonville, and the far western panhandle. The hottest competition between the two parties for registrants is in central Florida along the so-called I-4 corridor linking Tampa, Orlando, and Daytona Beach and along the central and southern Atlantic coast. This same area is also among the fastest growing in the state, which means we can expect both parties to concentrate substantial resources on recruitment and voter mobilization in this area in coming years.

Any discussion of Florida's political geography must also consider where Florida's residents come from. While the population of the South has grown significantly, the growth in Florida has surpassed that of other states. Florida has long been a popular retirement destination for citizens from the North-

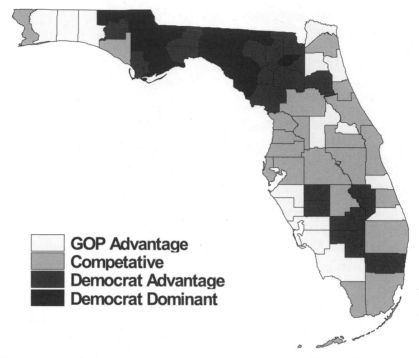

Figure 5.2. Distribution of Party Registration Advantage across Florida Counties, 2004. *Source*: Florida Department of State, Division of Elections, "Voter Registration Statistics," <http://elections.dos.state.fl.us/votereg/index.shtml>.

east, and retirement communities dominated by such folks are strongholds of the Democratic Party in South Florida. In 1988, Massachusetts governor Michael Dukakis won the Democratic primary in Florida based largely on support from retirees. More recently, residents from the Midwest and the Plains states have made up a growing share of Florida's new residents, bringing with them moderate to conservative political views.

Florida is also a major destination for Latino immigrants; the largest groups are of Cuban, Mexican, or Puerto Rican descent. The Cuban Americans concentrated in the Miami area have long been staunch supporters of the Republican Party because of its relatively strong anti-Castro position. The Mexican American and Puerto Rican populations in Florida have been growing most rapidly along the I-4 corridor. Both groups have shown divided loyalties between the two parties, with Puerto Ricans leaning somewhat more strongly toward the Democratic Party. The competition between the parties for support among these two growing demographic groups is a major part of the broader two-party competition taking place in the I-4 corridor.

Table 5.2. Results of State and National Chief Executive Elections in Florida, 1990–2004

Election	Republican Vote	Democratic Vote	Percent Republican	Percent Democratic
1990 Gubernatorial Election	1,535,068	1,995,206	43.5	56.5
1992 Presidential Election	2,173,316	2,072,709	40.9	39.0
1994 Gubernatorial Election	2,071,068	2,135,008	49.2	50.8
1996 Presidential Election	2,244,164	2,546,600	42.3	48.0
1998 Gubernatorial Election	2,191,105	1,773,054	55.3	44.7
2000 Presidential Election	2,912,790	2,912,253	48.8	48.8
2002 Gubernatorial Election	2,856,845	2,201,427	56.0	43.2
2004 Presidential Election	3,964,522	3,583,544	52.1	47.1

Source: Florida Department of State, Division of Elections, "Election Results," available online at http://election.dos.state.fl.us/elections/resultsarchive/index.asp.

The trend in party registration toward the Republican Party does not tell the whole story about the ideological and partisan composition of Florida. Election returns for gubernatorial and presidential races over the past decade help us understand more about this story. We look at chief executive races to illustrate this phenomenon because people often perceive presidents to have more power than they actually possess (Pfiffner 1994, 228). People would be reluctant to trust the broad overarching power they erroneously ascribe to the presidency to someone with whom they disagree, but they might be willing to trust that same person with the lesser powers of other offices. Thus, a voter's choice for president may be more likely to reflect her/his political beliefs than her/his choices for lower offices would.

The same trend might operate at the state level because governors also head the executive branch but at a lower level. The powers of governors vary, but people often fail to recognize the limits of those powers. This was exemplified by calls in the spring of 2005 for Governor Jeb Bush to intervene in order to have Terri Schiavo's feeding tube reconnected and his response that the limits of his powers constrained his ability to do so. Our general point, however, is that the results of recent presidential and gubernatorial races serve as good indicators of the ideological composition of the state (see Table 5.2).

Florida's gubernatorial race is held every four years during nonpresidential election years, and in both 1990 and 1994, Democratic candidate Lawton Chiles won. While George H. W. Bush won Florida's presidential electoral votes in 1992, Bill Clinton won them in 1996, demonstrating that the state of Florida was not solidly behind either party in national politics during the 1990s. However, since 1998, Florida has voted Republican in all four gubernatorial and presidential elections: Jeb Bush won the governorship of Florida in 1998 and 2002 and George W. Bush won Florida and the presidency in the presidential elections of 2000 and 2004. Also, except for the hotly contested and highly contentious 2000 presidential election, Republicans have won these contests in Florida by comfortable margins. This recent electoral success has occurred even while the Democratic Party maintains a slight advantage in party registration among voters.

Another way to examine what appears to be an incongruity between party registration and behavior at the polls on Election Day is to look at Florida's sixty-seven counties. Table 5.3 reports the percentage of all registered voters in Florida in October 2004 who registered as Democrats along with the percentage of the total votes cast in November 2004 for the Democrat's presidential nominee, John Kerry, for each county. While the percentage of Democratic Party registrants matches fairly well with the percentage of the presidential vote John Kerry received in several counties, there is a marked difference in many other counties. For example, 69 percent of the residents in Baker County who registered to vote in 2004 were Democrats, yet Kerry received only 22 percent of the votes cast there. The gap was even wider in counties such as Holmes, Lafayette, Liberty, and Union. In contrast, in several counties, the percentage of the presidential vote Kerry received in 2004 exceeded the percentage of voters registered as Democrats by more than ten percentage points; this happened in Broward, Charlotte, Martin, Monroe, Palm Beach, Pinellas, and Sarasota counties. In fact, the simple correlation between the percentage of the vote Kerry received and the percentage of registered voters who registered as Democrats across the sixty-seven counties is slightly negative (−0.03) and is not statistically significantly different from zero. This does not mean that Democratic registrants were not more likely to vote for Kerry compared to others. However, it does mean that looking at the distribution of party registration at the county level in Florida does not accurately predict the distribution of a party's support at the polls across counties.

This is not too surprising. State parties are not under the direct control of their national counterparts, and their positions on issues can differ from those of the national party as well as other state parties. Similarly, county parties and their partisans cannot necessarily be directed by the state party to vote the way state party leaders might prefer. As a result, membership in the Florida Democratic Party or Republican Party is not a perfect indicator of level of support for the policies of the national party. For example, in the 2004 elections, many Florida counties with ties to the Old South had large discrepancies between the percentage of votes that were cast for John Kerry and the percentage of voters who were registered Democrats. Most of these

Table 5.3. Democratic Party Registration and Votes for Democratic Candidate John Kerry in 2004 across Florida Counties, by Percent

County	Percent that Voted for Kerry	Percent Registered Democrat
Alachua	56.1	50.5
Baker	21.9	69.3
Bay	28.1	39.2
Bradford	29.9	61.4
Brevard	41.6	36.5
Broward	64.2	50.5
Calhoun	35.5	82.4
Charlotte	42.9	31.9
Citrus	42.1	38.9
Clay	23.3	25.6
Collier	34.1	24.4
Columbia	32.1	56.5
DeSoto	41.1	59.3
Dixie	30.4	77.5
Duval	41.6	46.2
Escambia	33.7	40.7
Flagler	48.3	38.1
Franklin	40.5	77.3
Gadsden	69.7	82.9
Gilchrist	28.8	58.6
Glades	41.0	64.8
Gulf	33.1	67.1
Hamilton	44.5	78.9
Hardee	29.3	63.8
Hendry	40.5	56.5
Hernando	46.2	38.8
Highlands	37.0	39.8
Hillsborough	46.2	41.7
Holmes	21.8	72.7
Indian River	39.0	30.0
Jackson	38.1	71.5
Jefferson	55.3	72.3
Lafayette	25.4	82.8
Lake	38.9	34.3
Lee	39.0	29.7
Leon	61.5	57.1
Levy	36.5	59.7
Liberty	35.4	88.3
Madison	48.8	79.5
Manatee	42.7	33.0
Marion	41.0	39.7
Martin	41.7	27.5
Miami-Dade	52.9	42.8
Monroe	49.7	36.1
Nassau	26.2	36.8
Okaloosa	21.6	24.7
Okeechobee	42.3	58.5
Orange	49.8	40.2

continued

Table 5.3.—*Continued*

County	Percent that Voted for Kerry	Percent Registered Democrat
Osceola	47.0	40.2
Palm Beach	60.4	45.1
Pasco	44.4	37.3
Pinellas	49.5	37.8
Polk	40.8	42.6
Putnam	40.1	57.7
Santa Rosa	21.8	28.1
Sarasota	45.2	31.2
Seminole	41.3	32.3
St. Johns	30.6	28.3
St. Lucie	51.8	41.4
Sumter	36.4	40.8
Suwannee	28.6	63.6
Taylor	35.5	75.6
Union	26.8	75.5
Volusia	50.5	40.8
Wakulla	41.6	66.9
Walton	25.9	36.8
Washington	28.1	67.0

Source: Florida Department of State, Division of Elections, "Election Results" available online at http://election.dos.state.fl.us/elections/resultsarchive/index.asp and "Voter Registration Statistics" available online at http://elections.dos.state.fl.us/votereg/index.shtml.

counties are located in Florida's Panhandle, which has supported Republican candidates in presidential elections since Barry Goldwater's candidacy in 1964. Democratic registrations in Panhandle counties are partially attributable to the legacy of the Dixiecrat Party that was once predominant throughout the South (CalTech/MIT Voting Technology Project 2004, 1–2, 6). Many of these voters call themselves Democrats but vote like Republicans. Gains Republicans have made in the state of Florida, then, are likely to be underrepresented by changes in the percentage of Republican registrants in the state.

Republicans have made electoral gains in other areas of Floridian politics that have altered congressional delegations and state legislative bodies in their favor (see Table 5.4). As recently as 1988, Republicans were minorities in Florida's delegations to the U.S. House, the state house, and the state senate. In 2002, however, Republicans constituted 65 percent of Florida's state senate, 67.5 percent of the state house, and 72 percent of Florida's delegation to the U.S. House (Knuckey 2003, 129). These are very solid majorities and reflect the gains Republicans have made in Florida in recent years.

In 2004, Republican Mel Martinez emerged from a closely contested race to replace retiring Democratic U.S. senator Bob Graham. Florida's current senior senator, Bill Nelson, is a Democrat, which makes the state's U.S. Sen-

Table 5.4. Republicans as a Percent of Florida's National and State Government
Bodies, 1980–2004

	Percent of Florida's	Percent of	Percent of
Year	Delegation to the U.S. House	State House	State Senate
1980	26.7	32.5	32.5
1982	36.8	30.0	20.0
1984	31.6	35.8	20.0
1986	36.8	37.5	37.5
1988	47.4	39.2	42.5
1990	52.6	38.3	42.5
1992	56.5	40.8	50.0
1994	65.2	47.5	52.5
1996	65.2	50.8	57.5
1998	65.2	60.0	62.5
2000	65.2	61.7	62.5
2002	72.0	67.5	65.0
2004	68.2	70.0	65.0

Source: Statistical Abstracts of the United States, various years.

ate delegation evenly split between the two parties. While Republicans do
not dominate the Senate delegation, Martinez's victory shows that they have
made some recent progress. Thus, the trend toward parity in the number
of registered Democrats and Republicans in Florida is far from a perfect
measure of the state's ideological orientation. The narrowing of this gap by
Republican registrants, though, has coincided with increases in the power
of the Republican Party in Florida's legislative and executive branches. More
Florida voters call themselves Democrats than Republicans, but most of
those elected to represent them are Republicans.

It is worth noting that the inconsistency between Democratic Party registration and Republican electoral success may stem in part from the nature of
the registration process. Many citizens who register initially with one party
do not bother to change their registration even after their party preferences
change (see Beck 1982).

Despite the increased number of Republican officeholders in the state,
voters have successfully advanced several liberal policies in Florida in recent years. While Republicans have been winning offices in Florida, citizens
have circumvented their elected officials and enacted several liberal policies
through the constitutional amendment process. The drift in party support
has not been fully matched by a conservative ideological shift on all issues
among voters. In Florida, citizens vote on amendments to the state constitution when they vote for state- and national-level officeholders. One of
the amendments voters supported required that public schools reduce the
number of students in each of their classes for young children (Friedman

2003, 4); another effectively banned smoking in all establishments other than bars. In the 2004 elections, Florida voters approved an amendment that increased the minimum wage (Friedman 2005, 3). Thus, while more Republicans have won elective office in Florida in recent years, they have faced some liberal citizen-imposed constraints on what they can do while in office.

Party Activist Behavior in Florida during the Transition

Party activists, by definition, play a more prominent role in shaping the respective agendas of the two political parties than do a party's rank-and-file members and their role in the party is more demanding than that of other members. Party members with strong ideological commitments to the party would be more likely to tolerate the additional demands of being an activist in order to have a larger role in the party. The ideological views of party activists, then, would closely mirror those of the party platform. Also, because of their heavy involvement in party activities, activists are credible sources of information about the internal dynamics of their parties.

While much has changed for the parties in relation to the balance of power in the South as well as in Florida, internal changes have occurred in the parties during the transition from Democratic dominance to two-party competition in which the Republicans have an advantage. In Florida, as in many other places, this transition was very noticeable in the 1990s. During this time period, the Florida Republican Party was well organized and strategically sought a majority of the seats in both houses of the state legislature. The Florida GOP discerned which legislative districts could be won, was involved in seeking individuals to run for office, and allocated resources toward districts where they had a chance of winning (Knuckey 2003, 131). The Florida Democratic Party, however, was bogged down by infighting and ideological factionalism that created divisions among both the party's activists and its elected officials. This made it more difficult for the Democratic Party to compete with the better-organized and more-focused GOP (Knuckey 2003, 131).

These differences in the behavior of the two state parties in the previous decade obviously contributed to the development of Florida's current party system. However, many other notable changes have occurred among party activists in recent years. Between 1991 and 2001, party activists in Florida became more polarized ideologically (Knuckey 2003, 134). This parallels developments at the national level (Layman, Carsey, Green, and Herrera 2005). Despite this increased polarization (Knuckey 2003, 134–35), sizeable minorities of activists in both parties still report holding views that are in opposition to their party's ideological orientation on certain issues (Knuckey 2003, 136). For example, in 2001, 44.4 percent of Florida's Democratic activists supported the death penalty, 35.4 percent supported prayer in schools, and 36.7 percent expressed support for a flat tax (Knuckey 2003, 135, Table 3). This independence on some issues extends to Republican Party activists in Florida as well; 40.2 percent of them were in favor of legal abortions (Knuckey 2003, 135, Table 3). These numbers show that while Democratic and Republican party activists on average are generally further apart from each other ideologically than they were previously, there is still a substantial amount of diversity in the opinions among activists in each party.

When they were polled, activists were also queried about some organizational aspects of their party. When asked how the strength of their party had changed over the previous decade, Republicans in Florida were more likely on all measures of party strength to assert that their party had gotten stronger (Knuckey 2003, 137, Table 4). This trend is best reflected by how the activists viewed the overall organization of their parties. While 85 percent of Republicans asserted that their party's overall organization had become "somewhat stronger" or "significantly stronger" in the previous decade, only 48.5 percent of Democratic activists made this claim about their party (Knuckey 2003, 137, Table 4). Because this data was obtained in 2001, though, the lack of confidence Democrats expressed in their party may have been influenced by their party's defeat in the 2000 elections. Furthermore, the confidence Republicans expressed in their state party in 2001 would also have been affected by their narrow victory in the state in the recent presidential election and the number of seats they held in both the state house and state senate. Whether GOP activists correctly perceive an increase in the strength of their organization or they are simply translating their electoral gains into the perception of greater organizational strength, they clearly feel much better about their party's organization and the direction it is heading as compared to activists in the Democratic Party.

Florida's Republicans would be justified in holding these views in 2007 because they are still more mobilized and better funded than their Democratic counterparts. For example, the victory in Florida for the Bush-Cheney ticket in the 2004 presidential race was attributed in part to the Republican Party's widespread mobilization of voters. The Bush-Cheney campaign mobilized conservatives by encouraging them to register to vote at gun shows and churches as well as other locations (Smith 2004, 1A). The dominance of the Republican Party over the Democratic Party in Florida, however, goes beyond election returns and voter registrations. In early 2005, "[Florida

Democrats] raised only $268,844 in the first quarter . . . compared to $3 million raised by the Republican Party of Florida" (Cotterell 2005, 1). While the chair who ran the Republican Party of Florida during the recent elections, Carole Jean Jordan, recently won a second term at that post (Branom 2005, 1), in 2005 the Democrats selected their fourth statewide chair since the 2000 election. Scott Maddox, who was the chair of the Florida Democratic Party during the 2004 campaign, left the post in order to run for governor in 2006. His pursuit of the Democratic nomination was derailed, however, after reports of financial mismanagement in the Democratic Party under his leadership surfaced. Thus, the Republicans have a strong electoral base from which to draw, ample funds to reach that base, and stable leadership, while the Florida Democratic Party has none of these attributes.

Although Florida's Democratic Party has historically been known for factionalism (Key 1949), factionalism exists to some extent in both state parties. However, the degree to which it affects each party differs, as do the issues that promote factionalism in each party. In a survey conducted in 2001, Republican activists cited fewer sources of factionalism in their state party than did Democrats. Abortion was the only issue that most Republican activists perceived to be a source of a "fair amount" or more of disagreement in their state party organization. Democratic activists reported many more sources of divisiveness within their party. Regional differences and urban-rural distinctions were the sources of factionalism Democrats acknowledged most often. However, 54 percent of Democratic activists also perceived that their party was divided along ideological lines. Most Democratic activists also stated that there were disagreements between members who supported different leaders (Knuckey 2003, 137–39). Such disagreements may be a manifestation of the party's ideological divisions.

While party activists in Florida became more polarized during the 1990s, the Democratic Party continues to retain a higher degree of ideological heterogeneity. This has the benefit of allowing the Democratic Party to draw its membership from people with a wide range of beliefs, but it comes with the drawback of allowing potential infighting to keep members from focusing their efforts on defeating Republicans. Although ideological differences do not affect the Republican Party of Florida as much as they do its Democratic counterpart, Florida Republicans are far from being in complete agreement about all issues. In 2001, 32.6 percent of Republican activists in Florida stated that ideological conflict among members of their state party was a cause of factionalism in that organization. In light of the party's divisions on abortion, this disagreement could be indicative of the existence of economically conservative and socially conservative factions in the party that some-

Table 5.5. Registered Voters by Party Affiliation in Florida, 1994–2004

Date	Percent Republican	Percent Democratic	Percent Independent	Percent Minor
October 11, 1994	41.88	49.48	8.04	0.60
October 7, 1996	40.97	46.16	11.49	1.38
October 5, 1998	40.05	44.91	13.50	1.53
October 10, 2000	39.19	43.45	15.46	1.90
October 7, 2002	38.69	42.56	16.50	2.26
October 4, 2004	37.79	41.37	18.31	2.54

Source: Florida Department of State, Division of Elections, "Voter Registration Statistics" available online at http://elections.dos.state.fl.us/votereg/index.shtml.

times come into conflict with one another (Knuckey 2003, 138–39). Thus, while Florida's Republican Party is not as affected by factional differences to the same degree as the state's Democratic Party, the gulf between its economically conservative and socially conservative members has a noticeable impact on the party.

Minor Parties and Electoral Politics

The American political system is primarily a two-party system in which two strong and ideologically wide-ranging parties compete with one another for power and influence. The party system in Florida is no different from the national one in this respect. Third parties, however, do exist and have managed to exercise some influence in both American and Florida politics. In fact, Table 5.5 shows that Florida has seen a slight increase in the percentage of citizens who register as members of minor parties, from less than 1 percent of registered voters in 1994 to about 2.5 percent in 2004. The influence of minor parties is exercised predominantly through "spoiling" an election for one of the major party's candidates and drawing the electorate's attention toward issues that the two major parties do not discuss. Florida's competitive party system has been especially impacted by third parties because of the close margins between the major parties in presidential elections.

Recently, it has become easier for third parties to perform these functions in Florida because it has become easier for them to obtain access to the ballot. A previous statute required minor parties to submit a petition with the signatures of 3 percent of registered voters before the ballot would list their candidates. Current Florida law, however, states that third-party candidates are required to gather signatures from only 1 percent of registered voters in the area that the office they seek represents (Florida Statutes 99.096[3b]). While it may sound easy to gather the signatures of 3 percent of registered voters, that requirement prevented many minor parties from acquiring access to the ballot. In a large district or in a race for a statewide office, a minor party on a shoestring budget found it very difficult to acquire that many signatures. The reduction of this requirement to 1 percent of registered voters allows more parties to have access to the ballot.

In elections, third parties generally have a negative impact on candidates from the major party whose policy positions are closest to theirs. In such circumstances, voters who might otherwise have voted for the major-party candidate cast their ballot for the ideologically proximate third party instead. Because minor-party candidates rarely win office in Florida or elsewhere in the United States, voting for a minor-party candidate effectively harms the candidate from the major party located closest to the voter's own ideology. Abramson, Aldrich, Paolino, and Rohde (2000, 497) examined the motives of minor-party voters in the presidential elections of 1968, 1980, 1992, and 1996 and found that voters supported third-party candidates when they were dissatisfied with the candidates nominated by the major political parties. People who vote for third-party candidates appear to do so based on whether they like the candidate—they do not seem to use the candidate's party affiliation to reduce the cost of gathering information about the views held by candidates before deciding for whom to vote. The labels of third parties do not provide readily understandable information to voters in the same way that the two major party labels do because the platforms of third parties are not as well known and they do not have a policy history. Most voters have a general conception of the differences between Democrats and Republicans, but few would be well versed in the differences between the platforms of the Libertarian Party and the Constitution Party. Thus, as a result of the low visibility of their party organizations, third parties must rely on running appealing candidates if they are to acquire a noticeable percentage of the vote (Abramson, Aldrich, Paolino, and Rohde 2000).

Ross Perot's third-party candidacies in 1992 and 1996 pulled votes away from a major-party candidate and drew the public's attention to an issue the major parties had not been addressing. Perot discussed the national budget deficit extensively during his campaign and illustrated the problem clearly with graphs and charts. If we assume that most voters who voted for Ross Perot would have voted for Bob Dole in 1996—admittedly a bit of a stretch—we can hypothesize that Perot may have cost Dole the state of Florida (see Table 5.6). A more convincing argument, however, can be made that Ralph Nader's Green Party candidacy cost Al Gore the state of Florida and the presidency in the 2000 election, assuming that most or all of the voters who

Table 5.6. Votes in Florida for Candidates in the 1996 Presidential Election, by Number and Percent

Votes for Dole (Republican)		Votes for Clinton (Democrat)		Votes for Perot (United States Reform Party)	
N	Percent	N	Percent	N	Percent
2,244,164	42.3	2,546,600	48.0	483,841	9.1

Source: Florida Department of State, Division of Elections, "Election Results," available online at http://election.dos.state.fl.us/elections/resultsarchive/index.asp.

Table 5.7. Votes in Florida for Candidates in the 2000 Presidential Election, by Number and Percent

Votes for George W. Bush (Republican)		Votes for Al Gore (Democrat)		Votes for Ralph Nader (Green Party)	
N	Percent	N	Percent	N	Percent
2,912,790	48.8	2,912,253	48.8	97,488	1.6

Source: Florida Department of State, Division of Elections, "Election Results," available online at http://election.dos.state.fl.us/elections/resultsarchive/index.asp.

chose Nader would have voted for Al Gore if Nader had not run (see Table 5.7).

Therefore, the assertion "the major parties monopolize power, while the minor parties use the elections as an occasion for a subsidiary political agitation that does not lead to power" (Schattschneider 1942, 68) is true only when power is defined as legal authority. If power is conceived as control over "who gets what, when, where, and how," then third parties exercise power by placing issues on the agenda and keeping certain major party candidates out of office by spoiling elections for them. The "power" of third parties, then, consists of their ability to stimulate debate on issues that the major parties refuse to discuss and pull valuable votes away from certain major-party candidates. The law in Florida makes it relatively easy for third parties to attempt to obtain and use this power.

Campaign Finance in Florida

At the national level, campaign finance reform has been an issue that has garnered a great deal of attention from the general public and the media in recent years. The issue of the influence of moneyed interests on politics to the detriment of the average citizen is as old as the practice of governing itself. However, the salience of this issue varies across different time periods. In his 2000 bid for the Republican nomination for president, Senator John McCain (R-Ariz.) made campaign finance reform one of his key issues.

Though McCain lost the nomination to George W. Bush, his emphasis on the need for campaign finance reform placed the issue on the national agenda and resulted in legislation designed to curb the influence of interest groups in national politics. The Bipartisan Campaign Reform Act of 2002 placed limitations on the behavior of interest groups in national elections. While this act was not directly aimed at state parties, it affected the state of Florida greatly. Because Florida is a swing state, during presidential elections Floridians are bombarded with advertisements from campaigns and interest groups. Provisions of the new law placed restrictions on these advertisements. Unions and corporations are forbidden from financing television commercials that discuss candidates for a national office and are aired in the 30-day period leading up to a primary or the 60-day period leading up to a general election. Their political action committees are permitted to finance these ads, but contributions to political action committees are constrained by legal limitations (Greenhouse 2003). Thus, the limitations on political advertising greatly impacts electoral politics in Florida. These restrictions not only affect presidential elections but can also indirectly affect what is known as the "coattails effect," in which candidates for lower offices from the same party follow a popular presidential candidate into office.

The state of Florida has also made great strides in the area of campaign finance. Attempts to regulate the financing of campaigns in Florida originated long before John McCain's 2000 presidential run or the Bipartisan Campaign Reform Act. A Florida law banned corporations from using money to influence politics in 1897. Another law passed in 1917 limited the campaign spending of candidates in elections for county and statewide offices. However, neither law was enforced diligently (Huckshorn 1998, 22–23).

Later in the twentieth century, the Florida legislature passed campaign finance legislation that could actually be enforced. The Campaign Finance Act of 1973 placed limits on campaign contributions ranging from $1,000 to $3,000 per election. The differences in the limits the law imposed were based on the authority of the office for which an election was held. The act required campaigns to report their expenses and contributions multiple times during both the primary campaign and general election campaign as well as after each of these time periods. The law also established the Florida Election Commission, which had little authority until a 1977 amendment to the law permitted the commission to fine violators of campaign finance laws. These fines could be as high as $1,000 per violation. Nine years later, in 1986, the Florida legislature gave the commission the authority to impose automatic fines of $50 per day for filing the necessary campaign finance reports after the deadline. The money to pay these fines had to come from the personal funds of the candidate in question, not from his or her campaign treasury (Huckshorn 1998, 23–24). Thus, Florida's campaign finance laws, like those of the United States, have gradually gotten stricter, and both of these sets of laws have affected how parties and campaign organizations raise money and encourage people to support their candidates in Florida.

Conclusion

Political parties in Florida have endured the same transitions as parties across the South and the entire country. Once part of the solidly Democratic South, Florida, like other southern states, now has a more competitive two-party system. Democrats maintain a slight advantage in party registration in Florida, but Republicans have had the upper hand in electoral contests in the state since 1994. The nationwide resurgence of the influence of parties and their importance in campaigns and governing has also occurred in Florida. So too has the increase in ideological polarization that characterizes national party politics. Institutional changes within Florida's state government have further contributed to the influence of parties and partisanship in the state. Finally, the role of minor parties has become increasingly important in the United States and in Florida in recent years. We began this chapter by noting the many functions parties perform in representative democracies. The various trends and developments nationally, regionally, and within the state have combined to increase the power of political parties to carry out these functions. It remains to be seen whether the growth in the importance of parties in Florida will continue to expand, whether it has reached a plateau, or whether some backlash will result in challenges to the authority and influence of parties and their leaders. While many scholars accept Schattschneider's claim "that modern democracy is unthinkable save in terms of the parties" (1942, 1), both scholars and citizens hear James Madison's famous warning in Federalist #10 about the dangers of "factions" ringing in their ears when they decry partisan bickering and gridlock. As of now, however, it is very clear that party politics is alive and well in Florida.

Notes

1. The Web site for the Florida Republican Party is available at <www.rpof.org>; the Web site for the Florida Democratic Party is available at <www.fladems.com>.

2. The collection of this data has been supported by the Earhart Foundation of Ann Arbor, Michigan; the Odom Institute for Research in Social Science of the University of North Carolina; and the Center for Governmental Services at Auburn University. We are grateful to Wright, Nelson, and Bowling for sharing their data with us.

3. All election return data was obtained from Florida Department of State, Division of Elections, "Election Results," available online at <www.election.dos.state.fl.us/elections/resultsarchive/index.asp>, unless otherwise specified. All voter registration data was obtained from Florida Department of State, Division of Elections, "Voter Registration Statistics," <www.election.dos.state.fl.us/voterreg/index.shtml>.

References

Abramson, Paul R., John H. Aldrich, Phillip Paolino, and David W. Rohde. 2000. "Challenges to the American Two-Party System: Evidence from the 1968, 1980, 1992, and 1996 Presidential Elections." *Political Research Quarterly* 53, no. 3: 495–522.

Aldrich, John H. 1995. *Why Parties? The Origin and Transformation of Political Parties in America*. Chicago: University of Chicago Press.

Bartels, Larry. 2000. "Partisanship and Voting Behavior, 1952–1996." *American Journal of Political Science* 44, no. 1: 35–50.

Beck, Paul Allen. 1982. "Realignment Begins? The Republican Surge in Florida." *American Politics Quarterly* 10, no. 4: 421–38.

Benton, J. Edwin. 2007. "The Interplay of Party Leadership and Standing Committees in a Competitive versus a Non-Competitive State Legislative Setting: The Case of Florida." *Florida Political Chronicle* 18: 25-39.

Black, Earl, and Merle Black. 2002. *The Rise of Southern Republicans*. Cambridge, Mass.: Belknap Press of Harvard University Press.

Bond, Jon R., and Richard Fleisher, eds. 2000. *Polarized Politics: Congress and the President in a Partisan Era*. Washington, D.C.: CQ Press.

Branom, Mike. 2005. "Jordan Re-Elected to Second Term as Chair of Florida Republicans." *Naples News.com*, January 30.

CalTech/MIT Voting Technology Project. 2004. "On the Discrepancy Between Party Registration and Presidential Vote in Florida." Available online at <www.vote.caltech.edu/media/documents/Florida_discrepancy3.pdf> (accessed March 2, 2007).

Carmines, Edward C., and James Stimson. 1989. *Issue Evolution: Race and the Transformation of American Politics*. Princeton, N.J.: Princeton University Press.

Cohen, Jeffrey E., Richard Fleisher, and Paul Kantor. 2001. *American Political Parties: Decline or Resurgence?* Washington, D.C.: CQ Press.

Cotterell, Bill. 2005. "Party-Leader Search Like a Coaster Ride." *Tallahassee Democrat*, April 30.

Downs, Anthony. 1957. *An Economic Theory of Democracy*. New York: Addison Wesley.

Dunkelberger, Lloyd. 2004. "Race for House Speaker of 2008 Heats up Early." *The Ledger* (Lakeland, Florida), November 28.

Friedman, Robert. 2003. "Mixed Messages in Florida." *Southnow* 4 (January): 4. <www.southnow.org/southnow-publications/southnow-chronicle/sn4.pdf> (accessed March 14, 2007).

———. 2005. "GOP Wins in Florida; Ideological Shift Less Certain." *Southnow* 8 (January): 3. Available online at <www.southnow.org/southnow-publications/southnow-chronicle/sn8.pdf> (accessed March 14, 2007).

Greenhouse, Linda. 2003. "The Supreme Court: The Ruling; Justices, in a 5-to-4 Decision, Back Campaign Finance Law That Curbs Contributions." *New York Times*, December 11.

Hernson, Paul S., and John C. Green. 2003. *Responsible Partisanship? The Evolution of American Political Parties in the Post-War Era.* Lawrence: University of Kansas Press.

Hershey, Marjorie Randon. 2005. *Party Politics in America.* 11th ed. New York: Pearson Longman.

Huckshorn, Robert J. 1998. "Political Parties and Campaign Finance." In *Government and Politics in Florida*, edited by Robert J. Huckshorn, 2nd ed. Gainesville: University Press of Florida.

Key, V. O., Jr. 1949. *Southern Politics in State and Nation.* New York: Alfred A. Knopf.

Knuckey, Jonathan. 2003. "Florida: Party Activists in a Two-Party System." *American Review of Politics* 24, no. 2: 127–43.

———. 2005. "Racial Resentment and the Changing Partisanship of Southern Whites." *Party Politics* 11, no. 1: 5–28.

Layman, Geoffrey C., and Thomas M. Carsey. 2002. "Party Polarization and Conflict Extension in the American Electorate." *American Journal of Political Science* 46, no. 4: 786–802.

Layman, Geoffrey C., Thomas M. Carsey, John Green, and Richard Herrera. 2005. "Party Polarization and 'Conflict Extension' in the United States: The Case of Party Activists." Paper presented at the Annual Meeting of the Southern Political Science Association, New Orleans, Louisiana, January 6–8.

Petrocik, John. 1987. "Realignment: New Party Coalitions and the Nationalization of the South." *Journal of Politics* 49, no. 2: 347–75.

Pfiffner, James P. 1994. *The Modern Presidency.* New York: St. Martin's Press.

Prier, Eric. 1997. "Exploring the Organizational Structure of the Florida House of Representatives." Ph. D. diss., Florida State University.

Salinero, Mike. 2001. "McKay's reforms: Difficult tax battle." *The Tampa Tribune*, July 1.

Schattschneider, E. E. 1942. *Party Government.* New York: Rinehart and Company, Inc.

Schreckhise, W. D., and T. G. Shields. 2003. "Ideological Realignment in the Contemporary U.S. Electorate Revisited." *Social Science Quarterly* 84, no. 3: 596–612.

Smith, Adam C. 2004. "GOP Strategy Turns Florida into Foothold." *St. Petersburg Times* (South Pinellas edition), November 4.

Stanley, Harold W. 1988. "Southern Partisan Change: Dealignment, Realignment, or Both?" *Journal of Politics* 50, no. 1: 64–88.

6

Interest Groups in Florida

MATTHEW T. CORRIGAN AND J. EDWIN BENTON

Interest groups historically have been associated with the performance of a number for functions that are integral to the healthy functioning of democratic government. For example, they educate the public about how government operates and about important issues, represent various segments of society, provide protection to numerical minorities, encourage participation in politics generally and in campaigns and elections specifically, and fill gaps in representation caused by a weak party system. However, interest groups are probably best known for their role in attempting to influence the proposal, passage, defeat, or modification of legislation and administration of government (Truman 1951).

It is in this latter role that some observers of American politics have expressed some concern. In 1787, in *The Federalist No. 10*, James Madison warned against the potential divisiveness of factions (the term he used for interest groups) and the pursuit of self-interests. Yet he believed that interests could be controlled through a system of separation of powers with checks and balances in which competing interests would serve as a check on one another. In spite of these early concerns about interest groups as well as those articulated by scholars (e.g., Key 1942; Lowi 1969; and Mahood 2000), they grew in both number and influence over the years and with little fanfare at the national and state level as the number of government activities increased.

Recently, however, two long-time students of interest groups (Thomas and Hrehenar 2003) reported that interest-group representation in virtually all state capitals had increased dramatically since the 1970s.[1] Florida was no exception. Estimates based on the number of groups registered with the legislature as of the 1990 session indicated that the number of interest groups represented in Tallahassee had almost quadrupled from 946 in 1968 to 3,488 in 1990 (Morris 1994). It is fair to say that the number of groups seeking influence in the state capital has grown exponentially since 1990, although more recent official statistics are not available to verify this.[2] Ben

Wilcox, the director of Common Cause, made this observation about interest groups and lobbying in present-day Tallahassee:

> It used to be just a little corps of the "good ol' boy" lobbyists. Now it's
> just mind-boggling. It's a huge amount of people coming here to try to
> influence the process. People get hired just because they have connec-
> tions with one specific legislator. (Kleindienst 2005, 1).

Many more groups seek access to government officials with the hope of
shaping policy decisions than was the case even three decades ago.

It is reasonable to speculate that much of this increase in interest-group
presence in Florida is a by-product of the state's rapid population growth and
the fact that politics in the state has been changing. Just as the state of Florida
has changed rapidly in the post–World War II era, interest-group politics in
the state have changed as well. This chapter describes the part interest groups
play in the formation of policy decisions in Florida. First, it provides a context
for understanding the growth in both the presence and influence of interest groups in the state. Second, it identifies and discusses the tactics interest
groups use to influence policy making and administration. Lastly, it identifies
the most prominent and influential interest groups in the Florida.

Florida and Interest Groups

Florida politics used to mirror politics in other southern states—agricultural
issues and courthouse politics ruled the day. As recently as the late 1960s,
this point was confirmed by *Florida Trend* (1969) magazine, which asserted
that the "Florida Establishment," a group of influential individuals in the
state that combined economics and politics, was governing the state. This
group included representatives from agriculture (e.g., Ben Hill Griffin and
Chester Ferguson), industry and utilities (e.g., Ed Ball and McGregor Smith),
banking (e.g., Harry Hood Bassett, Henry Dial, Frank Smathers, and Thomas
F. Fleming), attorneys and judges (B. K. Roberts and Millard F. Caldwell),
and politicians (Chesterfield Smith and William Augustine Shands—the
leader of the once-powerful "Pork Chop Gang" in the Panhandle). In his
description of Florida fifty years ago, Robert Huckshorn (1998) describes
a tacit agreement between these power brokers and the elected legislative/
executive branch officials to keep government regulation of business to a
minimum, thereby assuring that powerful business leaders and interests had
tremendous influence in Florida politics.

Over the last four decades, the "New Establishment" has supplemented
the "Florida Establishment." The coalition of interests influencing politics

and policy decisions in Florida has expanded to include not only the state's traditionally strong interests—the citrus, cattle, horse racing, phosphate, electric power, and liquor industries—but also new interests—representatives of the service and tourism industries, builders and contractors, foreign investors, advocates for the real estate industry and developers, advocates for the banking and insurance industries, health care providers, labor unions, teachers, public employees, environmentalists, feminists and civil rights groups, attorneys, and organizations such as the American Association of Retired Persons (Dye 1998).

The political culture and structure of government in Florida has always made the state a hospitable environment for interest groups. Florida's ineffective and noncompetitive political party system (remember that Florida was part of the solid Democratic South from the end of the Civil War until the early 1970s) resulted in a political void that interest groups gladly filled. Moreover, Democrats elected to the legislature or the governorship or to the other state executive offices in the old cabinet (attorney general, secretary of state, treasurer, comptroller, commissioner of agriculture, and commissioner of education) typically embraced the values and ideals found in Elazar's (1984) traditionalistic and individualistic cultures. They favored a government committed to maintaining the political, social, and economic power structure, thus promoting an elitist orientation in which government initiates only those policies designed to promote the interests of the governmental elites (traditionalistic culture). Yet Democrats pursued their own interests and those of their supporters rather than the general good with the ultimate goal of a political system that cleared the way for individuals to pursue their own self-interest (individualistic culture). Conservative Democrats had their own individual fiefdoms and believed in a government dedicated to preserving segregation and keeping the number of regulations that would affect their businesses to a minimum. In short, this hybrid culture favored the status quo.

More so than most states, the governmental structure in Florida aids and encourages the efforts of interest groups to influence policy making. The state's executive branch is composed of an elected governor and, until recently, a totally elected cabinet—secretary of state, attorney general, comptroller, treasurer, commissioner of agriculture, and commissioner of education.[3] Each of these independent departments—in addition to over 200 other separate and independent governmental agencies—has historically provided interest groups with a large number of access points from which they could monitor and create pressure for favorable treatment. The lack of executive leadership under this arrangement left an "influence vacuum" that interest groups were happy to fill (Kelley 1983). Furthermore, with the tremendous expansion of government functions since the end of World War II, groups have found it very advantageous to lobby executive agencies because their welfare may be directly affected by government actions. Interest groups attempt to isolate administrative agencies that affect them from the governor, unrelated cabinet offices, and the legislature in order to strengthen their influence with these agencies. The structure of the executive branch, which is characterized by its lack of control over state administration, and the incentives for interest groups to work to influence administrative agencies have combined to produce a situation in which interest groups have been able to gain extensive control over both the administrative process and the initiation of policies.[4]

Several features of the Florida legislature make it susceptible to the influence of interest groups. The legislature is a bicameral body that provides opportunities at many stages (e.g., when a bill is introduced; during the work of standing committees, subcommittees, conference committees, and select committees; and during action on the floor of the legislature) for interest groups to influence the outcome of legislation. In addition, lobbyists can provide a valuable service to legislators. The short duration of the legislation session (sixty days) makes instant access to technical and political information an indispensable ingredient of the work of part-time legislators and the legislative process. Lobbyists usually can provide the needed information in a condensed and easily digestible form, although what they provide is typically somewhat biased. Compounding the brevity of the 60-day session is the lack of adequate research staff and the inadequate expertise of legislators (and with the advent of term limits, this is likely to be in even shorter supply), and interest groups are quite willing to fill these gaps in information and expertise as well as inform policy makers about their policy preferences. The size of the legislative body also gives a distinct advantage to interest groups. The senate tends to be rather tightly controlled by its leadership, and thus the influence pressure groups can exert is partially dependent on access to the president of the senate and committee chairs. Interest groups face a large challenge in gaining access to the Florida House of Representatives because it is a much larger body. However, calculating lobbyists can take advantage of the confusion and mastermind the legislative process for their own purposes by getting several versions of a bill introduced during the same session of the legislature. Furthermore, the ability of interest-group lobbyists to successfully advance their agenda is enhanced when presiding officers appoint other legislators who share interest groups' interests to powerful or strategic committees.

The group affiliations of legislators is closely related with committee appointments. Members of each chamber lobby each other, and some interest groups have an advantage by virtue of the private interests and group affiliations of lawmakers. For instance, a large proportion of legislators are attorneys, meaning that the Florida Bar Association has "in house" influence. In addition, a considerable number of legislators are businesspersons, insurance agents, educators, farmers, real estate brokers/agents, and medical professionals. The private interests and group affiliations of these legislators are more likely to get the attention of the legislature than those of some other groups.

In summary, the rise of the "New Establishment," the political culture of the state, and the fragmentation of government structure means that ample opportunity has existed for many different types of interests to try to influence Florida politics. This led Kelley and Taylor (1992) to label Florida as a strong interest-group state. This description is still accurate.

Group Tactics for Affecting Policy in Florida

The relationship between interest groups and Florida's elected officials has changed dramatically over the last thirty years. But it is particularly important to recognize that—for good or bad—Florida politicians are more dependent on interest groups than ever before. Interest groups use several tactics or strategies in an effort to take advantage of this situation and influence public policy in Florida.

1. Lobbyists

If interest groups want to be a constant presence in Tallahassee, they hire lobbyists to represent them. It appears that interest groups in Florida have been doing that with increasing frequency over the last three decades. The number of registered lobbyists in Florida has grown tremendously since the mid-1970s. This increase in the number of lobbyists parallels the significant expansion in the state's population, and hence, the perceived need of elected public officials to keep pace with the demand for more government services. Consequently, the number of lobbyists in Florida increased by 652 percent in the late twentieth century, from an estimated 776 in 1976 to over 5,833 in 1990 (see Morris 1996).[5] These lobbyists are usually connected with law firms and provide strategies for influencing lawmakers and executive agencies. Professional lobbyists work the legislators at receptions, in private conversations and meetings, and at testimonial dinners (elaborate affairs to show appreciation for the lawmakers). This type of face-to-face interaction "affords lobbyists an access point to become acquainted with legislators, their aides, and their followers and to size up their abilities and positions on public issues" (Kelley 1983, 127). Since former legislators know the system the best, they often become lobbyists after they leave the legislature; notable examples are Sam Bell, John Grant, Mallory Horne, Ralph Haben, Lee Moffitt, Ken Plante, and Dale Patchett.

Lobbyists must register with the state of Florida and follow certain regulations. However, they operate in one of the most accommodating states in the nation. Thomas and Hrebenar (2003, 137) have classified Florida from the 1980s to the present as a state in which interest groups are dominant, meaning that they "as a whole are the overwhelming and consistent influence on policy making." Numerous attempts to toughen lobbying requirements in the state have failed. Lobbyists in Florida do not have to report how much they get paid from special interests. They are not required to report how they spend money on legislators and government bureaucrats. They also do not have to report what they spend on the family members of legislators. Therefore, the Center for Public Integrity has rated Florida in the bottom fifth of all states in terms of regulating lobbyists (Morgan 2005).

In response to reports of abuses connected to lavish spending by interest groups, the Florida legislature enacted a comprehensive ban on gifts in a special session in 2005 that prohibits lobbyists from giving gifts, dinners, and other gratuities to legislators.

2. Election Support

Money and grassroots organizations are two of the many ways groups help candidates get elected.

Money

While individuals are an important source of campaign contributions, groups that can bundle hundreds or thousands of contributions are vital to political parties and candidates. Money has become increasingly important in campaigns because of the need to buy television ads and send negative direct-mail pieces. Almost all competitive races now use a media saturation strategy that is very expensive. Parties and candidates have to depend on interest groups to raise this type of money. The average cost of a campaign for governor is now over $10 million per candidate, and competitive state senate races may reach up to $1 million per candidate (National Institute on Money in State Politics 2005). The 2006 governor's race in Florida nearly

Table 6.1. Campaign Contributions to 2002 Florida Gubernatorial Campaign by Major Industry

	William H. McBride (Democrat)	Jeb Bush (Republican)
Accountants	$41,608	$62,930
Automotive	$0	$54,685
Business associations	$52,018	$0
Business services	$45,887	$61,445
Commercial banks	$53,408	$55,935
Construction services	$74,157	$122,966
Crop production and basis processing	$0	$100,555
Education	$266,077	$0
General contractors	$39,153	$377,676
General trade unions	$29,680	$0
Health care professionals	$179,585	$513,460
Insurance	$44,803	$188,465
Lawyers and lobbyists	$1,247,739	$486,015
Miscellaneous finance	$50,865	$134,625
Miscellaneous health	$0	$140,961
Party committees	$2,036,105	$2,905,335
Public subsidy	$1,976,288	$0
Real estate	$182,937	$407,510
Securities and investment	$0	$60,451

Source: Institute on State Politics and Money. 2005. followthemoney.org. Website accessed in October 2005.
Note: Many individual contributions are not identified by industry.

topped $25 million in contributions. As Table 6.1 shows, Republican Jeb Bush received most of his contributions from business interests, including contractors, real estate, and agricultural interests. Democratic candidate Bill McBride received most of his contributions from education interests and lawyers. These interests attempt to influence policy by becoming active supporters in statewide campaigns. Florida is a large state with several expensive media markets, and these contributions have become the lifeblood of every statewide campaign.

Incumbents always have to be wary of potential challengers who have the ability to raise large amounts of money. The best strategy to scare off potential challengers is to raise enough money long before the next election. This means that campaigns for the next election begin immediately after the current election, a cycle that makes Florida politicians even more dependent on groups to raise money.

While Florida's Campaign Finance Act of 1973 limits contributions to $500 per candidate per election (that is, $500 for the primary and another $500 for the general election), groups and individuals that seek influence have made getting around these limits a high priority. First, individuals can bundle contributions. For example, the head of an insurance company may contribute $500 dollars to a state legislator's candidacy. He/she can also "suggest" that his entire company and his friends also contribute $500. If fifty friends can be persuaded, that $500 becomes $25,000. This type of bundling is a common practice among interest groups.

Political action committees (PACs) can also bundle. Florida law makes it legal for PACs to donate to candidates, but their donations are limited to $500. Thus, a PAC that represents education interests can give $500 to candidates per election cycle, but different PACs representing the same interest can bundle their contributions to candidates. In 1998, the Florida Education Association (FEA) gave state legislative candidate Buddy Dyer $5,000 in campaign contributions for a single election. They legally went over the $500 limit by splitting the contributions among different PACs that covered the same interest (Knott 2001). Thus, when a lobbyist for the FEA approaches a candidate, he or she knows that the lobbyist can bring more than $500 to their campaign.

Political parties strategize with interest groups to exceed the $500 limit and get more money to candidates from groups. Florida is one of thirteen states that has no limits on what can be contributed to political parties. Unions, corporations, PACs, and individuals can give millions of dollars to political parties. Parties use that money to contribute thousands of dollars to individual candidates. Parties can also use this money to buy advertising and campaign assistance on their own behalf. For example, the Center for Public Integrity found that telecommunications firms contributed over $4 million to the Florida Republican Party from 1999 to 2005. The timing of these contributions "coincided with the Legislature's approval of a controversial $355 million phone rate increase." The telecommunications industry is honest about why it contributed so much; a spokesman for them defended their contributions by saying "we are a highly regulated industry. . . . [and] being part of the political process gives us some access and an opportunity to be heard" (Kennedy 2005, B1).

Contributions to political parties probably are the fastest and most effective way interest groups can influence elected officials in Florida. This method easily destroys the intent of the $500 limit. Political parties, instead of striving to ignore interests and produce policy for the public good, cater to individual interests in order to raise more money. This is clearly illustrated by the different types of interest groups that donated money to Florida political parties in 2002. For Republicans, finance and real estate interests were the largest donors to the party. Health care interests, including insurance providers and hospital associations, were another major contributor to the

Republican Party. Because the state has so many senior citizens and because of the importance of development to the state's economy, how can the party ignore these interests? Lawyers and labor interests dominated the contributor lists to the Democratic Party. These contribution patterns helped set the stage for the battle between business interests and lawyers over tort reform. Other major contributors were communications and electronic interests. These types of contributions raise questions about whether political parties have coherent philosophies or have become simply extensions of major interest groups.

Another way groups get around this $500 limit is by producing their own television commercials or direct-mail pieces to try to influence citizens to vote for their candidates. A recent ruling by the Florida Election Commission has encouraged more independent groups to get involved. The commission ruled that independent groups may spend as much as they want on campaign support for candidates as long as their advertising does not explicitly ask the voters to vote for a particular candidate. Thus, if a business group wants to promote a Republican candidate, it can purchase an unlimited number of television or radio commercials or billboard ads. Independent groups can also attack candidates they do not like. Groups often send direct mail to the homes of likely voters that attacks candidates they do not support, and they can use their own resources to target legislators through negative media campaigns. They also can give an early boost to candidates. For example, a group called the Conservative Education Network funded a series of ads for gubernatorial candidate Tom Gallagher a full year before the gubernatorial election in 2006. This group gives money only to candidates that will support legislation to restrict lawsuits involving personal injuries and businesses. (Smith and Bosquet 2006).

Grassroots Support

Groups can also provide grassroots support for campaigns. They can mobilize their memberships to go door to door for candidates, make phone calls, take voters to the polls, provide babysitters while voters go to the polls, wave signs on roadways and at the polls, and organize Internet discussion groups. They also distribute posters, pamphlets, and leaflets on behalf of candidates and circulate newsletters, pamphlets, and journals to members of their group and to other groups with similar interests informing them about current political issues and urging them to take certain actions, including registering to vote, voting, signing petitions, writing letters, and talking to public officials. In addition, it is not uncommon for interest groups to fund voter-registration and get-out-the-vote drives. All of these activities are vital to successful campaigns.

In recent years, campaign strategists have realized that television ads and direct mail have a limited capacity to persuade voters. Person-to-person contact is more likely to convince supporters to vote. Activities such as hosting house parties, creating Internet discussion groups, soliciting for votes at church, and going door to door have all increased in recent years. Interest groups can provide the people on the ground to help with these activities and the organizational resources to coordinate this work. Some studies estimate that this grassroots work can increase the final vote count by 5 to 10 percent. The Florida chapter of the National Rifle Association historically has been heavily involved in these types of activities.

Christian conservatives have also aggressively employed grassroots tactics in election campaigns and have often become supporters of Republican candidates in Florida in recent years.[6] Organizing church groups is a good way of getting grassroots support. Church and religious groups are already organized, and their members share common ideas. Controversial issues such as abortion and gay rights have helped to unify Christian conservatives. This passion and organization has led church groups to issue voter guides, go door to door, and make phone calls for candidates.

3. Social Relationships

Personal relationships are extremely important when groups attempt to influence policy makers. In some instances, success in lobbying is determined by who you know. Lobbyists follow a strategy of making sure they are known to important legislators and their assistants. As a rule, skilled lobbyists have more than a passing acquaintance with the committee chair and each member of target committees directly related to their interests. They carefully discuss facts and figures on complex issues with members they are trying to influence. When direct contact proves difficult, lobbyists seek influential intermediaries or close friends to help them make contact with legislators. Often the contact is made though an influential person back home who is willing to work to move a legislator in the direction of the interest group that employs the lobbyist. These contacts may be a local banker or minister, the president of the local bar association, the president of the chamber of commerce, or the chair of the county Democratic or Republican executive committee.

Although we do not have definitive studies on the interaction between legislators and lobbyists in Florida, lobbyists frequently can be assets to legislators, and they are eager to take advantage of this coveted position. Because of common interests, legislators and lobbyists are sometimes interested in building coalitions to pass or block specific bills or public issues. As legislators are typically very busy during legislative sessions, lobbyists may help survey other members of the legislature, identify potential group support, coordinate a winning coalition of legislators and lobbyists, or shepherd a bill through the legislative process. Legislators need help in lining up support at many crucial points in the process, including when committee assignments are made, when committees take action on an issue, how the legislative calendar is set, during a floor vote, and during the actions of conference committees. Lobbyists can also provide innovative proposals for resolving public problems that could be advantageous to both legislators and the interest group that employs them. The position of the legislator could be elevated if the legislature adopts an innovative proposal, and the political status of the group that helped the legislator make this happen could be secured. It is not uncommon for lobbyists to provide legislators with proposals in the form of drafted bills.

As suggested earlier, interest groups also sponsor hundreds of events during the legislative session in Tallahassee. Lobbyists pay for events such as tributes to house and senate leaders. These events are usually held in fancy hotels and restaurants. According to legislative rules, the meal cannot be worth more than $100, but $100 can buy a very nice dinner for most individuals. This type of social interaction occurs both during the legislative session and after it has ended (Fineout 2005). In 2005, lobbyists even paid for engagement parties for two Florida state senators (Morgan 2005). Until the recent lobbying reforms passed in 2005 that banned free meals for legislators, all of these activities were legal. Many of these activities may shift to events sponsored by independent political groups.

Close personal relationships with policy makers can lead to lobbying success. For example, John Thrasher, former speaker of the Florida House, has used his personal relationship with Governor Jeb Bush to set up a successful and lucrative lobbying practice in Tallahassee. These personal relationships allow interest groups to get close access to important decision-makers.

4. Information

Interest groups also offer important information to policy makers. State legislators, who work only part time, and their staffs, which are small, must consider hundreds of bills in a legislative session. No practical way exists for legislators to understand every aspect of the hundreds of issues they encounter. Lobbyists provide technical information to legislators about specific proposals. The legislature often invites interest groups or their lobbyists to give testimony. When state legislative committees (and even state agencies) hold public hearings, representatives of various interest groups appear and present useful technical and political information about their policy preferences based on substantial research. This testimony and exchange of information often becomes the chief source of information for legislators, whose time and resources are limited.

Lobbyists also write speeches and talking points for legislators on issues. Interest groups use these opportunities to put forth their positions on issues. They perform the same function for executive agencies. Many times the well-paid lobbyist is able to focus on particular issues in a more comprehensive way than a government agency employee, who may have a huge workload.

An example of this type of relationship occurred with homebuilders in the state. Pro-development interest groups wrote most of the legislation that changed the regulation of wetlands in Florida. Working with eighteen lobbyists in Tallahassee, the homebuilders lobbied Florida's Department of Environmental Protection and the Army Corps of Engineers to make it easier for building to occur on environmentally protected wetlands. These lobbyists then persuaded the legislature to adopt the changes. During the bill's passage, the Florida Home Builders Association provided most of the technical expertise to legislators and the state agency (Pittman and Waite 2005).

5. Outsider Strategy

Groups advocate for their agendas in a variety of ways. Traditional lobbying is done through professional lobbyists. However, if groups are disappointed in the results of private lobbying, they can take their concerns public. They can rally members of associations or groups through e-mail, through the U.S. mail, by FAX, or by telephone. They can target TV and radio commercials to specific districts to try to raise enough public sentiment to get citizens to contact their legislators. Legislators do not like this type of pressure from constituents, and they may try to avoid it by listening to the lobbyists for these groups.

When interest groups become totally frustrated with the legislature, they can take the more drastic approach of sponsoring a constitutional initiative on a statewide ballot. This type of initiative requires its backers to get thousands of signatures from across the state to put a measure on the ballot. Most successful constitutional initiatives have been characterized by hired signature gatherers and professional public relations campaigns. Recent successful initiatives include a provision to protect pregnant pigs, an amendment to ban certain types of net fishing, and an amendment that mandates a certain class size for all primary and secondary education in the state. The ultimate interest group showdown in the initiative process occurred in the 2004, when medical doctors who had complained for years about rising medical malpractice rates put an amendment on the ballot to limit attorneys' fees in malpractice cases. The result was that multiple amendments on this topic passed and created more confusion about the topic.

In another dramatic use of the constitutional initiative, in 1982, senior citizens and their representatives in Florida were able to bring about the establishment of the Department of Elder Affairs. This department is devoted solely to senior citizens, who account for nearly 25 percent of the state's population. Florida is one of the most demographically diverse states in union, yet through their group association seniors managed to create a state agency devoted to their issues.

State legislators argue that this system of amending the constitution takes away their power to legislate. They have made a series of proposals to make the amending the constitution more difficult. In 2006, legislation was enacted that requires 60 percent of voters to ratify constitutional initiatives. However, it is not certain that this change will occur because it is the voters who ultimately approve changes in the initiative process. Citizens' groups maintain that the initiative process is a needed check on the legislature and should be left alone. Obviously, many interest groups agree with this position because the initiative process is another way for them to impact policy.

6. Using the Court

When groups cannot get what they want from the executive or legislative branches, they sometimes turn to the court system. At times, this takes the form of getting involved in judicial elections. By supporting or opposing candidates for judgeship, interest groups hope to create a judicial environment that is minimally respectful of, if not supportive of, their views on important issues. For example, in recent years, right-to-life and anti-abortion groups have supported judicial candidates that have voiced support for the sanctity of life and family values and have targeted candidates who do not support these views for defeat. An example of the latter was the campaign that was mounted against then Florida Supreme Court justices Rosemary Barkett and Leander Shaw for their controversial positions in support of abortion rights in the early 1990s.

Interest groups can also use test cases to try to advance a particular issue. This strategy involves identifying and providing legal support to an individual with standing to sue who represents a class of people who have been aggrieved in some way. Such was the case in 1997, when female employees of the Publix grocery chain, with the backing of the Florida chapter of the National Organization for Women, sued the company over promotion and pay policies they alleged were discriminatory against women. The grocery store chain agreed to pay the women workers $81.5 million to settle the class action suit Schottelkotte, 1997).

More often, however, interest groups write amicus curiae (friend of the court) briefs. Even though an interest group may not be a plaintiff or defendant in a case, it can write a brief to let a judge know how their interests will be impacted in judicial decisions involving the issue under court review. In recent years, groups that opposed Governor Bush's education voucher program have used the courts to block its implementation. Bush's proposal would have provided tax-funded vouchers to parents of students who attend schools that consistently receive a failing grade from the state. The money would have allowed parents to send their children to a private school of their choice. Teachers' groups and other education advocates have gone to state court to block the voucher program. They argue that the Florida constitution does not allow taxpayer funds to be used for private education. The groups have successfully blocked most of the program in the courts. Recently these groups have prevailed in the Florida Supreme Court (see *Bush v. Holmes* [2006]).

Types of Interest Groups

Who are the important interest groups operating in Florida? Major interest groups in Florida can be classified into several categories.

Business Interests

As the state shifted away from its dependence on agriculture as its primary economic activity, business interests found a receptive environment for expanding their endeavors in Florida. Because of the unevenness of Florida's economy in the first part of the twentieth century, state politicians have worked to make Florida more friendly to business. Florida's policy of no income tax has the made the state attractive for potential employees. Florida's constitution has a right-to-work clause that weakens unions. The state's environmental and safety regulations are minimal compared to states in the

Northeast and Midwest. This strong pro-business culture is demonstrated by the strength of business groups in Tallahassee. A listing of the largest businesses reveals that many of them are related to the real estate, building, trucking, and tourism industries as well as big agriculture (see Florida Trend 1969). Hundreds of business groups have received exemptions from Florida's sales tax. These exemptions make their products cheaper in comparison to others. Not surprisingly, the rise of the Republican Party in the state has aided business interests tremendously.

Single-Issue Interest Groups

Groups that advocate for a single interest they believe to be in the public interest have become an important part of Florida politics. These groups include the National Rifle Association, the Florida Christian Conference, the League of Conservation Voters, and Mothers Against Drunk Driving. The goal of these groups is to promote legislation specifically tailored to their concerns. They have been very successful in influencing Florida politics by a variety of methods. When personal lobbying of legislators fails, these groups do not hesitate to take their case to their members, who then flood the offices of state legislators with e-mails, faxes, and telephone calls advocating their positions. As mentioned above, groups that promote conservative social issues have been very effective in recent years. These groups have been instrumental in passing legislation about abortion; adoption of children by gay adults; the location of bars, strip clubs, and adult bookstores; the sale of alcohol and tobacco products; commercial and residential growth; sexual abstinence education; DUI penalties; and protection of the environment and endangered lands and animals. This success has coincided with the emergence of the Republican Party in the state.

Professional Associations

Professional associations lobby for the professional interests of their members. Support in the legislature is vital for these groups because the legislature creates the regulations that govern how their professions operate. For example, the Florida Chiropractors Association wants recognition of their work as an important medical profession. The Florida Bar wants the legislature to revise restrictions on how much money attorneys can make from malpractice cases. A wide array of medical professionals, from physical therapists to pain specialists, want limits on regulations and reimbursement for services given to the indigent. Both the Florida Bar and the Florida Medical Association want a strong voice in the admission policies and curricula of state-supported medical and law schools, and they want to control who is admitted to the practice of medicine and law through exams and other requirements.

Unions

The right-to-work provision in Florida's constitution means that labor unions have a difficult battle in the state. A much smaller proportion of the Florida workforce is unionized than is the case in other large states such as New York, Michigan, California, Illinois, and Pennsylvania. Union membership cannot be a condition of employment; there can be no closed shops in Florida. However, the presence of unions in the state is increasing. The Service Employees International Union (SEIU), which represents all types of service workers, has consistently tried to improve the standing of lower-wage workers in the state. The American Federation of State and Municipal Employees (AFSME) and the Teamsters have lobbied governments at all levels in Florida for better wages and conditions. The Florida Education Association, a labor union, has been heavily involved in several gubernatorial campaigns. In 2002, it was a strong supporter of Democrat Bill McBride in the race for governor. Even with this activism, unions have found it tremendously difficult to have influence in a state that is now governed by pro-business Republicans under a right-to-work constitution.

Government

In Florida, as in other states, government entities often lobby other government entities. Hundreds of local government entities across the state of Florida want to make sure that they are getting a fair deal from the legislature. Because local governments depend upon state government for their creation, their relationships with Tallahassee are crucial. School districts and universities want more money; water management districts want more authority to regulate the water supply. Both cities and counties want a larger share of state aid, more latitude in raising revenue, fewer restrictions on their ability to borrow money, and more authority over their affairs. In addition, cities and counties want relief from costly state mandates that reduce their flexibility to budget and ability to respond to the service needs of citizens. Since these topics are so important, local government entities spend millions of dollars lobbying the state's legislature and executive branch. Government entities frequently hire government-relations professionals to represent their interests, especially water-management districts, school districts, state universities, and executive departments and agencies. The Florida League of Cities and the Florida Association of Counties, as well as the Florida City/County Management Association, to which most cities and counties belong, are always looking out for the interests of the state's 412 municipalities and 67 counties, while many larger cities and counties hire lobbyists to push their agendas in Tallahassee and even in Washington. Moreover, numerous professional associations of elected and appointed officials in Florida's state and local governments (e.g., clerks of the circuit court, sheriffs, supervisors of elections, property assessors, tax collectors, mayors, city and county financial officers, and school superintendents) have a lobbying presence in Tallahassee.

The Media

The role the media in Florida plays in influencing policy differs from that of other major interests in the state. It influences public policy through information about public affairs, and the strength of the mass media is largely determined by its activities outside the government rather than through lobbying activities inside government. Media power in Florida is somewhat diffuse because of the wide variety of media markets (Dye 1998; Hill, MacManus, and Moreno 2004). Presently, Florida has over 45 daily newspapers, over 170 weekly newspapers, 695 radio stations, and 329 television stations.[7] All major television networks (CBS. NBC, ABC, FOX, CNN) as well as the Associated Press (AP), United Press International (UPI), the *New York Times*, the *Washington Post*, and the *Wall Street Journal* have representatives in Tallahassee.

While radio and television stations typically belong to national affiliates and national media corporations own some newspapers in the state (e.g., Knight-Ridder owns both the *Miami Herald* and the *Tallahassee Democrat*), media outlets have discretion regarding editorial decisions about state and local news and have the potential to influence public opinion and policy matters in the state. They can determine what will be selected as news, how it will be presented, and how much time or space will be allotted to stories. The mass media has the opportunity to express its opinion on matters of statewide or local importance through both editorials and commentaries. And when the *Miami Herald, St. Petersburg Times, Tampa Tribune, Jacksonville Times-Union,* or *Orlando Sentinel* expresses a point of view, public officials and the public do listen.

Case Studies

Terri Schiavo

The strange case of Terri Schiavo, a 41-year-old Pinellas Park woman who had suffered severe brain damage fifteen years earlier, captured the nation's attention in the spring of 2005. The case received extensive coverage in the national and state media because her husband and guardian, Michael Schiavo, wanted to remove the feeding tube that kept her alive, while her parents, the Schindlers, wanted the feeding tube to remain in place. This case became a test case for right-to-die issues, but it also illustrated the power of interest groups in Florida's political process. In 2003, when the feeding tube was removed, the Florida legislature passed a bill that gave the governor the power to order the feeding tube to be reinserted. The governor promptly exercised this power. The legislature's decision to pass a law about this case put the state of Florida in the middle of a family dispute.

The controversy did not end in Tallahassee. The Florida Supreme Court ruled that the bill that ordered the feeding tube reinserted was unconstitutional. When Michael Schiavo asked that the feeding tube be taken back out, many Christian conservative groups became mobilized. Using the media and the Internet to press their case, Christian Conservatives swamped the U.S. Congress. This pressure forced Congress to pass a bill in a late-night emergency session to give her parents more legal options to block the removal of the tube. The president of the United States signed the legislation. Even with that legislation, state and federal courts would not intervene. The tube was finally removed in March 2005, and Terri Schiavo died the next week.

How did this case reach the legislature and the governor? An unusual combination and coalition of groups pushed the case. Christian conservative groups such as Focus on the Family, National Right to Life, and the Family Research Council all solicited their members to contact Florida legislators. Since Christian conservatives are a vital part of Republican electoral victories, Republicans took the input of citizens aligned with these groups seriously. The Florida Baptist Convention was also a vocal proponent of reinserting the feeding tube, as were groups that represented disabled adults. When the controversy came up again in 2005, demonstrators flocked to the state capital to lobby for Terri Schiavo. They wore red tape over their mouths and distributed dozens of red roses to lawmakers. Florida legislators were inundated with letters, phone calls, e-mails, and personal visits. Washington

Post commentator Jeffrey Birnbaum noted the power of interest groups in a case like this:

> Their pleas touched a chord with millions of Americans and made Schiavo's case a cause celebre. The omnipresence of her situation in direct-mail communication from those groups and on talk radio made (the case) synonymous with the battle over life and death issues (Birnbaum 2005).

Even though most polls showed that Americans did not want the government to intervene in this case, well-organized advocacy groups received attention from all levels of government. In the end, the legislature rejected the second attempt to influence it in 2005, but Schiavo's case dominated the first half of the legislative session that year in Florida.

National Rifle Association

The National Rifle Association (NRA) was an undeniable power in U.S. politics in the second half of the twentieth century. However, the group's true success was at the state level. Florida has been a target for the NRA's legislative efforts. Section 8 of the Florida constitution has a strong provision about the right to bear arms, and the NRA has skillfully used this phrase to expand the rights of gun owners in the state since the 1970s. The association does not have a large lobbying corps, but it has 12,000 members statewide (Rushing 2005) who respond to the calls of their leadership to lobby legislators. Its membership brings an important ingredient to the lobbying process: passion. While polls show that most Floridians want more gun regulations, gun supporters are much louder and focused in their support than those who do not agree with them.

The NRA has been extraordinarily successful in its efforts in Florida with both Republican and Democratic lawmakers. Since the 1970s, the Florida legislature has passed laws allowing concealed weapons to be carried, prevented local governments from keeping records about gun owners, and enacted a law allowing citizens to use deadly force if they believe they are in danger, even if they are in a public place (Rushing 2005). Most important, these laws have made it almost impossible for local governments to place any of their own restrictions on gun owners. Local law enforcement officers have protested some of these changes, but the legislature has usually sided with the NRA. With organization, passion, and money, the NRA has had a profound impact on gun laws in Florida.

Even after several workplace shootings, the NRA in Florida pushed a bill in the 2006 legislation session to allow employees to carry guns in their cars as they drive to work. The NRA argues that employees need protection at work. The Chamber of Commerce and other business groups believe the bill is a bad incident waiting to happen. This battle has brought two powerful forces into opposition—the NRA and the Florida Chamber of Commerce.

Offshore Oil Drilling

Because of the dramatic success of the Republican Party in Florida since the 1980s, one might conclude that all conservative interest groups have a lobbying advantage. Yet Florida politics can still be difficult to categorize. The environmental issue of offshore oil drilling shows that interest-group politics cannot be easily predicted. Opposition to offshore oil drilling has persisted since the 1970s in Florida. The state that is usually so friendly to business has consistently said no to oil drilling. The coasts and beachfront property add an important economic and environmental benefit to the state. Florida residents have long been opposed to any type of drilling near the state's coasts. The League of Conservation Voters has continually monitored any attempts to drill near Florida. As oil supplies become scarce, the pressure to drill may increase, and the strength of the anti-drilling coalition will be tested in the state. In 2006, President Bush's administration was in conflict with Florida's governor Jeb Bush concerning oil drilling. In his 2006 State of the Union address, President Bush said that the country was far too reliant on foreign oil, an indication that the government and oil companies may begin pursuing drilling of oil reserves off Florida's coast.

Since the 1990s, both Republicans and Democrats from Florida have blocked efforts by oil companies to lobby the U.S. Congress to begin drilling there. Yet the federal government may force the state government of Florida to allow drilling; a U.S. Senate committee approved a bill that would allow the drilling of 3.6 million acres of natural gas and oil in the Gulf of Mexico. Both Senator Mel Martinez (R) and Senator Bill Nelson (D) have promised to filibuster the bill if it makes it to the Senate floor (Reiss 2006). Yet in 2007, legislation passed the Congress to expand drilling closer to the Florida coastline.

Doctors versus Lawyers

Medical doctors and trial attorneys have been in a prolonged political battle over malpractice insurance. Many doctors in the state have complained that they could not get malpractice insurance because so many lawsuits were being filed against them. The Florida Medical Association (FMA) strongly lobbied the Florida legislature to limit the fees attorneys can receive from malpractice cases. Although the legal profession has historically enjoyed good relations with the Florida legislature because many legislators were and are practicing attorneys, pro-business legislators have demanded action on tort reform. This reform would reduce personal injury settlements involving individuals and businesses.

Neither side has been satisfied with what the legislature has done about the malpractice issue. Both sides took their battle to the voters in 2004 in the form of three constitutional amendments. The FMA sponsored an amendment to limit the fees attorneys receive from malpractice cases. Trial lawyers sponsored two amendments, one to require doctors to publicly report incidents of medical malpractice and another making loss of a doctor's medical license mandatory if he or she is cited by the courts for malpractice three times. Both sides spent over $30 million on these initiative campaigns. All three amendments passed in November 2004 (Boulton 2004). Neither side could claim victory, but the Florida constitution may be the real loser. The constitution was amended three times by two groups of professional elites that clearly were not considering the interests of the citizens of Florida as a whole.

Conclusion

Florida is a state with strong interest groups, but the growth of the Republican Party and new methods of communication have changed the rules of lobbying. Lobbyists from the business sector are a potent force in Tallahassee; Florida is a business-friendly state and its laws reflect that philosophy. Until recently, the development and home-building industries were able to fight off many attempts to institute stringent laws to manage growth in the state. This clash between development interests and environmental interests will continue to be one of the most important political battles in the state. Other businesses receive generous exemptions from the sales tax, a practice that was denounced by the president of the Florida Senate in 2004. Professional associations such as the groups that represent lawyers and doctors constantly ask the legislature to do their bidding.

Conservative social groups have also increased their clout in Tallahassee. The state chapter of the National Rifle Association has an extremely successful record of getting pro-gun legislation enacted in Florida. Religious conservatives have lobbied to restrict more abortions, ban gay marriage, and block stem-cell research. In alliance with the Republican Party, these groups have substantial influence in Florida politics.

The methods of influence have also evolved. More and more, campaign contributions are funneled through individual political action committees and independent groups. When groups do not get what they want out of the legislature, they mount sophisticated pressure campaigns that ask members to contact their legislators through phone calls, letters, and e-mails. When groups become totally frustrated, they launch drives for amendments that attempt to change the Florida constitution to their liking.

In sum, the lack of institutionalized political culture in Florida allows interest groups to fill the political vacuum. As challenges mount in a state that is growing dramatically, battles among interest groups will only intensify.

Notes

1. In addition to confirming that interest groups have become much more numerous and powerful since the early 1960s, Cigler and Loomis (1998) have reported that new interest groups have brought about important changes in the way these groups affect public policy.

2. Prior to 1993, all lobbyists had to register with the Florida legislature. Now lobbyists must register only if they are employed and receive payment for lobbying or contract for economic consideration for the purpose of lobbying or if the person is principally employed by one government agency or department to lobby another government entity such as the legislature or governor's office (Morris and Morris 2006).

3. Since 2000, holders of only three cabinet posts—the attorney general, the chief state financial officer, and the commissioner of agriculture—are elected. The governor appoints the remaining members of the cabinet.

4. As Scher notes in Chapter 8, it is too soon to speculate about what the shift from election to appointment to cabinet posts will mean for gubernatorial power or about the access and influence interest groups will have with departments and agencies now under the governor's control.

5. Because of a change in registration requirements for lobbyists in 1993 (see note 2), there is no definitive accounting of the number of lobbyists in Florida. However, it is quite likely that the number in 2007 significantly exceeds the number in 1990.

6. For a good source on the political activities of conservative Christian groups in Florida, see Wald and Scher (2003).

7. These figures are derived from "RadioStationWorld," which provides information about broadcast and cable radio and television stations; <www.tvradioworld.com> (accessed March 26, 2007).

References

Birnbaum, Jeffrey. 2005. "The Forces That Set the Agenda." *Washington Post*, April 24.

Boulton, Guy. 2004. "Malpractice Showdown." *Tampa Tribune*, October 24.

Cigler, Allan J., and Burdett A. Loomis. 1998. *Interest Group Politics*. 5th ed. Washington, D.C.: CQ Press.

Dye, Thomas R. 1998. *Politics in Florida*. Upper Saddle River, N.J.: Prentice Hall.

Elazar, Daniel J. 1984. *American Federalism: A View from the States*. New York: Harper and Row.

Fineout, Gary. 2005. "Slot Lobbyists Woo Key Legislators." *Miami Herald*, August 11.

Florida Trend. 1969. "Special Report on Florida's Establishment." *Florida Trend*, November, 16–34.

Hill, Kevin, Susan MacManus, and Dario Moreno. 2004. *Florida Politics: Ten Media Markets, One Powerful State*. Tallahassee: Florida Institute of Government.

Huckshorn, Robert. 1998. "Introduction." In *Government and Politics in Florida*, edited by Robert J. Huckshorn. 2nd ed. 1–9. Gainesville: University Press of Florida.

Institute on State Politics and Money. 2005. <http://followthemoney.org> (accessed October 2005).

Kelley, Anne E. 1983. *Florida Government and Politics*. New York: Lanham.

———, and Ella Taylor. 1992. "Florida: The Changing Patterns of Power." In *Interest Group Politics in Southern States*, edited by Ronald J. Hrebenar and Clive S. Thomas. 125–51. Tuscaloosa: University of Alabama Press.

Kennedy, John. 2005. "Hello, Politicians? It's Politicians on the Line: The Phone Industry Has Poured Millions into Political Campaigns, a Study Finds." *Orlando Sentinel*, September 29.

Key, V. O., Jr. 1942. *Politics, Parties, and Pressure Groups*. New York: T. J. Crowell.

Kleindienst, Linda. 2005. "Florida Lobbyists Use Large Numbers, Freebies to Woo Lawmakers." *South Florida Sun-Sentinel*, March 8.

Knott, Alex. 2001. "Florida Legislators, Lobbyists Cozy in the Sunshine." *Center for Public Integrity*, February 23. <www.publicintegrity.org/report.aspx?aid=309> (accessed March 14, 2007).

Lowi, Theodore J. 1969. *The End of Liberalism*. New York: W. W. Norton and Company.

Madison, James, Alexander Hamilton, and John Jay. 1961. *The Federalist Papers: Number 10* (New York: Mentor Books).

Mahood, H. R. 2000. *Interest Groups in American Society: An Overview*. Upper Saddle River, N.J.: Prentice Hall.

Morgan, Lucy. 2005. "Soirees Sponsored by Lobbyists Decrease." *St. Petersburg Times*, April 16.

Morris, Allen. 1994. *The Florida Handbook 1993–1994*. Tallahassee: Peninsular Publishing Company.

———. 1996. *The Florida Handbook 1995–1996*. Tallahassee: Peninsular Publishing Company.

Morris, Allen, and Joan Perry Morris. 2006. *The Florida Handbook 2005–2006*. Tallahassee: Peninsular Publishing Company.

National Institute on Money in State Politics. 2005. *Follow the Money*. Online searchable database available at <www.followthemoney.org>.

Pittman, Craig, and Matthew Waite. 2005. "Wetlands Could Get Easier to Destroy." *St. Petersburg Times*, July 31.

Reiss, Cory. 2006. "Gulf Offshore Drilling Bill Easily Advances to Senate Floor." *Sarasota Herald-Tribune*, March 9.

Rushing, J. T. 2005. "Under the Gun." *Florida Times-Union*, April 17.

Schottelkotte, Suzie. 1997. "Publix Settles Sex Discrimination Suit." *Lakeland Ledger*. December 28.

Smith, Adam, and Steve Bosquet. 2006. "Gallagher Ads No Longer a Mystery." *St. Petersburg Times*, February 5.

Thomas, Clive S., and Ronald J. Hrebenar. 2003. "Interest Groups in the States." In *Politics in the American States: A Comparative Analysis*, edited by Virginia Gray and Russell Hanson. 8th ed. Washington, D.C.: CQ Press.

Truman, David. 1951. *The Governmental Process: Political Interests and Public Opinion*. New York: Knopf.

Wald, Kenneth D., and Richard J. Scher. 2003. "A Necessary Annoyance? The Christian Right and the Development of Republican Party Politics in Florida." In *The Christian Right in American Politics: Marching to the Millennium*, edited by John C. Green, Mark J. Rozell, and Clyde Wilcox. 79–100. Washington, D.C.: Georgetown University Press.

7

The Legislature and the Legislative Process in Florida

KEVIN MICHAEL WAGNER AND ERIC PRIER

Like every state except Nebraska, the structure of the legislative branch in Florida is similar to that of the national Congress. While there have been multiple changes and two significant revisions of the state constitution since 1838, the legislative branch continues to anchor state politics in Florida. The bicameral structure of the legislature requires the approval of a majority in each chamber to pass legislation. Legislative power can be checked by the executive branch through the use of the veto and by the state courts via judicial review.

The most recent revision of the Florida constitution, which occurred in 1968, updated the previous constitution of 1885 and still determines the structure and powers of Florida's government. While the 1968 constitution reflects a growth in support for popular sovereignty and citizen input and control of government, its underlying historical devotion to tempering popular sovereignty through the three branches of government is largely unchanged. Legislative power is still divided between two houses because of the slowing and deliberative effect of this structure. The state constitution vests the most authority in the legislature, including the power to make laws and the authority to tax and make appropriations.

The earliest incarnation of the legislative branch was the thirteen-member Legislative Council of the Florida Territory, which governed the peninsula prior to statehood and was made up of the "thirteen most fit and discreet persons in the territory." In 1850, Florida had a population of 87,445, which included about 39,000 slaves (Phelps 2002). In the days of the Legislative Council, legislators met every second year for only two months. They typically worked in crowded quarters, and each member's "office" consisted of only a desk (Francis and Williams 1998). However, by 1950, when the state's population had increased to approximately 2.4 million, the small council had become obsolete. The number of state legislators has changed in response to a burgeoning population, greater demand for government action, and technological advances.

The state's population growth after World War II necessitated change in the legislature. In 1976, legislators were provided personal office space in a newly completed state office building that also housed many of the offices of the executive branch. The house and senate chambers were fully computerized to make voting and the processing of bills more efficient. Today, Florida is regarded as having one of the most transparent legislatures in the country. For instance, the state along with Florida Public Broadcasting uses fixed television cameras in the galleries of each chamber to provide gavel-to-gavel coverage of all legislative sessions and airs summaries on its affiliate stations each evening on *Capitol Update*. The state also makes the coverage available online through a series of webcasts. In addition, the Legislative Information Division provides a statewide toll-free phone number that citizens can call to request free copies of and updates on the current legislative status of bills. For a fee, anyone can access the division online to track a bill (including its full text), the voting patterns of a legislator, the activities of a committee, voting records of the legislature, and session information (Francis and Williams 1998).

Despite the state's massive growth (by 2006, Florida's population had reached 17 million), the Florida legislature still meets part-time and continues to promote the "citizen-legislator" ideal. It meets for a regular 60-day session each year during the spring, beginning on the first Tuesday after the first Monday in March. Pressing matters can force legislators to return to the capital for extended or special sessions; the governor or leaders of both chambers acting jointly can call special sessions, which typically deal with specific issues that cannot wait for a regular session. Legislators are often in the capital long before the start of the session to meet with each other and plan and organize the upcoming session as well as review legislation, choose party and institutional leadership, and constitute the committee membership.

The Florida House is made up of 120 members elected from single-member districts. Each member is elected every two years during general elections held in even years. Typically, legislative districts are redrawn after each decennial census in a special reapportionment session in February. Each house district represents approximately the same number of voters. The senate's forty members are elected to four-year terms. The senate elections are staggered; half of the senate members are elected every two years. As is the case with the house, senators represent districts of roughly equivalent populations that are allocated based on data provided by the U.S. census.

Since each senate district contains approximately 400,000 Florida citizens, they tend to range over much larger geographic areas than house districts.

The Membership

Though the legislature still officially meets part-time, being a state legislator in Florida has increasingly become a job that requires full-time attention. Effective legislating often requires that the legislators be in Tallahassee long before the start of the regular session for committee meetings and to get legislation on the agenda. While the state's ability to maintain a part-time legislature is increasingly strained, legislators are helped by significant staff allocations. Each member of the house is provided one aide and one secretary who work full-time for that representative. Senators receive three to four full-time staff members. The facilities are modern and convenient; each legislator has office space adjoining the legislative chambers as well as an allocation for an office in their district. This has been one reason why Florida legislators have indicated that they are essentially satisfied with their legislative careers (Williams 1997). Despite the pressures of legislating in one of the most populous states in the nation, a job in the Florida legislature is still prized.

Most Florida legislators regularly maintain employment outside the legislature, and very few publicly declare themselves to be full-time lawmakers. This is curious, since close observers of the institution believe that the job increasingly requires legislators to devote more time to studying the needs of their constituents in such a diverse state. Table 7.1 shows the occupations of Florida House members in 2006; one can see that some of the declared occupations of legislators do not lend themselves to easy classification. For instance, twenty-two members identified themselves as engaged in "business," and an additional twelve considered themselves to be "consultants." Only four declared themselves to be full-time legislators.

The representativeness of Florida's legislators is questionable. In one of the grayest states in the nation, the legislature has only ten people, or 8 percent, who are retirees. This is about half of what would be expected; the U.S. Census Bureau estimates that almost 17 percent of Florida's citizens are aged 65 and older. Moreover, the legislature is overpopulated with members from the legal profession. In both Florida legislative chambers, the legal profession is a prominent source of legislators. In the senate, one-quarter of its members have law degrees; in the house, the percentage is slightly greater. A large number of attorneys is not uncommon in state legislatures for a number of reasons, including training and familiarity with the law and law-

Table 7.1. Fields of Occupations of Florida House Members, 2006

Field of Occupation	Number	Percent
Lawyer/Legal profession	34	27
Business	22	17
Education	13	10
Consultant	12	9
Retired	10	8
Agriculture	9	7
Construction, real estate, and development	9	7
Medicine	8	6
Insurance industry	5	4
State legislature	5	4
Total	127[a]	99[b]

Source: Florida Legislature.
Notes: a. The total number of occupations exceeds 120 because some members listed more than one occupation.
b. Total does not equal 100 due to rounding.

making, access to the resources required to take long absences from one's regular employment, and the ability to make the transition from lawyer to legislator to lawyer again. Even though the legal profession is one of the most common occupational backgrounds of legislators, the number of vocations represented in the Florida legislature is fairly diverse. In both chambers, members hold a wide array of jobs and employment in areas such as medicine, banking, business, agriculture, and industry.

Other demographic data such as educational achievement give us a clearer picture of the typical legislator. In the 2004–2006 Florida House of Representatives, only 6 of the 120 members lacked some college education, while 113 had earned a college degree. In the 2004–2006 Florida Senate, 31 of the 40 members held college degrees, and all 40 senators claimed at least some higher education. It is safe to say that Florida legislators are far more likely to have college degrees than the overall population. Moreover, if religious affiliation is any indication, more conservative religions such as Baptist and Catholic tend to be better represented in the legislature.

Table 7.2 shows that Protestant denominations are most common in the legislature and that Baptist is the most common Protestant denomination. Each chamber also includes a significant number of Jews and Catholics, though a number of different faiths are represented, especially in the house, where members follow eighteen different religions/denominations (Phelps 2002). In both chambers, Baptists and Catholics constitute over half of both the senate and house chambers. The patterns are generally reflective of the population in Florida, where Protestants are the plurality and Catholics are a close second. The number of Jewish legislators is proportionally higher than

Table 7.2. Religious Affiliations of Members of the Florida Legislature, 2006

Religious Affiliation	Number	Percentage
Baptist	42	26
Catholic	42	26
Methodist	18	11
Jewish	14	9
Episcopal	10	6
Presbyterian	8	5
Other	18	11
Not Reported	8	5
Total	160	99[a]

Source: Florida Legislature.
Note: a. Total does not equal 100 because of rounding.

the Jewish population of the state would suggest, especially in the senate chamber, where they hold 15 percent of the seats despite the fact that Jews constitute approximately 2.5 percent of the state population.

Florida continues to attract people from the north, and that is reflected in the makeup of the legislature. The minimum requirements to become a member of the legislature are that a person be over 21 years of age, a resident of the district from which he or she is elected, and a resident of the state of Florida for two years prior to the election. Unsurprisingly, a majority of Florida legislators were not born in Florida, though the distribution is broad and varied. A significant number of legislators are originally from New York, but members come from Connecticut to California and from several foreign nations, including Cuba, Peru, Canada, and the West Indies.

Historically, the Florida legislature has been dominated by whites. It was not until 1968 that the first post-Reconstruction African American was elected to the Florida House. While minority representation has increased, the racial makeup of the legislature, and of the state itself, consistently favors whites. Even so, minority representation in the current legislature is relatively close to the distribution in the actual population. Whites make up about 80 percent of the Florida population (white, non-Hispanic are 62.8 percent) and hold approximately 80 percent of the seats. This proportionality, which did not always exist, is largely the product of the adoption of single-member districts in 1982 and court intervention in redistricting in 1992. The growth of black representation led to the formation of the Legislative Black Caucus in 1982.

Leadership positions continue to be dominated by white males, though the Republican caucus shows increasing strength in members with Latino backgrounds, especially members from South Florida. The Cuban-American Caucus was formed in 1988 and is largely Republican and conservative. The largest minorities in both chambers continue to be members of African American and Latino heritage, which again parallels the general population of the state. Echoing national trends, African American legislators are almost exclusively Democrats and are represented in leadership positions within the Democratic Caucus in both the senate and house.

As is true in most state legislatures, the gender distribution in the Florida legislature strongly favors men. In recent sessions, women accounted for approximately one in four house members and about one in five state senators. Moreover, there appears to be a fairly strong partisan bias in electing women, especially in the senate, where Democrats are about twice as likely as their Republican counterparts to elect women. Indeed, 36 percent of the Democratic senators are women, compared to 15 percent of Republican senators who are women. In the most recent session of the Florida House, 34 percent of Democrats were women, compared to 21 percent of Republicans who were women.

Analyzing the backgrounds of the women serving in the 2006 legislative session reveals several patterns. Whether they are Republican or Democrat, women serving in both chambers often have a family history of participation in Florida politics. For example, relatives of many women members have served in the Florida House or Senate or have served as governor. Women members tend to follow similar paths into the upper chamber; like all of their Republican counterparts, women Democratic senators served in the house before getting elected to the senate. Some have been their party's whip, while one, Gwen Margolis, served as the senate president from 1990–1992. Several women also have committee leadership positions. For instance, in the senate, Republicans serve as chairs or co-chairs on six different committees, while Democratic women have five vice chair positions. In the House of Representatives, greater partisan differences emerge, where Republican women have ten chairs, co-chairs, or alternating chairs and four vice chair positions, while Democratic women have only one co-chair and two vice chairs.

In rank-and-file committee assignments as well, there are partisan differences for women. For example, in the senate, Republican women serve on nineteen different committees and have an average of 5.75 committee assignments, while Democrat women serve on twenty different committees with an average of 5.2 committee assignments. Moreover, Republican women in the house average 4.83 committee assignments, while their Democrat counterparts serve on an average of 5.25 committees. In the powerful Rules Committee, Republican women in the house have four slots to the

Democratic women's two, and in the senate, Democrat women have only one seat to the three for Republicans, one of which is a vice chair position.

Nonetheless, research on Florida legislators suggests that gender biases in politics are declining. Based on interviews with Florida legislators, Susan A. MacManus (1994–1995) determined that gender differences in political experience, political ambition, and family commitments were declining, especially among younger women. MacManus's research has not yet been supported by large shifts in the gender makeup of the Florida legislature, but generational shifts can be slow to develop.

Leadership

The presumption in Florida is that a legislative chamber populated by 120 members in the house and 40 members in the senate can adequately safeguard the interests of and represent the entirety of the state. But this conclusion requires a premise that may be empirically unsupportable, namely that all legislative members are comparably regarded and treated as equals. Indeed, representative democracy requires that the constituent represented by Legislator A should not have an advantage in the legislative process over a constituent represented by Legislator B. If this assumption is violated—if Legislator A has more political power or influence than Legislator B—the inequality of both legislators and citizen-constituents is institutionalized. The coordination problems that characterize any legislative organization are typically overcome by endowing a minority with power to expedite the legislative process. The end result is that coordinators, or leaders, wield more authority, thereby making some legislators more equal than others.

Institutionalized patterns of conduct and a legislative organization based on hierarchical modalities distort the capacity of legislators to equally represent their constituents. Selection of leaders in each chamber is critical, as the presiding officers in each body exercise significant discretionary power over floor proceedings and interpret the rules that govern how proposed legislation is processed. To a great degree, presiding officers (that is, the senate president and the speaker of the house) control what legislation ultimately gets to the floor and how it gets there. The presiding officers also have significant authority to select and remove members for standing committees and select committees, where bills are first heard.

By controlling the Rules Committee, the presiding officer may decide which committee hears a particular bill and therefore favor some legislation while blocking other bills. The presiding officer in each house also controls key administrative functions such as the allocation of parking privileges and the location of members' offices. While this might not initially appear important, presiding officers can use their control of such perquisites to sanction or reward voting behavior. Because legislators are unequal in the process, policy is determined to a great degree by presiding officers and committee chairs. Inasmuch as each citizen can cast only one vote for one legislator (as opposed to casting ballots for the whole legislature), accountability is minimized in terms of public policy.

The degree of control the leadership exercises in a state legislature can vary. Several factors intervene, including the size of the dominant party's majority. In cases where control of the chamber is close and the competition between the parties is high, the leadership exerts tight control. This trend was illustrated in Florida as the balance between Republicans and Democrats shifted from Democratic dominance to a competition between Democrats and Republicans. When this happened, leaders of the chambers and committees exercised tighter control over other members (Benton 2007). The competitive trend in Florida appears to be short lived; Republicans have gone on to dominate membership in both chambers. Whether this sizable Republican majority will lead to decreased influence of the leadership is not yet clear though there are some initial signs of small divisions in the Republican majority.

Since the members of the Florida legislature are limited by the state constitution to terms of eight years, the battle for leadership between members in the same party can be fierce. Each chamber chooses its officers every two years and adopts its own rules of procedure. These selections take place during organizational sessions after the biannual elections in November. Perhaps emphasizing the partisanship within each chamber, the presiding officers are really chosen in majority caucus, and the votes for each on the floor typically are made along party lines. By tradition, a new presiding officer is chosen every two years. Once presiding officers have served their single term, there are many incentives for them to leave the chamber, and they often become lobbyists of their former colleagues with great success.

This rotation system has the paradoxical effect of making house speakers and senate presidents more dictatorial in the sessions in which they hold the position. Often, this is expressed through the patronage system of appointing committee chairs. Because chairs often control committee business, it is likely that they will use these positions to their personal and partisan advantage. Traditionally, a committee chair will only serve one term in that position. Until the advent of term limits, the selection process was based on legislative tenure and committee service. But recently the ability of a legislator to raise funds to support fellow party members has become more important. The selection is done years in advance so that each upcoming legislature knows who its leaders will be before it actually meets for the session. Contenders for the leadership positions marshal their strength by accumulating pledges from party members, typically years ahead of the leadership term they are seeking.

Prior to 1992, speakers of the Florida House and presidents of the Florida Senate were Democrats and the battles for the leadership positions were largely internal matters within the Democratic caucus. However, this state of affairs began to reverse itself in 1992. In that year, Republicans split the senate by capturing twenty seats and ultimately entered a power-sharing agreement with the Democrats by which each party controlled the senate presidency for one year. In 1994 and in 1996, respectively, Republicans captured the Senate and House, and since then they have maintained a significant numerical advantage over Democrats, making the leadership issues in the legislature an internal matter within the Republican Party.

Because of their short tenure in office, members who wish to become a presiding officer in either chamber tend to engage in politicking. Because prospective speakers must plan ahead, they often begin by lining up votes and supporters among their legislative colleagues several years in advance. In the past, a grooming process placed future speakers in a queue for that office. For example, when Democrats were the majority party, house speakers would line up closely allied legislators; the next speaker had most likely just served as chair of the Rules Committee. Sometimes the queue went farther back to the second in line; those who became chair of the Rules Committee would first have served as chair of the Committee on Finance and Taxation or chair of the Appropriations Committee or another committee with similar prestige and power.

However, things have changed since the Republicans became the majority party in 1997. Although there are hints that future speakers will come up through the ranks of the majority party, it is too early to determine if this process has become institutionalized (that is, if there is a ladder of party leadership that leads to the presiding officer's chair). For example, Daniel Webster, who became the first Republican speaker in 1997, was the Republican minority leader in the session immediately preceding his reign. Yet because of the nature of the position, he had no specific committee assignments.

Before becoming his party's leader, Mr. Webster served on the Appropriations Committee, the Judiciary Appropriations Committee, the Rules & Calendar Council, and the Transportation Committee in 1995. When Mr. Webster became the speaker, Jim King became the Republican majority leader. Like Mr. Webster before him, his position did not have any specific committee duties. While Mr. King was the Republican majority leader, another Republican member, John Thrasher, was co-chair of Rules, Resolutions & Ethics. However, when Speaker Webster vacated his position, Mr. King was not elected speaker because he left the chamber and was subsequently elected to the Florida Senate. This series of events allowed Mr. Thrasher to become speaker of the house in 1999, but it is too early to discern whether or not holding a party leadership position will be more important than holding particular institutional positions if a member wants to become the presiding officer.

Because of the power associated with the leadership positions, the leadership battle can be bitter and divisive, even though it is between members of the same party. Consider the contest for leadership in the 2008 senate, which became openly bitter in 2005. Republican senator Alex Villalobos of Miami was thought to have secured the presidency of the 2008 senate based on written pledges from other Republican senators. The dynamics of the leadership race changed when Senator Jeff Atwater, a Republican from North Palm Beach, garnered the support of a group of Republicans who defected from Villalobos. Though this happened several years before the leadership spot was to be filled, the conflict in the intervening years could affect the ability of the caucus members to work together. As one Villalobos supporter noted, speaking of fellow party members, "It becomes very uncomfortable. People are less inclined to sit with you, less inclined to talk with you" (Bousquet 2006).

The Committee Structure

Most of the work of the legislature is done in committees, groups of persons chosen by the presiding officer to perform specific functions. Committees generally consist of two kinds. A standing committee has continuing authority to consider matters within its subject field. The name of the committee usually describes its policy jurisdiction. (Tables 7.3 and 7.4 list house and senate committees for the 2007–2008 session of the legislature.) Select committees are created to deal with a specific and typically narrow issue or event. Unlike standing committees, which continue for the duration of the term and tend to become permanent fixtures from session to session, a select committee usually disbands when the purpose for which it was created has been accomplished or its mandate has expired. Often a select committee will be an interim committee, meaning it will do its work between regular sessions of the legislature (Phelps 2002). Committees that are of limited

Table 7.3. Florida Senate Committees, 2007–2008

Agriculture
Banking and Insurance
Children, Families, and Elder Affairs
Commerce
Communications and Public Utilities
Community Affairs
Criminal and Civil Justice Appropriations
Criminal Justice
Education Facilities Appropriations
Education Pre-K–12
Education Pre-K–12 Appropriations
Environmental Preservation and Conservation
Ethics and Elections
Finance and Tax
General Government Appropriations
Governmental Operations
Health and Human Services Appropriations
Health Policy
Health Regulation
Higher Education
Higher Education Appropriations
Judiciary
Military Affairs and Domestic Security
Regulated Industries
Rules
Transportation
Transportation and Economic Development

Source: Florida Senate.

duration are also sometimes referred to as ad hoc, a Latin phrase meaning "for this." Like special committees, they also expire upon the completion of the specified tasks.

For the purpose of resolving disputes between the two houses of the legislature, conference committees are created and appointed from each chamber, and they typically address one piece of legislation. A majority of the members of the committee from each chamber must agree before committee members can submit a conference committee report to their respective chambers. Although neither chamber is obligated to accept these reports, they usually do, since the alternative would be the failure of the legislation for that session. This is a strict procedural process whereby amendments may not be offered to the conference report, and the report must be accepted or rejected in its entirety.

There is general continuity in the number and jurisdictions of standing committees from session to session, but other types of decision-making units can change. For example, the use of subcommittees varies over time.

Table 7.4. Florida House Committees and Councils, 2007–2008

Economic Expansion & Infrastructure Council

Committee on Economic Development
Committee on Ethics & Elections
Committee on Infrastructure
Committee on Tourism & Trade

Environment & Natural Resources Council

Committee on Agribusiness
Committee on Conservation & State Lands
Committee on Energy
Committee on Environmental Protection

Government Efficiency & Accountability Council

Committee on Audit & Performance
Committee on Military & Veterans' Affairs
Committee on State Affairs
Committee on Urban & Local Affairs

Healthcare Council

Committee on Health Innovation
Committee on Health Quality
Committee on Healthy Families
Committee on Healthy Seniors

Jobs & Entrepreneurship Council

Committee on Business Regulation
Committee on Financial Institutions
Committee on Insurance
Committee on Utilities & Telecommunications

Policy & Budget Council

Rules & Calendar Council

Safety & Security Council

Committee on Constitution & Civil Law
Committee on Courts
Committee on Homeland Security & Public Safety
Committee on Juvenile Justice

Schools & Learning Council

Committee on 21st Century Competitiveness
Committee on Education Innovation & Career Preparation
Committee on K–12
Committee on Postsecondary Education

Source: Florida House of Representatives.

In the past, joint committees were often used from session to session, as were select committees, which tended to be disbanded after one session. The most significant change in the system was the explosion from twenty-four to forty-three committees from 1995 to 1997. When Republicans took control of the Florida House in 1997, the first Republican speaker immediately initiated a new committee structure that funneled authority through supercommittees called councils. This new hierarchy eliminated all subcommittees and acted as a gatekeeper of legislation that came out of committees under each council's jurisdiction.[1]

Paradoxically, the loss of subcommittees as units of decision making may have increased centralized control over the legislative process. For example, if the 575 subcommittee assignments for 1995 are weighted the same as the 495 standing committee assignments for that year, the speaker actually appointed a total of 1,070 total positions for the 1995 session. Dividing this by the total number of standing committees plus their subcommittees yields an average size for decision-making units of 11.26. This figure is much closer to the average of 9.9 members per standing committee in 1997–1999, when Republicans had no subcommittees but had added more committees and the newly formed councils. Even though the organizational structure appeared to have changed dramatically when subcommittees were eliminated, the real impact on the size of decision-making units was negligible. Nonetheless, the majority party was able to pursue a strategy of maximizing influence by stacking the committees with its members.

Consider that if partisan influence within each chamber was based on the actual results of the state legislative elections and was distributed in an unbiased fashion within the legislative institution, the proportion of members from each party on each committee would mirror party representation in the full house and there would be no difference in the average number of assignments between the parties. However, differences in committee distributions have always favored the majority party on both subcommittees and committees. For example, in 1995, only 58 percent of legislators were Democrats, yet Democrats held an average of 61 percent of the seats on the legislature's seventy sub-committees. Although this seems like a slight advantage, consider that at least 70 percent of the membership of fifteen of the seventy subcommittees identified as Democrats. Moreover, each standing committee in the same year averaged 62 percent Democrats while fully one-fourth of the committees had 66 percent Democrats or more (Prier 2003).

When Republicans became the majority, they did the same. In 1997, the year subcommittees were abolished, 51 percent of the house membership won seats as Republicans. However, Republicans accounted for at least 57 percent on twenty-four of the fifty-one committees and councils. Indeed, these twenty-four committees and councils averaged 61 percent Republican. Majority parties have magnified their influence on legislation by controlling the agenda through the use of chairs and by stacking committees with their own members. In 1997 for example, the average number of assignments given to Democrats was 2.74, while the average for Republicans was 3.18 (Prier 2003). The ability to manipulate the assignment system to create systematic favoritism in not only the volume of assignments, but in the value of those placements is a key benefit for the majority party and a significant means of control for each chamber's presiding officer.

In the House, speakers have gone to great lengths to stack legislative committees with their own partisan members beyond what each party's representation in each chamber would suggest (see also Benton 2007). This is perhaps emphasized by the fact that when the Republicans took over in 1997 and partisan competition was at its highest, the systematic favoritism in assignments switched from benefiting the Democrats to favoring the Republicans. There are probably at least two reasons why this occurred.

First, it is likely that House speakers want to protect themselves and their proposed agendas against potential defectors in their party on any given piece of legislation. Second, speakers probably dole out favored assignments to supporters in their party. Because a speaker needs to bring together a coalition of supporters, it is plausible that he promises particular assignments to party members in return for support. Committee leadership positions are prized the most, but rank-and-file committee positions are also valued. There is some reward for holding and investing time in these positions, and speakers appear willing to accommodate their colleagues in this regard. Presiding officers set the number and size of committees and typically appoint people to each committee in a way that amplifies the power and influence of the majority-party members. It does not matter whether Democrats or Republicans controlled the chamber; the pattern is the same. Because of their ability to manipulate the placement of legislators on committees and councils, majority-party members have a greater ability to wield influence in the legislature than their numbers alone would suggest.

The importance of this maneuvering is evident in the distribution of the benefits that come with positions of influence in the legislature. The ability of members of the legislature to take home benefits to the districts is an important component of their political strength. Similar to "pork" in Congress, these benefits are called "turkeys" in Florida, pet projects placed in the state budget that tend to benefit narrow interests or local areas of members' districts.

In fact, since control over the legislature changed in 1997, the close relationship between membership in the majority party and the ability to bring home the turkeys may have led up to seven house Democrats to abandon their party ties and become Republicans.[2] Rudy Bradley switched parties and became the lone African American Republican in either house of the Florida legislature at that time. In describing his switch, Bradley said: "Most certainly the change in parties changed my relationship with the leadership, and it was very beneficial to my district in terms of getting needed funding."[3]

The Flow of Legislation

Legislation can come from many sources, but to be considered by the legislature it must be proposed by a member of the respective chamber in which it is introduced. Groups that support changes in Florida law seek a member to sponsor their legislation and help shepherd it into law. In theory, any person or group can approach a legislator with an idea. The Florida Senate, in the *Florida Senate Handbook,* includes an instruction list for making "considerable contributions to the process of creating public policy" (Blanton 2004). However, in practice, the source of new legislation is often a group or several groups that are organized to support a particular interest. The process of getting a bill through the legislature is complex and often requires more than one legislative session to gather enough support to push it through both chambers. As a result, groups with strong organizations and contacts in both houses and the executive branch are far more likely to achieve success in pushing their legislation.

Groups from industry are particularly active before and during the legislative session, though the lobbying groups in Florida can come from a large number of economic sectors, including manufacturing, real estate, law, labor, medicine, tourism, and finance and from a broad array of single-issue organizations. It is also common for local governments and elements of the state government such as the governor, attorney general, state agencies, or even universities to propose and lobby for legislation. While members of the legislature must often consider and weigh proposals from various sources, they can, and do, propose legislation themselves.

Once an idea is proposed, the first step in getting it made into law is writing it in the form of a bill. Since the legislative session in Florida is very short, most legislation is proposed and drafted long before either chamber comes into session. Many legislators have no particular skill in writing legislation and rely on others to put their proposals in the form suitable for consideration by the Florida House or Senate. Sometimes this process is accomplished by the group or groups supporting the legislation, as they often have access to lawyers and other resources that aid in drafting. Other times, a legislator relies on the chamber's Bill Drafting Service, which can write the bill or review a proposal for style and form. There are specific rules about the form of legislation, including beginning every bill with the phrase, "Be it enacted by the legislature of the State of Florida . . . ." The absence of this phrase is fatal to the legislation, and members who oppose a measure may attempt to strike the phrase as a means of defeating the bill.

After its drafting, the bill is filed with the secretary of the chamber, recorded in the daily record, and assigned by the presiding officer to a committee for consideration based on the subject matter. Between 2,200 and 2,700 bills are introduced in each legislative session. Over the last several sessions, the number of bills introduced has been fairly stable at about 2,300, though only about 400 to 500 are passed by the legislature. Indeed, the passage rate for bills has remained fairly constant at about 20 percent over the last decade (Phelps 2004). But these numbers are imprecise, either because similar bills are often combined under a single bill number or because proposals are incorporated into a larger committee report that makes it seem that a bill (as indicated by its designated number) failed to pass, even if the substance of the law is ultimately successful in another form. Nonetheless, what is clear in reviewing the success rate of bills is that since no more than 500 bills are likely to pass in a given session, successful legislation will likely remain a difficult prospect in the Florida legislature.

Legislators attempt to maximize the chances that their bill will pass by filing the legislation with the secretary before the legislative session begins. During the session, legislators propose most bills in both chambers simultaneously rather than waiting for them to be handled exclusively by one chamber before moving to the other. This is done largely for pragmatic reasons, as the short duration of the legislative session often requires that bills be on the agenda in both chambers for there to be enough time for them to make it through the deliberation process.

Assignment to the proper committee is a major factor in the success of any legislation. It is common for a bill to die in committee because the chair of the committee does not schedule the bill for hearings or consideration. Thus, the presiding officer can influence the passage or failure of legislation by selecting a committee with a predictable disposition on the legislation. Obviously, a bill stands a better chance of passage if the sponsor of the bill also sits on the committee where the bill is being considered, because he or she then has an opportunity to defend and champion the proposal.

Bills in the Florida legislature face many hurdles, as many as half of the bills proposed will never make it beyond the original committee. In order for the bill to move through the process, a positive report from the committee, meaning a formal vote in which a majority of the committee members vote for approval, is typically required, yet even getting a bill to a formal vote can be difficult. Within the committee, bills are subject to changes and amendments and may even be incorporated with other proposals into a "committee substitute bill" that will make it part of a larger package when it is finally considered by the full chamber. If some part of the measure makes it through the committee and is approved, the bill will then be moved to the calendar, where its progress may end. In the senate, the Rules Committee selects the bills that go to the floor, and in the house, a council decides whether to schedule a bill for the full chamber.

Though it is a substantial accomplishment to get a bill to the floor of either chamber, reaching the floor is no guarantee of passage. The bill is given a second reading, where amendments and ultimately the passage of the legislation are voted upon. Legislators can use amendments to defeat a measure by striking the required enacting clause or by adding or subtracting a provision that will cause the bill to lose majority support. Numerous procedural maneuvers and delays can help defeat or expedite a bill. For example, while the rules require that legislators be notified when a bill is under consideration with the understanding that members have a day to review it before it is read again on the next day, the rules are regularly waived, allowing for immediate consideration and passage of favored legislation. If the bill successfully makes it through the second reading, a final vote occurs at the third reading.

If a companion bill has been simultaneously passed in the other chamber, final passage can come rapidly, and the bill will then be forwarded to the governor for consideration. If there is no companion bill and if a bill that has already passed one chamber is then referred to the other chamber, the legislation will need to go through the entire process in the other chamber. When this happens, the odds that the bill will be passed are decreased considerably, and if it is late in the legislative term, failure of the bill is almost guaranteed. To avoid this outcome, representatives and senators who support the bill coordinate their efforts by reconciling differences through friendly amendments as it moves through each chamber.

If a piece of legislation passes both chambers with significant differences, the bill is sent to a conference committee, which consists of members from both chambers, in an attempt to resolve the differences. If the committee is able to resolve the differences, the compromise legislation, called the committee report, is returned to each chamber for an up or down vote. Conference committees are relatively uncommon for most legislation in Florida and are used primarily to resolve differences about the budget. This typically involves the most intense negotiations of the legislative session and concerns the funding of projects that affect many members and their districts. Because there is only a limited amount of time for consideration of bills, the budget and appropriations can, and often do, dominate the attention of legislators, especially toward the end of session.

The final hurdle for a piece of legislation is the governor, who can veto a bill. This sends it back to the legislature, where it can become law only with the approval of a two-thirds vote in each chamber. The governor also has authority to reject specific appropriations within a bill. This authority, called the line-item veto, allows the governor to trim special projects from the budget like turkeys mentioned previously. The governor can also punish members of the legislature by removing an appropriation in a specific district. Because the veto, especially the line-item veto, can be potent, the governor often plays an important role in shaping legislation by threatening vetoes or suggesting approval or dissatisfaction with legislation during the legislative processes.

Redistricting

While the population of each chamber's district is approximately the same, the final shape and physical size of districts can vary greatly. The process of creating districts to favor one party over the other, called gerrymandering, has historically been used by the majority party in power to capitalize on its electoral advantage. In the 2006 session, Republicans controlled 70 percent, or 85 of 120 seats, in the Florida House of Representatives, and 65 percent, or 26 of 40 seats, in the Florida Senate. This is striking when one considers that as of April 2006, 40 percent of voters in the state were registered as Democrat, 38 percent were Republican, 3 percent were registered with a minor party, and 19 percent were not affiliated with any party. Obviously, several factors affect the outcomes of individual elections, such as the strength of the candidates and the differential turnout rates for partisans in the electorate, among other things. But this data strongly suggests that the current electoral map for both houses of the legislature is comprised of single-member district boundaries that overwhelmingly favor the Republican Party.

While the battle over districting is certainly a contemporary issue, it is one of historical significance in Florida. Because the Democratic Party dominated state politics for much of the twentieth century, redistricting was not a partisan battle as much as it was a geographic one. Before term limits were instituted in 1992, rural legislators conspired to systematically disenfranchise and dilute the influence of the growing urban areas in the state. In 1955, James Clendinen, editor of the *Tampa Tribune*, dubbed a group of entrenched legislators who were determined to preserve their base of power the "Pork Chop Gang." The phrase technically referred to the rural members of the Florida Senate (legislators from metropolitan areas were known as "Lambchoppers"), but the term *Porkchopper* came to refer more specifically to rural North Florida members of both legislative chambers who maintained power in session after session.

North and South Florida legislators typically fought over control of the state's budget, and the increasing prosperity of the urban areas, especially in South Florida, served to further galvanize the Porkchoppers and their constituents. Because some rural incumbents were repeatedly returned to office before the imposition of term limits in 1992, sometimes for over twenty years, Porkchoppers were able to control their respective chambers through their grip on the presiding offices and their control over committee assignments. This system preserved rural dominance because Porkchoppers controlled the appropriations process that doled out money for local projects such as roads and bridges, and they successfully set up effective roadblocks to equal reapportionment based on population. Consequently, the system preserved the dominance of the white rural southerner.

To maintain their power, Porkchoppers needed to manipulate the drawing of legislative districts, which packed many more voters into some districts than others. Indeed, by 1960, districts were so malapportioned that a majority of state legislators were elected by less than 13 percent of the state's population (Dauer 1984, 141). Hugh Douglas Price (1962) called it "the state with the least representative legislature of any in the Union." The grip of the northern Porkchoppers was ultimately broken as a result of the U.S. Supreme Court's decisions in *Baker v. Carr* (1962) and *Reynolds v. Sims* (1964), which mandated the one vote per citizen standard for legislative districting. This forced the state of Florida to recognize the growth of urban areas such as Miami, Jacksonville, and Tampa and redistrict accordingly.

In Florida, federal courts at both the district and appellate levels handed down a series of judicial rulings in *Swann v. Adams* that invalidated several reapportionment plans put forth during successive Florida legislative sessions in the 1960s (*Swann v. Adams*, 263 F. Supp. 225 [1967]). The case ultimately went to the U.S. Supreme Court (*Swann v. Adams*, 385 U.S. 440

[1967]). When the U.S. Supreme Court issued one of its rulings rejecting Florida's legislative apportionment plan in 1967, legislators who had been elected in 1966 were already in session attempting to accommodate both state and federal courts with new reapportionment plans. The 1967 Supreme Court ruling in *Swann* rendered the legislature's existing reapportionment plan null and void despite the legislature having already begun its deliberations. Because of the court ruling, the existing legislature, which was elected in 1966 and seated, was actually not legitimate in the eyes of the law. Later, a report issued by the Florida House of Representatives Committee on Reapportionment (1991, 9) put it this way: "It was truly a remarkable, if not bizarre situation, having an unlawful legislature authorized to do nothing else except create another, more legal, group of lawmakers."

In spite of these legal difficulties, the legislature finally was able to adopt an acceptable reapportionment plan. The new plan and the subsequent redistribution of legislative seats did not end the political bloodletting that often surrounded reapportionment, but it did create a new balance in the legislature between urban and rural members and ultimately changed the state's public policies to be more responsive to the needs of citizens in metropolitan areas. For the first time, large metropolitan areas such as Miami and Tampa were able to wield significant influence in the state legislature and ultimately shift appropriations away from the more rural north.

At that time, the Florida legislature was a one-party legislature dominated by the Democratic Party. Hence, the battle over redistricting was not between parties but rather between incumbent legislators. However, as new immigrants began to change the partisan makeup of the state, Republicans made inroads in both houses. By 1997, Democrats were the minority party in Florida for the first time since Reconstruction. This change has tended to promote partisan polarization in the legislature, and the political stakes have been raised concerning redistricting. Under a one-party system, redistricting was a battle for geography. Under the two-party system, redistricting has become the means by which the majority party can maximize its seats in the legislature.

Today legislators use technology to help them redraw their districts to their liking. The party in power seeks to increase its voting strength and can do so with greater precision using computer programs that allow lawmakers to draw the boundaries of districts to the level of city blocks. The programs permit legislators to efficiently divide up voters based upon incumbent legislators' desires, a process that in effect allows incumbents to choose their voters. While there is some debate about how effective redistricting is as a partisan tool (see Niemi and Jackman 1991), the results in Florida are rather compelling as incumbents seeking reelection are rarely turned out in state or congressional elections.

This success may be a consequence of better technology and the increasing sophistication of the staffs of legislators, but the end result is that the electoral process for the Florida legislature has become increasingly noncompetitive, whether or not incumbents are personally responsible for the resulting partisan bias within each legislative chamber. This normally results in the assurance that winners of each party's primary will win the legislative seat, because just like in most states, when fewer voters show up to the polls during these elections, strong partisan voters tend to dominate primary elections disproportionately. Political rhetoric in Florida has become increasingly polarized because the legislators running for office need only appeal to strong partisans rather than the moderate party members for votes.

For these reasons, the party finding itself in the minority tends to favor a proposal pushed by the Florida chapter of Common Cause since the 1970s. The proposed state constitutional amendment attempts to establish additional standards for legislative and congressional districts by requiring that districts be compact and, where practicable, use existing political and geographical boundaries to preserve "communities of interest." Perhaps more important, an amendment if approved would urge that districts not be drawn to favor an incumbent, a political party, or a person. It would also propose that the reapportionment process be taken out of the legislature and put into the hands of a bipartisan redistricting commission with members appointed by legislative leaders and the Florida Supreme Court, which would rule in cases of a deadlock. The Florida Supreme Court rejected this effort to amend the constitution to remove the redistricting power from the legislature in March 2006, although it did so largely for technical rather than substantive reasons.

Designing districts to create equitable representation is neither simple nor easy, even when the political will to do so is strong. Although conventional wisdom conceptualizes partisan bias as the difference between the proportion of votes a party receives in the general election and the share of that party's members who take their seats in the chamber, in Florida the problem with this measurement stems from the lack of competition for seats across the state. It may seem that the voting population of a district favors one party or ideology, but it may be the lack of viable choices that drives the outcome. Because the legislature tends to redraw districts that favor the majority party in power, it is difficult to determine whether voters in Florida choose not to vote on Election Day because they are frustrated with the state's political system or because they are happy with the state of political affairs. Understandably, members of the majority party in the legislature have no particular desire to alter the current noncompetitive dynamic and continue to design districts that guarantee success for their party. That is why, in Florida, when politics is the topic, one often hears that "candidates pick voters more often than voters pick candidates."

Legislative Elections

A steep decline in competition for legislative seats is the current trend in elections in the state of Florida. State legislators generally are satisfied with their careers in the legislature, yet very few Floridians compete in elections for those seats. If the seats are as desirable as surveys suggest, then it follows that many people should be seeking the seats in competitive elections. Yet the evidence indicates that not only are most legislative elections not competitive, the amount of competition is actually declining. The end result of the practices of redistricting to make legislative seats secure along partisan lines is that most competitors are discouraged from challenging entrenched incumbents for the seats. This trend is clearly illustrated in the number of unchallenged candidates for the Florida legislature depicted in Table 7.5.[4]

The trend away from competition is difficult to miss in the data. In 2000, only eight Democratic seats and six Republican seats were unopposed in the Florida House. By the 2006 elections, fourteen Democrats and thirty-one Republicans faced no competition in their elections. The percent of candidates who ran unopposed shot up from 12 percent in 2000 to 43 percent in 2004, before leveling off at 38 percent of legislators who faced no electoral opposition in 2006. The numbers are even more significant in the Florida

Table 7.5. Unchallenged State Senators and Representatives, Florida, 2000–2006

	House				Senate			
General Election	Democrat	Republican	Total Races	Percent Unopposed	Democrat	Republican	Total Races	Percent Unopposed
2000	8	6	120	12	2	6	21	38
2002	11	7	120	15	6	12	40	45
2004	17	34	120	43	5	6	22	50
2006	14	31	120	38	2	6	20	40
Average	27	43						

Source: Florida Department of State, Division of Elections.
Note: 2006 estimates are based on the number of candidates who had filed as of March 1, 2006.

Senate, where the average percent of legislators who ran unopposed for election or reelection was 43 between 2000 and 2006. Despite larger senate districts with presumably larger pools from which challengers could be drawn, only eight of the twenty seats up for election fielded any challenger in the 2006 general election.

This finding is not limited to general elections; the competition for state legislative seats is extremely low in primaries as well. This suggests that the lack of competition is partly due to an incumbent advantage. This is clearly seen in the data in Table 7.6, which compares the amount of competition for available seats in the Florida House and Senate elections from 2000 to 2006. Broken down by chamber and by primaries and general elections, we created a competition score as a measure of competitiveness. It is computed as the ratio of the total number of candidates running for each chamber's seats divided by the total number of potential races in that election. Given that all 120 house seats are up for election every two years, there are potentially 120 races in each of the two major party primaries, for a total of 240 potential races in any given election cycle. However, in the general election, there are only 120 potential races after the nominees from the two parties have been chosen. In essence, if Florida was a two-party competitive system, the expected competition scores would average 4.0 in the case of house primaries (two candidates in each primary for each seat for a total of 480 candidates vying for the 120 seats). In the general election we would expect an average competition score of 2.0 with 240 candidates running for each of the 120 available seats. These expectations exclude those potential candidates who run as candidates of third parties or as write-ins.

The data in Table 7.6 illustrates the dearth of competition and the level of safety enjoyed by incumbents in Florida. In the 2006 house election primaries the competition score of 0.81 suggests that the candidates from the two major parties were largely safe from electoral challenges within their own party. Moreover, the competition score of 1.61 in the general election does not bode well for those citizens who believe in a thriving democracy, because it is far enough below the expected score of 2.0 to give one pause. Competition appears to be very rare as measured by this indicator, and the situation is little changed in the senate.

Overall, the average competition scores are similar in both chambers, with average scores of 0.88 and 0.78 in the house and senate primaries, respectively, and scores of 1.80 and 1.73 for the respective general elections. But without a fuller examination of year-to-year challenges across districts that might indicate whether seats in specific districts are safer from chal-

Table 7.6. Number of Candidates and Competition Score for Elections for Florida House of
Representatives and Senate, 2000–2004

	House Primary	General Election	Senate Primary	General Election				
	N	Competition Score[a]	N	Competition Score	N	Competition Score	N	Competition Score
2006	195	0.81	193	1.61	32	0.80	36	1.8
2004	175	0.73	196	1.63	26	0.59	34	1.55
2002	209	0.87	256	2.13	66	0.83	63	1.58
2000	263	1.10	217	1.81	38	0.90	42	2.0
Average	210.5	0.88	215.5	40.5		0.78	43.8	1.73	1.80

Source: Authors' calculations based on data from Florida Department of State, Division of Elections.
Note: a. Number of candidates running for each chamber's seat divided by the total number of potential races.

lengers than seats in other districts, we are left to speculate on whether this state of affairs is good for Florida.

We believe that there are multiple explanations for the security of incumbents and the diminished competition for seats in the legislature. While gerrymandering has doubtless had an impact, another contributing factor has been the failure of the Democratic Party to field viable candidates across legislative contests. This trend continued in 2006, as thirty-one Republican candidates in the Florida House and six Republican candidates in the Florida Senate were unopposed in the 2006 election, and there is little evidence that the Democratic Party will resurge any time soon. Moreover, candidates from third parties have not done well in either chamber historically, and that continues to be the case. Although candidates of seven different parties other than Democrats and Republicans have received at least one vote in house races from 2000 through 2004, candidates from only three other parties received such votes in the Florida Senate during that period. These other candidates include those from the Green Party, the Independent Party, the Libertarian Party, the Natural Law Party, and the Reform Party.

From 2000 to the 2004 elections, 5.8 percent of those who ran for house seats and an additional 10.3 percent of those who ran for the senate did so as write-in candidates. Nearly one-quarter of those brave enough to run in this way for the house literally receive no votes, while half receive fewer than twenty. However, one write-in candidate, D'Lorah Butts-Lucas, received a total of 2,664 votes (6.4 percent) when she was defeated by Democrat Joyce Cusak in the District 27 General Election in 2004.[5]

The trend away from competition should not be attributed entirely to the partisan districting efforts of incumbent legislators, as competition at the

Table 7.7. Ballot Rolloff for Elections for Florida House of Representatives and Senate, 2000–2004

	House Primary Rolloff	General Election Rolloff	Runoff Rolloff	Senate Primary Rolloff	General Election Rolloff	Runoff Rolloff
2000	39.3	67.6	46.4	16.9	30.0	16.2
2002	20.6	77.1	18.8	45.2		
2004	15.9	48.7	4.0	24.2		
2006	36.9	51.3	25.3	26.3		
Average	28.2	61.2	16.3	31.4		

Source: Authors' calculations based on data from Florida Department of State, Division of Elections.

primary level has declined as well (see Table 7.6). Nonetheless, the data suggest that incumbents are strongly situated to scare off potential challengers from both parties. No matter the reason for the lack of challengers, legislative elections in Florida are also characterized by the fact that Florida voters typically cast fewer ballots for candidates for the state legislature than they do for candidates for federal-level offices, such as president or U.S. Congress. Political scientists have termed this phenomenon *ballot rolloff.* The extent to which rolloff occurs can be measured by dividing the number of ballots cast for state legislators in a given election by the total number of people in the state who voted. Rolloff data for the primary and general elections from 2000 to 2006 is revealing (see Table 7.7).

In contrast to ballots they cast for other races on the same Election Day, a significant number of Florida's voters do not cast ballots for candidates for the state legislature. This may be because they do not have the ability to vote for the legislative candidate of their choice (because the candidates are running unopposed and thus do not appear on the ballot because they are automatically reelected) or because they simply choose to leave this portion of the ballot blank. The most egregious example was in the 2004 general election cycle when the rolloff was substantial across elections and across chambers. Indeed, the primaries show a rolloff in the house of 15.9 to 4.0 in the senate. Substantively, what this means is that of those Floridians who turned out to vote on August 31, 2004, in the primary election, only one in six (15.9 percent) voted for house legislative candidates. On that same day, only one in twenty-five voters (4 percent) cast a ballot for one of the candidates running in their senate district.

These trends are more pronounced for the senate than the house, despite the fact that some senate districts are large; a condition that political scientists have traditionally argued should generate more challengers (Mann and Wolfinger 1980). Typically, the senate generates more competitive elections in states because it attracts challengers who have political experience and name recognition. Moreover, while a challenger for a house seat can be overwhelmed by an incumbent's advantages, senate challengers tend to have a larger area from which to raise campaign funds and garner more publicity. Yet, the evidence from Florida elections defies this expectation.

This result is also found at the primary level, where one should see a higher percentage of interested voters (see Aldrich 1995) and therefore less rolloff. Yet at the primary level, the rolloff was more pronounced; only 4 percent of the primary voters in 2004 actually voted for a state senator. This trend is also significant in the house, which again suggests that the lack of partisan competition is not the only ingredient driving so many noncompetitive races in the Florida legislature. Moreover, the general election numbers are not very encouraging if one equates a healthy democracy with high voter participation. Though the general election in November 2004 saw a surge in turnout probably due to the contentious nature of the presidential election that year, only about one in two voters cast a ballot for a house candidate, while only one in four voters did so for senate candidates.

This section has made the case that there are several reasons why the Democratic Party is at such a disadvantage in Florida legislative elections. There are few challengers to incumbents despite the fact that legislative terms are limited. It is difficult to avoid pointing to the gerrymandering revolution of the 1990s as one culprit, because it is no longer a secret that because of the increased technological precision and sophistication of those who draw the legislative districts, politicians now control the distribution of the voting electorate to a large extent. The lack of competition between and within the two parties is likely attributable to the success of incumbents and parties in raising money as well as the strategic allocation of legislative resources for reelection efforts. The dearth of third-party alternatives and the inability of Democrats to field candidates across the state have probably contributed as well.

There is also a structural component to this trend. Competition may be on the decline because of the 2000 ballot initiative in Florida that implemented term limits. Legislators can serve only eight years in the house and eight years in the senate. Scholars have theorized that term limits will lead to a decline in challenges to incumbents in state houses (Cary, Niemi, and Powell 2000). This is largely because potential challengers for a seat will probably wait for the seat to open rather than compete against a popular and well-funded sitting legislator. It is an irony of politics that term limits are likely to keep an incumbent safe, at least during the length of the term. While the effects of term limits on the Florida legislature are still being studied and understood, the early trends suggest that the impact on competition may be significant (Wagner and Prier 2007). Initially, term limits forced substantial turnover in the legislature by forcing members out in 2000. Since that time, newly seated legislators have faced little opposition and have easily won reelection (Depalo 2006). The institutional influence of term limits on electoral patterns will be tested in 2008, when competition should increase for the seats that will open when the terms of legislators elected in 2000 expire.

Conclusion

The landscape of Florida politics is rapidly changing, and the political context in which the state legislature operates mirrors this broader trend. As the legislature changes from a Democratic-dominated branch to one increasingly populated by Republicans, larger questions should be raised concerning the kind of legislature Floridians want to have and whether that body should work more closely with the governor on important policy issues. While the state's political system is based on a republican ideal, much of the data presented in this chapter indicate a large gap between the representative democracy children learn about in school and the empirical reality embodied in the Florida legislature. The data illustrate that legislative seats in both chambers are increasingly noncompetitive. In an environment of majority-party control of institutionalized legislative procedures, it might be worth asking if the interests of Floridians can be effectively organized and attended to within the legislature. With issues facing the state ranging from its burgeoning population to other concerns related to health care, education, transportation, environmental protection, and resource management, Florida's part-time legislature may need renewed scrutiny to determine if it is still capable of representing the interests of the people.

Notes

1. Informal conversations with legislators and staff suggested that the councils were a key link between the leadership and the committees. The councils had the formal authority to rank bills coming out of committees under their jurisdiction and could send them back to committee for reconsideration.

2. These seven legislators (with their districts in parentheses) included Peaden (5), Goode (31), Kelly (42), Bradley (55), Murman (56), Spratt (77), and Bronson (79).

3. As quoted in Jo Becker, "Switching Party Ties Brings Home Bacon," *St. Petersburg Times*, May 27, 2000.

4. Although all members of the Florida House of Representatives must face the voters every two years, the terms of the Florida senators are set at four years by the Florida constitution in Section 15(a), and they are to have staggered elections whereby those from odd-numbered districts will be up for election in the years whose numbers are multiples of four while even-numbered districts will hold elections in the years whose numbers are not multiples of four. The constitution makes an exception for the next election after a reapportionment by which some senators are elected for terms of two years when it is necessary to do so to maintain staggered terms. Thus, the 2002 redistricting resolution passed by the legislature mandated that senators who represented odd-numbered districts had to stand for election in 2002. This is why half the senate seats are subject to change in most years.

5. Among senate candidates, 5.6 percent receive no votes, while half who run as write-ins receive fewer than ten votes. During the period 2000 to 2004, the most votes received for senate write-ins was 1,625 by Alex Schraff in the 2004 general election (Senate District 25).

References

Aldrich, John. 1995. *Why Parties?* Chicago: University of Chicago Press.

Benton, Edwin J. 2007. "The Interplay of Party Leadership and Standing Committees in a Competitive Versus a Non-Competitive State Legislative Setting: The Case of Florida." *Florida Political Chronicle* 18: 25-39.

Blanton, Faye W. 2004. *The Florida Senate.* Tallahassee: Secretary of the Senate.

Bousquet, Steve. 2006. "Power Plays in State Senate." *St. Petersburg Times*, March 20.

Carey, John M., Richard G. Niemi, and Lynda W. Powell. 2000. *Term Limits in State Legislatures.* Ann Arbor: University of Michigan Press.

Dauer, Manning J. 1984. *Florida's Politics and Government.* Gainesville: University Presses of Florida.

Depalo, Kathryn. 2006. "State Legislative Term Limits and the Law of Unintended Consequences: An Examination of Member Behavior, Power Structure and Legislative Organization in Florida." Ph.D. diss., Florida International University.

Florida House of Representatives, Committee on Reapportionment. 1991. *Reapportionment in Florida: Out of the 19th Century, into the 21st.* Tallahassee: Florida House of Representatives.

Francis, Wayne L., and Elizabeth G. Williams. 1998. "The Florida Legislature." In *Government and Politics in Florida*, edited by Robert J. Huckshorn. 2nd ed. 124–46. Gainesville: University Press of Florida.

MacManus, Susan A. 1994–1995. "Women in State Legislative Office." *Political Chronicle* 6: 10–18.

Mann, Thomas, and Raymond Wolfinger. 1980. "Candidates and Parties in Congressional Elections." *American Political Science Review* 74, no. 3: 617–32.

Niemi, Richard G., and Simon Jackman. 1991. "Bias and Responsiveness in State Legislative Redistricting." *Legislative Studies Quarterly* 16, no. 2: 91–110.

Phelps, John B. 2002. *The Florida House of Representatives Handbook.* Tallahassee: Office of the Clerk of the House of Representatives.

————. 2004. *The Florida House of Representatives Handbook*. Tallahassee: Office of the Clerk of the House of Representatives.

Price, Hugh Douglass. 1962. "Florida: Politics and the Pork Choppers." In *The Politics of Reapportionment*, edited by Malcolm E. Jewell. 81–97. New York: Atherton Press.

Prier, Eric. 2003. *The Myth of Representation and the Florida Legislature: A House of Competing Loyalties*. Gainesville: University Press of Florida.

Wagner, Kevin, and Eric Prier. 2007. "Absentee Elections: Measuring the Impact of Term Limits in Florida." Presented at the Annual Meeting of the Southern Political Science Association, New Orleans, La.

Williams, Elizabeth G. 1997. "The Impact of Increased Female Representation in U.S. State Legislatures." Ph.D. diss., University of Florida.

8

The Florida Governor in the Twenty-First Century

RICHARD K. SCHER

Between 1885 and 2000, the structure of the Florida executive branch remained fairly constant. The constitution of 1968 instituted a number of changes, especially in the governor's budget powers, but much of the rest of the executive structure remained the same. The governor's office was weak, even amazingly weak. In his classic study of the formal powers of U.S. governors carried out in the mid-1960s, Joseph Schlesinger ranked the Florida governor 46 out of 50; only the governor's offices of Mississippi, South Carolina, Texas, and North Dakota were deemed weaker (Schlesinger 1965, 229). It was astonishing if any Florida governors were able to accomplish anything. Most did not, but a few were able to transcend the weakness of the office and accomplish a great deal.

But in 2000, a number of reforms were initiated by the Constitution Revision Commission of 1997 that had been approved by the voters in 1998. These changes significantly changed the shape and politics of the Florida executive branch and strengthened the governor's office. When these changes were instituted, a powerful and activist governor, Jeb Bush, occupied the Florida governorship. Even before 2000, Bush had moved to consolidate power in his office and greatly expand the governor's way of doing business, especially regarding budget matters. The combination of his efforts and the structural changes in the office stemming from constitutional reform has increased the political assets of the Florida governorship and expanded its potential impact on state politics. Indeed, it is an open question whether it was the forceful actions of Mr. Bush or the constitutional reforms that were more important in reshaping the office. In any case, it is clear that if Professor Schlesinger were to do his analysis of the powers of governors today, the Florida executive would no longer occupy a position at the end of the list; it would move up significantly.

This chapter examines the history of Florida executive branch. Recent changes in the executive achieve significance for the student of Florida government only if they are seen in the context of what existed before. The chapter begins with an overview of Florida's gubernatorial politics during the twentieth century, the period governed by the 1885 constitution. It examines how the executive branch was structured during that period and how that structure so strongly influenced what governors did. We then move to a consideration of changes in the executive that the Constitution Revision Commission and Mr. Bush created late in the twentieth century. We conclude the chapter with an assessment of what difference these changes have made for the governor's role in Florida politics and whether they are adequate for the needs of the fourth most populous state, one that continues to grow rapidly and repeatedly demonstrates serious growing pains as it faces the twenty-first century.

The Florida Governor in Historical Perspective

Twenty-five men occupied the Florida governorship during the twentieth century. Among them are former senate president Charley Johns, who served as acting governor upon the death of Dan McCarty in 1953, and former lieutenant governor Buddy MacKay, who served for about a month when Lawton Chiles died late in his term in 1998. Almost all were lawyers; the rest were involved in business, finance, or agriculture. About half had served in the state legislature (usually in a leadership position); one had previously been a U.S. senator (Chiles); two had been members of the U.S. House (Caldwell and MacKay); and three had held no public office prior to assuming the governor's office (Catts, Kirk, and Bush). All but four were Democrats: Sidney Catts was nominally a Democrat but was actually affiliated with and nominated by the Prohibition Party, and Claude Kirk, Bob Martinez, and Jeb Bush were Republicans.

What kind of leaders were these twenty-five individuals? What were their goals as governors? To answer these and related questions, we have to examine the political context of the Florida governorship. That is, what kind of office was it? What did people expect of their governors? What was the position of the governorship in the political culture of the state?

We have to begin (as is so often the case in any examination of state politics in the South) with V. O. Key (Key 1949), who argued that there were many roots of the tremendous problems of racism and poverty that were the hallmarks of the South in the first half of the twentieth century. One root, of course, was the one-party political system of that region. But the weakness of southern political institutions was also very much to blame. Key singled out poor executive leadership in states as the strongest example of weak political institutions in the region. He held governors very much at fault for failing to address the social inequalities and pathologies racism and poverty caused. Executive leadership was so weak—often so nonexistent—in the region that it lead Schlesinger to the dour but accurate assessment that politics generally, and executive politics in particular, were major sources of the South's many problems. Key argued that they would not become part of the solution to southern social and economic pathologies until strong leaders emerged in the context of a robust, viable two-party system.

We must leave aside the question of whether a two-party system really has emerged, and helped, in the South and, in this case, in Florida specifically. But Key's assessment of southern leadership was accurate. The truth is that the office was staggeringly weak. Why and how this was true is a matter we will examine in the next section. But it should be noted now that the weakness of the office reflected the state's political culture, particularly public expectations about what the office should be and what the governor should do.

There are many conceptions and definitions of political culture and little professional consensus about which definition is best. For our purposes, political culture refers to the norms and rules and mores and styles that govern political activity. It is thus a reflection of what people want and expect from politics, what the range of acceptable political activity is, and what kinds of behaviors and styles are permissible and legitimate.

Political culture is not static; it evolves over time as the public changes its mind about what it wants from politics and how political activities should go forward. But it is also true that there is a core or center of gravity about a state's political culture that remains relatively constant over time. Certainly this was the case in Florida, and it strongly influenced gubernatorial behavior. Floridians during the twentieth century expected low taxes and few services from their state government. In contrast to other states (Minnesota comes to mind) where citizens demanded a high level of quality services and were willing to pay for them, Floridians preferred only the most minimal levels of services and taxation for many decades. It is not stretching the point to say that even at the outset of the twenty-first century this attitude figures prominently in the state's political culture and influences decision-making in Tallahassee.

In this minimalist view of governmental activity, citizens expected governors to do very little. The office of governor in Florida was weak because that's what Floridians wanted. The office was designed to ensure that governors faced severe constraints on virtually all sides. The functions governors were expected to fulfill followed directly from the state's minimalist political culture.

The governor in Florida was expected to perform two functions at most. The first was to hand out state patronage to the winning faction within the Democratic Party, the faction to which the successful gubernatorial candidate belonged. There was, of course, a great deal of patronage to be dispensed in the form of state contracts, appointments, and land purchased by the state. There were always state contracts to dispense for roads and bridges, schoolbooks, and parks and other forms of public works. It was the governor's job to make sure that as much of the patronage as possible became the spoils of the victors; the losers would have to wait for the next election. It was exactly this kind of activity that prompted Governor Millard Caldwell, who attempted to establish merit systems for appointments and competitive contracts for doing state business in the mid-1940s, to remark that "[t]he judgment evidenced by the [governor's] opportunities will determine whether the state will enjoy four years of politics or four years of capable government" (Scher 1997, 297).

The second, and more important, function of the Florida governor was to ensure that no one attacked or undermined dominant economic and social structures. It was the governor's job to maintain the privilege and power of the ruling elite. This meant, of course, keeping blacks and poor whites—by far the largest segments of the population—in their places.

Even though Florida shared a history of slavery with its neighboring states in the Deep South, to a large degree, it did not share the legacies of that institution—the plantation economy, a huge black population, and an even larger impoverished white population. Its black population was relatively small except in some panhandle counties.[1] While sharecropping and cash-crop agriculture were common in Florida, neither was as extensive as could be found in other southern states. Nor were they as economically disastrous as elsewhere; Florida farmers were relatively better off than most of the small dirt farmers in other parts of the region.[2]

And yet Florida shared many of the social norms and mores and structures of its neighboring southern states. Racism and discrimination were rampant, Jim Crow laws predominated throughout the state, and blacks were the objects of scapegoat politics. The state saw more than its share of lynchings, and the Ku Klux Klan and later the White Citizens' Councils were active. Poverty was widespread in Florida, and if it was not as severe as in Mississippi, Alabama, and Louisiana, its pathological corollaries of disease, malnutrition, poor education, and social violence were very much in evidence.

Economic, social, and political elites declined to respond to the pathologies of racism and poverty. Indeed, in Florida as elsewhere, elites actually

made them worse, either through neglect and a failure to address them seriously or by actively pursuing policies that exacerbated them. Examples of
the latter include racially discriminatory housing policies such as occurred
in Belle Glade and banks' lending policies that prevented small farmers from
having access to capital.[3] It was exactly these kinds of practices—and there
were many others—that led Key to his conclusion that politics was part of
the problem in the South, not a possible solution.

Governors were not always members of the Florida economic or social
elite; sometimes they were recruited by elites to represent their interests
in Tallahassee. But often they were members of the privileged class. In either case, the effect was the same. The task of governors was to ensure that
the position of social and economic elites was secure. This meant that the
governor's office was conservative by nature. Far from being an instrument
of policy making or broad-based improvement of the general welfare, the
governorship was dedicated to restraint in the extraction, distribution, and
use of public resources, to the extent that many of its occupants proudly pro-
claimed during their campaigns, inaugural speeches, and state of the state
addresses that they had no intention of raising taxes, expanding or improving public services, or engaging in any practice that enlarged the purview of
state government. Most claimed to run the state on a businesslike basis and
often compared themselves to CEOs. In fact, this comparison was not accurate; no business can survive for long without reinvestment, expansion, and
development. These kinds of statements were part of the game that characterized Florida politics for most of the twentieth century: the governor
talked about being the steward of the state and protecting the interest of all
but in fact protected the interest of the rich and (small) middle class, bought
off impoverished whites with smoke and mirrors and the rhetoric of racism,
and ignored blacks unless they became so disgruntled that repressive measures had to be taken against them.

The actions of most Florida governors during the twentieth century fit
this pattern, more or less. We can call them caretakers. They took pains to
conserve the interest of dominant elites because the political culture did not
encourage—indeed, it discouraged—executive activism or use of the public
weal to address serious state issues. They took office with the goal of handing
out patronage to members of their winning faction and keeping the social
and economic lid on.

But not all Florida governors were like this. A few were populists. Florida
populist governors were of a restrained sort, but they nonetheless were bona
fide populists. Suspicious of concentrations of wealth and conscious of the
plight of the poor, populist governors in Florida made modest efforts to re-

distribute resources. Napoleon Broward is perhaps the best example of this type. Fuller Warren, who grew up in abject poverty, is another example; he never lost sight of his roots. He was also sensitive to the problems Florida blacks faced, and in a small way he did his part to combat the discrimination they faced daily. He forced the unmasking of the Ku Klux Klan, for example, and was the first Florida governor in the twentieth century to invite blacks into the governor's mansion. A few other governors were not exactly populists but made occasional gestures in that direction; William Sherman Jennings, LeRoy Collins, Claude Kirk, and Lawton Chiles come to mind. The expectations of the Florida public (and the political culture generally) did not offer an environment in which populism could flourish in the state. In a sense it is remarkable that Florida had any populist or populist-leaning governors. The persistence of severe economic inequalities, lack of opportunity for some social groups, a poor education system, and pervasive racial discrimination undoubtedly account for the modest populist showing in the governor's office.

A third kind of Florida governor can be called the policy maker. This individual uses the powers of the governor's office boldly (and invents them if necessary) to address serious public issues in a serious way. Policy-maker governors can be considered architects of public policy; they want to attack public problems by creating structures and revenue streams that will outlast their own administrations. Some analysts assume that these governors are liberals. Nothing could be further from the truth. Some of Florida's most conservative governors—Caldwell and Bush come to mind—are also among the most energetic policy makers. Indeed, it is arguable whether Florida has ever had a liberal governor in the sense the term is used in, say, Massachusetts, New York, Minnesota, New Jersey, or California. Rather, there have been some moderate progressives who have been effective policy makers. Examples include William Sherman Jennings, LeRoy Collins, Reuben Askew, and Bob Graham.

Most of Florida's policy-maker governors have appeared only recently on the state's political stage. This is not surprising. As Earl Black pointed out, the civil rights movement, especially the 1965 Voting Rights Act, freed southern governors from many of the constraints and pressures they had faced in the past and allowed them to expand their range of interests and activity. After 1965, there were fewer pressures on the governor, including the Florida governor, to protect dominant elite interests and keep blacks and poor whites in their places (Black 1976). Obviously not all policy-maker governors responded to this opportunity in the same way; the approaches to policy development of governors Askew and Graham, on the one hand, and

Bush on the other, could not be more different. What is common to all in this category, however, is that they had a robust view of the governor's office, had a clear public agenda that they were willing to push vigorously, would not be intimidated or deterred by the structural limitations of the office, and felt that they were responsible for addressing public needs.

Of course, the civil rights movement and the Voting Rights Act were not the only reasons strong governors began to emerge in Florida. As the state's population grew, so did public needs. As Neil Pierce (1972) so aptly put it, by the 1970s, Florida had become one of the nation's megastates, and the need and demand for services there grew rapidly. The public began to demand that the state provide better public schools and universities, roads and highways, and health care and adequate law enforcement. The state's political culture began to change during this time. Governors became the focus of the public demand for services. By the late 1960s and early 1970s, the Florida governor had become much more the center of gravity of state politics than had been the case before. Public expectations that the governor "do something" grew almost as rapidly as the state's population. It was this changing set of public expectations about what the governor was expected to do that permitted—indeed, demanded—a more robust form of leadership from the governor than had been the case previously and allowed the policy-maker governor to emerge. It also provided the impetus for reform of the governor's office for the first time since 1885 in order to provide the executive with a better set of tools and more opportunities for addressing public issues.

The Office of Governor in Florida

Had U.S. history taken a different turn, Florida could have had a powerful gubernatorial office. The constitution of 1865 was created at the behest of President Andrew Johnson at the conclusion of the Civil War. That document called for the election of a governor and separately elected lieutenant governor, each of whom was elected for four years *with no limitation on reelections*. It also called for the election of a secretary of state, attorney general, comptroller, and treasurer, each of whom was also elected for four-year terms. However, this constitution was never put into place; the U.S. Congress rejected Johnson's plans for integrating the Confederate states back into the Union and instead imposed military governors in the region (Morris 1995, 678).

The Reconstruction constitution of 1868 in some respects offered the governor substantial appointive power. The executive could appoint all county offices; no county officials were elected. This constitution also was the first to use the term *cabinet* in conjunction with the executive branch; it included, besides the offices mentioned above, a surveyor general, superintendent of public instruction, adjutant general, and commissioner of immigration (Morris 1995, 679).

But it was the 1885 constitution that established the structure of the governor's office and executive branch that lasted, with a few modifications, until 2000. It was clearly a reaction to the two previous constitutions; it weakened the governor's office significantly and fragmented the executive branch. It abolished the office of lieutenant governor and reduced the governor's term to one four-year period with no possibility of reelection. This constitution formally established the cabinet—composed of secretary of state, attorney general, comptroller, treasurer, superintendent of public instruction (later changed to commissioner of education), and commissioner of agriculture (later this official was also made head of the Department of Consumer Affairs). It placed no limitation on the number of terms for which cabinet members could seek reelection; this is an important aspect of this constitution. It also cut the salaries of all members of the executive branch, including that of the governor (Morris 1995, 680).

Although the 1885 constitution created a weak governor, it reflected the historical tradition in U.S. states. This resulted in the classic dilemma whereby public expectations for the governor were high, but constitutions gave governors weak formal powers to meet those expectations. Some states—notably New York, New Jersey, Illinois, Minnesota, and California—moved in the direction of strengthening the governorship. However, as the 1885 constitution demonstrates, Florida was not among states that sought to strengthen the governor's powers.

How are we to view the office of governor the 1885 constitution created? What criteria can help us understand its few potentialities and its many weaknesses?

Our best approach is to follow the lead of Joseph Schlesinger (1965) who, as noted earlier, created an index of gubernatorial power based on formal authority of the office, which was usually (but not always) provided by the state constitution. Formal authority can be a useful guide to understanding the powers of the office, but it is not the only measure of power. Political contexts and circumstances; the governor's political skills, style, ability to create statewide consensus and a vision of the future, and sense of timing and relations with the legislature (and courts), party structure and discipline, interest-group structures, and just plain luck (among other factors) can strongly influence how powerful a governor appears to be. But in the end, all gubernatorial power has to rest on and emanate from the formal authority granted by the constitution, laws, and (sometimes) tradition.

Schlesinger (Schlesinger 1965, 219–34) lists the following as areas of formal authority by which to judge the governorship:

- Tenure potential
- Appointment potential
- Budget powers
- Veto power
- Administrative structure and its political impact

In two of these areas, the Florida governor fared comparatively well, at least relative to other southern states (Schlesinger 1965, 219–22, 227; Scher 1997). Unlike some other southern states, the Florida governor has always had a four-year term. The fact that Florida's executive could not be reelected for a consecutive term, however, presents a serious weakness in the Schlesinger index. As research on the impact of the four-year term of the Florida governor has shown, the governor really only had one short period, two years, to have much of an impact on the state. For the first two-thirds of the twentieth century, the legislature met only every other year. By the time of the second legislative session, backroom maneuvering by major players in the legislature for leadership positions or even a run at the governorship almost completely eclipsed the sitting governor, and the executive was reduced to little more than a figurehead for the final two years of his term (Colburn and Scher 1980).

It was not until 1968, when governors gained the power to succeed themselves for an additional term and the legislature began to meet annually, that much of the lame-duck problem for governors was eliminated. Of course, much also depended on the political style and legislative agenda of the incumbent governor in a second term; Reubin Askew, the first beneficiary of the change, remained active for all eight years, as did his successor Bob Graham. Lawton Chiles, whose health began to fail during his second term, almost disappeared from view in its latter stages, often quite literally; sometimes even his own staff could not find him. Jeb Bush represented a return to the Askew/Graham style in that he proved to be vigorous and active even in the latter stages of his administration.

The Florida governor also has a legislative veto—in fact, two types of vetoes. The governor can veto the bill or allow it to become law without signing it (that is, withhold the veto). Thus, in Florida, the act of vetoing a bill is a proactive one; bills that are not vetoed can become law even without the governor's signature.

The governor also has what is called a line-item veto that applies exclusively to appropriations measures. The governor can use the line-item veto to veto individual line items in a budget. For much of the twentieth century, governors used the line-item veto sparingly, less in a partisan mode than as a way of protecting the budget against the unwarranted use of "turkeys" (special pet projects inserted in the budget solely for the benefit of members' home districts). Former governor Jeb Bush greatly expanded the use of the line-item veto.

The legislature has the power to override gubernatorial vetoes; two-thirds of the members present in each house must vote to override the governor's veto. Overrides are fairly rare, however; toward the end of the Chiles administration, when Republicans became a majority of the legislature, there were several attempts to override Chiles's vetoes, and a few were successful. In general, observers felt that these were purely partisan moves from Republicans as they sought to assert their newfound legislative clout.

In the other Schlesinger measures of gubernatorial powers, the Florida governor has ranked very low. Of the remaining three, unquestionably the greatest problems were caused by the administrative structure of the Florida cabinet. Much has been written about this unique institution, but a brief overview is essential for grasping how much it constrained the Florida governor (Colburn and Scher 1980; Scher 1997).

The cabinet, which was established by the 1885 constitution, consisted of six separately elected members: secretary of state, attorney general, comptroller (who also served as banking commissioner), treasurer (who also served as the insurance commissioner and state fire marshal), superintendent of public instruction (later renamed the commissioner of education), and commissioner of agriculture. The governor was not a member of the cabinet; neither was the lieutenant governor when that office was created in 1968. But the governor sat with the members of the cabinet, deliberated, and voted with it. This arrangement was called the "cabinet system." The governor's voice was only one among seven on the cabinet system, and it would be wrong to assume that the he dominated it merely because he sat in the center of the cabinet table, generally presided at meetings, and was probably the most visible (and publicly accessible) member.

The name *cabinet* can be deceptive. Readers should not think of the president's cabinet or the Canadian cabinet. The Florida cabinet was a unique political structure. True, other states have had, and some still have, cabinet-type institutions, and of course most states have a fragmented, decentralized executive branch consisting of a number of officials, who are usually separately elected from the governor. But what made Florida's cabinet system unique was the way it took power away from the governor and put it into the hands of the other six members. Some powers devolved because individual members were heads of large public agencies; the commissioner of education, for example, was the head of the Department of Education, for decades the largest state agency. But in addition, the cabinet functioned as a collective decision-making unit that "deal[t] with a broad range of state issues" (Scher 1997, 283). Originally the cabinet sat as the governing body of some twenty-two boards and agencies; by the 1940s, the number had grown to thirty. Most important, not every cabinet member sat on the board of every agency; the governor, for example, sat on only nineteen of the thirty agencies. Thus, the governor had only the most indirect involvement in vast areas of state activity and in some instances no involvement at all (Scher 1997, 283).

More generally, the governor had to proceed carefully in relations with cabinet members. They would take umbrage if they felt that he was intruding too forcefully into matters they saw as rightfully within their purview and would support one another against him; the cabinet exhibited every evidence of the territorial imperative. Thus, everything that involved cabinet members, even if indirectly, had to be negotiated. Cabinet members did not always oppose the governor. They recognized that he was first among equals and in any case was the state executive with the widest range of responsibility and the state official to whom the public looked for leadership and guidance. But this did not obviate the tremendous effort governors had to put into communicating and negotiating with their cabinet colleagues; they expended great amounts of time and political capital to make even the smallest gains (Scher 1997, 283–84).

These matters were significantly compounded because unlike the governor, the terms of cabinet members were not limited. They could and did serve for decades, building close relationships with one another, members of the legislature (and its staff), interest groups, and county and city officials. At least some cabinet members regarded the governor's office as a revolving door—here today, gone soon. But meanwhile the cabinet retained continuous power over vast areas of state activity with only minimal input from the governor (and sometimes none at all).

Clearly the existence of the cabinet intruded on and limited gubernatorial authority. And it had a direct impact on the two remaining elements of Schlesinger's index: appointments and budget powers. Obviously, the governor could not make any appointments in areas controlled by the cabinet or to departments that cabinet members headed. But other administrative agencies outside the cabinet fell under the authority of the governor; indeed, prior to reorganization of the executive branch in 1969, there were more than 150 of these boards and agencies, known as the "little cabinet."

This vast array of state offices provided the governor with tremendous appointment opportunities; if nothing else, he could use them to dispense patronage. But the truth is that the little cabinet was mainly a nightmare for the governor. Because his executive branch was so poorly organized (the word *organized* really does not fit the helter-skelter arrangement of agencies and offices), so fragmented and disparate and messy, the governor had no hope of exercising administrative control. And the large number of appointments he had to make actually caused more problems than they solved. There was no way the governor could personally know all of the hundreds, even thousands, of individuals he was appointing; often he did not even know much about the board or agency to which he was making the appointment. As a result, governors often made mistakes. Unsuitable appointments—for a variety of reasons, including incompetence, lack of loyalty, conflict of interest, and unethical and even illegal behavior—were all too common. Thus, the weakness of the Florida governor in appointments ranged across the board: on the one hand, he could not make appointments to the most important state agencies and departments because of the cabinet, and on the other hand, he had to make so many minor appointments that there was usually no rhyme or reason to how he made them (Colburn and Scher 1980).

The cabinet also sharply limited the governor's budget powers. For most of the twentieth century (until 1968), the cabinet, sitting as the state budget commission, created the budget collectively every two years, corresponding to legislative sessions. Very little about the process of budget construction was systematic or forward looking; the idea of using the budget for state planning or as a tool for policy analysis simply did not exist. Rather, agency heads would attend budget commission meetings and make requests. If the agencies they represented fell under the purview of the cabinet or any member of the cabinet, those requests would be honored, perhaps increased; cabinet members rarely challenged the figures an agency head sought when a cabinet colleague oversaw that agency, and agencies the cabinet controlled would arrive with prearranged figures. The governor, if he bothered to attend the meetings at all, more or less sat in silence. He knew nothing of the individuals or agencies; many he had never heard of and most he would never see again because he would soon leave office. And in any case he too was disinclined to challenge budget requests that subordinates of cabinet members made; if he did, that challenge would come back to haunt him. For the most part the governor lacked knowledge even of his own little cabinet and the budget requests its members brought. The whole process was little more than back-scratching; while it may have been rational in the sense that it allowed the budget process to move forward, it certainly did not result in a budget proposal that reflected serious analysis or priority-setting (Colburn and Scher 1980).

In any case, the budget document, which the budget commission sent to the legislature, was always regarded as a draft—a starting point. The Florida legislature has been a strong, independent, and interventionist body for decades and has very rarely acceded meekly to the executive budget. Rather, it typically rewrote the budget on its own terms. When this happened, the close ties cabinet members had to key legislators and interest groups was crucial; they could be used to protect requests from cabinet agencies. For the governor, matters were different. Unless he had had long legislative service in a leadership position, he usually knew few of the members of the legislature. He had to rely on whatever powers of persuasion and political favors he could muster to secure his budget requests. Often the legislature would rebuff him anyway.

In 1968, a new constitution gave the governor the power to create an executive budget. This enabled Florida governors to introduce new management and budgeting techniques based on the latest research in public administration about the budget process. Governors hired professional staffs, and the governor's budget director became one of the most powerful—and respected—members of state government. As a result of these changes, the budget could be used as an instrument to make policy and set priorities.

Did this matter to the legislature? It barely noticed the structural changes. In spite of the new budgeting techniques and the fact that the legislature itself set up an office capable of systematically analyzing the executive budget, members of the legislature continued to regard the governor's budget document as a tentative first step toward a budget. The governor's executive budget was often called "the doorstop," because legislators had little use for the thick, heavy document other than to use it to keep doors from slamming shut. "DOA"—dead on arrival—was a common legislative reaction to the governor's budget; legislators preferred to construct the budget in their traditional way. And given the attitudes of legislators to the governor's budget—at best suspicious, at worst hostile—and their institutional jealousy of the governor's office, they simply moved ahead with their own budget document. The governor and his staff would have to hustle and cajole and plead to make sure anything resembling the document they originally sent over would eventually emerge. Often it did not, and it was for this reason that governors had to resort to the line-item veto to try to regain some semblance of control over the budget. On a number of occasions, gubernatorial use of the line-item budget resulted in threats by the legislature to sue the governor for breaching the separation of power, and sometimes the legislature actually filed such suits. While state courts upheld the governor's use of the line-item veto, the fallout in the form of resentment and hard feelings would last until the next budget cycle, when the whole process would begin again.

Recent Developments

Changes in the Florida governor's office and executive branch began to occur in the early 1990s. They were both structural and political. As noted earlier, some came because of efforts to streamline and modernize the executive branch, while other changes came because of the powerful activist leadership of incumbent governor Jeb Bush. Although each of these occurred independently, in fact they intertwined to such a degree that they significantly affected the powers of the governor's office. They undoubtedly will be very influential in how future governors conduct their office.

Term Limits

By the early 1990s, Florida was caught up in the fad for term limits that swept the U.S. political scene. It was part of the trend toward reinventing government that was supposed to return government to the people, make government more responsive and accountable, and ensure that citizens rather than professional politicians took charge of and operated the machinery of government (Osborne and Gaebler 1992). Much of the effort to create term limits was directed at legislative bodies, especially state legislatures, but these efforts also included local legislative bodies and even the U.S. Congress (although the U.S. Supreme Court disallowed the efforts of state legislatures to impose term limits on members of the U.S. House of Representatives and Senate, stating that they lacked the constitutional authority to do so).

Term limits were also imposed on state executives. In many states, including Florida, governors already faced term limits; two consecutive terms was common. But in 1992, voters in Florida approved a constitutional initiative that limited the terms of cabinet officials (as well as members of the legislature) to a maximum of eight consecutive years. As we will see, the imposition of term limits for cabinet officers has had significant implications for the governorship.

Structural Changes in the Cabinet

In 1997, the Florida Constitution Revision Commission met in accordance with the constitutional mandate to do so every twenty years. The commission proposed nine revisions, one of which dealt specifically with the state cabinet. Its summary statement described the new structure of the state cabinet:

> Merges cabinet offices of treasurer and comptroller into one chief financial officer; reduces cabinet membership to chief financial officer, attorney general, agriculture commissioner; secretary of state and education commissioner eliminated from elected cabinet; secretary of state duties defined by law; changes composition of state board of education from governor and cabinet to board appointed by governor; board appoints education commissioner; defines state board of administration, trustees of internal improvement trust fund, land acquisition trust fund.

The fact that the commission proposed such extensive cabinet revisions was at once surprising and not surprising. For decades, students of government and public administration had regarded the cabinet as an anomaly, an anachronism, a hindrance to effective executive leadership in the state. The fact that it was unlike anything else in any other state was sufficient to raise scholarly eyebrows and doubts. But there was more. Scholars saw the cabinet as diluting executive power, preventing the governor from serious coordinated efforts to address public needs and engage in long-range planning. In short, the cabinet was not the sort of political institution needed for an emerging megastate. Academics found many allies for their views in Florida's journalistic community; one did not have to read very many newspapers before encountering articles about the worthlessness of the cabinet and the cabinet system.

But academics and journalists were not the only critics. Governors rarely missed an opportunity to criticize the cabinet system. Usually this occurred after the governor had left office—why antagonize the persons one sat next to at regular meetings and on whose support so many gubernatorial initiatives relied? And, in truth, the cabinet was not always a stumbling block to the governor; sometimes it could actually be helpful (Colburn and Scher 1980; Scher 1997). But tensions and conflicts between governors and cabinet members sometimes became open and very public conflicts (one thinks especially of the Kirk administration),[4] and on more than one occasion over the years, fisticuffs between the governor and a cabinet member threatened to ensue.

But the problem for reformers was that the cabinet was well entrenched in the political tradition and culture of Florida. It had its defenders, of course—the legislature generally liked it and interest and clientele groups loved it, as did many local officials (states attorneys, for example, and sheriffs because they could appeal the budgets of their county commission if they thought they had been shortchanged), but there was little enthusiasm for making any changes to it elsewhere, including among the general public, which probably had little or no idea of what it was or how it worked. As a result, as one student of Florida politics wrote not long before the Constitution Revision Commission met, it appeared that the cabinet was entrenched for the duration and was not likely to disappear any time soon, because of inertia if for no other reason (Scher 1994, 1997, 1998).

For a variety of reasons, this prediction proved inaccurate. Probably the most important was the opposition of former governors to continuing the cabinet system. But there was also a bipartisan sense on the commission that the Florida government needed to modernize and allow the governor the potential for more executive authority. In the end, the proposals to modify the cabinet were relatively uncontroversial. They passed the commission members easily, and voters accepted them by a margin of more than 55 percent in the general election of 1998 (Florida Division of Elections 1998.

The effect of the revisions significantly affected the structure of the cabinet and, eventually, relations between the governor and the cabinet. Beginning in 2000, the secretary of state is no longer a member of the cabinet; the secretary is now appointed by the governor. Likewise, the commissioner of education is no longer a member of the cabinet and is instead appointed by the governor. The cabinet no longer sits as the state board of education, previously one of its most important roles. Instead, the governor now appoints a state Board of Education, over which the appointed commissioner sits. The two cabinet offices of comptroller and treasurer have been combined into a single office, the potentially powerful chief state fiscal officer. This individual also combines the tasks of the former banking and insurance commissioners. Only the attorney general and commissioner of agriculture remained untouched by revisions, probably a function of the power of law enforcement agencies and big agriculture in Florida, neither of which wanted to see a change in the cozy relationship they enjoyed with those offices.

As a result of the revisions, the size of the cabinet has shrunk significantly. From six members in the system, the governor now has only to deal with three—the attorney general, the chief state fiscal officer, and the commissioner of agriculture. The constitution requires that these individuals, with the governor, also constitute the State Board of Administration, serve as the trustees of the Internal Improvement Trust Fund and Land Acquisition Trust Fund, and serve as the head of the Department of Law Enforcement. Thus, not only does the governor have to deal with fewer separately elected state executives, he or she also sits as a member of the most important cabinet-controlled boards. In contrast to the former system, when the governor sometimes wondered what colleagues would decide during meetings of boards on which he did not sit, the governor now participates in cabinet board meetings.

The effect of all this has enhanced gubernatorial authority and consolidated power more fully in his or her hands. It is difficult to judge yet just how important these structural changes have been for the governor. Since 2002, all members of the cabinet have been Republicans and strong supporters of the governor (with the exception of Democrat Alex Sink, the new chief state financial who was elected in 2006), especially during the tenure of former governor Jeb Bush. At least publicly there were no obvious conflicts, or even significant areas of tension, between Mr. Bush and his cabinet colleagues. How much of this is attributable to structural change, Mr. Bush's powerful and activist political style, and partisan enthusiasm is not clear. Judgments about the impact of the new cabinet system on executive leadership in the state will have to wait until several more elections have occurred. Further insights will become apparent if partisan splits occur—that is, if the governor and at least one cabinet member are of different parties. Given the evolution of Florida politics from relatively nonpartisan to high-temperature partisan (and ideological) politics, such an eventuality may significantly reduce harmony between the governor and the cabinet. Whether it will result in the acrimony that characterized the administrations of former governor Kirk and other previous governors remains to be seen.

Term limits are another way that structural changes in the cabinet have affected members' relations with the governor. In the past, cabinet members saw governors come and go because they could run for as many terms as they wanted, whereas the governor was limited to one term until 1968 and two thereafter. It is also the case that cabinet terms are coterminous with the governor's; that is, cabinet candidates run in the same general election as the governor, and unless they die or are impeached or choose to resign, they will run for reelection with him or her as well.

It will be in this relatively new situation where they run at the same time that impacts relations between the governor and the cabinet. The cabinet is far more visible than previously. The offices of attorney general and chief fiscal officer, in particular, are now viewed as potential stepping-stones for the governorship. Obviously this will affect the relations of these cabinet officers with one another, and it undoubtedly will affect their positions on gubernatorial proposals. If one or both incumbents belong to a different party than the governor, their attitudes and positions might differ significantly from those of the governor as they seek to establish their own agenda and campaign grounds. In the past, the cabinet was not a viable stepping-stone to the governorship; in the twentieth century, no cabinet officer succeeded to the governorship—indeed, very few even tried (Colburn and Scher 1980, 49). But this is no longer true, and second-term governors or governors who chose not to run for reelection will need to recognize that collegial relations with the cabinet could change substantially depending on the future ambitions of cabinet members.

Appointments

Changes in the structure of the cabinet have also enhanced the Florida governor's appointment powers, especially in two key areas: elections and education.[5] The secretary of state has a number of functions, including chartering corporations, keeping official state records and archives, and overseeing public art. But unquestionably the secretary's most important (and sensitive) role is in overseeing state elections, including that for president of the United States. Perhaps at no other time has the importance of the secretary's role in elections been more visible or important than during the 2000 election, when the incumbent, Katherine Harris, became something of a celebrity—famous or infamous, depending on one's politics—as the events of that fiasco unwound.

At the time, Harris had served two years in office, having been elected in 1998. The fact that she was not a gubernatorial appointee was of no political consequence; she and the governor were close political allies, and they had served as co-chairs of the George W. Bush campaign effort in Florida. Harris stepped down from the office to run for Congress in 2002; Glenda Hood, whom Bush appointed in 2003, succeeded her in office. In 2004, once again a scandal arose—as it had in 2000—with accusations that the Division of Elections had provided a flawed list of convicted felons to local election officials; under Florida law, these individuals were not allowed to vote. Eventually the list had to be discarded after an investigation by the *Miami Herald* and public outrage. Other allegations of impropriety arose prior to the election, raising the same set of issues that had been raised four years earlier—namely, that state officials had intervened in the election process to such an extent that it affected the final results (Manjoo 2004).

What was significant about the shift from an elected to an appointed secretary of state is that it allowed Bush to deflect criticism. Whereas Harris became a lightning rod for all the electoral problems in 2000, hardly anyone paid attention to Glenda Hood four years later. Unlike Harris, she stayed out of the limelight, free to operate election machinery as she saw fit and in conjunction with whomever she chose to consult. Whether or not this included the governor or key officials in the Republican Party is not known, nor is it germane here. What is important is that once the defective list became publicized, the governor insisted that it be scrapped. He emerged occupying the high moral and political ground, and since he is largely exempt from media scrutiny and criticism, the whole matter had disappeared long before Election Day. The new system of appointing the secretary of state allows the governor to have a direct and immediate hand in how elections in Florida are run; the governor did not have this capability previously, at least not to such an extent.

The same is true in education. There too the governor's newfound powers of appointment allow much greater influence than in the past. Over the decades, education has been a morass for governors (Colburn and Scher 1980). Most governors have given at least lip service to its importance, and some—Bob Graham perhaps most of all—have embarked on elaborate plans to improve its quality in the state. Most have focused on K-12 education, leaving higher education aside and under the control of the old Board of Regents, an agency created by the legislature and largely distant from the governor, although he did appoint its members.

Most governors have had limited success in trying to upgrade the state's education system. There are many reasons for this: the highly decentralized system; the extraordinary variety of the sixty-seven different school systems (from extremely rural to high density, minority-dominated urban districts) that prevents any kind of "one size fits all" approach to policy; a powerful teachers' union; the enormous and stodgy education bureaucracy of the Department of Education; strong advocacy for private school advocates in the state, especially among Catholics but increasingly among fundamentalist Protestants; and the unwillingness of Floridians, as reflected in the state legislature, to make major investments in public education (likely a result of the large percentage of retirees among the Florida population). In addition, the cabinet and commissioner of education protected schools against any serious intervention by the governor unless he first secured their consent.

Much of this changed after cabinet restructuring in 1998. The commissioner of education left the cabinet and is now a gubernatorial appointee. The governor also appoints the seven-member State Board of Education, which has full authority over the state's educational system. It answers to the governor alone, a far cry from when the whole cabinet served as the state's board of education. While there are still the huge Department of Education and the sixty-seven different school systems to contend with, the state board is much more capable of holding them directly accountable (and the governor is indirectly capable of doing so) than was the case in the past. Governor Bush's campaign to weaken the state's teachers' union and dismantle public schools was possible because the new appointive structure greatly empowered the governor's role to carry out his proposals; all aspects of public education must now be approved by the board the governor appoints.

In higher education too Jeb Bush vastly increased his potential for control. In a lightning strike early in his tenure, Bush abolished the Board of Regents in 2001, largely because it opposed his executive order ending affirmative action in the state university system (although there were other, more political, reasons as well). This brought public higher education in the state largely under the control of the state board of education that the governor appoints, as well as individual boards of trustees that were established by the legislature and governor to supervise each of the ten institutions of the state university system, plus New College in Sarasota. The governor appoints about half the members of the individual boards of trustees, and the board of education appoints the remainder except for an ex officio member, usually the president of the student body of an individual campus.

There was a substantial public reaction against the governor's highhanded abolition of the old Board of Regents. To many it appeared to be a power grab by the governor, and others were concerned that universities might no longer be insulated from political pressures that could be brought against them. As a result, a petition to create a constitutionally recognized Board of Governors for higher education was approved, and a constitutional amendment was passed establishing it in 2002; it began operations the following year. There are seventeen members on the board: it includes the commissioner of education, fourteen members appointed by the governor, and two ex officio members.

Thus, when the dust settled, the governor found that his hand in higher education had been strengthened. The Board of Regents was gone, and he or his surrogates appointed all the other governing boards. As of this writing, there is considerable bickering about the relationship between the Board of Governors and the legislature, especially on funding issues. No doubt this will take time, and probably some lawsuits, to resolve. But however the political issues are resolved, the end result is that as a result of cabinet reform and enhanced appointive powers, the governor's authority in public education in Florida, from kindergarten through graduate and professional schools, has increased considerably.

State Budgeting

Earlier in the chapter we noted that budgeting for the governor used to be something of a no-man's-land filled with land mines. Prior to 1968, the cabinet system of budget-making limited gubernatorial influence over the whole process, and even after the 1968 constitution permitted an executive budget, the fiercely independent Florida legislature asserted itself as it revamped the budget document the governor had submitted.

In the late 1990s and early twenty-first century, how the state budget was created changed significantly. They occurred because the incumbent, Jeb Bush, was not satisfied with the budget traditions of the past. Relatively few structural changes had been made in the way budgeting went forward (other than the legislature's requirement that the budget be completed seventy-two hours before it adjourned sine die). Bush began two new major practices that changed how the budget document was perceived by the legislature and how that body dealt with it. The effect did not reduce legislative authority over the budget. That remained high, and the legislature was still an independent body in spite of its willingness to give former governor Bush almost everything he wanted, especially during the first five years of his administrations. Rather, as a result of changes Bush made, the legislature could no longer dismiss the executive budget out of hand as "dead on arrival." Nor could members continue the long-established, even cherished, tradition of adding turkeys—favorite projects—willy-nilly and expect the governor to allow them to go through.

The first of Bush's changes created the so-called e-budget. The budget no longer was simply a large, heavy document to be used as a doorstop. Rather, it was a streamlined, readily accessible electronic file that could be downloaded anywhere, anytime, by anyone. It was placed prominently on the governor's Web site, subject to inspection by anyone who cared to look.[6]

The effect of the e-budget is difficult to overstate. Whereas previously the budget was an arcane document accessible only to a relatively few cognoscenti, now it is open and accessible to everyone. The legislature can no longer hide as it creates the state budget. It has to do so far more transparently than it did in the past because so many more players are involved in examining the budget and pressing their claims in a knowledgeable manner than used to be the case. Other state officials, county and city officers, groups that advocate for good government, the media, the general public, and powerful interest groups all have instant access to the governor's budget proposals and can involve themselves directly and in an informed manner in legislative deliberations over the budget.

In Bush's second assault on the traditional budget process, he revitalized and aggressively used the line-item veto. In the past, governors had largely used it as a slap on the wrist against legislators who had been less than cooperative. Occasionally it had partisan overtones, and sometimes it seemed to be used merely to remind the legislature that the governor did, in the end, have a role in the budget process.

Bush's use of the line-item veto went beyond any of this. He used it as a means of redressing the balance of power between the executive and legislative branches over the state budget. It became for him a powerful weapon that would give legislators pause before they ignored his requests and priorities or asserted their wants and needs at the expense of those of the governor.

Bush did not waste any time using his newfound budget authority. In the 1999 budget, his first, he vetoed some 550 items totaling about $313 million. While this seemed like a drop in the bucket compared to the $48 billion state budget, in fact it was the largest total targeted by the line-item veto in two decades (Conley and Scher 2004). Nor did he stop there. Bush used the line-item veto to remove another $313 million from the 2000 budget, and he did so with $289 million in 2001. In 2004, Bush eliminated a record $349 million from the budget, but in 2005 the figure was a more modest $180 million.

Needless to say, Bush's liberal use of the line-item veto resulted in a great deal of complaining from legislators as pet projects were vetoed, especially in the first year or two. And the outcry was not just from Democrats. Bush did not use the item veto in a particularly partisan manner, and Republicans also were surprised to find that their turkeys had been vetoed. Media response was generally favorable but cautious, as it was not clear at first what kind of political game Bush was playing. Florida TaxWatch, which monitors state budgets and expenditures, was supportive as it engaged in its annual process of "turkey-watching."

Eventually the governor's actions became clear, and it was obvious that he was not playing a game at all. Instead, he was attempting to rationalize a budget process that had increasingly gotten out of control as the state budget grew rapidly during the 1990s because of increased population and swelling state coffers. The budget was filled with the prizes given to powerful state interests and lobbyists and the local turkeys so valued by individual legislators and county and municipal officials. Through his use of the line-item veto Bush could eliminate many of the political plums and favors that constituted the budget.

But he also sent a message to legislators about what he would and would not accept; it was in this sense that the governor was not playing a game because he made totally clear what the criteria were for acceptable line items in the budget (Conley and Scher 2004):

- The project had to include demonstrable public benefits;
- The project had to serve statewide, not purely local, needs;
- The project had to be rigorously reviewed in a competitive process that compared it to other proposals;
- The project had to be free of technical flaws

These changes were an attempt to bring some order and rationality to the large number of local and special-interest projects the budget had contained. But the impact was even greater, because for the first time in memory, the governor had seized control of a major portion of the budget process. The legislature still had the capacity to design the state budget, although given the powerful role that Bush played in the legislature as governor, and the willingness of Republicans to follow his lead, he generally got everything he wanted and sometimes more. The margins of the budget—the turkeys—was where previous governors had lacked control, and this is where Bush asserted himself. The message he sent to legislators was clear: if they did it Bush's way, their projects likely would be approved. If not, they were doomed. Either way, the governor was the final arbiter of what was in the budget. This consolidation of power in such a short time can only be described as remarkable.

Is this consolidation of budget power—through the e-budget and line-item veto—personal and limited to the Bush administration? Or has it been institutionalized to the extent that future governors, Democrats or Republicans, can seize it, use it, and build upon it? As of this writing it is impossible to say. What is clear, however, is that governor-watchers in Florida will be closely observing how the next governors of the state deal with the budget and whether or not the balance of power seems to have shifted once again away from the governor and back to the legislature.

Conclusion

At the outset, we noted that for the entire twentieth century, the Florida governorship was regarded as one of the weakest in the nation. In his comparative study of formal gubernatorial powers, Schlesinger ranked Florida near the bottom among the fifty states. A fragmented executive (highlighted by the existence of the cabinet system), weak appointive powers, and limited budgetary control were the primary reasons the Florida governorship lagged behind other states.

What effects have the recent changes discussed in this chapter had on the governorship? If the Schlesinger study were to be repeated today, where would Florida rank? Obviously we can't answer this question, since no other states have been investigated for this study. And other states have also made changes in their governorships, undoubtedly with the purpose of enhancing gubernatorial powers (Beyle 1999; Hedge 1998; Van Horn 1996), so it is not clear where Florida's governor stands relative to them, even though in absolute terms the power of the office has increased.

And yet it is very clear that the Florida governorship is not what it was. The changes in the cabinet cannot be overemphasized; the governor no longer faces executive competition and decentralization of authority. He or she is able to make, virtually unilaterally (only the consent of the senate is required), important appointments that give the executive powers over state election machinery and public education (kindergarten through graduate school), which are unprecedented in the Sunshine State, as well as in a host of other key areas such as welfare and health care. And former governor Bush seized control of the state budget process like no other governor before him.

All of this has raised the potential for the Florida governor to have an impact on the politics, indeed the life, of the state, as never before. But the key word in the previous sentence is "potential." In the end, the office is only what its occupant makes it. Governor Bush showed himself to be an activist, aggressive chief executive. Does this mean that all who come after him will be the same? Not at all. So much depends on the circumstances in which the state finds itself, the governor's views on what the governorship should be, the political climate of the state, and other matters (Scher 1997). As we saw, so much of what Bush has done regarding the budget is not necessarily institutionalized; it is not clear that the next governor will be able to control the budget process in the same way.

And there is room for continued change. It is possible that in the future the remnants of the cabinet will cease to exist and Florida's executive branch will look more like that of other states. Perhaps the needs of the state will require even more executive budget authority. None of this is clear at this time.

Perhaps we can conclude by paraphrasing a comment made by a black southerner during the civil rights movement who, when asked what it all meant, said, "We are not what we oughta be, we are not what we're gonna be, but thank God Almighty we are not what we was" (Scher 1997, 231). The Florida governorship is surely evolving, and no one knows what it will become. But it is surely a very different political institution from what it was during the twentieth century.

Notes

1. V. O. Key, *Southern Politics*. New York: Vintage, 1949, chapter 5.

2. Gavin Wright, *Old South, New South*. New York: Basic Books, 1986.

3. Expert Report of Professor Richard K. Scher, *Lillie Burton et al. v. Belle Glade City Council*, U.S. District Court Case No. 97-5091, 966 F. Supp. 1178 (S.D. Fla., June 25, 1997).

4. David Colburn and Richard K. Scher, *Florida's Gubernatorial Politics in the Twentieth Century*. Tallahassee: University Presses of Florida, a Florida State University Book, 1980, 107, 125–27.

5. The governor continues to have important appointive powers in areas other than these ones. The constitution allows for the possible existence of twenty-five executive agencies, to which the governor can appoint the heads. Currently, there are eighteen such agencies in existence: the Agency for Workforce Innovations and the departments of Business and Professional Regulation, Children and Families, Citrus, Community Affairs, Corrections, Elder Affairs, Environmental Protection, Health, Health Care Administration, Juvenile Justice, Lottery, Management Services, Military Affairs, State, and Transportation. These agencies direct important and often controversial policy initiatives, most of which begin in the governor's office.

6. As a brief but important aside, it is essential to note another of former governor Bush's major contributions. He brought the world of electronic and information technology to the governor's office to the extent that it is correct to say that Florida now has a virtual governorship in addition to the institutional one. Bush's governor's Web site included all significant proposals and reports of the office as well as links to a variety of other sites dealing with some aspect of state government. In addition, Bush was readily available by e-mail; he spent some time each day responding to questions and communicating directly with Floridians using this medium. The effect brought the governor's office closer to the portion of Florida's population with access to digital technology than at any time before.

References

Beyle, Thad. 1999. "The Governors." In *Politics in the American States*, edited by Virginia Gray, Russell L. Hanson, and Herbert Jacob. 7th ed. 191–231. Washington, D.C.: CQ Press.

Black, Earl. 1976. *Southern Governors and Civil Rights*. Cambridge, Mass.: Harvard University Press.

Colburn, David R., and Richard K. Scher. 1980. *Florida's Gubernatorial Politics in the Twentieth Century*. Tallahassee: University Presses of Florida.

Conley, Richard S., and Richard K. Scher. 2004. "'I Did It My Way': Governor Jeb Bush and the Line Item Veto in Florida." *Florida Political Chronicle* 15, no. 1: 1–18.

Florida Division of Elections. 1998. "1998 Elections Information." <http://election.dos .state.fl.us/election.shtml> (accessed June 5, 2007).

Hedge, David. 1998. *Governance and the Changing American States*. Boulder, Colo.: Westview Press.

Key, V. O., Jr. 1949. *Southern Politics*. New York: Vintage.

Manjoo, Farhad. 2004. "The Downloading of the President '04." *Salon.com*. <http://dir .salon.com/story/tech/feature/2004/08/24/machines/index.html> (accessed March 14, 2007).

Morris, Allen, ed. 1995. *The Florida Handbook 1995–1996*. Tallahassee: Peninsular Publishing Company.

Osborne, David E., and Ted Gaebler. 1992. *Reinventing Government: How the Entrepreneurial Spirit Is Transforming the Public Sector*. Reading, Mass.: Addison-Wesley.

Pierce, Neal R. 1972. *The Megastates of America*. New York: W. W. Norton.

Scher, Richard K. 1994. "Administrative Reform and Executive Policy Making." In *Reinventing Government in Florida*, edited by Jamail Jreisat and Frank P. Sherwood. 47–51. Tallahassee: Florida State University Center for Public Management.

———. 1997. *Politics in the New South*. 2nd ed. Armonk, N.Y.: M. E. Sharpe.

———. 1998. "The Governor and the Cabinet." In *The Florida Public Policy Management System*, edited by Richard Chackerian. 2nd ed. 73–106. Tallahassee: Florida State University Research Foundation.

Schlesinger, Joseph A. 1965. "The Politics of the Executive." In *Politics in the American States*, edited by Herbert Jacob and Kenneth N. Vines. 207–37. Boston: Little, Brown and Company.

Van Horn, Carl E., ed. 1996. *The State of the States*. 3rd ed. Washington, D.C.: CQ Press.

9

The Florida Courts

No Longer Obscure but Still Powerful

DREW NOBLE LANIER AND ROGER HANDBERG

Since the publication of the second edition of this volume, the Florida courts have appeared on the national and international stages in several high-level and controversial cases. The cases surrounding the 2000 presidential election (*Palm Beach County Canvassing Board v. Harris* [2000] and *Gore v. Harris* [2000]) and, most recently, the Terri Schiavo controversy (*Bush v. Schiavo* [2004]) have brought the Florida courts out of the obscurity in which they were once enshrouded (CNN 2005). The previous rather invisible state of Florida's courts, in which the state's tribunals wielded great policy-making power, yet were often overlooked by the public and in formal analyses of state politics (Handberg and Lawhorn 1998), was due, in part, to the fact that few controversies brought public or media attention to their importance. However, *Schiavo* and the presidential election cases, among others, have raised questions about the operation, independence, and accountability of the judiciary (see Handberg 1994).

Amid the shrill arguments that occurred in the wake of the 2000 election and the *Schiavo* rulings, Florida courts have been reluctantly dragged into the spotlight, bringing greater attention to their operations and rulings from the public and political leaders in Florida and elsewhere. In 2001, in response to perceived activism by the Florida Supreme Court in the presidential election cases in particular, the Florida legislature amended the statutes that control selection to the state's judiciary to undercut the independence of the courts, to some extent. Unlike the California Supreme Court in the 1980s, when its justices were publically forced from the bench, Florida courts have not been historically seen as being at the forefront of political reform. That view now appears to have changed in recent years (see Culver and Wold 1986).

This chapter updates much of the material covered in earlier versions and reviews changes in the machinery for selection to the state's courts, primarily at the appellate level. It examines how the courts have, largely unwillingly, become more politicized, and it analyzes the increasingly strained relationship that the Florida judiciary has developed with the state legislature and governor and the reasons underlying that tension.

Political Culture of the State

Like many other southern states, Florida has recently experienced rapid growth and industrialization, a process that continues. Florida currently ranks fourth in overall population and is expected to surpass New York within two decades. Indeed, about 700 additional people join the state's population daily, 85 percent of whom choose to live in urban areas within ten miles of either coast. The transitory population of Floridians has been described as "rootless" in that, in their new locales, they lack some of the traditional political anchors (e.g., church, labor unions) that may have influenced their political affiliations in their places of origin. As such, "they drift from candidate to candidate with little lasting loyalty" (Dye 1998, 5). Historically, the state's politics were "white, conservative, segregationist, and one-party Democratic" (Dye 1998, 2), but political power has steadily shifted from the northern part of the state, where the state capital is located, to the central (Orlando, Daytona Beach, Titusville, and Space Coast), Gulf Coast (Tampa, St. Petersburg, Clearwater, Fort Myers, and Naples) and southeast (Palm Beach, Miami, and Fort Lauderdale) regions.

Each of these areas has a distinct political culture. The northern part of the state largely reflects the conservative Democratic politics of the Old South. Central Florida is the most rapidly growing part of the state and tends to be Florida's political swing area; the area is largely conservative, but many retirees tend to vote for Democratic candidates. The Gulf Coast area is largely populated by retirees. They tend to be relatively wealthy, hail from the Midwest, and vote Republican. In contrast, the southeast region is a heavily populated "polyglot of cultures," including residents with Anglo-Saxon, Jewish, African-American, Hispanic, and Haitian roots (Dye 1998, 8).

Additionally, the state electorate has grown in its Republican affiliation during the recent past. Florida, like other states in the Solid South, has moved away from the historical dominance of Democratic candidates at the polls since 1964 (Carmines and Stimson 1989). This Republican ascendancy has been marked by Floridians' support of Republican candidates in several of the last presidential elections and by a growing diffuse Republican party affiliation among the state's voters (Jewett 1997, 2001; Stanley and Niemi 2000). This trend is mediated by the growing urbanism of the state; urban areas tend to have relatively higher proportions of residents identifying with the Democratic party. Between 1990 and 2000, the proportion of the state's population living in urban areas increased from 84.8 to 89.3 percent.

The Intersection of Law and Politics: The Impact on Florida Courts

This politico-cultural milieu produces a heterogeneous mix of political affiliations that affects the state's courts primarily through selection of judges and, ultimately, their decision making. Florida courts represent—for better or for worse—the peculiar political culture and geography of the state: a combination of southern traditionalism, midwestern Republicanism, and progressivism tinged with ethnic politics in certain regions of the state. Selection of judges in Florida is decentralized to a large extent to the local level, allowing both local political elites (e.g., the city council, county commission, or party leaders) and rank-and-file voters the opportunity to influence who is chosen for the bench. Accordingly, changing tides of public opinion, the partisan affiliation of the state's voters and the state's generalized political culture are all associated with state judges' decisions, in part because judges are subject to these same forces because they are residents of the state and their respective locales too. Judges ultimately have a large reservoir of discretion about which litigant to support, and their general political views impacts, to some extent, whose interests are supported and whose are not (see, e.g., Pritchett 1948). Hence, because of local control in the selection of state trial judges, judicial decision-making reflects, in some measure, the predominant local mores and values on key policy questions of the day, making the courts political institutions (Lanier 2002; Lanier and Handberg 2002b).

Growing Disjuncture of the Courts

The rather rapid political changes that Florida has endured underlie the strained relationship that has characterized the stance of the state courts with respect to the legislative and executive branches and the political affiliation of the state electorate as a whole. Unlike the judiciary, the state's governor and legislators have been popularly elected throughout Florida's history; thus, they are more closely tied to changes in public opinion and political shifts among the state's electorate. The state's shift away from one-party dominance began when the state's first Republican governor since Reconstruction, Claude Kirk, was elected in 1966. Kirk's appointees helped break the "Democratic stranglehold on [state] offices" (Handberg and Lawhorn 1998, 157). Yet the district courts of appeal and the state's supreme court were not as quick to respond to such changes because of the unique selection process extant for judges on those tribunals, who in the 1960s were appointed by the governor. These changes distanced the appellate bench both from dramatic changes in public opinion and from the shifting views of the other branches, which were riding a wave of ascending Republican power across the state (Lanier and Handberg 2002b).

This schism led to an increase in charges that some members of the Florida judiciary were judicial activists, particularly members of the state supreme court. One such target was Justice Rosemary Barkett, the first woman to serve on the court and its first female chief justice. She and Justice Leander Shaw (the second African-American judge on the court and its first chief justice of color) drew significant opposition from citizen groups, notably the National Rifle Association and several pro-life organizations. During Barkett's retention election one year after she was appointed, they asserted that she was too lenient in her rulings in criminal cases and that Shaw, who was the author of the state's leading pro-abortion privacy ruling, was out of step with the views of the public (Handberg and Lawhorn 1998). In July 2003, the Florida Supreme Court struck down a state statute requiring that parents of minor females seeking an abortion be notified of their child's intent to undergo the medical procedure (*North Florida Women's Health and Counseling Services, Inc. v. State of Florida* [2003]). The decision was widely criticized and caused some public uproar. Chief Justice Shaw led the court through that decision.

Due in part to such decisions and the structural isolation of the courts from changes in public opinion, the Florida Supreme Court (and, to some extent, the Florida judiciary overall) is thought, by many Floridians, to hold policy preferences inconsistent with those of the state and its elected leaders and citizens. This split has more recently been accentuated by the Christian right's increasing political influence recently. That interest group has sought to exert its growing power on who is selected for the bench at both the appellate and the trial court levels. It does so through organized opposition to candidates in retention elections or in the bodies that recommend judicial candidates to the bench, or both.[1] This growing rift has led to political conflicts within the state that have embroiled the state's courts in partisan debates and forced them out of the shadows of obscurity.

Current Court Structure and Operation

Like many state courts in the United States (except those in Louisiana), the Florida courts are common law courts whose decision making controls

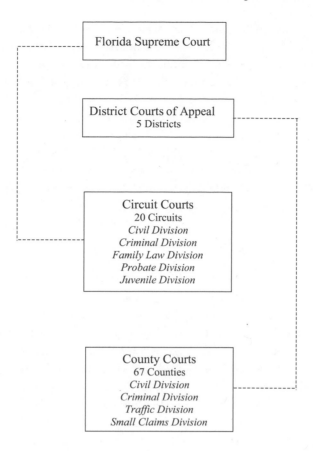

Figure 9.1. Current Structure of Florida Courts, 2007.

the resolution of similar subsequent cases, although they operate within a mixed legal framework that combines common law elements with statutory interpretation. Because laws are inherently vague, the creativity of the reviewing judges is important in deciding what meaning to bring to new or unique situations that were unforeseen by the drafters of the law (primarily the Florida legislature). Once a court issues a decision, the legislature can essentially overrule it by passing a new statute that clarifies the meaning and intent of the elected body (see Handberg and Lawhorn 1998). As a consequence of efforts in the 1970s to streamline state judiciaries, the Florida judiciary is now composed primarily of four levels (see Figure 9.1).

In some cases, litigants have the option of filing their case in one of the federal district courts (the national trial courts) in the state—the southern, middle (central Florida area), or northern districts. Once filed, a case usually runs to completion within that system. Hence, a dual court system exists in Florida, as in the rest of the United States; a state system operates side-by-side with the federal system, each autonomous and independent from the other to a large degree (see Lanier 2002). Several important federal cases originated in Florida. These include *Gideon v. Wainwright* (1963; establishing the right to counsel for felony defendants), *Argersinger v. Hamlin* (1972; establishing the right to counsel if it is possible that a defendant could serve jail time), and *Profitt v. Florida* (1976; reestablishing the death penalty by creating a new procedure to limit jury discretion in the wake of *Gregg v. Georgia* [1976]). The Florida state courts also were the originators of the presidential election cases in 2000 and *Schiavo* in 2004.

Florida Supreme Court

The Florida Supreme Court is the state's court of last resort. It primarily hears discretionary appeals from district courts of appeal's rulings in order to ensure uniformity in the interpretation of Florida law and of the state and federal constitutions. Under its mandatory jurisdiction, the court must hear death sentences before the accused is executed because of the clear need to ensure that the sentence is meted out in a manner following the dictates of due process. It also must hear cases involving bond validations, rulings of administrative agencies regarding statewide utility rates, and decisions of the district courts of appeal that strike down a state statute or a provision of the Florida constitution. The first two types of cases can be appealed directly from the circuit courts to the supreme court. (Figure 9.1 illustrates this relationship with the dashed line connecting the two courts). The supreme court's decisions construing the Florida constitution are binding on lower courts. The executive and the state attorney general may request advisory opinions from the court in certain matters (Bast 2005).

The court is currently composed of seven justices, and each of the appellate districts has at least one representative on the court. Supreme court judges must have been members of the Florida Bar for at least ten years, and they must retire at age 70.[2] The governor appoints the seven justices from a list of three to six potential appointees that the court's Judicial Nominating Commission composes. The justice serves an initial term of about one year and then stands in an unopposed retention election. If he or she is retained, the justice serves a six-year term. To date, every justice has been retained, although some members have garnered some organized opposition in their retention elections. Judges who do not receive a majority of votes to retain them are removed from the bench and a successor is chosen. This is the so-called merit system, or Missouri plan, of judicial selection that Florida adopted in the mid-1970s.

The court decides cases, after hearing oral argument in many cases, to determine if the lower court has interpreted the law correctly. The court is characterized by "collegial decision making by equals" (Handberg and Lawhorn 1998, 155), and no one justice has more influence than another. The chief justice position rotates on the basis of seniority; the most senior associate justice who has not previously served as chief justice becomes the next leader of the court. Exceptions to this custom can occur; for example, in the 1970s, a Florida justice who was required to undergo a psychiatric exam had to wait several years before assuming the position. A minimum coalition of four justices is necessary for the court to render a decision, and a quorum of five is necessary for it to consider a case (Lanier 2002).

In 2003–2004, the Florida Supreme Court received a total of 2,291 cases. It issued a total of eighty-one signed opinions and one hundred seventy per curiam opinions, which are short opinions that do not bear an individual justice's name as the primary author. The remainder of the cases were disposed of with memoranda or brief orders. These latter cases did not receive plenary consideration (Schauffler, LaFountain, Kauder and Strickland 2005).[3]

District Courts of Appeal

There are five district courts of appeal that currently have a total of sixty-two judges. These tribunals are intermediate courts of appeals and are geographically distributed across the state.[4] They primarily hear appeals from the lower courts; this significantly reduces the workload of the supreme court, enabling it to focus its attention on the state's most important legal and policy questions. County courts may certify questions for the district courts of appeal to review that are deemed to be of great public importance (which the dashed line on Figure 9.1 connecting the two levels represents). Like the supreme court, the district courts of appeal hear oral argument and decide questions of law. They sit in rotating panels of three judges drawn from the entire membership of the court. In cases of great importance, the entire circuit will sit (known as an en banc hearing). The size of each district court of appeal is set by statute: presently, the first district has fifteen judges; the second has fourteen; the third has eleven; the fourth has twelve; and the fifth has ten.

District court judges must have been members of the Florida Bar for at least ten years and must not be older than 70. As with supreme court justices, the governor appoints members from lists that the court-specific Judicial Nominating Commission composes. The judge then stands in retention election and, if successful, earns a full six-year term. The district court members choose a chief judge for each of the respective jurisdictions. In 2003–2004, the state's five intermediate courts of appeals received 24,089 cases (of which 19,440 were mandatory to be heard and 4,649 were discretionary). The courts disposed of 24,358 cases during the same period (of which 19,844 were mandatory and 4,514 were discretionary).[5] (Court Statistics Project 2006).

Circuit Courts

Florida has twenty circuit courts covering multiple counties, as Figure 9.2 demonstrates (the numbers in the figure represent these circuits). The total number of state circuit court judges (527) is distributed among the circuits based on the population and caseload of each subdivision.[6] Circuit courts are Florida's trial courts of general jurisdiction and are composed of a single judge, unlike the multimember appellate courts located above them in the state judicial hierarchy. Either a jury or the presiding judge serves to establish the facts in the case. They hear actions not addressed by the county courts, probate and equity matters, felonies, disputes over real property, domestic relations cases, juvenile adjudications, and administrative actions. They hear civil matters in which the amount in controversy exceeds $15,000. Each circuit may establish divisions within the circuit based on the subject matter of the case (see Figure 9.1). They also hear appeals de novo (anew) from the county courts with the exception of rulings that declare a state statute or constitutional provision invalid or decisions that are certified to the district courts of appeal as being of great public importance. Losing parties may appeal to the respective district court of appeal.

Circuit judges must have been a member of the Florida Bar for at least five years and must not be older than 70. They are elected in nonpartisan contests to six-year terms.[7] The governor may fill interim vacancies from a list of at least three persons that the Judicial Nominating Commission composes. The circuit members elect a chief judge who is responsible for various administrative matters and serves a two-year term, which is renewable. In 2003–2004, the state's twenty circuit courts received 859,452 cases (665,582 civil; 193,870 criminal) and disposed of 806,253 cases during the same period (619,098 civil; 187,425 criminal) (State Courts Administrator 2005).[8]

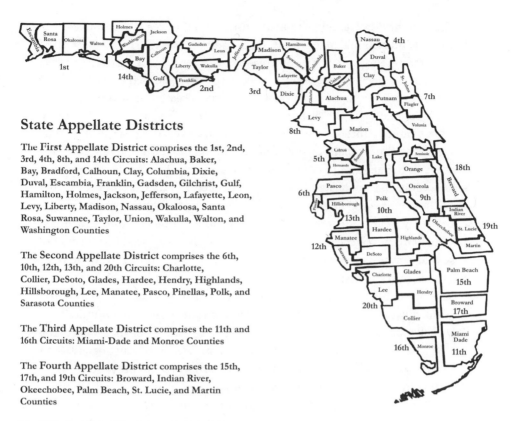

State Appellate Districts

The First Appellate District comprises the 1st, 2nd, 3rd, 4th, 8th, and 14th Circuits: Alachua, Baker, Bay, Bradford, Calhoun, Clay, Columbia, Dixie, Duval, Escambia, Franklin, Gadsden, Gilchrist, Gulf, Hamilton, Holmes, Jackson, Jefferson, Lafayette, Leon, Levy, Liberty, Madison, Nassau, Okaloosa, Santa Rosa, Suwannee, Taylor, Union, Wakulla, Walton, and Washington Counties

The Second Appellate District comprises the 6th, 10th, 12th, 13th, and 20th Circuits: Charlotte, Collier, DeSoto, Glades, Hardee, Hendry, Highlands, Hillsborough, Lee, Manatee, Pasco, Pinellas, Polk, and Sarasota Counties

The Third Appellate District comprises the 11th and 16th Circuits: Miami-Dade and Monroe Counties

The Fourth Appellate District comprises the 15th, 17th, and 19th Circuits: Broward, Indian River, Okeechobee, Palm Beach, St. Lucie, and Martin Counties

The Fifth Appellate District comprises the 5th, 7th, 9th, and 18th Circuits: Brevard, Citrus, Flagler, Hernando, Lake, Marion, Orange, Osceola, Putnam, St. Johns, Seminole, Sumter, and Volusia Counties

Source: Florida State Courts Annual Report, 2005-2006 (2006). The bold numbers represent the circuit court divisions. The smallest boundaries and names are counties.

Figure 9.2. Divisions for Florida District Courts of Appeal and Circuit Courts.

County Courts

Each of the state's sixty-seven counties has at least one county court whose geographic jurisdiction is demarcated by the county's boundary lines; there are presently a total of 280 county judges. Although each county has at least one judge, the number of judges in each county varies depending on the comparable workload and population in the county. Miami-Dade County, for example, has forty-one county judges, while several others have only one because of the relative lack of judicial business in the area. These judges hear both civil and criminal matters, although their jurisdiction is circumscribed most often by the amount in controversy or other subject matter concerns (that is, the subject of the dominant legal issue involved in the case). Several counties in highly populated urban areas have created divisions based on the subject matter of the dispute to facilitate the efficient resolution of the matter. County courts may hear civil cases not exceeding $15,000 in controversy, landlord-tenant disputes, simple divorces, and some real property matters. If the amount in controversy in a civil case is less than $5,000, the small claims division hears the case using procedures that are more informal than those employed in other divisions of the county court system. County courts may hear minor criminal matters too, including traffic violations. Like the circuit courts, either the judge or a duly-composed jury hears the case and serves as the fact finder. Losing parties may appeal to the circuit courts or, in some cases, directly to the district courts of appeal.

County court judges, sitting in counties with populations exceeding 40,000, must have been bar members for at least five years; in counties having smaller populations, county court judges must simply be members of the bar or have completed a law training program. They, too, must be less than 70 years of age and are elected to four-year terms in a nonpartisan process. The governor fills interim vacancies from a list that the Judicial Nomination Commission composes; the list must contain at least three names. In 2003–2004, the state's sixty-seven county courts received 2,851,814 cases (1,839,320 civil; 1,012,494 criminal). Collectively, they disposed of 2,674,454 cases (1,813,081 civil; 861,373 criminal) during the same period (State Courts Administrator 2005). The two levels of trial courts in Florida are reflective of a national trend to split trial functions; such courts complete the lion's share of judicial business in the nation, as compared to the relatively small number of cases disposed of by the federal courts in the land. The clearance rate for all of Florida's trial courts was 93.3 percent during the 2003 fiscal year, when 3,500,364 cases were filed statewide (Johnson 2004). In 2004, in contrast, the nation's ninety-four district courts in the federal system received only 352,360 cases, during which time they "terminated" 317,382 cases, finally resolving them. Their clearance rate was, therefore, 90.07 percent then (Mecham 2005).

Adjuncts to the Courts

Prosecutors and Public Defenders

In addition to the institutional courts that constitute the state judiciary, several adjuncts assist the courts in fulfilling their responsibilities. The offices of the state attorney and public defender are sited at the circuit court level. The incumbents of these two offices are elected to four-year terms and must have been members of the state bar for at least five years. State attorneys are charged with prosecuting cases on behalf of the state and conduct grand jury investigations, trials, and any initial appeals. The public defender's office represents poor individuals accused of crimes, unless there is a conflict of interest or if there are insufficient resources within the public defender's office to handle the case. If so, the trial court may appoint private attorneys who represent individuals on a case-by-case basis, usually for a substantially reduced fee that is paid by the state. Should the defendant be found guilty, the public defender's participation in the case certifies that the process conformed to due process demands. This tension between the public defender's role as advocate for the defendant and the fact that his/her presence essentially certifies the fairness of the proceedings makes the public defender position more difficult and less prestigious than the position of prosecutor. As most criminal defendants are found guilty, the public perceives the public defender to be tainted by association, a taint that extends to the prosecutor's office too.

The prosecutor's office has several distinct advantages over the public defender's office. In addition to the enhanced prestige of serving as a prosecutor, the state's attorney's office is usually twice as large as the public defender's in terms of the number of attorneys employed by that division, in addition to its having a significantly larger budget for investigations and other resources necessary to prosecute criminal defendants. Many state attorneys take that position as a stepping-stone to higher political office (Lundy 2006). However, in recent years, the position has become more of a long-term career choice because of the increased caseloads for prosecutors as well as the repercussions that criminal work has on an individual's professional reputation, as the taint that affects public defenders also follows prosecutors. The public is aware that many persons involved in criminal trials are rather unsavory characters and are typically not trustworthy community members. While this may be perceived to be an unfair burden, that is the unfortunate reality of law practice. Even criminal judges are affected by this relationship. Assistant prosecutors gain a significant amount of trial experience that can help them land a job with a private firm, and this leads to high levels of turnover among the young attorneys who tend to serve in those offices early in their careers (Handberg and Lawhorn 1998).

Capital Collateral Regional Counsels

Individuals convicted of capital crimes are presently represented by a state-funded attorney, the capital collateral regional counsel (CCRC), who challenges the verdict and the resulting death sentence on appeal. The state has three regional offices to handle capital appeals (Handberg and Lawhorn 1998). In 1985, the state created the capital collateral representative (CCR)—the precursor of the CCRC—after the state Supreme Court threatened to halt executions in the state because of the lack then of competent, qualified death penalty counsel representing those persons committed to Florida's death row. Like many other state agencies, the CCR was grossly underfunded. Following review by two special commissions, the legislature became increasingly frustrated with the CCR's putative "lack of financial accountability," arising from the belief that its attorneys were spending money without any direct benefit to the accused or to criminal justice system generally, actions that were alleged to be taken many times merely to slow down the process. The perceived underqualification of its attorneys also caused the legislature a great deal of concern (Coyle 1998).

Accordingly, the legislature in 1997, based in part on these concerns, carved the CCR into three independently run offices, each of which is known as the Capital Collateral Regional Counsel (CCRC). These three offices are headed by a regional counsel whom the governor appoints following recommendations of the Supreme Court Judicial Nominating Commission. The legislature also created a registry of private attorneys who are qualified to represent capital defendants in order to overcome the deficit of full-time, state-paid attorneys who are qualified to argue such appeals. Despite this pool of private advocates, the attorneys of the CCRC handle many more cases per person than they should, according to at least one advocacy group (Coyle 1998). Florida is only one of a handful of states in the nation to provide such representation, as the U.S. Supreme Court has held that such representation is not required by the U.S. Constitution (Coyle 1998).

The Florida Bar

The state supreme court supervises the Florida Bar as part of its mandated duties. Florida has an integrated, or mandatory, bar. However, attorneys may practice in one of the federal courts in Florida without gaining admission to the state bar if they are admitted in another state or the District of Columbia. Mandatory membership in the Florida Bar facilitates more effective discipline of attorneys who violate bar rules and ensures that clients are adequately protected from unqualified and perhaps unscrupulous individuals. Under the bar's statutory authority, it can censure, suspend, or even disbar attorneys who act unethically or incompetently.

State Courts Administrator

The state courts administrator was created in 1972 as part of the campaign to modernize and reform the courts. The administrator develops systematic data on workload in the judicial system for the chief justice to use as part of the courts' annual budgetary requests and in projections of the need for additional judges and specialized courts (see Johnson 2004). The administrator also serves as the liaison between the state judiciary, the other legislative and executive branches, and national organizations seeking to reform the courts. At the local level, the true power resides not in local court administrators, but in the clerk of the circuit court resident in each county. These officials, elected to four-year terms, are responsible for the filing and organizing of the paperwork that constitutes each lawsuit and other official actions. Although local court administrators, like the state courts administrator, were created in an effort to make the state judiciary more efficient, their power was undercut by the circuit clerks, who worked to retard political reform and ensure that changes would occur only with their cooperation (Handberg and Lawhorn 1998).

Judicial Qualifications Commission

Established in 1973, the Judicial Qualifications Commission (composed of six judges, two members of the bar, and five laypersons) investigates complaints filed against current judges at the circuit court level and above. The supreme court may review any action that the commission takes. After an initial investigation, which is confidential, the commission makes an initial finding about whether probable cause exists for further action. If it finds that probable cause exists, a formal public hearing is held on the charges. The penalty imposed can range from a reprimand to involuntary retirement. Usually, a judge who has been ensnared in an investigation resigns to limit bad publicity and public embarrassment over the matter. Over its history, the commission has removed ten circuit judges and reprimanded fifty-six others. County court judges may be suspended by the governor and removed by the state senate.

State Judicial Politics

In the conventional view of the law, courts have long been thought of as apolitical. However, we assert that the judiciary is no more, or no less, political than any other governmental unit. We employ the customary political science definition of "politics" as the understanding that the interpretive and constitutional power of the courts influences the policy-making process just as clearly as the executive and the legislative branches do. Under the state's prevailing power structure, Florida courts have authoritative discretion about what judgments to render, whose interests to protect, and what policies to oppose (Easton 1965; Lanier and Handberg 2002b; Lasswell 1938).

Judicial Reform: A National Trend

The view that courts are supposedly apolitical has driven many of the efforts to reform the judiciary. Although the campaign to reform courts nationally began in the early 1900s, the reform movement did not gain momentum until after World War II, when the nation began to grow substantially, not only in terms of population but also economically. With this unprecedented growth came calls for governmental reform that affected the judiciary and other branches. The efforts of public interest groups, such as the League of Women Voters and the state bar, were central to advancing such issues. Two trends were characteristic of this reform movement: unification and simplification (Handberg and Lawhorn 1998).

Before the reform process began, the judicial system in Florida was characterized by "essentially independent entities often tied together only loosely" (Handberg and Lawhorn 1998, 150). The relationship among the state's varied courts was tentative, and often there was little communication among the courts, even among those in adjacent counties. The state judiciary passively responded to daily needs without any underlying systematic plan or organization, a process reformers aptly criticized because of its inefficiency and inequity.

Accordingly, a central tenet of reformers was a simplified and streamlined hierarchy that had clear lines of appeal between a reduced number of court levels and the origination of full-time court administrators who could monitor the court's docket and manage it to some extent. A second reform was that the state judiciary would come under the aegis of the Florida Supreme Court, which would have the power to promulgate rules of procedure and evidence for all the state courts and would have budgetary authority over them. Making state funding the predominant fiscal source for the courts was central to this reform; this change would ensure an equitable flow of funds to the courts. In addition, reformers have advocated judicial selection methods that would depoliticize the courts, such as the merit system and a more centralized and systematized method of disciplining (and ultimately removing) judges for unprofessional or erratic behavior (Handberg and Lawhorn 1998; Hall 2001).

Judicial Reform Comes to Florida

Florida's judiciary in the 1960s reflected the then-existing national trend: the system was disjointed in many respects and included different variants of local courts, such as justices of the peace. In 1972, Article V of the 1968 constitution (dealing with the judiciary) was amended to implement many of the reformers' goals: the trial courts were reorganized into a uniform and less unwieldy system, and systematic standards and procedures were set down for the selection and disciplining of all state judges. In addition, court administrators were instituted to aid in the efficiency and timeliness of the disposition of the courts' business. Selection of judges was formally removed from local control to ensure that judges were not unduly swayed by the dominant political interests in a county.

In 1972, Florida voters supported a referendum to change judicial elections from partisan to nonpartisan methods. Partisan elections had been the selection system for many years in the state. This change to nonpartisan methods coincided with the rise of the two-party system in the state and the decline of the Democratic Party's historical hegemony over state politics, including the courts. The 1972 reforms also instituted a process whereby the governor may fill interim vacancies on the bench. This change enhanced the governor's power because appointed judges rarely encountered a significant (or even minimal) challenge and even more rarely went down to defeat because of the structural advantages that an incumbent enjoys.

Before this reform, there had been a "silent de facto conspiracy" across the state about filling judicial vacancies. According to Florida political tradition, judges would resign their office a year or so prior to their retirement. The governor would then be able to fill the vacancy based on the bar's recommendations and those of the retiring judge's political associates (Handberg and Lawhorn 1998, 157). The newly selected appointee could then stand in the next election with the benefits attendant to a judicial incumbent, whereas if the judge served out his full term, the state's voters would directly choose a successor without the governor's tacit stamp of approval on the candidate (Lanier and Handberg 2002b).

Incumbents in general are difficult to defeat. Judicial incumbents stand on even more solid ground when running for reelection. First, practicing attorneys are reticent to run against sitting judges in elections. If they lose the election, they run the risk of earning the ire of the judge whom they have just challenged. Also, the bar association tends to support the incumbent. Judicial elections tend to be low saliency events that do not draw much media or voter attention due to the principles of judicial ethics that prevent candidates from announcing their views on disputed issues of public policy. This dynamic makes it difficult for voters to distinguish rationally among candidates. Usually, judicial incumbents who are not reelected lose because of some personal scandal. Handberg and Lawhorn (1998, 157) report that one Florida judge encountered opposition during an election only after he was "found to be printing pornography on his office computer. Local attorneys and other judges had been aware of the drinking problem of another judge for years, but no effective action was taken [against him] until he hit a parked police car after a liquid lunch."

The 1972 amendments to Article V had the effect of distancing the courts from the rather abrupt changes then beginning to occur in the state's partisan affiliation. These reforms increased the lag time between changes in public opinion (which the executive and legislative branches feel more quickly and directly) and the composition and the decision-making of the state's judiciary. Although the Republican Party was then on the rise in the state, that change was not as promptly reflected in the judiciary, over which traditional political forces in the state, notably the Florida Bar, still held sway. While two Republican governors served in the 1960s (Claude Kirk) and 1980s (Bob Martinez), the governor's mansion was overall dominated by Democrats in that Republican governors who were elected during this period served only single terms.

The nonpartisan system of selecting judges continued until a series of incidents involving four of the seven Florida Supreme Court justices occurred in the mid-1970s. Two justices were accused of attempting to exert undue influence over separate decisions in lower courts. The legislature, influenced by the seriousness of the allegations, invoked the rarely-used impeachment process, but both justices resigned before they could be formally removed from office. They were both later disbarred, and one subsequently died as a fugitive from drug-smuggling charges (Handberg and Lawhorn 1998). About the same time, it became publicly known that the supreme court's chief justice was suffering from alcoholism to the point that his work was impaired. The state's Judicial Qualifications Commission stated that he would be removed from office if he did not seek assistance with his problem. The fourth scandal erupted when a justice was involuntary committed for a formal psychiatric evaluation "because of his erratic behavior under stress" (Handberg and Lawhorn 1998, 158). Fortunately, the justice was able to return to work eventually; he even later served as the chief justice until he reached mandatory retirement. Because four of the justices were under investigation or some disability at the same time, the court for a time lacked a quorum and it appointed judges from the lower courts so that the supreme court could meets its workload responsibilities.

Together, these events damaged the credibility and legitimacy of the Florida court system overall and the supreme court in particular. Many of Florida's political and legal elites grew uneasy in the wake of these scandals because they perceived that the apolitical nature of the judiciary was being eroded. The League of Women Voters led a movement, along with the Florida Bar, to amend the selection process for the supreme court and the district courts of appeal to make it less ostensibly partisan. In 1976, voters chose in a second referendum to use the merit plan to select all the state's appellate court judges (both at the supreme court and the district courts of appeal levels).[9] While the formal process continued of choosing judges for the two levels of state trial courts in nonpartisan elections, the long-standing practice of such judges resigning their posts prior to the end of their terms (thereby allowing the governor to appoint a successor who then could run as an incumbent) remained intact.

The legislature was not unaware of this customary practice and enacted a modified merit selection process to diminish, although not eliminate, the governor's influence over the interim selection of judges. Under the revised system, the governor must choose an interim successor from among a list of potential nominees that the judicial nominating commissions of the circuit courts compile, much like the system in place for the state's appellate courts.[10] This change, which limited the governor's discretion with regard to interim appointments, was part of the collection of changes made to Article V of the Florida Constitution pursuant to a 1972 referendum, by which judges became selected through nonpartisan elections, as noted above (Little 1989; *Nipp v. Smith* [1994]). Once the interim term expires, trial court incumbents stand in competitive elections (unlike appellate judges, who run unopposed) and, if elected, they serve a full six-year term.

Immediately following the successful 1976 referendum, reformers sought to extend the merit plan to all appointments to the trial bench, not simply interim ones. Opponents of this reform, notably racial and ethnic-minority community members, perceived that merit selection was a thinly veiled attempt by the state bar to disenfranchise their constituencies just as their turn at exerting their power over the state judiciary came at the political roulette wheel (Lanier and Handberg 2002b). Namely, these communities were then beginning to demonstrate some significant influence on elections for trial judges. For example, in North Florida, primarily the Jacksonville area, local political leaders of the African-American community opposed the proposed reform because they believed that its adoption would leave the courts hostage to lawyers, especially the defense-corporate bar, whose members they believed held policy views contrary to their own (see Dye 1998). Attorneys who customarily represent corporate defendants and other commercial interests against tort claims (such as personal injury) typically are Republicans, while voters who are racial and ethnic minorities are more often Democrats. In South Florida, Hispanic voters (primarily Cuban Americans) raised similar objections to the plan for fear that their traditional influence at the polls would evaporate.

Amid this opposition, the legislature passed two proposed referenda items authorizing amendments to the state constitution, thinking that only narrow groups opposed the extension of the merit system to the trial bench. The first was a local option under which voters residing in specific jurisdictions could choose to adopt the merit plan for all judges within that political district. In November 1998, voters went to the polls to consider this and other questions. Voters across the state's counties and circuits approved the option measure by a margin of about 14 percent (Lanier and Handberg 2002a). The second referendum was held in November 2000. In it, the state's voters considered the question of whether actually to adopt the merit system for judges serving in the state's twenty circuits and sixty-seven counties. Despite the efforts of reformers and at least some press coverage of the question, the reform was a resounding failure statewide. The closest vote occurred in Broward County, a traditional Democratic stronghold, where only 40 percent of voters supported the measure. This amalgam of sixty-seven different elections occurred at the same time as the 2000 presidential election but with much less fanfare and drama, yet with more far-reaching effects for Floridians. Presently, Florida's judiciary remains split; the two appellate court levels (comprised of the district courts of appeal and the Florida Supreme Court) operate under the merit plan, while circuit and county judges continue to be elected.

Apart from these institutional revisions, the chief justice delivers a "state of the judiciary" report each year to the legislature. It is modeled after a similar document that the U.S. chief justice provides to Congress. The address documents the accomplishments of the court system during the last year, suggests revisions in the law, and lobbies for a budget for the following fiscal year. It highlights the courts' dependence on the legislature, which has complete discretion as to whether it will adopt the chief justice's recommendations (see Johnson 2004; Schwartz 2005). As a result of the past efforts of chief justices and a recommendation from the Constitution Revision Commission, the responsibility for funding all Florida courts shifted primarily (although not exclusively) from the county level to the state level in 2004, which the state's voters adopted via referendum in 1998. This reform, which came to be known as "Revision 7" because of its relative placement on the ballot seeking voters' responses to it and other proposed amendments, to Article V of the Florida Constitution sought to equalize to a large extent the funding for state courts (Barnett 2000). Counties had previously been quite divergent in the resources that they committed to the local courts, as the population, tax base and economic development of each varies considerably. The change provided for a more equitable distribution of resources to ensure that the state's courts could fulfill their responsibilities without gross disparities in the quality and availability of court services, although counties still provide some funding for the state courts under their jurisdiction (Johnson 2004).

The supreme court is also working with each of the state courts to establish an electronic filing system to expedite case management, especially with capital cases, which typically have ten times the filing volume of noncapital cases (Johnson 2004). In 2004, the supreme court and the Fourth District Court of Appeal implemented this pilot project; it will be expanded as more courts submit plans to the supreme court for review. Three judicial circuits are also participating in digital court-reporting projects for trial courts in their respective jurisdictions to reduce the costs of that service, as court reporting currently costs the state $25 million annually.

An additional innovation for which Florida has been particularly known is the use of cameras in the courtroom. In the 1970s, the Florida Supreme Court authorized the most widespread use of cameras of any state court. (The camera remains in a fixed position; only the focus changes.) Floridians, thus, have easier access to what goes on in their courts than most Americans do, although judges may restrict the use of cameras in certain cases (those involving minors, for example) (Handberg and Lawhorn 1998).

Tort Reform

Beyond reforms of the judiciary, Florida has also struggled with reform of its tort laws, especially as they relate to medical malpractice cases. Tort reform is relevant to an understanding of Florida courts because tort cases represent demands on the state judiciary.[11] Which cases the judiciary hears and in what form affects the operation of the courts, broadly speaking. Moreover, many members of the public believe, rightly or wrongly, that such cases are without merit. Proponents of tort reform believe that many tort cases that are filed are without legal basis, but simply pursued to enrich the plaintiff and the plaintiff's lawyer at the expense of an innocent defendant, to the detriment of the economy, the legal system (that is already overburdened with cases) and to the defendant who has to bear the defense costs of the suit even if it is later dismissed. Further, such cases contradict the American sense of individualism and stoicism, under which one simply bears in silence the consequences of unfortunate injuries during life. Accordingly, in the 1970s, a national political movement emerged to restrict tort cases from being filed. Since 1986, 39 states have adopted some sort of revision to their tort laws (Neubauer and Meinhold 2007). Such reforms may influence the operation of the courts significantly. This movement highlighted the political nature of the courts, as we have defined it, because they are the institutions in which such broad societal disputes are resolved according to predetermined rules and guidelines.

Medical malpractice suits are one category of tort cases. In 1988, the state began its initial foray into the reform of medical malpractice lawsuits with an attempt to limit the extent of physician liability. Such suits were funneled to a special mediation panel to divert as many cases as possible from the costly, lengthy, and risky process of a civil trial (Handberg and Lawhorn 1998). Trials in general are risky ventures as the persons involved (witnesses, jurors and judges) may act in unexpected ways, to the detriment of the parties. Medical malpractice cases, in particular, are risky for plaintiffs as they are difficult to win due in part to the question of causation: that is, the plaintiff (in order to prevail) must show that the physician's negligence caused the injuries for which money damages are sought. They are also terribly expensive to litigate (Hensler 1993). Overall, plaintiffs in medical malpractice cases prevail only approximately 25 percent of the time; in automobile cases, by contrast (which are usually more straight-forward), plaintiffs prevail in approximately 60 percent of the cases (Cohen and Smith 2004). Recently, Florida reform proponents have pointed out that several physicians have left the state or stopped practicing medicine altogether because of the perception that medical malpractice insurance premiums were too high (see Greene 2004). Proponents of tort reform in the state have alleged that this systemic problem imperiled the quality of medical care provided in the state.

Thus, in 2004, the state's voters returned to the polls to consider a second set of referenda on tort reform. The proposed policies included one that limited that amount of a judgment or settlement that an injured claimant could receive from a medical liability suit. The idea underlying the referendum was that if the amount an attorney would receive for litigating a medical malpractice claim were limited, perhaps there he or she would have less incentive to bring such cases and fewer nonmeritorious, questionable cases will populate the courts' dockets. Also, the limited fee would protect the integrity of the process by not creating an incentive for an attorney to slant his or her professional advice. The proposal passed by a margin of about two-thirds.

However, on the same ballot, voters considered amendments to the state constitution that would withdraw the medical licenses of physicians who had committed three or more incidents of medical malpractice. An additional referendum sought to allow patients greater access to information about health care providers so they could make a more informed decision about whether to undergo a certain procedure. Both of these measures passed by a wide margin. Thus, Florida's voters have cast the law in two contradictory directions, which the state legislature (now dominated by Republicans) will most likely have to reconcile.

The Criminal Justice System

Because a large segment of Florida's population is transitory, the state has historically had a very high crime rate, indeed the highest in the nation per capita during several years. Despite the state's overall crime rate's having decreased in recent years, the state still retains the top rank in violent crimes (Dye 1998). This trend, therefore, presents a challenge to the state court system, which must process those accused of crime and sentence those found guilty.

Driven by drug-related crime (arising, in part, due to Florida's long coastline), the state's tough drug laws, and lengthy prison sentences for drug offenders, the state's per capita imprisonment rate was 463 per 100,000 in 2003, up from 445 in 1996; the 2003 national rate was 482 (Harrison and Beck 2004; Florida Department of Corrections 2005b). The incarceration rate grew by nearly 6 percent during 2003 alone; the average annual increase from 1995 to 2003 was 2.8 percent. At the end of 2003, only California (629) and Texas (453) had larger numbers of prisoners under sentence of death than did Florida (364) (Bonczar and Snell 2004). In July 1997, the state's death row was the largest in the nation.

In addition, Florida seeks to imprison individuals for a longer proportion of the time to which they are sentenced originally. A lingering concern among the public has been that criminals are released far too early and that they quickly lapse into recidivism after being released. The average proportion of a sentence that a prisoner serves belies the political concern that has been brought to bear on this question. In 1994, an average offender served 53.7 percent of the sentence. By 2004, that figure had risen to 84.9 percent. The state passed the "85 percent law" under which offenders were required to serve at least 85 percent of their sentence before being released. Certainly, the longer the time that an offender serves, the more strain that it places on the financial and physical resources of the state (Florida Department of Corrections 2005d). To keep pace with the political rhetoric about responding to the rising crime rate and the corresponding increase in average rate of sentence served, more prisons had to be built, but, in a state without a personal income tax and one currently having a Republican-controlled legislature, that was a problem, especially since parole was abolished in 1983 (Handberg and Lawhorn 1998). Overall, the state Department of Corrections supervised through community release programs 151,150 persons in addition to incarcerating 81,974 prisoners during FY 2004, up from 136,056 persons in community supervision programs during FY 1995, in addition to its housing 61,992 prisoners then (Florida Department of Corrections 2005e)

In 1989, in response to a federal court order to reduce the inmate population and overcrowding in the state's prisons, the state created drug courts. The rationale was that offenders who repeatedly appear in the state's courts need to deal with their underlying dependency issue as well as the legal ramifications of their actions. Rather than exclusively involving the judge and other court personnel in the adjudication of guilt, those courts attempt to create a solution to the basic problem. Neubauer and Meinhold (2007) refer to this process as "diagnostic adjudication," as the emphasis is on discerning what the fundamental issue is and not primarily on questions of guilt or innocence. The first drug court was located in Miami-Dade County, and they are now located throughout the state (Florida State Courts 2005).

In addition to fiscal considerations, the state has grappled with equity in sentencing. A touchstone of the legal system is the idea that similarly situated individuals are treated similarly. However, as Florida was (and is) a state touched by the politics of the Deep South, questions of sentencing inequities arose. A defendant in one circuit could be sentenced to probation, while another person charged with the same crime in another area might receive fifteen years. To limit the prevalence of sentence disparity, the legislature empowered the Florida Supreme Court to develop sentencing guidelines for certain offenses. Depending on the defendant's record, judges are allowed to impose minimum and maximum sentences. Several versions of the guidelines were adopted in 1983, 1994, and 1995 that in various ways restricted or limited the discretion of the judge imposing the sentence.

However, the Florida Supreme Court struck down the 1995 version of the guidelines as violating the single-subject rule required by Article III, section 6 of the Florida Constitution (*Heggs v. Florida* [2000]). That provision requires that "every law shall embrace but one subject and matter properly connected therewith, and the subject shall be briefly expressed in the title." During the 1997 legislative session, the legislature abolished the Florida Sentencing Commission and passed a new set of guidelines known as the Criminal Punishment Code, which became effective on October 1, 1998 (Florida Department of Corrections 2005a). These most recent guidelines, in effect, provide "a significant broadening of upward discretion in sentencing," which means that more offenders have a greater chance of receiving a sentence including some prison time than under previous law (Florida Department of Corrections 2005c).

The state still continues to experiment with community-based alternative sentences, including electronic monitoring. But convicted criminals with creative minds can circumvent alternative sentences and move through communities without regulation or monitoring. This situation may not be palatable to the public, especially as a number of high-profile and emotional cases involving the kidnapping and murder of young girls has recently occurred. Crime in Florida will continue to be a political hot-button issue, especially as the state climbs out of the budget deficit that has occurred since the decline in state tourism after the 9/11 attacks. Because much of the state's revenue is tied to taxes associated with tourism, its tax revenue collection significantly diminished following those attacks, which has created a budget shortfall in many areas. Moreover, while tourism is now rebounding to some extent, the state still is struggling to recover its prior level of tax revenue that is so vital to the operation of the state's agencies.

The Death Penalty in Florida

In 1972, the U.S. Supreme Court reviewed a death sentence handed down to a criminal defendant in Georgia and struck down capital sentences as being inherently unconstitutional under the Eighth Amendment to the U.S. Constitution; it held in *Furman v. Georgia* (1972) that such penalties constituted "cruel and unusual" punishment. In the wake of the U.S. Supreme Court's decision reinstituting the death penalty four years later in *Gregg v. Georgia* (1976), Florida revised its capital statute to reflect the procedural demands announced in that case. In short, *Gregg* required states that sought to enact death penalty statutes to fulfill several exacting steps before someone could be lawfully executed. The Court essentially stated that states may not constitutionally have laws that mandate a death sentence for certain offenses. Rather, states may impose the death penalty for certain offenses *only after* the jury has considered any mitigating and aggravating circumstances of the offense. Mitigating circumstances may include the crime's being the defendant's first offense or the defendant's being mentally challenged. Aggravating circumstances may include the offense's being committed in the process of the defendant committing another crime or the defendant's having a long record of prior crimes. Also, states must split the trial into two phases: one dealing with guilt or innocence, and a second (if the accused is found guilty) involving the question of sentencing.

In 1976, the U.S. Supreme Court upheld Florida's revised death penalty statute in *Profitt v. Florida* (hereafter "the *Profitt* statute"; State of Florida 2005). The Court upheld similar statutes in two other states, and these laws became templates for other states as they moved to revise their law to reflect the demands of the *Gregg* court (see Driggs 1999). The *Profitt* statute requires trial juries to determine guilt or innocence after hearing and considering all mitigating and aggravating evidence. If guilt is established, then the jury hears evidence about what sentence to recommend to the court, which then decides what penalty to impose on the defendant. The trial court must prepare a detailed order setting out the process of evidence-weighing that it completed in the determination of the sentence and an explicit discussion of the probative nature of any mitigating evidence (Driggs 1999, 2002; *Campbell v. State* [1990]).[12] The Florida Supreme Court has ruled that if the jury recommends a life sentence but the trial court ignores that recommendation and imposes a death sentence, such rulings will be upheld only if they are "so clear and convincing that virtually no reasonable person could differ" (*Tedder v. State* [1975], 910; quoted in Driggs 2002, 770). The state's revised death penalty statute also provided for direct mandatory appeal to the Florida Supreme Court for review of the death sentence and the procedures that the lower court followed in handing down the ruling.

Because of this strict procedure, the Florida Supreme Court has heard a number of cases reviewing capital sentences and, thus, has set death penalty policy in a number of areas. Driggs (1999, 212) asserts that it has completed its grim task "as seriously as any state supreme court in the country." Central to the court's review of death penalty recommendations is the question of proportionality: that is, whether the punishment is appropriate considering the severity of the offense and all the aggravating and mitigating circumstances in the case (see Driggs 1999, 2002). In essence, the court ensures that defendants are treated equitably—that is, similarly situated defendants receive similar sentences (Driggs 1999; *State v. Dixon* [1973]). The court will not conduct a proportionality review in so-called collateral attacks generally (*Williams v. Wainwright* [1987]), but it may do so when the defendant alleges ineffective assistance of counsel (*Hudson v. State* [1993]).[13] It will engage in such analyses even with pro se defendants (those who represent themselves without the benefit of an attorney), or one who does not oppose the death penalty (*Meyers v. State* [1997]). Once the proportionality review has been completed, the court may uphold the death sentence, it may reduce a death sentence to life imprisonment, or it may remand the case to the trial court to reweigh the evidence in line with the court's decision (Driggs 1999).

The state's supreme court brought itself into the public eye when it rejected a challenge, in *Jones v. Butterworth* (1997), to the constitutionality of the use of the electric chair as a method of capital punishment (Driggs 2002). In the wake of *Jones*, Florida legislators, in an attempt to ensure that later courts would not invalidate that method of imposing the death penalty, proposed as a referendum that the Florida Constitution be amended to prohibit "cruel *and* unusual punishment," rather than what the original language required (prohibiting "cruel *or* unusual punishment") (Driggs 1999). By so amending the Florida Constitution, its language would be made consistent with the language of the U.S. Constitution's Eighth Amendment as interpreted by the Court in *Furman*, *Gregg* and *Profitt* (among other cases), which are discussed above. The measure would, thus, have narrowed the breadth of prisoners' protection under Florida law. In November 1998, voters approved the measure. In *Knight v. State* (1998), the Florida Supreme Court addressed this change in the law and implicitly indicated that it would *not* consider the larger question as to whether that state constitutional amendment undermines its long history and tradition of conducting proportionality review in capital cases (Driggs 1999). Indeed, following the court's ruling in *Knight*, it once again reviewed the constitutionality of the electric chair as a means to carry out capital sentences after one defendant suffered a bloody nose during the execution. In *Provenzano v. Moore* (1999), the court upheld the use of that method. However, after yet another constitutional challenge in the U.S. Supreme Court to the electric chair, the Florida legislature adopted lethal injection as the preferred method of capital punishment unless the defendant elects electrocution (Driggs 2002).

Since 2000 (after the political firestorm that engulfed the court during the presidential election cases), the court has become less willing to overturn death sentences. Driggs (2002, 781) points out that the Florida Supreme Court affirms "a substantial majority" of the death sentences that it reviews; however, it reduces 20 percent of such penalties to life imprisonment. Driggs (2002) argues that the court prior to 2000 affirmed fewer death sentences and engaged in a more rigorous review of such rulings. Durham (2004) asserts that this change in policy (that is, the court's diminished likelihood of overturning death sentences during its post-conviction proportionality review) was due to the political pressure that was brought to bear by a Republican governor, a Republican-controlled legislature, and a change in membership on the court. The legislature passed the Death Penalty Reform Act of 2000, which would have created (among other provisions) a dual system in which direct appeal of the conviction and any post-conviction attacks on their death sentences (known collectively as collateral attacks, which are discussed above) would occur simultaneously (Durham 2004). However, in *Allen v. Butterworth* (2000), the Florida Supreme Court struck down the act as violative of the doctrine of separation of powers (Driggs 2002). These political incursions on the court may have undermined its judicial independence in its death penalty jurisprudence. The cost (measured in the loss of the defendants' freedom or their very lives) of the court's losing some amount of its institutional discretion falls most heavily upon those of very humble means and backgrounds (Durham 2004).

Florida Courts in the Eye of the Hurricane: The 2000 Presidential Election Cases and Reform of Judicial Selection

Before the political storm of 2000 occurred, Florida courts were generally unknown to the public. The public was more concerned with the executive and legislative branches. Controversy had touched the court system only sporadically, and then only the supreme court was at the center of a brief storm. The concerted campaign in 1992 by supporters of the death penalty and opponents of abortion against Justice Rosemary Barkett during her retention election is an example of such temporal attention given to Florida's courts. Barkett ultimately was retained by the voters, but she received only 60.9 percent of the vote that year; traditionally, vote totals in retention elections are much higher. In 1999, the supreme court again caught the attention of the state legislature (and, to some extent, the voters) when the court struck down laws that would have accelerated death sentences after one inmate suffered a bloody nose during an electrocution. Justice Leander Shaw was the target of organized opposition because of his vote in the case supporting the majority ruling that the use of the electric chair was unconstitutional and his posting on his personal website of a photo of the inmate with a bloody nose (Lanier and Handberg 2002b). Thus, "long-simmering resentments over decisions [of the courts] on the death penalty, abortion, gun control, school vouchers, affirmative action and taxation" were bubbling just below the surface in the days leading up to the 2000 election (Cooper 2001).

Many scholarly articles have been written about the legal and political ramifications of the disputed 2000 presidential election between George Bush and Al Gore. An extensive legal analysis and detained explanation of the events of that case are beyond the scope of this chapter. However, the Florida Supreme Court's decisions favoring Democrat Al Gore cast the court into a conflict with the governor (whose brother, George W. Bush, was the Republican Party candidate) and the legislature that was exacerbated by the growing disjuncture between changes in the partisan dynamics of the state and Florida's appellate courts. State courts all along the judicial hierarchy were involved in the lengthy process, which brought unprecedented media coverage and public attention to the judiciary for a time. Because of the hostility that had been brewing against the supreme court prior to the 2000 election and the perception that at least some of the justices then serving on the court were judicial activists, the legislature and the governor were quick to strike.

In the 2001 legislative session (which began in March following the election contest), Republican governor Bush and the Republican-controlled legislature made several changes to restrain what they believed was a runaway judiciary. One bill that the legislature considered revised the procedure for the selection of the Judicial Nominating Commission (JNC) members (who are responsible for selecting the slate of potential nominees that the governor considers for the state's appellate courts). Prior to 2001, the state's JNCs were composed of three members of the bar, three gubernatorial appointees, and three persons whom the bar and the governor jointly name. Under the revised bill, the Florida Bar merely *recommends* persons to be selected for the JNC, and the governor may reject all four if he or she so chooses. The governor alone selects the additional five members of each JNC, although two of these persons must be members of the bar. The proposal gave the governor essentially complete control of JNC membership (Lanier and Handberg 2002b). On June 19, 2001, Governor Bush signed the proposal into law, giving him untrammeled control over the selection of Florida's appellate judges (including those who serve on the state supreme court) and a heightened degree of influence over the state's two levels of trial courts in interim appointments. In addition, the influence of the bar has grown; now five of the nine members of each JNC must be attorneys. Governor Bush and the Republican-controlled legislature also threatened to reduce the staffing of state courts and reduce the budgetary allocation of the state court system by about 2.5 percent (Cooper 2001).

The legislature also debated, but did not ultimately pass, a proposed constitutional amendment that would have required district court of appeal judges and state supreme court justices to obtain two-thirds of the total votes in retention elections in order to remain on the bench, rather than the preexisting majority requirement. Recall that if a judge is not retained, then the governor nominates a successor for the position. Hence, the proposed revision would have inflated the governor's power over the state judiciary, especially the appellate bench, which reviews important policy questions for the state.

Under the proposal, however, the legislature sought to restrain the governor's power by requiring him to submit his judicial nominees to the senate for confirmation, just as the president must do in the federal system. It also sought to abolish the JNCs and nullify the requirement that Florida attorneys join the state bar (and thus nullify the bar's power in judicial selection in the state), hence expanding the governor's power over the bench even further. Although the bill died in committee in May 2001, it is a harbinger of the increased partisan influences being brought to bear on the state judiciary (especially the appellate courts) that seek to limit the discretion of Florida courts and imperil their political independence.

To some extent, the governor's discretion in making appointments to the state courts is constrained by the collective decisions of the court-specific JNCs, but the members of these nominating commissions are chosen by the governor alone and presumably share common policy views with him or her about which candidates are prepared and qualified to join the bench. While it is true that appellate judges have to stand in retention elections approximately one year following their initial appointment to the bench, such elections do not conform to the democratic ideal of informed voters choosing from among competing candidates; the voter simply chooses to retain or not retain the judge under consideration, a process discussed above. Thus, the Florida governor essentially acts alone in the choice of appellate judges and many trial court judges.

The irony of these changes is striking: they were imposed by the legislature and the governor because of charges that the state supreme court had become a "runaway tribunal," yet they may have served to politicize the courts permanently. Florida's judiciary may be damaged in its efforts to stand independent from the views of the other branches and exercise true discretion about what interests to support and what to oppose and which policies to continue and which policies to nullify. This change may tip the balance of power in favor of the executive branch to the detriment of the judiciary's overall independence, a central element of any democratic government. This shift may be manifested in lower levels of diffuse support in the state for the Florida courts as a whole, thus diminishing the critical levels of legitimacy that shore up the public's trust in their decisions. One could argue that as the Florida courts become more Republican in their composition, conflict should decline, possibly returning such courts to their previous obscurity.

Conclusion

Florida courts in recent years have been in transition. They have moved to center stage, both by choice and by political pressures within and beyond the state. This more visible face of the Florida courts is manifest in their involvement in the *Schiavo* case and in other controversial decisions, notably those involving the privacy rights of minors and the death penalty. Whether reform of the state judiciary will continue depends on the ever-evolving relationship between the courts and the elected branches. Whatever the course of history, the continuing challenge for the Florida courts is retaining their constitutionally delegated power and political independence. That will be indeed a daunting challenge in the years to come.

Notes

1. The merit plan in Florida works in the customary way: a Judicial Nominating Commission composes a list of three to six potential nominees from which the governor makes an ultimate selection. After the judge serves for about one year, the selected person stands in an unopposed retention election in which the voters in the jurisdiction decide if he/she should continue in office. Voters are presented with the sole question "Should Judge X be retained?" and provided two options: retain the judge or do not retain the judge. If by a simple majority of those who cast votes on the question agree that the judge should be retained, then the person continues on the bench and serves a six-year term. If the majority of voters decide not to retain the jurist, the governor then chooses another candidate and the process begins once again (Neubauer and Meinhold 2007).

2. Technically, a judge need not retire immediately once he or she reaches age 70. Article V, §8 of the Florida Constitution states that judges who reach the age of 70 who have completed at least one-half of their terms may remain on the bench until the terms are completed. Hence, judges may ultimately serve until they are 71 or 72, depending on when their birthday falls during their term of service.

3. The Court will give expedited review to cases that are legally important but yet

not of significant import to justify their receiving plenary consideration. For example, the Court may hear a case involving a criminal appeal and give it expedited review if the judges believe that it should be resolved by the Court but it is not so significant making it worthy for full consideration by the tribunal.

4. The First District Court of Appeal is headquartered in Tallahassee; the Second in Lakeland; the Third in Miami-Dade County; the Fourth in Palm Beach County; and the Fifth in Daytona Beach.

5. The number of cases received and disposed of during a particular time period are not necessarily equal as there may be some cases held over from a prior period that were not able to be resolved by the courts then, thereby contributing to the backlog of cases awaiting judicial resolution.

6. The largest judicial circuit (the 17th circuit) has fifty-three judges; the smallest (the 16th circuit) has only four.

7. Nonpartisan elections are those in which the candidates standing for election appear on the ballot without any identifying party affiliation associated with their name. Accordingly, voters must choose from among the candidates based on other factors, which makes the process more difficult for many voters.

8. "Civil cases" for the circuit courts includes not only traditional civil cases (those involving two private parties or nonpublic remedies) but also those pertaining to domestic relations, probate, and juvenile issues.

9. See note 1 above and associated text for a discussion of the merit plan selection method.

10. Article V of the Florida Constitution establishes twenty-six judicial nominating commissions, one for the supreme court, one for each of the five district courts of appeals, and one for each of the twenty judicial circuits. The judicial circuits JNCs have jurisdiction over appointments to both the circuit and county courts across the state.

11. A "tort" is a private civil wrong by a person against another person, other than a breach of contract. For example, negligence leading to the injury of another may be tortuous conduct. Such legal injuries are not limited to personal injury, for which money is typically sought as relief, but may also include property damage that is recognized by the law as an injury (Neubauer and Meinhold 2006).

12. "Probative" means that the evidence in question tends to prove an issue in question (Garner 2004).

13. After one has exhausted the initial appellate process, state and federal prisoners may challenge their convictions on specific legal grounds in addition to those already decided. These post-conviction attempts to seek some redress are known as "collateral attacks" as they are efforts to avoid the effects of a court's decision by filing a separate court proceeding from that of the direct appeal of one's sentence (Neubauer and Meinhold 2007, 419).

References

Barnett, Martha W. 2000. "The 1997–98 Florida Constitution Revision Commission: Judicial Election or Merit Selection." *Florida Law Review* 52:411–23.

Bast, Carol M. 2005. *Florida Courts.* 4th ed. Upper Saddle River, N.J.: Pearson Prentice Hall.

Bonczar, Thomas P., and Tracy L. Snell. 2004. *Capital Punishment, 2003.* Washington, D.C.: Bureau of Justice Statistics. <www.ojp.usdoj.gov/bjs/pub/pdf/cp03.pdf> (accessed March 14, 2007).

Carmines, Edward G., and James A. Stimson. 1989. *Issue Evolution: Race and the Transformation of American Politics.* Princeton, N.J.: Princeton University Press.

CNN. 2005. "Frist: Schiavo Rulings Won't Affect Dispute over Judicial Nominees." *CNN Inside Politics.* <www.cnn.com/2005/POLITICS/04/05/senate.judges.ap/index.html> (accessed April 11, 2005).

Cohen, Thomas, and Steven Smith. 2004. *Civil Trial Cases and Verdicts in Large Counties.* Washington, D.C.: Bureau of Justice Statistics. <www.ojp.usdoj.gov/bjs/abstract/ctcvlc01.htm> (accessed May 1, 2007).

Cooper, Claire H. 2001. "Fla. Court in the Crosshairs." *National Law Journal,* April 9.

Court Statistics Project. 2006. *State Court Caseload Statistics, 2005.* Williamsburg, Va.: National Center for State Courts.

Coyle, Marcia. 1998. "Suit: Death Defense Is a Sham." *National Law Journal,* December 21.

Culver, John H., and John T. Wold. 1986. "Rose Bird and the Politics of Judicial Accountability in California." *Judicature* 70 (August–September): 81–89.

Driggs, Ken. 1999. "'The Most Aggravated and Least Mitigated Murders': Capital Proportionality Review in Florida." *St. Thomas Law Review* 11:207–88.

———. 2002. "Regulating the Five Steps to Death: A Study of Death Penalty Direct Appeals in the Florida Supreme Court, 1991–2000." *St. Thomas Law Review* 14:759–823.

Durham, Philip L. 2004. "Review in Name Alone: The Rise and Fall of Comparative Proportionality Review of Capital Sentences by the Supreme Court of Florida." *St. Thomas Law Review* 17: 299–370.

Dye, Thomas R. 1998. *Politics in Florida.* Upper Saddle River, N.J.: Prentice Hall.

Easton, David. 1965. *A Systems Analysis of Political Life.* New York: Wiley.

Florida Department of Corrections. 2005a. "Executive Summary." In *Sentencing Guidelines 1996–1997 Annual Report.* <www.dc.state.fl.us/pub/sg_annual/9697/executives.html> (accessed March 17, 2007).

———. 2005b. "Inmate Admissions Rise Sharply (10.4%) This Fiscal Year." In *Florida Department of Corrections 2003–2004 Annual Report.* <www.dc.state.fl.us/pub/annual/0304/stats/im_admis.html> (accessed March 14, 2007).

———. 2005c. "Overview of Florida's Sentencing Policies." In *Florida's Criminal Punishment Code: A Comparative Assessment.* <www.dc.state.fl.us/pub/sg_annual/0001/intro.html> (accessed March 14, 2007).

———. 2005d. *Time-Served and Percentage of Sentence Served in Florida's Prisons.*

<www.dc.state.fl.us/pub/timeserv/monthly/timeserved.pdf> (accessed March 14, 2007).

———. 2005e. "How the Statistical Pages are Organized." In *Florida Department of Corrections 2003–2004 Annual Report.* <www.dc.state.fl.us/pub/annual/0304 /stats/index.html> (accessed May 2, 2007).

Florida State Courts. 2005. "Drug Court Program." <www.flcourts.org/gen_public /family/drug_court/index.shtml> (accessed March 17, 2007).

Garner, Bryan. 2004. *Black's Law Dictionary.* 8th ed. St. Paul, Minn.: West.

Greene, Lisa. 2004. "Fla. Doctors Cut Services over Malpractice Rates." *St. Petersburg Times* (South Pinellas edition), November 9.

Hall, Melinda Gann. 2001. "State Supreme Courts in American Democracy: Probing the Myths of Judicial Reform." *American Political Science Review* 95, no. 2: 315–30.

Handberg, Roger. 1994. "Judicial Accountability and Independence: Balancing Incompatibles?" *University of Miami Law Review* 49: 127–38.

———, and Mark Lawhorn. 1998. "The Courts: Powerful but Obscure." In *Government and Politics in Florida,* edited by Robert J. Huckshorn. 2nd ed. 147–68. Gainesville: University Press of Florida.

Harrison, Paige M., and Allen J. Beck. 2004. *Prisoners in 2003.* Bureau of Justice Statistics Bulletin NCJ205335. Washington, D.C.: Bureau of Justice Statistics. <www.ojp .usdoj.gov/bjs/pub/pdf/p03.pdf> (accessed March 17, 2007).

Hensler, Deborah. 2003. "Reading the Tort Litigation Tea Leaves: What's Going On in the Civil Liability System?" *Justice System Journal* 16:139–54.

Jewett, Aubrey. 1997. "Partisan Change in Southern State Legislatures." Ph.D. diss., Florida State University.

———. 2001. "Partisan Change in Southern Legislatures, 1946–1995." *Legislative Studies Quarterly* 26:457–548.

Johnson, Brenda G., ed. 2004. *Florida State Courts: 2003–2004 Annual Report.* Tallahassee: Office of the State Courts Administrator. <www.flcourts.org/gen_public/ pubs/bin/courts_annual_report04.pdf> (accessed March 14, 2007).

Lanier, Drew Noble. 2002. "Florida." In *Legal Systems of the World: A Political, Social and Cultural Encyclopedia,* edited by Herbert M. Kritzer. 545–49. Santa Barbara, Calif.: ABC-CLIO.

———, and Roger Handberg. 2002a. "Business as Usual: Judicial Reform in Florida, 1970–2000." Paper presented at the Annual Meeting of the American Political Science Association, Boston, Mass., August 29–September 1, 2002.

———. 2002b. "In the Eye of the Hurricane: Florida Courts, Judicial Independence, and Politics." *Fordham Urban Law Journal* 29:1029–52.

Lasswell, Harold D. 1938. *Politics: Who Gets What, When and How.* New York: McGraw-Hill.

Little, Joseph W. 1989. "An Overview of the Historical Development of the Judicial Article of the Florida Constitution." *Stetson Law Review* 19:1–41.

Lundy, Sarah. 2006. "A Revolving Door of Public Attorneys." *Orlando Sentinel,* October 23.

Mecham, Leonidas Ralph. 2005. *Judicial Business of the United States Courts, 2004*

Report of the Director. <www.uscourts.gov/judbususc/judbus.html> (accessed March 24, 2007).

Neubauer, David W., and Stephen S. Meinhold. 2007. *Judicial Process: Law, Courts, and Politics in the United States.* 4th ed. Belmont, Calif.: Thompson Wadsworth.

Pritchett, C. Herman. 1948. *The Roosevelt Court: A Study in Judicial Politics and Values 1937–1947.* Chicago: Quadrangle Books.

Schwartz, Beth C. 2005. *Florida State Courts: Annual Report 2004–2005.* Tallahassee: Office of the State Courts Administrator. <www.flcourts.org/gen_public/pubs/bin/annual_report0405.pdf> (accessed March 14, 2007).

Stanley, Harold W., and Richard G. Niemi. 2000. *Vital Statistics on American Politics, 1999–2000.* Washington, D.C.: Congressional Quarterly.

State Courts Administrator. 2005. *Trial Court Statistical Reference Guide, FY 2003–04.* Tallahassee: Office of the State Courts Administrator. <www.flcourts.org/gen_public/stats/reference_guide03_04.shtml> (accessed March 14, 2007).

State of Florida. 2005. "Sentence of Death or Life Imprisonment for Capital Felonies; Further Proceedings to Determine Sentence." Chapter 921.141 of *Criminal Procedure and Corrections.* <http://law.justia.com/florida/codes/TitleXLVII/ch0921.html> (accessed March 14, 2007).

Schauffler, Richard Y., Robert C. LaFountain, Neal B. Kauder, and Shauna M. Strickland. 2005. *Examining the Work of State Courts: A National Perspective from the Court Statistics Project.* Williamsburg, Va.: National Center for State Courts. <www.ncsconline.org/D_Research/csp/2004_Files/EWSC_Full_Report.pdf> (accessed April 27, 2007).

10

Local Governments

Institutions of Governance and Agents of Service Delivery

J. EDWIN BENTON AND RICHARD C. FEIOCK

It is a fairly settled legal principal that local governments in Florida are really parts of their state, since the U.S. Constitution establishes a federal form of government and recognizes only two levels of government—the national government and the states. As such, local governments have no right to self-government, and all of their governmental powers derive from state laws or constitutions. That is, local governments are creatures of their state (meaning that they exist in a unitary or dependent relationship to their state government) and therefore are subject to the obligations, privileges, powers, and restrictions that their state governments impose upon them. The state, in accordance with the constitution and law, may create or abolish any or all units of local government. Like their counterparts in other states, local governments in Florida—that is, counties, municipalities, and special districts[1]—were formalized to assist the state in performing state functions or delivering state programs and services at the local level and to provide a higher level and larger menu of uniquely local services to large concentrations of people. In the former role, local governments serve as political or administrative units of the state, while in the latter role, they perform as full-service local governments, especially counties and municipalities.

The everyday lives of Floridians are certainly touched and impacted by both the federal government and the state governments. However, the daily lives of Floridians are probably impacted more frequently and profoundly by some aspect of local government. It may be their county government, which oversees elections, assesses property for taxing purposes, collects taxes, distributes a variety of welfare benefits, issues birth or death certificates, inoculates preschool children against disease and adults against the flu, operates a criminal justice and court system, and issues titles for property or vehicles. Or it could be their city government, which provides fire and police services, streetlights, sidewalks, drainage for storm water, water and sewer services, parks and recreational facilities, or garbage pickup. Another possibility may be a special-purpose or service district that is charged with regulating water usage, protecting the environment, building and operating a hospital, constructing and managing low-income housing units, overseeing redevelopment in a highly urbanized and declining area, or even providing fire protection and utilities to residents of unincorporated areas. In short, there is only one federal government and one state government, but there are many local governments in Florida that perform a multitude of functions and provide countless services.

Florida residents receive services from four principal local government entities—cities, counties, school districts, and special districts. In Florida, these units of local government spend more money and employ more workers than the state government does. Florida has 67 counties,[2] 412 municipalities, 67 school districts, and 626 independent special districts (U.S. Bureau of the Census 2003). All municipalities have home rule,[3] while counties have the option of adopting home rule charters[4] (currently nineteen counties have opted to do so). The 67 school districts are governed separately, but since 1942, they have had coterminous boundaries with the county governments.

Every Floridian lives within the jurisdiction of at least two local governments—a county and a school district—and nearly half of all Floridians reside within the boundaries of a third local government—a municipality. Moreover, it is not unusual for Floridians to live within the jurisdiction of several special-service districts. In short, counties, municipalities, and special districts, as a result of their seemingly omnipresent existence, continue to be prominent players in government and politics in Florida, especially since they are critical institutions of local governance and important agents of service delivery. This chapter provides an overview of the history, structure, and roles of Florida counties, municipalities, and special districts. (School districts will be addressed in Chapter 13, which focuses on education policy in Florida).

The Relationship between the State and Local Governments in Florida

The state legislature was involved directly and often in the affairs of counties and municipalities until the state constitution was revised in 1968 to provide them greater home rule. For much of the nineteenth and twentieth centuries, the legislature's role in local governance emerged in special legislation, commonly called "local bill courtesy." Local bill courtesy ensured that the decisions of the local legislative delegation would almost always be adopted into law by the entire legislature through local bills. Thirty years ago, almost a third of the bills passed into law in Florida were local bills. While this percentage has declined, some local bills are still introduced and the vast majority of them are adopted.

"Special legislation" or local bills dominated local affairs throughout the nineteenth century and continues to play a role. Florida's five elected county constitutional officers (the sheriff, supervisor elections, clerk of the circuit and county court, property appraiser, and tax collector) have traditionally supported special legislation as a flexible, quick tool. Since county governments were restricted to general or special law, they often encountered problems that required legislative authority to resolve, and county commissioners often needed assistance from the state legislature. In some instances, special laws allow them to bypass the county commission. Achievement of county home rule has lessened demand for special legislation, but even in large home rule cities, local officials still may request special legislation in controversial matters.

Home rule was made an option for counties by the 1968 constitution and the County Administration and Optional County Charter Law in 1974 (Florida Statutes, Chapter 125.84). Charters have to be approved by the state legislature before they are submitted to the voters. Once a charter is passed, the community is free to amend it as it sees fit, with one exception. A community does not have the power to recall local officials; that is regulated by state statute.

County Governments

County governments in Florida (like counties or their equivalent in forty-seven other states[5]) were originally established to assist the state government in the administration of state programs at the local level. Florida's counties were designed to be subdivisions of the state and were to serve as local "branch" or "satellite" offices around the state with responsibility to perform what has been referred to as traditional government services and function as the administrative arm of the state (see Salant 1991). Performance of many of the latter group of services was mandatory, and counties functioned primarily as political and administrative extensions of the state. In fact, prior to the Florida's 1968 constitution, counties had limited autonomy because of the common application of the legal precedent commonly referred to as Dillon's Rule, and thus they could not act without the state's express permission.

County Services

In their role as administrative arms of the state, all counties in Florida traditionally have been responsible for implementing the state's health care and welfare programs (although there has been a tremendous growth in the state's implementation responsibilities since the mid-1950s), constructing and maintaining roads, enforcing the law in unincorporated areas, operating the state's court system, housing prisoners awaiting trial and those sentenced to less than one year, collecting taxes, appraising property, recording legal documents and keeping vital statistics, supervising elections, maintaining public buildings, and providing agricultural information and advice. Florida's twenty-four rural counties (those with populations of less than 50,000 persons) still continue to function in large measure as administrative arms of state government. Occasionally, rural counties may also provide services typically provided by municipalities in urban areas.

However, the state's forty-three urban counties (those with 50,000 or more persons) are more likely to operate as full-service local governments (see Benton 2002; Benton and Menzel 1991, 1993). This means that they are more likely to have been granted home rule charters and usually provide a longer list of services (that is, municipal-type and urban-type services) in addition to the services associated with being administrative arms of the state. It is not unusual for urban counties to be involved in providing fire and police protection, public housing, emergency medical services, library services, sewage and solid waste collection and disposal, and emergency management. They also contribute to extended health care, planning and zoning, construction of civic and cultural centers and marinas and sports stadiums, mass transit, provision of utilities, management of storm water, preservation of natural resources, protection of the environment, airport construction and operation, and redevelopment of urban areas.

Counties have developed a number of administrative and fiscal tools to provide increased services to residents in densely populated unincorporated areas. For instance, in 1978, Hillsborough County (Tampa) became the first county to establish a municipal services taxing unit. Under this arrangement, the county government could identify areas of the county that warranted the provision of urban-type services and provide an appropriate mechanism to pay for the service (i.e., taxes and/or fees). This innovation was a response to litigation accusing the county of double taxation. Today, most urban counties in the state use this innovative device.

Organization of County Government

Generally speaking, county government organization in Florida is reflective of a bygone era typified by a fragmented and headless government structure. Policy decisions continue to be made by an array of independently elected officers as well as a five- to seven-member board of county commissioners that is the county's legislative body. Commissioners are elected on a partisan (i.e., party labeled) ballot for four-year staggered terms with no term limits and on either an at-large (i.e., countywide) or district basis, although some charter counties use a combination system. Florida's five elected constitutional officers at the county level are also elected on a partisan ballot for four-year terms. In addition, counties are served by elected state attorneys (criminal prosecutors) and public defenders. Unless otherwise specified by county charter, constitutional officers as well as state attorneys and public defenders are elected on a partisan ballot for four-year terms and can serve an unlimited number of terms. The role each of these seven separately elected officials fulfills relates to the county's role as an administrative arm of state government, and each official administers his/her own office, although each must secure budgets and facilities from the board of commissioners. This can often lead to conflict between elected officials and the board. A sheriff who is unhappy with the board's budgetary allocation for his/her department can create a public-relations nightmare for the board by painting it as being soft on crime. Moreover, under the Florida constitution, sheriffs can appeal directly to the governor to mediate their differences with the board of county commissioners.

Historically, county governments in Florida and in other states had no executive head of the government comparable to the president (national level) or the governor (state level) who was charged with the responsibility of implementing policy decisions of the legislative body. In Florida, the board of commissioners collectively oversaw the execution of their policy decisions, while the five constitutional officers saw to it that the orders and decisions of their units were carried out. Consequently, county governments were sarcastically referred to as "headless wonders."

As a result of the Florida legislature's enactment of the County Administration and Optional County Charter Law in 1974 (Florida Statutes, Chapter 125.84), counties have the opportunity to adopt one of three types of executive structure: a county executive elected countywide to serve in an administrative and policy/political capacity (county executive form); a county administrator/manager appointed by the board of county commissioners (commission/administrator plan); and an elected chair of the board of commissioners and an appointed administrator who reports to the chair (county chair/administrator plan). No county has opted for the county manager form, while three counties (Orange, Dade, and Duval) have adopted the county executive form. Most counties (forty-eight[6]) have chosen the county administrator model. The remaining counties (fifteen) still retain the traditional commission form of government, an arrangement that fuses executive and legislative powers.

County Charters

In addition to granting counties the authority to select their form of government, the 1974 County Administration and Optional County Charter Law permitted counties to adopt home rule charters. The strengthening of home rule in Florida has meant that the state legislature has had to deal with fewer special laws, which has led to a diminished and different role of state legislators in local government affairs.[7] Home rule charters can be thought of as local constitutions; they offer opportunities to expand the powers and functions of counties, reorganize constitutional and other county functions, determine the means of electing and appointing local officials, establish methods of finance, and strengthen county management practices and procedures.

As of 2005, nineteen counties had adopted some form of home rule charter. They are Dade (1957), Duval (1967), Volusia (1970), Sarasota (1971), Broward (1975), Pinellas (1980), Hillsborough (1983), Palm Beach (1984), Charlotte (1985), Alachua (1986), Orange (1986), Seminole (1989), Clay (1991), Osceola (1992), Brevard (1995), Lee (1996), Polk (1998), Columbia (2002), and Leon (2002).

County charters may be proposed by a charter commission or the board of county commissioners, and voters must approve them through a referendum (Florida Statutes, Chapter 125). Charters permit—but do not mandate—a reallocation of functions between counties and cities. County charters can empower counties with the authority to provide certain services to an urban population on a countywide basis to facilitate an improvement in service delivery and take advantage of economies of scale. County charter governments also may be empowered to transfer responsibility for providing a service from a municipality to the county through the countywide voter referendum that creates the charter (see *Broward County v. City of Ft. Lauderdale*, 480 So., 2d 631 [Fla. 1985]). Streamlining the roles of county constitutional officers is one way to increase administrative efficiency in charter counties. Charters may describe the administrative responsibilities of these officers and may stipulate the method of selection (elected or appointed) and the extent of sovereignty (autonomous and elected by the public to appointed and serving under the county administrator). Changes may be made for one or more of the constitutional officers by amending the charter. As independently elected officials with a great deal of autonomy, constitutional officers usually oppose changes to the charter that reduce their autonomy or independence. In spite of such resistance, several county charters have made changes in the responsibilities of constitutional officers, ranging from totally eliminating elected officials (e.g., Dade) to abolishing one or more constitutionally elected offices and shifting their duties to administrative units under the county manager or administrator (e.g., Broward and Volusia). These kinds of changes permit county governments to reallocate revenues and rethink spending priorities and may radically improve organizational efficiency by eliminating duplication of managerial and financial functions.

While only a limited number of counties have successfully used charters as a means to eliminate the position of constitutional officers, many have used their charters to deal with specific issues. Several counties have shifted from countywide election of county commissioners to a single-member district approach (that is, where one legislator is elected from each commission district). Other counties have created countywide planning councils to supervise regulation of land use. In addition, several charter counties have moved to a countywide approach to financing and planning for transportation programs.

Success in the adoption of county charters hinges on several factors, including the support or neutrality of constitutional officers who may be adversely affected by the change, the effect on the existing powers of the county vis-à-vis cities (or vice versa), and the level of community support. Support for noteworthy changes may materialize only when a crisis brings a community together and results in communitywide education and efforts to reform the county's system of government. An example would be the crisis that occurred in Duval County prior to its consolidation with the City of Jacksonville amid charges of county and city corruption. Oftentimes a county charter is portrayed as a "no change" or "starter" charter, one that alters county government only minimally but provides an opportunity for structural and functional change in the future. Presenting a charter as a "no change" document may lessen the political conflict over its adoption.

Municipal Governments

From a purely legal perspective, cities in Florida are municipal corporations that have been granted charters from the state government delineating their boundaries, governmental powers and functions, structure and organization, methods of finance, and authority to elect and appoint officials and employees. In a sense, the state's grant of a charter to a community may be viewed as a license to operate as a city (officially called a municipality). However, the powers of self-government granted by the municipal charter are not unlimited. Under Florida's constitutional home rule provisions, Florida municipalities may "perform municipal functions and provide municipal services, and may exercise any power for municipal purposes except as otherwise provided by [state] law (Florida Constitution, Article VIII, Section 2(b))." The Florida legislature reinforced this limitation of municipal powers when it enacted the Municipal Home Rule Powers Act in 1973.

Charters grant municipalities in Florida a considerable amount of latitude in how they govern and provide services to residents. That is, they have discretion except as limited by law in almost every arena except taxation, where the constitution restricts their authority. In addition, municipalities are normally responsible to enforce state law within their boundaries and have the power to make local laws (called ordinances) that operate only within their boundaries.

Municipal Services

Florida's municipalities have always provided a menu of staple services that typically are not available to residents of unincorporated areas. The range of municipal services varies with the size of the city. Most all of Florida's 412 cities, regardless of size, provide police and fire services, utilities (e.g., water, sewer, etc.), parks and recreational facilities, and garbage collection, and maintain sidewalks, city streets and rights of way. Medium- to large-size cities are likely to provide environmental protection, planning, zoning, growth management, solid and hazardous waste disposal, airports, mass transit, housing and community development, consumer protection, neighborhood beautification, sports stadiums, theaters, museums, cultural centers, golf courses, tennis courts, and marinas. Over thirty municipalities provide electrical services through their own power utilities (e.g., Tallahassee, Jacksonville, Orlando, Gainesville, Lakeland, Bartow). At one time, several large municipalities (e.g., Tampa, Miami, Jacksonville, Tallahassee) operated city hospitals, but in the 1980s, they began to turn over control of these facilities to special districts or legislative authorities because of the high cost of malpractice insurance.

Structure of Municipal Government

Municipalities in Florida can choose between a mayor-commission (mayor-council) and a commission-manager (council-manager) type of government. The first option can be divided into two types. In the mayor-commission or mayor-council structure, the methods of selecting a mayor and extent of his or her powers vary. Under the weak mayor-commission system, commissioners choose one of their fellow commissioners to serve as mayor, often for a one-year term. The mayor presides over the commission but exercises no executive powers separate from the commission's power other than special duties that are primarily ceremonial. In a strong mayor-commission system (in which the mayor is directly elected), executive and legislative responsibilities are split: the mayor serves as the chief executive and occasionally appoints a chief administrative officer, and the commission is in charge of legislative matters. The mayor appoints department heads—often subject to the approval of the commission—and typically has the power to veto ordinances the commission adopts. The municipal charter spells out these and other powers and duties of the mayor and commission.

The commission-manager (or council-manager) plan, which is based on recommendations made by advocates for national municipal reform in the United States in the late 19th and early 20th centuries, attempts to separate the policy-making and administrative functions of city government. The commission appoints a city manager as chief administrator for the city, who serves at the pleasure of the elected commissioners and (through them) the public. The manager has day-to-day flexibility to implement council policy, administer city services, execute the city budget, and enforce city ordinances in a professional nonpartisan manner. The administrative bureaucracy is headed by a professionally trained manager rather than the mayor or council. Some commission-manager cities have an independently elected mayor as well as a city manager. Often in commission-manager systems, the municipal charter spells out the relationship of commission members and city employees, describing the separation of the political and administrative functions.

Regardless of the type of structural arrangement municipalities adopt, both commissioners (or council members) and separately elected mayors serve four-year terms with no limit on reelection and can be elected on either a partisan or nonpartisan ballot; most cities hold partisan elections.

Table 10.1. Population and Forms of Municipal Government in Florida, 2007

Population	Commission/ Strong Mayor	Commission/ Weak Mayor	Commission	Commission/ Manager	Hybrid	Total
Under 1,000	7	60	1	18	0	86
1,000–2,499	11	18	3	21	0	53
2,500–4,999	6	17	3	30	3	59
5,000–9,999	2	4	1	47	0	54
10,000–24,999	3	2	0	72	0	77
25,000–49,999	1	0	0	37	0	38
50,000–100,000	2	1	0	25	0	28
Over 100,000	6	0	0	11	0	17
Total	38	102	8	261	3	412

Source: Lynn Tipton, Florida League of Cities, June 14, 2007.

Commission (or council) members whose terms are staggered can be elected on either an at-large or district basis, although a number of municipalities use a combination (or mixed) system.

As Table 10.1 indicates, the council-manager system is the most popular form of municipal government among Florida municipalities. Newer and medium-size municipalities prefer the council-manager plan that relies on professional administration rather than political factions and adapts easily to the changing conditions rapid growth brings (DeGrove and Turner 1998). The smallest municipalities in Florida are less likely to have adopted the city manager system; they usually opt for the weak mayor-commission plan, in which the mayor usually serves part-time and a city clerk or a coordinator carries out the few functions of city government. However, a considerable number of these smaller jurisdictions (especially those with a higher proportion of residents with money and some college education) use the city manager system.

Six of the largest cities in Florida (Orlando, Tampa, Miami, St. Petersburg, Hialeah, and consolidated Jacksonville) have adopted a strong mayor system but may appoint a chief administrative official who is directly accountable to the mayor. Several other large cities, particularly those in densely populated urban areas (Fort Lauderdale and Hollywood) have opted for the city manager system. The smallest cities with city managers tend to use them as generalists who can administer a city efficiently without having to create a large bureaucracy of specialists.

Municipal Reorganization and Boundary Change

The successful reorganization efforts of Florida counties—Miami-Dade County in 1957 and Jacksonville-Duval County in 1968—attracted great attention nationally (Sofen 1963; Martin 1990). The Dade County reorganization is called a modified two-tier or federated system because the county is the sole provider of services in the unincorporated areas. Twenty-six municipalities still provide services, and those areas have two levels of government. Dade County has abolished the office of sheriff and other constitutional officers and placed all of them under the county manager. Its county commission is made up of nine members elected at large. A ceremonial mayor (that is, one who officially represents the county at major functions but has no more power than other members of the commission) is elected at large presides over the commission. This system was adopted in 1957 through an amendment to the Florida constitution that brought about a home rule charter with features that even present-day home rule counties are not allowed to have.

Dade County's charter empowers it to "set reasonable minimum standards for all governmental units in the county for the performance of any service or function." Where minimum standards are set, cities cannot choose to forego a service or set a lower standard. They can only choose to meet the standards or transfer the service to the county. "Metro," as the Dade County government is known, also has the power to abolish special districts and in fact exercised this power in the case of the Miami Housing Authority. The charter also has elastic clauses that give the county the authority to do everything necessary to carry out the work of a central metropolitan government and go beyond its specified powers. Municipalities are not allowed to expand and annex new territory. New cities can incorporate, though, and since 1990, nine cities in the county have done so.

Dade County's responsibilities are much wider than those of most counties. Many functions performed by special districts and legislatively created service authorities in other counties are part of the Dade County government. The Miami International Airport and the Port of Miami are examples. The county government rather than independent authorities directly controls mass transit and hospitals; this contrasts with how most other counties in Florida administer transportation and health care. In September 1997, voters defeated a referendum to dissolve the city of Miami. Dissolution would have had the effect of fully consolidating the city with the unincorporated territory Metro-Dade County governs.

The Jacksonville-Duval County consolidated government was adopted in 1967 by local popular vote and placed in the state constitution. The Jacksonville consolidation charter features a strong mayor who appoints all executive officials except the county sheriff. The charter includes a 21-member council elected by district and two distinct areas of property taxation (one for the urban core and one for the outlying previously unincorporated areas). All county elected constitutional officers including the sheriff were retained. Six small preexisting cities have been allowed to exist but not expand. The new system has been very popular with most voters. Jacksonville had been facing severe difficulties (a polluted river, discredited schools, local politicians who were suing each other), and the contrast in government effectiveness since the charter was instituted could not be more pronounced. Yet total spending, spending for public safety (i.e., police and fire), and taxes over fourteen years have not been affected by the consolidation (Benton and Gamble 1984). Furthermore, the unified approach of the consolidated government has enabled it to get more federal aid and recruit businesses and an NFL franchise.

Incorporation and Annexation

The land boom of the 1920s created a first wave of incorporations, but it ended with the crash in land values in 1926 and the onset of the Great Depression several years later. Many newly created municipalities incurred huge debts and struggled to remain solvent. A second wave of incorporations took place after 1945 as service people who had been stationed in Florida during World War II settled in new cities. Miami and the surrounding area boomed, and many new municipalities were created both in Dade and Broward counties. A third wave took place after 1962, but it was already running out of steam by the early 1970s, when the legislature changed the rules of incorporation and made it more difficult to create new cities.

Only four new cities were created through the end of the 1980s, but twenty-three new municipalities have incorporated since 1990, most of which are in the southeastern part of the state. Two new municipalities were incorporated from private homeowner developments (Wellington in Palm Beach County and Weston in Broward County), while two others (Palm Coast in Flagler County and Deltona in Volusia County) were incorporated from community development districts after their county governments could not provide adequate services to them. Nine new municipalities emerged in Dade County (Key Biscayne, Aventura, Pinecrest, Sunny Isles Beach, Miami Lakes, Palmetto Bay, Doral, Miami Gardens, and Cutler Ridge); these cities elected to incorporate rather than rely on the Metro-Dade service delivery system. Another three new municipalities (DeBary, Fort Myers Beach, and Southwest Ranches) used incorporation as a means to replace countywide comprehensive plans with plans tailored to their unique communities. Palm Beach County has the most municipalities with thirty-eight, followed by

Dade and Broward Counties, with thirty-five and thirty-one municipalities, respectively.

Annexation statutes in Florida make it difficult for existing cities to annex territory unless the land is almost uninhabited or is owned by only a few individuals. In all cases, the law requires that a majority of the voters in the area to be annexed approve of the proposed annexation. As is the case elsewhere, majority approval does not happen often. Nonetheless, the device of voluntary annexation, which permits 100 percent of the owners of certain lands to petition for annexation, circumvents the requirement of voter approval. Rules about voluntary annexation expressly forbid the creation of "enclaves," "islands," or "fingers," yet these rules are routinely ignored, even in interpretations by the state attorney general. Cities use the device of voluntary annexation to bargain with owners and future developers of unsettled territory. The bargaining may include giving special permission for higher population densities for future developments or special districts that may make the area more attractive to high-income homeowners or investors. Wealthy enclaves may thus emerge just as easily within cities as they might through incorporation. Residents in these areas may pay slightly higher taxes.

Special-District Governments

Special districts are the most widely used form of government in Florida; 626 have been created to date. A special-district government is a mechanism to permit a service to be provided in a geographical area that (supposedly) uniquely fits the service requirements and at the same time the tax burden to those who receive the service. This form of local government, while not authorized by any specific part of the Florida constitution, is recognized and implicitly authorized by a number of references in articles that pertain to finance and taxation and local government.

There are two types of special districts—ones that operate on a regional basis and ones that are confined to a county or city or some portion of them. Regional (or intergovernmental or metropolitan-wide) special districts can offer a limited solution to the problem of fragmented government by operating across county or city boundaries. They are especially useful where urban problems spill beyond traditional legal jurisdictional lines and cannot be solved by counties or cities acting on an individual basis. This is likely the case for issues related to pollution, transportation, housing, and deteriorating infrastructure. Consequently, a number of regional-type districts have been created with a singular focus on soil and water conservation, mass transit, community development, and drainage and flood control.

The most common type of special district is created to transfer direct responsibility for a function from a city or county to a district. Counties often use this device to ensure that municipal services (e.g., fire protection, water supply, sewage, solid waste collection, parks and recreation) are available to densely populated unincorporated areas. Some cities have chosen to use special districts to perform urban-type functions that they are no longer willing or able to handle financially (e.g., airports, hospitals, urban renewal, construction and operation of sports facilities, solid waste management, parking, and low-income housing).

Special districts are popular for a number of reasons. The most obvious is that they provide a means to provide desirable and needed services. In addition, special districts can collect their own revenue (e.g., state and federal grants, charges for services, fees, taxes, rent) and spend money and conduct operations without the oversight of county or city officials. Special districts and authorities can also issue their own revenue bonds, and the resulting indebtedness does not count against any county or city debt limits. In addition, districts that are granted taxing authority can piggyback their bill for property taxes onto the tax bill sent out each year by the county tax collector. Under this arrangement, county and city commissioners (or council members) are insulated from the potential political fallout from these additional taxes. And perhaps more important, it permits the combined local governments in an area to exceed the 10-mill tax limit to which each county and each municipality is subject under the state constitution (see Article VII, Section 4).

The governing structure of special districts and authorities varies considerably. Most are governed by boards whose members are appointed by the cities and counties in which the district or authority operates or are city or county officials who sit on boards as ex officio members (Dye 1998, 162). The governor typically has the power to appoint some of the members of metropolitan-wide districts or authorities. In some instances (particularly community development districts), the public may elect board members.

Special districts or authorities may create more problems than they solve, however. Once established, district or authority boards or commissioners, whose members for the most part are appointed, often operate on a quasi-independent basis and seem immune to public pressure for change. This situation can be exacerbated when a board or commission hires a professional administrator, who is largely out of the public spotlight, to oversee district operations. Professional administrators, who are often not connected to popular control and close political responsibility, often wield immense power over a service that is being provided. The structure and selection of boards or commissions as well as the manner in which districts and authorities operate often confuses the public and makes it difficult for the average citizen or other local governments within the district's jurisdiction to hold districts or their officials accountable for their decisions.

Local Government Services

Local governments in Florida provide three basic types of services—traditional, municipal-type, and regional- or urban-type. Traditional services are some of the oldest and most familiar services local governments provide and include such broad functions as maintaining roads and highways, protecting the public welfare, providing health care and hospitals, providing police protection, operating and overseeing corrections, operating a judicial/legal system, maintaining public buildings, and administering finances. Counties historically have provided many of these services, which are usually mandated by the state. Municipal-type services include providing utilities (e.g., water supply, electric power, and natural gas), fire protection, libraries, and a host of consumer or protective inspections (e.g., food, building, mechanical, and safety inspections). Regional- or urban-type services include airports, mass transit, public parking facilities, sewage treatment, solid waste disposal, water and air pollution control, natural resource conservation and environmental protection, housing and community development, parks and recreational facilities, and water transportation and terminals. Residents of highly urbanized, densely populated areas expect these services. They have also typically been associated with the list of services municipalities provide.

Since the early 1960s, local governments in Florida have been sorting out which branch of government is responsible to provide which services. How have Florida's counties, municipalities, and special districts sorted out who is responsible to provide a large and increasing menu of services in an ever-changing environment? That is, do counties, municipalities, and special districts provide the same services they have always provided or has there been a shifting of responsibility for service among these local governments?

Traditional Services

In 1962, counties in Florida were the major providers of traditional services; counties accounted for 53 percent of all local government expenditures in

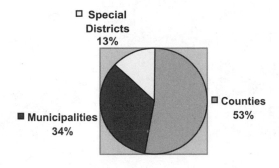

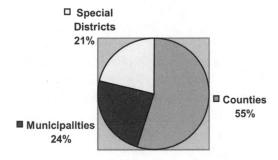

Figure 10.1. Local Government Providers of Traditional Services in Florida by Proportion, 1962 and 2002. *Source:* U.S. Bureau of the Census, 2002 Census of Governments, *Compendium of Government Finances.* Washington, D.C.: Government Printing Office, 2005.

this area (see Figure 10.1). Municipalities accounted for the second largest proportion (34 percent), and special districts accounted for the remaining 13 percent. In 2002, counties were still the major providers of traditional services; 55 percent of all local government spending for these type services was attributable to counties. However, the roles of municipalities and special districts as providers of traditional services had changed markedly by 2002. Municipalities were accounting for a smaller proportion of local government spending for traditional services (34 percent in 1962 versus 24 percent in 2002), while the special-district proportion had increased noticeably from 13 to 21 percent. This means that special districts now rival municipalities as deliverers of traditional services.

County governments continue to play an important role in the delivery of traditional services, as evidenced by the fact that counties still account for a

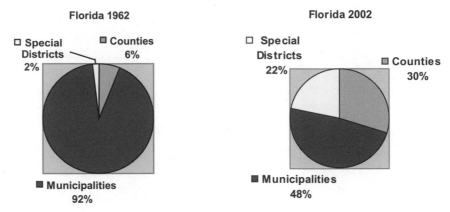

Figure 10.2. Local Government Providers of Municipal-Type Services in Florida by Proportion, 1962 and 2002. *Source:* U.S. Bureau of the Census, 2002 Census of Governments, *Compendium of Government Finances.* Washington, D.C.: Government Printing Office, 2005.

significant proportion of all local government spending for the most costly traditional services—public welfare (74 percent), health care other than in hospitals (83 percent), judicial/legal (90 percent), corrections (100 percent), highways (66 percent), and financial administration (78 percent)(U.S. Bureau of the Census, 2005). The county share of hospital expenditures, however, declined somewhat from 1962 to 2002, as did the share municipalities pay for this service. By 2002, the county share of police expenditures exceeded that of municipalities (53 percent for counties; 47 percent for municipalities). The municipal share of local government spending in several other service areas (health care other than in hospitals, judicial/legal, corrections, hospitals, highways, and financial administration) also declined noticeably between 1962 and 2002. Special districts now play an enhanced role in providing traditional services because they have assumed responsibility for the operation of former city and county hospitals and, to a lesser extent, because they have begun to participate in the delivery of public welfare and health care services (other than in hospitals).

Municipal-Type Services

Municipalities in Florida—like municipal governments nationally—were the dominant providers of municipal-type services in 1962 (see Figure 10.2). In fact, municipalities accounted for an overwhelming proportion of total local government spending for municipal-type services—92 percent. Counties and special districts accounted for only 6 and 2 percent, respectively. However, dramatic changes in the roles counties, municipalities, and special districts play in the delivery of municipal-type services occurred between 1962 and 2002. In 2002, municipalities accounted for less than half (48 percent) of all local government expenditures for municipal-type services, while the share counties and special districts contributed to the provision of these services had increased substantially. By 2002, counties were responsible for 30 percent of all municipal-type spending, and special districts accounted for another 22 percent. Simply stated, in 2002, counties and special districts collectively were spending more to provide municipal-type services than municipalities were.

These sharp changes in financial responsibility for municipal-type services are also reflected in individual government spending proportions for the four specific service areas included in this category. Over the period 1962 to 2002, the county share of local government expenditures jumped significantly for libraries (from 9 to 76 percent), fire protection (from 2 to 42 percent), and utilities (from 6 to 23 percent). In 2002, counties also accounted for 54 percent of all spending for protective inspections.[8] The special district share for utilities increased markedly from 2 to 27 percent between 1962 to 2002. The proportion special districts contributed to fire protection and libraries increased modestly—that is, from 2 to 8 percent and from 0 to 3 percent, respectively. While municipalities were spending more money for each of these services in 2002 than they were in 1962, the municipal share of local expenditures decreased drastically for each of them—that is, from 96 to 50 percent for fire protection, from 91 to 21 percent for libraries, and from 92 to 50 percent for utilities.

Urban-Type or Regional Services

Municipalities were also the major providers of urban-type (regional) services in 1962 (see Figure 10.3). Municipalities accounted for almost two-thirds (62 percent) of total local government expenditures in this area. In contrast, counties contributed 23 percent to the delivery of urban-type services. Special districts were responsible for the remaining 15 percent of local government spending for urban-type services. By 2002, the roles of municipalities and counties in the provision of urban-type services had been reversed; counties had replaced municipalities as the most important providers of these services, accounting for 47 percent of all local government spending in this area. The municipal proportion of total local government spending for urban-type functions was only about half of what it was in 1962 (i.e., 34 percent in 2002; 62 percent in 1962). The proportion special

Florida 1962

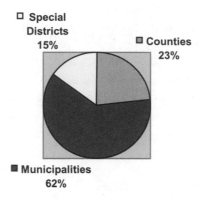

□ Special
Districts
15%

▣ Counties
23%

■ Municipalities
62%

Florida 2002

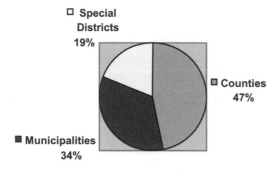

□ Special
Districts
19%

▣ Counties
47%

■ Municipalities
34%

Figure 10.3. Local Government Providers of Urban-Type Services in Florida by Proportion, 1962 and 2002. *Source:* U.S. Bureau of the Census, 2002 Census of Governments, *Compendium of Government Finances.* Washington, D.C.: Government Printing Office, 2005.

districts contributed to urban-type functions had increased slightly from 15 to 19 percent.

County governments were playing a greater role in several specific service areas by 2002. For example, the county portion of total local government expenditures for sanitation increased from 10 to 60 percent between 1962 and 2002, and it rose from 0 to 57 percent for mass transit. Other significant increases took place in the categories of sewage (from 11 to 46 percent), housing/urban development (from 0 to 35 percent), and parks and recreation (from 17 to 43 percent). Counties also continued to be responsible for the largest proportion of local government dollars spent for airports (69 percent) and for such things as marinas, docks and shipping terminals, and water ferries (54 percent). Yet municipalities still accounted for a larger proportion than counties did for sewage (50 versus 46 percent) and parks and recreation (56 versus 43 percent) and accounted for almost all local government funds expended for parking facilities. While significant shifts in the roles municipalities and counties play were occurring in a number of service areas between 1962 and 2002, special districts maintained their position as the major providers of housing/urban development services and services for natural resource conservation and environmental protection. The proportion special districts contributed for these two service areas was 40 and 62 percent, respectively. In addition, special districts have been playing a larger role in the construction and operation of airports in recent years, accounting for 22 percent of total local government expenditures in 2002, compared to only 1 percent in 1962.

Explaining Changes in Service Responsibilities

A number of factors seem to have been responsible for the changes in the roles counties, municipalities, and special districts play in the provision of traditional, municipal-type, and urban-type services since the early 1960s. The rapid increase in the state's population is a key factor, but even more important has been where people in Florida have chosen to live. In 1960, approximately two out of every three Floridians (68 percent) lived in municipalities; the remaining 32 percent resided in the unincorporated areas of the state. Over the last forty years, living patterns have changed; now 51 percent of all Floridians live in unincorporated areas.[9] Municipalities are no longer the main providers of such services as fire protection, libraries, utilities, and a number of protective and safety inspections. Residents of unincorporated areas are now demanding that these services, once usually only available to city dwellers, be provided to them. Municipalities are still important players in the provision of these services, but not to the extent they were four decades ago.

The rapid growth in Florida's population has also resulted in greater urbanization. Sometimes it is nearly impossible to distinguish where a city ends and the unincorporated area of a county begins (e.g., where the city of Tampa ends and where unincorporated Hillsborough County begins as one is driving out of the city) or where one municipality ends and another municipality starts (as one drives from the city of St. Petersburg to Gulfport to Pinellas Park to Seminole, for example). Issues such as traffic control and signalization, housing and urban redevelopment, sewage disposal, solid waste management, environmental protection, parks and recreation, and air transportation know no political or jurisdictional boundaries. These and other urban-type problems often defy a one- or two-city or even a one-county solution. A government with legal authority to fashion comprehensive or regional solutions is needed to effectively address vexing urban-type problems. More and more, this has meant that Floridians are looking to their county governments to provide urban-type services directly or for their counties to establish special districts for these purposes; municipalities are the last choice among residents for delivery of these services.

Another reason that municipalities play a smaller role as providers of urban-type services is because they have been unwilling or unable to provide newer services (e.g., mass transit, urban renewal, environmental protection) or to continue providing services for which they once were responsible. The declining role of municipalities in providing services at airports or for parks and recreation is a case in point. Why should a city continue to provide these kinds of services when a majority of the users live in the unincorporated areas of counties and do not pay city taxes to support them? Furthermore, the growing fiscal problems of some of the state's largest and oldest cities has meant that they can no longer bear the financial burden of providing costly urban-type services.

The greater availability of federal grants-in-aid as well as the exponential growth in federal and state mandates can also help explain the greater involvement of all local governments in several service areas, especially the larger roles of counties and, at times, special districts. The growth of federal entitlement programs has led to a greater role for counties in the areas of public welfare and health care, while a combination of federal aid and federal and state mandates are largely responsible for a bigger role for counties and special districts in areas such as sanitation and solid waste management, sewage treatment and disposal, housing/urban redevelopment, and mass transit.

The greater involvement of county governments in all service areas—but particularly in the provision of municipal- and urban-type services—is also attributable to efforts to modernize the structure and operations of county governments. County governments were created primarily to deliver traditional services; they were never intended to provide municipal- and urban-type services and become full-service local governments like municipalities. As a way to reinvent themselves and be better able to provide a wider menu of traditional services and undertake a variety of municipal- and urban-type services, many counties in Florida have adopted more modern forms of structure and operating procedures. For instance, county governments now routinely employ an administrator who is in charge of running day-to-day operations, implementing policy decisions, and developing plans to expand services. A smaller number of counties (nineteen at this writing) have adopted home rule charters that give them much greater latitude to raise the larger sums of money they need to finance additional services or expand older ones. In fact, two recent studies (Benton 2003a, 2003b) report a statistically significant relationship between counties that have modernized in Florida (that is, those that have an administrator and a charter) and 1) the ability to raise additional revenue to expand the level and menu of services, and 2) increased spending for traditional and urban-type services. In addition, the legislature and the courts have facilitated the expansion of the service role of counties by providing mechanisms such as municipal services taxing units.

Arrangements for Delivery of Services

Local governments in Florida are responsible for producing a long list of services, meaning that they must make sure that these services are available to the public. However, *production* is different from *provision*. Whenever Florida local governments provide a service, they typically elect to do so by using an existing department or by creating a new one (that is, in-house provision). However, they may choose some alternative arrangement for delivering these services (for example, through contracts with other service providers or franchises or through interlocal agreements). Inadequate attention has been paid to the issue of how local governments in Florida choose to deliver services. Benton and Menzel (1992) conducted a systematic inventory of service provision and production arrangements for counties, but no similar research has been done at the municipal level.

While local governments can choose from a large range of options to deliver services, the four primary categories are in-house production, contracts with for-profit service vendors, service contracts with nonprofit organizations, and interlocal agreements with neighboring local government units. In Florida, like most states, contracting out to for-profit firms is the most controversial arrangement for producing services. Contracts with for-profits can reduce costs because of the generally lower wage and benefit levels in the private sector. Municipalities are likely to be involved in privatization because local services tend to be the more mundane routine tasks such as collecting garbage, maintaining roads, and providing legal services. Nevertheless, because the outcomes of public services are difficult to measure, private firms have incentives to act opportunistically. The profit motive creates incentives for efficient production, but it may also motivate firms to cut corners in various ways, including limiting access to services or allowing the quality of services that are costly to produce to decline.

Contracting out with private firms is fundamentally different from contracting out with nonprofit organizations or other units of government. Contracts with nonprofit organizations are particularly popular for social and human services because it is typically difficult to define, measure, and monitor the quality of these services (Jang 2006). Moreover, consumers tend to trust nonprofit providers more than profit-seeking enterprises because they fear that profit-seekers will exploit information advantages that result from the difficulty in measuring service outcomes to shortchange consumers.

Service contracts or interlocal agreements with other local government units are ubiquitous in Florida. Intergovernmental service production can take a variety of forms, ranging from formal service contracts to memoranda of understanding, mutual aid agreements, and informal "handshake" agreements (U.S. ACIR 1985, 1). Interlocal agreements are authorized and encouraged by the Inter-local Cooperation Act of 1969 (Florida Statutes, section 163.01), which provides a broad legal framework for local governments to work together and reduces the risk of litigation (Andrew 2005). Florida's 1985 Growth Management Act also requires an "intergovernmental coordination element" in the comprehensive plans of local governments. Andrew (2005) has identified 2,251 different types of contractual arrangements to provide public safety in thirty-three county governments.

Conclusion

Counties, municipalities, and special districts are destined to continue to have significant and expanding roles as instruments of local governance and service deliverers to Florida's burgeoning population. Approximately 1,000 new residents move to Florida every day, making it the third-fastest-growing state in the nation. Florida's local governments are certain to be challenged in their quest to provide more and better services for this rapidly growing population. But population increase alone will not be the only reason for the continuing—indeed, increasing—importance of local governments in the Sunshine State. Devolution of responsibilities by federal and state governments, the continued flow of federal and state aid, the persistence of federal and state mandates, the preference of many citizens for local government action, and even international concerns related to terrorism and global warming will keep local governments alive and well in the twenty-first century.

However, it is likely that the roles various local governments play as service providers will continue to evolve and change. Counties and special districts are expected to initiate new services and programs and expand their roles as service deliverers into areas that historically were reserved for municipalities, while counties will probably continue to function in their time-honored role as administrative arms of the state. In this regard, it will be interesting to note the extent to which local governments in Florida will rely on nonprofit organizations or resort to various forms of privatization, intergovernmental agreements, co-production arrangements, and volunteerism to augment how they deliver staple and new services.

Notes

1. Townships, a fourth unit of local government, are commonly found in New England and parts of the Midwest.

2. In 1968, Duval County and the City of Jacksonville consolidated to form one government that was designated the City of Jacksonville. However, Duval County is counted here as one of sixty-seven counties and the city of Jacksonville as one of 412 cities, although the U.S. Bureau of the Census recognizes Jacksonville only as a municipal government.

3. Home rule typically refers to the power of local communities to choose their own form of government, provide services, tax their residents, and exercise governmental powers not specifically denied them by state law.

4. The specific legally adopted document that permits local governments to exercise self-determination.

5. In Alaska, they are called boroughs, while in Louisiana they are referred to as parishes. Rhode Island and Connecticut originally established counties but abolished them in 1842 and 1958, respectively, and since 1997, Massachusetts has abolished seven of its twelve counties.

6. This includes all nineteen of the charter counties.

7. However, state legislators continue to hold a reservoir of local power. Since state law supersedes county ordinances, legislators have the power to reverse county actions.

8. There is no comparison with 1962, since the *Compendium of Government Finances* of the U.S. Bureau of the Census did not report data on this service area at that time.

9. Demographers project that an even smaller proportion of Floridians will be living in municipalities by 2020 and that between 55 and 60 percent of the state's population will be living in unincorporated areas. This would help explain the greater role counties (and, in some cases, special districts) now play in delivering municipal-type services.

References

Andrew, Simon A. 2005. "Inter-local Contractual Arrangements in the Provision of Public Safety." Paper presented at Creating Collaborative Communities: Management Networks, Services Cooperation, and Metropolitan Governance, Wayne State University, Detroit, October 31, 2005.

Benton, J. Edwin. 2002. *Counties as Service Delivery Agents: Changing Expectations and Roles*. New York: Praeger.

———. 2003a. "County Government Structure and County Revenue Policy: What's the Connection?" *State and Local Government Review* 35:78–89.

———. 2003b. "The Impact of Structural Reform on County Government Service Provision." *Social Science Quarterly* 84, no. 4: 858–74.

Benton, J. Edwin, and Darwin B. Gamble. 1984. "City/County Consolidation and Economies of Scale: Evidence from a Time-Series Analysis in Jacksonville." *Social Science Quarterly* 65, no. 1: 190–98.

Benton, J. Edwin, and Donald C. Menzel. 1991. "County Service Trends and Practices: The Case of Florida." *State and Local Government Review* 23:69–75.

———. 1992. "Contracting and Franchising County Services in Florida." *Urban Affairs Quarterly* 27:436–56.

———. 1993. "County Services: The Emergence of Full-Service Governments." In *County Governments in an Era of Change*, edited by David R. Berman. 53–69. Westport, Conn.: Greenwood Press.

DeGrove, John, and Robyn Turner. 1998. "Florida. Local Government: Coping with Massive and Sustained Growth." In *Government and Politics in Florida*, edited by Robert J. Huckshorn. 2nd ed. 169–92. Gainesville: University Press of Florida.

Dye, Thomas R. 1998. *Politics in Florida*. Upper Saddle River, N.J.: Prentice Hall.

Jang, HeeSoun. 2006. "Contracting Out Local Government Services to Nonprofit Organizations." *International Journal of Public Administration* 29:799–818.

Martin, Larry. 1990. "States and Counties: Adversaries or Partners? The Florida Perspective." Paper presented at the Annual Conference of the American Society for Public Administration, Los Angeles, Calif., April 7–11.

Menzel, Donald C., and J. Edwin Benton. 1991. "Service Trends and Practices in Florida Counties." *Journal of STAR Research* 1:16–37.

Salant, Tanis J. 1991. "County Governments: An Overview." *Intergovernmental Perspective* 17 (Winter): 5–7.

Sofen, Edward. 1963. *The Miami Metropolitan Experiment*. Bloomington: Indiana University Press.

U.S. Advisory Commission on Intergovernmental Relations. 1985. *Intergovernmental Service Agreements for Delivering Local Public Services: Update 1983* (A-103).

U.S. Bureau of the Census. 2003. *2002 Census of Governments*. Vol. 1-1. *Government Organization*. Washington, D.C.: Government Printing Office.

U.S. Bureau of the Census, 2005. *2002 Census of Governments, Compendium of Government Finances*. Washington, D.C.: Government Printing Office.

11

Intergovernmental Relations in Florida

ROBERT B. BRADLEY AND J. EDWIN BENTON

Intergovernmental relations (hereafter referred to as IGR) involve and result from the formal and informal interactions and activities of governments and their officials. In the United States, this encompasses the activities of and interactions between and among governmental units of all types and levels within the U.S. federal system—that is, national, state, and local. Therefore, one could envision several distinct IGR scenarios: national-state-local relations, national-state relations, national-local relations, state-local relations, interstate relations (that is, relations between two or more state governments), and interlocal relations (that is, relations between various local governments). From a national perspective, the potential exists for many opportunities for various combinations of governments to work together to develop, fund, and implement public policies. Even if we focus only on Florida, one can image a seemingly infinite number of possibilities for officials of the national (federal) government, the state government, and local governments in Florida (67 counties, 412 municipalities, 67 school districts, and 750 special districts) to come into contact and interact with one another.

The Setting of IGR

In order to understand how IGR plays out nationally as well as in Florida, it is instructive to look at the setting within which this happens. An important part of the context of IGR is the number and growth of governmental units. In 2002, the *Government Organization* report of the *U.S. Census of Governments* (U.S. Bureau of the Census 2002) identified almost 88,000 independent governmental units in the United States. The federal and fifty state governments were just a small portion of the total; most were local governments. However, less than half of all local governments were formed to serve a broad range of general functions; these included counties, municipalities, and townships. In all, there were 3,034 county governments, over 19,400 municipalities, and approximately 16,500 townships in the United States.

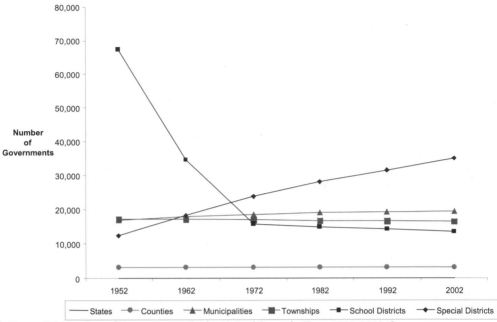

Figure 11.1. Number of Governments in the United States by Type, 1952–2002. *Source*: U.S. Census, *Statistical Abstract of the United States, 2003*, no. 421, p. 276.

Most local governments were special-purpose governments, designed with enough administrative and fiscal authority to qualify as separate governments that fulfill a limited number of designated functions. Across the nation, these included over 13,500 school districts and more than 35,000 special districts.[1]

Over the last half-century, the number of units in the intergovernmental system in the United States has changed. As Figure 11.1 demonstrates, the number of general-purpose governments (that is, municipalities and counties) has remained relatively the same since the 1950s. However, there was considerable change in the number of special-purpose governments in that period. Between 1952 and 1972, the number of independent school districts dropped dramatically. That decline has continued since 1972, but at a much slower pace. The number of school districts is 20 percent of what it was in the early 1950s. The number of independent special districts, on the other hand, has almost tripled in that time. Such districts typically provide a single service. Sometimes they are regional governments that provide a service for broad swaths of counties and municipalities. Other times, they are narrowly confined, occasionally serving only a few blocks within a city. Their activities range from providing water and fire protection to sewer collection/disposal to libraries and even to low-income housing and lighting.

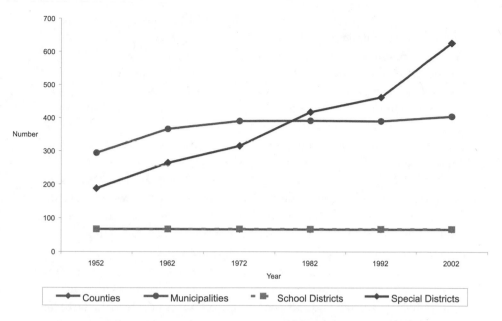

Figure 11.2. Number of Florida Governments by Type, 1952–2002. *Source*: U.S. Census, *Statistical Abstract of the United States, 2003*, no. 422, p. 277.

The number of governments throughout the country and the types of changes that have occurred are impressive. And while the situation in Florida bears some similarities to national trends, there are notable differences. For instance, as of 2002, Florida—the fourth most populous state in the nation—ranked 25th among the states in number of local governments; it has 1,192.[2] The state has 66 counties, 1 city-county consolidated government (Jacksonville-Duval), 412 municipalities, 67 school districts, 28 community college districts, and 626 independent special districts. Since 2002, 6 new municipalities have been incorporated, while around 150 new special districts have been created.

Furthermore, the pattern of change in Florida does not mirror that of the nation. Since the establishment of Gilchrist, Gulf, Martin, and Indian River counties in 1925, the number of counties in the state has remained the same. And since the boundaries of school districts in Florida are co-terminal with county boundaries, no new school districts have been created. Florida law does not allow townships, but the number of municipalities has grown. The state registered an increase of seventy municipalities in the 1950s, forty-four in the 1960s, and twenty-six in the last fifteen years. Figure 11.2 shows that special districts account for the greatest growth among types of local governments; their number has almost quadrupled since 1952.

A second part of the context of IGR that must be considered is people—that is, the key public officials who strongly influence the direction of IGR actions. The *human* as opposed to the *governmental* aspect of IGR focuses on the actions and attitudes of the persons who hold official positions in the units of government under consideration. As Anderson (1960, 4) aptly put it: "It is human beings clothed with office who are the real determiners of what the relations between units of government will be. Consequently, the concept of intergovernmental relations necessarily has to be formulated largely in terms of human relations and human behavior." From this, we, like Wright (1988, 17), must conclude that in reality "there are no relationships among *governments*; there are only relations among *officials* who govern different units." Simply put, the singular and collective actions and attitudes of public officials are the heart of IGR. Their actions are heavily influenced by how they perceive the actions and attitudes of other IGR participants.

To get a sense of the importance of the human aspect of IGR, it is useful for us to consider the growth in the number of IGR players, which includes both popularly elected and full-time employed officials. Over the last half-century, the number of elected state and local officials has not changed that much; in 2007, it amounts to approximately 500,000 persons. Nevertheless, the multiplicity of these officials introduces a great deal of variety and complexity into the relationships among the several jurisdictions and planes of government. Not all of the approximately half-million elected officials are important or influential in their relations with officials from other governmental units. However, even a conservative estimate would probably place the number of such elected officials at around 10 percent of this total or 50,000! To this large number, of course, we add the 537 popularly elected national officials—president, vice-president, senators, representatives—plus nine Supreme Court justices and several hundred federal judges. All are significant IGR actors.

Elected officials, obviously, are not the only officials who interact in and play important roles in the intergovernmental arena. In 2002, nearly 18.2 million full-time equivalent (FTE) employees worked for national, state, and local governments. Of that total, state and local governments employed 15.6 million, while the remaining 2.6 million worked for the national government.

While the number of popularly elected officials has remained fairly constant over the last five decades, this has not been the case for full-time equivalent (FTE) employees. Let's examine the trends in public sector expansion with the assistance of Figure 11.3, which charts the FTE employment for

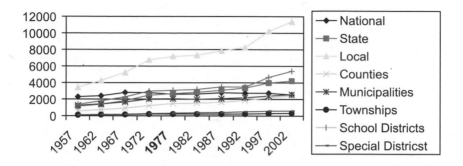

Figure 11.3. Trends in Full-Time Employment in National, State, and Local Governments, 1957–2002 (in millions). *Source:* U.S. Bureau of the Census, 2002 Census of Governments, *Compendium of Public Employment*. Washington, D.C.: Government Printing Office, 2004.

each type of governmental unit from 1957 through 2002. Just like popularly elected officials, these workers fall under Anderson's rubric of "human beings clothed with office." They are actual or potential participants in IGR.

The topmost trend is one of the most striking features in Figure 11.3. In 1957, total local government employment was around 3.5 million (FTE). By 2002, the local government FTE workforce had increased to 11.4 million, or by an average of 5.1 percent per year over this 45-year period. If we disaggregate the top line, we can view the trends for each of the five jurisdictions under the rubric of local government (that is, counties, municipalities, townships, special districts, and school districts). FTE employment in special districts grew at the fastest rate between 1957 and 2002 (around 10 percent per year), although the aggregate number of special-district employees is fairly small when compared to the number of county, municipal, and school district employees. County employment had the next highest growth rate, averaging about 7.5 percent per year. School district and township employment also increased over the last five decades, but at a more modest pace—6.4 and 4.8 percent per year on average, respectively. Municipal FTE employment grew the least—2.3 percent per year on average—over this period.

Who are IGR actors in the United States? First, the list would include all national government officials—that is, popularly elected officials, appointed members of the federal judiciary, and FTE employees. Second, the list would include the nearly 6,000[3] popularly elected and nearly 789,000 state and local government full-time employed officials in the state. In addition, the

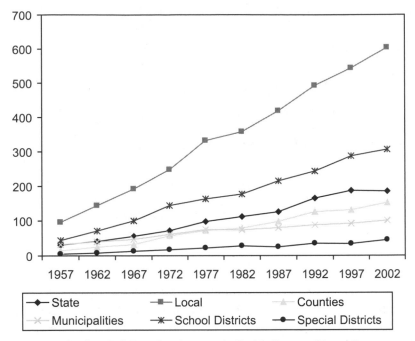

Figure 11.4. Trends in Full-Time Employment in Florida State and Local Governments, 1957–2002 (in thousands). *Source:* U.S. Bureau of the Census, 2002 Census of Governments, *Compendium of Public Employment.* Washington, D.C.: Government Printing Office, 2004.

list could potentially consist of popularly elected and full-time employed officials in the states that might interact with their counterparts in Florida.

While the list of IGR participants in Florida would be smaller, it has grown in size as the state's population has grown over the last five decades. Unlike most other states, the number of popularly elected officials—especially those at the local level—has increased with the growth in the number of municipalities and special districts in the state. And, of course, there has been a significant increase in the number of FTE state and local employees in Florida. This trend is clearly evident from the employment data depicted in Figure 11.4, which illustrates that public-sector employment in the state has grown phenomenally. The FTE workforce at the state level grew from just under 31,000 in 1957 to almost 185,000 by 2002, while the number of local government FTE employees increased from nearly 96,000 in 1957 to over 604,000 by 2002. In short, state and local employment increased six-fold over this 45-year period. While the individual growth rate in county, special and school district, and municipal FTE employment is not as dramatic, the number of county, special district, and school district employees was growing at an annual rate of 21.2, 19.3, and 13.2 percent, respectively. Even the number of municipal FTE employees increased, on average, by about 5 percent per year over this period.

A final part of the IGR context is the constitutional or legal framework of federalism, which sets the tone for what units of governments can (or cannot) do constitutionally or legally and lays the foundation for the types of interaction various units may undertake. The legal relations among the national, state, and local governments are embedded in and flow from the federal model. As a set of relationships, federalism changes over time. As a structure, federalism is the division of power between the individual states and the national government that spells out the authority of local governments within each state. The U.S. Constitution grants relatively elastic powers to the national government. Among other enumerated powers, the Constitution grants Congress the power to "make all Laws which shall be necessary and proper for carrying into Execution [these] Powers." While the supremacy clause of Article 1 of the Constitution limits federal authority, it establishes the Constitution as the supreme law of the land. This binds the judges in every state to the federal constitution, notwithstanding "any Thing in the Constitution or Laws of any State to the Contrary." At the same time, the Tenth Amendment provides that "[t]he powers not delegated to the United States by the Constitution, nor prohibited by it to the States, are reserved to the States respectively, or to the people."

This tension between federal and state authority is integral to the Constitution's design. Geographically distinct governments have overlapping authority. As Bradley and Hosack have noted, "What links state and nation, locality and state is the representation of people in complementary institutions" (1998, 244). Neither level of government can abolish the other. Moreover, policy concerns raised within one level can be redressed at other levels within the federal framework. The concurrent powers that both the federal and state governments hold in areas such as taxation and spending for the general welfare create and allow for overlapping governmental actions. As a consequence, the legal concept of federalism fosters and, in fact, encourages relationships between governments and their officials.

All fifty states also have their own constitutions. Some predate the U.S. Constitution. The Constitution does not require and does not prohibit states from establishing local governments. In fact, local governments often predate state governments. The provisions of state constitutions vary greatly and, like the legal relationships in the U.S. Constitution, have changed over time. The relations between a state and its local governments do not necessarily mirror those between the states and the national government. For instance, the Florida constitution assigns a broad array of power and duties to a variety of local governments that range from municipalities and counties to school districts and special districts. But state and local relations in Florida or in the other forty-nine states are not exempt from national considerations, and the course of state and local relations often echoes developments between the state and the national government. The relations among governments range from compulsory orders, mandated actions, and preemptions to memoranda of understanding, joint agreements, and grants of aid.

Florida has fewer local governments than most states of its size. Texas and Pennsylvania, for example, each have almost 5,000 governments. Likewise, Florida has fewer popularly elected and full-time employed officials than some other states do. The numbers might lead one to the mistaken conclusion that intergovernmental relations are likely to be less confusing in Florida than elsewhere. But neither numbers nor the constitutional and legal framework of the national and state governments determine the structure of IGR. The relations among and between the various levels of government are quite involved and complex, even when just a few governments are involved. Conflict and confrontation are as common as coordination and cooperation. As suggested above, the relations involve the dealings of political leaders and administrative officials, institutional arrangements, and the purposes of the various governments and how governments interpret those aims.

Opportunities for Cooperation and Conflict

Opportunities for cooperation and conflict among governments arise from the overlap of both the geographical division of power and functional authority. States are part of the overall geography of the nation; counties reside within states; municipalities typically fall within counties; and districts can transverse cities and counties. Geography matters. As significant, the functions each of these governments perform within the overall system are not settled. Even traditionally territorial-based services relating to roads, sanitation, water, parks, utilities, public health, education, and personal and property protection can be provided by several overlapping jurisdictions. The same holds true in the area of regulation of the use of property, the exercise of rights, public safety, general welfare, and conditions of aid. Overlapping governments often claim powers, privileges, duties, and responsibilities when concerns emerge; this is equally true in policy arenas that involve the distribution of resources such as unemployment, health care, welfare, concern for the disabled, and treatment of the elderly and in policy areas that involve development and regulation.

Table 11.1 provides some insight into the overlap of functional interests among Florida's governments. In 2002, the various governments in Florida spent slightly more than $95 billion. State government was responsible for the direct provision of services that accounted for almost 39 percent of the total—almost $37 billion. The state's role is especially important in the provision of public welfare, public health, social insurance, veteran's services, highway funding, corrections, and the protection of natural resources. Counties take a leading role in providing for libraries, airports, port facilities, and solid waste management, and municipalities are primary providers of parking, transit, fire protection, parks and recreation, and sewerage. School districts concentrate on education, while special districts are especially significant in providing hospitals and, to a lesser extent, utilities, housing and community development, natural resources, and airports.

Table 11.1 shows that even though each type of government specializes in providing some types of services, other services are not dominated by any single level of government. Cities and counties both provide substantial police protection; both help operate roads; and both, along with the state, are actively involved in inspections of all kinds within their boundaries. The state, counties, and municipalities are all involved in judicial matters. Virtually each type of government is involved to some degree in housing and community development. This broad range of activity and concern gives rise to conflicts and the need for cooperation among the state's governments.

The implications for overlapping authority within a system where the division of power among governments is coupled with geographical representation is best seen in the efforts of governments to share and compete for tax and fee revenues. Revenue can be raised from three main bases of economic activity: income, consumption, and wealth. In Florida, the personal income tax is prohibited by the state constitution, although the state is allowed to levy corporations for income taxes. As a result, governments must raise most of their revenue from taxes on wealth such as personal tangible or intangible property or on consumption such as general sales transactions, regulatory activities, or selective sales activities (see also Chapter 12).

Table 11.2 lists the percentage of revenue each type of government raised from the sources available to it in 2002. School districts, for example, are heavily dependent upon property taxes. The state relies on general and selective sales. Almost half of the revenue of special districts comes from direct charges for their services. Counties and municipalities turn to a variety of sources that often reflect the circumstance of the governments. Local prop-

Table 11.1. Percentage Direct Expenditure by Florida's Governments by Type of Government Function, 2002

Functional Area	Total Expenditures (in thousands of dollars)	State (%)	Counties (%)	Municipalities (%)	Special Districts (%)	School Districts (%)	Total
Education	$25,793,994	20	0	0	0	80	100
Libraries	$390,917	1	75	20	3	0	100
Public Welfare	$12,500,047	95	4	1	1	0	100
Hospitals	$4,306,698	4	25	1	71	0	100
Health	$3,184,348	83	14	2	1	0	100
Social Insurance Administration	$129,579	100	0	0	0	0	100
Veterans' Services	$25,331	100	0	0	0	0	100
Highways: Capital Outlay	$4,560,851	81	14	5	0	0	100
Highways: Operation	$2,159,633	47	32	20	0	0	100
Airports	$1,593,289	0	69	9	22	0	100
Parking Facilities	$86,030	0	1	99	0	0	100
Sea and Inland Port Facilities	$341,916	3	52	26	18	0	100

Transit Subsidies	$5,260	0	26	74	0	100
Police Protection	$4,392,951	10	48	43	0	100
Fire Protection	$1,856,088	0	42	50	8	100
Corrections	$3,364,963	65	33	1	0	100
Protective Inspections	$567,580	42	31	26	0	100
Natural Resources	$2,401,664	58	15	1	26	100
Parks and Recreation	$1,836,837	10	39	50	1	100
Housing and Community Development	$1,179,014	6	33	23	38	100
Sewerage	$1,714,078	2	26	68	4	100
Solid Waste Management	$1,851,558	11	53	34	1	100
Financial Administration	$1,773,190	42	39	19	0	100
Judicial and Legal	$1,645,988	48	47	5	0	100
Public Buildings	$425,414	29	32	39	0	100
Other Administration	$1,041,522	25	40	34	0	100
Interest on General Debt	$3,740,477	28	41	16	16	100
Utilities	$7,189,737	1	23	49	27	100
Insurance Trusts	$5,035,414	89	0	11	0	100

Source: Calculated using Bureaus of the Census, State and Local Government Finances 2002 Census of Governments as updated October 2005 found at http://www.census.gov/govs/estimate/0210flsl_2.html, http://www.census.gov/govs/estimate/0210flsl_1.html.

Table 11.2. Source of Own-Source Revenue by Percent, Florida Governments, 2002

	State	Counties	Municipalities	Special Districts	School Districts
Property Taxes	1.3	32.5	18.7	16.6	76.2
General Sales	42.0	2.6	1.8	0.0	0.0
Selective Sales	15.0	8.6	12.5	0.0	0.0
Individual Income	0.0	0.0	0.0	0.0	0.0
Corporate Income	3.6	0.0	0.0	0.0	0.0
License Taxes	4.6	0.1	0.0	0.0	0.0
Other Taxes	8.0	1.6	3.1	0.6	0.0
Current Charges	8.7	29.4	21.7	49.6	16.1
Miscellaneous General Revenue	16.6	19.4	12.6	14.3	7.7
Utility Revenue	0.0	5.7	29.6	18.9	0.0
	100.0	100.0	100.0	100.0	100.0

Source: Calculated using Bureaus of the Census, State and Local Government Finances 2002 Census of Governments as updated October 2005 found at http://www.census.gov/govs/estimate/0210flsl_2.html, http://www.census.gov/govs/estimate/0210flsl_1.html.

erty owners, for example, who have a considerable stake in local schools, contribute to the well-being of the school district they live in. State governments serve a broader constituency and levy taxes on corporations, whose income can be reasonably attributed to economic activity within the state.

However, the geographic extent of economic activity and the interests of the various types of governments preclude some neat parceling of revenues to even various levels of government, as Table 11.3 demonstrates. Several governments tap most sources. For example, each type of government relies to some extent on property taxes. The personal property of a single taxpayer can fall under the authority of the state, county, municipality, special district, and school district. This situation demands intergovernmental resolution. Governments must reach some arrangement about how they share and use the bases of revenue available to them.

In Florida, the state constitution provides a basic road map. Among its many provisions, it prohibits the personal income tax, secures the corporate income tax for the state, limits the intangible personal property tax and directs its use to the state, reserves the personal tangible property tax to local governments, and generally limits the power of local governments to levy taxes by confining taxing decisions to the legislature. In short, the ability of local governments to raise revenue for their operations is narrowly constrained by the state constitution. Florida's constitution is quite clear in this regard; Section 1(a), Article VII, states: "No tax shall be levied except in pursuance of law. No state ad valorem taxes shall be levied upon real estate or tangible personal property. All other forms of taxation shall be preempted to the state except as provided by general law." With the exception of the lo-

Table 11.3. Governments Source of Own-Source Revenue by Percent, Florida, 2002

Source of Revenue (in millions of dollars), 2005	Total	State	Counties	Municipalities	Special Districts	School Districts	Total
Property Taxes	$15,754,214	2.7	33.4	13.9	7.2	42.9	100.0
General Sales	$14,734,278	95.8	2.8	1.4	0.0	0.0	100.0
Selective Sales	$7,902,139	63.9	17.7	18.5	0.0	0.0	100.0
Individual Income	—	—	—	—	—	—	
Corporate Income	$1,218,864	100.0	0.0	0.0	0.0	0.0	100.0
License Taxes	$1,573,652	98.9	1.0	0.0	0.0	0.0	100.0
Other Taxes	$3,357,302	80.2	7.9	10.6	1.2	0.0	100.0
Current Charges	$15,022,456	19.5	31.6	16.9	22.4	9.5	100.0
Miscellaneous General Revenue	$11,844,227	47.1	26.5	12.4	8.2	5.8	100.0
Revenue from Utilities	$5,689,187	0.2	16.1	61.0	22.6	0.0	100.0
Total	$77,096,319	43.5	21.0	15.2	8.8	11.5	100.0

Source: Calculated using Bureaus of the Census, State and Local Government Finances 2002 Census of Governments as updated October 2005 found at http://www.census.gov/govs/estimate/0210flsl_2.html.

cal property tax and several constitutionally authorized revenue programs they share with the state, local governments depend on the legislature for the authority to levy any other forms of taxation. This increases the relative importance of the property tax for local governments.

The constitution restricts taxation in several ways. It limits the rate at which counties, municipalities, and special districts can tax personal property; prohibits taxation of motor vehicles, boats, airplanes, trailers, trailer coaches, and mobile homes, even though they are tangible personal property; limits the rate of increase of personal property taxes; and restricts overall growth of state revenues.

These restrictions have dramatic and lasting impacts on intergovernmental relations. They help explain why Florida's counties and municipalities raise more of their revenue from charges and user fees than counties and municipalities in other states do. They suggest an explanation for the increased use of special districts as service providers across the state. But constitutional decisions are only one piece of a larger puzzle. They are interpreted, implemented, and modified annually, sometimes through changes in law, often through informal arrangements, and typically through the ongoing efforts of concerned individuals. State and local officials work almost continually to adjust and retune the intergovernmental system. But officials are not the only group that is concerned about intergovernmental relations in Florida. Many organizations, covering a broad array of issues, are also concerned about the ongoing nature of intergovernmental decisions that are made in Tallahassee and in courthouses, city halls, and offices throughout the state. (See Appendix A in this chapter for a sample of organizations that work with local governments.) They worry about new court decisions that will change the rules under which they operate; about new mandates and preemptions that will change both the services they can provide and the ways in which they can provide them; and about their ability to conduct local affairs within ever changing rules and shifting policy directions.

This high level of interaction with all levels of government in the state, both among officials and among interest groups, can be traced to the demographics of a state that has experienced decades of sustained growth. In 1970, only one county in Florida had a population greater than one million and only 15 counties had populations greater than 100,000. In 2005, these figures were 5 and 32, respectively. In 1970, 60.4 percent of the population lived in municipalities; by 2005, it was 47.0 percent. Florida's population has become increasingly nonwhite over the last two decades. In 1980, 14.7 percent of the population was nonwhite; in 2000, 17.8 percent was nonwhite. The population is also becoming increasingly Hispanic (persons of Hispanic origin may be any race). In 1980, 8.8 percent of the population was Hispanic; by 2000, the figure was 16.8 percent, or 2.7 million people.[4]

The changes in population both respond to and help create shifts in the economic realities governments face. During the 1990s, for example, five historically rural counties (Flagler, Sumter, Collier, Wakulla, and Osceola) increased their population by more than 60 percent. Officials at all levels and throughout the state both cooperate and compete for economic growth. Even within a single metropolitan area, economic issues influence intergovernmental relations in significant ways. Local officials scramble to meet the demands of new and changing residents and to keep abreast of changes in the economy that affect their residents and influence their ability to raise the revenue they need to solve ever-changing problems.

Responding to Intergovernmental Challenges: Revenues

The differences in the economic and demographic circumstances of governments as well as the need to come to some common arrangement regarding the sources of revenue available to governments generates the need for one level of government to provide financial assistance to another. The scale of intergovernmental revenue transferred from one level to another in Florida is substantial, as seen in Table 11. 4.

The federal government and the state government provide almost $15 billion apiece to other governments in Florida. These contributions dwarf

Table 11.4. Intergovernmental Revenue in Florida, 2001–2002 (in thousands of dollars)

Intergovernmental Revenue	To State Government	To County Governments	To Municipal Governments	To District Governments	To School Districts
From Federal Government	12,785,500	847,015	306,263	811,244	206,235
From State Government	0	2,298,880	1,037,508	374,358	11,221,603
From Local Governments	355,484	90,307	251,512	103,048	43,820
	13,140,984	3,236,202	1,595,283	1,288,650	11,471,658

Source: U.S. Bureau of the Census, "State and Local Government Finances by Level of Government and by State: 2001–02: Florida," available online at http://www.census.gov/govs/estimate/0210flsl_1.html.

the funds local governments distribute to other governments, which totals less than $1 billion. Most of the state's assistance goes to school districts and is intended to help boost the amount of funding available for K-12 education and to counter the unequal resources available to counties through the property tax. The state provides more aid to poor counties than it does to wealthy ones. In a similar fashion, much of the assistance from the federal government goes to the state Medicaid program, another redistribution to equalize resources; more federal aid goes to poorer states than to wealthy ones.

Governments transfer funds to each other to ameliorate the competition and conflict inherent in the federal system. These transfers help address the problems that arise from the need to share common revenue bases and solve problems of interest to more than one governmental jurisdiction. Over time, the system of grants-in-aid the federal and state governments use has become rather complex. The solution to revenue problems cannot be divorced from other considerations in the intergovernmental system. Consider the form that federal and state aid takes.

Federal intergovernmental aid goes largely to state governments, but it also provides much-desired assistance to the other types of governments. The assistance comes in various forms and is given under differing conditions. The federal government mostly distributes aid on the basis of either block and categorical grants, but it also uses other types of grants such as project, formula, matching, and entitlement grants. In 2000, there were approximately 750 categorical grant programs for state and local governments. However, this estimate can only be approximate because programs often contain elements of several different types of grants. Grant programs can be generally classified according to the amount of discretion they give the recipients:

- Project grants—Provide the least amount of discretion to recipients and fund specific services or projects for fixed periods of time. The federal officials who make the awards usually have substantial discretion about who gets the money (e.g., minority business development grants).

- Categorical grants—Provide a narrow range of discretion and are typically designated for a specific use in fairly general categories of activities. They may be distributed using a formula or with the discretion of federal agencies (e.g., flood mitigation assistance grants).
- Formula grants—Provide funds according to a distribution formula set out in federal law. Typically, they are not designed for specific projects but are intended to address policy issues written into the formula (e.g., the National Bioterrorism Hospital Preparedness Program).
- Block grants—Provide broad discretion to the recipients with minimal administrative requirements and typically address a general policy area (e.g., the federal government's Community Development Block Grant Program, the Temporary Assistance to Needy Families program of the U.S. Office of Family Assistance, and grants for the treatment and prevention of substance abuse).
- Entitlement grants—Provide automatic payments (in accord with statutory benefit levels and the number of recipients) to any person or government that meets the eligibility requirements (e.g., many of the elements of the Medicaid Program).

Virtually all forms of federal assistance come with some conditions. Some are matching grants that require recipients to contribute cash, services, or the like to match a percentage of the grant. For example, the federal-aid highway program requires recipients working on interstate projects to provide matching funds worth 10 percent of the total grant. They may also include requirements that participating governments not change the amount of revenues that they put into a program (maintenance of effort) or that the federal funding will diminish each year over the life of a program and the participating recipient governments are required to provided increasing matches over time. Another set of conditions is designed to promote a public policy, such as citizen participation, as a condition of receiving federal funds; these are referred to as cross-cutting requirements.

Often federal grant programs allow for waivers of conditions or provide mechanisms to increase flexibility in how funds can be used. The conditions for such waivers or flexibility are typically written into the legislation creating the program and then are implemented by the county executive. Typically, flexibility in the requirements associated with the administration of the grant is provided when recipients meet other accountability requirements. The No Child Left Behind legislation, for example, provides waivers for increased accountability on the part of the recipient government, but similar provisions are absent in the Disabilities Education Act.

The scope of federal grant activity is enormous. Less than 20 percent is distributed in block grants. Most is distributed through categorical and entitlement grants. For example, in 2003, the Department of Health and Human Services administered 282 grant programs totaling $246 billion. However, some federal efforts are quite limited. The National Endowment for the Arts handled only three grant programs in 2003 that disbursed about $95 million.

In 2003, Florida ranked 45th in per capita receipt of funds from federal grants. Over 90 percent of the aid was designated for health and human services programs such as Medicaid and Temporary Assistance for Needy Families; transportation activities and highways; education programs such as Special Education, Title 1, No Child Left Behind Act, Rehabilitative Services, and Adult and Vocational Education; housing activities such as low-rent housing assistance and the community development block grant; and agriculture programs such as Child Nutrition Programs, Special Supplemental Food Program (or WIC), and the Food Stamp Program (Florida Legislative Committee on Intergovernmental Relations 2005).

Florida state government has a somewhat similar though much less diverse set of intergovernmental funding mechanisms. Most of the state's aid is distributed through formula appropriations or shared revenues. Local school districts receive most of their annual appropriation under the Florida Education Finance Program, which establishes revenue allocations to support the constitutionally required uniform system of free public schools. The purpose of the state's funding formula is "to guarantee to each student in the Florida public educational system the availability of programs and services appropriate to his or her educational needs which are substantially equal to those available to any similar student notwithstanding geographic differences and varying local economic factors."[5]

Counties and municipalities both receive funds through shared revenue programs (see Chapter 12).

Responding to Intergovernmental Challenges: Authority

Intergovernmental transfers provide an opportunity to mitigate problems within the intergovernmental system. The opportunities for cooperation and conflict take several other forms, however. They involve concerns over mandates, preemptions, delegation, and devolution. Mandates are the requirements to act that one government places on another; preemptions are the requirement against acting that one government imposes on another; delegation is the authorization to act on its behalf that one government extends to another; and devolution is the grant of authority that one government confers on another.

Consider again the case of revenues in Florida. Under Florida law, a number of revenue sources are authorized for use by counties or municipalities.[6] Under this arrangement, in order to levy a tax, the local government must first enact an ordinance providing for the levy and collection of the tax. Even then general law may restrict the use of the funds generated. By and large, such sources yield quite limited funds.

The legislature has devised some special taxing opportunities in another way. Local-option taxes must be enacted by a majority or majority-plus vote of the governing body or through approval by the voters in a referendum. Such sources usually raise substantial sums, and state law typically restricts the use of funds raised through local-option taxes to specific purposes.[7]

The constitutional requirement adopted in Florida that "[a]ll other forms of taxation shall be preempted to the state except as provided by general law" is not unusual within the federal scheme. This sort of preemption of authority is common. The U.S. Constitution, for example, implicitly limits the states' sovereignty and places restrictions on their ability to act autonomously. The nature of these limits changes over time as courts, legislatures, and executives emphasize different solutions to the problems the system of governments face.

Two Supreme Court decisions over the last three decades appeared to first tilt authority toward the states and then moved toward strengthening the hand of the federal government. Both involved interpretation of the Tenth Amendment, which specifies that "powers not delegated to the United States by the Constitution, nor prohibited by it to the States, are reserved to the States respectively, or to the people." In 1976, in *National League of Cities v. Usery*, the Court reserved control of wages of state employees to the states and ruled that it was beyond the authority of the federal government to regulate them. But almost a decade later, *Garcia v. San Antonio Metropolitan Transit Authority* overturned *National League of Cities*, arguing that most conflicts over state sovereignty involved political questions that should be resolved through political processes. More recently, the Court has limited federal action that falls under the purview of the commerce clause and the Eleventh Amendment (*United States v. Lopez* [1995] and *Seminole Tribe of Florida v. Florida* [1996]). In the words of Kenneth Thomas, "It would appear that the status of the state in the federal system has been strengthened by recent Supreme Court opinions."[8]

Such changes in how federal authority is understood affect the ability of the federal government to mandate or preempt state action. The Supreme Court's opinion in *The United States v. Lopez* (1995), for example, ruled that the Gun-Free School Zones Act was an unconstitutionally broad use of the commerce clause and limited congressional authority. However, Supreme Court actions do not of their own accord limit the use of such legislative policy by the Executive Branch since it often takes specific action by concerned parties asking lower courts to stop the implementation of activities previously declared unconstitutional by the Supreme Court.

In the mid-1990s, members of Congress who were concerned about the number and scope of federal mandates tried another approach to restrict the passage of such legislation and to minimize the impact of congressional actions on private firms, and state and local governments. In 1995, Congress enacted the Unfunded Mandates Reform Act, which was designed to limit federal requirements that were not accompanied by appropriate funding. While the law includes preemptions of the authority needed by a state, local or tribal government or the private sector to engage in some activity, it does not cover conditions of grants-in-aid that impose costs on these entities. Between 1996 and 2004, 12 percent of all legislation enacted by Congress contained mandates. Over 90 percent of these did not meet the thresholds established in the Unfunded Mandates Reform Act and therefore went into effect without accompanying aid from the Congress. These thresholds include the requirement that direct costs (to state, local, or tribal governments) of all mandates contained within the mandate must equal or exceed $50 million (in 1996 dollars) in any of the first 5 fiscal years that the relevant mandates would be effective. About half of the mandates were preemptions on state or local authority and were not compensated.[9]

Overall, attempts to limit federal mandates or reduce preemptions have been unsuccessful. As a result, federal mandates, preemptions, and conditions of aid are more common than ever. In legislation about issues ranging from consumer safety and homeland security to transportation and energy, the state and its localities must contend with restrictions on their ability to frame and implement policy.

Similar concerns about authority have arisen in Florida. As early as the late 1970s, local officials began to push for statutory limitations on state mandates. In fact, the Legislature deployed a number of mechanisms including a statutory limitation on unfunded mandates, a new fiscal note process, and a new oversight body that were successfully put in place, although their overall impact was limited. In response, city and county officials worked in the 1980s to gather support for an amendment to the state constitution that would limit the ability of the state to enact unfunded mandates. In 1990, they succeeded, and Article VII, Section 18(d) was approved by the voters and incorporated into the Florida constitution. It requires state mandates to include: 1) laws that require municipalities and counties to spend funds or take an action that requires the expenditure of funds; 2) laws that reduce their authority to raise revenue; or 3) laws that reduce the percentage of a state tax shared with them. Unfunded mandates are prohibited unless two-thirds of the members of each house of the legislature vote to enact them.

After more than a decade, the process appears to be working with some measure of success, though unfunded mandates still are enacted and implemented. In 2004, for example, the Florida Legislative Committee on Intergovernmental Relations identified 103 mandates in 76 separate bills enacted in the general legislative session. Most were procedural in nature; only two were estimated to have a significant fiscal impact on cities and counties. Of these two, one provided sales tax relief for Floridians on selected items with a purchase price of $50 or less. This provision limited the authority of cities and counties to raise revenues under tax options delegated to them and as such is an unfunded mandate. However, the provision took effect because two-thirds of the members of each legislative chamber had voted for it. The other significant unfunded mandate increased the fiscal responsibility of county governments for public safety issues by requiring them to provide juvenile detention services that cost an estimated $90 million. In this case, the law was challenged and subsequently overturned as unconstitutional because it did not receive the required two-thirds vote in each chamber.

Florida has not addressed preemptions explicitly, as the federal unfunded mandates law does. But the state legislature regularly enacts legislation that displaces local laws already in place. These preemptions are limits on the home rule authority provided to municipalities and counties in the state's constitution and statutes. In Florida, municipal and county governments have relatively broad discretionary authority over their affairs, with the exception of taxing authority. The legislature enacted thirteen preemptions in 2004. One, for example, prohibits counties and municipalities from issuing or taking disciplinary action against an elevator inspection certification (Laws of Florida, Chapter 2004-12). Another prohibits local government entities from keeping a record of privately owned firearms or a list of owners of such firearms (Laws of Florida, Chapter 2004-56).

While the legislature limits the authority of local governments in some areas, it can also expand their authority in other areas. In 2004, eight legislative provisions provided new or expanded revenue sources for counties or municipalities. Most are relatively minor, but some are likely to generate substantial revenue (e.g., the increase in the amount clerks of court may charge per page for recording instruments for Florida residents). Another thirty-four provisions in twenty-five different bills enacted in 2004 provide new or additional explicit discretionary authority to counties and municipalities. Typically, such measures provide flexibility within limitations imposed by statute.

The division of authority in Florida is often negotiated in the state's legislature, city halls, county courthouses, and district offices. A range of intergovernmental coordination mechanisms exists, but typically state statutes and local ordinances structure how governments work together. In Florida, for example, section 163.01 of Florida Statutes authorizes local governments to enter into interlocal agreements with public and private entities to improve their efficiency or effectiveness. Section 163.07 of Florida Statues, promoting Efficiency and Accountability in Local Government Services, provides a voluntary process for municipalities, counties, and special districts to resolve conflicts about the delivery and funding of local services on a county or regional basis. Such laws encourage the development of several types of intergovernmental coordination agreements, which the Florida Legislative Committee on Intergovernmental Relations (LCIR) classifies as informal interlocal agreements, memorandums of understanding, intergovernment agreements, joint planning agreements, and mutual aid agreements.

At the state level, several agencies are explicitly authorized to enter into interagency agreements to improve coordination and efficiency in the delivery of services. They too use the whole range of intergovernmental coordination agreements the LCIR has laid out. In addition, the state has worked extensively to build statewide intergovernmental purchasing and information technology systems. Florida statutes also now encourage the use of alternative techniques to resolve conflicts in areas ranging from land use and housing to transportation and health care. Nevertheless, intergovernmental tools can only accomplish so much. These mechanisms are deployed in the context of political considerations that cannot be ignored.

Other Intergovernmental Challenges in Florida

Another type of intergovernmental challenge confronting the state and/or the state and local governments in Florida is the continuing decrease in federal funding and changes in which programs federal grants-in-aid fund.

This affects the state government in Florida directly and local governments indirectly. Another challenge is coping with the rifts that are occurring with increasing frequency between municipalities (or would-be municipalities) and the counties where they are located.

Uncertainty of Federal Aid

Although the national government has made grants to state and local governments since the beginning of the republic, the federal grants system expanded substantially during the New Deal years and solidified the use of categorical grants. By the end of the Eisenhower administration, grant programs existed in areas ranging from vocational education and public health to agricultural research and housing. A large proportion of grants were intended for capital infrastructure. The interstate highway program became the prototype of large and broadly distributed categorical federal grants that provided assistance to state governments.

The number of categorical grants grew during the Lyndon Johnson's Great Society, but the federal government also experimented with block grants in health care and law enforcement and with a variety of coordination mechanisms. Federal administrators and state officials alike complained about the regulatory headaches imposed by the conditions associated with the aid. In addition, federal officials became disenchanted by the unwillingness of state governments to address pressing problems in the nation's urban areas. Increasingly large proportions of the federal assistance went directly to local governments, bypassing state governments.

Under the New Federalism of Richard Nixon's administration, the welter of categorical grants that had been created during the 1960s gave birth to revenue-sharing proposals and consolidations such as community development block grants. These innovations were designed to provide state and local officials with the flexibility they needed to ensure that funds were put to their most effective use. During this period, local governments continued to receive relatively large amounts of funding directly from the federal government.

The Reagan administration continued the effort to simplify the overall grants system, consolidating seventy-seven categorical grants into nine block grants in 1981. Despite such efforts, the grants-in-aid system continued to grow. Categorical grants continued to increase in number and expense. It was only under the pressure of continuing budget deficits that the expansion of the grant system slowed. However, the character of the system changed in several distinct ways during the Reagan administration. First, the number and amount of funds that provide assistance directly to local governments decreased significantly. Second, conditions of aid involved more mandates that linked unrelated policy issues. Federal highway funding, for example, was tied to the elimination of drinking ages below the age of 21, a specific practice the Supreme Court sanctioned as part of a more general approach to federal conditions of aid in *South Dakota v. Dole* (1987). Finally, during the Reagan years, the grants system turned away from an emphasis on funding infrastructure. Gradually, social welfare assistance activities and individual entitlement grants became more important.

These trends continue. The second Bush administration has sought changes ranging from proposing grants that are linked with faith-based initiatives to recommending further consolidation and reduced funding for community and economic development in the Strengthen America's Communities initiative. Notably, though, while the federal grants system still emphasizes payments to individuals, the overall growth in the system in relation to total federal outlays has slowed since 2000. In other words, federal aid to state and local governments as a proportion of total federal outlays—in both actual and constant dollars—has shrunk since 2000 (see Benton 2007).

The slowing growth of the federal fiscal grants system has exacerbated another feature of the current system; federal grants-in-aid now emphasize health concerns, especially through the Medicaid program. And since Medicaid requires matching state or local funds, it has indirectly put enormous pressure on the revenue systems of virtually every state government. The mandatory entitlement of most Medicaid services has forced a change in state priorities since 1988 (see National Association of State Budget Officers 2005). The changes have been dramatic both nationally and in Florida. Only spending for health services has increased significantly over the period. Spending for corrections has held its own, but all other spending is down. Even public education, which has been at the top of the list of concerns for almost fifteen years, receives a smaller share of total state spending in Florida now than it did in 1988. Transportation spending has been hit especially hard.

So while the federal government has directed more of its intergovernmental spending toward the states rather than to local governments, the ability of states to foster their own public policies has increasingly been preempted indirectly through the Medicaid program. States have sought relief in several ways. There are growing calls for waivers and additional flexibility in the conditions of federal aid. States have sought, and to some extent received, greater deference in the courts. But the intensity of the Medicaid dilemma has forced them to both redirect their own priorities and to call indirectly upon local governments to assume a greater portion of the burden in providing some services.

In Florida, Medicaid has grown from 12.5 percent of the budget in 1990 to 22.4 in 2005. During this period, the share of local education funding the state provides dropped from 51.2 to 43.6 percent.[10] State policy makers have used the real estate bubble and the property tax calculations included in the Florida Education Finance Program to increase the share local school districts pay for education.

Conflict between Florida Counties and Their Municipalities

In spite of the growth in interlocal cooperation and coordination in Florida, there has also been a marked increase in both the number of conflicts between county governments and the municipalities located within their boundaries over the last two to three decades. This has been especially the case in rapidly growing areas of the state. Population growth, as suggested throughout this book, has placed a tremendous amount of pressure on cities and counties to keep pace with the steadily escalating service demands of both older and newer residents and has forced them to find the additional revenue necessary to pay for new or expanded services. It has also created the need to wisely manage or control growth so as to protect a fragile environment and the quality of life for present and future generations of Floridians.

In one scenario, county governments are in conflict with their municipalities over land use and planning. Municipalities are ever vigilant and are frequently seen as jealously guarding their power—or, as they see it, their right—to chart out and determine their own destinies. As a result, pro-growth municipal officials, developers, and citizens are increasingly at odds with county officials who assert their responsibility and authority to control growth and dictate land use plans within cities. County officials typically assert that the overall good of the county supersedes the peculiar interests of the city when they construct the local comprehensive plan, and it is not unusual for the state to support counties in this regard. On the other side, municipal officials argue that the county needs to stay out of their business and tend to matters pertaining to the unincorporated areas of the county, as municipalities have been granted corporation status by the state so they can guide their destinies and development apart from the rest of the county. Such a situation has been brewing for the past few years between Manatee County and its municipalities and has led to intense bickering and even the threat of lawsuits.

A similar though somewhat different scenario has recently emerged in Sarasota County. The cities of North Port and Venice each have plans to annex massive parcels of undeveloped land, which has evoked a critical and threatening response from Sarasota County officials. The county has gone on record as strongly opposing these announced intentions, held public forums to educate the public about the negative affects of the cities' plans, has gotten the pertinent state agencies to side with it, and has even stated that it will challenge any annexation plans in court if necessary. County officials claim that neither of these cities has the capacity now (nor will they in the near future) to provide critical services (e.g., roads, water supply, sewage disposal, storm-water management, parks and recreation, environmental protection) and that the result will be more urban sprawl. Moreover, county officials fear that if these annexations are allowed to go forward, Sarasota County will be expected to provide and finance a significant portion of the cost of the needed infrastructure. At this writing, the controversy in Sarasota County is at the simmering point and is likely to escalate further; it appears that North Port and Venice are prepared to go forward with their annexation plans.

Another related kind of conflict scenario has been unfolding across the state for several decades and promises to exacerbate friction between counties and cities. This situation also involves aggressive municipal annexation of undeveloped real estate in unincorporated parts of counties, and the fear is that it will impede or compromise the quality of service delivery for many local government functions, increase service costs to most residents, and prevent the realization of economies of scale by most local governments. The annexation of some highly coveted land in northern Hillsborough County and bordering Pasco County by the city of Tampa serves as a case in point. This annexation has cut off a sizable area of unincorporated territory from a much larger part of unincorporated Hillsborough County and has led to an untenable situation with regard to fire protection. From a strategic and ISO (that is, insurance underwriters') perspective, the isolated area is too far away from the nearest county fire station to expect firefighters to respond within an acceptable time frame. Ideally, a county fire station could have been built in the newly annexed area to service both this area and the area that is now too far from an existing station. But annexation has preempted this option, and the county is faced with the choice of building and operating a station that is not cost effective or permitting this area to have less-than-adequate fire protection; in that case, the areas' residents and businesses will have to pay higher insurance premiums. Moreover, the city has been unwilling to contract with the county at a reasonable price to provide fire protection to the area in question, since it has always had designs on annexing the area in spite of the county's consistent efforts to rebuff its attempts to do so. For the foreseeable future, conflict is likely to characterize relations between the City of Tampa and Hillsborough County as the city seeks to enlarge its boundaries while county fire service areas that previously were able to realize economies of scale have been balkanized and property tax revenue that used to be earmarked for county fire protection now goes into the city treasury. Similar scenarios can be found around the state involving fire protection or the provision of other types of critical services.

Other issues are destined to generate intergovernmental conflict in Florida. These include the use of state sales tax revenue to fund local health care, which will pit communities against one another and against the state; preemption of franchise regulation and the drive to produce a more uniform business environment (for example, by preempting local regulation of cable TV or by compromising the ability of local governments to collect taxes for communication); and property tax reform that will pit businesses against residential areas.

Conclusion

The drama of intergovernmental relations in Florida is likely to feature a mosaic of cooperation and conflict. And, as suggested at the outset of this chapter, these relations should be seen as interactions among officials (both elected and appointed) at the state and local government level in Florida and of state officials with federal officials. Governments are but a conduit through which intergovernmental relations and interactions occur. Another dimension of intergovernmental relations not really addressed in this chapter but one to pay close attention to is the relationship between government officials and employees of nonprofit and for-profit organizations who provide services and programs via contract or franchise agreement (or what some have referred to as the "fourth face" of intergovernmental relations). But in the end, while we take note of the interactions and exchanges among the various actors in intergovernmental relations, we should never lose sight of or appreciation for the substance of policy decisions and subsequent provision of services that are the product of day-to-day intergovernmental relations, for this is what is really important to the public.

Appendix A. Examples of Organizations That Work with Local Governments in Florida

Association of Directors of Florida Animal Services Agencies
Association of Pretrial Professionals of Florida
County Veterans Service Officers Association
Florida Administrators of Volunteers in Government
Florida Animal Control Association
Florida Association for Intergovernmental Relations
Florida Association of City Clerks
Florida Association of County Agricultural Agents
Florida Association of County Attorneys
Florida Association of County Emergency Medical Services Educators
Florida Association of County Engineers & Road Superintendents
Florida Association of County Health Officers
Florida Association of County Social Services Executives
Florida Association of Nonprofit Organizations
Florida City and County Management Association
Florida Economic Development Council
Florida Emergency Preparedness Association
Florida Extension Association of Family & Consumer Sciences
Florida Festivals and Events Association
Florida Government Communicators Association
Florida Government Finance Officers Association
Florida Housing Coalition
Florida Local Environmental Resource Agencies
Florida Local Government Information Systems Association
Florida Municipal Electric Association
Florida Public Employers Labor Relations Association
Florida Public Personnel Association
Florida Recreation & Parks Association
Florida Redevelopment Association
Florida Regional Councils Association
Florida Section American Water Works Association
State Association of County Aging Services Providers
Florida Government Finance Officers Association, Florida Planning and Zoning Association

Notes

1. The census figures do not count a range of less-autonomous governmental entities, usually known as legislative authorities or commissions.

2. This figure does not include 590 dependent special districts in the state, as identified by the Florida Department of Community Affairs. Dependent districts are created

by or rely upon another general-purpose government for the appointment of a major portion of its membership or the approval of its budget.

3. The number was last estimated in 1992 by the U.S. Bureau of the Census at 5,588 (1992). The figure of 6,000 includes the officials of newly created districts and municipalities.

4. See <http://edr.state.fl.us/population/popsummary.pdf> and <www.floridalcir.gov/dataMtoR.html>.

5. §236.012 (1) Florida Statues, 1999.

6. These include the 911 fee, the communication services tax, the discretionary surtax on documents, the green utility fee, the gross receipts tax on commercial hazardous waste facilities, the insurance premium tax, the intergovernmental radio communications program, the municipal pari-mutuel tax, the municipal parking facility space surcharges, the occupational license tax, the public service tax, and the vessel registration fee.

7. These include local discretionary sales surtaxes, local-option food and beverage taxes, local-option fuel taxes, and local-option tourist taxes.

8. Kenneth R. Thomas, "Federalism, State Sovereignty and the Constitution: Basis and Limits of Congressional Power," updated June 17, 2005, Congressional Research Service Report for Congress, p. CRS-21.

9. This information is derived from testimony given by Elizabeth Robinson, deputy director of the Congressional Budget Office, on April 14, 2005 (Congressional Budget Office 2005).

10. The "Digest of Education Statistics" is the federal source for comparable data, <http://nces.ed.gov/programs/digest/d05/tables/dt05_153.asp>. The latest figures are for FY 2002–2003.

References

Anderson, William. 1960. *Intergovernmental Relations in Review*. Minneapolis: University of Minnesota Press.

Benton, J. Edwin. 2007. "George W. Bush's Federal Aid Legacy." *Publius: The Journal of Federalism* 37: 371–89.

Bradley, Robert B., and Marsha Hosack. 1998. "Intergovernmental Relations in Florida: Issues and Alternatives." In *Florida Public Policy Management System: Growth and Reform in America's Fourth Largest State*, edited by Richard Chackerian. 2nd ed. Dubuque, Iowa: Kendall/Hunt Publishing Company.

Congressional Budget Office. *A Review of CBO's Activities Under the Unfunded Mandates Reform Act: Statement of Elizabeth Robinson, Deputy Director, before the Subcommittee on Oversight of Government Management, the Federal Workforce, and the District of Columbia Committee on Homeland Security and Governmental Affairs, U.S. Senate*. Washington, D.C.: Congressional Budget Office, 2005. <http://hsgac.senate.gov/_files/CBOTestimonyRobinsonUMRAdoc.pdf>.

Florida Legislative Committee on Intergovernmental Relations. 2005. Steve McCain, memorandum to LCIR members, Federal Grant Expenditures to Florida in 2003. <www.floridalcir.gov/meetings/jan2405fedgrants.pdf> (accessed March 14, 2007).

National Association of State Budget Officers. 2005. *State Expenditure Report 2004.* Washington, D.C.: National Association of State Budget Officers.

U.S. Bureau of the Census. 1992. *Elected Officials of State and Local Governments by State: Census Years 1977 to 1992,* Table 2. Washington, D.C.: U.S. Department of Commerce. <www.census.gov/prod/2/gov/gc/gc92_1_2.pdf>.

———. 1995. *1992 Census of Governments.* Vol. 1. *Government Organization.* No. 2. *Popularly Elected Officials.* Washington, D.C.: U.S. Department of Commerce. <www.census.gov/prod/2/gov/gc/gc92_1_2.pdf (accessed March 21, 2007).

———. 2002. *2002 Census of Governments.* Vol. 1, no. 1. *Government Organization.* Washington, D.C.: Government Printing Office.

Wright, Deil S. 1988. *Understanding Intergovernmental Relations.* 3rd ed. Belmont, Calif.: Duxbury Press.

12

The Economics and Politics of Financing Florida's Many Governments

SUSAN A. MACMANUS WITH THOMAS A. WATSON
AND ANDREW F. QUECAN

The Florida of today faces many challenges: continued population growth, a diverse population (as measured by race/ethnicity and generational makeup), a changing economic base, projections that hurricane seasons will be more intense, above-average homeland security vulnerabilities and mandates, increased use of constitutional amendments as a way to dictate budget priorities, and a politically divided electorate.

Each of these trends affects the budgets of Florida's many governments but not always in the same way. The economies, population makeup, and politics of various regions of the state vary considerably, as they do among different types of governmental units (state, county, municipal, school district, special district). The fiscal pressures facing these governments differ by their location—rural, suburban, or metropolitan. There is no "one size fits all" approach to raising money or paying for state and local governments in the Sunshine State.

A Crowded Governmental Landscape: Fiscal Challenges

Florida, the nation's fourth-largest state, is home to over 1,800 governmental units. In addition to the state government, 67 counties, 67 school districts, 408 municipalities, and 1,352 active special-district governments serve the people of Florida.[1] It costs billions of dollars to operate these governments, which deliver a multitude of services and programs to the public. People must be hired; buildings, facilities, equipment, and supplies procured and maintained; insurance purchased; monies set aside for emergencies; and so forth. When annual revenue does not keep pace with spending needs, governments either have to raise taxes or fees, borrow money, cut back spending, or do a little of each to make ends meet.

The politics of raising money (or the politics of taxation) is always contentious. For quite some time, Floridians have been hostile to new and/or higher taxes, particularly property taxes. Younger people perceive them as a deterrent to home ownership, while many older Floridians view property taxes as threats to their fixed incomes (MacManus 1996). Over the years, the animosity toward property taxes has sent counties, cities, and school districts scrambling for new sources of revenue such as impact fees and user charges. It has also sent local governments in search of broader authority from the state to impose local-option sales taxes that, on occasion, have been granted.

Population Growth Projections to 2030

Florida's population will continue to grow in each of the next three decades (see Chapter 1). Some counties can expect higher growth rates than others. The "in-filling" trend that began in the late 1990s will continue; the state's interior counties will grow faster than the coastal counties that are already densely populated. Lower taxes, more-pristine environments, and lower housing costs in these areas are attracting new residents to the noncoastal areas. These new residents are coming from other states, other countries, and other Florida counties. Florida residents who live in congested areas are increasingly choosing to move to less crowded parts of the state. For others, interior county locations are perceived as safer from the direct hit of hurricanes.

High growth creates political tensions in the affected areas. It often pits old-timers against newcomers and pro-growth proponents against those who opposed growth and development. It also forces governments to budget proportionately more for capital projects (infrastructure) than low- or no-growth localities, which can appropriate a greater portion of their spending for services and programs. The political tensions sparked by growth can be politically costly for elected officials. A study of local elections in Florida found that budget decisions about infrastructure were often the reason incumbents were defeated when they ran for reelection (MacManus 2004a). But the same tensions exist at the state level as legislators in Tallahassee grapple with how to balance the budgetary needs of fast-growing parts of the state and the needs of poorer, more rural counties whose economies are not expanding as rapidly. State lawmakers are also subject to intense cross-pressures from citizens demanding that they cut local property taxes and from local governments fiercely opposing such actions and complaining about unfunded state mandates.

A More Diverse Population

Florida's growth has been fueled by in-migration from other states and other countries. Two-thirds of the state's residents were not born in Florida (U.S. Bureau of the Census 2000). Consequently, the state has become more diverse, in terms of both race/ethnicity and generations. The U.S. census reports that during the 1990s, Florida was one of seventeen states where the rate of increase in racial and ethnic diversity exceeded that of the nation at large. Racial and ethnic minorities are especially drawn to the state's metropolitan areas, particularly in South and Central Florida. Others are attracted to Florida for different reasons. Historically, retirees have been enticed to the state by the sunshine, low taxes, and affordable housing; Latin and South American immigrants by the opportunity for freedom; and young adults and baby boomers by jobs.

Racial/Ethnic Diversity

The biggest change in recent years has been in the Hispanic population, which is now larger than the black population. Many of the new Hispanic residents have migrated from Latin and South American countries, often in search of economic opportunities or to escape from a repressive political regime (Moreno 2004). Florida has also attracted a number of African Americans from the North who have moved back home after migrating out during the 1960s—a pattern characterizing black population growth in many southern states (Hill 2004)—and blacks from the Carribean. The state's Asian population is growing as well.

Such demographic developments have political implications. By and large, Florida's black population is solidly Democratic, its Cuban population is solidly Republican, its non-Cuban Hispanic population is divided but leaning toward the Democratic Party, and its Asian population is more independent. In many municipal and school board elections, which are nonpartisan, tensions emerge between these racial/ethnic groups over who gets what and when in the budget.

Immigrants' Impact on the Budget: An Asset or a Liability?

The percentage of Floridians who were born in the United States is declining. According to the 2000 census, 16.7 percent of the state's population is foreign born, the fifth highest of any state, and that percentage is rising. The influx of immigrants into Florida has put tremendous pressure on budgets at the state and local levels, particularly in the areas of education, health care, and affordable housing. One study has estimated that "in Florida the net burden on state and local governments from immigrants is on the order of $2,000 per immigrant household" annually (Zannis with Denslow 2005). Why? Because immigrant households pay less in taxes (because they make less) but have higher demands in terms of services. However, another study (Boswell, Nogle, Paral, and Langendorf 2001, 141) arrived at a very different conclusion: "There is no question that immigrants are carrying their fair share of the tax burdens in Florida and Miami." The Boswell, Nogle, Paral, and Langendorf study also found that per capita spending on services was nearly the same for immigrants as for natives.

Political and budgetary tensions over immigration, especially illegal immigration, can be intense, especially at times when revenue growth is marginal. The business community tends to be more pro-immigration because immigrants often are willing to do jobs that others will not do, especially in Florida's service and agricultural sectors, and because language and cultural diversity are an asset to the state's growing international trade sector.

Age/Generational Diversity

When people think of Florida, many think of retirees. While it is true that Florida's senior population is the largest of any state, the gap between the oldest and youngest portions has shrunk since 1970, primarily due to higher birth rates among Florida's new immigrant populations and a flatter rate of retiree in-migration. These two age-extreme populations are often referred to as the "dependent populations" because they pay in less in taxes while requiring more government services than the working-age population.

On many state and local issues, the young and the old among voting-age populations actually agree on what the big problems are. Where they differ is on which problems should be tackled first and on the causes and cures of these problems. For example, more young adults feel that the economy and jobs are higher priorities than seniors, who focus more on taxes and government spending. Young adults favor budgets that emphasize programs to prevent problems while older Floridians favor budgets that feature reactive programs (MacManus 1996).

Florida's younger population is trending toward the Democratic Party while its older population is trending slightly toward the Republican Party as the oldest, most solidly Democratic FDR generation is replaced by younger seniors who are healthier, wealthier, and better educated than the oldest old (MacManus 2004b, 17). Voter turnout among Florida's senior population is considerably higher than that of younger citizens, especially in state and local elections (MacManus 2005a). However, the 45–64 age cohort now makes up the largest portion of the voting age population (MacManus 2005b).

Florida's Changing Economy

Florida's economy, once heavily dominated by agriculture and tourism, has become somewhat more diversified in recent years with the growth of the state's high-tech, financial services, and international trade sectors. However, tourism- and agriculture-related industries are still considered to be significant, as is Florida's defense sector.

Important regional economic differences are evident across the state. As economist Carole Taylor-West (1995, 2) has observed:

> Florida has emerged not as a homogeneous economic entity but as a collection of disparate regional economies, highly diversified in economic base structure, demographic composition, growth rates, level of economic well-being and vulnerability to swings in the national and international economies.

The state's service and finance, insurance, and real estate sectors have grown the fastest over the past ten years, as measured by their proportional makeup of the state's *gross state product* (GSP). (GSP is the value of goods and services produced by the state; it is frequently used as a broad measure of the state's economy.) The sharpest declines have been in governmental activities and public utilities/transportation (see Figure 12.1). *Note*: Information was a new category added in 2005.

Measuring levels of *employment* is another way to gauge sector size. By 2005, the service and trade sectors accounted for about 62 percent of the state's employment (the national average was 54 percent). Professional and business services are the largest sector in Florida (17 percent of all employment), followed by government (14 percent), retail trade (13 percent), education and health services (12 percent), and leisure and hospitality services (11 percent).[2]

State leaders have implemented a number of tax credits and tax breaks to attract different types of businesses and industries to Florida. For example, in 2003, the state launched a successful plan to entice California-based Scripps Research Institute (with its high-tech, high-paying jobs in the biotechnology sector) to open a Florida site in Palm Beach County. However, state-adopted business incentive policies may generate controversy, particularly at the lo-

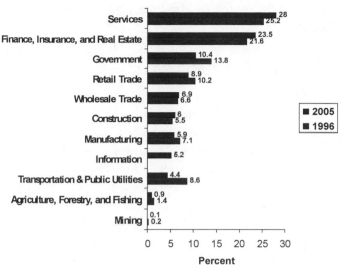

Figure 12.1. Change in Florida's Gross State Product by Economic Sector, 1996 and 2005.

Note: Information was a new category added in 2005.

Source: State of Florida, Full Faith and Credit, State Board of Education, Public Education Capital Outlay Bonds, 2006 Series B, pg. A4. Available at http://www.sbafla.com/bond/pdf/programs /education/PECO.pdf, accessed May 18, 2007.

cal level, even when the motive for enacting them is economic diversification. Such has been the case in Palm Beach County (Hafenbrack 2005). Tax credits and tax reductions for businesses as a means of sparking economic development have long been controversial not just in Florida but across the United States, more so at the local than at the state level.

The good news is that as the state's economy has diversified, it has become more resilient in the face of major economic or political shocks (Morrell 2005). Florida has weathered several in recent years: uncertainty about the state's tourist sector following September 11, 2001; declines in the stock market; the weakness of economies in Central and South America; unprecedented and costly major hurricane seasons in 2004 and 2005; and periodic dips in consumer confidence. The state has lead the nation in job creation for nearly a decade.

Many economists believe that Florida's economic future depends on the state's ability to continue to diversify its economy and attract high-value-added jobs. The state plans to focus on expanding its life sciences (biotechnology, medical device manufacturing, pharmaceuticals, and health care), information technology, aviation/aerospace, homeland security, financial/ professional services, and manufacturing sectors. To do this, Florida must invest more in educating its work force (Denslow 2005, 423–24.) Others argue that tax reform and the related issue of housing affordability are also keys to the state's continued economic growth.

Intensifying the Demand for Emergency Preparedness: Hurricanes and Homeland Security

The demand for emergency management on state and local government budgets has intensified in recent years (Caruson and MacManus 2006a). Florida's vulnerabilities to natural disasters (hurricanes) and breaches of homeland security are greater than those many other states face (Caruson and MacManus 2006b). The vulnerabilities became apparent after the September 11, 2001, terrorist attacks (which greatly affected Florida's tourist-centered economy) and the staggering 2004 and 2005 hurricane seasons, during which the state was hit by a record-breaking eight major hurricanes. In 2004 alone, the cost of recovery and relief efforts was estimated to be $4.3 billion, $387.7 million of which was not reimbursable.

The Constant Fight for a Fair Share of Federal Funds

In the continuing scramble for revenue, Florida's state and local government officials are well aware of how important federal funds are to their economies. They frequently lobby national officials hard to make sure Floridians get back a fair share of the federal tax dollars they send to Washington. Billions of federal funds flow into Florida annually from a variety of sources (Hovey and Hovey 2005).

- *Grants to state and local governments* (9 percent of all federal money coming into Florida). Examples: child nutrition programs, the special milk program funded under the Child Nutrition Act of 1996, state and private forestry management, disaster relief, construction of wastewater treatment facilities, low-income home energy assistance, Medicaid, public housing grants, a highway trust fund, and an airport trust fund.
- *Salaries and wages paid to federal employees working in Florida* (9 percent). Examples: military and civilian employees working for the Department of Defense and employees of the U.S. Postal Service and other federal agencies.
- *Direct federal payments to individuals living in Florida* (66 percent). Examples: Social Security, Medicare, veterans' benefits programs, federal retirement and disability payments, food stamps, housing as-

sistance, unemployment compensation, Pell grants, and national guaranteed student loan interest subsidies.

- *Purchases made in Florida by federal agencies* (10 percent). Examples: purchases of goods and services made by the Department of Defense, the U.S. Postal Service, and other federal agencies.

In addition, the federal government issues or backs billions of dollars' worth of loans to individuals, businesses, and governments in the state.

Historically, Florida has received less back in federal grants than most other states, whether measured in terms of per capita grants or in relation to the state's federal tax burden. Florida ranks thirtieth among the states in the amount of federal funds received relative to the amount of federal income taxes Floridians paid.

Some analysts attribute this federal aid "inequity" to uncoordinated efforts by various state agencies, decisions by Congress to use old census figures (which greatly disadvantages high-growth states such as Florida), and the general redistributive nature of many federal grant programs designed to aid poorer entities and individuals. Those who believe Florida is still being short-changed, especially on transportation funds, advocate pushing harder for more federal funds on the premise that Florida deserves a more equitable share of federal aid. Others warn that too much reliance on federal funds can backfire. They argue that if Congress suddenly decides to reduce or redirect federal aid, too much reliance on federal funds could put state and local governments in a fiscal squeeze, especially if the federal monies cut are funding essential or politically popular programs.

In the opinion of many local government officials, the State of Florida should pick up some of the slack in federal funding when it occurs by increasing state aid to local governments. But state officials are quick to point out that they have enough difficulty meeting *state* spending needs. Over time, the percentage of the state's total direct revenue transferred to local governments has decreased. In the early and mid-1980s, the state typically transferred 10–11 percent of its revenue to local governments each year. By the mid-1990s, state transfers had fallen to around 7 percent annually. By the early 2000s, it had shrunk to 4 percent for cities and counties; if we count aid to school districts, that number increases slightly to 6 percent.[3]

An Increasingly Divided Electorate

Florida is regarded as one of the nation's most competitive states in terms of partisan politics. Statewide elections are generally expensive, close, and fiercely fought contests. Democrats and Republicans are almost at parity in terms of voter registration (see Chapters 3 and 5). However, the fastest growth is in the percent who do not register as either a Democrat or a Republican. The southeast part of the state is the most heavily Democratic, followed by counties with large universities (Leon, which hosts Florida State University, and Alachua, which hosts the University of Florida). The southwest is the most heavily Republican. The I-4 corridor, the state's midriff, is the most politically competitive part of the state and has the largest concentration of independent, or swing, voters (MacManus 2004b, 165–94). A divided electorate makes it more difficult to secure consensus on both the taxing and spending sides of the budgetary ledger. Republicans are more anti-tax and pro-privatization than Democrats; they are fiscally conservative and are oriented toward market forces.

Growing Use of Constitutional Amendments: A Voter Mobilization Tool with Major Budgetary Consequences

Some say Florida is becoming "California lite" due to the escalation in the number of amendments placed before voters for their approval. Constitutional amendments can be placed on the ballot for voter approval in several ways, but the two primary methods are by the state legislature and by voter petition (citizen initiative). Many of these have major budget consequences, such as the amendment passed in 2002 that reduced the size of school classrooms.

Amendments are being used more frequently in Florida as tools to get voters to the polls. Even the public is becoming frustrated with the trend (Pritchett and McClure 2005). A statewide survey of Floridians[4] found that 82 percent think amendments get put on the ballot that really should not be there; 72 percent believe that well-financed special-interest groups are generally responsible for putting amendments on the ballot rather than average citizens banding together. Perhaps the most alarming finding from a budget perspective is that 73 percent admitted they did not recall having seen the estimated cost of any of the proposed amendments they voted on.

The voting patterns on proposed constitutional amendments over the last twenty years affirm what many have concluded about the Florida electorate—they are generally anti-tax but pro-spending. A majority tends to vote against proposals that increase taxes and for amendments that promise to limit taxes, reduce spending, or improve fiscal management and productivity. At the same time, Floridians are likely to vote for measures requiring substantial commitments of state funds in areas ranging from court costs and statewide pre-kindergarten programs to smaller class sizes. Thus, a major challenge facing Florida's public sector in the 2000s is how to meet the rising expenditure demands associated with rapid population growth in a fiscally conservative, anti-tax political environment.

Financing Florida's State Government

Florida law requires that financial operations of the state be maintained through the General Revenue Fund, various trust funds, and the Budget Stabilization Fund (the "rainy day fund"). Managing the state's finances involves elected officials, economists, policy analysts, and the public.

The State Budgeting Process

Preparing Florida's budget is quite complex, as are the adoption phases of the process (see Table 12.1). Article IV, Section 1 of the Florida constitution provides that the "[g]overnor shall be the chief administrative officer of the state responsible for planning and budgeting for the state." It requires the governor to submit a balanced budget to the legislature each year based on the budget requests of various state agencies. But Article III, Section 19(a)(1)of the constitution gives the legislature the statutory authority to set forth the requirements for creating, considering, and passing the budget: "General law shall prescribe the adoption of annual state budgetary and planning processes and require that detail reflecting the annualized costs of the state budget and reflecting the nonrecurring costs of the budget requests shall accompany state department and agency legislative budget requests, the governor's recommended budget, and appropriation bills." Article VII, Section I of the Florida constitution also gives the legislature the final responsibility to determine appropriations (adopt the budget): "No money shall be drawn from the treasury except in pursuance of an appropriation made by law." The same Article "generally grants the Legislature the preeminent authority among all other branches and levels of government to levy taxes and appropriate revenues" (Office of the Majority Whip Representative Ellyn Bogdanoff, 2007:2).

In the late autumn before the beginning of a new fiscal year, the legislature's appropriations staff and the governor's budget office send the budget guidelines to each state agency. This happens after the Consensus Revenue Estimating Conference (comprising a representative from the Office of the Governor, the Senate, the House of Representatives, and the legislature's Office of Economic and Demographic Research) releases its

Table 12.1. Florida's Budget Process Timetable

Governor/Office of Policy and Budget and the Legislature	State Agencies	Governor/Office of Policy and Budget	Legislature	Governor/Office of Policy and Budget
Provide Instructions to Departments for:	Prepare Long-Range Program Plan	Receive/Analyze:	Prepare Appropriations Act	Governor May Line Item Veto Specific Appropriations
•Long-Range Program Plan	Prepare Legislative Budge Request	•Long-Range Program Plans	Review Governor's Recommendations	Governor Signs Budget into Law
•Legislative Budget Request	Prepare Capital Improvements Program Plan	•Legislative Budget Request	Review/Analyze/ Revise Budget	Create Operating Budgets for Agencies from General Appropriations Act
•Capital Improvements Program Plan	Prepare Information Technology Plan	•Capital Improvements Program Plan	Appropriations Act Passed by Both Houses	
•Information Technology Plan	Prepare Internal Operating Budget	•Information Technology Plan		
		Hold Public Hearing		
		Develop Recommendations Based on Governor's Priorities and Available Revenues		
May–June	May–September	August–January	December–May	May–July

Source: Executive Office of the Governor, "Florida's e-Budget Process Overview," available online at http://peoplesbudget.state.fl.us/overview.aspx (accessed April 2, 2007).
Note: Chart does not include the implementation or audit phases of the budget process.

revenue projections. The agreed-upon revenue figure (by the Consensus Revenue Forecasting Estimating Conference) is the baseline number against which proposed spending is judged to ensure that a balanced budget is proposed. Other consensus forecasts provide the economic, demographic, and caseload estimates needed to develop critical economic and demographic information vital to the budget process.

By September, the joint Legislative Budget Commission (LBC) issues a long-range financial outlook to assist the legislature and the state agencies in preparing their spending need estimates. In 2006, Florida voters approved a constitutional amendment creating the LBC in order to improve the state's long-range budget planning. The Legislative Budget Commission consists of an equal number of members of the House and Senate, appointed by the

House Speaker and Senate President respectively (Office of the Majority Whip, 2007).

By October 15, agencies must submit their requests to the governor and the legislature. Unlike the process in most states, agencies submit budget requests directly to both the legislature and the governor, and their requests must be based on their independent judgment of their needs. The governor, with his/her Office of Planning and Budgeting, integrates these requests into two budget documents ("The Governor's Budget Recommendations" and "The Governor's Budget Recommendations: Summary"). The governor must submit these documents to the legislature no later than thirty days before the regular session begins. Naturally, the governor does not give every agency exactly what it originally requests (see Table 12.2). It is the governor's role as the state's chief executive to prioritize these agency requests along the lines of his/her own preferences and priorities. The governor's proposed expenditures must not exceed projected revenue. No later than fourteen days after the governor gives the legislature the budget recommendations documents, he/she must submit "The Governor's Recommended Appropriations Bill." Article III, Section 19 of the Florida constitution requires an itemization of specific appropriations that exceed $1 million (in 1992 dollars). The legislature updates the dollar threshold every four years using the Consumer Price Index.

The state legislature is responsible for passing the General Appropriations Act (GAA) each year. The constitution (Article III, Section 19) requires the appropriations bill to contain seven major program areas: 1) education enhancement lottery trust fund items; 2) all other education funds; 3) human services; 4) criminal justice and corrections; 5) natural resources, environment, growth management, and transportation; 6) general government; and 7) judicial branch.

Prior to the convening of the annual legislative session (the first Tuesday after the first Monday in March), another Consensus Revenue Estimating Conference is held to determine the revenues available for appropriation during the legislative session. Also prior to the session, the President of the Senate and the Speaker of the House provide spending allocation and policy guidelines to their respective committees and councils. During the session, each committee/council formulates its own specific budget proposal based on its allocation and projected expenditure needs. All council and committee budget proposals are then forwarded to the umbrella committee/council in each chamber charged with consolidating the requests into a General Appropriations bill. In the Senate, it is the Fiscal Policy and Calendar Com-

Table 12.2. Comparison of Agency Requests with Recommended Appropriations, FY 2007–2008

Agencies	Governor's Recommendations 2007–2008	Agency Request 2007–2008	Difference ($)	Difference (%)
Administered Funds (Statewide)	$247,204,785	$8,506,056	238,698,729	2806.22
Agency for Health Care Administration	$16,950,161,745	$16,631,710,252	318,451,493	1.91
Agency for Persons With Disabilities	$1,243,344,059	$1,138,808,180	104,535,879	9.18
Agency for Workforce Innovation	$1,543,053,508	$1,547,186,307	-4,132,799	-0.27
Agriculture and Consumer Services	$357,673,092	$431,661,560	-73,988,468	-17.14
Business and Professional Regulation	$141,742,576	$141,348,210	394,366	0.28
Children and Family	$3,004,387,625	$2,946,059,500	58,328,125	1.98
Services	$3,004,387,625	$2,946,059,500	58,328,125	1.98
Citrus	$67,329,861	$67,266,983	62,878	0.09
Community Affairs	$1,617,853,498	$1,610,274,904	7,578,594	0.47
Corrections	$2,516,534,100	$2,479,421,938	37,112,162	1.50
Education	$23,945,881,047	$26,724,637,582	-2,778,756,535	-10.40
Elder Affairs	$393,288,267	$378,146,841	15,141,426	4.00
Environmental Protection	$2,214,545,163	$2,057,906,010	156,639,153	7.61
Executive Office of the Governor	$577,282,906	$156,926,573	420,356,333	267.87
Financial Services	$307,386,180	$305,758,313	1,627,867	0.53
Fish and Wildlife Conservation Commission	$291,595,760	$271,125,017	20,470,743	7.55
Health	$2,766,390,352	$2,617,277,399	149,112,953	5.70
Highway Safety and Motor Vehicles	$435,781,955	$463,999,224	-28,217,269	-6.08
Justice Administration	$787,595,165	$894,211,674	-106,616,509	-11.92
Juvenile Justice	$699,789,058	$699,086,913	702,145	0.10
Law Enforcement	$288,997,962	$293,149,182	-4,151,220	-1.42
Legal Affairs	$175,757,113	$175,783,631	-26,518	-0.02
Legislative Branch	$215,606,098	$215,663,432	-57,334	-0.03
Lottery	$161,528,767	$164,576,719	-3,047,952	-1.85
Management Services	$542,871,201	$536,163,260	6,707,941	1.25
Military Affairs	$63,504,557	$56,318,829	7,185,728	12.76
Parole Commission	$10,106,611	$12,893,552	-2,786,941	-21.61
Public Service Commission	$28,312,382	$28,326,415	-14,033	-0.05
Revenue	$562,899,326	$566,669,639	-3,770,313	-0.67
State	$154,530,300	$114,488,214	40,042,086	34.97
State Court System	$478,677,220	$533,526,765	-54,849,545	-10.28
Transportation	$8,379,712,477	$7,747,594,818	632,117,659	8.16
Veterans' Affairs	$63,875,765	$58,894,378	4,981,387	8.46
Total	$71,235,200,481	$72,075,368,270	-840,167,789	-1.17

Source: Executive Office of the Governor. Available at http://www.ebudget.state.fl.us/bdagencies.aspx?full=1, accessed May 18, 2007.

mittee and in the House, the Policy and Budget Council. Throughout the process, committees and councils conduct hearings where they invite input about the budget requests from individual citizens, special-interest groups, and the governor's office.

Ultimately each house must pass the same version of the General Appropriations Act before it can be sent to the governor to be signed into law. A majority vote in each house is needed to pass the Act. Should the two chambers initially pass different bills (which is almost always the case), a conference committee will be appointed to negotiate a final appropriations bill. The resulting compromise appropriations bill is called the Conference Report. It must be approved by both the Senate and the House and cannot be amended on the floor (Office of the Majority Whip, 2007).

A constitutional amendment passed by Florida voters in 1992 requires a 72-hour waiting period between the introduction of the final proposed General Appropriations Act and its passage by the legislature in order to allow more careful scrutiny (Article III, 19[d]). Copies must be furnished to each legislator and each cabinet member, the chief justice of the Florida Supreme Court, and the governor. (The press usually gets a copy as well.)

Once passed, the General Appropriations Act is sent to the governor for his/her signature. Florida's governor has a line-item veto (Article III, Section 8), which means that specific items, or lines, in the budget can be deleted. Often the mere threat of a veto by the governor may cause legislators to think twice about funding levels for a particular item. Overturning the governor's line-item veto and restoring funding for that item requires a two-thirds vote of each house of the legislature. In a diverse state such as Florida, this is often difficult.

Once the governor receives the General Appropriations Act passed by the legislature, disgruntled agencies, industries, local governments, or individuals who "lost" during the budget process may have one more chance to prevail if they can convince the governor to exercise the line-item veto. Some taxpayer groups such as Florida TaxWatch publish their own list of suggested items to veto. (Florida TaxWatch's widely circulated list of what it judges to be "frivolous" appropriations is called the "Turkey Watch.")

After the budget has been adopted, the Office of Planning and Budgeting develops the Initial Approved Financial Plan and timetables for releasing appropriated funds to state agencies. Throughout the fiscal year, the Legislative Budget Commission is responsible to oversee the budget. Strict rules limit this body's power to release funds or authorize the transfer of appropriated funds for alternative uses.

Several times in Florida's history, legislators have challenged mid-year adjustments the governor has made. Usually the courts have ruled in favor of the legislators because the major responsibility for appropriating funds is constitutionally granted to the state legislature.

State Revenue: Types of Funds Used

The state of Florida finances its operations and infrastructure through three types of funds, all of which are in the custody of the state's elected chief financial officer: 1) the General Revenue Fund; 2) trust funds designated for a specific purpose either by state law, the state constitution, or a trust agreement; and 3) the Budget Stabilization Fund.

About 42 percent of all state funds end up in the General Revenue Fund (GR Fund) (see Figure 12.2.) Revenue not designated for a specific program is placed in this fund. Most of this is tax revenue; the major source is the sales tax. In the FY 2005–2006 budget, about 71 percent of the GR Fund came from the sales tax, 9 percent from the corporate income tax, and the rest from a variety of other smaller revenue sources, including taxes on alcoholic beverage, intangible personal property, estates, and cigarettes (see Figure 12.3). Note: The intangible personal property tax was eliminated as of January 1, 2007.

The remaining 58 percent of all state moneys are placed in trust funds, which hold monies that are designated for a specific purpose, either by general law, the state constitution, or trust agreement. For example, much of the state's motor fuel tax revenue is earmarked for transportation, a certain portion of lottery proceeds goes into the Educational Enhancement Trust Fund, and a portion of a number of state taxes are earmarked for Florida's local governments. Some funds hold monies received from other governmental entities, like the federal government.

The state's largest trust funds are those earmarked for Medicaid, transportation, education, workers' insurance, land conservation, and administration. But there are hundreds of small state trust funds. All trust funds, with limited exceptions, terminate after four years unless they are reenacted. New trust funds may not be created without the approval of three-fifths of the membership of each house of the legislature.

The Budget Stabilization Fund is an emergency-type fund financed by transfers from the General Revenue Fund. It was created by an amendment to the Florida constitution approved by voters in November 1992. It must be funded at a rate of at least 5 percent of the previous year's GR Fund collections. Withdrawals from this fund are allowed only for GR Fund shortfalls

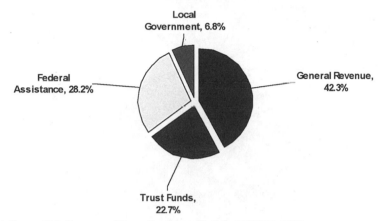

Total $63,470.3 million

Local Government, 6.8%

Federal Assistance, 28.2%

General Revenue, 42.3%

Trust Funds, 22.7%

Figure 12.2. Sources of State Revenue, Florida, FY 2005–2006.

Source: Florida Tax Handbook, 2007, pg. 16. Available at http://edr.state.fl.us/reports/taxhandbooks/taxhandbooks.htm, accessed May 17, 2007.

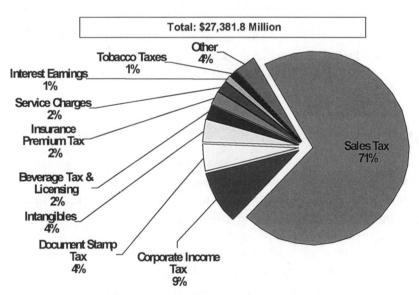

Total: $27,381.8 Million

Other 4%

Tobacco Taxes 1%

Interest Earnings 1%

Service Charges 2%

Insurance Premium Tax 2%

Beverage Tax & Licensing 2%

Intangibles 4%

Document Stamp Tax 4%

Corporate Income Tax 9%

Sales Tax 71%

Figure 12.3. Sources of Revenue, Florida General Fund, 2005–2006.

Source: Actual data for FY 05–06 from Revenue Estimating Conference, April 2006. The Florida Legislature, Office of Economic & Demographic Research "Detailed Revenue Report for FY 2005–2006." Available at http://edr.state.fl.us/reports.htm (accessed May 17, 2007).

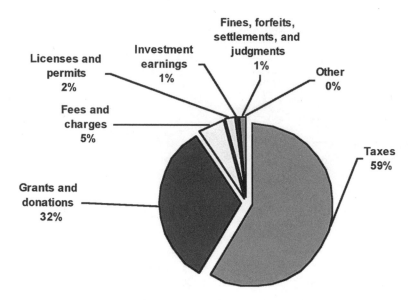

Figure 12.4. Composition of Total State Revenue by Source, Florida, FY 2006.

Source: Florida Department of Financial Services, Comprehensive Annual Financial Report, 2006, pg. 28–29. Available at http://www.fldfs.com/aadir/statewide_financial_reporting/index.htm, accessed May 17, 2007.

and emergencies and must be repaid from general revenues in five equal annual installments, commencing in the third fiscal year after monies are taken out of the Fund, unless the legislature dictates a different repayment schedule.

A Closer Look at Florida's Revenue Structure and Tax History

Florida has nineteen major state taxes and sixteen minor state revenue sources.[5] However, tax revenue makes up only 59 percent of the state's total revenue. Other revenue sources include grants and donations, licenses and permits, fees and charges, investment earnings, fines, forfeitures, judgments, and other sources (see Figure 12.4).

The bulk of Florida's taxes are based on consumption rather than on income or wealth. The state's major income-based tax is the corporate income tax, which contributes around 4 percent of all direct state taxes. In 2005, the two major wealth-based taxes—the intangible personal property tax and the estate tax—together contributed approximately 3 percent of all direct state taxes. However, in 2006, the Florida Legislature abolished the intangible personal property tax, effective January 1, 2007. And because of changes in the federal tax law, Florida's estate tax is expected to be eliminated by 2007.

Florida is one of only seven states without a state personal income tax; the others are Texas, South Dakota, Wyoming, Nevada, Washington, and Alaska. Florida's constitution prohibits a state personal income tax. Therefore, before the state could impose such a tax, a majority of the state's electorate would have to vote to amend the constitution. Most political analysts believe this is not very likely to occur any time soon, especially in a state with an anti-tax reputation. Surveys have consistently shown little support for a personal income tax (Weissert 2005a, 2).

Over the years, the state's tax structure has been altered as its economy and the makeup of its population have changed. The authors of *Florida's Tax Structure* conclude that "Florida's tax structure has changed significantly since 1949 when Florida received 41.4 percent of state revenues from gasoline and motor vehicle taxes and 30.3 percent from so-called 'sin [alcoholic beverage, cigarette and tobacco, pari-mutuel] taxes.'" In 1949, a 3 percent sales and use tax was enacted. Today, sales taxes make up a far larger proportion of the state's revenue than either "sin taxes" or gas taxes.

Florida: A Low-Tax State

Analysts agree that Florida's state and local taxes per capita are lower than those in many other states. So too is its tax burden (calculated by dividing total state and local tax payments by total income). Florida's combined state and local tax burden, 10.0 percent, ranks 38th among the states (The Tax Foundation 2007). Many point to Florida's low tax burden as one of the primary reasons for its economic growth. Others see it in a less positive light, believing that in the long run, higher taxes could help produce greater economic productivity through development of a better-educated work force and improved infrastructure.

Public finance reformers continue to press for a revenue system for the state that is fairer, more diversified, and more broad-based. They favor more wealth-based taxes, more graduated (needs-based) rate structures on existing fees and taxes, and the elimination of various loopholes.

Exemptions, or tax expenditures, as they are formally known, cost the state a lot. A 2005 estimate of the lost revenue from all current tax exemptions, deductions, allowances, exclusions, credits, preferential rates, and deferrals contained in Florida's tax laws put the figure at $47.2 billion (Florida Senate 2005, 181). But reformers' attempts to close these loopholes, such as the attempts that occurred in the early 2000s, have largely been unsuc-

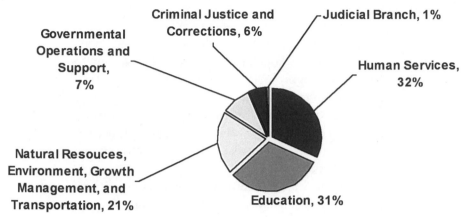

Figure 12.5. Spending Priorities of Florida's General Fund Budget, FY 2006–2007

Source: Florida Tax Handbook, 2007, pg. 17. Available at http://edr.state.fl.us/reports /taxhandbooks/taxhandbooks.htm, accessed May 17, 2007.

cessful. Because many of the loopholes are designed to spur the growth of certain sectors of the economy or areas of the state, proposing that they be closed usually evokes fierce political battles in Tallahassee and/or in the courts.

The Public's Spending Preferences

Ironically, while Floridians want their state elected officials to hold the line on taxes, they expect the state to solve major problems in meeting the needs of Florida's residents. The state spends the most of its General Fund Budget on health and human services (32 percent) and education (31 percent) (see Figure 12.5).

This spending pattern seems to reflect the citizenry's priorities. Numerous monthly surveys of Floridians have found that Floridians favor spending more for health care programs for the poor and near-poor (e.g., Medicaid) and K-12 education than for highways or even higher education (Weissert 2005a, 2–3). In 2002, voters approved constitutional amendments that reduced class size in public education and provided for a free voluntary prekindergarten program for four-year-olds. But the spending categories of health care and primary education represent potential threats to the state's credit rating. Fitch, a bond rating firm, identified as key credit risks for the state "large, primarily growth-related capital needs, especially for schools, and very rapid growth of Medicaid spending, which will need to be contained."[6]

Medicaid is a tremendously complex federal-state program for the poor, elderly, and disabled. It is the fastest-growing element of most states' budgets. It has been labeled "the 800-pound gorilla" by some (Weissert 2005b, 83). To its credit, Florida has been in the forefront of Medicaid reform. In fall 2005, the state received a Medicaid waver to allow it to experiment with a program in two test counties that would allow enrollees to choose among managed care plans and to create individual benefits accounts that offer extended benefits if they take steps to improve their health (Denslow with Dai 2005, 81).

Earmarked Revenue Dictates Some Spending Patterns

Certain revenue sources are dedicated to specific spending categories. For example, lottery monies are earmarked for education but not for any of the other major spending categories, while the more unrestricted general revenue monies help support a portion of virtually every major spending category. Once a revenue source becomes linked to a specific function (or functions), it is quite difficult politically to reverse this linkage. The more earmarks are in place constitutionally or statutorily, the more difficult it becomes to adopt significant shifts in budgetary priorities.

Efforts to Contain Costs

Finding more efficient and effective ways of providing public services can help control spending. Over the years, the state's governors and legislators have turned to high-profile, high-powered commissions, task forces, and study groups made up of leaders from across the state to find ways to improve government operations. This approach began with the creation of the Tax and Budget Reform Commission (constitutionally mandated by Florida voters in 1988) and has continued with Partners in Productivity, the Productivity Measurement and Quality Improvement Task Force, the Governor's Commission for Government by the People, the Commission on Accountability to the People, the Governor's Commission on Workers' Compensation Reform, the Study Committee on Public Records, the Property Tax Reform Committee, and others.

Evaluation units have also been set up within government. In 1994, the legislature created the Office of Program Policy Analysis and Government Accountability (OPPAGA) to regularly examine how much programs cost and measure their efficiency and effectiveness. The office has become "a leader in performance evaluation" with "a reputation for high-quality independent performance audits" that "include baseline data that allows one to compare actual program or agency performance to past or targeted performance levels" (Government Performance Project 2005).

Privatization is another cost-containment technique that has been used by state and local governments in Florida, albeit with mixed results (see Baker 1996). The 1994 Government Accountability and Performance Act required the governor and cabinet, sitting as the State Council on Competitive Government, to consider whether certain state services can be best provided by private enterprise. Efforts were made to privatize sections of the state government, some of which were more successful than others. Negative findings from early OPPAGA analyses about some of the privatization efforts prompted the governor to issue an executive order in 2004 creating the Governor's Center for Efficient Government, which is housed in the Department of Management Services. The center is charged with "providing a more transparent and deliberative review of state contracts with private companies."[7]

In an effort to get rid of agencies or programs that are no longer needed (one of the most difficult tasks politically), the legislature passed the Florida Government Accountability Act in 2006. It is, in effect, a "sunset law" that calls for various state agencies to be automatically abolished unless the legislature decides to continue them. The act set a timetable for each state agency's legislative review and mandated the creation of a Legislative Sunset Advisory Committee to advise the legislature in its sunset decisions. But getting rid of an agency is easier said than done; each agency has its own significant groups of supporters.

State Borrowing

Florida's voters historically have been more likely to vote for bond issues (borrowing) than for new or higher taxes, especially for infrastructure (roads, bridges, schools, water-related projects) and for the purchase of environmentally sensitive land.

As of 2006, the state's outstanding debt totaled $23 billion. Over three-fourths of this debt is in the form of full faith and credit bonds (tax-backed general obligation bonds) that must be approved by Florida voters. Examples of things funded by these bonds include Public Education Capital Outlay

(PECO), improvement of the university system, Preservation 2000/Florida Forever, Save Our Coast, acquisition of right of way and bridges and funding for construction of ports, prisons, and affordable housing. The remainder of the outstanding debt is in revenue bonds (self-supporting debt) backed by a specific tax or revenue source. These do not require voter approval. Examples of projects funded in this way are the state's toll roads and facilities and projects to control water pollution and construct auxiliary facilities at universities.

By law, the state's Division of Bond Finance must conduct an annual debt affordability study to be used as a tool for measuring, monitoring, and repaying the state's debt.[8] Explicit rules govern the amount the state can borrow. For example, the amount borrowed through full faith and credit bonds may not exceed 50 percent of total state tax revenue for the two preceding fiscal years. The state debt fiscal responsibility policy (Florida Statutes, Chapter 215.98) establishes debt service to revenue as the benchmark ratio that must be used to estimate future debt capacity. The target ratio is 6 percent; the cap ratio is 7 percent.

Florida's credit rating has always been good. But in 2005, its full faith and credit bond rating was upgraded from AA+ to AAA, thereby saving the state millions in interest costs. Standard & Poor's applauded the state for its "strong and conservative financial and budget management practices, coupled with substantial budget reserves and economic trends that have been among the strongest nationally." It also cited 1) stable revenue performance over the past several years, setting Florida apart from most other states; 2) budget pressures that have been effectively managed as the state continues to fund various constitutional amendments and the service demands of a growing population; 3) a service-based economy with growth that continues to outpace the national economy as measured by employment, population, and gross state product; 4) solid economic growth prospects over the long term and a strong competitive position in the Southeast; 5) average income levels; and 6) a moderate debt burden that will remain stable because of legal guidelines. Another key factor identified by Standard and Poor's that contributed to Florida's excellent credit rating is the actuarial soundness of the Florida Retirement System, which is "contrary to trends for many other states."[9]

Borrowing remains a popular way of bridging the gap between insufficient current revenue and the revenue needed to fund capital projects. We can expect continued use of borrowing to meet growth- and security-driven infrastructure demands, especially for new schools, roads and turnpikes, airport and port security, and correctional facilities.

Financing Florida's Local Governments

Public opinion polls consistently show that Floridians believe their local governments are more responsive than the state or the national government. Taxpayers also feel that local governments give them the most for their tax dollars. On the other hand, when things start falling apart, local governments are much easier to access with complaints via initiatives, referenda, protests, and boycotts than the other government structures.

Many local officials find it frustrating that decisions made by higher levels of government sometimes produce less-than-desirable results at the local level. Often the public does not understand how or why these results have happened. Local officials, like state officeholders, often represent constituents who have little or no interest in paying higher taxes or fees to address certain problems. Many genuinely believe that governments take in far more than enough revenue and could solve most problems if they would just use the revenue on hand more efficiently and effectively (MacManus 1995; Benton and Daly 1992). The situation is described perfectly in *A Profile of Florida Municipal and County Revenues*: "In the face of state-imposed revenue-raising and revenue-expenditure constraints, state mandates, burgeoning population growth, as well as citizen expectations for expanded services [but not higher property taxes], Florida's municipalities and counties struggle to fund their budgeting needs" (Advisory Council on Intergovernmental Relations 1989, 10)

Over the past several decades, local government officials have pressured the state for greater authority to raise revenue and more state aid and have pressured the state to restrict the number of unfunded mandates and regulations. Some progress has been made, although not as much as local governments would like. The wish lists of county commissioners and city council members remain the same: fewer state mandates, more money for capital projects (particularly in high-growth areas), more unrestricted revenue sources, regulatory relief, fewer restrictions on interlocal agreements, and more local control over growth management plans.

Periodically, state-local government relations become quite strained, as was the case in 2007 when the governor and the Republican-controlled state legislature proposed a radical revamping of local property taxes—a restructuring perceived by local officials to be highly punitive and fiscally devastating. For many local governments, the property tax is their major source of revenue.

Fearing major budget shortfalls, local government officials vehemently opposed a legislature-sponsored constitutional amendment that proposed doubling the homestead exemption (except for school district taxes), allowing homestead property owners to transfer up to $500,000 of their Save-

Our-Homes benefits to their next homestead (portability), giving businesses a $25,000 exemption for personal tangible property, and capping annual property assessment increases for non-homesteaded property at 10 percent (except for school district taxes).

Revenue Restrictions Facing Florida's Local Governments

Florida's constitution imposes major revenue-raising constraints on local governments. It preempts to the state all tax sources not specifically provided by law except for the ad valorem (property) tax (Article VII, Section 1). This means that the state has first rights on all revenue sources except the property tax. But the state limits the collection of local property taxes in a number of ways.

State Limits on Local Property Taxes

First, the state sets a maximum property tax, or millage, rate. (A mill is defined as 1/1000th of a dollar or $1 per $1000 of taxable value.) The Florida constitution caps the millage rate for Florida's local governments at 10 mills for county purposes, 10 mills for municipal purposes, and 10 mills for school purposes. It allows the legislature to set the millage rate for a county that is furnishing municipal services. The legislature also sets the millage rate limits for special districts, but they must be approved by voters. Interestingly, Duval County–City of Jacksonville has a 20-mill cap since it operates as both a county and municipal government. Some of the smaller rural jurisdictions are close to the 10-mill cap.

Second, the legislature requires school districts to levy a certain millage rate or face loss of state funds from the Florida Education Finance Program. This required local effort is determined annually by the General Appropriations Act.

Third, the state constitution or statutes mandate certain exemptions for property taxes or rate differentials that take away revenue from local governments. The biggest of these is the constitutionally guaranteed homestead exemption. This permits any homeowner to exempt $25,000 of the assessed value of the property from property taxation. The exemption hits smaller and poorer local governments hardest. But it is a very popular exemption, and all attempts to reduce it have failed miserably at the hands of the state's voters. In fact, Floridians keep voting to offer more exemptions. In 1998, they voted to offer an additional homestead tax exemption for those 65 and older with limited income, and in 2002 they voted to offer an exemption to home owners who improved their property by constructing living quarters for parents or grandparents (the "granny flat" amendment).[10] In 2006, Florida voters approved an amendment that allows local governments to double the homestead exemption for low-income seniors from $25,000 to $50,000 and an amendment authorizing a property tax discount for a partially or totally permanently disabled veteran who is 65 or older, was a Florida resident at the time he entered military service, and whose disability is combat-related. And, as previously noted, in 2008 Florida voters were asked to approve property tax–related exemptions for homeowners and businesses.

A constitutional amendment approved by voters in 1992 limits the annual growth rate of assessments on homestead property to 3 percent or the inflation rate (the increase in the Consumer Price Index), whichever is greater; this amendment has greatly affected high-growth counties. Another amendment, the Save Our Homes amendment, has taken a lot of potential property tax revenue out of the coffers of local governments, particularly in recent years when housing values have increased sharply. It is designed to prevent homeowners from having to sell their homes because they cannot pay the increasing property tax. Local governments must wait until the home is sold to begin taxing at the current market value. Meanwhile, there is a gap between the property-tax monies local governments *can* collect and those they *do* collect. There is also a gap between the assessed value of a homestead property and the actual market value that effectively reduces the amount of property tax that can be generated by local governments. In 2004, Save Our Homes saved individual Florida homeowners $2.9 billion in county property taxes. The homestead exemption saved them another $2.2 billion. Together, they cost local governments over $5 billion in lost revenue (Tamman 2005).

Over time, the Save Our Homes amendment created a property tax system that is perceived to be highly unfair by many, most notably new homeowners, people with second homes, especially "snowbirds," nonresidents who have vacation homes in the state, and business owners. Some 68 percent of all the state's property owners fall into one of these categories (Whitehouse, 2007).

Save Our Homes, beloved by many homeowners with no plans to move, was not so revered by those who wanted to move to another home but feared loss of the Save Our Homes property tax growth cap. This prompted some legislators to propose making the Save Our Homes provision portable while at the same time it evoked loud cries of opposition from local officials fearing more revenue losses. Revamping Save Our Homes proved to be one of the most painful and difficult fiscal tasks ever to face state legislators. It was a central element in the property tax revolt that swept through Florida in the mid-2000s, as through much of the nation. It pitted state and local government officials against each other, just as it did different classes of property owners.

A wide range of other property tax exemptions, tax rate differentials, and assessment rate differentials (e.g., for property owned by governments, churches and nonprofits, widows/widowers, or disabled persons; property being used for economic development, agricultural property, parks and recreational lands; and property used to control pollution) also takes tax revenue away from local governments. Proponents argue that these exemptions make the property tax less regressive and/or prevent environmental problems associated with the elimination of open space.

Exemptions and rate differentials reflect a community's values, as does tax policy in general. But once exemptions and rate differentials are put in place, they are virtually impossible to get rid of, even if values and conditions change. Attempts to eliminate them are painted as property tax increases by beneficiaries—a political kiss of death in many Florida communities. This is why local government officials resent it when state officials impose them on localities.

State Limits on Local Sales Taxes

For years, local governments in Florida were considerably more restricted in their ability to impose local sales taxes than their counterparts in many other states; the only way they could raise local sales tax revenue was by piggybacking the local tax on the state tax. But between 1976 and 1996, the Florida legislature authorized fifteen new local sales tax options. While these were an important step in the right direction, these options are still much more restrictive than local officials believe they should be in terms of which local governments can use them, how the funds must be spent, and how they are adopted. Larger jurisdictions are generally given more authority to levy these local option taxes than smaller jurisdictions.

Most local-option general sales taxes permitted by the Florida legislature have been earmarked for limited purposes (e.g. transit systems, indigent care, public hospitals, the homeless, infrastructure, conservation and acquisition of recreation land, tourism development, school construction, professional sports facilities). They can be adopted only by voter approval or, in some cases, by an extraordinary majority vote of the local legislative body. Generally, counties have broader authority to use these taxes than cities or special districts.

Occasionally, the legislature has granted local governments the right to impose sales taxes of a selective nature (e.g., on fuel, hotel and motel rooms, and restaurant food and beverages). But these too must be approved by voters or extraordinary votes of the county commission or city council and be used for specific purposes. Many are limited to jurisdictions that meet certain size thresholds.

The state legislature did not grant school boards the right to impose any kind of local-option sales tax until 1995. Now districts can propose a half-cent general sales tax, but the tax cannot be levied without voter approval and it must be used for school construction. The electoral successes of these sales tax votes have been mixed.

State Prohibition of Local Personal Income Taxes

Florida prohibits its local governments from imposing a local personal income tax or payroll tax. (As noted earlier, the state itself is constitutionally prohibited from levying a personal income tax.) The truth is that almost no local officials have requested this taxing authority. Polls show that an income tax is even less popular with voters than the property tax.

State Aid: Locals Want More, the State Offers Less

Local officials *have* asked the state for more state aid, in the form of general shared tax revenue or grant money, although a number of state revenue sources are already shared in some measure with Florida's local governments. Generally, state-shared revenue programs authorize the state to allocate a portion of a state-collected tax to specified local governments based on eligibility requirements. State law determines how much of a particular state tax or fee will be shared with local governments (if any) and for what purpose. In general, Florida's counties and cities get considerably more money from state-shared revenue than they do from the federal government.

Florida's counties receive shares of the state's revenue from beverage license taxes; various gas, fuel, and road taxes; cigarette taxes; insurance license taxes; general sales taxes and user fees; intangible property taxes; mobile home license taxes; oil, gas, and sulfur production taxes; the phosphate rock severance tax; and the wireless enhanced 911 fee.

The state's municipalities receive shares of the state's taxes on beverage licenses; cigarettes; insurance premiums; intangible property; gas, fuel, and road usage; general sales; and mobile home licenses. As with counties, municipalities generally have unrestricted use of many of these revenue sources (with the exception of gas, fuel, and road usage taxes, which are earmarked for roads and transportation, and the documentary stamp tax, which is earmarked for affordable housing).

The state's school districts receive portions of the state's lottery proceeds, fuel taxes, and mobile home license taxes. Of these revenue sources, the most misunderstood and controversial is the lottery. It was approved by Florida's voters in 1986 following an expensive high-profile marketing campaign, but many citizens soon became somewhat disillusioned with the lottery. They discovered that lottery funds were being substituted for tax dollars that had previously been earmarked for education. In other words, rather than increasing the overall proportion of the state's budget going to education, lottery funds were merely being substituted for other state funds, which were transferred elsewhere. There was no net gain in the percentage of the state's budget going to education.

The lottery has become a symbol of the state government's failure to spend Florida taxpayers' dollars as promised. It has made it very difficult for local governments to use earmarking strategies to get voters to approve new local revenue sources. Surveys asking voters why they would (or did) vote against a half-penny sales tax earmarked for school construction often find that their disillusionment with the lottery is a major reason for voting "no."

In 1997, Florida's lawmakers enacted the Bright Futures Scholarship Program, which is funded by the lottery proceeds, in an attempt to restore the public's faith in the lottery. The program, an idea borrowed from Georgia, rewards graduating high school students for their academic achievements by providing lottery funding to help them pursue postsecondary educational and career goals in Florida. The legislature has also passed laws that give more authority to local school districts, community colleges, and universities to decide how they will spend the funds instead of leaving the decision to the State Department of Education in Tallahassee.

Revenue Reliance and Expenditure Patterns of Local Governments

Florida's local governments vary in their revenue reliance patterns primarily for three reasons. First, the State of Florida does not permit all local governments to tap the same revenue sources at the same rate. Second, local governments have different functional responsibilities. Third, the socioeconomic and political makeup of Florida's communities varies considerably, thereby affecting revenue assessment and collection patterns.

Overall, Florida's counties are the most dependent on taxes (primarily property taxes), school districts on state aid, and cities and special district governments on service charges. (See Figure 12.6, which does not include school districts.) Many of the services municipalities and special districts deliver are amenable to user fees and charges, including parks and recreation, water, sewers, solid waste collection, and utilities. In contrast, counties in Florida deliver a larger proportion of public-good services such as courts, corrections, roads, health, welfare, voter registration, and libraries, which are not associated with fees (Bradley 1989). And school districts deliver education, also a public good.

Most of the state's local governments have fairly good credit ratings (A

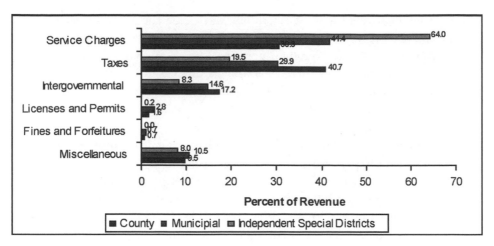

Figure 12.6. Florida's Local Government Revenues by Type of Income, FY 2005.

Source: Florida Legislative Committee on Intergovernmental Relations. Available at http://www .floridalcir.gov/stwidefiscal.html, accessed May 18, 2007.

or higher). Increasingly, more of Florida's governments are buying insurance to protect their borrowing and to secure a higher bond rating. But the City of Miami nearly collapsed fiscally in 1996 and 1997 (following widespread corruption involving elected officials and city financial managers), which has caused the state, local government auditors, and national credit rating firms to scrutinize bond sale offerings by local governments more carefully.

Challenges Ahead: Blue or Gray Skies or a Little of Both?

Florida's state and local governments face some formidable fiscal challenges in the years ahead. Revenue will not grow as fast as demands for expenditures (especially for education, health and family matters, prisons, transportation, and environmental protection), which are driven by the state's changing population demographics, spending-related constitutional amendments, federal mandates, and lawsuits.

Governments, too, face spending needs of their own, primarily for technological improvements. In an era of taxpayer animosity toward higher taxes and more government, governmental agencies must find other ways to improve their efficiency to reduce the rate of growth in spending. Up-to-date technology that is more in line with what the private sector has is seen as an important way to streamline operations, reduce paperwork, and hold down costs. Rising health insurance costs for government workers is another serious problem with major fiscal consequences. Finally, the state may face a knowledge gap among its employees as the baby boomers retire and not enough younger workers enter state government jobs to replace the retiring generation.

In the years ahead, Florida's public sector must face the challenge of raising enough revenue to meet the needs associated with continued, albeit slower, population growth. Raising more revenue without creating disincentives to further economic development or fueling another taxpayers' revolt will not be easy. To date, the state's efforts to diversify revenue have had limited success for both constitutional and political reasons. The state remains heavily dependent on consumption-based taxes that fluctuate considerably as the economy moves. But a clash between public and private sector officials is likely if the only new revenue sources proposed are aimed exclusively at businesses. At the same time, the public is becoming increasingly weary and resentful of the tax breaks given to big corporations and wealthy business owners, especially sports team owners.

Raising more revenue could become a bigger problem for small rural county governments, large municipalities, and many school districts as they approach the 10-mill limit on property taxes they can levy. It will be virtually impossible to raise the limit because it is established in the Florida Constitution and because voters would need to consent to change the constitution, not a likely prospect. This could force the state to rewrite formulas to share taxes and/or distribute state aid.

The issue of the unused capacity of local governments to levy taxes could become a point of greater tension between the state and its local governments, especially if local governments that are not at their millage caps continue to complain about state aid levels. State officials, who have their own fiscal stress, are not likely to be sympathetic to requests for more aid from local governments that have not taken full advantage of the taxing options available to them under state law. Local officials say this is an unrealistic expectation, tantamount to political suicide, particularly since the need for higher local taxes is often a consequence of more state mandates and regulations.

Another challenge the state faces is the development of fiscal policies that adequately address the vastly different and widening demographic, socio-economic, and political profiles of the state's high-growth and low-growth areas. This will be difficult because cities and counties in different economic circumstances will likely end up working against each other when they pressure state officials to alter revenue-sharing formulas and spending requirements.

Always worrisome is the status of federal support for military bases, defense contracts, and the NASA space program, each of which brings in billions of dollars to Florida. Emergency management demands are becoming more intense, especially on local governments, which must fund the first responders and bolster vulnerable infrastructure. It is difficult to gauge federal fiscal support for homeland security and disaster relief.

Finally, the search for solutions to Florida's future fiscal problems will have to take into account the state's aging population, which is already sparking some intergenerational tensions between older and younger constituents and its increasingly diverse racial/ethnic population. These tensions often pit groups against each other in the struggle for funding. Reaching a consensus on budget priorities is likely to become more difficult.

The good news is that Florida continues to be a magnet for people and jobs—the key ingredients of Florida's economy.

Notes

1. The source for the number of cities as of October 2005 is www.flcities.com. The source for the number of special district governments is a report by Florida Department of Community Affairs (2005).

2. Figures are from Standard & Poor's Public Finance, RatingsDirect, February 25, 2005.

3. *Florida Consensus Estimating Conference Book 2, Revenue Analysis FY 1970–71 through FY 2005–06*, 6; Florida Legislative Committee on Intergovernmental Relations, "State Revenues Shared with Local Governments and School Districts, 1974–2003," www.floridalcir.gov/dataStoZ.html (accessed May 17, 2007).

4. A telephone survey of a random sample of 800 adult Floridians was conducted December 7–24, 2004, by Susan Schuler & Associates for the Collins Center For Public Policy, Inc., and the James Madison Institute, both of Tallahassee.

5. The major state taxes are auto title and lien fees; beverage tax; cigarette and other tobacco products tax; communication services tax; corporation income tax; documentary stamp taxes; taxes on drivers' licenses; estate tax; gross receipts tax on utilities; insurance premium tax; intangibles tax; funds from the state lottery; motor fuel taxes; taxes on motor vehicle and mobile home licenses; pari-mutuel tax; pollutant taxes; sales and use tax; severance tax—oil and gas; severance tax—solid minerals. Minor taxes are taxes on beverage licenses; citrus taxes; corporation fees; dry cleaning tax; taxes on health care assessments; hotel and restaurant licenses and fees; hunting and fishing licenses; inspection licenses and fees; taxes on insurance licenses; taxes on motorboat licenses; professional and occupational licensing fees; securities fees; service charges; unemployment compensation tax; and workers' compensation assessments. (Note: In 2007, the occupational license tax became a "local business tax," the estate tax and taxes on intangibles were abolished, and the surcharge on alcoholic beverages sold for consumption on premises was repealed.)

6. "Fitch Ratings Upgrades $11.7B Florida GOs to 'AA+,'" *Business Wire*, March 3, 2005, www.thefreelibrary.com/Fitch+Ratings+Upgrades+%2411.7B+Florida+GOs+to +'AA%2b'-a0129636206 (accessed on May 17, 2007).

7. [Florida] Department of Manage Services, "Governor's Center for Efficient Government Introduces New Process to Management State Procurement and Contracting," press release, July 8, 2004.

8. Standard & Poor's Public Finance, RatingsDirect, February 25, 2005.

9. Ibid.

10. The estimated loss of revenue in FY 2005 from these two sources of revenue was $25.8 million (Florida Senate 2005, 143).

References

Advisory Council on Intergovernmental Relations. 1989. "A Profile of Florida Municipal and County Revenues." www.floridalcir.gov/reports/profile89.pdf (accessed on May 18, 2007).

Baker, Keith G. 1996. "Privatization: Two Opinions." In *Florida TaxWatch* (April).

Benton, J. Edwin, and John L. Daly. 1992. "The Paradox of Citizen Service Evaluations and Tax Preferences: The Case of Two Small Cities." *American Review of Public Administration* 22, no. 4: 271–87.

Boswell, Thomas, June Nogle, Rob Paral, and Richard Langendorf. 2001. *Facts about Immigration and Asking "Six Big Questions" for Florida and Miami-Dade County*. Gainesville: University of Florida, Bureau of Economic and Business Research.

Bradley, Robert. 1989. "Intergovernmental Design, Legislative Mandates, Revenue Flexibility, and Local Relations." Paper presented at the Governor's Conference on Local Government in the 1990s, Clearwater, Florida, January 18–19.

Caruson, Kiki, and Susan A. MacManus. 2006a. "Funding Homeland Security and Hurricane Preparedness: Florida's Local Governments Face Formidable Fiscal Pressures." *Municipal Finance Journal, July 2006*, 27, no. 2: 75–93.

———. 2006b. "Mandates and Management Challenges in the Trenches: An Intergovernmental Perspective of Homeland Security." *Public Administration Review, July/ August 2006* 66, no. 4: 522–36.

Denslow, David. 2005. "The Structure of Employment in Florida." In *Tough Choices: Shaping Florida's Future*, edited by David Denslow and Carol Weissert. 417–42. Gainesville and Tallahassee: University of Florida and Florida State University.

Denslow, David, with Chifeng Dai. 2005. "Expenditure Projections: Medicaid." In Tough Choices: Shaping Florida's Future, edited by David Denslow and Carol Weissert. 61–82. Gainesville and Tallahassee: University of Florida and Florida State University.

Executive Office of the Governor. 2005. *Long-Range Program Plan Fiscal Years 2006– 2007 through 2010–2011 (Trends and Conditions Statement)*. Tallahassee, Fla.: Executive Office of the Governor.

Florida Department of Community Affairs. 2005. "Special District Information Program." www.floridaspecialdistricts.org/OfficialList/numbr_of.asp (accessed March 15, 2005).

Florida Department of Management Services. 2004. "Governor's Center For Efficient Government Introduces New Process to Manage State Procurement and Contracting." Press release, July 8.

Florida Legislative Committee on Intergovernmental Relations. 2003–2005. *Local Government Financial Information Handbook*. Tallahassee: FLCIR.

Florida Senate. 2005. *2005 Florida Tax Handbook*. Tallahassee: Florida Senate.

Government Performance Project. 2005. "Florida: Information." In *Grading the States 2005: Florida*, 10–12, www.gpponline.org/StateOverview.aspx?relatedid=1&statec onst=STATE_FL (accessed March 15, 2007).

Hafenbrack, Josh. 2005. "Scripps Land May Be Sold to Developers to Keep Business Deals Secret." *South Florida Sun-Sentinel*, August 12.

Hill, Kevin. 2004. "Florida's Black Voters: Regional Concentration, National Origin Diversity, and Partisanship." In *Florida Politics: Ten Media Markets, One Powerful State*, edited by Kevin A. Hill, Susan A. MacManus, and Dario Moreno. 65–82. Tallahassee: Florida Institute of Government.

Hovey, Kendra A., and Harold A. Hovey. 2005. *CQ's State Fact Finder 2005*. Washington, D.C.: CQ Press.

MacManus, Susan A. 1995. "The Constituents Are Mad: Just Ask Florida's Local Government Budget Chiefs." *Government Finance Review* 11 (August 1): 11–16.

———. 1996. *Young v. Old: Generational Combat in the 21st Century*. Boulder, Colo.: Westview Press.

———. 2004a. "'Bricks and Mortar' Politics: How Infrastructure Decisions Defeat Incumbents." *Public Budgeting & Finance* 24:96–112.

———. 2004b. "Florida Overview: Ten Media Markets, One Powerful State." In *Florida Politics: Ten Media Markets, One Powerful State*, edited by Kevin A. Hill, Susan A. MacManus, and Dario Moreno. 1–64. Tallahassee: Florida Institute of Government.

———. 2005a. "Florida's Senior Voters in Election 2004: Results, Top Issues, Reforms, & New Concerns." *Public Policy & Aging Reports* 15:10–14.

———. 2005b. "Florida: The South's Premier Battleground State." *American Review of Politics* 26 (Summer): 155–84.

Moreno, Dario. 2004. "Florida's Hispanic Voters: Growth, Immigration, and Political Clout." In *Florida Politics: Ten Media Markets, One Powerful State*, edited by Kevin A. Hill, Susan A. MacManus, and Dario Moreno. 83–100. Tallahassee: Florida Institute of Government.

Morrell, Stephen O. 2005. "The Less Risky Florida Economy." *Florida TaxWatch* (July), www.floridataxwatch.org/centers/ccf.php (accessed March 15, 2007).

Office of the Majority Whip Representative Ellyn Bogdanoff. 2007. "Whip's Policy Brief," April 11.

Pritchett, Mark, and Bob McClure. 2005. "Poll Shows Public Distrust of Amendment Process." *Journal of the James Madison Institute* 30 (Winter): 4–6, 11.

Tamman, Maurice. 2005. "State's Homestead Cap Creates Rigid Tax Caste System." *Sarasota Herald-Tribune*, September 18, http://search.theledger.com/apps/pbcs. dll/article?AID=/20050918/NEWS/509180417&SearchID=73281272241559 (accessed on May 17, 2007).

Taylor-West, Carole. 1995. "Regional Heterogeneity of the Florida Economy." In *The Economy of Florida*, edited by J. F. Scoggins and Ann C. Pierce. 1–31. Gainesville: Bureau of Economic and Business Research, University of Florida.

The Tax Foundation. 2007. "Florida's State and Local Tax Burden, 1970–2007." www.taxfoundation.org/taxdata/show/447.html (accessed May 28, 2007).

U.S. Bureau of the Census. 2000. www.census.gov. http://factfinder.census.gov/servlet/QTTable?_bm=y&-geo_id=04000US12&-qr_name=DEC_2000_SF3_U_QTP22&-ds_name=DEC_2000_SF3_U_.

Weissert, Carol. 2005a. "Introduction." In *Tough Choices: Shaping Florida's Future*, edited by David Denslow and Carol Weissert. 1–6. Gainesville and Tallahassee: University of Florida and Florida State University.

———. 2005b. "Medicaid: The 800-Pound Gorilla." In *Tough Choices: Shaping Florida's Future*, edited by David Denslow and Carol Weissert. 83–119. Gainesville and Tallahassee: University of Florida and Florida State University.

Whitehouse, Mark. 2007. "Florida Hones Plan to Overhaul Property Taxes." *The Wall Street Journal*, May 29.

Zannis, J. C., with David Denslow. 2005. "International Immigration." In *Tough Choices: Shaping Florida's Future*, edited by David Denslow and Carol Weissert. 373–86. Gainesville and Tallahassee: University of Florida and Florida State University.

13

Florida's Education System

LYNNE HOLT AND BABAK LOTFINIA

Florida's public education system includes all levels of education in the state: pre-kindergarten, kindergarten, grades 1 through 12, two-year community colleges, and four-year colleges and universities. In 2002, the Florida legislature articulated the following vision and goals for the educational system: that it be coordinated and seamless from kindergarten through graduate school, that it be student centered, that it provide for maximum access and high-quality education, that it safeguard equity, and that it provide local operational flexibility while promoting accountability. All levels of the educational system in Florida are responsible for adhering to these expectations, but they have their own distinct missions, institutional oversight bodies, enrollment profiles, funding issues, financial pressures, and challenges. This chapter will highlight and discuss these fundamental differences among the components of Florida's public education system.

Florida's K-12 Public Education System

Mission

Florida's public school system is a large part of the state government, consisting of 67 school districts, almost 4,100 schools, 320,225 full-time staff, and over 2.6 million students (Florida Department of Education 2007a). Its objective is to provide, in the words of the Florida constitution, a "uniform, efficient, safe, secure, and high quality system of free public schools that allows students to obtain a high quality education." Education is mandatory in Florida for children ages 6 to 16, but they have a wide array of choices in how they fulfill that requirement. Students may attend public, parochial, or private schools, and they may be educated in home-schooling or private tutoring programs.

Institutional Oversight

The public school system falls under the jurisdiction of the State Board of Education, which is authorized by statute to set broad policies and standards for Florida's schools and to submit annual budget requests for the entire education system to the governor and the legislature. The Florida Department of Education, which is within the State Board of Education, administers K-12 programs and initiatives and disseminates information to the public about the K-12 public education system. Pursuant to a constitutional amendment adopted in 2002 and enabling legislation enacted in 2004, the department is also responsible for creating standards, curricula, and the accountability regime for the Voluntary Pre-Kindergarten Education Program, which provides early learning experiences for Florida's four-year-old children. Below the board and department are the local school districts, each of which is geographically identical to the county it serves and is governed by an elected school board. The school boards are required to implement and supplement state laws and rules and generate plans required by the state. Each school board also is required to operate and maintain its district's school system and have a superintendent, who functions as the executive officer of the school board and who is responsible for the administration, management, and supervision of the schools and instruction in the district. The school board is also required to create a school advisory council for each school in its district. Each council's membership consists of the principal and representatives of the teachers, support employees, students, parents, businesspeople and the wider community. Each council prepares and evaluates the school improvement plan required by state law and helps prepare its school's annual budget.

Enrollment

Projections

In 2005–2006, enrollment in Florida's public primary and secondary school system was well over 2.6 million (Florida Department of Education 2006d). Enrollment declined throughout the second half of the 1970s but then increased by almost 76 percent from the period 1984–1985 to 2005–2006. Much of that increase—about 31 percent—occurred between 1990 and 2000. However, enrollment is expected to slow down in coming years and has even dipped slightly in 2006–2007 from the previous year.[1] Part of the reason for the projected slow-down is demographic, but part may be attributable to accelerated graduation and growing enrollment in private and home schools.

Student Profile

Since 1980–1981, there has been a shift in the grades most affected by enrollment increases in Florida's public schools. For example, enrollment in the ninth grade has almost doubled from 127,000 students in 1980–1981 to 246,000 in 2005–2006, an increase of over 70 percent in the past fifteen years, compared to an increase of less than 40 percent for Florida's public schools overall. The racial and ethnic composition of K-12 students in Florida's public schools has also changed over the years: in the 28-year period from 1978 to 2006, the share of white students in Florida's public schools fell from almost 70 percent of the total enrollment to less than 47 percent. During that time period, the share of minority students rose from 30 percent to 52 percent; the Hispanic student population accounted for the largest enrollment gains (Florida Department of Education 2007c).

Funding

According to the state's constitution, public schooling in Florida is freely provided to students. The state and school districts fund their obligations from proceeds from tax revenue and federal resources.

Operating Expenses

In fiscal year 2004–2005, the state's share of public education funding for operating expenses, such as wages and supplies, was 43.26 percent, the districts collectively contributed 46.38 percent, and federal funds covered the remaining 10.36 percent (Florida Department of Education 2006b, 1). Most of the state and local funding for operational costs is determined by the Florida Education Finance Program (FEFP), which was established by the legislature in 1973 to equalize school funding among Florida's districts.[2] It consists principally of proceeds from property and sales taxes from the school districts and a broad mix of state revenues, although the calculations that determine the share of total funding the state and districts are responsible for are closely related.

The FEFP is designed to provide an equal base level of educational resources across Florida's sixty-seven school districts, primarily by redistributing funds from counties with a high tax base per student to counties with a low tax base per student. The FEFP also adjusts for differences in costs inherent in various programs (for example, for exceptional and special education students) and for differences in personnel costs among counties. The FEFP also includes a number of programs to help schools provide supplemental instruction, establish reading programs, and cope with declining enrollment among other activities. In addition to the FEFP, the state provides funds for transportation, school safety, technology, and other programs related to instruction (known as "categorical programs"), including allocations to districts for operating expenditures to meet new requirements about smaller class sizes. In 2006–2007, state and local funding for operating expenses totaled $18.3 billion and was comprised of $9.9 billion in state funds and $8.4 billion in local funds. Of the state's share, categorical programs accounted for more than $2.9 billion, most of which, $2.1 billion, was designated for the operating expenditures associated with meeting requirements that schools reduce class sizes (Florida Department of Education 2006b, 20, 34).

Capital Outlay

The construction, maintenance, and repair of schools and other facilities (i.e., capital outlay) are not funded from the FEFP but from a mix of proceeds from the Florida Lottery, appropriations from the state tax on retail consumption of utility services (known as gross receipts tax), and other state and local taxes and fees. Appropriations by the legislature for capital outlay totaled $1.57 billion in 2006–2007. Of that total, more than two-thirds were designated for the construction and maintenance costs associated with meeting requirements imposed by the 2002 Class Size Reduction Amendment (Florida Department of Education 2006b). In 2003–2004 the last year for which the data were available at this writing, local sources generated roughly $4.2 billion for capital purposes, with another $5 billion retained from previous years (Florida Department of Education 2006a).

Accountability

Accountability is one of the guiding principles of Florida's education system, and it is a major component of the federal No Child Left Behind Act of 2001, under which reading and math proficiencies at the fourth and eighth grade levels have been assessed by standardized tests since 2002–2003. States are now required to assess science proficiencies at the fourth and eighth grade levels and writing at the eighth grade level as part of the testing program required by No Child Left Behind. That testing initiative is called the National Assessment of Educational Progress. Although accountability is popular with policy makers, assessment as practiced is not without detrac-

Table 13.1. Annual Proficiency Goals of Adequate Yearly Progress by Target Subject and Year

	Percent of Students Proficient	
School Years	Math	Reading
2001–2002 to 2003–2004	38	31
2004–2005 to 2006–2007	53	48
2007–2008 to 2009–2010	68	65
2010–2011 to 2012–2013	83	82
2013–2014	100	100

Source: Florida Department of Education, "Fact Sheet: NCLB and Adequate Yearly Progress," 3, available online at http://www.firn.edu/doe/flbpso/pdf/nclbfactsheet.pdf (accessed March 16, 2007).

tors, because time used to prepare and administer tests can reduce the time available for other types of learning. No Child Left Behind is up for reauthorization in 2007 and is therefore subject to change.

One of the terms coined in the No Child Left Behind program is *adequate yearly progress* (AYP), which measures the academic performance and participation of all students as well as eight subgroups of students based on race or ethnicity, socioeconomic status, disability, and English proficiency. No Child Left Behind set the goal of 100 percent proficiency in math and reading among the nation's students by 2013–2014, where "proficiency" is defined by the state governments. In Florida it is defined as attaining a score of three, four, or five on the Florida Comprehensive Assessment Test, more commonly known as the FCAT (Florida Department of Education, n.d.a.). Florida's proficiency goals from 2001–2002 through 2013–2014 are outlined in Table 13.1. Schools whose students fail to make AYP face the following interventions by the State Board of Education: technical assistance (after two consecutive years of failing to make AYP), additional education services to disadvantaged students (after the third consecutive year), and "corrective measures," such as the replacement of certain faculty and staff (imposed by the school district after four consecutive years). After the fifth consecutive year, the noncompliant school is identified by the Board for restructuring, which can include replacement of the principal and other staff or the contracting out of educational services. Additionally, after a school fails for two consecutive years, its students may transfer into another public school in the district, provided there is space to accept them. Districts whose schools fail to make AYP are subject to a similar series of consequences (Florida Department of Education n.d.a.).

Since 1998, Florida has used the FCAT to show progress toward meeting performance benchmarks of the Sunshine State Standards, which were established by the state and are independent of the requirements set by No Child Left Behind. FCAT assessments currently measure progress toward meeting state standards in reading, math, science, and writing. Reading and math assessments are administered in grades three through ten. Florida has seen an upward trend over the years 2000–2006 in math and reading achievement on the FCAT in most of those grades (Florida Department of Education 2007a).

Another controversial aspect of educational accountability in Florida is school choice, where the parents of K-12 students have the legal right to transfer their children to the school of their choice, provided space is available. School choice programs are intended to meet students' needs without penalizing families financially and to spur innovation and performance in education. Options include public school choice (i.e., enrollment in charter schools, controlled open enrollment among public schools, and relocation from a failing school to a different public school), private school choice, home education, and private tutoring. School vouchers are another part of the choice regime, but they serve very few students and have recently come under judicial scrutiny (Florida Department of Education n.d.a., 5). In 2005–2006, more than 540,000 schoolchildren in Florida participated in the state's voucher programs, were home-schooled, and attended private or charter schools. Of these students, roughly 367,000 attended private schools (Florida Department of Education n.d.b).

Graduation rates provide another measure of accountability. In 2002, Florida, with a high school graduation rate of 59 percent, ranked behind the populous states of New York, California, Texas, and Illinois and 49th among the 50 states and the District of Columbia (Department of Education 2007a).

Challenges

Public schools in Florida face many formidable challenges. Chief among them from a funding perspective are the need to increase teacher salaries, low levels of funding per student compared to per-student funding in other states, growth in property tax valuation, and the class size reduction mandated by the 2002 constitutional amendment.

Teacher Salaries

No matter how one looks at it, low pay for teachers in Florida poses a significant obstacle to improvement of education in the state. Average teacher salaries in Florida have lagged behind the national average. From 1992–1993 to 2002–2003, average teacher salaries in the nation grew by 31 percent, whereas Florida's grew only by 29 percent. It would be better, however, to compare Florida to the other southern states, where teacher salaries grew at a student-weighted average rate of 37 percent for the time period between 1992–1993 and 2002–2003. In 2003–2004, teacher salaries in Florida had fallen to 98 percent of the average of teacher salaries other southern states pay. A similar pattern exists for per-student spending. Between 1997 and 2002, the per-student operating expenditures likewise grew over 31 percent in both the South and in the nation; in Florida, per-student spending increased only 16 percent (Dewey 2005).

Florida will likely experience great difficulty in meeting both federal and state requirements for the number and quality of teachers if this trend continues. Long hours, increasing accountability requirements at the state and federal levels, and uncompetitive pay are likely to put pressure on Florida to retain seasoned and dedicated teachers. Alternative routes to teacher certification might be a partial solution, and this idea is currently supported at the national and state levels. However, there appears to be little incentive for large numbers of well-paid professionals (such as lawyers, accountants, and engineers) to give up lucrative careers to pursue teaching, and this is the pool from which new teachers would be drawn in alternative certification policies.[3]

Relative Funding for Students

Like funding for teachers' salaries, per-student funding is a rough measure of the state's commitment to public education. Per-student funding in Florida has fallen 26 percent below that of the nation and 13 percent below that of the South. As Table 13.2 indicates, for Florida to simply maintain its position in terms of per-student funding relative to the South and the rest of the nation, the state would have to provide increases in total state and local funding averaging 6.35 percent annually by 2014–2015. If the state wants to improve its position and provide approximately the same per-student funding level as the South and nation does, it will need to increase its average annual spending by 7.74 and 8.98 percent, respectively, by 2014–2015. This is important because comparatively lower spending on teachers' wages and other aspects of student instruction may hurt the state's goal of attracting families headed by young professionals (Dewey 2005, 146–50).

Growth in Taxable Value of Schools

Recent funding increases for Florida's public schools have come disproportionately from increases in property tax revenues, which in turn have been

Table 13.2. State and Local Operating Expenditure Targets for Education, Florida, 2009–2010 and 2014–2015

Scenario	2009–2010 State and Local Funds (billions of dollars)[a]	Percent Average Annual Increase	2014–2015 State and Local Funds (billions of dollars)[a]	Percent Average Annual Increase
Maintain Current Relative Position	20.4	6.43	27.6	6.35
Catch the Southern Average	23.5	9.00	31.9	7.74
Catch the National Average	26.7	11.31	36.1	8.98

Source: James Dewey, "Funding Florida's Educational Standards," in Tough Choices: Shaping Florida's Future, edited by David Denslow and Carol Weissert (Gainesville and Tallahassee: University of Florida and Florida State University, 2005), 150.
Note: a. Constant 2004 dollars.

driven by rapid population growth and an appreciation of housing prices that have far exceeded Florida's averages over the past two decades. Such unusually strong growth rates are unlikely to persist; estimates by the Bureau of Economic and Business Research at the University of Florida suggest that average annual population growth will decrease from above 2 percent in the period 2000–2005 to around 1.6 percent in 2010–2015. Slower population growth will reduce growth of property tax revenue by reducing both new home construction and the growth in the value of existing real estate (Dewey 2005, 155–62.) However, a projected slowing of Florida's property tax base tells only part of the story, because other sources of revenue typically used to fund building construction and maintenance at public schools—lottery proceeds and proceeds from the gross receipts tax—are unlikely to increase enough to offset lower property tax proceeds. We might also expect general revenues, mostly derived from sales tax proceeds, to come under greater pressure to fund the cumulative costs associated with No Child Left Behind and requirements of the Class Size Amendment. This scenario assumes approximately the same allocations to public schools as now and also assumes that the requirements to fully implement No Child Left Behind and the 2002 Class Size Reduction Amendment will continue to apply (Holt and Denslow 2005, 271).

Class Size Reduction

Funding the Class Size Reduction Amendment adopted by Florida voters in 2002 is another daunting challenge. The Florida constitution sets out the following requirements for maximum class size in core classes: eighteen in grade three and below, twenty-two in grades four through eight, and twenty-five in grades nine through twelve. The amendment requires that these objectives be met by the beginning of the school year 2010–2011. The schedule for implementing the class size amendment was outlined by statute. All grades must comply at the school district–level average by 2005–2006, at the school-level average by 2007–2008, and at the class-level average by 2009–2010. The cost of fully implementing the amendment for operations and classroom and building construction and maintenance varies depending on which estimate is used: the state's Revenue Estimating Conference's projections range from a low of $20 billion to a high of $28 billion, but the Florida Department of Education's estimates range from a low of $22 billion to a high of $26.5 billion. The largest portion of those costs will be for operating expenditures such as overhead and hiring new teachers (Blomberg 2006).

School districts will face another challenge as they look for enough qualified teachers to fill the new classrooms. The number of new teachers needed is projected to be almost 20,000 for the period from 2004–2005 to 2010–2011 (Council for Education Policy, Research and Improvement 2005). This need for new teachers comes at a time when Florida is experiencing teacher shortage problems, particularly in the fields of math, special education, and the sciences. One option to respond to that challenge is through differential pay schemes. School districts could offer pay raises and bonuses to recruit and retain teachers in schools that have been traditionally hard to staff or for subjects like high-school math and science in which there are critical teacher shortages. During 2005–2006, 17 Florida school districts offered higher pay for those purposes (Office of Program Policy Analysis and Government Accountability 2007).

Community Colleges

Mission and Responsibilities

Florida's community college system is a significant segment of the state's postsecondary education system, consisting of 28 colleges spread over 61 campuses at 177 sites in 2006–2007. In 2005–2006, these colleges served almost 800,000 students, the majority of whom were part-time (Florida Department of Education 2007b). The primary mission and responsibility of Florida's community colleges is to respond to community needs for postsecondary academic education and education culminating in career degrees. The colleges provide lower-division undergraduate instruction leading to associate degrees (associate in arts, associate in science, and associate in applied science) and vocational instruction leading to certificates. Their role in providing vocational and professional training is particularly important in light of Florida's status as the nation's leader in job growth, much of it in occupations that require some postsecondary education or training. In recent years, several community colleges have been authorized to award four-year baccalaureate degree programs in the fields of education or applied sciences.

Institutional Oversight

As with Florida's public school system, community colleges are under the jurisdiction of the State Board of Education. Each community college is governed by a local board of trustees. These boards of trustees are granted a great deal of oversight and autonomy because community colleges are locally based and locally governed entities even though they are tied to state government funding and policies. Reflecting this mix of community-driven autonomy and state government affiliation, each local board of trustees is statutorily "authorized to adopt rules, procedures, and policies, consistent with law and rules of the State Board of Education, related to its [statutory] mission and responsibilities, its governance, personnel, budget and finance, administration, programs, curriculum and instruction, buildings and grounds, travel and purchasing, technology, students, contracts and grants, or college property" (Florida Statutes Annotated 1001.64 (4)(b)). Each board of trustees is authorized to hire a president, who is responsible for the overall operation and administration of the community college.

Enrollment

Projections

For budgeting purposes, community college enrollment is computed using the number of full time-equivalent (FTE) students. Because so many students attend community college on a part-time basis, the number of individual students enrolled in a given year is actually almost three times greater than the FTE enrollment number. As Figure 13.1 shows, enrollment has increased steadily from 175,063 FTE students in 1982–1983 to 287,714 in 2005–2006. Because of the hurricane seasons of 2004 and 2005, estimated enrollment dipped in 2005–2006 for the first time in recent years as students were lured away from their studies to take advantage of construction and other hurricane-related jobs. Moreover, Florida's military bases furnish

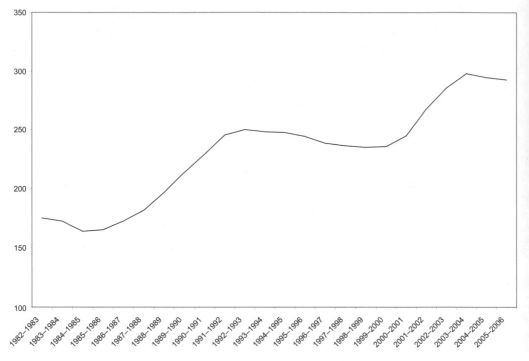

Figure 13.1. FTE Enrollment at Florida's Community Colleges, 1984–1985 to 2004–2005 (in thousands).

community colleges with students, and thus operations in Afghanistan and the war in Iraq have affected enrollment in the state's community colleges.

Enrollment numbers are expected to climb again in future years because the number of first-time students entering Florida's community colleges has continued to grow, increasing by over 77 percent in the past ten years. However, in the foreseeable future, we might expect enrollment at Florida's community colleges to grow much more slowly than in the past, in response to the slowing growth trend in the projected number of Florida's high school graduates, many of whom will ultimately enter the state's community college system.

Student Profile

Females represent over 60 percent of all community college students in Florida, and the percentage of females relative to males has been increasing over the years. The typical community college student is now 30 years old (25 years old if she is seeking college credit), but the average age has been declining in recent years. Florida's community colleges tend to admit a higher percentage of minority students than do the state's universities, and that percentage has continued to increase at a slow but steady rate. According to the fall headcount for 1996–1997, minority enrollment represented one-third of all community college students. In 2005–2006, it had climbed to 40 percent. The greatest percentage increase has been in the Hispanic student population. Students with disabilities account for 2 percent of the overall community college population. Although the majority of students continue to be part-time (63 percent), the percentage of full-time students relative to part-time students has been growing (Florida Department of Education 2004, 2007b).

Community college students are more at risk for not succeeding in college and for dropping out than are students at four-year colleges and universities. Students from disadvantaged families are more likely than their university counterparts to be academically underprepared for the rigors of college work, face competing work and family obligations, and have high financial needs (Boswell and Wilson 2004). Community colleges are attempting to respond to those challenges in various and often creative ways through collaborative efforts with government, businesses, and foundations.

Funding

The operating budget of community colleges is comprised predominantly of state general revenue funds, lottery proceeds, and fees. The Florida legislature annually appropriates general revenue funds in line-item appropriations for each community college; these appropriations represented 62 percent of the community college system's operating budget in 2006–2007. Lottery proceeds represented 7 percent and student tuition and fees represented the remaining 31 percent. Student tuition must fall within a range of a standard amount annually established by the legislature. The fee per credit hour is a flat fee that does not reflect program costs or actual student needs. Community colleges have the statutory authority to set their fees within 10 percent below or 15 percent above that standard. The average community college student must pay tuition and several other fees: a student financial aid fee, a student activity fee, a capital improvement fee, and a technology fee. In fall 2006, for example, the average amount for tuition and fees for thirty credit hours was less than $2,034 for resident students. Nonresidents pay much more (Florida Department of Education 2007b). In contrast to community college systems in most states, Florida's system is not authorized to levy or access local sales and property taxes.

General revenue appropriations have not kept up with enrollment growth in recent years, and funding from lottery proceeds has been critical to community college programs. Lottery proceeds were first appropriated for Florida's community colleges in 1987–1988, when they received almost $10 million; this figure increased to over $128 million in 1994–1995. Since then, community college funding from the lottery has dipped and in recent years has hovered around $100 million annually until 2006–2007, when it increased to over $115 million (Florida Department of Education 2007b). The demand for these funds has continued to escalate, but revenue from this source has remained mostly flat.

In contrast, student tuition and fees have continued to increase over the years. Whereas student tuition and fees comprised only 22 percent of the operating budgets of the community college system in 1984–1985, they represented 31 percent of the operating budget in 2006–2007 (Florida Department of Education 2007b). Tuition and fees for Florida's community colleges are also lower on average than for community colleges in most other states in the region and lower than the national average (College Board 2006).

Challenges

Florida's community colleges will face many challenges as they attempt to meet state accountability outcomes within their respective operating budgets. Some of the most notable challenges include meeting workforce needs, providing quality faculty, managing fiscal pressures to provide higher-cost programs to meet student and local community demand within existing budgets, managing enrollment growth, and expanding the mission of community college education.

Meeting Workforce Needs

By law, the State Board of Education is required to give the highest priority to workforce programs that train people to enter high-skill/high-wage occupations identified by the Workforce Estimating Conference, which establishes a list of occupations that demand workers at the state level. A report by the Office of Program Policy Analysis and Government Accountability (2004) examined how efficiently community colleges use the funding allotted to them to meet that workforce objective. Students at Florida's community colleges earn adult vocational certification, associate degrees, or college credit certification. Both wages and earning potential were positively related to completion of programs. However, many students never complete their degrees, particularly students pursuing the associate in science. Students who fail to complete these programs can expect to earn lower wages on average. Most community college students who completed their degrees were enrolled in programs that prepared them for high-skill/high-wage or targeted occupations.

Providing Quality Faculty

The proportion of faculty in Florida's community college system who are part-time was almost 76 percent in fall 2006—roughly three part-time instructors to every one full-time faculty member (Florida Department of Education 2007b). Part-time instructors allow community colleges to respond quickly to programmatic demands of communities and are also significantly less expensive than full-time faculty, thus enabling the colleges to enroll more students at less cost per student. However, there may be a negative effect on student retention if part-time instructors teach more than half of the courses taken by students attending college for the first time. In response to 1994 recommendations by the State Board of Community Colleges, most of Florida's community colleges initiated policies to better integrate and retain qualified part-time instructors, but a few have encountered financial and other obstacles in doing so (Florida Department of Education 2005).

Incentives to Offer Lower-Cost Programs

Community colleges might save money by offering more low-cost programs, such as remedial education, instead of higher-cost programs, even if the latter might result in higher-wage jobs that are in demand at the local and state level. Because Florida's tuition is a flat fee per credit hour, community colleges would appear to have an incentive to offer lower-cost programs that will generate greater revenue for them. Remedial education is certainly one of the important missions of Florida's community colleges. In fact, community colleges are responsible by statute for delivering remedial programs, often under contract with Florida's public universities. At the same time, the Florida Department of Education's most recent long-range plan calls for the stabilization or reduction in the number of students receiving remedial (college preparatory) instruction (Florida Department of Education 2006c).

This raises a number of policy questions. Are remedial courses being offered disproportionately to offset higher-cost programs? Are they structured in such a way that they will improve the prospects for student retention and program completion? State funding subsidizes approximately two-thirds of the annual cost of educating Florida's community college students. Students who are already prepared for community college courses when they enter are twice as likely to earn associate degrees or certificates as students who need some type of remedial education course. Community colleges typically must pay instructors more to teach postsecondary vocational courses and courses leading to advanced or professional degrees than they pay instruc-tors to teach college preparatory courses. So they are forced to some extent to depend on the revenues generated from courses in less costly programs to offset the expense of their higher-cost programs.[4]

Enrollment Growth

Curbing enrollment is certainly one way to respond to fiscal constraints. This approach would have implications for the equity objective promoted by Florida's open-door admission policy for community colleges. Moreover, it runs counter to one of the outcome goals of the Florida Department of Education for community colleges—to increase the proportion of students seeking postsecondary education in the state's community college system. However, the pressure to curb enrollment may have abated somewhat be-cause total enrollment for the community college system has declined since 2003–2004 and is expected to grow much more slowly in future years. In-dividual campuses will undoubtedly experience enrollment changes differ-ently depending on their respective missions and locations.

Mission Expansion

The Florida legislature enacted legislation in 2001 that allows all community colleges to apply to the State Board of Education for permission to provide upper-division coursework and award baccalaureate degrees for four-year programs. Seven community colleges currently offer baccalaureate degrees in education or applied sciences. Almost 2,500 students pursued a commu-nity college baccalaureate in 2005–2006 (Florida Department of Education 2007b). Florida law makes it clear that the primary mission for community colleges offering baccalaureate degrees must continue to be the provision of associate degrees that lead to a university education. Therefore, the question becomes whether community colleges can continue to expand their course offerings and programs and stay true to their statutory mission.

Florida's University System

Mission and Responsibilities

Florida has ten public four-year universities and one public liberal arts college in its university system. In 2004–2005, Florida's public universities served over 280,000 students, while the private institutions served almost 162,000 students (Chronicle of Higher Education 2005). As reflected in Table 13.3,

Table 13.3. University Enrollment in Florida by Enrollment Level and University, Fall 2005[a]

University	Undergraduate	Graduate	Unclassified	Total
University of Florida	34,028	14,310	1,378	49,725
Florida State University	30,418	7,926	1,308	39,652
Florida A&M University	10,372	1,529	278	12,179
University of South Florida	32,968	7,910	2,143	43,021
Florida Atlantic University	19,951	3,386	2,367	25,704
University of West Florida	7,828	1,239	634	9,701
University of Central Florida	37,568	6,328	1,057	44,953
Florida International University	28,406	5,085	3,484	36,975
University of North Florida	13,077	1,618	658	15,353
Florida Gulf Coast University	5,978	762	524	7,264
New College of Florida	761	0	1	762
Total	221,355	50,093	13,841	285,289

Source: Board of Governors, State University System of Florida, "State University System of Florida Facts and Figures: Quick Facts," 2005, available online at http://www.flbog.org/factbook/quickfacts.asp#headcount (accessed March 15, 2007).

Note: a. Preliminary headcounts.

Florida's public universities with the largest enrollments are the University of Florida (with almost 50,000 students), the University of Central Florida (with almost 45,000 students) and the University of South Florida (with just over 43,000 students).

Each public institution in the state university system submits a mission statement to the Board of Governors, which has ultimate authority to approve these missions. The board's most recent strategic plan, which it adopted in June 2005, articulated a shared mission of the constituent universities: "The State University System of Florida consists of ten public universities and one public liberal arts college, each with its distinctive mission, collectively dedicated to serving the needs of a diverse state through excellence in teaching, research and public service" (Board of Governors, State University System of Florida 2005c, 5). Several universities have regional missions, while others have expansive missions that serve state, national, and international constituencies or students in graduate and professional school as well as undergraduates. The mission of each institution drives how it meets certain system-wide goals. These include providing access to its programs and producing degrees, meeting statewide professional and workforce needs, and building world-class academic programs and research capacity. Measurable goals are thus used to evaluate each university's progress toward meeting specified efficiency and equity objectives, and the Board of Governors reviews this progress periodically.

Institutional Oversight

Control of Florida's public university policy has been subject to much change in recent years. The Florida Board of Regents was eliminated in 2000 as the oversight board for Florida's public university system. Oversight of that system was then consolidated under the State Board of Education, which also provides policy direction to the state's community colleges, vocational institutions, independent school options, and public pre-K–12 education. However, a constitutional amendment adopted by Floridians in November 2002 created the Board of Governors, which consists of seventeen members and has policy oversight for the operation, regulation, control, and management of the entire state university system. The Board of Governors is responsible for, but is not limited to, defining the distinctive mission of each university in the state system and their coordination agreements with Florida's public schools and community colleges. It also must ensure that coordination and operation of the system is well planned and avoids duplication of facilities or programs. Strategic planning, budget submittals, and accountability for the expenditures of the constituent universities also are under the purview of the Board of Governors.

Separate boards of trustees were established under the 2000 legislation. These boards of trustees have continued to operate following adoption of the 2002 constitutional amendment. They are expected to implement policies that boost the performance of their respective universities.

Enrollment

Projections

The recent rapid growth in student enrollment at Florida's public universities has put pressure on Florida's postsecondary education system. For budgeting purposes, enrollment growth in Florida's public universities, as in the state's community colleges, is computed using numbers of FTE students. Over 180,000 FTE students were enrolled in Florida's public universities in 2004–2005, where enrollment has increased by 140 percent in the past twenty-four years and by 24 percent since 2000. Figure 13.2 shows total FTE student enrollment for Florida's public universities since 1984–1985.

FTE enrollment is always a substantially lower number than the head-count enrollment number. In 2004–2005 the head-count enrollment was approximately 280,000, compared to over 180,000 FTE at Florida's public universities. The head-count enrollment computation is particularly useful for planning for facilities use and expansion, parking and transportation

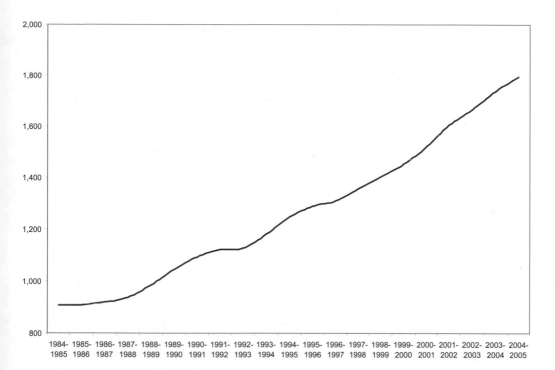

Figure 13.2. FTE Enrollment at Florida's Public Universities, 1984–1985 to 2004–2005 (in thousands).

services, course sections, supply of teaching personnel, and support services needed for students, among other issues.

Florida's legislature determines annually the number of students funded at each of the state's public universities, in contrast to funding practices for the state's public schools and community colleges. Therefore, it is difficult to project reliably enrollment at Florida's universities. The growth in the number of high school graduates is expected to slow in future years. Correspondingly, the Board of Governors projects little growth in the state's public university enrollment from 2005–2012: from as little as 4 percent to as much as 23 percent during this period depending on the combination of legislatively-funded enrollment and students' access to financial aid (Board of Governors, State University System of Florida 2007b).

Student Profile

Since 1995 the profile of students at Florida's public universities has changed somewhat. Today, the typical student is a female, white, full-time undergraduate pursuing a business or management degree (Board of Governors,

State University System of Florida 2005a). However, students are becoming younger, and there are slightly more women enrolled now than in the past. These students are more likely to be attending school full-time than part-time (Board of Governors, State University System of Florida 1995–1996, 2005–2006).[5] These trends suggest that financial assistance strategies may be working better than in the past, at least for many in-state students.

Business and management degrees were the most pursued undergraduate degrees at Florida's public universities in both 2004–2005 and 1995–1996, although a slightly higher proportion of students received them in 2004–2005 than in 1995–1996. Education was the second most popular field of study, although a proportionately smaller percentage was awarded that degree in 2004–2005 compared to nine years earlier (Office of Program Policy Analysis and Government Accountability 2005a). One reason for this shift may be that education degrees are less remunerative than business degrees. This observation has implications for efficiency objectives that link production of degrees to areas of critical state need.

Fifty-eight percent of Florida's public university students graduate in six years. Although there is certainly room for improvement, this percentage compares favorably to the average of 53 percent of students at public institutions nationwide. Factors contributing to the relatively high graduation rate in Florida include a higher percentage of graduates from minority populations in Florida than in the nation as a whole and a smaller gap between the percentages of whites and minorities graduating in Florida than in the nation as a whole (Board of Governors, State University System of Florida 2005b).[6]

Funding

The state universities' operating budgets are funded from general revenue, lottery proceeds, major-gift trust funds, the phosphate research trust funds, and tuition and fees. The Florida legislature annually appropriates general revenue and trust funds in line-item appropriations for each public university. For 2005–2006, general revenue funds represented almost 63 percent of total funding; lottery proceeds, 4 percent; tuition and student fees, 32 percent; and other trust funds, less than 1 percent. The total funding from all sources was over $2.7 billion for state public universities in 2005–2006 (Board of Governors, State University System of Florida 2006b).

Since 1990, general revenue appropriations have stayed roughly at the same level per student in inflation-adjusted dollars. The greatest increase has come from tuition and student fees, which grew from 22 percent of funding in 1990–1991 to over 32 percent of funding in 2005–2006. Resident tuition fees are set annually by the legislature in appropriations bills, but the Board of Governors was authorized in the appropriations bill for 2005–2006 to set tuition for nonresident students and graduate students, provided it did not increase by more than 5 percent from the previous year. This authorization is delegated to the Board of Governors in the appropriations process and must be renewed annually. For 2005–2006, the legislature set the maximum tuition for resident undergraduates at $71.57 per credit hour, meaning that students who took an average of 12 credits a semester that year paid $1,718 in tuition. Until recently, Florida was only one of two states where the legislature establishes tuition; the other is Louisiana.[7]

The overall picture of funding for Florida's public university system, like university systems in other states, is one of increasing reliance on tuition and fees. In recent years, undergraduate tuition has increased steadily, although tuition increases have been less dramatic in Florida than in other states in the region and in the nation as a whole (Southern Regional Education Board 2005).[8] With the exception of Nevada, Florida has the lowest average resident undergraduate tuition and fees for public four-year universities in the nation. Table 13.4 compares Florida's average tuition and fees to those of

Table 13.4. Average In-State Enrollment-Weighted Tuition and Fees in Public and Private Colleges and Universities, Southern States, 2006–2007

States	Public	Private
Alabama	$4,915	$13,437
Arkansas	$5,298	$13,569
Florida	$3,336	$21,189
Georgia	$3,913	$20,124
Louisiana	$3,796	$21,748
Mississippi	$4,455	$12,320
North Carolina	$4,063	$20,882
South Carolina	$7,916	$17,529
Tennessee	$4,974	$18,497
Texas	$5,940	$19,225
Virginia	$6,558	$20,536
South (excluding Florida)[a]	$5,183	$17,787
United States	$5,836	$22,218

Source: College Board, "Trends in College Pricing 2006," 22, available online at http://www.collegeboard.com/prod_downloads/press/cost06/trends_college_pricing_06.pdf (accessed May 4, 2007).
Note: a. Average for the South calculated by the authors.

several states in the region and the nation as a whole. The average tuition for private four-year universities is also lower in Florida than in most other states in the nation but not in the South.

Challenges

Florida's public universities will face several challenges in the foreseeable future in meeting their equity and efficiency goals: they will need to balance institutional supply and student and employer demands; compete internationally with other institutions and systems; and ensure adequate access to postsecondary education (Board of Governors, State University System of Florida 2005c). Other challenges include increasing the number of first-generation college students as a means of improving prospects of disadvantaged Floridians and maintaining student diversity on campus. The coupling of tuition to the Bright Futures Program and, more indirectly, to the Florida Prepaid Program has arguably hampered flexibility in responding to these challenges.

Tuition and Financial Aid Programs

Two state programs have been instrumental in improving student access to Florida's postsecondary institutions—the Bright Futures Program, the largest state scholarship program, and the Florida Prepaid Program. Bright Futures bases its awards on a percentage (either 100 percent or 75 percent) of tuition and fees at Florida's public colleges and universities. Since 1997–1998, the first year that Bright Futures scholarships were awarded, total expenditures have risen from $70 million to $346.2 million in 2006–2007 for postsecondary students in two-year and four-year institutions, while the number of Bright Future recipients increased from nearly 42,500 to 148,509 (Office of Economic and Demographic Research 2007).

A major challenge in securing adequate funding for Florida's public universities is the extent to which the Bright Futures Program and the Florida Prepaid College Program are linked to tuition. Although tuition has been increasing steadily in recent years, it still remains among the lowest in the country, particularly for public university undergraduate programs. If tuition increases so that it is closer to the national average, lottery proceeds needed to cover scholarships for Bright Futures will also need to increase. A growing reliance on the lottery for Bright Futures, in turn, will leave less funding for other purposes. Because the lottery is mature and transfers to education have been fairly stagnant, funding for education programs other than Bright Futures would need to come from different funding sources or the costs for Bright Futures would need to be contained. At this writing, several proposals to change the program are under consideration.

The Florida Prepaid College Plan Program also assists the families of students who contribute to plans that may cover the tuition, fees, room and board, books, supplies, computers, and equipment at Florida's public universities and community colleges. Family members purchase prepaid plans for their children, typically when the children are young. These plans lock in the total cost of tuition for up to 120 credit hours, dormitory costs, and required local fees. Over one million plans have been purchased since the program's inception in 1988, making it the largest prepaid program in the country (Florida Prepaid College Board 2005). The money for these plans is managed based on certain assumptions about future tuition and fees and room and board expenses. If any of these assumptions are understated and tuition and fees rise more rapidly than the estimates used to keep the program solvent, the fiscal integrity of the program may become a more pressing concern.[9]

Balancing Supply and Demand

Floridians with baccalaureate degrees can expect to earn more on average than their counterparts with associate degrees, if all things are equal. Advanced degrees are likewise associated with higher average earnings than baccalaureate degrees. From the perspective of the state's economy, some degrees have value that exceeds earnings because certain skills are in greater demand, like teaching and nursing, because they provide much-needed services, or because they expand or attract technological development, like computer science or engineering. Four obstacles prevent Florida's universities from supplying enough graduates to meet state demand in critical fields: low student interest in pursuing a career trajectory; stringent program requirements for which students are often unprepared (e.g., engineering); licensure or accreditation requirements that have contributed to shortages in fields such as nursing; and high program costs, particularly in engineering and laboratory sciences. A task force created to review ways of improving access to Florida's postsecondary education system recently focused on these issues of supply and demand; its report proposes certain broad measures for expanding the supply of graduates in targeted program areas. For example, the state might offer incentives through financial assistance programs. Specifically, the Bright Futures Program might provide supplemental funding to students enrolled in programs that prepare them for critically needed occupations (Office of Program Policy Analysis and Government Accountability 2005b).

International Competition

The missions of some of Florida's public universities are based on regional needs, but other universities, most notably the University of Florida and Florida State University, have research interests that make them globally competitive in certain fields. An ongoing concern of Florida's research universities is how to compete with research universities elsewhere to attract the funding needed to build and equip research facilities and attract world-class faculty and students to work on projects of national and international importance.

To increase research capacity, however, universities need adequate support staff and resources to submit grants and administer them. Operating funds for universities have increasingly come from tuition and fees that are still among the lowest in the nation. In terms of core funding for public universities, which includes both tuition and state appropriations, Florida ranked 34th among 48 states that used the same accounting standards in FY 2005 (Board of Governors, State University System of Florida 2007c). Meanwhile, as noted, increases in state funding for university operations have been constrained by relatively flat general revenue funding over the years (when adjusted for inflation).

Adequate Access to Postsecondary Institutions

The Board of Governor's Strategic Plan 2005–2013 calls for providing adequate access to undergraduate and graduate education and promoting diversity. At the same time, the plan calls for universities to increase per capita research expenditures (state and sponsored), and provide competitive financial packages to recruit faculty, graduate students and post-doctorates. Realizing those and other objectives costs money.

To increase student accessibility to universities, policy makers will either need to keep tuition relatively low or find other ways to make Florida's postsecondary education more affordable. Low tuition, of course, impedes progress toward the objectives of improving faculty salaries and increasing research activity because the underlying infrastructure (equipment, supplies, lab space, and graduate students) needed for research and even for pursuing external research grants is expensive. On the other hand, for many students and their families, the greatest barrier to improving access to Florida's public and private universities is the expense of a college education. Florida's students and their families must pay 83 percent of approximately $16,000 needed for full-time undergraduate attendance at a public university in the state and three-quarters of all undergraduates benefit from financial aid (Board of Governors, State University System of Florida 2007a). At this writing, policy makers are proposing various measures to make more needs-based assistance available to students from lower-income families. Because access to postsecondary education is an endorsed policy objective, such measures will become even more necessary as tuition increases. Of course, another and not mutually exclusive way of keeping university costs down is to improve efficiency in the delivery of university programs and services through improved graduation and retention rates. Because the state subsidizes roughly two-thirds of the cost of a typical undergraduate student's education at a public university, graduation and retention rates are arguably a good measure of efficiency. And retention rates are likely to increase if students are adequately prepared at the secondary level for university programs.

Maintaining Diversity

Minority enrollment in Florida's public universities has increased steadily since 1990, but that trend has shown signs of tapering off in recent years. Enrollment of undergraduate African Americans was almost the same in fall 2004 as it was in fall 2005. But Hispanic undergraduate student enrollment has almost tripled since 1990 and has increased by 8.5 percent from 2004 to 2005. One explanation for the generally flat growth in enrollment overall among minority students in recent years is a decrease in enrollment among African American and Hispanic students from out of state. Florida A&M University, Florida's historically black university, enrolled 1,116 fewer black out-of-state undergraduates in 2005 than in 2000. Fewer out-of-state Hispanic students have also enrolled in Florida's universities, but the reduction is not as dramatic for this group as it is for African American students (Board of Governors, State University System of Florida 2006a). This may be because nonresident tuition has increased from $233 per credit hour in 2000 to $501 per credit hour in 2005.

Concluding Observations

What are the pressures facing Florida's K-20 education system as it looks toward the future? At all levels, rapid enrollment growth that is not matched by funding increases is a unifying theme. Enrollment in Florida's public elementary and secondary schools has increased by 76 percent from 1984–1985 to 2005–2006, and of all states, Florida is projected to experience the highest net migration from other states and, following only California and New York, the third highest number of foreign immigrants during the period 1995–2025 (Florida Department of Education 2007a). Although enrollment will continue to grow, this tells only part of the story. The proportion of young people in Florida will decline relative to people 65 years and older. Florida's public school districts will need to garner support from a proportionately larger percentage of elderly people who no longer have children in the school system or will retire in Florida and may not have deep affiliations to the state.

Meanwhile, Florida's school districts will continue to juggle fiscal pressures, accountability pressures, and teacher supply pressures while they try to meet federal and state mandates. They also will continue to provide services to increasing numbers of children who need special or additional services in efforts to realize the legislature's guiding principle to "maximize access to education and allow the opportunity for a high quality education." Access and equity concerns are inherent in Florida's K-12 public school system, and they will continue to coexist, sometimes uneasily, with calls for greater efficiency in the delivery of public education services.

The state's community colleges have historically been creative in attracting new types of programs, partnering with high schools and four-year colleges and universities, and serving a diverse population that includes academically and vocationally oriented students, students interested in pursuing careers in fields with critical needs such as teaching and nursing, students who need flexible course schedules, students who are still in high school and want to begin their postsecondary coursework, students who need to acquire certain competency levels before enrolling in college-level courses, and students in apprenticeship programs.

At the same time, accountability measures for greater efficiency and equity have been developed at the state level that exert pressure on community colleges to demonstrate how they are responding to present and anticipated challenges. Whether they can keep their primary missions intact as they respond to these often-competing challenges remains to be seen. Finally, as long as the legislature continues to set tuition and fees and appropriate most of the funding for community colleges, and as long as those colleges have no access to local tax proceeds, fiscal constraints may continue to be an issue for them.

Like Florida's K-12 schools and community colleges, Florida's universities and colleges are facing many daunting challenges. Businesses are demanding highly skilled workers and there is a critical need for educated Floridians in education, health care, engineering, computer sciences, and other critically needed fields. There is always debate about what exactly Florida's universities should be accountable for and to whom. To date, many of the accountability measures revolve around outputs such as the number of degrees granted or the percent of faculty engaged in teaching or the number of published articles by faculty.

Florida's universities are in the midst of competing expectations about equity as they try to provide greater access to students from poorer families and improve retention and graduation rates and student diversity and at the same time identify ways to increase funding for faculty and research endeavors to improve their competitive stance. Meanwhile, energy costs, health insurance costs, building construction costs, and costs for faculty to establish research programs and laboratories, particularly in the sciences, will continue to put pressure on their budgets. It is a tough balancing act and one that is expected to continue in future years.

Notes

1. Enrollment in Florida's public schools totaled 2,668,337 in fall 2005 and 2,662,701 in fall 2006, a reduction of 5,636 students (Florida Department of Education 2006d at Table 4).

2. School funding in Florida, like in many other states, is complex, and we refer to only the most prominent aspects, omitting from our discussion important features of the FEFP. The Florida Department of Education (2005b) discusses the 2006–2007 FEFP allocations, by funding program, in detail. In general, the FEFP is governed by Part II of Chapter 1011 of Florida Statutes, "Funding for School Districts," and FEFP expenditures are authorized in annual state appropriations acts.

3. The traditional route to teacher certification is through an undergraduate degree from a college of education followed by certification after graduation. In order to address chronic teacher shortages, recent policy has favored expanding the pool of potential teachers by crafting accelerated programs that condense the traditional teaching curriculum into a period of several months to two years of intense study and supervised classroom practice. Alternative-route programs tend to focus on one of three main clienteles: 1) "mid-career changers," typically college-educated professionals, such as accountants and lawyers, who wish to take up teaching; 2) "para-professionals" already working in the education system, such as teachers' aides, secretaries, and bus drivers, who seek a degree and certification to teach; 3) trained and certified teachers seeking certification in another subject area, such as in special education. See United States Department of Education (2004) for an overview of the policy advocating alternative routes, and Dewey (2005, 150–53) for a discussion of some of the limitations of these programs.

4. See Table 23, "Cost Analysis Summary, 2005–2006," in Florida Department of Education 2007b. The cost per FTE student based on 30 credit hours for postsecondary vocational courses totaled $6,640,and for college preparatory courses, $4,748.

5. The average age of undergraduates for the first two years of university was and remains 19, but the average age for the last two years of university has decreased by a year

since 1995 from 23 years old to 22 years old in 2005 (Board of Governors, State University System of Florida, Table 22, Factbook, 1995–1996, 2005–2006). A slightly higher proportion of women (57 percent of all students) attended Florida's public universities in 2005 than in 1995 (55 percent) (Board of Governors, State University System of Florida, Table 18, Factbook, 1995–1996, 2005a). In 2005, 29 percent of the students were part-time; in 1995 the proportion of part-timers was a higher 37 percent (Board of Governors, State University System of Florida, Table 18, Factbook, 1995–1996, 2005–2006). In 2005, 59 percent of all students were white and 35 percent were minority, with Hispanics constituting the largest portion. In 1995, 67 percent were white and Hispanics also constituted the largest portion of minorities (Board of Governors, State University System of Florida, Table 18, Factbook, 1995–1996, 2005a).

6. This information compared the graduation rates of all full-time first-time-in-college students in Florida's public universities who began in 1997 and graduated in 2002–2003 to the data compiled by the National Center of Education Statistics of students graduating from four-year public institutions in that time frame.

7. At the time of this writing, another lawsuit challenging the authority of the legislature to set tuition is pending. On March 13, 2006, a Leon Circuit Court judge issued a decision authorizing the Florida Board of Governors to set tuition and fees for the state university system.

8. Tuition and required fees for public four-year colleges and universities increased by 30 percent from 1994–2004, compared to 48 percent in the United States and 62 percent in the 16 states represented by the Southern Regional Education Board (2005).

9. See Weissert (2005) for a discussion of Bright Futures and Florida's Prepaid Tuition Program.

References

Blomberg, Jeanine. 2006. "Class Size Reduction Cost Estimates." Presentation to the Senate Committee on Education Appropriations, February 16. <www.firn.edu/doe/arm/pdf/021605senate.pdf> (accessed March 15, 2007).

Board of Governors, State University System of Florida. 1995–1996. Factbook. <www.fldcu.org/factbook/> (accessed May 15, 2007).

———. 2005–2006. Factbook. <www.fldcu.org/factbook/> (accessed May 15, 2007).

———. 2005a. *Florida Quick Facts.* <www.fldcu.org/factbook/quickfacts.asp#gender>.

———. 2005b. "State University System Graduation Rates: How Are We Doing?" *Information Brief* 2, no. 1 (January 27). <www.flbog.org/borpubs/GradRates/2005-01GradRates.pdf> (accessed March 15, 2007).

———. 2005c. "Strategic Plan, 2005–2013." <www.flbog.org/StrategicPlan/pdf/StrategicPlan_05–13.pdf> (accessed March 15, 2007).

———. 2006a. "Fall Student Enrollment in State University Institutions." <www.flbog.org/factbook/enrollment.asp> (accessed March 15, 2007).

———. 2006b. "Summary of State Appropriations and Actual FTE Students, Excludes UF-IFAS, UF-HSC, USF-HSC and FSU-MS, 1981–1982 through 2005–2006." <www.flbog.org/borpubs/FundingHistory/univFundHist82_06.pdf> (accessed March 15, 2007).

———. 2007a. "How Do Students Meet the Cost of Attending a State University?" <www.fldcu.org/factbook/quickfacts/2007_02FinAidInfoBr.pdf> (accessed April 25, 2007).

———. 2007b. "Impact of Changing Population, School Enrollment, and High School Graduate Projections on SUS Enrollments."

———. 2007c. "State University System Funding: How Do We Compare?" <www.flbog .org/factbook/quickfacts/2007_01FundingCompInfoBr.pdf> (accessed April 20, 2007).

Boswell, Katherine, and Cynthia D. Wilson. 2004. "Keeping America's Promise: A Report on the Future of the Community College." <www.ecs.org/clearing-house/53/09/5309.pdf> (accessed March 15, 2007).

Chronicle of Higher Education. 2005. *Almanac of Higher Education 2005–6*. Washington, D.C.: Chronicle of Higher Education.

College Board. 2006. Trends in College Pricing. <www.collegeboard.com/prod_down-loads/press/cost06/trends_college_pricing_06.pdf> (accessed April 30, 2007).

Council for Education Policy, Research and Improvement. 2005. "Impact of the Class Size Amendment on the Quality of Education on Florida." <www.cepri.state.fl.us /pdf/2005%20Class%20Size%20Impact%20Full%20Report.pdf> (accessed May 7, 2007).

Dewey, James. 2005. "Funding Florida's Educational Standards." In *Tough Choices: Shaping Florida's Future*, edited by David Denslow and Carol Weissert. 137–73. Gainesville and Tallahassee: University of Florida and Florida State University.

Florida Department of Education. N.d.a. "Fact Sheet: NCLB and Adequate Yearly Progress." <www.firn.edu/doe/flbpso/pdf/nclbfactsheet.pdf> (accessed March 16, 2007).

———. N.d.b. "School Choice Options." <www.floridaschoolchoice.org/district/files /School_Choice_Options.pdf> (accessed May 7, 2007).

———. 2004. "Analysis of Student Characteristics, 1998–99 Compared to 2003–2004." Data Trend #29. <www.fldoe.org/CC/OSAS/DataTrendsResearch/DT29.pdf> (accessed March 15, 2007).

———. 2005. "Part-Time Faculty in Florida Community College System: A Status Report." <www.fldoe.org/CC/Vision/PDFs/PR2005_2.pdf (accessed March 15, 2007).

———. 2006a. "2003–2004 Profiles of Florida School Districts—Financial Data." <www.fldoe.org/fefp/pdf/0304profiles.pdf> (accessed May 2, 2007).

———. 2006b. "2006–07 Funding for Florida School Districts: Statistical Report." <www.fldoe.org/fefp/pdf/fefpdist.pdf> (accessed May 1, 2007).

———. 2006c. "Long-Range Program Plan FY 2006/2007–FY 2011/12." Draft. <www .fldoe.org/strategy/pdf/0712lrpp.pdf> (accessed April 23, 2007).

———. 2006d. "Membership in Florida's Public Schools: 2006–2007." <www.firn .edu/doe/eias/eiaspubs/xls/pk-12mem0607.xls> (accessed April 30, 2007).

———. 2007a. *Change, and Response to Change, in Florida's Public Schools*. <www.firn .edu/doe/eias/eiaspubs/pdf/changes0207.pdf> (accessed April 30, 2007).

———. 2007b. *The Fact Book: Report for the Community College System*. <www.firn .edu/doe/arm/cctcmis/pubs/factbook/fb2007/fb2007.pdf> (accessed April 25, 2007).

————. 2007c. "Growth of Minority Student Populations in Florida's Public Schools." Florida Information Note. <www.firn.edu/doe/eias/eiaspubs/pdf/minority.pdf> (accessed April 30, 2007).

Florida Education Access Task Force. 2006. "Report of the Joint Task Force of the Florida State Board of Education and the Florida Board of Governors." <www.fldoe.org/OSI/meeting_2006_01_18/pdf/final.pdf> (accessed March 15, 2007).

Florida Prepaid College Board. 2005. "Florida Prepaid College Plan Reaches the 1 Million Mark." <www.florida529plans.com/News/press022805.html> (accessed March 15, 2007).

Holt, Lynne, and David Denslow. 2005. "PK-12 Education Trends." In *Tough Choices: Shaping Florida's Future*, edited by David Denslow and Carol Weissert. 175–82. Gainesville and Tallahassee: University of Florida and Florida State University.

Office of Economic and Demographic Research. 2007. "Student Financial Aid Estimating Conference: Action Minutes." <http://edr.state.fl.us/conferences/financialaid/sfa030507_Minutes.pdf> (accessed May 8, 2007).

Office of Program Policy Analysis and Government Accountability. 2004. "Students Benefit from Workforce Education Programs, but Performance Can Be Improved." *OPPAGA Progress Report* (June). <www.oppaga.state.fl.us/reports/pdf/0442rpt.pdf> (accessed March 15, 2007).

————. 2005a. "Florida's University Graduates Tend to Stay in State Workforce after Completing Their Degrees." *OPPAGA: Office of Program Policy Analysis & Government Accountability* (December). <www.oppaga.state.fl.us/reports/pdf/0559rpt.pdf> (accessed March 15, 2007).

————. 2005b. "Individuals with Baccalaureate Degrees have Positive Outcomes: Increasing Production in Critical Areas Poses Challenges." *OPPAGA: Office of Program Policy Analysis & Government Accountability* (December). <www.oppaga.state.fl.us/reports/pdf/0558rpt.pdf> (accessed March 15, 2007).

————. 2007. "17 School Districts Offered Differentiated Pay Policies to Support Staffing Needs During 2005–2006 School Year." *OPPAGA: Office of Program Policy Analysis & Government Accountability* (January). <www.oppaga.state.fl.us/reports/pdf/0702rpt.pdf> (accessed April 30, 2007).

Southern Regional Education Board. 2005. *Florida Featured Facts*. Atlanta, Ga.: Southern Regional Education Board. <www.sreb.org/main/EdData/FactBook/2005StateReports/Florida05.pdf> (accessed March 15, 2007).

U.S. Department of Education. 2004. "Innovations in Education: Alternative Routes to Teacher Certification." <http://www.ed.gov/admins/tchrqual/recruit/alroutes/index.html> (accessed May 1, 2007.)

Weissert, Carol. 2005. "The Squeeze Facing Higher Education." In *Tough Choices: Shaping Florida's Future*, edited by David Denslow and Carol Weissert. 283–317. Gainesville and Tallahassee: University of Florida and Florida State University.

14

Florida's Health Care Policy

Making Do on the Cheap

CAROL S. WEISSERT AND WILLIAM G. WEISSERT

On a summer day in 2005, Florida secretary of health and state health officer Dr. John O. Agwunobi strode briskly into one of the conference rooms of the Florida Department of Health to address a group of master's degree interns selected from nearby Florida State University and Florida A&M University, their professors, and Florida Department of Health staff. "Welcome to the best state department of health in the country," Dr. Agwunobi said in a voice familiar to Floridians, who have often heard him discussing health-related hurricane information, disease outbreaks, vaccine shortages, and other health emergencies on the radio. "After you've completed your training and begun your careers, as you go to work and visit professionals in other states, you will find that there is widespread agreement that you have experienced the best—Florida has the best department of health in the nation."

Dr. Agwunobi did not take time to explain the criteria he was using to judge his department the best in the nation. Whatever measure he might have had in mind, he would no doubt have wanted to adjust it for a variety of factors crucial to the delivery of health services, including Florida's very large population, making it the fourth-largest in the nation, estimated to have been 18,089,888 in 2006 (U.S. Census Bureau State and County Quick Facts, updated May 7, 2007). That population is ethnically and racially diverse and growing rapidly: three-quarters of population growth comes from in-migration rather than births. It is an elderly population as well. Those aged 65 and over make up nearly 17 percent of the state's population—the largest population of this age group of any state in the nation (U.S. Census Bureau 2006). Florida's warm weather and vast stretches of white-sand beaches are a favorite destination of tourists from around the world, but thanks to its mild temperatures and high humidity, the state is also host to many varieties of organisms that would be less likely to survive in colder climates (Florida Department of Health 2006).

Its challenges are numerous and serious. Many people outside the state believe that Florida is rich and simply chooses not to spend its wealth on public services, but that belief is only half right. It is true that the state is stingy compared to other states in its spending on public services such as health care. Combining spending for health from all sources—public and private—Florida ranks thirty-ninth out of fifty states in the percentage (2.8 percent) of its state domestic product spent on health care programs.

But Florida is far from wealthy. Florida ranks thirty-fifth in median household income among fifty-one states and territories. In 2003–2005, the state's median income was $42,079, or about 8.6 percent below the U.S. median of $46,037 and nearly 30 percent below that of the nation's richest state, New Jersey, at $59,989. For fiscal year 2005, thirty-six states raised more state tax dollars per resident than Florida (Kaiser Family Foundation 2005a).

In keeping with the state's desire for low taxes, recent state leaders have called for major cuts in state programs and agencies as a way to promote market-based approaches and reduce the size of government. Health is one of many areas where programs are being cut or growth is being constrained even as the demands from an expanding population increase (Denslow and Weissert 2005).

In this chapter, we evaluate health care policy and outcomes in Florida in the context of Florida's political history and current reality. We often compare Florida's health care status, programs, and spending with other states and with past years. Since health care policy is such a large area, we focus on a few specific programs—Medicaid, children's health, pharmacy assistance programs, malpractice insurance, anti-smoking programs, and the state's response to the growing problem of people who lack health insurance. Although Florida is often in the middle of the pack in outcome measures for public health, its contributions to health care programs such as Medicaid, child health, and anti-smoking efforts are at the bottom or close to the bottom compared to other states. We attribute this to the state's low-tax–low-services history and political culture. While some might argue that very low spending and moderately low results is a good trade, others might say that given the state's population and natural resources it could be doing much more for the health care of its citizens. Also problematic is the ever-growing demand for services that is outpacing the state's willingness to fund them. Ironically, perhaps because of its low-tax–low-services constraint, Florida is often a leader in innovation in health care policy—at least initially, until demands for resources encounter political constraints on spending.

Health Status Indicators

Statisticians use a wide variety of measures to evaluate the overall health status of a jurisdiction. Typical measures include morbidity and mortality rates for common diseases and conditions, infectious disease rates, indicators of adequacy of access to health care providers and facilities, indicators of the quality of health care facilities, patterns of health care consumption, and indications of the effort state agencies are making to address pressing problems. Overall, the picture in Florida turns out to be rather complicated. Of course Florida has problems, as all states do. One marker of problems and the priority the state gives them is the goals for health improvement that are listed prominently on the Florida health department's Web site and further elaborated in its Long-Range Program Plan (Florida Department of Health 2006). These goals are to improve maternal and infant health, improve the health of children, control infectious diseases, reduce births to teenagers, reduce chronic diseases, increase access to dental care, control environmental health threats, reduce injuries and deaths from violence, and ensure that health care practitioners are competent. The department also provides links to Florida Charts, its high-quality and user-friendly interactive report-generating tool that permits assessment of disease prevalence at the statewide and county-by-county levels for a wide variety of diseases and conditions for several recent years. Combining these with national measures provides a reasonably thorough profile of how the state measures up against other states.

Florida and National Mortality and Morbidity Measures

Table 14.1 illustrates how Florida compares to other states in selected mortality statistics for 2001–2003. In overall deaths per 100,000, Florida ranks twenty-ninth (meaning that twenty-one states have lower death rates). The state ranks nineteenth in the incidence of infant deaths (thirty-one states have lower rates), and twenty-sixth in child deaths (twenty-four states have lower rates). In some disease-related deaths (cancer, stroke, and diabetes), the state's performance is respectable. However, the number of motor vehicle deaths in Florida is higher than in all but nineteen other states.

Table 14.2 provides Florida's national ranking on key indicators of morbidity, including premature births, obesity, AIDS, smoking, visits to the physician and dentist, and asthma. Florida has a laudable ranking in asthma among adults (33rd). It ranks 29th in percent of people overweight or obese

Table 14.1. Florida's Ranking on Mortality Measures, 2003 (deaths per 100,000 population)

Measure	Ranking among 50 States
Overall Death Ranking[1]	29
Infant Death (per 1,000 births)[2]	19
Child Death	26
Teen Death from Accidents, Homicide, or Suicide	26
Death from Heart Disease	28
Death from Cancer	40[2]
Death from Diabetes	41
Death from Stroke	47
Occupational Fatalities[2, 3]	23
Death due to Firearms	24
Motor Vehicle Death	19

Source: Kaiser Family Foundation, "State Health Facts," available online at http://statehealthfacts.org (accessed April 2, 2007).
Notes: 1. 2004 data.
2. 2002 data.
3. Per 100,000 workers.

Table 14.2. Florida's Ranking on Morbidity Measures, 2005

Measure	Ranking among 50 States
Low Birthweight Infants[1, 2]	16
Percent Children Ages 0–18 Who Are Uninsured[3]	3
Percent Adults Who Are Overweight or Obese	29
Percent of Adults Who Participated in Physical Activity in the Past Month	38
AIDS Case Rate (all ages)[4]	4
Percent Adults 65 and Over Who Had a Flu Shot in the Past Year	49
Percent Mothers Beginning Prenatal Care in First Trimester[5]	18
Percent Children Aged 19–35 Months Who Are Immunized[2]	1
Violent Crime Offenses Rate[4]	4
Percent of Adults Who Have Been Told They Have Asthma	33
Percent of Adults Who Smoke	19

Source: Kaiser Family Foundation, "State Health Facts," available at http://statehealthfacts.org (accessed April 2, 2007).
Notes: 1. As a percent of all births.
2. Data for 2004.
3. Data for 2004–2005.
4. Per 100,000 population.
5. Data for 2002.

even though more than half (58.2 percent) of Floridians are obese or overweight, according to the Centers for Disease Control and Prevention. Only the fact that the rest of the nation is so heavy makes Florida rank moderately well despite its high prevalence. Moreover, the prevalence of being overweight has increased nearly 70 percent since 1986, while the prevalence of obesity has doubled (Florida Department of Health 2006).

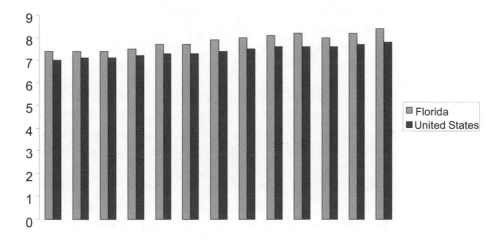

1990 1991 1992 1993 1994 1995 1996 1997 1998 1999 2000 2001 2002

Figure 14.1. Percent of Low Birth Weight Babies: Florida and the United States, 1990–2002.

Obesity rates are no doubt aggravated by the fact that the state's population has an extremely poor level of physical activity. Despite its temperate weather, it is the twelfth worst in the nation for the measure of physical activity rates. Another challenge is HIV/AIDS. Florida ranks fourth in the nation in AIDS cases per 100,000 population and is fourth in the nation in new cases per year (4,666 in 2003).

In 2004, Florida ranked a regrettable sixteenth in percentage of low birth-weight infants. Its rate of 8.5 percent is above the U.S. average of 8.1 percent. Perhaps more troubling is the fact that the gap between Florida and the U.S. average for low birth-weight babies has increased since 1990 (Annie E. Casey Foundation 2006). (See Figure 14.1.) Florida ranks an extremely disturbing forty-second among forty-four states in the percentage of children who are uninsured. Seventeen percent of Florida's children are uninsured, compared to 12 percent nationally (Kaiser Family Foundation 2005a).

Florida's preventive care, the hallmark of public health, is also mixed, according to national measures. Florida ranked forty-ninth among fifty-one states and territories in its rate of annual influenza vaccination for adults age 65 and over in 2005. It actually had a negative rate of improvement of −8 percent three years before the nationwide shortage of flu vaccine (Centers for Disease Control and Prevention 2002, 2003). This is a disturbing indicator of neglect of the most basic public health practice. Yet it ranked first in childhood immunizations (89 percent compared to a US average of 81 percent). This measure is widely recognized as one of the most basic indicators of preventive health efforts.

Combating Smoking

The state's worst recent performance is probably in combating smoking. It has more smokers per capita than the nation at large, and more Black smokers per capita than the nation. Moreover, it has mortgaged its future: The state ranked extremely low (forty-third) in spending for tobacco prevention in 2005 (Campaign for Tobacco-Free Kids 2004, iii). Its $1 million budget in 2005 for tobacco prevention represented just 1.3 percent of the Centers for Disease Control's (CDC) recommended spending for that year and only 0.10 percent of its tobacco settlement revenues. Across the nation, the average spending of tobacco settlement revenues was 33.6 percent of the CDC's recommendation. Florida was once held up as a model for all states of how to decrease teen and adult smoking rates. In fiscal year 2001, it spent $44 million on tobacco prevention. It is now labeled one of the "most disappointing states" (Campaign for Tobacco-Free Kids 2004, iii) by the Campaign for Tobacco Free Kids for its cuts to programs that were once highly successful.

This designation of most disappointing is ironic given Florida's leadership role in successfully suing the nation's tobacco companies for costs the state incurred for caring for residents who smoke. Although Mississippi, which was led by its activist attorney general, was the first to file suit in 1993, Florida was close behind, filing suit in 1995. Florida's action was pivotal to the future of tobacco settlements, since in 1994 the legislature enacted a law that almost guaranteed that the industry could not win in the state's courts. The law stipulated that "principles of common law and equity . . . are to be abrogated to the extent necessary to ensure full recovery by Medicaid from [tobacco companies]" (Derthick 2002, 79). A spokesman for the Tobacco Products Liability Project described the law as "the most important legislation ever adopted anywhere in the United States on the subject of holding cigarette manufacturers financially responsible for the health care costs their products and conduct produce" (Derthick 2002,167).

In August 1997, before any trial could begin, the industry settled with the state for $11.3 billion over twenty-five years. In addition, the industry agreed to pay for costs and fees of the private lawyers who prepared Florida's case and a number of public health measures, including removing all billboard and transit advertisements and financing a pilot program aimed at reducing youth smoking. This settlement was key because of its size (Mississippi settled for $3.4 billion) and the inclusion of the public health components, which set the stage for those contained in the 1998 Master Settlement Agreement between the major cigarette manufacturers and attorneys general of forty-six states. (Florida was not included because it had signed a separate agreement.)

One side note concerning Florida's leadership is telling, however. A year after passing the path-breaking law, Florida's legislature repealed it, apparently in response to strong lobbying by business interests. Democratic governor Lawton Chiles vetoed the repeal (perhaps as the legislature knew he would). The Florida supreme court upheld the law, and the U.S. Supreme Court declined to revisit the decision. (Derthick 2002). In 1998, Florida moved to implement an aggressive anti-tobacco education program that had rather spectacular results. Smoking among teens in the state fell from 23.3 percent to 20.9 percent in less than a year. In spite of this success, the 1999 Florida legislature, under Republican leadership, reduced the funding by nearly half as the new Republican governor, Jeb Bush, indicated that he was shifting the policy goals of the program (Givel and Glantz 2000).

Health Providers and Services

A final key to understanding Florida's health picture relates to use of services and availability of health professionals. Florida has a relatively high rate of hospital admission. Adjusted for population, the state's 203 hospitals experienced 134 admissions per 1,000 population in 2004 (this rate is the twelfth highest in the nation), placing it above the national average of 119 admissions. This rate is one and one half to twice the rate of admission of states with the lowest rates. Lengths of stay were more modest, however, at 696 days per 1,000 population, making the state twenty-second in the nation. The national average was 673 days (Kaiser Family Foundation 2005a).

In 2004, 390 people per 1,000 population visited Florida emergency rooms, roughly 2 percent above the national average of 383. This ranks the state at twenty-seventh in such visits. The fact that a third of the population—or at least a number of visits equivalent to one-third of the population (some probably were repeat users)—visited emergency rooms in 2004 suggests that health care facilities might not be optimally available when patients want to use them. Florida has a larger than average number of physicians:55,858 physicians (not counting those who work for the federal government in one capacity or another); only two states (New York and Texas) have more doctors. Florida also has an above-average number of primary care physicians, and it has an above-average number of black and Hispanic physicians, though these ethnicity statistics do not control for population size or ethnic makeup (Kaiser Family Foundation 2005a).

The state also ranks high in number of hospitals, rural health clinics, federally qualified health centers (available principally to poor and near-poor citizens), nursing home residents, and physician's assistants, and it ranks close to average in number of hospital beds per 1,000 population. But it ranks very low in outpatient visits and nursing home residents per 1,000 elderly people, despite its large absolute number of nursing home beds and residents (Kaiser Family Foundation 2005a).

Indeed, nursing home residents adjusted for its large elderly population ranks the state forty-fifth in the nation; just 2.2 percent of its 65 and over population lives in nursing homes. Observers in other states have long speculated that Florida deliberately keeps its bed supply low relative to its elderly population so that those who need nursing homes will return to the states where their children live rather than enter nursing homes that eventually will likely be subsidized by Florida's Medicaid program. Other possible explanations are that people consciously choose to return to other states when they need a nursing home or that they are healthy enough to make less frequent use of nursing home beds than other states' elderly people. (That is, they are active and functional until very close to death—a scenario long hoped for as a vision for everyone's old age but generally not achieved, at least not by most elderly people.) Most likely the low rate of use reflects a long-term public policy choice by state government to discourage private nursing home bed construction so the availability rate will not be high enough to meet demand.

In short, looking at health status, costs, and use measures, Florida's population is in as good or better standing than the populations of many states. Exceptions are its high levels of AIDS cases, high incidence of low birth-weight infants, rising rate of syphilis cases, high incidence of nonviolent criminal offenses, poor efforts to reduce the incidence of obesity and high levels of physical inactivity, poor performance on adult immunization, high rate of motor vehicle deaths, high rate of stroke among blacks, and high rate of deaths among cardiovascular disease victims, teens, and those who are casualties of firearms. Florida generally chooses policies that keep its expenditures as low as possible. It tends to favor minimal reliance upon the public purse for solutions, even in those areas where the policy outcomes are positive, as in its anti-smoking campaign in the late 1990s.

This self-reliant attitude is evident in other ways too, some of which may have public health consequences. Public health experts consider violence in general and gun violence in particular to be an important public health concern on a par with smoking because its effects are devastating, its incidence high, and its costs quite burdensome to public facilities and agencies. Consequently, when the 2005 state legislature passed a bill—which the governor signed—relaxing constraints on violent response by residents who feel themselves threatened in their homes or in public places or in private places where they have a right to be, public health advocates felt they had suffered a policy defeat. Retreat is no longer required and the venue where encounters can be legally responded to with force was expanded so much that it is now virtually unlimited. This development broadly expands upon the policy about carrying permits for concealed weapons adopted years earlier by the state.

In recent years, few new dollars have been allocated to public health prevention programs, and the state is increasingly relying on local public health departments and county governments to fund and implement preventive health care programs.

Florida's Health Policy Response

Florida has often been known as an innovator in health policy. In the early 1980s, it was one of the first states to tax hospitals to supplement matching state funds for Medicaid expansion; in the early 1990s, it was a leader in suing tobacco companies and setting up innovative anti-smoking campaigns; in the 1990s, it was early in pursuing the idea of managed competition and encouraging Medicaid to cover managed care and led the way for other states in developing programs to control Medicaid drug costs and to provide needed drugs to elderly poor and near-poor people. Its provision of health coverage for children in near-poor families helped define the national State Children's Health Insurance Program. In 2004–2005, Florida was the focus of national attention on right-to-die issues raised by the tragic case of a young, long-incapacitated woman named Terri Schiavo. In 2005, it was a national leader in entirely overhauling its Medicaid program.

In the 1990s, Florida revamped state health and human sources administration by separating its once-mammoth Department of Health and Rehabilitative Services (DHRS) into four new health and human services agencies: Department of Elder Affairs (1991), Agency for Health Care Administration (1992), Department of Juvenile Justice (1994), and Department of Health (1997). Finally in 1997, DHRS was renamed the Department of Children and Families (OPPAGA 2000). These changes were made to save money and improve the efficiency of government under a Democratic governor, Lawton Chiles (Crew 1992).[1]

In the section below, we discuss some of these programs, focusing on Medicaid, prescription drug assistance, child health, medical malpractice, and health insurance. The biggest story is Medicaid, a policy that has bedeviled Florida and all other states for several decades. At issue is not the program's value, but its rising and seemingly unsustainable costs.

Medicaid

Unquestionably the most important health policy program in Florida—and in all other states—is Medicaid, the federal-state program targeted to the poor and disabled.[2] Every legislative session, the Florida legislature enacts at least a dozen laws further shaping, often curtailing, programs and services in an effort to slow rising costs. Yet the costs continue to rise, even in the face of federal and state efforts at containment. In fiscal year 2006, health care and social services made up the biggest slice of Florida's budget—nearly $23 billion of a $70 billion budget. Most of that—$15 billion—came from state and federal Medicaid funds.

Florida's Medicaid program covers 2.2 million people, including some of the state's most vulnerable and frail citizens. It pays for 44 percent of all births, the health care of over one-fourth of the state's children, and the cost of care for two-thirds of all nursing home residents in the state (Alker and Portelli 2005). It is not one program but several, providing services for

- low-income uninsured children, some low-income parents, and low-income pregnant women
- disabled persons, including those with mental illness and low-income elderly
- those who are too poor to pay the premiums and co-pays required for Medicare, the federal program for elderly people
- safety-net hospitals and community health centers that serve the poor

Not surprisingly, given the scope of Medicaid, it is expensive; it accounts for around 25 percent of the total state budget each year. In Florida, costs of Medicaid increased at an annual average of 12.5 percent from 2000 to 2005 (Alker and Portelli 2004a). As Figure 14.2 shows, Medicaid spending rates rise and fall over time, reflecting a variety of factors that include the number of individuals enrolled in the program, advances in health care technology,

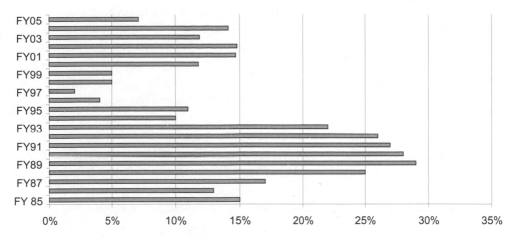

Figure 14.2. Annual Medicaid Expenditure Growth Rate in Florida, FY 1985–FY 2003.

changes in provider treatment involving drug and technology choices, and level of payments to providers.

The biggest increases were in the late 1980s and early 1990s, a time when enrollments were up due to economic problems. Growth since 1999 is substantial but less than that of a decade earlier. Perhaps most problematic is the increase in Medicaid costs over the past few years compared to the increase in state revenues. Former governor Jeb Bush liked to point out that Medicaid costs in Florida had grown by 88 percent since 1998, while tax dollars collected by the state during that same period had grown by only 24 percent (Gomez 2005).

Another way to gauge Medicaid's importance in Florida's state policy is to examine the percentage of the state budget allocated to the program. Medicaid has long been a major component of state spending (nearly 15 percent in fiscal year 1992), but in recent years the percentages have been increasing and now constitute around 25 percent of the Florida budget (including both federal aid and state dollars). Former governor Bush estimated that if left unchecked, the Medicaid budget would account for 60 percent of the state budget by 2015 (Lauer 2005a).

Another concern is the fact that this growth has taken place in a program that, compared to other states, is very conservative, if not cheap. Florida spending per Medicaid recipient is thirty-ninth out of the forty-eight states on which data are available. This statistic is in line with similar spending patterns in the state for other measures of health care provision. Florida is forty-fifth in spending per child, forty-second in spending per adult, thirty-ninth in spending per disabled person, and forty-fourth in spending per elderly in Medicaid (Alker and Portelli 2004b).

Since the federal government pays almost 60 percent of Florida's Medicaid bill, in some regard it makes sense for Florida to provide for the health care of needy citizens (and voters). For each state dollar spent on Medicaid, the federal government sends $1.44 to Tallahassee (Alker and Portelli 2004b).

Several aspects of the Medicaid program involve policy choices that affect costs. The first is the number of persons eligible for the program (it is an entitlement program, which means that all eligible individuals will be provided for under the program). Also important is the scope and level of the benefits those recipients receive. A third important component is the level of payment to providers of the health care service.

Florida's Enrollment

The federal government sets a minimum standard for eligibility for a number of components of the Medicaid program. But the state can voluntarily provide for individuals whose income and assets are above the federal standard. For example, all states must pay for pregnant woman who have incomes of up to 133 percent of the poverty level; states can opt to pay for pregnant women who have incomes of up to 185 percent of the poverty level. States can also choose to cover groups of people. Florida covers the medically needy, those with medical expenses so large that they reduce their income to near the eligibility level for Medicaid.

Typically, when the economy declines and citizens lose their jobs, the need for public assistance and Medicaid increases. Indeed, there was a substantial increase in enrollment in the late 1980s and early 1990s, when the country and the state was in the midst of a recession. Another increase that began in the late 1990s was thought to reflect in part the loss of employer-provided health coverage as many small employers curtailed their health insurance expenses in Florida and across the nation.

Enrollment is also important because the costs vary by enrollment category. For example, children are the largest percentage of Medicaid enrollees but make up the smallest percentage of costs compared to other groups; children account for over half of all Medicaid enrollees but only 16 percent of the cost. In contrast, elderly people make up less than 10 percent of enrollees but account for 18 percent of the cost of Medicaid in Florida. People who are blind or otherwise disabled represent 19 percent of enrollment but nearly 58 percent of spending (Alker and Portelli 2005). While these percentages are common across the states, the rates of growth in the categories are not.

In programs for those who are elderly and disabled, Florida Medicaid has seen growth rates that are higher than rates in other states. Between 1992 and 2002, growth in Medicaid recipients who are blind or disabled grew 3.1 percent in Florida, compared to 1.2 percent across all states, and the cost of providing care for low-income elderly people grew by 2.3 percent in Florida, compared to less than 1 percent across all states.

Florida's Benefit Package

Priorities in Florida's Medicaid program can be gauged by looking at how the program dollars are allocated. Nursing home care and prescriptions accounted for 16 and 19 percent, respectively, of spending in fiscal year 2005. Hospital inpatient care accounted for 14 percent of Medicaid spending. Health maintenance organizations accounted for 11 percent of Medicaid spending. The remaining spending was for physicians, home- and community-based care, out-patient hospital care and a number of smaller targeted programs such as graduate medical education, home health services, and case management services (Agency for Health Care Administration 2006). If we compared the spending patterns for Medicaid twenty years ago, we would see less spending for outpatient hospital care, prepaid plans and, prescriptions. In Florida, as in other states, paying for prescription drugs has taken a steadily larger share of the Medicaid budget, in spite of efforts to curtail that spending. Nationwide, we know that these increases flow from the growing number of prescriptions used by Medicaid beneficiaries, changes in the types of drugs used, and manufacturers' price increases.

Fraud and Abuse

Cases of fraud and abuse in Florida's Medicaid program make good copy for newspapers but are difficult to quantify across the program. What we do know is that the administrative costs of Medicaid are lower than those of other health programs. Nationwide, administrative costs of Medicaid are 4 to 6 percent of the cost of claims paid, compared to 8 to 12 percent of the cost of claims paid for non-Medicaid reimbursed HMOs and 15 to 20 percent of the cost of claims for private health insurers (Smith and Moody 2005). And the cost of paying providers of Medicaid services in Florida is low. A commonly used standard of assessing the generosity or stringency of Medicaid programs is comparing a state's Medicaid payment rate to the payment rate of Medicare, the national health care program for the elderly and disabled. Florida pays physicians 65 percent of what Medicare pays nationally. The fifty state Medicaid average is 69 percent of what Medicare pays (Alker and Portelli 2005).

Florida's Efforts to Control Medicaid Spending

Florida has been a leader in incremental efforts to curb Medicaid spending. In the late 1990s the state recognized the significance of rising drug costs and led the nation in efforts to curtail those costs. Florida's strategies for keeping drug costs down have included using a pharmacy benefit manager to buy drugs in bulk for all Medicaid providers, requiring prior authorization for nondiscounted drugs, setting monthly limits on brand-name drug use, making use of generic drugs mandatory, requiring patients to share costs, and demanding supplemental rebates or management of patient care. Some of these strategies are subject to alteration under the federal Medicare Prescription Drug Improvement and Modernization Act of 2003, and other aspects may be altered in the short or long term as the state's plans for shifting Medicaid patients to a new system for purchasing health care coverage are implemented. But whatever specific changes are enacted, Florida is likely to remain a leader in innovations to improve efficiency in prescription drug assistance for its poor and near-poor populations.

Florida has also been a leader in its efforts to manage diseases since 1997. Its goal is to improve outcomes and control costs among high-risk Medicaid clients suffering a variety of conditions (asthma, diabetes, HIV/AIDS, hemophilia, hypertension, cancer, end-stage renal disease, congestive heart failure, and sickle-cell anemia). The state discontinued contracts with large drug companies who provided disease management, but it has maintained disease-management programs in selected areas such as high-risk obstetrics that are operated by health management companies.

The state has also periodically eliminated or curtailed its medically needy program, reduced provider fees, adopted strategies to combat Medicaid fraud, and imposed or raised co-payments. Like other states (but not as enthusiastically), Florida has maximized federal payments by levying provider taxes on hospitals that serve the poor (using this money as the state's matching funds, which then leads to more federal dollars. The state then repays the hospitals for their provider taxes, but pockets most or all of the federal match, which in Florida is 59 percent. A related program maximizes payments through the upper payment limits program where designated providers can receive funding from the state that exceeds the regular Medicaid reimbursement. A state makes the enhanced Medicaid payment to county nursing homes or hospitals. The providers give back much or all of the extra payment to the state and the state keeps the federal match. In both programs the state does not put up additional money but benefits from a generous federal match (Weissert 2005).

Reforming Florida's Medicaid Program

The state's most recent effort to reform health care provision is by far the boldest. In 2005, Governor Jeb Bush announced his plan to reform Medicaid by essentially privatizing it—limiting the state's role and giving private entities the ability to compete for recipients armed with vouchers for care. Privatization was a major focus of Bush's leadership in the state, and expansion into the state's largest program area seemed only natural. In October 2005, the U.S. Department of Health and Human Services approved the state's request for a waiver of Medicaid provisions in order to change the program from one that pays providers for services rendered to participants to one that pays premiums to health maintenance organizations and other entities that are managing the health care of recipients. State legislation signed in December 2005 launched the program, which began its first phase in Broward and Duval Counties.

Instead of providing defined benefits or services, the plan features defined contributions, or premiums, that the state pays at risk-adjusted rates for each Medicaid recipient to plans those recipients select. Ideally, these plans will compete for clients, thus assuring both diversity of choices and quality care. Providers will be different as well. Managed-care organizations will compete for the Medicaid vouchers as well as new entities such as provider service networks and community networks (which are not fully defined). The idea is that turning the program over to the private sector will save the state money and improve access (and quality) through competition.

Among the most innovative components of the privatization proposal are the three separate components that managed-care organizations and other insurers can provide. The services managed-care organizations offer must provide a comprehensive care component that includes the services the federal government now requires for all Medicaid patients such as hospital and physician care and pharmaceuticals. The plan includes a catastrophic component—assurance that if the Medicaid consumer falls victim to illness or an accident that requires very large expenses, the insurer or the state will cover these costs. The most innovative component is called enhanced benefits. In this component, Medicaid customers who demonstrate positive and beneficial health behavior can quality for flexible spending accounts that can be used to purchase additional services or employer-based insurance.

The overall plan is innovative in five ways. First, it relies on defined contributions. Medicaid consumers are given risk-adjusted premiums that vary by such factors as the recipient's age, health status, and medical history. Second, all of the various plans within the privatization program must offer a package of benefits that is equivalent to the value of the current state Medicaid package for the average member of the population. While plans must offer all mandatory benefits, the levels and amounts of services may vary under the new program. Some plans might focus on certain types of recipients or those with specific needs as a way to attract clients. Third, the plan will feature enhanced benefits, such as flexible savings accounts. Fourth, privatization will change the entitlement program into a block grant, where the state commits a defined amount of money to the program and no more. In addition, the plan is developing a new type of provider for Florida. We do not know yet what types of community provider networks might emerge, nor do we know who will oversee the licensing of these new entities. Finally, the waiver will allow recipients to opt out of Medicaid and receive a voucher they can use to purchase private coverage (for example, buying in to an employer's health insurance program).

What is clear is that Florida's Medicaid proposal represents a major change in governmental oversight over this key health program in the safety net. Early descriptions from the governor's office outlined the role of the government as threefold: protecting consumers (including a rating system for plans and service networks), providing information to Medicaid consumers who might need extra help in evaluating options and selecting the ones most suitable for them, and making a budget that sets the state's spending level for Medicaid. What seemed to be missing from the initial plan was oversight and efforts to assure accountability from the private entities that would be providing this key health care service to a vulnerable population.

The initiative has proceeded slowly—beginning with two counties in September 2006 and expanding to three more in 2007. The expectation is that the program will be in place across the state in 2009 or 2010. Medicaid recipients in the counties selected for the program who are children, their parents, and Supplemental Security Income (SSI) beneficiaries will be required to enroll. Those who are dually eligible for Medicare and Medicaid are not required to participate in the initial years of the program. The state was granted a separate waiver proposal to set up a new long-term managed care program to be rolled out the year after the waiver program of the Medicaid reform plan.

The Politics of Medicaid

Governor Jeb Bush has compared reforming Medicaid to eating broccoli and enduring a root canal—neither are enjoyable activities but supposedly both have worthwhile results. But the politics of Medicaid are not straightforward, they are not necessarily good for all involved, and they are not fun for anybody. While Medicaid customers are often not the most politically active group, the providers of their care—physicians, hospitals, and administrators of managed-care plans, nursing homes, drug stores, and pharmaceutical companies—are. So choosing between consumer interests (weakly represented) and provider interests (strongly represented) can be quite easy for legislators and the governor. However, there are other factors at play—namely the federal contribution to Medicaid and its economic implications. One study estimated that for every cut of $100 million in Medicaid, there is a loss of $303 million in business activity and 3,123 jobs (Alker and Portelli 2005). No wonder not a single legislator applauded when Governor Bush called Medicaid reform his first priority in his 2005 state of the state address (Hollins 2005).

KidCare

While Medicaid has long helped provide health care services to poor children, most states, including Florida, limit eligibility for these services to very poor children. In 1990, Florida set up the public-private Florida Healthy Kids Corporation to operate a family health insurance plan based on school enrollment. When the federal State Children's Health Insurance Program was created in 1997, Florida's was one of three preexisting state programs grandfathered into the national program, and the state's existing benefit package for Healthy Kids served as the initial benefit package for the new federal-state program. The Florida KidCare Program includes Medicaid (for children 0–19); the Healthy Kids program (for children of the working poor aged 5–19); the Children's Medical Services Network (for children 0–19 with special behavioral or physical health needs); and the Behavior Health Network (for children 5–19 with serious behavioral needs). Families with incomes below 150 percent of the federal poverty level whose children are eligible for the Healthy Kids program pay a monthly premium of $15, regardless of the number of children in the family. Families with incomes below from 151 to 200 percent of federal poverty level pay a $20 monthly premium. Families that earn more than 200 percent of federal poverty can buy in at a full price. Florida's counties participate in the program with a local match of up to 20 percent of the funding.

Unlike the Medicaid program, Healthy Kids is a block grant, not an entitlement, which means that the state has broad discretion in who to serve and what to provide to them. There is no obligation to serve every client who meets a particular set of eligibility criteria. Florida qualifies for around $300 million each year of funding from block grants. In recent years the legislature has made changes in the program that have affected it greatly. In 2003, the legislature limited KidCare enrollment so much that by early 2004, there was a waiting list of 90,000 children. In March 2004, the legislature offered spots for the 90,000 children but then stopped most new enrollments after that month, allowing only two enrollment periods. (Previously, families could enroll at any time). The new law also changed enrollment procedures, calling for more detailed information about family income and whether the family could get private insurance through their jobs. The rationale for that change was concern about fraud and making sure that the program was going to deserving children. But the legislature was also concerned about rising costs. When the waiting list was abolished, enrollment swelled to 358,000, but then it began to drop and fell to 248,000 in February 2005 (Saunders 2005).

In 2005, the legislature passed a law allowing year-round enrollment but did not change the cumbersome paperwork process that many argued was a constraint on enrollment. In June 2005, the number of children had fallen to 208,018—slightly more than half the number of children enrolled in the program in June 2004. In fact, in June 2005, almost $35 million in unspent funds were returned to the state treasury and another $88 million of federal money was not spent (Lauer 2005b).

Lack of Health Insurance in Florida

In Florida, as in much of the nation, many citizens lack health insurance. More than 3.5 million nonelderly Floridians had no health insurance in 2004–2005. (Most, though not all, elderly have insurance from Medicare, Medicaid, or both.) Over 72 percent of Florida's uninsured were members of families in which at least one member worked full-time, and another 10 percent had at least a part-time worker in the family. Many worked in small firms. About one-third (32 percent) of Florida's non-elderly uninsured are poor—falling at or below the federal poverty level (Kaiser Family Foundation 2005a).

According to a state-funded survey (Duncan, Porter, Garvan, and Hall 2005), most of the state's uninsured lived in South Florida and most were working. People 35–54 years old constituted more than a third of those without health insurance, while almost a quarter were 18–24. Hispanics and blacks were more likely than whites to be uninsured, though due to their larger numbers in the population, most uninsured residents are white. More than a third had been uninsured for at least two years by the time of the survey, and a fifth had never been insured.

The large number of people who are uninsured is a long-standing problem in Florida. In 1985, 25 percent of Floridians under the age of 65 had no health insurance; the percentage of state residents who lacked insurance was the third highest in the nation. In 2004–5, the percentage of uninsured under age 65 was 23 percent, and the state with New Mexico were tied at the second highest in the nation(Kaiser Family Foundation 2005a). Over that twenty-year period, Florida policy makers enacted several innovative policies to deal with the problem, most of which were never implemented or were implemented without adequate funding:

- In 1984, Florida's Public Medical Assistance Trust Fund, funded through a 1.5 percent assessment on operating revenues and general revenues of hospitals, was established to pay for the state's share of indigent health care services and primary care programs for low-income persons and for funding expansion of Medicaid to additional groups. Since 1996, those funds have been used solely to pay for in-patient hospital services for Medicaid patients, not for the uninsured.
- A 1988 program for the medically indigent that was designed to share state and local responsibilities has not been funded by the state since 1991.
- Mandates in the 1992 Florida Health Care Reform Act that would have ensured that all unemployed low-income citizens in Florida have access to basic health care were never implemented.
- A MedAccess program designed for individuals and families who had incomes at 250 percent or less of the federal poverty level who had been without health insurance for the preceding twelve months and who were not enrolled in Medicare or Medicaid was never implemented (National Health Law Program 1997).
- Florida's high-risk pool for citizens who cannot afford individual health insurance policies has been closed since 1991.

One important program launched in 1992 remains in place, but it is poorly funded. The Healthy Start Program provides newborns and their mothers with resources, support, and help in such areas as childbirth and parenting education, nutritional counseling, smoking cessation, and support groups. In fiscal year 2006, $1.5 million of the $28 million program was redirected to an abstinence program. This was a year when the legislature had over $1 billion in excess funds it did not anticipate when it convened in January 2005 (*Tallahassee Democrat* 2005).

Thus, in spite of some good intentions on the part of the state, county governments are primarily responsible for providing health care services to uninsured indigent persons in Florida. Counties in Florida are authorized to provide primary care services to those unable to obtain such services due to lack of income or other circumstances beyond their control. These services must be free to those with a family income of 100 percent or less of the federal poverty level and must have a sliding scale for those at higher levels of income. In addition, the state authorizes counties to establish special funding districts for indigent health care and to levy property taxes to fund such care with majority approval from the voters. State law also permits most counties to impose a half-cent sales tax by referendum to fund indigent care. The result is a patchwork quilt of programs with differing structures, approaches, and funding. Among the exemplary programs are the following:

- Hillsborough County uses the discretionary sales tax to fund an extensive managed-care program that has won national awards for innovation. The managed-care networks provide primary and preventive care as well as mental health, dental, and other ancillary services for the uninsured through contracts with a number of public and private providers.
- Broward County has established two special taxing districts that fund a network of hospitals and other health care facilities and services.
- Miami-Dade uses general revenues from property taxes, along with the sales surtax, to fund two tax-supported hospitals governed by the Public Health Trust.
- Palm Beach County set up a health care district, funded by local property taxes, to provide an insurance plan for eligible low-income county residents (Jackson and Beatty 2004).
- JaxCare is a local public-private partnership that provides care for the uninsured in Duval County (JaxCare 2007).

Meanwhile, in many counties, privately and charitably funded clinics and emergency department visits continue to be a major source of care for the uninsured.

Medical Malpractice: Interest-Group Politics

While much of health care policy takes place below the political radar screen, certain key issues invariably become major points of contention. Sometimes the battle is nested in ideological differences (such as in the Terri Schiavo case, in which the debate was about whether a young woman in a persistent vegetative state should be kept alive), and sometimes the political parties choose an issue as grounds for a battle to define their differences and motivate supporters (such as with the issue of abortion). At other times, major interest groups stake out positions and mount a battle to attract support either in the legislature or at the ballot box to serve their interests. Medical malpractice insurance premiums are an example of the latter. Physicians claim that rates rise due to the cost of defending practitioners against frivolous lawsuits and the cost of large damage settlements. Lawyers say that lawsuits have little connection to premium rates; they blame insurance companies and other factors.

Both sides—and a third player, insurance companies—tend to exaggerate their claims. A U.S. Government Accounting Office report (2003) found that claims that physicians were moving out of Florida to other states to obtain lower premiums were not accurate or involved very few physicians. There is also evidence that the real cause of rising malpractice rates is insurance companies that raise rates when they lose money from their investments. In telling testimony before a Florida Senate committee, where witnesses were placed under oath (an unusual practice), an insurance company executive admitted that his firm would thrive whether malpractice reform passed or not (Clark 2003).

Florida has been a battleground over the issue of malpractice premiums for several years. In 1989, Florida was one of the first two states in the nation to enact a no-fault program for birth-related neurological injuries. (Virginia enacted a similar program in 1988.) While the program was rated a success by external evaluators, it did not fully solve the malpractice insurance premium increase problem (Robert Wood Johnson Foundation 2002).

By 2004, when the issue of malpractice premiums returned to the political arena, it took three special legislative sessions to craft a solution, evidence of the high stakes for key interest groups. During the legislative deliberation, lawyers and patient groups took to the streets to oppose caps on damages (Boulton 2003). Physicians also closed their offices in some Florida cities, refusing to work until the legislature gave them some relief from non-economic damages (damages for pain and suffering). The law now sets non-economic damages at no more than half a million dollars per injured party, though in the special case of death or damage resulting in a persistent vegetative state, damages can go to one million dollars. Punitive damages cannot be awarded for more than triple the amount of compensatory damages, and in all events except deliberate harm punitive damages are capped at $500,000.

Yet neither side was satisfied. Physicians and attorneys decided to change tactics and go directly to the state's voters for more complete relief. Three constitutional amendments were placed on the November 2004 ballot, and all three passed. One limited lawyers' fees so that most of the money from court settlements would go to patients, not lawyers. The others would require doctors and hospitals to disclose medical mistakes and would revoke the license of physicians found guilty of malpractice in three court judgments (Royse 2004a, 2004b).

But the issue endures, in large part because the amendments conflict (one would make it harder to sue, the other two would make it easier) and because the state legislature—which was required to interpret the two anti-doctor amendments—interpreted the amendments much more restrictively than their plain language seemed to suggest. In addition, lawyers were reportedly poised to make the fee-restricting amendment moot by seeking client approval to waive its effects in their suits. Both sides filed new suits (Lamendola 2004). Commenting on the outcome of the turmoil, Dr. Paul Barach, director of the University of Miami Center for Patient Safety, observed: "We have not made it safer for patients in Florida, despite all the money and all the rhetoric" (Galewitz 2005, 10).

Other Issues

In an area as broad as health care policy, it is impossible to cover in any detail all issues of importance. What follows are brief summaries of other recent health care policies or issues:

- The 2004 Affordable Health Care for Floridians Act created new high-risk health insurance, required health care facilities to publish their prices, required the Agency for Health Care Administration (AHCA) to develop a physician information system for consumers to use to assess health care quality, required AHCA to publish retail prices for a 30-day supply of the fifty most commonly prescribed drugs and their generic equivalents, and required carriers that offer small-group coverage to offer a high-deductible plan that meets federal standards. In 2005, the prices of the fifty most popular drugs on the market in Florida for drug stores in every county were available on a state Web site.
- A 2005 law increased state oversight of abortion clinics that provide second-trimester abortions, including new rules covering a clinic's building, equipment, and staffing; the procedure itself; and post-abortion care (Hallifax 2005). Critics said the law was intended to intimidate and burden abortion providers, while supporters said the law was needed to assure the quality of the health care provided to recipients.
- A Governor's Health Information Infrastructure Advisory Board was

created in 2004 to help develop a plan for a statewide network that would exchange health care data. Staff worked with federal officials and a few other states to develop a blueprint other states may follow.

- A 2003 law set up a drug pedigree system that requires a certificate of authenticity (or pedigree) for prescription drugs sold in the state. The law was the result of a scandal in 2001 in which wholesale firms in South Florida were adulterating popular medicine. Over three years later, the federal Food and Drug Administration issued regulations requiring documentation or pedigree of drugs nationwide (FDA 2006).

Florida's Health Care Innovations: A Concluding Assessment

While it is difficult to define Florida's health care system as "the best," as Secretary Agwunobi would have it, it is less difficult to argue that Florida can boast about its innovations in the field of public health. The state's leadership over the years has found new ways to deal with uninsured children from near-poor families, disclose important health care information for consumers, and control Medicaid prescription drug costs. The state can also claim some leadership in early adoption of malpractice reforms, programs to stop teen smoking, and programs to manage certain diseases. Certainly the 2006 effort to reform Medicaid falls under the rubric of innovative policy. Florida legislators and their staff members often think of themselves as leaders in health care policy and of Florida as a place where other states come for ideas and advice.

However, Florida is hampered by the fact that is it a low-tax–low-services state. One could argue that the state has been forced to be innovative because of its limited revenues and staunch resistance to higher taxes. Without financial resources to solve problems, the state has had to find ways to be efficient and clever, relying on new approaches and new ideas instead of more money. However, this brief history also shows the downside of this approach. In area after area, the state has had to postpone or fail to begin implementation, reduce funding, and/or turn the program over to local governments or other entities for funding. This is not a problem of recent vintage. Under both Democratic and Republican governors and legislatures, policies have been simultaneously innovative and shortchanged, and they have often been short lived, a situation that can be described as innovation with little follow-through. This has been what Florida citizens and policymakers want and have gotten. Perhaps the reform of the Medicaid program will be a different story. Only time will tell.

Notes

1. The state legislature also changed the nature of community involvement in health and human services issues. In 2000, it abolished the statewide health and human services board that advised the secretary and changed the makeup of regional boards set up to provide public input (Florida Health and Human Services Board Inc. 2007).

2. Medicaid is a federal–state matching funds program. The percentage of costs paid by the federal government varies from state to state by each state's per capita income. The federal government pays for more than three-fourths of Mississippi's Medicaid spending, while it pays only half of spending for California and other high-income states. In exchange for these federal dollars, states must meet a number of federal standards in their Medicaid program, including offering a number of required services and serving citizens who meet maximum income and asset standards. States also have discretion under federal law to provide extra services and serve broader populations. So long as these optional choices do not exceed federal upper limits on the range of services and the income and wealth of patients served, the federal government will pay its share of Medicaid dollars spent on these optional services and clients.

References

Agency for Health Care Administration. 2006. *A Snapshot of Florida Medicaid.* <http://ahca.myflorida.com/Medicaid/deputy_secretary/recent_presentations/florida_medicaid_snapshot_100406.pdf> (accessed March 16, 2007).

Alker, Joan, and Lisa Portelli. 2004a. "Florida's Medicaid Budget: Why Are Costs Going Up?" <www.wphf.org/pubs/briefpdfs/Medicaid2.pdf> (accessed March 16, 2007).

———.2004b. "What Could a Waiver to Restructure Medicaid Mean for Florida?" <www.wphf.org/pubs/briefpdfs/Medicaid.pdf> (accessed March 16, 2007).

———. 2005. "Issues to Consider in Governor Bush's 'Florida Medicaid Modernization Proposal.'" <http://wphf.org/pubs/briefpdfs/Medicaid3.pdf> (accessed March 16, 2007).

Annie E. Casey Foundation. 2006. *2006 KIDS COUNT Data Book.* Baltimore, Md.: Annie E. Casey Foundation. <www.aecf.org/kidscount/sld/databook.jsp> (accessed March 16, 2007).

Boulton, Guy. 2003. "Cap Foes Take to Streets, Television." *Tampa Tribune,* July 2, 1.

Campaign for Tobacco-Free Kids. 2004. *A Broken Promise to Our Children: The 1998 Tobacco Settlement Seven Years Later.* Washington, D.C.: Campaign for Tobacco-Free Kids. <www.tobaccofreekids.org> (accessed May 28, 2007).

Clark, Lesley. "Florida Senate Panel Grills Experts about Rise in Medical Malpractice Rates." *Miami Herald,* July 15, 2003 (Lexus-Nexus, accessed May 31, 2007).

Crew, Robert E., Jr. 1992. "Florida: Lawton M. Chiles, Jr., Reinventing State Government." In *Governors & Hard Times,* edited by Thad Beyle, 15–27. Washington D.C.: CQ Press.

Derthick, Martha. 2002. *Up in Smoke: From Legislation to Litigation in Tobacco Politics.* Washington D.C.: CQ Press.

Duncan, R. Paul, Colleen K. Porter, Cynthia Wilson Garvan, and Allyson G. Hall. 2005.

"A Profile of Uninsured Floridians: Findings from the 2004 Florida Health Insurance Study." <http://fcmu.phhp.ufl.edu/pdf/2_reports_and_chartbooks/fl_health_ins_study_reports/Report02-02-2005-UninsuredFloridianProfile.pdf> (accessed March 16, 2007).

Food and Drug Administration. 2006. Compliance Policy Guide 160.900. Prescription Drug Marketing Act—Pedigree Requirements under 21 CFR Part 203. <www.fda.gov/cder/regulatory/PDMA/PDMA_CPG.pdf> (accessed May 28, 2007).

Florida Department of Health. 2006. "Long Range Program Plan Fiscal Years 2007–08 through 2011–12." <www.doh.state.fl.us/planning_eval/Strategic_Planning/LRPP.htm> (accessed March 17, 2007).

Florida Health and Human Services Board Inc. 2007. Historical Background. <www.fhhsb.org/Background.html> (accessed May 28, 2007).

Galewitz, Phil. 2005. "The Legislature Makes an End Run Around Medical Malpractice Amendments." *Florida Underwriters* (May): 10. <web.lexis-nexis.com (accessed June 15, 2005).

Givel, Michael S., and Stanton A. Glantz. 2000. "Failure to Defend a Successful State Tobacco Control Program: Policy Lessons from Florida." *American Journal of Public Health* 90, no. 5: 762–67.

Gomez, Alan. 2005. "Medicaid Plan Seen as Helpful—or Dangerous." *Palm Beach Post*, February 24.

Hallifax, Jackie. 2005. "Increase in Clinic Oversight Approved." *Tallahassee Democrat*, June 1.

Hollins, Mark. 2005. "Gov. Bush Gets Cool Reception from Legislators on Medicaid, Tax, School Plans." *Orlando Sun-Sentinel*, March 9.

Jackson, Catherine A., and Amanda Beatty. 2004. *Organization and Financing of Indigent Hospital Care in South Florida*. Santa Monica, Calif.: Rand Corporation. <www.rand.org/pubs/technical_reports/2004/RAND_TR106.pdf> (accessed March 16, 2007).

JaxCare. 2007. JaxCare's History and Mission. <www.jaxcare.org/mission_rev_1020.aspx> (accessed May 28, 2007).

Kaiser Family Foundation. 2005a. "State Health Facts." Available online at http://statehealthfacts.org (accessed March 24, 2007).

———. "State Medicaid Program Coverage of Tobacco Dependence Treatments by Type of Coverage, 2005." <http://statehealthfacts.org/cgi-bin/healthfacts.cgi?action=compare&category=Health+Status&subcategory=Smoking&topic=Cessation+Treatment+Under+Medicaid&gsaview=1>.

Lamendola, Bob. 2004. "Parties File Suits on Medical-Malpractice Amendments Passed by Florida Voters." *South Florida Sun-Sentinel*, November 4.

Lauer, Nancy Cook. 2005a. "Medicaid: Reform Is a Must." *Tallahassee Democrat*, March 9.

———. 2005b. "KidCare Enrollees Falling Steadily." *Tallahassee Democrat*, June 11.

National Health Law Program. 1997. "NHeLP's Analysis of State and Local Responsibility for Indigent Health Care in Florida." <www.healthlaw.org/search.cfm?q=Florida&fa=search> (accessed March 16, 2007).

Office of Program Policy Analysis and Government Accountability. 2000. "Progress

Report: Agencies Are Following through by Consolidating Administrative Ser-vices." <www.oppaga.state.fl.us/reports/health/r00–14s.html> (accessed March 16, 2007).

Robert Wood Johnson Foundation. 2002. "Can the No-Fault Approach Contain Mal-practice Insurance Costs?" <www.rwjf.org> (accessed May 31, 2007).

Royse, David. 2004a. "Voters to Decide Three Medical Malpractice Issues." *St. Augus-tine Record*, October 17.

———. 2004b. "Florida OKs Three-Strikes Malpractice Law." Associated Press State and Local Wire, October 15. <web.lexis-nexis.com> (accessed June 15, 2005).

Saunders, Jim. 2005. "More Changes Sought for Subsidized Health Insurance." *Tal-lahassee Democrat*, March 3.

Smith, Vernon K., and Greg Moody. 2005. *Medicaid in 2005: Principles & Proposals for Reform*. Lansing, Mich.: Health Management Associates.

———. 2007. "Medicaid Services Expenditures." Office of Economic and Demographic Research. <http://edr.state.fl.us/conferences/medicaid/medhistory.pdf> (accessed May 28, 2007).

Tallahassee Democrat. 2005. "Editorial: Babies in the Budget." *Tallahassee Democrat*, May 31.

U.S. Census Bureau State and County Quick Facts. <http://quickfacts.census.gov/qfd /states/12000.html> (updated May 7, 2007, accessed May 28, 2007).

U.S. Government Accounting Office. 2003. *Florida Medical Insurance Crisis May Be Exaggerated*. Associated Press State and Local Wire, September 5. <web.lexis-nexis .com> (accessed June 15, 2005).

Weissert, Carol S. 2005. "Medicaid: The 800-Pound Gorilla and Florida." In *Florida's Tax Services Tradeoff: Trends and Choices*, edited by Carol S. Weissert and Da-vid Denslow, 83–119. Gainesville and Tallahassee: University of Florida and Florida State University.

15

Welfare Policy in Florida

RENÉE J. JOHNSON AND DAVID M. HEDGE

Privatization and contracting out are the watchwords for understanding Florida's overall approach to social services, whether for children, single parents, the elderly, or two-parent working families. Even before the national impetus for welfare reform began in 1996, Florida was experimenting with the delivery of its social services. Since that time, Florida has implemented two welfare programs in the state. Each of these initiatives has resulted in an increasingly complex organizational structure that relies more and more on the private and not-for-profit sectors. Two public agencies in Florida have primary responsibility for traditional welfare services: the Department of Children and Families (DCF) and the Agency for Workforce Innovation (AWI).

The DCF's primary responsibilities include cash payments and social services to poor families in need, protection of abused and neglected children, and help for those with substance abuse and mental health problems. AWI is responsible for implementing policy in the areas of workforce development, welfare transition, unemployment compensation, labor market information, and early learning and school readiness.

Despite this important list of responsibilities, very few of these services are actually delivered by state employees. While the term *privatization* is often used to describe many of Florida's social services programs, this does not accurately describe the structure of its programs. When a government privatizes a public service, it no longer uses public funds to provide services. In other words, responsibility for providing the service is left completely to the market. Instead, Florida relies on contracting out these services. That is, state monies are used to ensure that public services are being provided, but these funds are given to for-profit or nonprofit organizations to implement public goals.

Virtually all social welfare services in Florida are delivered by for-profit and nonprofit providers who have contracts with the state to perform these services. Thus, one of the primary functions of state government in the area of welfare services is to ensure that there are contracts to perform the necessary services and to monitor and enforce compliance with these contracts.

The primary motivation behind the move toward the use of contracts is the belief that government efficiency is improved when fewer services are provided by state government employees. Thus far, Florida's track record with respect to contracts has been very mixed at best. According to a report by the Office of Program Policy Analysis and Government Accountability (OPPAGA—a research office of the Florida legislature),

> There have been long-standing concerns regarding the department's contract management and monitoring systems. In recent years, reports by the Governor's chief inspector general, the department's inspector general, and OPPAGA have identified serious weaknesses in the department's contracting processes. These reported weaknesses have included: (1) failure by department management to safeguard its ability to make objective, fair, and impartial decisions with department contracting actions; (2) improper use of the governmental agency exemption to contract with a state university, which skirted procurement laws and resulted in additional costs for the department; (3) inadequate training for department contracting staff in procurement and contract management; and (4) insufficient monitoring of contracted community-based lead agencies. (Office of Program Policy Analysis and Government Accountability 2006c)

In this chapter, we will discuss three primary aspects of Florida's social welfare programs: Welfare Transition, workforce development, and child protection. In each of these sections, we will briefly discuss the legislative history of the program, describe the current program in place, and analyze how that program is performing. First, though, we will discuss the substantial changes in the national approach toward welfare that have helped shaped the character of Florida's programs.

Welfare in a National Context

For nearly sixty years, the federal government essentially guaranteed that the majority of America's poorest families would receive some form of cash assistance for as long as they needed it. Although originally envisioned as a temporary program of aid, by the mid-1990s, Aid to Families with Dependent Children (AFDC) had become an integral part of federal social policy.

The guaranteed safety net changed in 1996 with the passage of the Personal Responsibility and Work Opportunity Reconciliation Act (PRWORA).

Intended to "end welfare as we know it," the legislation significantly altered the nature of welfare in the United States. For America's poor this meant a new set of rules and requirements and, perhaps most important, an end to the entitlement that had been in place for over half a century. In replacing the decades-old AFDC program with a new program, Temporary Assistance to Needy Families (TANF), federal welfare policy became more focused on moving welfare recipients into the workforce. Recipients were required to find at least part-time employment within two years of receiving aid and were, with few exceptions, limited to a lifetime total of sixty months of federal cash assistance.

For the American states, welfare reform in the 1990s meant a new set of responsibilities and the promise of much more control over welfare within their borders. In replacing AFDC with TANF, the 1996 legislation eliminated what had been an open-ended entitlement program and replaced it with a program of block grants to states. The amount of federal aid for the poor no longer depends on the number of families that are eligible. Instead, states receive a fixed amount of federal support. For most states, this shift in funding produced an initial windfall by guaranteeing the states an amount of federal aid pegged to funding levels that had existed during periods of higher poverty and unemployment (called maintenance-of-effort funds). However, as the economy weakened in the late 1990s and as the number of Americans in poverty increased, the states began to feel the pressure of having to provide welfare assistance on a fixed federal allocation. This chapter examines how Florida, the nation's fourth largest state, has addressed those and other issues in the wake of the historic reforms of the 1990s.

Temporary Assistance to Needy Families in Florida

Florida's welfare programs since 1990 can largely be described as transitory. The state has created and dismantled a host of public, private, and nonprofit bureaucratic institutions charged with implementing state welfare programs. Florida developed two similar programs in response to the passage of PRWORA in 1996. The first program was passed in 1996 by the Florida legislature and was called Work and Gain Economic Self-Sufficiency. This program provided transportation, child care, financial assistance, and other forms of assistance designed to help citizens find and keep employment. In 2000, the Florida legislature reexamined Florida's welfare programs, paying close attention to their structural design. This resulted in the passage of the Workforce Innovation Act of 2000 and the creation of the Welfare Transition program.

Prior to welfare reform, Florida organized its AFDC program in the Department of Health and Rehabilitative Services (DHRS). This department was responsible for managing all of the state's social services programs, including welfare, employment, health care, and many others. In the early 1990s, DHRS was reputed to be the largest agency of state government in the nation and had been reformed numerous times in its thirty-year history (Crew and Davis 2000). However, when Governor Lawton Chiles was elected in 1992, DHRS became a primary target of the reinventing government initiatives of this period. His efforts and the state legislature's interest in changing the underlying premise of welfare as an entitlement resulted in the first stage of welfare reform in Florida.

In 1993, the Florida legislature passed the Family Transition Act of 1993. It was one of the first time-limited AFDC programs in the nation. The act directed the state to seek waivers from the federal government to implement changes to the existing AFDC system in Florida. The act also funded two pilot reform projects that combined a time limit of twenty-four to thirty-six months for welfare benefits with a range of services, requirements, and financial incentives designed to encourage employment (Crew and Davis 2000). At this stage of the welfare transition process, many skeptics worried that work requirements and time limits might endanger families who truly needed financial assistance. However, early analysis of these pilot projects suggested that time limits and work requirements did not necessarily destroy families (Bloom 1995). As a result, Governor Chiles included plans for a substantial overhaul of the welfare system in his 1996 budget.

On May 16, 1996, the Work and Gain Economic Self-Sufficiency Act (WAGES) was signed into law by Governor Chiles. It preceded the national welfare reform legislation signed by President Clinton in August 1996. The WAGES act gave primary responsibility for the implementation of welfare reform to three state agencies and a new organization. The WAGES program emphasized work requirements and strict time limits that were shorter than what TANF would allow. The Department of Children and Families, which was newly created from the old DHRS, was responsible for economic services to poor children, families, and the elderly; adoption services; disability services; homelessness; and domestic violence. The Department of Labor and Employment Security took over responsibility for poverty issues related to employment such as unemployment insurance, career services, and the job-requirement portion of welfare. The Department of Health became responsible for poverty issues that intersected with health issues, such as medical care for indigent children, adults, and the elderly. The new organization, the WAGES state board, was designed as a partnership between the public and private sectors. It had a locally based organizational structure of twenty-four multicounty jurisdictions that were directly responsible for providing services under the WAGES legislation.

The current TANF program in Florida is called Welfare Transition (WT). In 2000, the Florida legislature passed the Workforce Innovation Act that created the WT program. Like WAGES, the goal of WT is to reduce dependency on welfare by enforcing time limits and work requirements. The primary difference in the WT program is its complete reorganization of the workforce development program. Additionally, WT allows exceptions to the stringent WAGES rules about time limits and creates more opportunities for clients to avoid penalties (Botsko, Snyder, and Leos-Urbel 2001).

The contemporary welfare structure in Florida is quite large and complex despite the primary goal of simplifying the welfare structure of the old DHRS (see Figure 15.1). Instead of one large governmental agency that implements welfare programs, the state now has three state agencies, one advisory council, twenty-four regional workforce boards, 96 one-stop career centers, and many independent contractors. Additionally, each of these different entities is now responsible for carrying out their specific responsibilities while also coordinating with the other agencies. Layered onto this complexity is the diversity of organizational types involved. Welfare policy in Florida is now implemented not only by traditional government agencies employing state workers but also by a variety of nonprofit and for-profit businesses with contractual relationships to the state and each other that must be administered and monitored for effectiveness and compliance. The organization of Florida's welfare programs is unique both in the nature and the degree of contracting out the state uses to implement its welfare program.

The Elements of Florida's Welfare Program

The national welfare reform that occurred in 1996 gave the states considerable leeway in dictating the terms of welfare. The result is substantial variety in state welfare programming. For example, while the federal legislation sets a lifetime limit of sixty months on the receipt of cash assistance, the states are allowed to set a shorter lifetime limit, can exempt a percentage of recipients from that limit, and can provide state-funded assistance after recipients have reached the federal time limit. As of 1999, nineteen states had adopted shorter lifetime limits and another six states had set no limits at all. Similarly, over half the states required recipients to work sooner than the federally prescribed twenty-four months (National Governors' Association Center for Best Practices 1999). States also have considerable discretion in determining who is exempted from the federal work requirement. Most states exempt individuals responsible for caring for a child under the age of 1, but as of 1999, five states (Georgia, Idaho, Utah, Montana, and Iowa) chose not to exempt mothers of newborns (McCallum 1999).

State programs also vary in the length and severity of sanctions they impose for failing to meet the new requirements. Under the 1996 legislation, states have the option of withholding some or all TANF benefits if a recipient failed to meet work participation requirements. For a majority of states, the most severe sanction is the loss of the entire TANF benefit for at least one month, and in a handful of instances failure to comply can result in the permanent loss of benefits. States can also limit who is eligible for aid and the amount of aid a family can receive. Twenty-one states have a family-cap provision that limits the amount of assistance to families that have additional children while the family is receiving public assistance (Urban Institute 2003). States also have the option of denying benefits to individuals convicted of a drug-related crime and to legal aliens, although few exclude the latter.

Another important way the states vary is in terms of programs of support intended to make getting and keeping a job easier for recipients. The most important of these provide childcare assistance to recipients and former recipients. Three-fifths of the states guarantee child care for families on TANF and for those who have left TANF. Nearly every state provides transitional Medicaid to families leaving TANF. In addition, states have used their maintenance-of-effort and other funds to offer additional programs of support, including programs aimed at reducing teenage pregnancy, services to low-income fathers, programs for teenage parents, homeless shelters, domestic violence programs, and post-employment services and training (Reichert and Tweedie 1999).

Finally, PRWORA's emphasis on work and enhanced state responsibility has led a number of states to revisit several fundamental organizational issues, including the degree to which state programs will be centralized, the role of the private sector, and how TANF will be coordinated with other programs of support, including food stamps, Medicaid, childcare programs and, most important, programs aimed at moving individuals off welfare and into work. Most states have chosen a more decentralized structure, often relying on regional boards and local organizations to coordinate and administer TANF and related programs. An increasing number of those organizations are outside the public sector and include nonprofit and for-profit organizations.

Florida's current TANF state plan contains a variety of programs and services to assist families in need. The overarching mission of Florida's TANF plan is to encourage work and promote traditional family structures. However, neither of these goals has been established without controversy.

One of the primary benefits of Florida's welfare plan provides temporary cash assistance to families in need. In order to qualify for cash assistance, an individual must generally make below 185 percent of the federal poverty level ($17,170 for a family of three in 2007); this policy makes extra allowances for victims of domestic violence, mental illness, and abuse or neglect. Florida provides a cash payment of $303 per month to a family of three that qualifies for welfare assistance. As can be seen from Table 15.1, this is lower than all but thirteen other states in the country. Although cash payments are often thought of as the primary benefit of welfare programs, Florida's cash benefit is quite modest.

However, cash benefits are not the only amenity provided by state welfare programs. Welfare programs today encompass a wide range of services designed to prevent individuals from needing welfare services or to help them leave welfare programs by becoming self-sufficient. Depending on the state, these services may include childcare assistance, transportation assistance, job-placement and job-training services, diversion payments, and many other services. These transitional elements of welfare programs began to be implemented in states around the country in the 1990s in recognition that many families who tried to leave welfare were plunged back into welfare status because of their inability to save for an emergency such as a car breakdown, a death in the family, or a housing emergency. Because earlier welfare programs required that individuals receiving cash assistance have no assets, families who had recently left welfare found themselves vulnerable. One of the major differences between Florida's older WAGES program and today's WT program is that WT now incorporates many of these transitional services in its welfare program. For example, the state of Florida provides for transitional health care and child care, allows recipients to own vehicles worth less than $8500, and permits modest savings accounts in order to prevent people from having to rely on cash assistance from the government.

States vary significantly in the generosity of their programs and the breadth and type of services they provide (Johnson, Hedge, and Currinder 2004). Thus, another way to measure the generosity of Florida's welfare programs is to compare its average expenditures per person on social welfare services to those of other states. As can be seen from Table 15.1, Florida ranks quite low in comparison to other states on its total welfare expenditures per person. Only seven states in the country rank lower than Florida

Table 15.1. Ranking of State Governments by Per Capita Expenditures on Public Welfare Programs, Percentage of People in Poverty, and Maximum Monthly TANF Payment for a Family of Three with No Income, 2003

Rank	Per Capita Expenditures on Public Welfare, 2003		Percentage of People in Poverty, 2001–2003 Average		Maximum Monthly TANF Payment for Family of Three with No Income, July 2003[1]	
1. Alaska	$2,025.92	Alaska	18.5		Alaska	$923
2. New York	$2,024.44	New Mexico	18.0		California[2]	$704
3. Rhode Island	$1,676.44	Mississippi	17.9		Vermont	$639
4. Minnesota	$1,558.16	Louisiana	16.9		Wisconsin[3]	$628
5. Maine	$1,520.60	West Virginia	16.9		New Hampshire	$625
6. Vermont	$1,476.21	Texas	15.8		Massachusetts[4]	$618
7. California	$1,366.84	Alabama	15.1		New York	$577
8. Tennessee	$1,306.11	Tennessee	14.3		Hawaii	$570
9. Pennsylvania	$1,300.24	New York	14.2		Rhode Island	$554
10. Mississippi	$1,287.72	North Carolina	14.2		Washington	$546
11. New Mexico	$1,283.07	Montana	14.0		Connecticut	$543
12. West Virginia	$1,231.71	Oklahoma	14.0		Minnesota	$532
13. Kentucky	$1,205.46	South Carolina	14.0		Montana	$507
14. South Carolina	$1,150.96	Arizona	13.9		Oregon	$503
15. Ohio	$1,095.29	Kentucky	13.7		Maine	$485
16. Connecticut	$1,085.57	California	12.9		South Dakota	$483
17. Oregon	$1,071.28	Florida	12.7		North Dakota	$477
18. Wisconsin	$1,053.93	Georgia	12.0		Utah	$474
19. Nebraska	$1,041.68	Illinois	11.8		Maryland	$473
20. North Dakota	$1,029.04	Maine	11.8		Michigan	$459
21. Washington	$1,019.44	North Dakota	11.7		West Virginia	$453
22. Alabama	$1,006.17	Oregon	11.7		Kansas	$429
23. Arkansas	$991.69	Washington	11.4		Iowa	$426
24. Missouri	$977.79	Idaho	11.0		New Jersey	$424
25. Hawaii	$974.07	South Dakota	10.9		Pennsylvania	$403
26. Iowa	$950.17	Michigan	10.8		Illinois	$396
27. Georgia	$928.94	Hawaii	10.7		New Mexico	$389
28. North Carolina	$927.81	Rhode Island	10.7		Ohio	$373
29. New Hampshire	$919.98	Ohio	10.4		Nebraska	$364
30. Maryland	$916.53	Kansas	10.3		Colorado	$356
31. Delaware	$914.50	Missouri	10.1		Nevada	$348
32. Illinois	$907.47	Nebraska	9.9		Arizona	$347
33. Michigan	$906.39	Pennsylvania	9.9		Wyoming	$340
34. Oklahoma	$906.25	Utah	9.8		Delaware	$338
35. Wyoming	$887.37	Massachusetts	9.7		Virginia	$320
36. Indiana	$867.39	Colorado	9.4		Idaho	$309
37. Texas	$836.92	Vermont	9.4		Florida	$303
38. Massachusetts	$824.44	Virginia	9.3		Missouri	$292
39. South Dakota	$812.57	Indiana	9.2		Oklahoma	$292
40. New Jersey	$810.58	Wyoming	9.1		Indiana	$288
41. Arizona	$803.41	Alaska	9.0		Georgia	$280
42. Idaho	$799.28	Nevada	9.0		North Carolina	$272
43. Florida	$788.26	Wisconsin	8.8		Kentucky	$262
44. Colorado	$756.95	Iowa	8.5		Louisiana	$240
45. Utah	$747.60	New Jersey	8.2		Texas	$213
46. Montana	$722.89	Connecticut	7.9		South Carolina	$205

continued

47. Virginia	$710.79	Delaware	7.7	Arkansas	$204
48. Kansas	$699.32	Maryland	7.7	Tennessee[5]	$185
49. Louisiana	$623.11	Minnesota	7.1	Mississippi	$170
50. Nevada	$530.78	New Hampshire	6.0	Alabama	$164
United States	$1,083.30	United States	12.1		

Sources: U.S. Census Bureau, "2003 Survey of State Government Finances," February 2005, http://www2.census.gov/govs/state/03statess.xls; U.S. Census Bureau, Current Population Survey, "2002 to 2004 Annual Social and Economic Supplements," http://www.census.gov/Press-Release/www/2004/IncPov04slides1–3.pdf; Urban Institute, "Welfare Rules Database" available online at http://anfdata.urban.org/wrd/maps.cfm.

Notes: 1. Maximum benefits are calculated assuming that the unit contains one adult and two children who are not subject to a family cap, has no special needs, pays for shelter, and lives in the most populated area of the state.
2. Nonexempt families.
3. W-2 Transition.
4. Nonexempt Families.
5. Time-limited family units.

in per capita welfare expenditures. In spite of this, only 12.7 percent Florida's population lives in poverty; the state ranks seventeenth among the fifty states for this statistic.

Florida limits cash welfare assistance to a lifetime cumulative total of forty-eight months for an adult. This is more restrictive than the 60-month limit the federal government has established. In addition to this lifetime limit, a family may receive benefits for only twenty-four cumulative months in any consecutive 60-month period (although a family may receive an extension to thirty-six cumulative months out of a consecutive 72-month period under special circumstances). A participant may earn up to twelve months of eligibility for each month he or she fully complies with state TANF rules by working a minimum of thirty hours per week in subsidized or unsubsidized employment or remains in full compliance with a substance abuse or mental health treatment program.

Florida also provides for a hardship extension, which will extend the time limit during which an individual can receive cash assistance. The regional workforce board is responsible for scheduling an appointment six months before the end of the time limit to interview the participant and assess his or her employment prospects and determine if a hardship extension should be recommended. This may occur if the participant has demonstrated diligent participation in work activities and faces extraordinary barriers to employment such as lack of education/work experience, domestic violence, medical incapacity, and certain teen-parent circumstances and he or she has not had more than one work sanction imposed in the last eighteen months (work sanctions impose a time-limited reduction in welfare benefits for failure to comply with the work requirements of the Welfare Transition program).

Families who move to Florida from another state are subject to the same time limitation as Florida residents. The number of months the family received assistance in another state will count toward the 48-month lifetime cumulative total. Florida also participates in a program titled Learnfare that reduces cash assistance benefits when a participant's dependent school-age child is determined to be a habitual truant or school dropout or the parent fails to attend a school conference each semester without good cause. Applicants/recipients with a preschool child are also required to begin and complete appropriate childhood immunizations.

Florida also institutes what is called a family cap on cash benefits. Family caps limit the cash benefits a family can receive if they give birth to a child while on assistance. In Florida, additional assistance is limited to 50 percent of the maximum incremental increase for a child born ten months or more after the family begins receiving public assistance and no benefits for any additional children after that.

The Workforce Innovation Act of 2000, which created Florida's WT program, established a number of new programs designed to help people in need on a short-term basis. These programs seek to prevent people from receiving ongoing public assistance and are often referred to as diversion programs. Florida's TANF plan includes a variety of diversion programs. Up-front diversion is designed for families who experience an unexpected circumstance or emergency situation that requires immediate assistance to help them secure or retain employment or child support. This program provides families a one-time cash payment in the hope that it will prevent them from entering the welfare system. In order to qualify for up-front diversion, families must meet all of the usual welfare program requirements and must agree not to apply for financial assistance for three months.

The state also provides emergency shelter to individuals eligible for TANF who are victims of domestic violence. The Healthy Families Florida program provides a community-based home visiting program for expectant families and families of newborns who are experiencing stressful life situations. Families with characteristics associated with a high risk of child abuse or neglect are contacted (often when a child is born) and offered the services of this program. Participation in the program is voluntary. The Temporary Financial Assistance for Homeless Families Program provides for a one-time payment of up to $2,000 per family for payment of first month's rent, security deposits, and utility deposits. The state runs diversion programs for families affected by substance abuse or mental health problems as well as relocation assistance for families who wish to move to communities where there will be greater opportunities to attain self-sufficiency.

Florida is also experimenting with privatizing eligibility determination. Currently, eligibility determination for cash benefits is still determined by the Department of Children and Families. However, given the pervasive atmosphere in favor of contracting, the 1997 Florida legislature determined that this aspect of welfare provision might be a good candidate for contracting out. As an experiment, the legislature allowed the Palm Beach Workforce Development Board to make eligibility determinations for the population in its jurisdiction. In 2001, the legislature expanded this program to incorporate two more locations in the Palm Beach area. Proponents of private eligibility programs argue that they place the potential recipient in an atmosphere focused on employment and self-sufficiency and provide job-seeking assistance.

Another recent change in the delivery of welfare services is the implementation of application for welfare services via the phone, the Internet, or local community agencies or churches. This was traditionally accomplished by applying at a local welfare agency, but the secretary of DCF, Lucy Hadi, proposed this plan in 2005 as a way to increase efficiency in the delivery of social welfare services. Reactions to this move have been mixed. Some view this as a move toward more efficiency because it eliminates several thousand DCF jobs. It also allows individuals to apply using a convenient streamlined method. However, the populations that use these services are those least likely to have Internet or phone access from home. Additionally, those living in rural areas may be left without any other options. The transition to this organizational structure has been problematic because many nonprofit social service providers were not even informed of the organizational change and were unable to inform their clients of how to access appropriate welfare services (Dunkelberger 2004; Kelly 2004).

Under certain circumstances, Florida permanently disqualifies individuals who meet all other requirements of the WT program from receiving benefits. For example, conviction after July 1, 1997, for drug trafficking in the amount of $500 or more will result in the permanent disqualification for Temporary Cash Assistance benefits with the first violation. Fraudulent statements or representations about identity or residence in order to receive multiple benefits will result in a disqualification period of ten years for each violation. Individuals are automatically disqualified if they are fleeing felons or if they violate probation.

Florida's Workforce Development Program

Typically, a discussion of workforce initiatives is not part of a review of social welfare services. It is usually presented as a separate analysis or included as part of a discussion of economic development policies. However, the passage of TANF and the implementation of WT in Florida have changed this. Because both the federal and state welfare programs make receiving cash benefits contingent on work effort, Florida's workforce development program is now integral to its welfare program.

Prior to 2000, Florida's workforce development system was highly fragmented, consisting of over 270 state and local organizations responsible for planning and delivering workforce services (Office of Program Policy Analysis and Government Accountability 2003). In the spring of 2000, the Florida legislature passed the Workforce Innovation Act, which created Workforce Florida, Inc. and the Agency for Workforce Innovation and ultimately led to the elimination of Florida's Department of Labor and Employment Services. The objectives of the legislation included better integration of the wide variety of employment services in the state, development of a comprehensive plan for marketing employment services to Florida employers, the creation of strategies to meet the increasing demand for workers with technical skills, and the provision of training programs to improve the skills of current workers. Thus, the goals of the Workforce Innovation Act of 2000 were not all related to welfare recipients. In this chapter, we focus only on those elements of the workforce development system that directly relate to Florida's welfare program.

One of the central purposes of this legislation was to explicitly link ongoing welfare reform efforts with employment efforts. By 2000, approximately 70 percent of former welfare recipients had left the welfare rolls, but many of those were working in low-paying or temporary positions. Approximately 60 percent of that group was in low-paying, temporary positions, and most of them made less than $10,000 a year (Cotterell 2000). Additionally, those who remained on the welfare rolls were often considered the hardest to employ. One of the stated purposes of the legislation was to focus efforts on helping low-income families find full-time work.

At the time of the debate over the Workforce Innovation Act, legislators and the governor emphasized that they had no intention of dismantling the Department of Labor and Employment Security (Cotterell 2000). The bill provided $62 million to train hard-to-place welfare recipients and helped with transportation and family transition costs for people moving from welfare to work. The legislation passed with only one negative vote and was supported by an unusually broad coalition that included the Florida Chamber of Commerce, administrators of welfare-to-work programs, and several key Democratic lawmakers (Yardley 2000). Primary opponents of the legislation included state labor unions. Others criticized the bill as another example of corporate welfare because private employment agencies would receive federal money for placing welfare clients in jobs (Yardley 2000).

The Workforce Innovation Act of 2000 is another example of Florida's reliance on government by contract. Under the new structure, the state Workforce Development Board and the state's old WAGES program were combined into Workforce Florida, Inc., whose primary responsibility is to handle all policy-making functions related to workforce development in Florida. Workforce Florida, Inc. is a nonprofit public-private partnership run by a president and a 45–member board that is appointed by the governor. By law, the majority of members of the board must be members of the business community (see Figure 15.1 for an organizational chart).

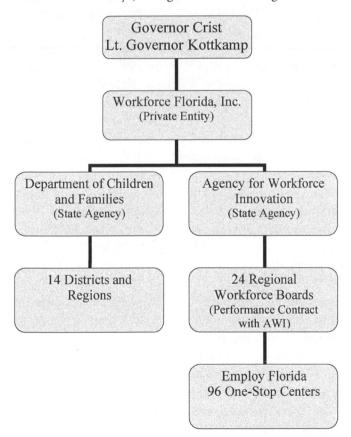

Figure 15.1. Organizational Chart of Welfare Services in Florida, 2007.

The Agency for Workforce Innovation is charged with implementing the policies developed by Workforce Florida, Inc. The agency is responsible for the administrative functions associated with employment services, unemployment compensation, and labor market statistics (all of which were previously housed in the Department of Labor and Employment Security). It receives the federal funds for employment-related programs such as TANF and distributes these funds to the state's twenty-four regional workforce boards. It is also responsible for monitoring the regional workforce boards and their contractors to ensure that they comply with all federal and state rules.

The majority of members of the twenty-four regional workforce boards are composed of members from the regional business community appointed by the county commissioners from their region. The regional workforce boards operate under a performance contract with the Agency for Workforce Innovation. In turn, the regional workforce boards contract with the ninety-six one-stop career centers that directly provide employment services to job seekers and employers (Agency for Workforce Innovation 2005). The one-stop centers, under the auspices of AWI, also are responsible for coordinating and delivering many social welfare services, such as transportation and childcare services for people on welfare and the School Readiness Program.

The Workforce Innovation Act of 2000 requires that all employment services be provided through the regional workforce boards. However, federal funding rules under the Wagner-Peyser Act require that state job-assistance programs be run by state employees and not be privatized. The U.S. Department of Labor warned Florida that it could lose up to $1.9 billion in federal funding for unemployment compensation, employment and training programs, and vocational rehabilitation if it dismantled and privatized Florida's Department of Labor and Employment Security (Kaczor 2000). Florida responded by creating the dual layer of authority that includes Workforce Florida, Inc. and AWI.

The state petitioned the U.S. Department of Labor for a waiver of the federal rule requiring that only publicly funded merit-system employees provide Wagner-Peyser services. In October 2002, the department responded that it did not have the authority to grant such a waiver but would continue to investigate the issue. If Florida is granted the waiver, it would allow private-sector employees to provide Wagner-Peyser services, which might allow more of the funds the federal government provides for these services to be funneled into programs that provide other employment services. This proposal is controversial, however, because labor groups are concerned about the future of merit-system employees in state government agencies as well as a potential lack of accountability in how federal funds for job assistance are being utilized. They worry that a business-dominated workforce agency will channel federal funds away from helping hard-to-employ individuals find jobs and toward job services for those who may be able to enter higher-wage jobs (Parks 2000).

Applicants for Temporary Cash Assistance in Florida are required to register for work with the regional workforce board service provider as a condition of eligibility (unless exempted for prespecified circumstances). Work activity is required under federal welfare rules, but each state defines what constitutes work activity. Participants must perform work activities for at least the minimum number of hours required under federal law, and the amount of time in a work activity is not to exceed that permitted under federal law or regulation. Work activities include looking for work; preparing for work; participating in training for new job skills; working at subsidized public-sector jobs; participating in subsidized private-sector employment/work supplementation programs (in which an employer is paid the participant's temporary cash assistance benefits to hire the individual); on-the-job training; working in unsubsidized jobs; taking classes directly related to employment; or satisfactory attendance at a secondary school, a GED class, or an English class for speakers of other languages.

The state also provides support services that remove barriers to participation in work activities. These services are authorized by the regional workforce boards. The inability of a regional board to provide support services is considered good cause for not participating in work activities but does not extend the 48-month lifetime limit on the receipt of cash assistance. Support services include child care (each family contributes to the cost of child care through a parent co-payment), transportation, ancillary expenses, personal and family counseling therapy, Medicaid, and employment-related education and training.

The state may waive work requirements or portions of work requirements because of medical incapacity, domestic violence, or other good cause. Good cause may include a family emergency caused by a family's inability to find suitable child care for a sick child under age 12, the hospitalization or death of an immediate family member, a natural disaster, lack of transportation or child care, a court appearance, provision of temporary care for a disabled family member, or domestic violence.

The state welfare plan also institutes penalties when an individual fails to comply with work requirements. These penalties are determined by a case manager located at one of the one-stop career centers operated by the regional workforce boards. For a first sanction, cash assistance is terminated for the entire family for a minimum of ten days or until the individual complies, whichever is later. For a second sanction, cash assistance is terminated for the entire family for one month or until the individual complies, whichever is later. For a third sanction, cash assistance is terminated for the entire family for three months or until the individual complies, whichever is later. Food stamps may also be removed. If a participant fully complies with work activity requirements for at least six months without any new penalties, all prior penalties will be forgiven. This means that a family's number of previous penalties will go to zero. Penalties do not generally affect the time limit. If a family does not receive assistance due to a penalty, they are "off the clock" with respect to TANF time limits.

The Workforce Innovation Act of 2000 has generally been judged to have been effective in reaching many of its goals. According to the Office of Program Policy Analysis and Government Accountability, "The workforce development system has achieved most legislative goals of the Workforce Innovation Act of 2000. The current system is less fragmented, has a performance accountability system, and is developing a unified automated information system to better manage participant data" (Office of Program Policy Analysis and Government Accountability 2003).

Nevertheless, many concerns remain. During the formulation of the Workforce Innovation Act, concerns were raised that Senator Jim King (R-Jacksonville) had a conflict of interest in pushing the legislation because he was a former staffing executive. The new workforce development structure implicitly involves many of the private staffing firms in Florida (Parks 2000). On the other side, staffing agencies have complained that the new structure presents unfair competition in the marketplace as public funds are being used to perform some of the functions that private staffing firms have traditionally provided.

In the state's transition from the Department of Labor and Employment Security to Workforce Florida, Inc., many civil service employees lost their jobs and their benefits. Many of these employees were ultimately hired into the new organizational structure but at lower rates of pay and with limited health insurance and retirement benefits (Graham 2000).

Since implementation of the act in mid-2000, many of the one-stop centers around the state have been closed due to budget constraints. When the act was first implemented, there were 144 local one-stop centers around the state. As of this writing, only 96 centers remain. While this may reduce the administrative costs of workforce development programs, it also makes it much more difficult for individuals and employers to use the services provided. This is especially challenging for unemployed and underemployed individuals who rely on the one-stop centers to access job-related TANF services designed to help them find and improve their employment status.

Despite the fact that the primary goal of the legislation is to streamline the disparate job programs in the state, more than three years after the implementation of the 2000 act, employers still report a lack of awareness of the various employment programs administered through the Agency for Workforce Innovation. In 2001, Workforce Florida, Inc. conducted a survey of 284 employers who did not use the services provided by the Agency for Workforce Innovation. Sixty-one percent of those surveyed report being unaware of the availability of services through the Agency for Workforce Innovation (Office of Program Policy Analysis and Government Accountability 2003). As a result, Workforce Florida, Inc. created a new "linking brand" entitled Employ Florida as a vehicle for connecting all of the services provided by the state's various workforce development offices (Office of Program Policy Analysis and Government Accountability 2003; Fishburne 2004).

Assessing Florida's Welfare to Work Programs

The number of families receiving Temporary Cash Assistance fell from 200,292 in September 1996 to just 50,831 in June 2006 (Winstead 2006). Of those remaining on the rolls in 2004, 40.4 percent were engaged in some form of work activity (Administration for Children and Families 2006). Few adults have come close to the time limits imposed by the WT program. In June 2006, about 58 percent of the caseload had been receiving cash assistance for twelve months or less. Only 4 percent of adults have more than the maximum sixty cumulative months of cash assistance, and 85 percent of these have been medically verified to be caring for disabled family members (Winstead 2006). Florida also has one of the highest rates of job growth and lowest rates of unemployment in the nation. And, effective May 2005, the minimum wage in Florida was $1.00 higher than the national wage. All of that bodes well for the state's poor who are able to work.

Findings from studies of those who have left public assistance programs that were conducted in the late 1990s and early part of the twenty-first century shed additional light on how former recipients in Florida have fared once they leave welfare. Because of the difficulties of tracking welfare leavers, estimates are that roughly half of those who left welfare in the first few years after TANF's enactment were employed. Crew and his colleagues at FSU found that only 31 percent of "leavers" held jobs in each of the four yearly quarters beginning in early 1997 (Crew and Davis 2000). During that period, leavers who worked one of the quarters earned on average $6,900, and those who were employed in each of the four yearly quarters averaged around $11,000. The evidence also suggests that nearly half of former recipients were able to leave the welfare system. According to Crew and Davis, 46 percent of leavers did not receive any form of social assistance (TANF, Medicaid, or food stamps) during 1997 and 1998 (Crew and Davis 2000).

Taken together, the evidence suggests that reforms "worked" for about half of those who left welfare in the late 1990s. But even among "successful" leavers, problems remain. Based on a review of the evidence in Massachusetts and Florida, Kim (2001, 2) concludes that "simply being out in the workforce does not mean being out of poverty. Both the Massachusetts and Florida studies found that time-limited leavers still faced substantial financial hardship and were mostly employed in low-wage jobs with few benefits."

Four years earlier, analysts at Florida's Office of Program Analysis and Government Accountability (Office of Program Policy Analysis and Government Accountability 2002) reported that the average of $7.00 an hour working recipients earned was just 68 percent of what officials estimated to be a "financial self-sufficient wage."

A number of obstacles make gaining and keeping a job difficult. Research reported by Crew and Davis (2000) suggests that a significant number of leavers have had a financial problem, did not have adequate transportation, and, perhaps most crucially, had problems finding and affording quality child care. According to their survey of leavers in the late 1990s, roughly a third of respondents reported problems getting to work, and equal numbers indicated problems with child care. Over half reported falling behind on their rent and utility bills, nearly half lost their phone service, and over 40 percent indicated that there had been times when they could not afford food. And like the rest of the nation, Florida has a significant number of families who are falling between the cracks. According to Crew and Davis (2000), nearly a quarter of those who had left welfare were not employed or receiving social services. After a comprehensive review of the performance of the new workforce development system, OPPAGA reported that program participants tend to lack the skills they need to get better-wage jobs and that few of them complete programs designed to improve their skills. According to the study, the majority of individuals (51 percent) that remain on welfare have only completed high school and another substantial set of individuals (29 percent) has less than a high school education (Office of Program Policy Analysis and Government Accountability 2003).

Subsequent revisions in the state's welfare laws have addressed some of those obstacles. During the 2000 legislative session, for example, Florida lawmakers expanded eligibility for transportation, child care, and training and educational services (Office of Program Policy Analysis and Government Accountability 2002). The savings from caseload decline have been reinvested in services that support work. One of the primary services Florida has invested in is child care. Childcare funding increased from $0.28 per dollar of welfare payments in fiscal year 1995–1996 to $3.57 per dollar of welfare payments in fiscal year 2005–2006 (Winstead 2006).

Florida's Child Welfare Program

In Hillsborough County, Florida, 2-year-old Quin-Shayla Gorden was beaten to death by her father fifty-four days after she was taken away from her mother because of her mother's drug-use relapse. In Jacksonville, Florida, an 8-year-old boy was placed in a foster home where he suffered cigarette burns on his back, beatings with belt buckles, spit in his food, and ligatures tied around his sexual organs. His younger sister was murdered in the same foster home. An investigation revealed that DCF never checked into the many abuse complaints against the foster family or on their previous record as a foster home in Michigan. In Tallahassee, DCF was sued in 2006 for housing four children in a conference room of one of its buildings without adequate beds, food, supervision, or sanitary facilities.

All of these stories underline Florida's troubled child welfare system. The state has received nationwide attention for its poor track record in protecting children. According to Ira Lustbader, associate director of Children's Rights Inc., a New York nonprofit organization that has sued Florida's child welfare agency, "Florida is clearly among the most dangerous and dysfunctional child welfare systems we've seen, and we've seen a lot" (quoted in Roig-Franzia 2002). The Annie E. Casey Foundation, a private foundation that conducts research and gathers data on child welfare, ranks Florida thirty-third out of fifty states in overall child welfare (Annie E. Casey Foundation 2006). This ranking is based on seventy-five measures of child welfare in the areas of employment and income, health, education, population and family characteristics, poverty, and youth risk factors. Stories abound of abused, murdered, and missing children in Florida's child welfare programs (Aguayo 2004; Goodnaugh 2005; Roig-Franzia 2002; Washington Post 2005a, 2005b). The most prominent story in recent memory was the disappearance of 5-year-old Rilya Wilson from her foster home in Miami in 2001. She had been missing from her home for fifteen months before case managers discovered that she was gone. Eventually her foster mother was arrested for her murder. Additionally, the previous secretary of DCF, Jerry Regier, had to resign in 2004 due to an inspector general's report that found that he and his top aides had accepted gifts from private contractors doing business with the department (Date 2004). Though he and his top aides were cleared of any criminal wrongdoing in July 2005, the criminal investigation found "the appearance of improper influence and favoritism" (Chapman 2005).

In the aftermath of these incidents, it was discovered that 400 children were missing from the state's child welfare system and that efforts to find them had been meager at best. By the end of 2002, Governor Jeb Bush proudly announced that the state had found all but 102 of the 400 children that had gone missing. Soon after, he announced an initiative to privatize the entire child welfare system in an effort to improve its lackluster performance. By the summer of 2006, the number of children missing from the state's system had skyrocketed to 652 (Miller 2006). As a result, the governor's office, the state legislature, the privately run contracted agencies, DCF, and child advocates are debating serious questions about Florida's child welfare system.

Florida's current child protection program, the Child Welfare and Community-Based Care Program, is administered by DCF. The state provides family support services designed to keep families together to remedy some of the underlying conditions that lead to abuse, neglect, or abandonment of children; the goal of these services is to strengthen families. In order to qualify, families served by this program must have cases open to Protective Investigations or Protective Services within DCF. While child protection services such as foster care, adoption, and emergency shelter are no longer directly provided by DCF, child protective investigations that determine whether a child has been abused or neglected and should be removed from the home are still provided by DCF. Protective Investigations is responsible for investigating reports of maltreatment and to ensure the safety and well-being of children who have been alleged to be abused, neglected, or abandoned. Children must be under age 18 and have a family income less than 200 percent of the federal poverty line to receive services funded by TANF. TANF funds are also used for the administrative costs associated with the Florida Abuse Hotline and Protective Investigations staff.

The Relative Caregiver Program provides financial assistance to relatives who are caring full-time for an eligible child who is adjudicated dependent and ordered by the court into the custody of that relative. The goal of the program is to lessen the potential that the child will be placed in foster care and avoid trauma to the child that could result from such a placement. The caregiver must be within the fifth degree of relationship and must also meet the technical requirements of the TANF program.

Florida's TANF plan explicitly states that "marriage is a critical factor to the well-being of children and families, as well as to society as a whole" (Florida Department of Children and Families 2005, 43). For this reason, the state developed the Strengthening Families Initiative to support healthy family formations, prevent family disruptions, and secure permanent families for children. The state uses funding to research, evaluate, develop, and implement public policy initiatives that are designed to provide couples with the necessary skills and support to form and sustain healthy marriages. It also provides both faith-based and secular programs to help those with troubled marriages. For example, TANF funds marriage and relationship education that includes instruction in parenting skills, financial management, conflict resolution, and job and career advancement for unmarried pregnant women and unmarried expectant fathers. Florida's high school curriculum mandates the teaching of the value of marriage, abstinence awareness, communication and relationship skills, and family budgeting skills. Finally, many divorce reduction programs as well as public advertising campaigns promote the value of marriage and the skills needed to enhance marital stability. The hope is that the Strengthening Families Initiative will prevent the need to use child protective services, the abuse hotline, foster care, and domestic violence services DCF provides.

As has been the trend in the other social service areas discussed in this chapter, child protection services in the state have been increasingly privatized through contracting out. Florida is the first state in the country to attempt almost complete privatization of child protective services. DCF remains responsible for overseeing programs, operating an abuse hotline, and performing child protective investigations that determine whether abuse or neglect has occurred. The remaining child welfare functions are provided by entities that contract with the department.

Advocates of contracting out hope that moving all child protective services into the private or nonprofit sectors will create incentives to provide reliable and effective services. Critics of this approach argue that contracts do not have as much accountability as government-provided services once did. Additionally, given Florida's recent troubled history with contracting, some officials have warned of the distinct possibility that unethical behavior will continue (*Palm Beach Post* 2005). Despite this debate, Florida became the first state to contract out all of its childcare services in the spring of 2005.

Prior to 1999, DCF was responsible for providing all child welfare services through a mix of state employees and private providers. Beginning in 1996, the Florida legislature demanded that DCF establish pilot programs to privatize child protection services through contracts with community-based agencies. One of the first programs was implemented in Pinellas and Pasco counties over the unanimous objections of local legislators (Smith 1998). This program involved contracting out child abuse investigations to the county sheriffs' departments. The sheriffs in both counties wholeheartedly endorsed the program, but after implementation began they found that they needed much more money than was originally budgeted to operate the program. Both county sheriffs threatened to withdraw from the program if additional funds were not allocated to run their programs. While additional funds were provided, the sheriffs' departments have pulled out of their child abuse investigation responsibilities because progress reports demonstrated a poor track record in properly documenting, following up, and closing cases (St. Petersburg Times 2001).

The legislature expanded DCF's privatization efforts in 1998 and 2000 and required the department to submit a plan for completely privatizing services by July 1, 1999. In 1998, the state began experimenting with privatization using smaller pilot programs. At the request of the Florida legislature, the Office of Program Policy Analysis and Government Accountability conducted ongoing analyses of these pilot projects. In a series of reports, OPPAGA concluded that there were many difficulties with these pilot programs and that child welfare outcomes were not improved under the contracted services. It concluded that "the Department of Children and Families is the appropriate state agency to be responsible for providing child protection services, and there is no compelling reason to transfer this responsibility to any other state agency" (Office of Program Policy Analysis and Government Accountability 2001, ii). Nevertheless, the state has forged ahead with the privatization of its child protection services.

In April 2005, the devolution of child welfare services was completed; each of the state's twenty-two regions had a contract with a community-based lead agency. Each of these agencies is responsible to provide a complete range of child protective services in its region, including in-home services, out-of-home services, emergency shelter, foster care, relative care, and adoption. Most of these agencies carry out these functions by using subcontractors. In December 2005, the lead agencies maintained sixty-four subcontracts for case-management services and 436 subcontracts for direct-care services such as placement in foster care, supervision of adoptions, and intervention in cases involving substance abuse and mental health issues (Office of Program Policy Analysis and Government Accountability 2006b). This large degree of subcontracting has created further problems in monitoring the performance of child welfare programs. Quality assurance and the monitoring of subcontractors in several lead agencies have been inadequate (Office of Program Policy Analysis and Government Accountability 2006a).

Funding for child welfare programs has increased substantially during the transition to community-based care. Statewide funding per child served has risen from $11,314 in fiscal year 1998–1999 to $17,966 in fiscal year 2004–20005 (in constant dollars) (Office of Program Policy Analysis and Government Accountability 2006b). Despite the substantial increase in funding per child, many child welfare outcomes have declined. The percentage of children experiencing repeated abuse has increased steadily since the state began using contracts. In 1999, 6 percent of children experienced re-abuse within six months of investigation; by 2004–2005 that statistic had increased to 11 percent (Office of Program Policy Analysis and Government Accountability 2006b). Additionally, children now move more frequently among foster care placements. Nevertheless, the program has increased the number of foster children who are adopted and has reduced the length of time children spend in foster care before achieving permanent placements (Office of Program Policy Analysis and Government Accountability 2006b). Part of the reason why the re-abuse number is increasing may be related to the reduced length of time children spend in foster care and the shorter amount of time before they are reunited with their families. Thus, reuniting children with their families more quickly may not necessarily be an appropriate measure of success if the child's family still poses a danger to him or her.

Since 1999, the state has increased the capacity of licensed foster homes statewide, and fewer foster homes are over capacity now than in 1999. This reduction has often been attributed to the lead agencies' successful efforts to recruit new foster parents combined with a decrease in the number of children in licensed foster care. However, foster parents have expressed many concerns about the foster program, including low payment rates, insufficient information about their foster children, and poor communication with lead agencies, case managers, and foster care providers (Office of Program Policy Analysis and Government Accountability 2006b). Despite the large increases in spending for child welfare and community-care services since 1999, the state has not increased the basic board rate provided to foster families since that time. Thus, the board rate is not even keeping up with the rate of inflation.

Caseloads have also decreased from an average of 35 cases per case manager in 1998–1999 to 24 per case manager in 2004–2005. Despite this substantial decrease in cases per worker, only two of the twenty-two lead agencies were meeting the statutory guidelines of fourteen to seventeen children per case manager. The agencies reported that they implement prevention services to keep families from unnecessarily entering the child welfare system in order to keep their caseloads down. Thus, there are incentives to keep children out of the child welfare system in order to improve an agency's performance. Case manager turnover rates remain high under the new structure; they increased from 29 percent in 1998–1999 to 31 percent in 2004–2005 (Office of Program Policy Analysis and Government Accountability 2006b). The high turnover rate among case managers appears to be attributable to several factors. Since the advent of the contract system, there is increased competition among case management organizations to attract qualified and experienced case managers. Despite the significant increase in state expenditures on child welfare, the average starting salaries for case managers are almost $2,000 lower statewide than what DCF paid case managers in 2004–2005 (the last year in which DCF employed case managers). At the same time that case managers are being paid less, they are also receiving fewer benefits than the state provided in terms of health care and retirement plans. Thus, the lead agencies report that case managers experience high levels of stress, work at emotionally draining jobs, and put in long work hours, all of which leads to widespread job dissatisfaction.

Thus far, the state's experience with contracting out its child welfare services has been mixed. The state has significantly increased its expenditures on child welfare programs since 1998. This is comforting to those who have been calling for increased resources in order to improve the state's dreadful record in child protection. Since the funding increases and the reorganization of the programs, some outcomes have improved. However, the state clearly has not improved its track record in many areas, and in fact, the number of children who are missing from the system and are abused while they are in the system has increased significantly since the program was reorganized.

Conclusions

Social welfare policy in Florida has changed significantly over the past two decades. Florida has made major changes in the character of welfare assistance that aims to move families off welfare and into jobs. These substantial changes in policy have been matched by equally significant changes in how welfare programs are carried out. Welfare assistance, workforce development, and child welfare have been considerably reorganized and decentralized, and they rely increasingly on the private sector to implement some or all of their programs. Not surprisingly, those changes have sparked considerable controversy and have had mixed results. Because many of these organizational changes have only recently been implemented, it will be important for the state to continue to evaluate the outcomes of these programs and whether they have been implemented appropriately. Poverty remains a reality for a significant number of Floridians, and the state is still struggling to learn how to manage a decentralized system of welfare that relies on dozens of private contractors and vendors.

References

Administration for Children and Families. 2006. "TANF Work Participation Rates: Fiscal Year 2004." <www.acf.hhs.gov/programs/ofa/particip/2004/table01a.htm#fnl> (accessed June 4, 2007).

Agency for Workforce Innovation. 2005. "One-Stop Center Directory." <www.florida-jobs.org/onestop/onestopdir/OneStopDirList.asp> (accessed August 23, 2006).

Aguayo, Terry. 2004. "National Briefing South: Florida: Report Faults Child Welfare Officials." *New York Times*, July 16.

Annie E. Casey Foundation. 2006. *2006 KIDS COUNT Data Book*. Baltimore, Md.: Annie E. Casey Foundation. <www.aecf.org/kidscount/sld/databook.jsp> (accessed March 16, 2007).

Bloom, Dan. 1995. *The Family Transition Program: An Early Implementation Report on Florida's Time Limited Welfare Initiative*. New York: Manpower Demonstration Research Corporation.

Botsko, Christopher, Kathleen Snyder, and Jacob Leos-Urbel. 2001. "Recent Changes in Florida Welfare and Work, Child Care, and Child Welfare Systems." <www.urban.org/publications/310184.html> (accessed March 16, 2007).

Chapman, Kathleen. 2005. "Probe of DCF Contract Scandal Faults Actions, Finds No Crime." *Palm Beach Post*, July 14.

Cotterell, Bill. 2000. "State Employees Column." *Tallahassee Democrat*, March 30.

Crew, Robert E., Jr., and Belinda Creel Davis. 2000. "Florida Welfare Reform: Cash Assistance as the Least Desirable Resource for Poor Families." In *Managing Welfare Reform in Five States: The Challenge of Devolution*, edited by Sarah F. Liebschutz. 25–42. Albany, N.Y.: Rockefeller Institute Press.

Date, S. V. 2004. "Bush Names Aide Interim DCF Chief." *Palm Beach Post*, September 9.

Dunkelberger, Lloyd. 2004. "DCF Closing Welfare Offices; Advocates for the State's Neediest People Fear Reduced Access to Medical Care and Food Stamps." *Sarasota Herald-Tribune*, November 20.

Fishburne, Lucia. 2004. "New 'Employ Florida' Link." *Florida Employment Law Letter* 15, no. 5 (January).

Florida Department of Children and Families. 2005. "Temporary Assistance for Needy Families State Plan Renewal, October 1, 2005–September 30, 2008." <www.dcf .state.fl.us/ess/TANF-Plan.pdf> (accessed March 16, 2007).

Goodnough, Abby. 2005. "Woman Accused of Killing a Missing Child in Florida." *New York Times*, March 17.

Graham, George. 2000. "Redistribution of Labor: A State Agency Is Hobbled by Budget Cuts, Reassigned Duties, and Employees Left in Limbo." *The Ledger*, November 19.

Johnson, Renée J., David M. Hedge, and Marian Currinder. 2004. "Bootstraps and Benevolence: A Comparative Test of States' Capacity to Effect Change in Welfare Outcomes." *State and Local Government Review* 36, no. 1: 118–29.

Kaczor, Bill. 2000. "Feds Warn State May Lose Funding if Labor Department Folded." The Associated Press State and Local Wire, April 27.

Kelly, Donna. 2004. "Office Closes; Needy Affected." *The Ledger*, December 19.

Kim, Anne. 2001. "Welfare Reform Progress Report: Two New Studies Show That Time Limits Deliver the Right Message without Harsh Effects." <www.dlc.org/ndol_ci.cf m?contentid=2956&kaid=114&subid=143>.

McCallum, Heather. 1999. "Welfare as We Know It Now. . . . State Approaches to TANF." Paper delivered at the Annual Meeting of the American Political Science Association, September.

Miller, Carol Marbin. 2006. "Florida Has a Skyrocketing Total of Foster Kids Who Have Vanished." *Miami Herald*, June 6.

National Governors' Association Center for Best Practices. 1999. "Round Two Summary of Selected Elements of State Programs for Temporary Assistance." <www.nga.org /Files/pdf/TANF1998.pdf> (March 16, 2007).

Office of Program Policy Analysis and Government Accountability. 2001. "Justification Review: Child Protection Program, Florida Department of Children and Families." Report No. 01-14 (March). <www.oppaga.state.fl.us/reports/pdf/0114rpt.pdf> (accessed March 16, 2007).

———. 2002. "Legislature Improves Welfare Reform in Florida." Report No. 02-48 (September). <www.oppaga.state.fl.us/reports/pdf/0248rpt.pdf> (accessed March 16, 2007).

———. 2003. "Special Examination: Review of the Workforce Development System." Report No. 03-10 (January). <www.oppaga.state.fl.us/monitor/reports/pdf/0310rpt .pdf> (accessed March 16, 2007).

———. 2006a. "Additional Improvements Are Needed as DCF Redesigns Its Lead Agency Oversight Systems." Report No. 06-05 (January). <www.oppaga.state.fl.us /reports/pdf/0605rpt.pdf> (accessed March 16, 2007).

———. 2006b. "Child Welfare System Performance Mixed in First Year of Statewide Community-Based Care." Report No. 06-50 (June). <www.oppaga.state.fl.us /reports/pdf/0650rpt.pdf> (accessed March 16, 2007).

———. 2006c. *The Department of Children and Families Has Taken Steps to Address*

2005 Contracting Law. Report No. 06-16 (February). <www.oppaga.state.fl.us /reports/health/r06–16s.html> (accessed March 16, 2007).

Palm Beach Post. 2005. "Abusing DCF Contracts." *Palm Beach Post,* January 1.

Parks, Kyle. 2000. "State Bill Reshapes Job Development." *St. Petersburg Times,* May 5.

Reichert, Dana, and Jack Tweedie. 1999. "Programs and Services Funded with TANF and MOE." <www.ncsl.org/statefed/welfare/tanfuses.htm> (accessed March 16, 2007).

Roig-Franzia, Manuel. 2002. "No Easy Fix for Florida's Troubled Child Welfare System: Persistent, Growing Problems Become a Key Issue in the Race for Governor." *Washington Post,* August 15.

Smith, Adam C. 1998. "Vote Favors Child Service Bill." *St. Petersburg Times,* April 22.

St. Petersburg Times. 2001. "Child Protection Is a Work in Progress." *St. Petersburg Times,* May 18.

Urban Institute. 2003. "Welfare Rules Databook: State TANF Policies as of July 2003." <http://anfdata.urban.org/WRD/WRDWelcome.cfm>.

Washington Post. 2005a. "Nation in Brief." *Washington Post,* April 8.

——. 2005b. "Nation in Brief." *Washington Post,* April 18.

Winstead, Don. July 11, 2006. "1996 to 2006: Ten Years of TANF in Florida." A Capitol Hill Briefing by Don Winstead, Deputy Secretary of the Florida Department of Children and Families. <www.floridajobs.org/pdg/wt/TANF_TenYrsInFl_NAWRS _Final082106_091206.ppt> (accessed June 5, 2007).

Yardley, William. 2000. "Bill Targets Welfare's Hard Cases." *St. Petersburg Times,* March 30.

16

Florida's Unfinished Agenda in Growth Management and Environmental Protection

LANCE DEHAVEN-SMITH

Florida's efforts to keep public services and facilities abreast of phenomenal growth and protect the state's fragile environment, although extensive, have been only marginally effective. Until just a few decades ago, Florida actively sought development and paid little if any attention to its environmental and social implications (Colburn and deHaven-Smith 1999). Growth was slow and the state needed jobs and residents. Attitudes shifted in the late 1960s as expressways, air conditioning, and the rising living standards of retirees brought an unexpected population explosion. State and local planning and other land-use controls were introduced in the early 1970s and then were significantly reformed, first in the mid-1980s and again in the early 1990s (Ben-Zadoc 2005). Despite these frequent adjustments, Florida's growth management system has failed to adequately protect Florida's environment and quality of life. Urbanization continues to intrude into wetlands and wildlife habitats; urban runoff pollutes lakes, rivers, and bays; severe water-supply shortages plague some regions all the time and all regions during droughts; the state's highway system is clogged with traffic, not just in the urban centers but statewide; and schools in the urban areas are so crowded that a constitutional amendment was enacted in 2002 to limit class sizes.

Yet another set of reforms to Florida's growth management laws was enacted in 2005, but the changes were similar to those of the past and hence are unlikely to prove more effective. The 2005 growth management legislation provided $1.5 billion in new state monies for local infrastructure and sought to strengthen planning and development controls related to schools and water supplies. Although well intentioned, the reforms perpetuated the weakness that has plagued Florida's growth management framework from the beginning, namely, the failure to contain urban sprawl with some sort of statewide urban growth boundary. Until the state places strict spatial limits on urbanization, efforts to tie urban development to the provision of roads, schools, and water supplies may help local governments avoid overloaded infrastructure, but they will actually exacerbate the sprawling pattern of development that is at the root of most of Florida's environmental and urban problems.

This chapter is divided into five sections. The first describes Florida's population growth and shows why urbanization in the state tends to be sprawling, undercapitalized, socially problematic, and harmful to the environment. The second discusses Florida's growth management challenges and the policies that are needed to preserve Florida's environmental resources and quality of life. The third examines the policy framework Florida established in the 1970s to begin planning for population growth and managing the impacts of development. The remaining sections chronicle Florida's repeated but largely unsuccessful efforts to reform this growth management framework to assure environmentally sensitive and economically sound urbanization.

Growth and Its Consequences

The 2000 census found that Florida had almost 16 million residents, an increase of almost 8 million since 1970. By 2005, the figure had already reached 17 million. Figure 16.1 depicts state population data from 1970 through 2000 and projections at five-year intervals through 2035.[1] If growth continues as expected, Florida will have 26.5 million residents in 2035. Past experience suggests that the vast majority of this population increase will be from in-migration rather than births. In the 1990s, there were about 500,000 more births than deaths, while the net gain from in-migration—2.6 million—was more than five times that number.

The most serious challenges Florida's population growth poses are caused not by the pace or magnitude of growth but by its spatial form and geographic location. Sprawling and polycentric, Florida's urbanization disrupts and sometimes destroys older communities, leaving behind a trail of urban blight as it extends outward into the state's large water-dependent ecosystems. Development is concentrated along the coast and in an urban corridor running across the center of the state from Tampa through Orlando to Daytona Beach. Figure 16.2 shows the geographic distribution of population at the block-group level of the 2000 census. Over the next thirty years, population growth will continue at about the same pace as the previous thirty years, but the pressures fueling urban sprawl will intensify, and the growth management challenges Florida faces will be even more difficult than those the state experienced in preceding decades.

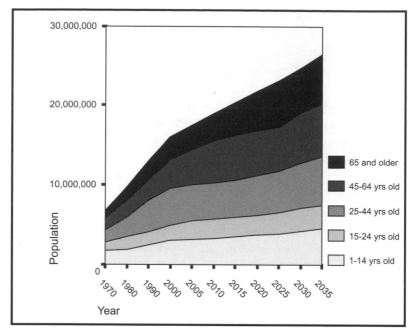

Figure 16.1. Florida's Population, Actual and Projected, 1970–2035, by Age Groups.

Sources: Data for 1970 to 2000 are from county-level census figures reported in the Florida Statistical Abstract of 1983 and 2003. Population estimates for 2005 and projections to 2030 come from Detailed Bulletin 145, Florida Population Studies 2006, Bureau of Economic and Business Research. Projections to 2035 were computed by the author as a rolling average from preceding trends.

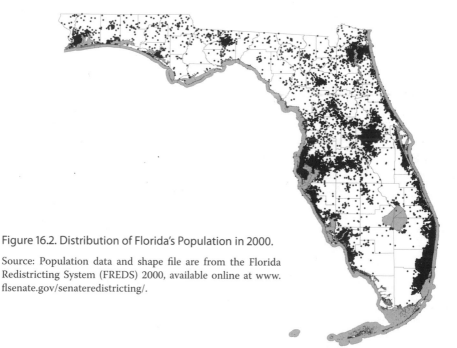

Figure 16.2. Distribution of Florida's Population in 2000.

Source: Population data and shape file are from the Florida Redistricting System (FREDS) 2000, available online at www. flsenate.gov/senateredistricting/.

The Demography of Urban Sprawl

Florida's population will become markedly older and more racially and ethnically diverse in upcoming decades (Colburn and deHaven-Smith 2002). Today about 32 percent of Florida's population are minorities, and the minority population is divided more or less evenly between blacks and Hispanics. By 2025, minorities will be 40 percent of the state population, with blacks making up about 17 percent and Hispanics 23 percent.

Florida's population will become steadily older as the large generation born between 1946 and 1964—the so-called baby boom generation—enters retirement. Figure 16.3 shows the age composition of Florida's population from 1970 through 2035. Significantly, the senior age group will constitute almost 40 percent of the projected increase in population between now and 2035. Today, about 18 percent of Floridians are 65 years old or older. This is already the highest percentage for any state in the nation. However, the Bureau of Economic and Business Research (BEBR) at the University of Florida projects that by 2025, that statistic will increase to 26 percent. If the trend continues for another decade, in 2035 Florida's seniors will constitute almost 30 percent of its population.

The expected influx of baby boomer retirees will exert a powerful influence on the rate, character, and location of Florida's urbanization, because retirees can choose where to live without concern about their place of employment (deHaven-Smith 1991). As shown in Figure 16.3, which is shaded according to the percentage of each county's population that is at least 65 years old, seniors frequently opt to live on the fringe of major employment centers, where they can be close to urban amenities while avoiding the noise, traffic, crime, and higher taxes of the inner cities.[2] Consequently, retirees extend urban sprawl even farther than middle-class commuters who work in the city but live in the suburbs usually do. Because retirees will dominate Florida's population growth for the next thirty years, they will continue to stretch and extend regional settlement patterns.

The Blight Belt

Because Florida's urbanization has been poorly regulated, residential and commercial development for the state's burgeoning population has caused many problems. The problems fall into three basic categories: environmental, social, and political. Table 16.1 lists the basic problems within each of these categories. Most of the problems either are caused directly or are exacerbated by the state's sprawling pattern of land use.

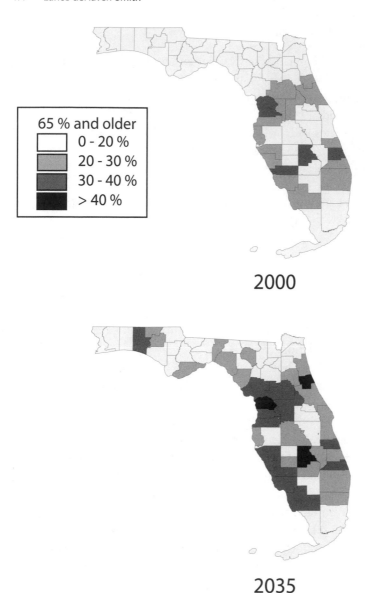

Figure 16.3. Percent Adults Aged 65 and Over in Florida, 2000 and 2035.

Sources: Population data for 1970 to 2000 are from census figures reported in the Florida Statistical Abstract of 1983 and 2003. Population estimates for 2005 and projections to 2030 come from Detailed Bulletin 145, Florida Population Studies 2006, Bureau of Economic and Business Research. Projections to 2035 were computed by the author as a rolling average from preceding trends.

Table 16.1. Problems Caused by Florida's Sprawling Growth

Environmental Problems	• Water pollution
	• Water shortages
	• Destruction of wildlife and wildlife habitats
	• Degradation of intact ecosystems
Social Problems	• Urban blight
	• Racially segregated schools
Political Problems	• Recurring fiscal crises
	• Inadequate public facilities and services

Florida's diffuse pattern of land development is responsible for two very serious and always-intractable social problems: urban blight and racial segregation of public schools. Urban sprawl causes urban blight and racial segregation in Florida because of the way the state's cities were laid out. Thirty or forty years ago, when most of Florida was agricultural and the coastal towns were small, the main north-south highway on each coast—U.S. 41 on the west and U.S. 1 on the east—was an informal border with clear-cut social implications. The wealthiest residents and virtually all of the urban whites lived on the coastal side of the highway, while African Americans lived further inland. The north-south highways were the "Main Streets" around which the small rural towns developed. The downtowns—if they could be called downtowns—had concentrations of restaurants, motels for the tourist season, and a variety of retail shops to serve both tourists and local residents.

Population growth and urbanization have been placed like a lattice atop this old pattern of land use. Expressways and malls have been built far inland, pulling most of the shoppers from the old coastal downtowns, and suburbs have spread inland all the way to the Everglades, leaving the old urban centers and their indigenous African American populations behind. Today, U.S. 41 from Tampa south through Naples and U.S. 1 from Jacksonville to Miami weaves through a belt of urban blight that extends along most of Florida's coastline. At almost any point on these roads the same pattern is found: Warehouses, new commercial development and upscale residential areas are punctuated roughly every five miles by poor predominantly African American neighborhoods. In a few instances, such as Pearl City in Boca Raton, these minority neighborhoods are stable and well kept, but more often they are run down and ridden with crime. Pockets of African American poverty are evident in almost every older town along Florida's east and southwest coasts.

Florida's blight belt exists because the economy that at one time supported the state's urban black population has all but disappeared. Many of the steadier agricultural jobs were lost to mechanization and urban sprawl, while household conveniences, fast foods, and dry cleaners have replaced the need for housekeepers and those who used to perform other domestic tasks. African Americans who could take advantage of new opportunities did so. Those who were too old, too young, too sick, or just unlucky became trapped in a narrow strip of land between the old Florida and the new.

The problem of racially segregated schools follows from urban sprawl in a similar way. In most parts of Florida where the population is growing, the vast majority of newcomers are white. Because most of Florida's growth is both white and sprawling, high-growth counties quickly become segregated. Whites live in inland suburbs far from the old cities, while African Americans live in the blight belt along the coastal highways.

School districts are confronted with a conflict between the desire of parents to have neighborhood schools and the legitimate demand of the courts that segregation be avoided. If the school districts provide neighborhood schools, the schools will be segregated because the coastal counties they serve are segregated. However, if the districts maintain their commitment to racial balance, they must implement a busing policy, which is widely opposed.

Because of judicial rulings, most of Florida's urban school districts have had to implement busing, but often they have done so in a manner that actually exacerbates the problems of the blight belt by contributing directly to the destruction of integrated schools in the coastal cities. In response to the pattern of white settlement in the inland areas, school boards have not bused white children to the coast; instead, they have turned to a policy of building schools equidistant between the coastal cities and the inland suburbs and then busing everyone to the center. This has minimized travel time for the students on the buses, but it has also led to the current tendency to close coastal schools, which adds to the problems of the coastal cities and promotes "white flight." Furthermore, the policy of busing African American students to the white suburbs is terribly unfair. It makes African Americans—the victims of years of racism and segregation—pay the price for integration.

Inadequate Public Facilities and Services

An endemic fiscal crisis is the most serious political problem caused by growth. Growth places a burden on state and local governments to provide roads, water and sewer systems, schools, and other public facilities (Fishkind, Milliman, and Ellson, 1978), but Florida's tax structure is such that the state's leaders cannot meet this challenge without constantly going back to the voters for increases in the tax rate, a request that is often met with opposition. State and local governments can raise tax revenues in three basic ways. They can tax property, they can tax income, and they can tax transactions or sales. Florida's tax structure is slanted heavily toward taxes on transactions. Florida is one of only ten states in the nation without an individual income tax, and its property tax is restricted by both a 30-mill cap (10 mills for any single taxing unit) and a $25,000 homestead exemption (Clarke 1988). In contrast, its sales tax is quite high. Only seven other states have sales taxes above Florida's rate of 6 percent.

Because people are subject to a transaction tax regardless of whether they live or earn their living in the taxing jurisdiction, this reliance on the sales tax was appropriate when Florida was a rural state dominated by tourism and seasonal residents. There were not many residents, but many people visited and spent money and hence were subject to the tax. However, in a rapidly growing urban state, heavy reliance on a sales tax inevitably leads to the kinds of revenue shortfalls Florida has been experiencing periodically since the early 1970s. Sales tax revenues rise only gradually with population growth because taxable expenditures per person are relatively constant regardless of the extent of urbanization. In contrast, costs increase rapidly in growing areas because urban facilities and services are much more expensive than their rural equivalents. Wastewater treatment plants cost more than septic tanks, SWAT teams and vice squads cost more than road patrols, and highways with overpasses and traffic signals cost more than two-lane roads with stop signs. With costs rising faster than revenues, Florida is unable to pay the bill for growth, at least for growth that requires substantial amounts of services but generates limited taxes.

Environmental Degradation

Urban sprawl is also responsible for many of the state's environmental problems. A diffuse pattern of urbanization is problematic in Florida because large parts of the state are marshes and wetlands. When the latter are drained or when roads are run through them, the environmental damage is extensive, far greater than what first meets the eye.

Florida's most serious environmental problem is the destruction of its natural system of water supply (Carter 1974; DeGrove, 1979,1984). The southern region of the state depends for its water supply on underground aquifers, which are replenished by shallow surface waters flowing down the center of the state into the Everglades, a vast "river of grass."[3] As population growth has occurred in the coastal areas and as fringe areas of the Everglades have been drained and developed, the water supply in the southern part of the state has been depleted. Government restrictions on water use are common during periodic droughts. Moreover, coastal communities experience saltwater intrusion into their well fields as inland communities tap the water supply and reduce the underground flow of water toward the coast.

Water pollution is a related problem. Urbanization brings with it the use of hazardous materials. Dry cleaners and gas stations pose a threat to Florida's environment because their waste products can easily contaminate the state's aquifers. Similarly, the high-tech industry, which is generally but incorrectly viewed as a clean industry, also produces waste that is dangerous to local well fields. Even seemingly innocuous actions by residents—pouring paint on the ground, flushing pesticides or glue down the toilet, throwing old car batteries into canals—can have serious effects. Unlike surface-water pollution, which can be tracked to its source and prohibited, groundwater pollution moves slowly through the aquifer, showing up at some distant point years later with no visible signs of its origins.

A third environmental problem traceable to urban sprawl is the destruction of wildlife species and habitats. Florida's state animal, the Florida panther, has been driven almost to extinction; it is estimated that only thirty panthers are alive today. Most have been killed while crossing highways that run through their habitats. Also threatened are manatees and numerous bird species, including eagles, which live on fish and other wildlife in the state's wetlands. The manatees are being killed by boaters, and the bird species are at risk because drainage of wetlands is destroying the habitat of their food supply.

A fourth problem is degradation of intact ecosystems, notably lakes and bays. Some of the state's largest lakes have been destroyed by waste washed into them from nearby agriculture, which has been pushed out of the urban areas into undeveloped wetlands. Rainwater from farms acts like fertilizer in the lakes, causing algae blooms that deprive the lakes of oxygen, ultimately killing their fish. Similarly, bays in metropolitan areas are polluted by urban runoff and by excessive amounts of freshwater flowing in from the canals necessary to prevent inland flooding. The high levels of freshwater are a threat to ocean fish and plants.

Managing Growth

Although at times they seem insurmountable, the urban and environmental problems caused by Florida's rapid population growth have relatively straightforward solutions. Of central importance is altering the geographical distribution of development. Florida's environmental and urban problems stem not so much from growth itself as from the pattern of land use that growth is taking. Development tends to sprawl outward from existing urban centers into agricultural areas and wetlands because rural land is comparatively inexpensive and easy to develop. However, urban sprawl is unattractive, it increases the cost of roads and other public facilities that must be extended, and it paves over wildlife habitats, well fields, and water recharge areas. Much of the degradation of the environment and decline in quality of life that Florida is experiencing could be avoided if growth were compact, contiguous, and centralized rather than scattered and diffuse.

The policy needed to achieve compact urbanization is generally referred to as an urban growth boundary. Local, regional, or state authorities designate areas for city-like growth, draw a boundary around the areas, and then zone the land outside them at a very low density. Both Hawaii and Oregon have successfully managed their growth with this approach (DeGrove 1984). Urban growth boundaries are also used widely in Europe and are one reason why European cities are well planned and attractive.

The barrier to an urban containment policy in Florida is not insufficient knowledge but political opposition, particularly from builders, realtors, bankers, and local governments. While business interests in the development industry usually support tax increases because taxes pay for roads, drainage, and other infrastructure essential for economic activity, they generally oppose restrictions on land use because such restrictions limit their ability to secure rural land for their projects. Likewise, local governments often resist such restrictions because they are actively involved in promoting growth; they are competing with one another to bring the best industries and most affluent residents to their areas. The history of growth management in Florida is one of conflict between development interests and a widespread desire among voters for well-planned and orderly growth.

Florida also needs to modernize its tax structure. This does not mean so much that taxes must be raised as that they must be fairly and clearly assigned. Government finance must be structured in such a manner that decisions about taxes and services are made transparently, the units of government responsible for delivering services are given adequate and appropriate sources of revenues, and responsibilities for service provision are clearly assigned to governmental units that are accountable to the populations being served.

Florida's Growth Management Framework

Florida began to deal comprehensively with rapid population growth in the early 1970s, when it put in place a combination of regulations that attempted to restrict land development. This legislation was effective in protecting some very important environmental resources and in making large-scale development more environmentally sensitive, but it had virtually no effect on the state's untoward pattern of urbanization. A second wave of legislation in the mid-1980s produced similar results. The legislation evolved along a path of least political resistance, and in the process the aspects of proposed bills dealing with urban sprawl were lost. A third wave of growth management reforms was launched in the 1990s, but these reforms, too, did not work out well. Another set of changes was introduced during the 2005 legislative session. Although it is too soon to know how well they will perform in practice, they follow the same general strategy as earlier reforms and are not likely to be more successful.

Framework of the 1970s

The growth management system Florida introduced in the 1970s had three components: a framework of planning for state, regional, and local land use; a process for regional review of developments with a regional or statewide impact; and a program to designate and protect areas of the state in which unsuitable land development would endanger resources of regional or statewide significance (Pelham 1979). The planning system was designed to make local land use planning and zoning consistent with a state comprehensive plan (Bartley 1975). Local planning was mandated under the Local Government Comprehensive Planning Act of 1975. Mandatory elements of local comprehensive plans included making decisions about future land use; planning for good traffic circulation; providing general sanitary sewers; handling of solid waste; ensuring adequate drainage; protecting potable water; conserving natural resources; planning for recreation and use of open space; housing; coordinating with other governments; siting of electric utilities; and constructing a plan to protect coastal zones. Through the development, adoption, implementation, and revision of its local comprehensive plan, each local government was supposed to identify and manage the consequences of growth in its area. State direction was to be provided by a state plan mandated under the State Comprehensive Planning Act of 1972.

The Development of Regional Impact (DRI) review program provided for regional review, local approval, and state appeal of plans for certain large-scale developments. Under state law, a DRI was defined as "any development which, because of its character, magnitude or location, would have substantial effect upon the health, safety, or welfare of the citizens of more than one county" (Florida Statutes, Chapter 380.06[1]). State guidelines and standards identified twelve types of activities that were large enough to have a regional impact: large residential developments, regional shopping centers, office parks, phosphate mining projects, schools, airports, amusement and recreational areas, industrial plants and industrial parks, port facilities, electrical transmission lines, petroleum storage facilities, and hospitals (Florida Administrative Code, Chapter 27-F-2).

A developer who wanted to build a project categorized as a DRI was required to apply for development approval to the local government with jurisdiction, to the appropriate Regional Planning Council, and to the Department of Community Affairs. The Regional Planning Council prepared an advisory report for the local government on the regional impacts of the proposed development. The local government then held a hearing and made a decision to approve, approve with conditions, or deny the development. In turn, the local development order for a DRI could be appealed by the Regional Planning Commission, the developer, or the Department of Community Affairs to the governor and cabinet, sitting as the Land and Water Adjudicatory Commission. This appeal mechanism enabled the state to override city or county land use decisions where regional or state interests had not been adequately considered (Thomas and Griffith 1974).

The Area of Critical State Concern (ACSC) program protected areas of the state where unsuitable land development would endanger resources of regional or statewide significance. Under state law, areas could be considered for ACSC designation if they had environmental, natural, historical, or archaeological resources of regional or state significance or if they were threatened by major public facilities (Florida Statutes, Chapter 380.05[2]). No more than 5 percent of the land area of the state could be subject to ACSC designations at any one time. Regional planning councils, local governments, and any other party could recommend suitable areas for designation to the Department of Community Affairs, which screened the proposals and, where appropriate, recommended areas for designation to the governor and cabinet, sitting as the Administration Commission. After 1979, an area designated by the commission had to be submitted to the state legislature for review and approval.

Once an area had been designated, affected local governments were required to prepare land development regulations that complied with the principles for guiding development set forth in the area designation rules or complied with state regulations. The Administration Commission could repeal the rule designating an Area of Critical State Concern if local land development regulations met state development principles for the area.

Problems with the 1970s Framework

The main inadequacy of the state's first growth management system was in the planning component (deHaven-Smith 1984). The requirement for local planning had virtually no effect on local land use decisions, and development continued to proceed willy-nilly. Moreover, the other two components of the state's growth management system—the DRI and ACSC programs—became distorted as state and regional agencies tried to compensate. The result was a combination of controls that produced many unintended but nevertheless pernicious impacts.

The system of state, regional, and local planning broke down because it lacked clear direction at the state level. The state plan was developed over a period of five years by state agencies working with advisory councils composed of interested citizens and public officials (Pelham 1979). It satisfied many conflicting interests precisely because it was comprehensive, general, and internally contradictory. The governor approved the plan in 1977 but the state legislature never adopted it; hence it did not have the force of law. The plan gradually faded from administrative concern and eventually was not even recognized as a relevant planning document (Stroud and Abrams 1981).

Lacking clear state policy, Florida's growth management system evolved strong thumbs but weak fingers, a system capable of squashing or redirecting selected types of land uses but not able to guide development in desired directions. The system's weak fingers were the local planning, amendment, and review processes. Plans exerted very little influence over local land use regulation (deHaven-Smith 1983). When there was a conflict between the plan and a desired zoning decision, often the plan rather than the zoning decision was adjusted. Many local governments amended their comprehensive plans as often as every few weeks. A rule that required regional and state review of amendments affecting more than 5 percent of a jurisdiction's land was simply circumvented; zoning decisions and amendments were disaggregated so that even though the 5 percent rule applied to them cumulatively, separately it did not. Likewise, although every five years local governments were required under the Local Government Comprehensive Planning Act to evaluate their comprehensive plans against stated objectives, there was no requirement that amendments be adopted to correct any shortcomings in the plan identified by the mandated review process.

The thumbs of the system were the state and regional permitting processes. Florida's statutes require permits or development orders for a wide range of projects; these statutes include Beach and Shore Preservation (Chapter 161); Dredge and Fill (Chapter 253); Water Resources Act, which involves surface and groundwater permitting (Chapter 373); Land and Water Management (Chapter 380), and Environmental Control (Chapter 403). Under these and other statutes, hundreds of permits are issued annually.

Unable to exert much influence over local planning and zoning through the state and local comprehensive planning frameworks, state and regional agencies tried to exert control over local land use decisions by attaching conditions to their permits. Virtually all permit applications were eventually granted, but most permits or development orders contained conditions that were often quite burdensome and frequently addressed issues that were not truly of regional or statewide concern (DeGrove 1984). This was particularly true of large projects captured by the DRI process. Each agency involved in the DRI review required modifications of proposed developments to accommodate its concerns. Typical adjustments included setting aside more land for open space or public use, expanding affected roads, and helping pay for off-site public facilities.

The ACSC program evolved along similar lines. Actual designations of Areas of Critical State Concern were rare, but state agencies began to use the threat of designation as a tool to counterbalance weaknesses in the comprehensive planning process (DeGrove and deHaven-Smith, 1988). To date, four Areas of Critical State Concern have been designated: the Big Cypress Swamp (to protect a major water-flow wetland); the Green Swamp (to protect a significant water recharge area and pine flatwood); the Apalachicola Bay area (to review a proposed dam); and the Florida Keys (to protect state historic and environmental resources). The program has been very effective in protecting environmental resources that are in isolated areas, but less effective in areas that are urbanizing. Of the ACSC designations to date, only the Keys had been experiencing much pressure from growth at the time of the designation, and there, because of intense local opposition to state intervention, it took over a decade for the ACSC program to have much effect.

Because of the imbalance in the 1970s growth management system, the system fostered some perverse development patterns. The rigorous requirements of the DRI process, which were put in place to compensate for weaknesses in local planning, ultimately became counterproductive. The process applied only to very large projects, and developers began to break their projects into small parcels that did not trigger the DRI review. The net effect was that the growth management system discouraged large-scale, highly capitalized development, which is easy for local governments to plan for, while it promoted small-scale, piecemeal development, which tends to creep up on local governments and produce cumulative impacts that cannot be accommodated. It was as if in trying to get a grip on growth, Florida had squeezed it through its fingers.

Growth Management Reforms of 1984–1987

In an effort to correct these problems, the annual legislative sessions from 1984 through 1987 enacted two far-reaching packages of changes to Florida's growth management system. One set of changes involved the regulatory framework for controlling development. The legislature revised the DRI program and strengthened the local, regional, and state planning process in an effort to correct the imbalances discussed above. The other changes addressed the state's tax structure. A blue-ribbon commission was established to assess and quantify Florida's obvious inability to keep public facilities abreast of growth, and a process was set in motion to expand significantly the range of items to which Florida's sales tax was applied. Overall, the objective was to establish a growth management system that would discourage urban sprawl and assure that public facilities were available as growth occurred.

DRI and Planning Reforms

In 1984 and 1985, the legislature relaxed the DRI review program and tried to give clear state-level direction to the local comprehensive planning process (O'Connell 1986). Changes to the DRI included 1) clarification of the DRI thresholds; 2) creation of an option by which local governments could become certified to do their own DRI reviews; 3) legislation stating specifically that small and large developments must be treated equivalently in the permitting process; and 4) prohibitions against breaking projects into smaller parts to avoid the DRI review. The intent of many of these changes was to remove or at least mitigate disincentives for large-scale development.

The revisions to the comprehensive planning framework were much more extensive. First, a process was established to develop a State Comprehensive Plan, which would be adopted by the state legislature. The governor's office and the state planning agency, the Department of Community Affairs, were given responsibility for developing a draft plan. The law further stated that if the legislature did not act on the plan thus drafted, the plan would automatically become law.

A second revision to the state planning process required major state agencies to prepare functional plans that were consistent with the State Comprehensive Plan. The agencies included in this revision were the Department of Transportation, the Department of Community Affairs (which deals with land use), the Department of Natural Resources, the Department of Environmental Regulation, and the Department of Health and Rehabilitative Services. The objective behind this new requirement for functional agency plans was to interject the state's growth management priorities into the state's budget process.

The third major change authorized Regional Planning Councils to write regional comprehensive policy plans. Regional Planning Councils are multicounty boards composed of local elected officials and gubernatorial appointees. Prior to 1980, their main responsibility was to review DRI applications. The regional comprehensive policy plans were to be consistent with the State Comprehensive Plan and were to be used in the review of local plans. The intent was for the state plan to frame the regional plans and for the regional plans to frame the local plans, thus inserting state concerns into local land use decisions.

The fourth reform created new components of the comprehensive plans of local governments. In addition to many new data requirements to document traffic levels, current and projected water consumption, and other local conditions important to future development, all local plans were required to have a capital facilities element that would establish acceptable levels of service for all major fixed-capital investments by the local government, identify ways to pay for those facilities at the levels of service established, and outline a method to assure that roads, sewers, jails, parks, and other public facilities would be constructed concurrent with new development. Local governments were to approve development only if they could demonstrate that their capital facilities element was capable of providing the public facilities the new growth would need. This requirement was referred to as "concurrency" because public facilities were to be made available at the same time development created impacts in a community or region.

Finally, all local governments were required to have land-development regulations as they implemented their plans. This entailed having a land use map, zoning ordinances, and a capital improvement budget to implement the capital facilities element.

Tax and Budget Reform

After adopting the State Comprehensive Plan, which had been prepared by the governor's office and other state agencies, the 1985 legislature created the State Comprehensive Plan Committee to calculate the costs of implementing the state plan and to recommend specific ways of paying for those costs. The committee included twenty-one civic leaders, legislators, and business leaders, and it was supported by a professional staff of economists and lawyers. It became known as the Zwick Committee after its chairman, Charles J. Zwick of the Southeast Banking Corporation. The committee presented its final report in February 1987.

Before the Zwick Committee completed its work, the legislature laid the foundation for a major tax increase. In 1986, it decided that on July 1, 1987, tax exemptions for sales of items other than food, medicine, feed, seed, and fertilizer would sunset. This meant that unless new laws were passed to maintain the exemptions, in July 1987 the state sales tax would begin to be applied for the first time to purchases of legal, advertising, medical, engineering, accounting, banking, and other services.

In its final report(State Comprehensive Plan Committee, 1987), the Zwick Committee endorsed applying the sales tax to services and called for a number of other tax increases. The committee estimated that the cost of achieving the goals of the state plan through 1997 would $52.9 billion more than existing tax revenues at state and local levels of government. This figure did not include many billions more that would be required if the state wanted to pay for the backlog of services and facilities that had accumulated from the inadequately financed growth of previous decades.

In the 1987 legislative session, the state legislature followed through on its intent to extend the sales tax to services. Despite a storm of protest from attorneys, doctors, the media, and others who would be affected, the exemptions on services were allowed to sunset. It appeared in June 1987, when the legislature adjourned, that the final component needed to manage Florida's growth had been put in place.

Failure of the 1984–1987 Reforms

Unfortunately, the state fell short of its ambitions once again. After they were enacted, the regulatory reforms were modified in subtle ways that robbed them of much of their strength, and support for the tax increase to pay for growth dissolved when a Republican was elected governor.

The unraveling of the new growth management system did not take place in a single stroke but occurred through a series of adjustments, only one of which was clearly recognized at the time as a major shift. The growth management system of the 1980s began to crumble almost as soon it was passed; the system was weakened behind the scenes in the hallways of the legislature and in the back rooms of administrative agencies. The sales tax on services was lost through a very visible and partisan process.

Just a few months after the sales tax exemptions on services were allowed to sunset, Florida's new governor—Bob Martinez, a Republican who had been in office less than one year—completely reversed his position. After polls showed significant public opposition to the "services tax," as it had come to be called, Governor Martinez decided that he had made a mistake in supporting the tax and began negotiating with state legislators to repeal it. In December 1987, the legislature went into a special session, repealed the services tax, and raised the state sales tax from five to six cents. The increase in the sales tax took care of immediate revenue needs but did not offer a long-term solution to Florida's fiscal problems.

Adjustments in the Regulatory Reforms

The regulatory component of the new growth management system was weakened very subtly over a period of several years. The first significant adjustment occurred when the legislature adopted the State Comprehensive Plan. One of the central aims in writing the plan was establishing a set of goals and policies that would allow local and regional plans to be rejected if they condoned urban sprawl. An important theme running through the draft state plan was a combination of policies designed to promote compact, contiguous, centralized urban development and to limit the urban sprawl that is so harmful to Florida's natural environment, agricultural industry, and wildlife habitats.

However, when the state legislature looked at the draft plan, it added language in a preamble that greatly limited the ability of the state Department of Community Affairs—the agency that would review local plans—to use the state plan to force local governments to contain urban development in their jurisdictions. In its preamble, the legislature said that no single policy in the state plan could be applied independently of all the plan's other policies (Florida Statutes, Chapter 187.101). Thus, the plan's policies of trying to reduce crime, stimulate business growth, and keep housing costs down were given weight equal to the policies related to promoting compact urban development. In principle, a local government could come forward with a plan that clearly would produce a pattern of urban sprawl and successfully defend it as being consistent with state policy inasmuch as it would promote business development or avoid the social problems associated with dense urbanization.

The second weakening of the regulatory framework occurred as the comprehensive regional policy plans were developed. One might have expected these regional plans to become a substitute for the state plan; they could have been framed with enough specificity to assure that local plans could be held accountable to objectives of compact development, even though the state plan was weak. However, the Governor's Office of Planning and Budgeting, which established the process for the development of the regional plans, adopted a cookbook approach that left the regional plans looking very much like watered-down versions of the state plan. The governor's office broke the state plan into a number of "policy clusters" and required each of the state's regional planning councils to address all policies in all clusters. This meant that a highly urbanized region had to address the policies appropriate to rural areas, and rural areas had to address policies pertinent only to urban areas. It became very difficult, if not impossible, for the regional planning councils to develop regional plans that were distinctive and directive.

A third undermining occurred in 1986, when the state legislature passed what was commonly referred to as a "glitch bill." The bill seemed harmless enough; all it was supposed to do was to correct some minor technical problems with growth management legislation. However, one of these minor changes turned out to be very significant. The original legislation was ambiguous about who set the levels of service required in the capital facilities elements of the local governments' comprehensive plans. Most people who favored strict growth controls wanted these levels to be set by the regional planning councils to assure that all local governments in each region would keep their public facilities up to minimal acceptable levels. This would avoid the situation, common throughout Florida's urban areas, of local governments continuing to approve development even after roads, schools, water systems, and other public facilities have been stretched to the limit.

However, in the "glitch bill," the legislature revised the Growth Management Act to say that levels of service for any given facility would be established by the particular unit of government that has responsibility for constructing and maintaining that facility. For example, the level of service on state roads would be set by the state, on county roads by the county, and on municipal roads by the cities. Obviously, the legislation raised doubts about exactly where the levels of service established by the regional planning councils would come into play. Furthermore, the Department of Community Affairs developed rules that made local governments responsible to set levels of services only for the facilities dealt with by select elements in their plans. The effect of these rules was to exclude schools, hospitals, libraries, jails, and social services from the requirements of the planning legislation.

Overall, these twists and turns in the evolution of Florida's growth management system made the system something of a developer's dream. On the one hand, all requirements for an urban growth boundary at the local level were effectively eliminated. Local governments facing intense growth pressures in their rural areas could not be required to restrict development, nor could they cite state policy as an excuse if they wanted to contain development. Further, the concurrency requirement tended to push development out of the cities, where roads were overloaded, and into the countryside, where road capacity was not yet overburdened. Without a considerable amount of local resolve, a continuation of urban sprawl was inevitable.

On the other hand, the growth management legislation required local governments to maintain public facilities that served new development at predetermined levels of service. Because health and human services were exempted from this requirement, county and city expenditures were diverted from social services to roads, drainage, and other land use improvements directly associated with construction. Moreover, because the services tax was repealed and the state was unable to provide significant additional funding to local governments, the capital facilities that cities and counties were required to maintain in line with growing demand had to be financed largely by property taxes. Thus, at the risk of oversimplifying the outcome, the net result of the growth management legislation of the 1980s raised property taxes on existing residents to pay for roads and drainage so that developers could continue to expand into rural areas.

Growth Management since 1990

As the growth management laws of the 1980s were implemented, the Department of Community Affairs (DCA) tried to deal with urban sprawl through its rule-making powers. DCA introduced rules requiring local governments to mitigate urban sprawl, and it declared some local plans unacceptable on the grounds that they did not do enough to contain development. However, although DCA worked diligently within the limits of its legislative mandate to limit the conversion of wetlands and rural lands to urban use and to provide exceptions to the concurrency requirement in some of Florida's downtowns, it could not overcome the tendency of the planning framework to promote urban sprawl, hurt older cities, and place local governments in the dilemma of having either to raise taxes to pay for infrastructure or harm their economic futures by greatly restricting development. Further, DCA's actions caused a political backlash. Developers and local governments claimed it had established its rules without sufficient legislative backing. Hostility to growth management and to DCA mounted.

These widely recognized problems and the rising tide of opposition did not immediately lead to reforms. Quite the opposite; those who supported the growth management system recognized its problems but were afraid to, in their words, "open up the legislation" because they thought the whole system might be repealed. For several years little or no progress was made in correcting the obviously undesirable effects of the concurrency requirement.

The ELMS III Reforms

Finally, in 1992, a third Environmental Land Management Study Commission was appointed to review the growth management framework and recommend changes. The commission was generally referred to by the acronym ELMS III. It recommended keeping the basic growth management framework but making adjustments that would enable it to function as originally envisioned. Most of the recommendations from ELMS III were enacted into law in 1993.

Viewed in historical context, the ELMS III legislation can be seen as another attempt to accomplish the goals of the growth management legislation of the mid-1980s. The ELMS III legislation would have phased out the DRI program in most counties and made the state, regional, and local planning frameworks more meaningful (Pelham 1993). The state plan would develop a growth management element with *objectives* (rather than just goals and policies). Regional plans would become strategic, focusing on regional resources and facilities. And local plans would include a written vision of the community's development, closer attention to affordable housing, a much-strengthened element on intergovernmental coordination, and (at the option of each local government) areas designated as exempt from concurrency.

Implicit in the new planning framework was a substantive conception of how Florida's growth was to be planned for and controlled. Under the old (mid-1980s) system, the focus was on *infrastructure*; the DRI program as well as the concurrency requirement allowed urbanization to occur almost anywhere as long as public facilities could and would be constructed to serve it. The ELMS III system emphasized *patterns of urbanization*. The new system was designed to channel growth away from environmentally sensitive areas and into existing urban centers, even if the latter had large infrastructure deficits (Ben-Zadoc 2005).

The ELMS III legislation had the potential to greatly improve Florida's system of growth management, but much depended on implementation, especially at the regional level. The whole system hinged on the efforts of the state's regional planning councils to insert state objectives for regional growth patterns into the comprehensive plans of local governments. To do this, regional planning councils needed their own plans for the evolving urban pattern as a whole that identified points where development should be encouraged and points where it should be prohibited and provided a template for evaluating each local plan as one piece of a larger composite.

Repeal of the ELMS III Reforms

Unfortunately, this new growth management initiative in Florida quickly collapsed, in almost exactly the same way as the two previous tries had. The first implementation problems occurred when the governor's office began to prepare a growth management element for the state plan. Many growth management advocates were concerned that any real change to the state plan might undermine DCA's existing rules and the local comprehensive plans that were based on them. Eventually, the governor's office abandoned its effort to produce a growth management element. Although the ELMS III legislation left open the option for the governor to revise the state plan every two years, revision proved to be politically impractical. Efforts to amend the state plan were undertaken more than once by the governor's office during the Chiles administration, but all of these initiatives ended in frustration.

The strengthened role for regional planning councils suffered a similar fate. Initially, developers and local governments thought that the ELMS III legislation would give them greater freedom. But as the new legislation was examined by local governments, developers, and other stakeholders during implementation, it became apparent that ELMS III might be more onerous than the DRI program that was to be phased out. Clear rules existed under the latter, and developers were accustomed to going through the review process. Also, the DRI review focused primarily on issues of traffic, drainage, and water supply. Under the new ELMS III legislation, regional planning councils began to position themselves to review developments of all sizes for potential interjurisdictional impacts of development. Suddenly, developers and local governments both began to see that regional planning councils might target all sorts of issues, including the impact of development on school integration, competing economic development goals of other areas, and future annexation plans.

These fears led to a reversal of policy. In 1996, under pressure from developers and local governments, the legislature repealed the provision in the ELMS III laws that would have phased out the DRI review process. At the same time, it eliminated the requirement that regional planning councils and local governments develop processes to determine if development proposals have significant impacts on other local governments or state or regional facilities. Overall, ELMS III did little beyond allowing exceptions to concurrency (Ben-Zadoc and Gale, 2001). It did not change the state plan, and the legislature reinstated the DRI program. Once again, the solution to urban sprawl remained elusive.

Growth Management in the Bush Era

When Jeb Bush was elected governor of Florida in 1998, he harbored hopes of overhauling the state's growth management system. Given his background, this was to be expected; when not engaged in public service, Bush is a real estate speculator and developer. Governor Bush made an initial push for change in July 2000, when he appointed a Growth Management Study Commission. To bring in new perspectives and ideas, he deliberately appointed few of the people who had served on the three ELMS commissions.

The Growth Management Study Commission's recommendations were uncontroversial, but during his first term the governor was unsuccessful in his efforts to turn them into growth management legislation. Again, the main impediment to reform was distrust. Environmentalists feared that the whole growth management system might be gutted if it was sent to the legislature for major adjustments. These concerns were not unreasonable. During the 1980s and 1990s, development interests had demonstrated that they were capable of using the legislative process to weaken growth management laws at strategic points when the laws came under legislative review. In addition, the potential for significant weakening had increased in the 1990s because Republicans had gained control of the governor's office and both houses of the legislature.

Moreover, the governor and legislature soon demonstrated a willingness to entertain radical proposals without first soliciting input from stakeholders and developing a general consensus on reform. The governor did not object when legislation was introduced to greatly restrict the legal standing of residents to challenge development orders. (This legislation was ultimately stalled.) Likewise, the governor expressed tentative support for a plan proposed by business leaders to allow water to be transferred from North Florida to other parts of the state.

The Reforms of 2005

Significant growth management reform did not become possible in the legislature until the 2005 session, when a new speaker of the house and president of the senate came into office and demonstrated a willingness to work together to limit the governor's influence. In the previous four legislative sessions, senate presidents had successfully blocked several gubernatorial initiatives that in their view would not have been good for the state, but they had been unable to enact much of their own agendas because they had not had cooperative house speakers. One speaker had been Jeb Bush's running mate in the 1994 gubernatorial election, and the other had launched a bid for the U.S. Senate in 2002 and obviously needed the governor's support. The situation changed in 2005, and the president and speaker announced early on that growth management was one of their top priorities. At this point, Governor Bush became willing to consider reforms that in the past he had contemptuously dismissed, such as increasing taxes to pay for public facilities and urban services.

The 2005 reforms focused on infrastructure. The legislature appropriated $1.5 billion in new money for various transportation, water, and school infrastructure programs. At the same time, it amended the growth management laws to add concurrency requirements for water and schools and to require that capital improvements elements of local comprehensive plans ensure that standards for levels of service are achieved and maintained.

In effect, the growth management legislation of 2005 was an effort to move beyond the concurrency system introduced in 1986. Under that system, applications for development approval were reviewed on a case-by-case basis and approval was contingent on roads being expanded sufficiently to keep traffic down to acceptable levels. The problem with this choke-point approach is that it does not require restrictions on development until traffic becomes apparent, at which point the community's quality of life has already been degraded. The concurrency management system can also be unfair in apportioning infrastructure costs (Boggs and Apgar, 1991). Developers who obtained approval for their projects while road capacity was sufficient were not required to pay to expand the road system, whereas those who came in later often had to scale back their projects and were also required to pay the full cost for expanding the community's infrastructure to accommodate another increment of growth. The Intergovernmental Coordination Element was strengthened in 1992–1993 in order to examine the cumulative impacts of regional development up front through intergovernmental negotiation, as opposed to assessing the impacts incrementally as new development actually came on line. The idea was that local governments would plan collaboratively for a level of development that could be accommodated by regionally significant facilities. However, this proved to be politically impractical when developers realized that many interjurisdictional impacts would be considered, not just traffic. If it had worked, the Intergovernmental Coordination Element would have forced local governments to plan for development and infrastructure comprehensively so they could avoid the bottlenecks of choke-point concurrency management and could apportion development rights and infrastructure costs equitably over time.

The approach adopted in 2005 seeks to use the capital improvements element to achieve the same end. The basic idea is that local governments will examine their zoning and projected population growth and will fully plan for the schools, water, roads, and related facilities and services that will eventually be required at build-out. In the past, there was no requirement that comprehensive plans synchronize authorized future land use and planned capital improvements. To be sure, both elements (future land uses and capital improvements) were included in the plan, but the future land use elements of local governments in high-growth areas often allowed for far more development than the local infrastructure could handle. The 2005 legislation attempted to correct this weakness by requiring the capital improvements element to jive with projected land uses.

The new legislation did not establish an urban growth boundary, but it did encourage local governments to adopt an urban service boundary beyond which urban services would be limited or unavailable. Such areas must be appropriate for compact contiguous urban development within a 10-year planning time frame. After DCA has improved an urban service boundary, most plan amendments within the urban services area can be made without DCA review. Also, developments within approved urban service areas are exempt from DRI reviews under certain conditions.

The concurrency requirement for water was tied to water-supply planning of water management districts. The potable water element must incorporate water-supply projects from the regional water-supply plan of the relevant water management district. Before a building permit can be approved, a local government is also required to consult with the applicable water supplier to determine whether adequate water supplies will be available to serve the new development at the certificate of occupancy.

School concurrency is mandated through required interlocal agreements between general-purpose local governments (cities and counties) and school districts. Each local government must adopt a public school facilities element and enter into an interlocal agreement with school districts to assure that schools are planned and constructed as development is approved.

The 2005 growth management legislation also addressed problems with the state plan. The legislation created the Century Commission for a Sustainable Florida, the members of which are to be appointed by the governor, the president of the senate, and the speaker of the house of representatives. The commission is required to send an annual written report to the governor and the legislature about the state's growth-management challenges and opportunities.

The growth management reforms of 2005 are a step in the right direction, but they are vulnerable to the same implementation problems that similar reforms have encountered in the past. Just as the 1986 reforms did, the present effort to tie development to infrastructure capacity is likely to contribute to urban sprawl as developers gravitate to areas where roads and schools have not yet become overcrowded and water supplies are plentiful. Similarly, the $1.5 billion in new state monies for local capital facilities is a much-needed boost, but comparable funding in the future is unlikely. It remains to be seen whether the Century Commission for a Sustainable Florida will be any more successful than previous state planning initiatives in forging the policies and political will necessary to contain urban sprawl.

Notes

1. The Bureau of Economic and Business Research at the University of Florida has issued population forecasts by age group and county through 2025 (Smith and Nogle 2003, 72). Growth has been forecast beyond 2025 by extrapolating trends from the bureau's projections.

2. Defined as individuals 65 years of age or older.

3. This was the title of an influential book by Marjorie Stoneman Douglas, one of the state's leading environmentalists.

References

Bartley, Ernest R. 1975. "The Local Government Comprehensive Planning Act of 1975." *Florida Environmental and Urban Issues* 3 (October): 1–3.

Ben-Zadoc, E. 2005. "Consistency, Concurrency and Compact Development: Three Faces of Growth Management Implementation in Florida." *Urban Studies* 42, no. 12: 2167–90.

————, and D. E. Gale. 2001. "Innovation and Reform, Intentional Inaction, and Tactical Breakdown: The Implementation Record of the Florida Concurrency Policy." *Urban Affairs Review* 36, no. 6: 836–71.

Boggs, G. H., and R. C. Apgar. 1991. "Concurrency and Growth Management: A Lawyer's Primer." *Journal of Land Use and Environmental Law* 7, no. 1: 1–27.

Carter, Luther J. 1974. *The Florida Experience: Land and Water Policy in a Growth State*. Baltimore, Md.: Johns Hopkins University Press.

Clark, Wayne A. 1988. "Sources of Revenue and Managing Growth." In *Growth Management Innovations in Florida*, edited by Westi Jo deHaven-Smith, 73–88. Fort Lauderdale: Florida Atlantic University/Florida International University Joint Center for Environmental and Urban Problems.

Colburn, David R., and Lance deHaven-Smith. 1999. *Government in the Sunshine State: Florida since Statehood*. Gainesville: University Press of Florida.

————. 2002. *Florida's Megatrends*. Gainesville: University Press of Florida.

DeGrove, John M. 1979. "The Political Dynamics of the Land and Growth Management Movement." *Law and Contemporary Problems* 43, no. 2: 111–43.

————. 1984. *Land Growth and Politics*. Chicago: American Planning Association.

————, and Westi Jo deHaven-Smith. 1988. "Resource Planning and Management Committees: Implementing Florida's Critical Area Program." In *Growth Management Innovations in Florida*, edited by Westi Jo deHaven-Smith, 34–47. Fort Lauderdale: Florida Atlantic University/Florida International University Joint Center for Environmental and Urban Problems.

deHaven-Smith, Lance. 1983. "Emergent Issues in Growth Management: Proceedings of a Policy Conference." *Florida Environmental and Urban Issues* 10 (April): 2–5.

————. 1984. "Regulatory Theory and State Land Use Regulation." *Public Administration Review* 44, no. 5: 413–20.

————. 1987. *Environmental Publics: Public Opinion on Environmental Protection and Growth Management*. Boston: Lincoln Institute of Land Policy.

————. 1991. *Environmental Concern in Florida and the Nation*. Gainesville: University of Florida Press.

————. 1998a. *The Atlas of Florida Voting and Public Opinion*. Tallahassee: Florida Institute of Government.

————. 1998b. "Collective Will-Formation: The Missing Dimension in Public Administration." *Administrative Theory and Praxis* 20: 126–40.

Fishkind, H. H., J. W. Milliman, and R. W. Ellson. 1978. "A Pragmatic Econometric Approach to Assessing Economic Impacts of Growth or Decline in Urban Areas." *Land Economics* 54, no. 4: 442–60.

O'Connell, Daniel W. 1986. "New Directions in State Legislation: The Florida Growth Management Act and State Comprehensive Plan." In *Perspectives on Florida's Growth Management Act of 1985*, edited by John M. DeGrove and Julian Conrad Juergensmeyer, 5–17. Boston: Lincoln Institute of Land Policy.

Pelham, Thomas G. 1979. *State Land-Use Planning and Regulation*. Lexington, Mass.: Lexington Books.

Smith, Stanley K., and June Marie Nogle. 2003. "Population Projections by Age, Sex and Race for Florida and Its Counties, 2002–2025." *Florida Population Studies* 36, no. 3 (July).

State Comprehensive Plan Committee. 1987. "Keys to Florida's Future: Winning in a Competitive World." Tallahassee: State Comprehensive Plan Committee. <www .dca.state.fl.us/fdcp/DCP/publications/index.cfm> (accessed March 16, 2007).

Stroud, Nancy E., and Kathleen Shea Abrams. 1981. *A Report on a Proposed State Integrated Policy Framework.* Fort Lauderdale: Florida Atlantic University/Florida International University Joint Center for Environmental and Urban Problems.

Thomas, Joseph M., and George Griffith. 1974. "DRI." *Florida Environmental and Urban Issues* 1 (October): 3–5.

17

Florida's Government and Politics: The Road Ahead

J. EDWIN BENTON

As noted at the outset of this volume, it is probably accurate and safe to conclude that the only constant in Florida government and politics is change. But that has not always been the case. At the close of World War II, Florida was a slow-growth state with a population of around 2.3 million, ranking it twenty-fourth among the forty-eight states and making it the third least populous southern state. Jacksonville, Tampa, and Miami were the state's largest cities, but they were hardly cosmopolitan and fast-paced metropolitan areas or bustling centers of commerce and culture like a number of cities located in other regions of the United States. Most Floridians lived in small rural towns, fishing camps, or American Indian reservations. Education and income levels of Floridians were below the national average (though higher than elsewhere in the South), and many persons barely eked out a living in nonindustrial pursuits. Cattle, agricultural, and landed interests had a lock on state and local politics and institutions. Politically, Florida was a mirror reflection of the Old South. That is, only white Floridians were permitted to vote, and they were conservative in their views, continued to endorse Jim Crow, and supported the southern wing of the Democratic Party. Women voted in much smaller numbers than men, and they rarely ran for or were elected to public office. A strong-willed and rural-dominated legislature that perfected the art of good-old-boy politics overshadowed even the most popular governors, while the state judiciary was stacked with political cronies and operated under the most archaic conditions with judges acting like the masters of their own fiefdoms. State and local government funding for education, health care, public welfare, roads and highways, and public safety paled in comparison to the financial effort of northern, midwestern, and western states.

Nevertheless, change was on the way. By the 1950s, Florida's population had begun to soar as thousands of new residents and tourists flocked to the state on a daily basis. Florida's population would increase by more than sevenfold over the next six decades. Places like Fort Lauderdale, West Palm Beach, Boca Raton, Miami Beach, Naples, Fort Myers, Daytona Beach, St. Petersburg, Sarasota, Cape Coral, Bradenton, Vero Beach, Orlando, Winter Haven, and Melbourne and hundreds of smaller, less well known communities became popular retirement destinations for northerners and midwesterners seeking a respite from cold winters, high taxes and living costs, rising crime rates, urban decay, congested roadways, and polluted environments. Needless to say, the rush to Florida by both transplants and tourists transformed the state's economy from a fairly homogeneous base to a much more diversified and internationally driven one. The service component of the economy increased exponentially, and the manufacturing, banking and investment, real estate, international trade and tourism, and space industry sectors grew substantially. Changes in politics, however, were slower in coming.

By the mid-1970s, the political winds in Florida were beginning to shift. This was due in part to the massive influx of new residents to the state—many of them confirmed Republicans from other parts of the country—who packed up their party affiliation and brought it with them to Florida. At the same time, young people coming into the electorate were more inclined to register and vote Republican than their parents and grandparents, while an increasing number of longtime state residents (many of them conservative New Deal Democrats) began to shift their party loyalty and vote Republican unless given a good reason not to do so. Thus, Floridians, whose flirtations with the national Republican Party can be traced back to the 1928 presidential contest between Al Smith and Herbert Hoover, were now voting more Republican in state and local elections as well. This pattern of increasing support for the Republican Party and its candidates was to continue and even accelerate during the 1980s, 1990s, and the early years of the twenty-first century.

Overlaying the political changes of the last thirty to forty years was a striking degree of stability in ideological self-identification. Approximately two-thirds of all Floridians think in ideological terms, and most classify themselves as either conservative or middle of the road (roughly 40 percent in each category), with the remaining 20 percent identifying as ideological liberals. These results are in line with those obtained in national polls, thus indicating that Floridians are quite similar ideologically to the American public as a whole. Nonetheless, survey data suggest that Floridians have exhibited some signs of political moderation in the opinions they hold. For example, Floridians appear to hold more moderate opinions on abortion, school prayer, and assistance to the poor and minorities, while they maintain rather conservative views on the death penalty, gay and lesbian rights, and military and defense policy. It is quite possible that these moderating views may be explained by the increasing diversity, size, and metropolitan character of the state's population.

As this book goes to press well into the first decade of the twenty-first century, it is clear that a metamorphosis has occurred in Florida government and politics over the last half-century. In the mid-1990s, the Democratic Party was supplanted by the Republican Party as the majority party in the Florida legislature, and Republicans presently have claim to approximately three-fourths of the seats in both chambers. With the election of Charlie Christ as governor in November 2006, Republicans are assured that they will control the executive branch for another four years, following Jeb Bush's eight years in office. Prior to Bush's reelection in 2002, no Republican governor had served more than one four-year term. Other evidence of a metamorphosis can be seen in the results of state cabinet and congressional elections. For the last six years, with the exception of recently elected State Chief Financial Officer Alex Sink, all three elected members of the cabinet have been Republicans, while an overwhelming majority of the state's U.S. House delegation (that is, eighteen out of twenty-five) and one of two U.S. senators are Republicans. In addition, a majority of elected local government officials in the state who run in partisan elections are Republicans. This is quite a change, given that not too long ago the state was considered to be part and parcel of the Solid Democratic South.

So what does the present political landscape portend for Florida's future? As noted in Chapter 1, the authors of this volume do not have a crystal ball that enables us to predict what Florida's state and local governments and their officials will choose to do or not to do in the years ahead. Governments are known to be fickle entities, and government officials (whether elected or appointed) tend to come and go with little advance notice and fanfare. This greatly limits our ability to make predictions about future political and governmental happenings in Florida with any degree of precision. However, we can confidently point to some things (not discussed in any priority order below) that warrant close attention as the drama of constant change continues to unfold.

Points of Interest for the Road Ahead

Evolving Political Party Politics

At this writing, it appears that the Republican Party has come close to achieving parity with the Democratic Party in terms of voter registration and voter self-identification. But neither party can lay claim to majority status, as about one in five of all Floridians say they are independents or identify with a minor party. This puts Florida in that grouping of states classified as competitive, and given current trends, it would appear that Florida will remain competitive for the foreseeable future in spite of the fact that Republicans are winning substantially more elections than Democrats. However, it is reasonable to predict that political party affiliation may begin to tip in favor of the Republican Party as old New Deal Democrats die out and are replaced by younger individuals or Republicans who migrate to the state.

Given this characterization of party politics, it is important to watch closely in the years ahead how independents and third-party identifiers vote in general elections, for they have the ability to play the role of kingmaker. Will they make Democrats or Republicans winners? Will they consistently throw their support to one party or will their support change from election to election or vary from one candidate to another? To date, they have tended to support Republican candidates more so than Democratic ones, but will this continue? At a minimum, this will mean that state and local election outcomes will not be easy to predict and election coalitions will remain fluid. Moreover, candidates will increasingly feel the need to gravitate toward the center of the political spectrum so as to attract the largest number of voters.

The role Florida will play in national politics over the next several decades also bears watching. First, beginning in 2008, the state's voters will have the opportunity to determine the early frontrunners for the Democratic and Republican nomination for president after the legislature in 2007 voted to move up the state's presidential primary date to January 29. This now means that voters only in the New Hampshire primary and the Iowa and South Carolina caucuses will have an earlier voice as to who the nominees will be. In short, this places Florida in the enviable position of potentially being able to determine who stays in and who exits the primary campaign at a very early stage. Second, as was seen in the 2000 election, Florida could be considered a must-win state for presidential candidates and could even make some favorite-son politicians (e.g., Jeb Bush and Bill Nelson) credible presidential or vice-presidential candidates. The state has the fourth largest number of votes in the Electoral College and increasingly is viewed as a bellwether state. Third, since Florida's delegation to the U.S. House of Representatives is the fourth largest among the states, Floridians potentially could have considerable influence on policy decisions in the Congress. The specific partisan nature (that is, Democratic or Republican) of this influence could begin to crystallize over the next several years, although it is decidedly Republican at the present time.

Legislative-Executive Politics and Relations

Are the roles historically ascribed to and played out by Florida's governor and the state legislature in the area of policy leadership likely to be altered appreciably in the decades ahead? This is another matter that bears close scrutiny. Beginning in 2000, the number of elected members of the Florida cabinet was reduced from six to three, and the governor now appoints the department heads in two key areas—elections and education. In addition, Governor Bush was able to elevate the role of the governor vis-à-vis the legislature with respect to the state budget by creating the e-budget (which made it more difficult for the legislature to obscure the budgetary process) and by aggressively using the line-item veto. These gubernatorial actions, along with a growing desire among citizens for decisive leadership in policy-making generally and the beginning of legislative term limits in 1994, would seem to present a greater opportunity for future governors to assume a much more important—indeed, pivotal—role in policy matters than heretofore has been the case. The critical question, however, is whether the consolidation of budget power and the expanded appointive powers are personal and limited to the Bush administration or whether the governor's new power has been institutionalized to the extent that future governors, Democrats and Republicans, can seize it, use it, and build upon it.

The manner of operation of and influences on the Florida legislature are also subjects that deserve careful scrutiny as we look into Florida's future. Simply put, the internal organization of the Florida legislature and folkways characteristic of this body will have a significant bearing on what interests will be most represented and will influence policy decisions. Who will call the shots in the legislative process, what interests will predominate, and what will be the role of ethnic groups such as Hispanics and African Americans?

At present, a centralized model seems to govern the operation of the legislature. The two presiding officers of the two chambers (that is, speaker of the house and the senate president) wield considerable power and committee chairs act as agents for the leadership. Without doubt, term limits have contributed to the loss of influence of standing committees vis-à-vis the leadership. But will the current centralized system persist or will a more decentralized arrangement replace it? Outputs by the legislature are also determined by the degree of influence exercised by a large constellation of interests such as real estate developers, conservationists, bankers, members of the gaming industry, investors, representatives of the entertainment/tourism industry, lobbyists for big agriculture, senior citizens, and service sector and government employee groups. Will these interests still be major players a decade or two from now or will they be replaced by new interests? Furthermore, Hispanics and African Americans are destined to play a greater role in legislative politics through their affiliation with the Republican and Democratic parties, respectively. The prospect for greater Hispanic influence appears to be more likely, given that Republicans currently control the legislature. Additionally, Hispanic influence is destined to increase with the selection of Marco Rubio from Dade County as the speaker of the house (2007–08). But things could change if Hispanic unity were to dissipate, if Democrats were to regain control of the Legislature, or if some African American legislators were to switch to the Republican Party.

Changing Demographics

Florida's population, while still growing, has shown signs of slowing down in recent years. What will this mean for the immediate and long-range future? The effects could be positive in that they will allow the state and its local governments to catch up with unmet infrastructure needs (e.g., roads, traffic control, water supply, storm water management, sewage disposal) and the need for more services in the areas of education and health care. It also could provide a reprieve to the threat to Florida's fragile environment or even save it. On the negative side, it could slow down the state's economy, which heretofore has seemed not immune to national recessionary forces. In addition, it means that the state and its local governments must engage in the tricky and inexact science of determining the optimal time to curtail infrastructure construction before overbuilding or overexpanding.

Another important dimension of Florida's demographics is the changing composition of the state's population. First, there has been a conspicuous graying of the population. Second, there continues to be a marked increase in the state's Hispanic population as well as in the number of illegal aliens. Third, fairly recent statistics indicate a slowing of the growth in the school-aged population. Fourth, Floridians are more inclined to live in the unincorporated areas of counties rather than in cities. Are these trends likely to change in the future, and if so, when? These trends, like population trends generally, deserve to be closely monitored, for they could have major implications for service delivery, revenue choices, election outcomes, and political decision making.

Another possible demographic change that could loom on the horizon is a substantial influx of new residents to the Panhandle area of the state. Could this be the next major destination for retirees as the southern and central parts of the state become more and more congested and less desirable places to live? If this were to happen, it could change the dynamics of politics in the state and establish new battle lines between pro-development and environmental groups.

Local Government Service Delivery and State-Local Relations

Florida's exponential growth has thrust county and municipal governments into the spotlight, and the expectations of both citizens and the state government have increased markedly about what local governments should be doing. Small towns and cities have greatly expanded their boundaries and their populations have exploded, while communities that were not even incorporated twenty or thirty years ago now have over 100,000 residents. Counties that have experienced tremendous growth in their unincorporated environs have taken on the character of and service delivery responsibilities usually associated with large cities. The result has been that their capacity to deliver services and the revenue available to these governments has been stretched to the limit and the state has had to resort to the creation of special districts to handle the overflow of service demands. Indeed, it is possible that a crisis in service delivery already exists or is imminent.

This characterization of the situation prompts us to ask several questions. Will the unincorporated areas of counties continue to grow and thus be called upon to provide an expanded array of municipal- and urban-type services? Will more new cities be incorporated or will existing cities annex more territory and assume a larger share of the responsibility for these type services? Will we see renewed interest in the ideas of city-county consolidation, intergovernmental cooperation, or various forms of privatization as a means to address the challenge of effective and efficient service delivery? Answers to these questions should provide insight not only into the how local governments respond to the challenge of providing more and better services to their residents but also how well they do it.

The ability and willingness of local governments to respond to the challenge of service delivery hinges in part on what the state government will do in three key areas: revenue restrictions, revenue sharing, and mandates. Local government officials frequently complain that they cannot tap new sources of revenue (e.g., a payroll tax for counties and cites and a local-option sales tax for cities) and the property tax is capped at 10 mills, thus hindering their ability to raise sufficient revenues. To make matters worse, local governments are facing the loss of millions of dollars in property tax as a result of the legislature and governor carrying through on their pledge during the 2007 legislative session and two special sessions to require local governments to roll back these tax levies. Local officials often mention that the state has an obligation to share a larger portion of its revenue with them, especially since the money is derived locally and that is where the service needs are. Finally, local governments must bear the burden of costly state mandates in addition to the ones imposed by the federal government. Will local governments receive adequate relief and/or assistance in the years to come?

"Tough Choice" Policy Issues

Whether the growth rate in Florida's population continues to slow down or not, the fact remains that the state will have some tough choices and decisions to make in the foreseeable future in the areas of education, public welfare, health care, and land use and environmental quality. Education and health care consume a considerable part of the state's budget, and Florida is confronting an unprecedented dilemma. Can the state afford to adequately fund these two programs at a much higher level than in previous years and continue to deliver other necessary staple services? Health care costs for the state are soaring due in large measure to the federal Medicaid program, while the No Child Left Behind mandate and the rising student population are sending education costs to record levels. Then there is the recurrent need to do more for the truly needy in the form of welfare assistance even as we attempt to redefine and reform welfare as we knew it prior to 1996. The choices are not easy—indeed, they are usually painful—because the state must balance the needs of those with little or no medical insurance with the needs of a society that has one of the highest high school dropout rates and students who score below the national average on most achievement tests. Can the state pull a rabbit out of the hat to meet the challenge ahead? We can be sure that the world—and most Floridians—will be watching and waiting to see what happens.

There is also the continuing struggle to sustain the current level of development while protecting the environment and preserving an acceptable quality of life in Florida for future generations. Are the Florida Everglades lost forever, or can they be reclaimed? Will there be enough water for drinking and cooking purposes and yet enough left to adequately sprinkle our lawns? Will there be any natural, pristine beauty left in Florida in twenty or thirty years, or will the state be one large conglomerate of asphalt, concrete, steel, glass, and stucco?

Conclusion

Exciting and interesting times—as well as the constancy of change—are a certainty for government and politics in the Sunshine State in the next few decades. But significant and critical challenges and demands lie ahead as well. How the state will respond is the subject of widespread speculation and anticipation as we approach the end of the first decade of the new century. All we can do is to stay tuned and take note of what happens and as good scholars accurately record, describe, and analyze these happenings in a follow-up to this volume.

Contributors

Roger Austin is a Gainesville, Florida–based political consultant specializing in all areas of state and local campaigns. Between campaign cycles, he is an adjunct lecturer in the Political Campaigning Program at the University of Florida as well as a Ph.D. student at UF, where he is writing his dissertation on campaign finance reform. From 1989 to 1992, Austin served as the political director and legal counsel for the Republican Party of Florida.

J. Edwin Benton is professor of political science and public administration at the University of South Florida. He has published extensively in the areas of state and local government and politics, intergovernmental relations, and Florida politics, and is the coeditor of *State-Local Relations in Florida* (1987) and author of *Counties as Service Delivery Agents* (2002). He is also a past president of the Florida Political Science Association.

Robert B. Bradley is professor in the Askew School of Public Administration and Policy, vice president for_planning and programs, and director of the Institute of Science and Public Affairs (ISPA) at Florida State University. He has served as director of the Florida Advisory Council for Intergovernmental Relations, the Florida Constitutional Commission on Taxation and Budget Reform, and the Florida Executive Office of Planning and Budgeting.

Thomas M. Carsey is the Thomas J. Pearsall distinguished professor of political science at the University of North Carolina—Chapel Hill. A former faculty member in the political science department at Florida State University, Professor Carsey has published two books and numerous articles in the areas of state politics, political parties, legislative politics, and campaigns and elections.

Matthew Corrigan is associate professor and chairperson of the department of political science and public administration at the University of North Florida. Dr. Corrigan's research interests include the presidency, southern politics, and survey methodology. His recent works have appeared in *State and Local Government Review*, *Journal of Urban Affairs*, and *Political Communication*.

Stephen C. Craig is professor and chairperson of political science department at the University of Florida, as well as director of the university's graduate program in political campaigning. He is author of *The Malevolent Leaders: Popular Discontent in America* (1993), editor of *The Electoral Challenge: Theory Meets Practice* (2006), coeditor of *Ambivalence and the Structure of Political Opinion* (2005) and *Ambivalence, Politics, and Public Policy* (2005), and has published numerous articles in professional journals, including *American Political Science Review, American Journal of Political Science, Journal of Politics*, and others.

Lance deHaven-Smith is professor of public administration and policy at Florida State University. A former president of the Florida Political Science Association, he is the author, coauthor, or editor of over a dozen books on Florida government, growth management, and environmental protection. His most recent book is *The Battle for Florida*, which analyzes the disputed 2000 presidential election.

Richard C. Feiock is the Augustus B. Turnbull Professor in the Askew School of Public Administration and Policy and he directs the Devoe Moore Center Program in Local Governance at Florida State University. His recent books include *Institutional Constraints and Local Government* (2001), *City-County Consolidation and Its Alternatives* (2004) and *Metropolitan Governance: Conflict, Competition and Cooperation* (2004). His current research on local government networks and institutions is supported by the National Science Foundation, Aspen Institute, and the Fulbright Scholar Program.

Roger Handberg is professor of political science and department chair, University of Central Florida. Dr. Handberg's work has been published in the *American Journal of Political Science, Law & Society Review, Political Research Quarterly*, and *American Politics Quarterly*.

David M. Hedge is professor of political science at the University of Florida and academic program director at the Bob Graham Center for Public Service. He has written extensively on state politics and public policy.

Kevin A. Hill is associate professor in the department of political science at Florida International University in Miami. He is the coeditor (with Susan MacManus and Dario Moreno) of *Florida Politics: Ten Media Markets, One Powerful State* (2004) and the author of dozens of articles and papers on Florida and southern politics.

Lynne Holt is a policy analyst, affiliated with the Askew Institute, the Public Utility Research Center, and the Bureau of Economic and Business Research, at the University of Florida. Dr. Holt writes about and helps organize meetings on various public policy issues affecting Florida and the nation. She coauthored with David Denslow a book chapter in *Tough Choices: Shaping Florida's Future* on Florida's PK-12 education trends.

Renée J. Johnson is assistant professor of political science at Kent State University in Kent, Ohio. Her current research focuses on the political economy of welfare policy in the United States. Her research has appeared in the *American Journal of Political Science*, the *Journal of Public Administration Research and Theory*, *Policy Studies Journal*, *State and Local Government Review*, as well as numerous book chapters.

Drew Noble Lanier is associate professor of political science and associate director of the Lou Frey Institute of Politics and Government at the University of Central Florida. His work has appeared in *American Journal of Political Science, Social Science Quarterly, Judicature and State Politics and Policy Quarterly*, among other journals. His book *Of Time and Judicial Behavior: United States Supreme Court Agenda-Setting and Decision-Making, 1888-1997* (2003) spans one of the longest periods of analysis among monographs on the Court.

Bob Lotfinia is a research coordinator at the Bureau of Economic and Business Research at the University of Florida. He has contributed to a series of publications relating to Florida's education system and the state's future, most recently its *Quality of Florida's Job Structure* report and a chapter on economic development for the state's Century Commission.

Susan A. MacManus is the Distinguished University Professor of Public Administration and Political Science in the department of government and international affairs at the University of South Florida. She is the author of *Targeting Senior Voters, Young v. Old: Generational Combat in the 21st Century,* co-author of *Politics in States and Communities*, 12th ed., co-author of *Politics in Florida*, and the co-editor/contributor to *Florida's Politics: Ten Media Markets, One Powerful State.* MacManus has served as the political analyst for WFLA-TV, Tampa's NBC affiliate for a number of election cycles.

Dario Moreno is the director of the Metropolitan Center and associate professor of political science at Florida International University. He writes and does research on Miami politics, Florida politics, and Cuban-American politics, and has published over twenty scholarly articles and book chapters and three books. Professor Moreno is a nationally recognized expert on Florida and Miami politics and is often quoted in both the national and local media.

James P. Nelson is a Ph.D. student in the political science department at Florida State University. His interests lie in the fields of American politics and public policy. His work includes papers on state political parties and campaigns.

Suzanne Parker is associate professor of political science at Purdue University. Her most recent publications are: "The Question of Committee Bias Revisited" in *Political Research Quarterly* (2004), and "Increasing Distrust of the United States in South Korea" in *International Political Science Review* (2006). She is the former director of the Survey Research Center at Florida State University and a past president of the Florida Political Science Association.

Eric Prier is associate professor of political science at Florida Atlantic University. Since his first book on the Florida legislature in 2003 (*The Myth of Representation and the Florida Legislature: A House of Competing Loyalties*), his current research examines global anticorruption efforts in public procurement and the social and institutional barriers to enhancing accountability and good governance.

Richard K. Scher is professor of political science at the University of Florida. His fields of interest include southern politics, Florida politics, campaigns and elections, and voting rights. He was a visiting professor in the department of political science, Central European University, Budapest, Hungary, in the winter and spring, 2007.

Terri L. Towner is assistant professor of political science at Georgia State University. She is currently involved in research examining the link between the unequal burdening of the Iraq war and the trends in public support.

Kevin Wagner is assistant professor of political science at Florida Atlantic University. His most recent publication is "Bayesian Inference in Public

Administration Research: Substantive Differences from Somewhat Different Assumptions" in the *International Journal of Public Administration* (2005). His research and publications focus on political development and the evolution of political institutions.

Carol S. Weissert is LeRoy Collins Eminent Scholar Chair and professor of political science at Florida State University. She joined the FSU faculty in 2003 from Michigan State University where she was professor of political science and director of the Institute for Public Policy and Social Research. She is editor of *Publius: The Journal of Federalism* and coauthor of *Governing Health: The Politics of Health Policy*, 3rd edition (2006).

William G. Weissert is professor of political science and director of the master's program in public health at Florida State University, and professor emeritus and former department chair at the University of Michigan School of Public Health. His most recent book is coauthored with his wife, Carol, entitled *Governing Health: The Politics of Health Policy*, 3rd edition (2006).

Index